Fodor's UP CLOSE

SAN FRANCISCO

the complete guide, thoroughly up-to-date

SAVVY TRAVELING: WHERE TO SPEND, HOW TO SAVE

packed with details that will make your trip

CULTURAL TIPS: ESSENTIAL LOCAL DO'S AND TABOOS

must-see sights, on and off the beaten path

INSIDER SECRETS: WHAT'S HIP AND WHAT TO SKIP

the buzz on restaurants, the lowdown on lodgings

FIND YOUR WAY WITH CLEAR AND EASY-TO-USE MAPS

FODOR'S   TRAVEL   PUBLICATIONS

NEW YORK • TORONTO • LONDON • SYDNEY • AUCKLAND

www.fodors.com

Second Edition

ISBN 0–679–00386–X

ISSN 1098–6243

FODOR'S UPCLOSE SAN FRANCISCO

Editor: Hannah Borgeson

Editorial Contributors: Lotus Abrams, Stephanie Adler, Chris Baty, Deke Castleman, Melisse Gelula, Lisa Hamilton, Constance Jones, Jennifer Kasoff, Denise Leto, Clark Norton, Marty Olmstead, Sharon Silva

Editorial Production: Stacey Kulig

Maps: David Lindroth Inc., *cartographer*; Robert Blake, *map editor*

Design: Fabrizio La Rocca, *creative director*; Allison Saltzman, *cover and text design*; Jolie Novak, *photo editor*

Production/Manufacturing: Mike Costa

Cover Art: Mark E. Gibson/The Stock Market

SPECIAL SALES

CONTENTS

I. BASICS *1*

2. EXPLORING THE BAY AREA 28

3. SHOPPING 86

4. FOOD 98

5. CAFÉ CULTURE 127

6. AFTER DARK 133

7. WHERE TO SLEEP 157

8. THE GREAT OUTDOORS 178

9. DAY AND WEEKEND TRIPS 196

INDEX 238

TRAVELING
UPCLOSE

H ave a picnic on a hilltop park. Go to a festival. Commune with nature. Memorize the symphony of the streets. And if you want to experience the heart and soul of San Francisco, whatever you do, don't spend too much money.

The deep and rich experience of San Francisco that every true traveler yearns for is one of the things in life that money can't buy. In fact, if you have it, don't use it. Traveling lavishly is the surest way to turn yourself into a sideline traveler. Restaurants with white-glove service are great—sometimes—but they're usually not the best place to find the perfect clam chowder with sourdough bread. Doormen at plush hotels have their place, but not when your look-alike room could be anywhere from Dusseldorf to Detroit. Better to stay in a more intimate place that truly gives you the atmosphere you traveled so far to experience. Don't just stand and watch—jump into the spirit of what's around you.

If you want to see San Francisco up close and savor the essence of the city, this book is for you. We'll show you the local culture, the offbeat sights, the bars and cafés where tourists rarely tread, and the B&Bs and other hostelries where you'll meet fellow travelers—places where the locals would send their friends. And because you'll probably want to see the famous places if you haven't already been there, we give you tips on losing the crowds, plus the quirky and obscure facts you want as well as the basics everyone needs.

OUR GANG

Who are we? We're artists and poets, slackers and straight arrows, and travel writers and journalists, who in our less hedonistic moments report on local news and spin out an occasional opinion piece. What we share is a certain footloose spirit and a passion for the City by the Bay, which we celebrate in this guidebook. Shamelessly, we've revealed all of our favorite places and our deepest, darkest travel secrets, all so that you can learn from our past mistakes and experience the best part of San Francisco to the fullest. If you can't take your best friend on the road, or if your best friend is hopeless with directions, stick with us.

LOTUS ABRAMS has lived in the Bay Area nearly her whole life. She updated the South Bay section and writes for *Sunset* magazine, where she is a fact checker.

CHRIS BATY has been writing about holes-in-the-walls and out-of-the-ways in the East Bay since he moved there in 1991. A resident of the Lake Merritt neighborhood, Chris spends his free time stalking the lake's egrets and publishing his Oakland-centric zine, *Frolic.*

DEKE CASTLEMAN learned his budget-traveler skills in the mid-1970s in Alaska, the most expensive state in the country, waiting for a job on the Trans-Alaska Pipeline. Now he divides his time between Las Vegas, where he edits the *Las Vegas Advisor,* and the Sierras, where he indulges in the free pleasures of nature. He updated the Lake Tahoe section of this guide.

MELISSE GELULA, our lodging expert, is a frequent contributing writer to Fodor's guides and a former Bay Area resident.

Armed with pen, paper, and a tank of gas, **LISA HAMILTON** set out to conquer the wilds of Marin and Santa Cruz counties and emerged, weeks later, with a recipe for lemon meringue pie and a new fascination for jellyfish. Now fully recuperated, she spends most days stuck in traffic on the Golden Gate Bridge, hoping the earthquake will wait until she gets home.

Berkeley-based writer and editor **DENISE M. LETO** shopped, quaffed, and thoroughly explored her way through San Francisco as she updated several sections of the guide. When she's not working, she can be found roaming the city's back streets in search of the perfect gin gimlet or squeezing *zampanos* at her favorite Berkeley haunt, the Cheese Board.

CLARK NORTON, who updated the Yosemite National Park section, divides his time between New York and California. He is the author of *Fodor's Where Should We Take the Kids? California,* and has contributed to numerous Fodor's guides.

MARTY OLMSTEAD is the former travel editor of *San Francisco Focus* magazine, for which she crisscrossed the state many times. Accounts of her voyages around the globe have appeared in *Travel and Leisure,* the *Los Angeles Times, Diversion, Glamour,* and *Odyssey.* She is also the author of *Hidden Tennessee* and *Hidden Georgia.* Marty, who lives in Sonoma County, writes a column about the Wine Country for the *Marin Independent Journal;* she updated the wine country section of this book.

Bay Area–native **SHARON SILVA,** who has been supping in San Francisco restaurants since her Gerber days, is an occasional contributor to the food pages of *San Francisco* magazine and other local publications and has coauthored two books on eating out in the Bay Area.

A SEND-OFF

Always call ahead. We knock ourselves out to check all the facts, but everything changes all the time, in ways that none of us can ever fully anticipate. Whenever you're making a special trip to a special place, as opposed to merely wandering, always call ahead. Trust us on this.

And then, if something doesn't go quite right, as inevitably happens with even the best-laid plans, stay cool. Missed your train? Stuck in the airport? Use the time to study the people. Strike up a conversation with a stranger. Study the newsstands or flip through the local press. Take a walk. Find the silver lining in the clouds, whatever it is. And do send us a postcard to tell us what went wrong and what went right. You can e-mail us at: editors@fodors.com (specify the name of the book on the subject line) or write the San Francisco editor at Fodor's upClose, 201 East 50th Street, New York, NY 10022. We'll put your ideas to good use and let other travelers benefit from your experiences. In the mean time, bon voyage!

ON-LINE SURVEY

Tell us what you think of this guide and get a free Fodor's How to Pack *guidebook. Our on-line reader survey can be found at* **www.fodors.com/ upclose/upclosesurvey.html**

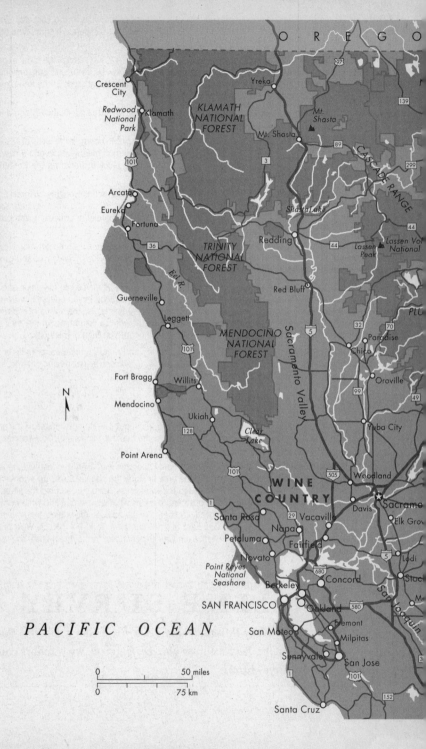

NORTHERN CALIFORNIA

OREGON

Crescent City

Redwood National Park

Klamath

KLAMATH NATIONAL FOREST

Yreka

97

Mt. Shasta

Mt. Shasta

89

CASCADE RANGE

299

3

Arcata

Eureka

Fortuna

36

TRINITY NATIONAL FOREST

Eel R.

Shasta Lake

Redding

44

Lassen Peak

Lassen Vol. National

44

Red Bluff

Guerneville

Leggett

MENDOCINO NATIONAL FOREST

101

Sacramento Valley

5

32

70

PLU

Paradise

Chico

Fort Bragg

Willits

Mendocino

Ukiah

128

Clear Lake

99

Oroville

49

Yuba City

Point Arena

101

505

Woodland

WINE COUNTRY

Santa Rosa

29

Vacaville

Davis

Sacramo

Elk Grov

Napa

Petaluma

Fairfield

Novato

680

5

Lodi

Point Reyes National Seashore

Berkeley

Concord

Stoc

SAN FRANCISCO

Oakland

580

San Joaquin

Me

San Mateo

Fremont

Milpitas

Sunnyvale

San Jose

1

101

Santa Cruz

152

N

PACIFIC OCEAN

0 — 50 miles
0 — 75 km

VIII

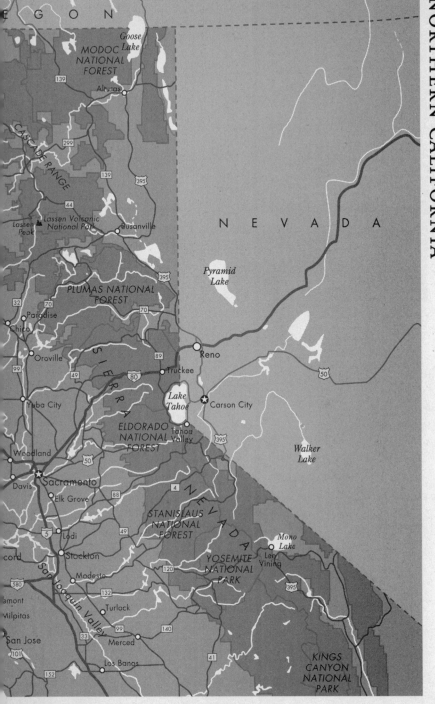

OREGON

Goose Lake

MODOC NATIONAL FOREST

Alturas

139

CASCADE RANGE

299

139

395

44

Lassen Peak

Lassen Volcanic National Park

Susanville

N E V A D A

Pyramid Lake

32

70

PLUMAS NATIONAL FOREST

Paradise

Chico

70

Oroville

89

Reno

80

Truckee

99

49

Yuba City

SIERRA

Lake Tahoe

50

Carson City

Walker Lake

Woodland

ELDORADO NATIONAL FOREST

Tahoe Valley

395

50

Davis

Sacramento

Elk Grove

88

4

N E V A D A

5

Lodi

49

STANISLAUS NATIONAL FOREST

Stockton

Mono Lake

Modesto

120

Lee Vining

395

580

San Joaquin Valley

132

YOSEMITE NATIONAL PARK

emont

Turlock

Milpitas

99

33

140

San Jose

Merced

101

152

Los Banos

41

KINGS CANYON NATIONAL PARK

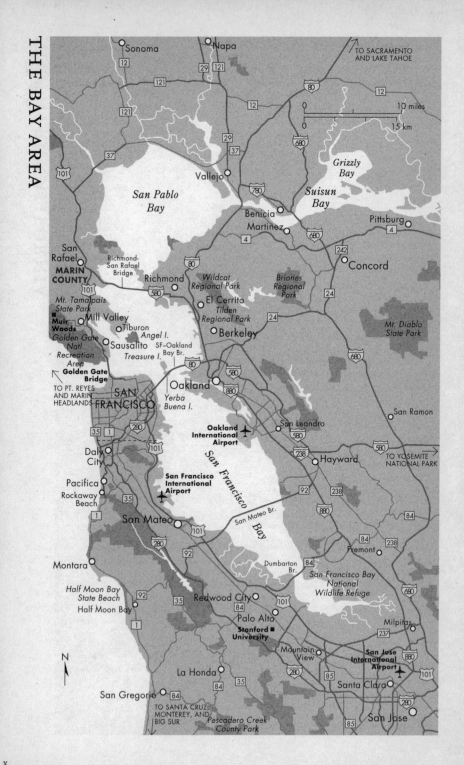

Sonoma

Napa

TO SACRAMENTO
AND LAKE TAHOE

12

29   121

121

80

12

121

29

680

0   10 miles

15 km

37

37

101

San Pablo
Bay

Vallejo

Grizzly
Bay

780

Suisun
Bay

Pittsburg

San
Rafael

MARIN
COUNTY

Richmond–
San Rafael
Bridge

Richmond

Benicia

Martinez

4

680

242

Concord

4

101

Mt. Tamalpais
State Park

Muir
Woods

Golden Gate
Natl.
Recreation
Area

Golden Gate
Bridge

TO PT. REYES
AND MARIN
HEADLANDS

580

Mill Valley

Tiburon

Sausalito

Angel I.

Treasure I.

SF–Oakland
Bay Br.

SAN
FRANCISCO

35   1

280

Wildcat
Regional Park

El Cerrito

Tilden
Regional Park

Berkeley

Briones
Regional
Park

24

24

Mt. Diablo
State Park

680

80

Oakland

Yerba
Buena I.

880

580

San Leandro

San Ramon

Daly
City

101

Oakland
International
Airport

580

238

Hayward

TO YOSEMITE
NATIONAL PARK

Pacifica

Rockaway
Beach

35

1

San Mateo

San Francisco
International
Airport

San Francisco
Bay

92

238

880

92

San Mateo Br.

84

238

280

101

Montara

92

Dumbarton
Br.

84

Fremont

84

680

Half Moon Bay
State Beach

Half Moon Bay

1

92

35

Redwood City

84

101

Palo Alto

Stanford
University

San Francisco Bay
National
Wildlife Refuge

Milpitas

237

La Honda

San Gregorio

84

84

35

Mountain
View

280

85

San Jose
International
Airport

880

101

Santa Clara

TO SANTA CRUZ,
MONTEREY, AND
BIG SUR

Pescadero Creek
County Park

85

280

San Jose

N

BASICS I

I f you've ever traveled with anyone before, you know that there are two types of people in the world—the planners and the nonplanners. Travel brings out the worst in both groups. Left to their own devices, the planners will have you goose-stepping from attraction to attraction on a cultural blitzkrieg, while the nonplanners will invariably miss the flight, the bus, and maybe even the point. This chapter offers you a middle ground; we hope it provides enough information to help you plan your trip to San Francisco and the Bay Area without nailing you down. Be flexible and remember that the most hair-pulling situations turn into the best travel stories back home.

AIR TRAVEL

BOOKING YOUR FLIGHT

When you book look for **nonstop flights** and **remember that "direct" flights stop at least once.** Try to avoid connecting flights, which require a change of plane.

CARRIERS

MAJOR AIRLINES • From the U.S.: **Alaska Airline** (tel. 800/426–0333) to Oakland, San Francisco. **America West** (tel. 800/235–9292) to Oakland, San Francisco. **American** (tel. 800/433–7300) to Oakland, San Francisco. **British Airways** (tel. 800/247–9297) to San Francisco. **Continental** (tel. 800/231–0856) to San Francisco. **Delta** (tel. 800/241–4141) to Oakland, San Francisco. **Northwest** (tel. 800/225–2525) to San Francisco. **Southwest** (tel. 800/435–9792) to Oakland, San Francisco. **TWA** (tel. 800/892–4141) to San Francisco. **United** (tel. 800/538–2929) to Oakland, San Francisco. **US Airways** (tel. 800/428–4322) to San Francisco. From the United Kingdom: **British Airways** (tel. 0345/222–111). **United** (tel. 0800/888–555). **Virgin Atlantic** (tel. 01293/747–747). **American** (tel. 0345/789–789) flies via New York or Chicago, and **Delta** (tel. 0800/414–767) flies via Los Angeles or Cincinnati. From Australia: **United** (tel. 800/538–2929) to San Francisco.

SMALLER AIRLINES • **Midwest Express** (tel. 800/452–2022) to San Francisco. **Reno Air** (tel. 800/736–6247) to San Francisco.

CHECK-IN & BOARDING

Assuming that not everyone with a ticket will show up, airlines routinely overbook planes. When that happens, airlines ask for volunteers to give up their seats. In return these volunteers usually get a certificate for a free flight and are rebooked on the next flight out. If there are not enough volunteers, the airline must choose who will be denied boarding. The first to get bumped are passengers who checked in late and those flying on discounted tickets, so **get to the gate and check in as early as possible,** especially during peak periods.

Always **bring a government-issued photo ID to the airport.** You may be asked to show it before you are allowed to check in.

CUTTING COSTS

The least-expensive airfares to San Francisco must usually be purchased in advance and are nonrefundable. It's smart to **call a number of airlines, and when you are quoted a good price, book it on the spot**—the same fare may not be available the next day. Always **check different routings** and look into using different airports. Travel agents, especially low-fare specialists (*see* Discounts & Deals, *below*), are helpful.

Consolidators are another good source. They buy tickets for scheduled international flights at reduced rates from the airlines, then sell them at prices that beat the best fare available directly from the airlines, usually without restrictions. Sometimes you can even get your money back if you need to return the ticket. Carefully read the fine print detailing penalties for changes and cancellations, and **confirm your consolidator reservation with the airline.**

When you **fly as a courier** you trade your checked-luggage space for a ticket deeply subsidized by a courier service. There are restrictions on when you can book and how long you can stay.

CONSOLIDATORS • Cheap Tickets (tel. 800/377–1000). **Discount Airline Ticket Service** (tel. 800/ 576–1600). **Unitravel** (tel. 800/325–2222). **Up & Away Travel** (tel. 212/889–2345). **World Travel Network** (tel. 800/409–6753).

ENJOYING THE FLIGHT

For more legroom **request an emergency-aisle seat.** Don't sit in the row in front of the emergency aisle or in front of a bulkhead, where seats may not recline. If you have dietary concerns, **ask for special meals when booking.** These can be vegetarian, low-cholesterol, or kosher, for example. On long flights, try to maintain a normal routine, to help fight jet lag. At night **get some sleep.** By day **eat light meals, drink water** (not alcohol), and **move around the cabin** to stretch your legs.

FLYING TIMES

Flying time is six hours from New York, four hours from Chicago, and one hour from Los Angeles.

HOW TO COMPLAIN

If your baggage goes astray or your flight goes awry, complain right away. Most carriers require that you **file a claim immediately.**

AIRLINE COMPLAINTS • U.S. Department of Transportation **Aviation Consumer Protection Division** (C-75, Room 4107, Washington, DC 20590, tel. 202/366–2220). **Federal Aviation Administration Consumer Hotline** (tel. 800/322–7873).

AIRPORTS & TRANSFERS

The major gateway to San Francisco is San Francisco International Airport, just south of the city, off U.S. 101. Several domestic airlines serve the Oakland Airport, which is across the bay but not much farther away from downtown San Francisco (via I–880 and I–80), although traffic on the Bay Bridge may at times make travel time longer. Fourteen carriers, most notably American Airlines, fly into San Jose International Airport.

AIRPORT INFORMATION • San Francisco International Airport (tel. 800/736–2008). **Oakland Airport** (tel. 510/577–4000). **San Jose International Airport** (1661 Airport Blvd., off I–880 near U.S. 101, tel. 408/277–4759).

TRANSFERS

Construction has begun on the long-awaited extension of BART to San Francisco International Airport, but until it is actually complete, **buses are the best way into the city.** From the airport you can take SamTrans Bus 7B (55 mins, $2.20), Bus 7F (35 mins, $3) to San Francisco's Transbay Terminal, or Bus 3X (20 mins, $1.10) to the Colma BART station. From here you can catch a train to downtown San Francisco (20 mins, $2.25) or Berkeley (45 mins, $3.05). The buses run every half hour—Bus 3X from 6 AM to 11:30 PM. Buses 7B and 7F from about 5 AM to 1 AM. Bus 7F restricts you to one small carry-on bag. (Bus 7F will also tote you to Palo Alto, stopping near the Stanford Shopping Center.) Locals tend to rely on private shuttles for their convenience and reliability (*see* Airport Shuttles, *below*). Long-term parking is $11 per day up to seven days and then $14 for each additional day. The lot tends to fill up during peak travel times, especially three-day weekends; call the Parking Hotline to check on availability before you set out and plan for extra time to take the free shuttle from the lot to the terminal.

From Oakland International Airport, the Air-Bart shuttle runs to the Coliseum BART station every 15–20 minutes from 6 AM to 12 PM Monday through Saturday and 8:30 AM to 11:45 PM on Sunday. Buy tickets ($2) at the BART station or airport terminal before you board. AC Transit Bus 58 ($1.25) follows the same route, continuing on to downtown Oakland, a 50-minute trip. Another money-saving option is a van company (*see* Airport Shuttles, *below*). A taxi to downtown Berkeley from Oakland International costs about $30–$35. Long-term parking is $10 for 24 hours or $8 in the economy lot next to Terminal 1. A free shuttle will take you to the terminals.

From the San Jose International Airport, VTA Bus 65 ($1.10) departs every 30–60 minutes for downtown San Jose before continuing south to Almaden. To reach San Francisco or the East Bay, take a private shuttle (*see* Airport Shuttles, *below*). Short-term parking runs 75¢ per half hour and $17 per day; long-term is $8 per day.

RESOURCES • **Parking Hotline** (tel. 650/877–0227). **Air-Bart Shuttle** (tel. 510/562–7700).

AIRPORT SHUTTLES

Airport shuttles will pick you up at your doorstep at any time of day or night and whisk you to the airport. The fare from San Francisco to SFO runs $10–$12; expect to pay $20–$35 from San Francisco to the Oakland Airport. There's often a reduced rate for a pickup of two or more people. You can save a few more bucks (up to $10) by boarding the shuttle at a major hotel.

The king of airport service is Super Shuttle, with service from San Francisco and the Peninsula to SFO and the Oakland airport. Quake City is a smaller, friendlier, employee-owned service: It runs to SFO and the Oakland Airport for a few dollars less than Super Shuttle. The BayPorter Express serves primarily the East Bay but also runs to SFO. The Marin Airporter will take you from Marin County to SFO.

TAXIS & SHUTTLES • **Super Shuttle** (tel. 415/558–8500). **Quake City** (tel. 415/255–4899). **Bay-Porter Express** (tel. 415/467–1800). **Marin Airporter** (tel. 415/461–4222).

BART

See Subway Travel, *below*.

BICYCLING

Though San Francisco's hills will undoubtedly give you thighs of steel and infinitely more respect for bike messengers, there are plenty of bicycle routes that can keep you away from traffic and get you around the larger hills. In 1996 the S.F. Bicycle Program began marking the most bicycle-friendly of its streets with numbered route signs. Follow them, and your biggest challenge may be to **keep an eye out for the opening doors of parked cars.** Berkeley TRiP (*see* Transportation around San Francisco, *below*) has great biking maps, including the *San Francisco Biking/Walking Guide* ($2), which shows street grades and bike routes. Bike enthusiasts can join the local pedaling scene at the **Critical Mass** ride on the last Friday of every month. While the ride began as a lighthearted group commute of just 45 riders in 1992, the crowds now number up to 1,000 and the attitudes range from friendly to revolutionary as traffic lights and motorists defer to the power of this unstoppable procession of cyclists. To join the ride, meet at 5:30 PM at Justin Herman Plaza (The Embarcadero at Market St.). For suggested cycling routes around San Francisco and the Bay Area, *see* Hiking and Biking *in* Chapter 8.

Professional bike thieves abound in the Bay Area. **Always use U-shape locks to secure both the wheels and the frame** to a sturdy post. You can get a good bicycle for around $50 at any flea market or police bike auction, where unclaimed bikes are sold.

BIKES ON PUBLIC TRANSIT

You can take your bicycle on Bay Area transit systems with varying degrees of hassle. CalTrain allows bikes on all trains, save some express trains. All ferries, except the Blue and Gold Fleet's bay cruises, take on bicycles at any time of day.

HALLIDIE'S SAN FRANCISCO TREAT

One rainy evening in 1873, young engineer Andrew Hallidie witnessed a horrible sight: One of four horses drawing a streetcar slipped and went barreling down a steep hill, dragging the other helpless horses behind it. This tragic incident inspired Hallidie to devise the era's most complex and industrious transportation system: the cable car—the world's first large-scale mechanized street transportation. In 1964 San Francisco's cable cars were declared a National Historic Landmark, the first moving entity to receive that honor.

Bikes on BART: Bikes are allowed in all but the first car of each train. During commuter rush hours, 6:30–9 AM and 3:30–6:30 PM, bikes are allowed only between the Embarcadero and East Bay stations (but not in the 12th and 19th Street stations in Oakland). During these hours a bike shuttle ($1) operates every 30–45 minutes between MacArthur BART and the Transbay Terminal; call CalTrans for more information. Bicycle lockers, available at some stations, rent for three months ($15) or one year ($30); call the BART Pass Office.

By autumn of 2000, East Bay AC Transit's entire fleet of 700 buses will be outfitted with bike racks, and until then most routes have at least some buses equipped to carry cycles. AC Transit allows bikes on all lines from midnight to 5:30 AM and on Buses 65 (weekdays) and 67 (weekends) for transit to Tilden Park. Golden Gate Transit has bike racks on all its buses. S.F. Muni allows bikes on nine bus lines, including Bus 76, which travels into the Marin Headlands.

RESOURCES • BART Office of Passenger Service (tel. 510/464–7127). **CalTrans** (tel. 510/286–0669). **BART Pass Office** (tel. 510/464–7133). **AC Transit** (tel. 510/839–2882 for information on bike racks).

BOAT & FERRY TRAVEL

For a change of pace, pack a thermos of coffee and a warm jacket and hop aboard one of the many ferries plying the bay's waters. Ferries are comparable to other forms of transport in speed (though not in price), and you can drink your java while taking in a lovely view. Your ferry ticket acts as a free transfer to buses on both sides of the bay. In the city the main point of departure is the landmark San Francisco Ferry Building.

The Blue and Gold Fleet sends ferries to Tiburon, Sausalito, Angel Island State Park, and Alcatraz. The weekday commuter ferry to Tiburon (20 mins) departs from the SF Ferry Building. All other departures are from Pier 41 at Fisherman's Wharf, including weekend service to Tiburon (30 mins) and daily service to Sausalito (30 mins), Angel Island (40 mins), and Alcatraz. One-way fare to Sausalito or Tiburon is $6. To Angel Island, round-trip fare (including park admission) is $11. Bikes are allowed on board at no additional charge, though space is limited. To Alcatraz, the fare is $7.75, or $11.25, including a worthwhile audio tour. Call for current schedules.

The Blue and Gold Fleet's Oakland/Alameda Ferry leaves from Jack London Square (Embarcadero and Broadway) in Oakland or the Alameda Ferry Dock (2990 Main St., Alameda) for the San Francisco Ferry Building (30 mins) or Pier 39 (40 mins). Ferries run every one-two hours from 6 AM on weekdays, 10 AM on weekends and holidays, until 8:50 PM. This ride gives you great views of Oakland's harbor and the Bay Bridge. The fare is $4.50

The Blue and Gold Fleet's Vallejo Ferry has a commuter run ($7.50) and an excursion fare to Six Flags Marine World ($40 round-trip, which includes park admission and shuttle to and from the park). In San Francisco ferries leave from the San Francisco Ferry Building and Pier 39; call for a current schedule.

Golden Gate Ferry crosses the bay between the San Francisco Ferry Building and Larkspur (45–55 mins; $2.75 weekdays, $4.70 weekends) or Sausalito (30 mins, $4.70). Ferries depart hourly, from 7 AM to 8 PM.

INFORMATION • Blue and Gold Fleet's **Tiburon, Sausalito, Angel Island, and Alcatraz Ferries** (tel. 415/773–1188 for 24-hr recorded information or 415/705–5555 for tickets). Blue and Gold Fleet's **Oakland/Alameda Ferry** (tel. 415/705–5555 or 510/522–3300 for 24-hr recorded information). Blue and Gold Fleet's **Vallejo Ferry** (tel. 415/705–5444). **Golden Gate Ferry** (tel. 415/923–2000).

BUS TRAVEL TO AND FROM SAN FRANCISCO

Greyhound travels to and from Bay Area cities all day, to farther-flung destinations. In San Francisco Greyhound operates out of the third floor of the Transbay Terminal, where many Muni lines (*see above*) begin. Plan your departure for daytime, as this terminal is dicey at night. In the East Bay the Greyhound office is in Oakland; in the South Bay it's in San Jose; and in Marin County you'll find it in downtown San Rafael.

BUS INFORMATION • **Greyhound** (tel. 800/231–2222). In San Francisco: **Transbay Terminal** (1st and Mission Sts., tel. 415/495–1569). In the East Bay: **Oakland** (2103 San Pablo Ave., at 20th St., tel. 510/834–3213). In the South Bay: **San Jose** (70 Almaden Ave., at Santa Clara St., tel. 408/295–4151). In Marin County: **San Rafael** (850 Tamalpais St., at 3rd St., tel. 415/453–0795).

FARES & SCHEDULES • Tahoe (7–12 hrs, $20 one way), Santa Cruz (2–4 hrs, $14 one way), Los Angeles (7–12 hrs, $32 one way), Seattle (20–26 hrs, $48 one way).

"Flat" streets in San Francisco: Stockton, Polk, Broadway Tunnel, Geary/Post, Market, and Valencia.

GREEN TORTOISE

Green Tortoise Adventure Travel is a cheap, funky alternative to humdrum bus travel. Buses come equipped with sleeping pads, kitchens, and stereos to ensure their slogan that you'll "arrive inspired, not dog-tired." The journey to Seattle (24 hrs, $59 one way) features a cookout ($4) and skinny-dipping. Regularly scheduled runs also go from the Bay Area to Los Angeles (12 hrs, $35), Eugene, Oregon (17 hrs, $39), and Portland (20 hrs, $49), with select stops along the way. Make reservations before you show up at their pickup point in San Francisco (1st and Natoma Sts.) or Berkeley (Berkeley Marina, across from the bait shop). **Bring cash or traveler's checks** because you can't pay with plastic.

INFORMATION • **Green Tortoise Adventure Travel** (494 Broadway, San Francisco 94133, tel. 415/956–7500 or 800/867–8647).

BUS & STREETCAR TRAVEL WITHIN SAN FRANCISCO

Despite all the griping about graffiti and rising fares, most Bay Area residents will admit the city bus systems are actually quite good. Bus passes and discount tickets are available at most grocery stores and check-cashing venues. The only regional pass available is BART Plus (*see* Subway Travel, *below*).

SAN FRANCISCO

Muni is forever improving its bus service, and its fares have stayed low as others have risen, but if you choose this public transit you run the risk of frequent breakdowns, disgruntled drivers, and belligerent passengers. Though buses are scheduled to run every 10–15 minutes, chronic delays often make it quicker to walk if you're not going far. Perhaps Muni's one saving grace is its owl service, which has nine lines running every 30 minutes between 1 AM and 5 AM.

The fare is $1. Your fare entitles you to one free transfer, good for 90 minutes. Passport passes allow unlimited access to Muni (including cable cars) for one day ($6), three days ($10), or seven days ($15). A special Weekly Pass ($9) is good only for Muni buses; with this you pay $1 for each cable car ride. The Fast Pass ($35) allows one month of unlimited travel on Muni buses, streetcars, and cable cars, as well as on BART and CalTrain routes within San Francisco. **Purchase passes at the Powell Street visitor center** (*see* Visitor Information, *below*).

If you don't mind crowds, cable cars are a great way to get the flavor of San Francisco's hills—or to feel like you're in a Rice-A-Roni commercial, depending on your point of view. They run at a pace straight out of the early 1900s (the cables that propel the cars move at 9.5 mph), so if you're a Type A, take the bus. For great views take the Hyde and Powell line, which travels from Fisherman's Wharf to Powell and Market streets downtown. Along the way you'll get a gander at Alcatraz and pass right by Lombard Street, the so-called crookedest street in the world. The line to board at the Hyde Street turnaround often requires a wait of more than an hour, making the less scenic California line from the Embarcadero BART station an attractive alternative. The fare is $2, and all passes except the $9 Weekly Pass are accepted.

INFORMATION • Muni (tel. 415/673–6864 or 415/923–6168 for lost and found).

EAST BAY

With more than 100 lines, AC Transit covers the East Bay from north of Richmond to south of Fremont. The fare is $1.25, and 25¢ transfers are good for two hours. Monthly passes run $45. A book of 10 tickets costs $10; a book of 10 transfer tickets costs $2.50.

The AC Transit lines designated by letters rather than numbers cross the Bay Bridge to San Francisco's Transbay Terminal (1st and Mission Sts.). Most only run from dawn to dusk; exceptions include the F (Berkeley), T (Oakland, connecting to Berkeley on Bus 40), and N (Oakland) lines, which operate until midnight. The Transbay fare is $2.20. Monthly Transbay passes cost $75.

INFORMATION • AC Transit (1600 Franklin St., Oakland, tel. 510/817–1717).

NORTH BAY

Golden Gate Transit provides service almost everywhere in the North Bay. Buses connect San Francisco with Sausalito, Mill Valley, Tiburon, San Rafael, Novato, Rohnert Park, and Santa Rosa every half hour during the week. Many buses run weekdays only, from dawn to dusk, but some routes (including the 20 and 50, which stop in Sausalito) run on weekends until 1 AM. Within San Francisco, buses leave the Transbay Terminal and make stops throughout the city. Fare costs $1.50–$5.30, depending on the length of your trip; a Ride Value Discount Ticket Book, with 20 tickets at a 20% discount, is available for purchase at the Golden Gate Ferry Terminal (on the Embarcadero at the foot of Market St.); at the Golden Gate Transit Administration Office (1011 Andersen Dr., San Rafael); and at many bookstores, gas stations, and grocery stores.

INFORMATION • Golden Gate Transit (tel. 415/923–2000 or 415/257–4476 for lost and found).

SOUTH BAY

SamTrans runs buses regularly throughout San Mateo County, south of San Francisco. Buses depart from the Daly City BART station, from downtown San Francisco, and from San Francisco International Airport (*see* Airports & Transfers, *above*) and go as far as Año Nuevo State Reserve, at the southern end of the county (*see* South Bay *in* Chapter 2).

The Valley Transportation Agency (VTA) operates buses and one light-rail line throughout San Jose and the Silicon Valley.

BUS INFORMATION • SamTrans (tel. 800/660–4287). **VTA Information Center** (4 N. 2nd St., San Jose, tel. 408/321–2300 or 800/894–9908).

FARES & SCHEDULES • SamTrans Bus 1L travels from Daly City BART along the coast to Half Moon Bay about five times daily. Most other buses run weekdays only, though some heavily trafficked routes are covered all week; **call SamTrans for help planning your trip.** The fare is $1.10 and $3 for express routes; no transfers are issued. Monthly passes cost $38 or $102 for an express route pass. Basic fare on VTA buses is $1.10; express buses cost a flat $1.75. The VTA Information Center sells day passes ($2.50 and $4 for express routes) and monthly passes ($35).

BUSINESS HOURS

SHOPS

Although many stores in San Francisco and Berkeley stay open seven days a week until 8 PM or 9 PM, stores in Oakland tend to close by 7 PM, and they remain shuttered on Sunday.

CAMERAS & PHOTOGRAPHY

PHOTO HELP • Kodak Information Center (tel. 800/242– 2424). *Kodak Guide to Shooting Great Travel Pictures,* available in bookstores or from Fodor's Travel Publications (tel. 800/533–6478; $16.50 plus $4 shipping).

EQUIPMENT PRECAUTIONS

Always **keep your film and tape out of the sun.** Carry an extra supply of batteries, and **be prepared to turn on your camera or camcorder** to prove to security personnel that the device is real. Always **ask for hand inspection of film,** which becomes clouded after successive exposures to airport X-ray machines, and **keep videotapes away from metal detectors.**

CAR RENTAL

To fully experience the best of the Bay Area—the Wine Country, for example, or coastal beaches—a rental car is practically a necessity. Your best bet is to **rent a vehicle at one of the region's airports.** The cheapest rates are available to those who can present a plane ticket, but even residents can save as much as $15 a day over the rates at downtown rental franchises. If you absolutely can't make it to the airport, almost all rental-car agencies have pickup and drop-off spots in downtown San Francisco within five or six blocks of Union Square. No matter where you pick up your car, you'll always pay a heavy surcharge (starting at about $25) if you don't return it to the same spot.

Rates in San Francisco begin at $36 a day and $123 a week for an economy car with air-conditioning, an automatic transmission, and unlimited mileage. This does not include tax on car rentals, which is 8.25%. All Bay Area car-rental companies require a credit card for deposit purposes. Some cards—American Express, for example—provide liability and damage insurance, so check with your credit card company before paying for the rental agency's insurance policy. You'll usually pay less if you **reserve in advance, and always ask about specials and discounts**—some rental agencies, for example, offer 10%–20% discounts if you have AAA membership or frequent-flier miles on certain airlines. Small, independent agencies generally have cheaper daily rates than the national chains but usually impose mileage charges. However, if you're planning on going far, **consider using the national companies** (Avis, Hertz, Budget, etc.); they usually give you unlimited mileage, which may cut your total cost.

You wouldn't be the first driver to shudder as you sit at a stoplight on a steep San Francisco hill, hoping your stick shift car won't slide 200 ft backward as soon as you lift your foot off the brake and engage the clutch.

MAJOR AGENCIES • Alamo (tel. 800/327–9633; 020/8759–6200 in the U.K.). **Avis** (tel. 800/331–1212; 800/879–2847 in Canada; 02/9353–9000 in Australia; 09/525–1982 in New Zealand). **Budget** (tel. 800/527–0700; 0144/227–6266 in the U.K.). **Dollar** (tel. 800/800–4000; 020/8897–0811 in the U.K., where it is known as Eurodollar; 02/9223–1444 in Australia). **Hertz** (tel. 800/654–3131; 800/263–0600 in Canada; 0990/90–60–90 in the U.K.; 02/9669–2444 in Australia; 03/358–6777 in New Zealand). **National InterRent** (tel. 800/227–7368; 0345/222525 in the U.K., where it is known as Europcar InterRent).

CUTTING COSTS

To get the best deal **book through a travel agent who will shop around.** Also **price local car-rental companies,** although the service and maintenance may not be as good as those of a major player. Remember to ask about required deposits, cancellation penalties, and drop-off charges if you're planning to pick up the car in one city and leave it in another. If you're traveling during a holiday period, also make sure that a confirmed reservation guarantees you a car.

Do **look into wholesalers,** companies that do not own fleets but rent in bulk from those that do and often offer better rates than traditional car-rental operations. Payment must be made before you leave home.

LOCAL AGENCIES • Enterprise (tel. 800/325–8007). **Reliable** (tel. 415/928–4414). **Bob Leech Auto Rental** (tel. 800/325–1240) at San Francisco International Airport rents cars at bargain prices. **Sunbelt** (tel. 415/771–9191) specializes in BMWs and Corvette and Miata convertibles.

WHOLESALERS • Auto Europe (tel. 207/842–2000 or 800/223–5555, fax 800/235–6321).

INSURANCE

When driving a rented car you are generally responsible for any damage to or loss of the vehicle as well as for any property damage or personal injury that you may cause. Before you rent **see what coverage your personal auto-insurance policy and credit cards already provide.**

For about $15 to $20 per day, rental companies sell protection, known as a collision- or loss-damage waiver (CDW or LDW), that eliminates your liability for damage to the car. Some states, including California, have capped the price of the CDW and LDW. In most states you don't need a CDW if you have personal auto insurance or other liability insurance. However, **make sure you have enough coverage to pay for the car.** If you do not have auto insurance or an umbrella policy that covers damage to third parties, purchasing liability insurance and a CDW or LDW is highly recommended.

REQUIREMENTS & RESTRICTIONS

In California you must be 21 to rent a car, and rates may be higher if you're under 25. You'll pay extra for child seats (about $3 per day), which are compulsory for children under 5, and for additional drivers (about $2 per day). Non-U.S. residents will need a reservation voucher, a passport, a driver's license, and a travel policy that covers each driver, in order to pick up a car.

SURCHARGES

Before you pick up a car in one city and leave it in another **ask about drop-off charges or one-way service fees,** which can be substantial. Note, too, that some rental agencies charge extra if you return the car before the time specified in your contract. To avoid a hefty refueling fee **fill the tank just before you turn in the car,** but be aware that gas stations near the rental outlet may overcharge.

CAR TRAVEL

Stick to public transportation if you want to avoid frustrations such as high tolls on the Golden Gate Bridge, traffic jams at any time, and a notable lack of parking.

From San Francisco I–80 heads east over the Bay Bridge to Oakland and Berkeley, then continues toward Sacramento and Lake Tahoe. Heading north across the Golden Gate are Highway 1 (19th Ave. and Park Presidio Blvd.) and U.S. 101 (Van Ness Ave. and Lombard St.). Highway 1 then splits off for a beautiful drive (complete with stunning views and treacherous curves) to Stinson Beach and north along the coast. U.S. 101 continues through Marin County toward the Wine Country. South along the peninsula, U.S. 101 (known here as the Bayshore Freeway) passes San Francisco International Airport on the way to San Jose. I–280 heads south, going farther inland. This route is a bit longer milewise but sees less traffic and is fairly accurately called "The World's Most Beautiful Freeway." Highway 1 hugs the coastline south to Half Moon Bay and beyond. In the East Bay I–880 links San Jose with Oakland, where it connects with I–80 to San Francisco or Berkeley and Sacramento. AAA's "San Francisco Bay Region" road map will keep you on track.

BRIDGE TOLLS

The toll on the Golden Gate Bridge is $3, collected only when you travel south into San Francisco. Discount ticket books are available at the toll office next to the bridge, at many city Safeway stores, and at some gas stations. For $16 you get six crossings (available at the toll office only); $40 gets you 15 crossings. Carpoolers (three or more people per car) pay no toll 5–9 AM and 4–6 PM weekdays. All the state bridges, including the Bay Bridge, San Mateo Bridge, Dumbarton Bridge, and Richmond/San Rafael Bridge, have the same toll ($2), collected in the westbound direction. A discount book ($74 for 40 crossings), good for four months from date of purchase, is available at the toll booths and Lucky supermarkets. Carpoolers cross free 5:30–10 AM and 3–6 PM weekdays in specially marked lanes.

PARKING

If you actually find a parking space in San Francisco, it may be on the side of a sheer precipice. Should you succeed in the hideous task of parallel parking on this 90-degree slope, **remember to curb your wheels.** Here's how: turn the wheels so they point toward the curb (to the left when facing uphill, to the right when facing downhill), set the emergency brake, and if you're in a stick shift, leave the car in gear. Not only will this keep you from rolling into other cars, it will also help you avoid a $23 ticket from the San Francisco Police Department.

The large Sutter-Stockton Garage (444 Stockton St.) has reasonable rates and is within walking distance of Union Square, Chinatown, and North Beach. The cheapest lot near Fisherman's Wharf is the Wharf Garage (350 Beach St., between Taylor and Mason Sts.). Parking in the East Bay is less difficult, though finding a spot near the UC Berkeley campus is no easy task. Try Sather Gate Garage (2450 Durant Ave., just west of Telegraph Ave.).

CHILDREN IN SAN FRANCISCO

If you are renting a car don't forget to **arrange for a car seat** when you reserve.

FLYING

If your children are two or older **ask about children's airfares.** As a general rule, infants under two not occupying a seat fly at greatly reduced fares or even for free. Experts agree that it's a good idea to use safety seats aloft for children weighing less than 40 pounds. Airlines set their own policies: U.S. carriers usually require that the child be ticketed, even if he or she is young enough to ride free, since the seats must be strapped into regular seats. Do **check your airline's policy about using safety seats during takeoff and landing.** And since safety seats are not allowed just everywhere in the plane, get your seat assignments early.

When reserving, **request children's meals or a freestanding bassinet** if you need them. But note that bulkhead seats, where you must sit to use the bassinet, may lack an overhead bin or storage space on the floor.

LODGING

Most hotels in San Francisco allow children under a certain age to stay in their parents' room at no extra charge, but others charge for them as extra adults; be sure to **find out the cutoff age for children's discounts.**

Circled North Beach for half an hour? Ready to dump your car any place it fits? Think again. The city issues 2.4 million parking tickets a year—and the number is only expected to increase.

CONCIERGES

Concierges, found in many hotels, can help you with theater tickets and dinner reservations: a good one with connections may be able to get you seats for a hot show or prime-time dinner reservations at the restaurant of the moment. You can also turn to your hotel's concierge for help with travel arrangements, sightseeing plans, services ranging from aromatherapy to zipper repair, and emergencies. **Always tip** a concierge who has been of assistance.

CONSUMER PROTECTION

Whenever shopping or buying travel services in San Francisco, **pay with a major credit card** so you can cancel payment or get reimbursed if there's a problem. If you're doing business with a particular company for the first time, **contact your local Better Business Bureau and the attorney general's offices** in your state and the company's home state, as well. Have any complaints been filed? Finally, if you're buying a package or tour, always **consider travel insurance** that includes default coverage (*see* Insurance, *below*).

LOCAL BBBS • Council of Better Business Bureaus (4200 Wilson Blvd., Suite 800, Arlington, VA 22203, tel. 703/276–0100, fax 703/525–8277).

CUSTOMS & DUTIES

When shopping, **keep receipts** for all purchases. Upon reentering the country, **be ready to show customs officials what you've bought.** If you feel a duty is incorrect or object to the way your clearance was handled, note the inspector's badge number and ask to see a supervisor. If the problem isn't resolved, write to the appropriate authorities, beginning with the port director at your point of entry.

IN AUSTRALIA

Australia residents who are 18 or older may bring home $A400 worth of souvenirs and gifts (including jewelry), 250 cigarettes or 250 grams of tobacco, and 1,125 ml of alcohol (including wine, beer, and spirits). Residents under 18 may bring back $A200 worth of goods. Prohibited items include meat products. Seeds, plants, and fruits need to be declared upon arrival.

INFORMATION • Australian Customs Service (Regional Director, Box 8, Sydney, NSW 2001, tel. 02/9213–2000, fax 02/9213–4000).

IN CANADA

Canadian residents who have been out of Canada for at least 7 days may bring home C$500 worth of goods duty-free. If you've been away less than 7 days but more than 48 hours, the duty-free allowance drops to C$200; if your trip lasts 24–48 hours, the allowance is C$50. You may not pool allowances with family members. Goods claimed under the C$500 exemption may follow you by mail; those claimed under the lesser exemptions must accompany you. Alcohol and tobacco products may be included in the 7-day and 48-hour exemptions but not in the 24-hour exemption. If you meet the age requirements of the province or territory through which you reenter Canada, you may bring in, duty-free, 1.14 liters (40 imperial ounces) of wine or liquor or 24 12-ounce cans or bottles of beer or ale. If you are 16 or older you may bring in, duty-free, 200 cigarettes and 50 cigars. Check ahead of time with Revenue Canada or the Department of Agriculture for policies regarding meat products, seeds, plants, and fruits.

You may send an unlimited number of gifts worth up to C$60 each duty-free to Canada. Label the package UNSOLICITED GIFT—VALUE UNDER $60. Alcohol and tobacco are excluded.

INFORMATION • Revenue Canada (2265 St. Laurent Blvd. S, Ottawa, Ontario K1G 4K3, tel. 613/ 993–0534; 800/461–9999 in Canada).

IN NEW ZEALAND

Homeward-bound residents 17 or older may bring back $700 worth of souvenirs and gifts. Your duty-free allowance also includes 4.5 liters of wine or beer; one 1,125-ml bottle of spirits; and either 200 cigarettes, 250 grams of tobacco, 50 cigars, or a combination of the three up to 250 grams. Prohibited items include meat products, seeds, plants, and fruits.

INFORMATION • New Zealand Customs (Custom House, 50 Anzac Ave., Box 29, Auckland, tel. 09/ 359–6655, fax 09/359–6732).

IN THE U.K.

From countries outside the EU, including the United States, you may bring home, duty-free, 200 cigarettes or 50 cigars; 1 liter of spirits or 2 liters of fortified or sparkling wine or liqueurs; 2 liters of still table wine; 60 ml of perfume; 250 ml of toilet water; plus £136 worth of other goods, including gifts and souvenirs. If returning from outside the EU, prohibited items include meat products, seeds, plants, and fruits.

INFORMATION • HM Customs and Excise (Dorset House, Stamford St., Bromley Kent BR1 1XX, tel. 020/7202–4227).

IN THE U.S.

INFORMATION • U.S. Customs Service (inquiries, 1300 Pennsylvania Ave. NW, Washington, DC 20229, tel. 202/927–6724; complaints, Office of Regulations and Rulings, 1300 Pennsylvania Ave. NW, Washington, DC 20229; registration of equipment, Registration Information, 1300 Pennsylvania Ave. NW, Washington, DC 20229, tel. 202/927–0540).

DINING

The restaurants we list are the cream of the crop in each price category.

RESERVATIONS & DRESS

Reservations are always a good idea: we mention them only when they're essential or are not accepted. Book as far ahead as you can, and reconfirm as soon as you arrive. None of the restaurants in this guide have particularly formal dress requirements.

DISABILITIES & ACCESSIBILITY

The Bay Area is an important national center for resources for people with disabilities, thanks mostly to Berkeley's Center for Independent Living—a group of people with disabilities who in the early '70s began fighting for their right to be accepted at UC Berkeley.

There are now more than 300 independent living centers nationwide, designed to help people with disabilities discover their potential; you'll find them throughout the Bay Area (see below). In addition, the American Foundation for the Blind has brochures and catalogs to help people access resources. Lighthouse Center for the Blind and Visually Disabled has assisting devices (canes, talking watches) and can direct people to support groups. Lion's Center for the Blind, in Oakland and San Jose, also has resources. Peninsula Center for the Blind has orientation and mobility specialists, social workers, and short-term counseling. For people with hearing impairments, the Hearing Society for the Bay Area provides social services, interpreting, vocational rehab, and referrals.

SAN FRANCISCO RESOURCES • **Independent Living Center** (649 Mission St., Third Floor, San Francisco, tel. 415/543–6222). **American Foundation for the Blind** (111 Pine St., Suite 725, San Francisco, tel. 415/392–4845). **Lighthouse for the Blind and Visually Disabled** (214 Van Ness Ave., at Grove St., San Francisco, tel. 415/431–1481). **Hearing Society for the Bay Area** (870 Market St., Suite 330, tel. 415/693–5870, TDD 415/834–1005).

EAST BAY RESOURCES • Berkeley's **Independent Living Center** (2539 Telegraph Ave., tel. 510/841–4776). Oakland's **Lion's Center for the Blind** (3834 Opal St., at 38th St., tel. 510/450–1580). In Marin County: San Rafael's **Independent Living Center** (710 4th St., tel. 415/459–6245).

SOUTH BAY RESOURCES • Santa Clara's **Independent Living Center** (1601 Civic Center Dr., Suite 100, tel. 408/985–1243). San Jose's **Lion's Center for the Blind** (101 N. Bascom Ave., tel. 408/295–4016). Palo Alto's **Peninsula Center for the Blind** (2470 El Camino Real, Suite 107, tel. 650/858–0202).

THE GREAT OUTDOORS

In San Francisco the nonprofit Environmental Traveling Companions organizes cross-country skiing, kayaking, and rafting trips for people with disabilities. Their prices are very reasonable: One-day trips start at about $40 per person. In the East Bay the Bay Area Outreach and Recreation Program organizes sports events and outdoor activities for people with disabilities, with programs for youth, adults, and senior citizens. California State Parks has a discount pass ($3.50) that gets you 50% off all parking and camping fees (provided the fees are more than $3). You can purchase the pass at any state park visitor center, or by mail.

RESOURCES • **Environmental Traveling Companions** (Fort Mason Center, Bldg. C, tel.415/474–7662). **Bay Area Outreach and Recreation Program** (tel. 510/643–9103). **California State Parks** (Disabled Discount Pass Program, Box 942896, Sacramento 94296-0001, tel. 916/653–6995).

LODGING

When discussing accessibility with an operator or reservations agent **ask hard questions.** Are there any stairs, inside *or* out? Are there grab bars next to the toilet *and* in the shower/tub? How wide is the doorway to the room? To the bathroom? For the most extensive facilities meeting the latest legal specifications **opt for newer accommodations.**

TRANSPORTATION

Transit organizations in the Bay Area have joined ranks to create an ID card, called the Regional Transit Connection (RTC) Discount Card, which gives people with disabilities discounts on travel throughout nine Bay Area counties; each transit company decides what kind of a discount to give (*see* Bus Travel to and from San Francisco, *above, and* Subway Travel, *below*). You can **get a pass at any transit office** by filling out a form and getting proof of disability from your doctor.

The RTC Discount Card is available at the BART Customer Service Office, open weekdays 9–11:30 and 2–4:30. With the ID you may purchase a $16 BART ticket for $4. All BART stations have elevators; call for a daily update on which elevators are out of service. Most Muni buses are wheelchair accessible; with the discount ID you pay 35¢ instead of $1, and a monthly pass is $8; contact the Muni Discount Office for access information. All AC Transit buses are wheelchair accessible; contact AC Transit Customer Service for information on obtaining a disability ID card, which allows the bearer to pay 60¢ instead of the regular $1.25 bus fare. All Golden Gate Transit buses are wheelchair accessible, and riders with disabilities are entitled to 50% off the fare.

Some major car-rental companies are able to supply hand-controlled vehicles with a minimum of 24-hours advance notice. Avis will install hand-control mechanisms at no extra charge if given a day's notice. Hertz asks for 48-hour notice (except at San Francisco International Airport, where a day will suffice). Rental companies often can't install hand controls on economy cars.

Apria Healthcare rents manual wheelchairs starting at $10 per day or $80 per month. In the East Bay, Grand Mar rents and repairs wheelchairs. Manual wheelchairs rent for $15 the first day, $5 each subsequent day, or $50–$100 a month; power wheelchairs are $20 a day, $400–$500 a month.

RESOURCES • BART Customer Service Office (800 Madison St., at the Lake Merritt BART station, Oakland, tel. 510/464–2133, TDD/TTY 510/839–2220; 510/834–5438 for elevator information). **Muni Discount ID Office** (tel. 415/923–6070, TDD/TTY 415/923–6366). **AC Transit** (tel. 510/817–1717; 510/891–4706 for customer service). **Golden Gate Transit** (tel. 415/332–6600). **Avis** (tel. 800/331–1212). **Hertz** (tel. 800/654–3131, TDD 800/654–2280). **Apria Healthcare** (480 Carlton Ct., South San Francisco, tel. 415/864–6999). **Grand Mar** (1311 63rd St., at Doyle St., Emeryville, tel. 510/428–0441).

COMPLAINTS • Disability Rights Section (U.S. Department of Justice, Civil Rights Division, Box 66738, Washington, DC 20035-6738, tel. 202/514–0301; 800/514–0301; 202/514–0301 TTY; 800/514–0301 TTY, fax 202/307–1198) for general complaints. **Aviation Consumer Protection Division** (*see* Air Travel, *above*) for airline-related problems. **Civil Rights Office** (U.S. Department of Transportation, Departmental Office of Civil Rights, S-30, 400 7th St. SW, Room 10215, Washington, DC 20590, tel. 202/366–4648, fax 202/366–9371) for problems with surface transportation.

TRAVEL AGENCIES

In the United States, although the Americans with Disabilities Act requires that travel firms serve the needs of all travelers, some agencies specialize in working with people with disabilities.

TRAVELERS WITH MOBILITY PROBLEMS • Access Adventures (206 Chestnut Ridge Rd., Rochester, NY 14624, tel. 716/889–9096), run by a former physical-rehabilitation counselor. **Accessible Journeys** (35 W. Sellers Ave. Ridley Park, PA 19078, tel. 610/521–0339 or 800/846–4537, fax 610/521–6959). **Accessible Vans of Hawaii, Activity and Travel Agency** (186 Mehani Circle, Kihei, HI 96753, tel. 808/879–5521 or 800/303–3750, fax 808/879–0649). **Accessible Vans of the Rockies, Activity and Travel Agency** (2040 W. Hamilton Pl., Sheridan, CO 80110, tel. 303/806–5047 or 888/837–0065, fax 303/781–2329). **CareVacations** (5-5110 50th Ave., Leduc, Alberta T9E 6V4, tel. 780/986–6404 or 877/478–7827, fax 780/986–8332) has group tours and is especially helpful with cruise vacations. **Flying Wheels Travel** (143 W. Bridge St., Box 382, Owatonna, MN 55060, tel. 507/451–5005 or 800/535–6790, fax 507/451–1685). **Hinsdale Travel Service** (201 E. Ogden Ave., Suite 100, Hinsdale, IL 60521, tel. 630/325–1335, fax 630/325–1342).

TRAVELERS WITH DEVELOPMENTAL DISABILITIES • New Directions (5276 Hollister Ave., Suite 207, Santa Barbara, CA 93111, tel. 805/967–2841 or 888/967–2841, fax 805/964–7344).

DISCOUNTS & DEALS

Be a smart shopper and **compare all your options** before making decisions. A plane ticket bought with a promotional coupon from travel clubs, coupon books, and direct-mail offers may not be cheaper than the least expensive fare from a discount ticket agency. And always keep in mind that what you get is just as important as what you save.

DISCOUNT RESERVATIONS

To save money **look into discount-reservations services** with toll-free numbers, which use their buying power to get a better price on hotels, airline tickets, even car rentals. When booking a room, always **call the hotel's local toll-free number** (if one is available) rather than the central reservations number—you'll often get a better price. Always ask about special packages or corporate rates.

AIRLINE TICKETS • Tel. 800/FLY–4–LESS. Tel. 800/FLY–ASAP.

HOTEL ROOMS • Accommodations Express (tel. 800/444–7666). **Central Reservation Service (CRS)** (tel. 800/548–3311). **Hotel Reservations Network** (tel. 800/964–6835). **Quickbook** (tel. 800/789–9887). **Room Finders USA** (tel. 800/473–7829). **RMC Travel** (tel. 800/245–5738). **Steigenberger Reservation Service** (tel. 800/223–5652).

PACKAGE DEALS

Don't confuse packages and guided tours. When you buy a package, you travel on your own, just as though you had planned the trip yourself. Fly/drive packages, which combine airfare and car rental, are often a good deal. In cities, ask the local visitor's bureau about hotel packages that include tickets to major museum exhibits or other special events.

DIVERS' ALERT

Do not fly within 24 hours of scuba diving.

EMERGENCIES

HOSPITALS • San Francisco General Hospital and the Medical Center at the University of California both have 24-hour emergency rooms. Physician Access Medical Center is a drop-in clinic in the Financial District. Access Health Care provides drop-in medical care at Davies Medical Center.

RESOURCES • **San Francisco General Hospital** (1001 Potrero Ave., tel. 415/206–8000). **Medical Center at the University of California, San Francisco** (505 Parnassus Ave., at 3rd Ave., near Golden Gate Park, tel. 415/476–1000). **Physician Access Medical Center** (26 California St., tel. 415/397–2881); open weekdays 7:30–5. **Access Health Care** (Davies Medical Center, Castro St. at Duboce Ave., tel. 415/565–6600); open daily 8–8.

24-HOUR PHARMACIES • **Walgreens** (498 Castro, at 18th St., tel. 415/861–3136; 25 Point Lobos, near 42nd Ave. and Geary St., tel. 415/386–0736; 3201 Divisadero St., at Lombard St., tel. 415/931–6417).

GAY & LESBIAN TRAVEL

San Francisco's gay community, particularly in the Castro district, is extremely supportive and close-knit. If you're trying to find your niche (be it a support group or a political organization), some friendly asking around at one of the Castro cafés or diners should get you helpful advice, if not a pal. Café Flore (*see* Castro District *in* Chapter 5), despite all the winking and whispering going on, is actually a great spot to start getting down to business with those in the know. If you're wired, the *Gay Guys' Guide to San Francisco* (www.niche.net/GayGuide2SanFran) is an excellent, humor-packed guide to gay life in the big city—and it lists dozens of local gay clubs, with interests from hiking to painting to political action.

Though the lesbian community doesn't center around a single district or neighborhood, Valencia Street in San Francisco's Mission District (*see* Mission District *in* Chapter 2) has several women's bookstores and organizations. Red Dora's Bearded Lady (*see* Mission District *in* Chapter 5) is a café and performance space frequented by young women, primarily in their twenties. In Berkeley the bookstore and coffeehouse Mama Bears hosts readings and social events in a warm, supportive environment.

LOCAL ORGANIZATIONS

In San Francisco, Communities United Against Violence provides crisis counseling and referrals for gays and lesbians who are victims of antigay violence. The Lavender Youth Recreation and Information Center is a social and support organization for gays, lesbians, and transgenders 23 years old and younger. If you call Monday through Saturday 6:30 PM to 9 PM, you can talk to other young gays and lesbians or a counselor (during off-hours you get recorded information). In Berkeley, the Pacific Center for Human Growth is a well-known gay and lesbian gathering place. The organization offers counseling, social gatherings, rap sessions, and support groups covering topics such as coming out. Check out the bulletin boards, which advertise everything from apartment rentals to social invitations. Drop-in hours are weekdays 10–10, Saturday noon–4, and Sunday 6 PM–10 PM. Their Lavender Line: Lesbian and Gay Switchboard and Counseling Services gives out information and referrals. In Palo Alto, the Stanford University Lesbian/Gay/Bisexual Community Center knows all about gay and lesbian happenings around campus and can refer you to a vast number of support groups and resources. During the school year the center is generally open weekdays from noon until 6; hours vary during summer.

INFORMATION • In San Francisco: **Communities United Against Violence** (973 Market St., Suite 500, tel. 415/777–5500 or 415/333–4357 for 24-hr emergency hot line). **Lavender Youth Recreation and Information Center** (3543 18th St., Second Floor, tel. 415/863–3636 or 800/246–7743). In Berkeley: The **Pacific Center for Human Growth** (2712 Telegraph Ave., at Derby St., tel. 510/548–8283). Pacific Center's **Lavender Line: Lesbian and Gay Switchboard and Counseling Services** (tel. 510/841–6224). In Palo Alto: **Stanford University Lesbian/Gay/Bisexual Community Center** (Fire Truck House, Santa Teresa St., Stanford Campus, Palo Alto, tel. 650/725–4222).

AIDS SUPPORT GROUPS & ACTIVISM

The San Francisco AIDS Foundation is an umbrella organization that will refer you to whichever of the city's AIDS-related group best suits you. They also operate a trilingual AIDS Hotline. For late-night counseling or information, call the AIDS/HIV Hotline, open nightly 5 PM–5 AM. The newly opened AIDS Health Project (AHP) Castro Center, run in conjunction with UCSF's AIDS Health Project, provides emotional support and counseling; every Friday they offer free, confidential HIV testing.

San Francisco has two chapters of the AIDS Coalition To Unleash Power (ACT UP), a national organization that advocates "militant, nonviolent, direct action" for increased AIDS research and an end to discrimination against those living with AIDS. ACT UP rallies in San Francisco have frequently made headlines because of their confrontational tactics. ACT UP SF meets every Monday at 7:30 PM at their community center; ACT UP Golden Gate holds meetings in its offices every Tuesday at 7:30 PM.

INFORMATION • San Francisco AIDS Foundation (1 6th St., tel. 415/487–3000; for hot line, 415/863–2437 or 800/367–2437 in northern California). **AIDS/HIV Nightline** (tel. 415/434–2437 or 800/273–2437 in northern California). **AIDS Health Project** (AHP) **Castro Center** (400 Castro St., at Market St., tel. 415/476–3902). **ACT UP SF** (1884 Market St., at Laguna St., tel. 415/522–2907). **ACT UP Golden Gate** (592B Castro St., tel. 415/252–9200; for hot line, 415/281–0680).

GAY- AND LESBIAN-FRIENDLY TRAVEL AGENCIES • Different Roads Travel (8383 Wilshire Blvd., Suite 902, Beverly Hills, CA 90211, tel. 323/651–5557 or 800/429–8747, fax 323/651–3678). **Kennedy Travel** (314 Jericho Turnpike, Floral Park, NY 11001, tel. 516/352–4888 or 800/237–7433, fax 516/354–8849). **Now Voyager** (4406 18th St., San Francisco, CA 94114, tel. 415/626–1169 or 800/255–6951, fax 415/626–8626). **Skylink Travel and Tour** (1006 Mendocino Ave., Santa Rosa, CA 95401, tel. 707/546–9888 or 800/225–5759, fax 707/546–9891), serving lesbian travelers.

PUBLICATIONS

The weekly *Bay Area Reporter (B.A.R.)* and the biweekly *Bay Times* are the two main gay and lesbian papers. Both have excellent news (local, national, and international), though the *B.A.R.* is heavier on news coverage and lighter on events and listings. The biweekly *Outnow* is a thin, San Jose–based forum for gay and lesbian news and local events; it also comes out in South Bay and East Bay editions. *The Slant* covers regional and county news for Marin's gay and lesbian community.

A Different Light (*see* Books *in* Chapter 3), the Bay Area's best gay bookstore, stocks a wide selection of "queerzines," including *Bear* ($7), which bills itself as "the magazine for hairy gay men"; *Girl Jock* ($4), the tongue-in-cheek magazine for girls who like sports; and *Drummer* ($7), for the leather fetishist. Also look for *On Our Backs* ($6) and *Girlfriends* ($5), two popular bimonthly lesbian pseudoporn mags, both based in San Francisco. The quarterly *Anything That Moves* ($6) is written specifically for bisexuals.

HOLIDAYS

Major national holidays include New Year's Day; Martin Luther King Jr. Day (3rd Mon. in Jan.); President's Day (3rd Mon. in Feb.); Memorial Day (last Mon. in May); Independence Day (July 4); Labor Day (1st Mon. in Sept.); Thanksgiving Day (4th Thurs. in Nov.); Christmas Eve and Christmas Day; and New Year's Eve.

INSURANCE

The most useful travel insurance plan is a comprehensive policy that includes coverage for trip cancellation and interruption, default, trip delay, and medical expenses (with a waiver for preexisting conditions).

Without insurance you will lose all or most of your money if you cancel your trip, regardless of the reason. Default insurance covers you if your tour operator, airline, or cruise line goes out of business. Trip-delay covers expenses that arise because of bad weather or mechanical delays. Study the fine print when comparing policies.

British and Australian citizens need extra medical coverage when traveling overseas.

Always **buy travel policies directly from the insurance company**; if you buy it from a cruise line, airline, or tour operator that goes out of business you probably will not be covered for the agency or operator's default, a major risk. Before you make any purchase **review your existing health and home-owner's policies** to find what they cover away from home.

TRAVEL INSURERS • In the United States **Access America** (6600 W. Broad St., Richmond, VA 23230, tel. 804/285–3300 or 800/284–8300), **Travel Guard International** (1145 Clark St., Stevens Point, WI 54481, tel. 715/345–0505 or 800/826–1300). In Canada **Voyager Insurance** (44 Peel Center Dr., Brampton, Ontario L6T 4M8, tel. 905/791–8700; 800/668–4342 in Canada).

INSURANCE INFORMATION • In the United Kingdom the **Association of British Insurers** (51–55 Gresham St., London EC2V 7HQ, tel. 020/7600–3333, fax 020/7696–8999). In Australia the **Insurance Council of Australia** (tel. 03/9614–1077, fax 03/9614–7924).

LODGING

The lodgings we list are the cream of the crop in each price category. We always list the facilities that are available—but we don't specify whether they cost extra: When pricing accommodations, always ask what's included and what costs extra.

APARTMENT RENTALS

If you want a home base that's roomy enough for a family and comes with cooking facilities **consider a furnished rental.** These can save you money, especially if you're traveling with a group. Home-exchange directories sometimes list rentals as well as exchanges.

INTERNATIONAL AGENTS • Europa-Let/Tropical Inn-Let (92 N. Main St., Ashland, OR 97520, tel. 541/482–5806 or 800/462–4486, fax 541/482–0660). **Hideaways International** (767 Islington St., Portsmouth, NH 03801, tel. 603/430–4433 or 800/843–4433, fax 603/430–4444; membership $99). **Hometours International** (Box 11503, Knoxville, TN 37939, tel. 423/690–8484 or 800/367–4668). **Rental Directories International** (2044 Rittenhouse Sq., Philadelphia, PA 19103, tel. 215/985–4001, fax 215/985–0323). **Rent-a-Home International** (7200 34th Ave. NW, Seattle, WA 98117, tel. 206/789–9377 or 800/964–1891, fax 206/789–9379). **Vacation Home Rentals Worldwide** (235 Kensington Ave., Norwood, NJ 07648, tel. 201/767–9393 or 800/633–3284, fax 201/767–5510).

HOME EXCHANGES

If you would like to exchange your home for someone else's **join a home-exchange organization,** which will send you its updated listings of available exchanges for a year and will include your own listing in at least one of them. It's up to you to make specific arrangements.

EXCHANGE CLUBS • HomeLink International (Box 650, Key West, FL 33041, tel. 305/294–7766 or 800/638–3841, fax 305/294–1448; $93 per year). **Intervac U.S.** (Box 590504, San Francisco, CA 94159, tel. 800/756–4663, fax 415/435–7440; $83 for catalogs).

HOSTELS

No matter what your age you can **save on lodging costs by staying at hostels.** In some 5,000 locations in more than 70 countries around the world, including the Bay Area, Hostelling International (HI), the umbrella group for a number of national youth-hostel associations, offers single-sex, dorm-style beds and, at many hostels, couples rooms and family accommodations. Membership in any HI national hostel association, open to travelers of all ages, allows you to stay in HI-affiliated hostels at member rates (one-year membership is about $25; hostels run about $10–$25 per night). Members also have priority if the hostel is full; they're eligible for discounts around the world, even on rail and bus travel in some countries.

ORGANIZATIONS • Australian Youth Hostel Association (10 Mallett St., Camperdown, NSW 2050, tel. 02/9565–1699, fax 02/9565–1325). **Hostelling International—American Youth Hostels** (733 15th St. NW, Suite 840, Washington, DC 20005, tel. 202/783–6161, fax 202/783–6171). **Hostelling International—Canada** (400–205 Catherine St., Ottawa, Ontario K2P 1C3, tel. 613/237–7884, fax 613/237–7868). **Youth Hostel Association of England and Wales** (Trevelyan House, 8 St. Stephen's Hill, St. Albans, Hertfordshire AL1 2DY, tel. 01727/855215 or 01727/845047, fax 01727/844126). **Youth Hostels Association of New Zealand** (Box 436, Christchurch, New Zealand, tel. 03/379–9970, fax 03/365–4476). Membership in the United States $25, in Canada C$26.75, in the United Kingdom £9.30, in Australia $44, in New Zealand $24.

HOTELS

All hotels listed have private bath unless otherwise noted.

TOLL-FREE NUMBERS • Best Western (tel. 800/528–1234). **Choice** (tel. 800/221–2222). **Comfort** (tel. 800/228–5150). **Days Inn** (tel. 800/325–2525). **Doubletree and Red Lion Hotels** (tel. 800/222–8733). **Holiday Inn** (tel. 800/465–4329). **Howard Johnson** (tel. 800/654–4656). **La Quinta** (tel. 800/531–5900). **Marriott** (tel. 800/228–9290). **Quality Inn** (tel. 800/228–5151). **Radisson** (tel. 800/333–3333). **Ramada** (tel. 800/228–2828). **Sheraton** (tel. 800/325–3535).

MAIL & SHIPPING

POST OFFICES • San Francisco's Civic Center post office will hold letters addressed to general delivery for 10 days. In Berkeley the main post office also holds mail for 10 days. A passport or valid ID is required to pick up general delivery mail. The Postal Answer Line is a 24-hour automated service that provides post office hours, postal rates, and more.

ALTERNATIVE AIRWAVES

A number of alternative broadcasters air political back-and-forths, eclectic music playlists, and radical chitchat from undisclosed (sometimes mobile) locations on unoccupied frequencies. Due to their low broadcasting power, you need to be nearby to pick up the following stations' broadcasts. Radio Libre (103.3 FM) is heard in the Mission, parts of Noe Valley, and in the SoMa area; San Francisco Liberation Radio (93.7 FM) can be picked up in the Richmond and Sunset districts; North Beach Radio (88.1 FM) transmits in the area between Columbus Avenue and Pier 39 in San Francisco; and Free Radio Berkeley (104.1 FM) can be heard in north Oakland and Berkeley.

Berkeley-based KPFA (94.1 FM), a much-loved listener-sponsored station, broadcasts classical, reggae, rap, soul, folk, and blues music as well as national news. Also tune in for interviews with artists and members of special-interest groups you didn't know even existed. KPOO (89.5 FM), the only African-American-owned and -operated radio station west of the Mississippi, has great DJs spinning everything from Coltrane to salsa. Listener-sponsored KCSM (91.1 FM), out of San Mateo, is 100% jazz. In the South Bay Foothill Junior College's KFJC (89.7 FM) beams out all kinds of music plus some outstanding shows.

News junkies have a few options. On the AM dial, San Francisco–based KCBS (740 AM) has rapid-fire news bites around the clock. They may not have the most in-depth coverage, but they certainly have the fastest. For higher-quality reporting, try San Francisco's public radio station KQED (88.5 FM), which broadcasts a lot of National Public Radio programming. All Things Considered starts at 4:30 PM weekdays and is repeated at 11 PM (weekends 2 PM and 5 PM). The BBC News Hour airs weekdays at 9 PM and is repeated at 1 AM (weekends 11:30 AM and 3 PM). San Francisco–based KALW (91.7 FM) also plays NPR and BBC throughout the day.

INFORMATION • General Delivery: Recipient's name, General Delivery, San Francisco, CA 94142). **Postal Answer Line** (tel. 800/725–2161). **San Francisco's Civic Center post office** (101 Hyde St., at Golden Gate Ave., 94142). **Berkeley's main post office** (2000 Allston Way, Berkeley 94704).

MEDIA

NEWSPAPERS & MAGAZINES

The Bay Area's two big dailies, the *San Francisco Chronicle* (morning) and the *San Francisco Examiner* (afternoon), are equally unremarkable. The *Chron* does have some great columns, and it has strangely endeared itself to local readers despite its lightweight coverage. The combined *Chronicle-Examiner* Sunday paper comes with the "Pink Section," useful for its extensive movie reviews and listings of all sorts of upcoming events.

The *Oakland Tribune,* formerly one of the country's premier African-American–owned dailies, has been reduced to a small-town rag. Many Berkeleyans read the student-produced *Daily Californian,* but it, too, wavers in the quality department. The *Marin Independent Journal* focuses mainly on Marin County but also tackles some more general issues. The big surprise in Bay Area dailies is the *San Jose Mercury News,* a paper that's read throughout the area and is highly respected in the journalism community.

You'll find better local coverage (and often better writing) in the Bay Area's many free weekly newspapers. The *San Francisco Bay Guardian* has run daring investigative pieces that the dailies don't dare print; also look for the *Guardian*'s "Best of the Bay Area" special in late July or early August and the "Insider's Guide" issue in February. While the *SF Weekly* occasionally comes up with great cover stories, it's popular for its extensive events listings and writers' biting wits. You'll find a lot of good information in the Bay Area's many gay and lesbian publications (*see* Gay & Lesbian Travel, *above*).

The *East Bay Express* comes in two parts: The front section has the East Bay's best local coverage of politics and issues, and the varied front-page articles (which may discuss Oakland history, highlight current issues, or showcase active locals) are usually well written and researched. The "Billboard" section has the best events listings in the East Bay as well as a huge classified section. Marin County's *Pacific Sun* has an events calendar and decent (if scant) local news. The much better *Metro* covers the whole South Bay, with high-quality feature articles and events listings.

If you're in the mood to hear a good yarn, call the Public Library's Dial-a-Story (tel. 415/437–4880), where the tale changes once a week.

ON-LINE RESOURCES

Do **check out the World Wide Web** when you're planning your visit. You'll find everything from up-to-date weather forecasts to virtual tours of famous cities. Fodor's Web site is a great place to start your on-line travels. For more information specifically on the Bay Area, your first stop should be the San Francisco Bay Resource Net, which has up-to-date links with more than a hundred Web sites covering Bay Area government, transportation, media, entertainment, museums and other points of interest, the arts, sports, restaurants, and more. Virtually San Francisco offers links to everything from ballroom dancing in the Bay to home pages for some of the area's most bizarre personalities. In line with its print and television incarnations, SF Gate offers pithy news stories but does showcase excellent photographs of the area along with up-to-date visitors' information. Yahoo has a whole subsection devoted to San Francisco and is chock-full of links to entertainment, art, housing, travel—you name it. Equally useful is the Bay Area Transit Info Project, which offers maps, schedules, and fares for all Bay Area transport lines (a total of nine counties). The current issues of the *Bay Guardian* and *SF Weekly* are yours to peruse on-line, while KUSF (*see* Radio, *below*) runs a Web site with information on Bay Area clubs, upcoming shows, and other goodies. The *San Jose Mercury News* has received praise as one of the best on-line newspapers in the country, and it's chock-full of local reports. The Gay Guys' Guide to San Francisco (*see* Gay & Lesbian Travel, *above*) is a humor-packed guide to gay life in the city.

What about when you're in town without a laptop computer? Most public libraries have terminals, but those at the San Francisco Main Library (100 Larkin St.), are brand new and state-of-the-art, with Net and Web access; check out its on-line catalog. For on-line access in cafés, *see box* Overcaffeinated on the Information Superhighway *in* Chapter 5.

WEB SITES • San Francisco Bay Interactive (www.sftoday.com). **Virtually San Francisco** (www.virtually.com/san_francisco). **SF Gate** (www.sfgate.com). **Yahoo** (sfbay.yahoo.com). **Bay Area Transit Info Project** (www.transitinfo.org). **Fodor's** (www.fodors.com). **Guardian Online** (www.sfbg.com). **SF Weekly** (www.sfweekly.com). **KUSF** (web.usfca.edu/kusf). *San Jose Mercury News* (www.sjmercury.com). *San Francisco Main Library* (sfpl.lib.ca.us).

RADIO

The Bay Area radio scene is largely dominated by Top 40, classic rock, and soft rock megastations. Set your dial to live 105 (105.3 FM) or KOME (98.5 FM) for modern rock, for classical music tune to KDFC (102.1 FM), and for country tunes, KSAN (94.9 FM). Browse the far left end of the FM range to find some less conventional programming. And keep in mind that the Bay Area's many hills mean that not all the stations listed here will be in range all the time. A few of the Bay's best: UC Berkeley's KALX (90.7

FM), a cool, alternative college station run by an all-volunteer staff, can be counted on for the eclectic, the avant-garde, and the noisy. KUSF (90.3 FM) comes out of the University of San Francisco, playing new music, ethnic music, and specialty shows.

MONEY MATTERS

Prices throughout this guide are given for adults. Substantially reduced fees are almost always available for children, students, and senior citizens. For information on taxes, *see* Taxes, *below*.

ATMS

ATM LOCATIONS • Cirrus (tel. 800/424–7787). **Plus** (tel. 800/843–7587).

CREDIT CARDS

REPORTING LOST CARDS • American Express (tel. 800/528–4800). **Discover** (tel. 800/347–2683). **Diners Club** (tel. 800/234–6377). **MasterCard** (tel. 800/307–7309). **Visa** (tel. 800/336–8472).

PACKING

When packing for a vacation in the San Francisco Bay Area, **prepare for temperature variations.** An hour's drive can take you up or down many degrees, and the variation from daytime to nighttime in a single location is often marked. The city can be chilly at any time of year, especially in summer when the fog is apt to descend and linger. Bring sweaters, jackets, and clothes for layering; you'll also want shorts or cool cottons for summer. Always tuck in a bathing suit, since many lodgings have pools and hot tubs.

In your carry-on luggage **bring an extra pair of eyeglasses or contact lenses** and **enough of any medication you take** to last the entire trip. You may also want your doctor to write a spare prescription using the drug's generic name, since brand names may vary from country to country. In luggage to be checked, **never pack prescription drugs or valuables.** To avoid customs delays, carry medications in their original packaging. And don't forget to copy down and carry addresses of offices that handle refunds of lost traveler's checks.

CHECKING LUGGAGE

How many carry-on bags you can bring with you is up to the airline. Most allow two, but not always, so **make sure that everything you carry aboard will fit under your seat, and get to the gate early.** Note that if you have a seat at the back of the plane, you'll probably board first, while the overhead bins are still empty.

If you are flying internationally, note that baggage allowances may be determined not by piece but by weight—generally 88 pounds (40 kilograms) in first class, 66 pounds (30 kilograms) in business class, and 44 pounds (20 kilograms) in economy.

Airline liability for baggage is limited to $1,250 per person on flights within the United States. On international flights it amounts to $9.07 per pound or $20 per kilogram for checked baggage (roughly $640 per 70-pound bag) and $400 per passenger for unchecked baggage. You can buy additional coverage at check-in for about $10 per $1,000 of coverage, but it excludes a rather extensive list of items, shown on your airline ticket.

Before departure **itemize your bags' contents** and their worth, and label the bags with your name, address, and phone number. (If you use your home address, cover it so that potential thieves can't see it readily.) Inside each bag **pack a copy of your itinerary.** At check-in **make sure that each bag is correctly tagged** with the destination airport's three-letter code. If your bags arrive damaged or fail to arrive at all, file a written report with the airline before leaving the airport.

PASSPORTS & VISAS

U.K. CITIZENS • U.S. Embassy Visa Information Line (tel. 01891/200–290; calls cost 49p per min, 39p per min cheap rate) for U.S. visa information. **U.S. Embassy Visa Branch** (5 Upper Grosvenor Sq., London W1A 1AE) for U.S. visa information; send a self-addressed, stamped envelope. Write the **U.S. Consulate General** (Queen's House, Queen St., Belfast BTI 6EO) if you live in Northern Ireland. Write the **Office of Australia Affairs** (59th Floor, MLC Centre, 19-29 Martin Pl., Sydney NSW 2000) if you live in Australia. Write the **Office of New Zealand Affairs** (29 Fitzherbert Terr., Thorndon, Wellington) if you live in New Zealand.

PASSPORT OFFICES

The best time to apply for a passport or to renew is during the fall and winter. Before any trip, check your passport's expiration date, and, if necessary, renew it as soon as possible.

AUSTRALIAN CITIZENS • Australian Passport Office (tel. 131–232).

NEW ZEALAND CITIZENS • New Zealand Passport Office (tel. 04/494–0700 for information on how to apply; 04/474–8000 or 0800/225–050 in New Zealand for information on applications already submitted).

U.K. CITIZENS • London Passport Office (tel. 0990/210– 410) for fees and documentation requirements and to request an emergency passport.

SAFETY

In any city, personal safety is often a matter of using common sense. It's a wise idea to carry all cash, traveler's checks, credit cards, and your passport in a money belt or some other inaccessible place, such as a front or inner pocket or a bag that fits underneath your clothes. Waist packs are safe if you keep the pack part in front of your body. Even if you're only planning to be gone for only a minute, **never leave your belongings unguarded.**

Looking like you're lost singles you out as prey to unsavory predators, but sometimes you can't help it. Nonetheless, there are some basic guidelines for where not to be if you want to avoid trouble. While police cars are ubiquitous in the SoMa and Mission nightclub areas around the clock, once the bar-hoppers head home at closing time this is a dangerous area. And though parking can be maddening on weekend nights, it's never a good idea to take advantage of the many alleys and side streets around the clubs. The Tenderloin and the Civic Center are generally sketchy areas, and despite the bustle during the day your wallet may get hustled if you aren't alert. Stay away from this part of town after dark unless you are arriving and departing in a taxi. The promenades of The Embarcadero and China Basin are great for walking during the day, but their wide, open spaces turn risky after the commuters clear out. The Outer Mission and the Western Addition are also places where outsiders can be targets for crime. In any neighborhood, however, it's important to know where you're going, and show it.

SENIOR-CITIZEN TRAVEL

To qualify for age-related discounts **mention your senior-citizen status up front** when booking hotel reservations (not when checking out) and before you're seated in restaurants (not when paying the bill). When renting a car ask about promotional car-rental discounts, which can be cheaper than senior-citizen rates.

EDUCATIONAL PROGRAMS • Elderhostel (75 Federal St., Third Floor, Boston, MA 02110, tel. 877/426–8056, fax 877/426–2166).

SIGHTSEEING TOURS

See box Walk This Way, *below.*

STUDENTS IN SAN FRANCISCO

STUDENT IDS & SERVICES • Council on International Educational Exchange (CIEE, 205 E. 42nd St., 14th Floor, New York, NY 10017, tel. 212/822–2600 or 888/268–6245, fax 212/822–2699) for mail orders only, in the United States **Travel Cuts** (187 College St., Toronto, Ontario M5T 1P7, tel. 416/979–2406 or 800/667–2887) in Canada.

SUBWAY TRAVEL

Relatively clean and quiet, Bay Area Rapid Transit (BART) is a smooth subway and commuter rail system that's better at moving you from one town to another than getting you around town. Its five lines serve San Francisco, Daly City/Colma, and the East Bay from Richmond to Fremont, out to North Concord and Dublin/Pleasanton. Trains run every 10–20 minutes until midnight, with service starting up again at 4 AM weekdays, 6 AM Saturday, and 8 AM Sunday. Evenings, Sunday, and holidays only the Daly City–Dublin/Pleasanton, Pittsburg/Baypoint–Colma and Richmond–Fremont lines operate. For information on the Air-BART Shuttle to the Oakland Airport, *see* Airports & Transfers, *above*.

FARES & SCHEDULES
The cost of a BART ticket ranges from $1.10 to about $4 depending on the length of the journey. Machines at each station allow you to buy tickets worth between $1.10 and $40; new machines allow purchases with ATM cards and credit cards as well as cash. Insert your ticket into the fare gate, then hold onto it when it pops out the top—you'll need it to exit. The fare is automatically deducted from your ticket at the gate. Any amount left unused can be used on your next ride, as you can add value to old tickets. A 15-minute ride from San Francisco's Embarcadero station to Oakland's MacArthur station costs $2.35; from downtown San Francisco to Berkeley (20–25 mins) you'll pay $2.65.

BART is seriously lacking in discount fares. You can purchase one of two high value tickets: $48 worth of rides for $45 or $32 worth of rides for $30. A bus transfer to Muni or AC Transit is available from the white machines near the BART gate. The two-part ticket gets you on the bus and is also good for a ride back to the same station within three days. In San Francisco put four quarters in the machine—both bus rides are then free. In the East Bay the transfer reduces the fare to $1 for each trip. The BART Plus ticket gives a discount on local bus systems: A $28–$61 ticket entitles you to unlimited rides on any Bay Area bus system for either the first two or last two weeks of the month, plus $15–$50 worth of BART rides.

SUBWAY INFORMATION • BART (tel. 650/992–2278 or 510/465–2278, 510/464–7090, www.bart.gov for lost and found).

TAXES
HOTEL TAX
In San Francisco, hotel tax is a high 14%. It's not much better in Berkeley, at 12%. In San Jose it's 10%.

TAXIS
You can occasionally hail a cab in San Francisco, but this is not New York City: **Phone for faster service.** The metered rates for Bay Area taxis are set by each city; you may be able to negotiate a flat rate to the airport or for travel between San Francisco and the East Bay. In San Francisco the rate is $1.70, plus 30¢ each additional sixth of a mile and 30¢ for every minute of waiting time or traffic delay. In the East Bay you'll pay a $2 base fee plus $2 a mile; a ride to San Francisco can cost $25 or more. Don't forget to tip the driver (15% is typical).

TAXI COMPANIES • Veteran's Cab (tel. 415/552–1300) or **Yellow Cab** (tel. 415/626–2345). In the East Bay: **Friendly Cab** (tel. 510/536–3000) or **Yellow Cab** (tel. 510/841–8294).

TELEPHONES
The explosive growth of Silicon Valley has changed the meaning of a local call in the Bay Area. Before unintentionally racking up your very own Pacific Bell bill, be aware that calling somewhere seemingly nearby can incur toll charges, even if it's within the same area code.

The area code for Oakland, Berkeley, and the East Bay is 510; for San Francisco and Marin County it's 415; for Palo Alto and San Mateo County, 650; for San Jose it's 408; and for Santa Cruz, Monterey and Carmel, the area code is 831.

TOURS & PACKAGES
On a prepackaged tour or independent vacation everything is prearranged so you'll spend less time planning—and often get it all at a good price.

BOOKING WITH AN AGENT
Travel agents are excellent resources. But it's a good idea to collect brochures from several agencies because some agents' suggestions may be influenced by relationships with tour and package firms that

reward them for volume sales. If you have a special interest **find an agent with expertise in that area**; ASTA (*see* Travel Agencies, *below*) has a database of specialists worldwide.

Make sure your travel agent knows the accommodations and other services of the place they're recommending. Ask about the hotel's location, room size, beds, and whether it has a pool, room service, or programs for children, if you care about these. Has your agent been there in person or sent others whom you can contact?

Do some homework on your own, too: Local tourism boards can provide information about lesser-known and small-niche operators, some of which may sell only direct.

BUYER BEWARE

Each year consumers are stranded or lose their money when tour operators—even large ones with excellent reputations—go out of business. So **check out the operator.** Ask several travel agents about its reputation, and try to **book with a company that has a consumer-protection program.** (Look for information in the company's brochure.) In the United States, members of the National Tour Association and United States Tour Operators Association are required to set aside funds to cover your payments and travel arrangements in case the company defaults. It's also a good idea to choose a company that participates in the American Society of Travel Agent's Tour Operator Program (TOP); ASTA will act as mediator in any disputes between you and your tour operator.

Remember that the more your package or tour includes the better you can predict the ultimate cost of your vacation. Make sure you know exactly what is covered, and **beware of hidden costs.** Are taxes, tips, and transfers included? Entertainment and excursions? These can add up.

TOUR-OPERATOR RECOMMENDATIONS • American Society of Travel Agents (*see* Travel Agencies, *below*). **National Tour Association** (NTA, 546 E. Main St., Lexington, KY 40508, tel. 606/226–4444 or 800/682–8886). **United States Tour Operators Association** (USTOA, 342 Madison Ave., Suite 1522, New York, NY 10173, tel. 212/599–6599 or 800/468–7862, fax 212/599–6744).

PACKAGES

The companies listed below offer vacation packages in a broad price range.

AIR/HOTEL/CAR • American Airlines Fly AAway Vacations (tel. 800/321–2121). **Continental Vacations** (tel. 800/634–5555). **Delta Dream Vacations** (tel. 800/872–7786). **United Vacations** (tel. 800/328–6877). **US Airways Vacations** (tel. 800/455–0123).

HOTEL ONLY • SuperCities (139 Main St., Cambridge, MA 02142, tel. 800/333–1234).

CUSTOM PACKAGES • Amtrak's Great American Vacations (tel. 800/321–8684). **Budget World-Class Drive** (tel. 800/527–0700, 0800/181181 in the U.K.) for self-drive itineraries.

FROM THE U.K. • British Airways Holidays (Astral Towers, Betts Way, London Rd., Crawley, West Sussex RH10 2XA, tel. 01293/723–121). **Jetsave** (Sussex House, London Rd., East Grinstead, West Sussex RH19 1LD, tel. 01342/312–033). **Key to America** (1–3 Station Rd., Ashford, Middlesex TW15 2UW, tel. 01784/248–777). **Kuoni Travel Ltd.** (Kuoni House, Dorking, Surrey RH5 4AZ, tel. 01306/742–222). **Premier Holidays** (Premier Travel Center, Westbrook, Milton Rd., Cambridge CB4 1YG, tel. 01223/516–688). **Trailfinders** (42–50 Earls Court Rd., London W8 6FT, tel. 020/7937–5400; 58 Deansgate, Manchester, M3 2FF, tel. 0161/839–6969).

FOR CHEAP FARES • Trailfinders (42–50 Earls Court Rd., London W8 6FT, tel. 020/7937–5400), specialists in around-the-world fares and independent travel. **Travel Cuts** (295A Regent St., London W1R 7YA, tel. 020/7637–3161), the Canadian Students' travel service. **Flight Express Travel** (77 New Bond St., London W1Y 9DB, tel. 020/7409–3311).

THEME TRIPS

ADVENTURE • Trek America (Box 189, Rockaway, NJ 07866, tel. 201/983–1144 or 800/221–0596, fax 201/983–8551).

BALLOONING • Above the West Hot Air Ballooning (Box 2290, Yountville, CA 94599, tel. 707/944–8638 or 800/627–2759). **Bonaventura Balloon Company** (133 Wall Rd., Napa, CA 94558, tel. 707/944–2822 or 800/359–6272, fax 707/944–2220).

BICYCLING • Backroads (801 Cedar St., Berkeley, CA 94710-1800, tel. 510/527–1555 or 800/462–2848, fax 510/527–1444).

GOLF • Golf Pacific Coast (1267 Saratoga Ave., Ventura, CA 93003, tel. 800/335–3534).

WALK THIS WAY

Wok Wiz Chinatown Tours and Cooking Company (654 Commercial St., San Francisco 94111, tel. 415/981–8989) leads several culinary/historic tours, including the popular "I Can't Believe I Ate My Way Through Chinatown" tour ($65). Despite the cheesy name, this is a great way to single out some great restaurants and learn about Chinese cuisine from cookbook author Shirley Fong-Torres. Tours usually start on Saturday morning at 10 and end, according to Shirley, "when the first person explodes."

Trevor Hailey (tel. 415/550–8110), a prominent member of the San Francisco lesbian community, leads a highly recommended tour of the city's famous gay neighborhood called "Cruisin' the Castro" ($40). The four-hour tour includes brunch; call for reservations.

The Victorian Home Walk ($20) follows a relatively hill-free course past over 200 meticulously restored Victorian buildings on streets from which tour buses are prohibited. Longtime San Francisco resident and tour leader Jay Gifford (www.victorianwalk.com, tel. 415/863–7577) narrates the stroll with historical and architectural insight as well as local lore about famous Painted Ladies. The tour lasts 2½ hours and is tailored with opportunities for shopping and lunch as tour goers please.

The "Walking to a Latin Beat" tour ($20) explores the Mission District's Latin community through its markets, murals, and music stores. In three hours, this walk from Mission Dolores to York Street with guide Brenda Chapel (tel. 415/921–0625) shows the transported heart of Central and South America in a nearly unvisited neighborhood with the best weather in the city.

For a tour of the Mission's murals, call Precita Eyes Mural Arts Center (tel. 415/285–2287) for information on its weekly walking tours ($5). Bicycle tours are also offered biweekly.

To be led around San Francisco for free (donations appreciated), call City Guides (tel. 415/557–4266), whose guided walks are sponsored in part by the San Francisco Public Library. They offer 25 tours each week covering almost every corner of town: Roof Gardens and Open Spaces, the Telegraph Hill Hike, Art Deco Marina, History of Haight-Ashbury, and the Mission Murals are just a few tour topics.

LEARNING • **Earthwatch** (Box 9104, 680 Mount Auburn St., Watertown, MA 02272, tel. 617/926–8200 or 800/776–0188, fax 617/926–8532) for research expeditions. **Oceanic Society Expeditions** (Fort Mason Center, Bldg. E, San Francisco, CA 94124, tel. 415/441–1106 or 800/326-7491).

MUSIC • **Dailey-Thorp Travel** (330 W. 58th St., Suite 610, New York, NY 10019-1817, tel. 212/307-1555 or 800/998-4677, fax 212/974-1420).

SAILING • **5 Star Yacht Charters** (85 Libertyship Way, Suite 12, Sausalito, CA 94965, tel. 415/332-7187).

TRAIN TRAVEL

AMTRAK

Amtrak trains stop at five Bay Area stations: in Richmond; Berkeley (where you can board but can't buy tickets); Oakland; Emeryville; and San Jose. From the Emeryville and Oakland stations, ticket holders can catch a free Amtrak bus to the San Francisco Ferry Building, on Embarcadero at the foot of Market Street.

AMTRAK STATIONS • **Richmond** (16th St. and MacDonald Ave.). **Berkeley** (3rd St. and University Ave.). **Oakland** (245 2nd St., at Jack London Sq.). **Emeryville** (5885 Landregan St.). **San Jose** (65 Cahill St.).

FARES

Amtrak's fares vary according to the time of year and other factors; a Bay Area–Seattle round-trip (24 hrs each way) runs from $180 to $330, while Bay Area–Los Angeles round-trips (12 hrs each way) are from $78 to $155.

Historic Black Landmarks: A Traveler's Guide (Visible Ink Press; $18) and African American Historic Places (Preservation Press; $26) are two solid travel books that include information on African-American landmarks in California.

TRAIN INFORMATION • **Amtrak Information** (tel. 800/872-7245).

CALTRAIN

CalTrain offers regular service from San Francisco (4th and King Sts.) to downtown San Jose (65 Cahill St.). A one-way trip costs $5.25 and takes 1½ hours; trains leave hourly between 5 AM and 10 PM, more frequently during commuter hours. Along the way the trains stop at a number of peninsula cities, including Burlingame (30 mins, $2.75), Palo Alto (1 hr, $4), Mountain View (70 mins, $4), and Santa Clara (80 mins, $4.75). Prices are lower during off-peak (midday) hours. Not all trains stop at all stations, so **check schedules carefully.**

INFORMATION • **CalTrain** (tel. 800/660-4287).

TRANSPORTATION AROUND SAN FRANCISCO

The San Francisco Bay Area has one of the most comprehensive public transportation systems of any U.S. region, making it easy for commuters and travelers to get around without contributing to traffic jams. For the lowdown on public transit, call the TravInfo hot line, which has up-to-the-minute information on public transit lines, highway traffic conditions, carpooling, parking, and airport transit for all nine Bay Area counties. Additionally, the free *Regional Transit Guide* is an excellent resource listing Bay Area transportation agencies, lines, and frequency. It's available in bookstores as well as at the San Francisco Visitor Information Center and the Berkeley TRiP Commute Store, or by mail from the Department of Technical Service. You can also buy public transit passes for the whole Bay Area at the TriP store. For information on how to maneuver through the city and its public transit system with a bicycle, *see* Bicycling, *above.*

INFORMATION • **TravInfo hot line** (tel. 415/817–1717, 510/817–1717, or 408/817–1717). **Berkeley TRiP Commute Store** (2033 Center St., 1 block west of Berkeley BART, tel. 510/644-7665). **MTC, Department of Technical Services/Regional Transit Guide** (101 8th St., Oakland 94607).

TRAVEL AGENCIES

A good travel agent puts your needs first. Look for an agency that has been in business at least five years, emphasizes customer service, and has someone on staff who specializes in your destination. In addition **make sure the agency belongs to a professional trade organization.** The American Society of Travel Agents (ASTA), with 27,000 agents in some 170 countries, is the largest and most influential in the field. Operating under the motto integrity in Travel, it maintains and enforces a strict code of ethics and will step in to help mediate any agent-client disputes if necessary. ASTA also maintains a Web site that includes a directory of agents. (Note that if a travel agency is also acting as your tour operator, *see* Buyer Beware *in* Tours & Packages, *above*.)

LOCAL AGENT REFERRALS • American Society of Travel Agents (ASTA, www.astanet.com, tel. 800/965–2782 24-hr hot line, fax 703/684–8319). **Association of British Travel Agents** (68–271 Newman St., London W1P 4AH, tel. 020/7637– 2444, fax 020/7637–0713). **Association of Canadian Travel Agents** (1729 Bank St., Suite 201, Ottawa, Ontario K1V 7Z5, tel. 613/521–0474, fax 613/521–0805). **Australian Federation of Travel Agents** (Level 3, 309 Pitt St., Sydney 2000, tel. 02/9264–3299, fax 02/9264–1085). **Travel Agents' Association of New Zealand** (Box 1888, Wellington 10033, tel. 04/499–0104, fax 04/499–0786).

VISITOR INFORMATION

TOURIST INFORMATION • For general information, there are dozens of chambers of commerce and convention and visitors bureaus in the San Francisco Bay Area. For information about the Wine Country, redwood groves, and northwestern California, contact the Redwood Empire Association Visitor Information Center. For $3 they'll send you a visitor guide; or pick up one at the center for $1. You can get information about Silicon Valley from the San Jose Visitor Information Center.

IN SAN FRANCISCO • San Francisco Convention and Visitors Bureau (201 3rd St., Suite 900, 94103–3185, tel. 415/974–6900). **SFCVB Visitor Information Center** (900 Market St., at Powell St., Hallidie Plaza, San Francisco 94102, tel. 415/391–2000 or 415/391–2001 for 24-hr recorded information).

IN GREATER BAY AREA • Berkeley (2015 Center St., First Floor, Berkeley 94704, tel. 510/549–8710 or 800/847–4823). **Oakland** (1000 Broadway Ave., Suite 200, Oakland 94607, tel. 510/839–9000 or 800/262–5526). **San Jose** (333 W. San Carlos St., Suite 1000, San Jose 95110, tel. 408/295–9600). **Santa Clara** (1850 Warburton St., Santa Clara 95050, tel. 408/244–9660).

WINE COUNTRY & SILICON VALLEY • Redwood Empire Association Visitor Information Center (2801 Leavenworth St., 94133, tel. 415/394–5991 or 888/678–8507, fax 415/394–5994). **San Jose Visitor Information Center** (150 W. San Carlos, Santa Clara, 95110, tel. 408/283–8833).

STATEWIDE • California State Office of Tourism (801 K St., Suite 1600, Sacramento, CA 95814, tel. 916/322–2882 or 800/862–2543) has a free visitor's guide.

IN THE U.K. • California Tourist Office (ABC California, Box 35, Abingdon, Oxfordshire OX14 4TB, tel. 0891/200–278); calls cost 50p per minute peak rate or 45p per minute cheap rate; send for brochure.

WHEN TO GO

San Francisco is often cold and windy, even in summer. Things warm up in September and October, the Indian summer months, and in May. The yearly average high temperature is 69°F, the average low 46°F. The East Bay tends to be a few degrees warmer than San Francisco: Highs average 72°F, lows 43°F. Marin County's weather varies from town to town: The coast is usually fogged in, the bay-side towns of Tiburon and Sausalito get a cool breeze, and San Rafael checks in at a solid few degrees warmer than most of the Bay Area, with an average summer high of 82°F. In the South Bay average summer highs, both on the coast and inland, hover in the 80s. In winter things cool down to a medium rare, with lows dipping to 40°F.

CLIMATE

FORECASTS • Weather Channel Connection (tel. 900/932–8437), 95¢ per minute from a Touch-Tone phone. For ski conditions in northern California, Tahoe, or the Sierras: **California State Automobile Association's Ski Report Hotline** (tel. 415/864–6440).

What follows are the average daily maximum and minimum temperatures for San Francisco.

Jan.	56F	13C	May	64F	17C	Sept.	70F	21C
	46F	8C		51F	10C		56F	13C
Feb.	60F	15C	June	66F	19C	Oct.	69F	20C
	48F	9C		53F	11C		55F	13C
Mar.	61F	16C	July	66F	19C	Nov.	64F	18C
	49F	9C		54F	12C		51F	10C
Apr.	63F	17C	Aug.	66F	19C	Dec.	57F	14C
	50F	10C		54F	12C		47F	8C

FESTIVALS

JANUARY • The **whale-watching** season runs through April. Patient watchers bundle up and pull out their binoculars at Point Reyes (*see* Hiking and Biking *in* Chapter 8). The rangers at the Point Reyes lighthouse (tel. 415/669–1534) can tell you how many whales have swum past in the days before your visit.

The one-day **Tet Festival** street fair (tel. 415/885–2743) is held on the Saturday nearest the Vietnamese New Year (the first new moon after January 20). The streets around the Civic Center come alive with performances by Vietnamese, Cambodian, and Laotian singers and dancers, and numerous booths sell Southeast Asian delicacies.

FEBRUARY • North America's oldest Chinese community celebrates the **Chinese New Year and Golden Dragon Parade** (tel. 415/982–3000) with cultural events, fireworks, and costumes. Festivities take place around January 28; this year, they'll celebrate the dawn of the Year of the Tiger (year 4696 on the lunar calendar).

Don't miss the huge weeklong Chinese New Year's festival, held during the first new moon in February. Come early to get a spot for the final parade—a riotous celebration of Asian culture, featuring firecrackers, lion dancers, and painted dragons.

MARCH • During the two-week **Tulipmania** (tel. 415/705–5500) more than 40,000 tulips bloom around Pier 39 at Fisherman's Wharf. You can walk around on your own or join one of the free guided tours.

With shamrocks, Guinness stout, and enough green to make even Mother Nature envious, the **St. Patrick's Day Parade** (tel. 415/661–2700) on March 15 at 12:30 PM is a party in motion. Despite the recent politicization of the parade, with "Gaylic Pride" and "IRA All the Way" banners popping up, the emphasis for San Francisco's Irish community is still firmly on green beer and folk tunes.

APRIL • Japantown's **Cherry Blossom Festival** (tel. 415/563–2313) features nearly 400 Japanese performers along with numerous exhibits of Japanese art. The most popular attractions are the *taiko* drum performance and the 2½-hour parade. For a schedule of events, send a self-addressed, stamped envelope to Cherry Blossom Festival, Box 15147, San Francisco 94115.

San Francisco International Film Festival (tel. 415/929–5000), the nation's oldest, features two full weeks of seminars and films ranging from the almost-mainstream (Pedro Almódovar, Wayne Wang) to the truly obscure. Screenings take place near the end of April at the Kabuki 8 and the Castro Theatre in San Francisco, the Pacific Film Archive in Berkeley, and other locations in the South Bay and Marin.

If your energy needs to be rechanneled, come to the **Whole Life Expo,** an annual, weekend-long New Age fest, held at San Francisco's Fashion Design Center (8th and Brannan Sts., tel. 800/551–3976). More than 250 booths display energy pyramids, massage tools, and healing crystals. Another exposition is held the third week in October, when the emphasis is on food and health.

MAY • Vibrant mariachi bands and colorful Mexican folklórico dancers congregate in the Mission District the weekend nearest May 5 to celebrate **Cinco de Mayo** (tel. 415/826–1401), the anniversary of Mexico's defeat of the French at the Battle of Puebla. On Sunday floats, bands, and salsa dancers wearing little more than feathers parade through the Mission, starting at 24th and Bryant streets and ending with a festival at the Civic Center.

Taste home-brewed beer at Berkeley's Civic Center Park at the **Berkeley Beer and Music Festival** (tel. 510/548–1067), and you may never drink anything else. A $15 tasting kit includes a beer mug and 10 drink coupons.

The weekend-long **Festival of Greece,** at the Greek Orthodox Cathedral (4700 Lincoln Ave., at Hwy. 13, Oakland, tel. 510/531–3400), emphasizes food—moussaka, dolmas, baklava—and wine, though music and Greek crafts also make an appearance. Costumed dancers perform for the crowds, but when the bands pull out their bouzoukis, everyone gets in on the action.

Listed in the *Guinness Book of World Records* as the world's largest footrace, the zany 100,000-person **Bay to Breakers** (tel. 415/777–7770) pits world-class runners against costumed human centipedes and huge safe-sex condom caravans in a 12k (7½-mi) race from the Financial District to Ocean Beach. The race takes place the third Sunday of May (May 21 in 2000). Entry forms start appearing in the *San Francisco Examiner* (*see* Media, *above*) on March 1.

On Memorial Day weekend, long after Mardi Gras and Carnaval celebrations in New Orleans and Rio de Janeiro are over, the Mission District revives the party with **Carnaval** (tel. 415/826–1401). Dozens of Latin American musical groups, including the Caribbean All-Stars and Xiuhcoatc Danza Azteka, keep the energy at top levels. The parade along Mission Street starts at 10 AM Sunday and terminates near the fair on Harrison Street (between 16th and 22nd streets), with food, craft booths, and performances.

JUNE • Summer brings out the neighborhood festivals. On the first weekend in June the **Union Street Spring Festival** (tel. 415/346–9162), near the upscale Marina district, features big bands, wine and food, tea dancing, and a waiters' race. The following weekend the **Haight-Ashbury Street Fair** (tel. 415/661–8025) has two stages, both featuring mostly local bands playing rap, jazz, and rock. Come see the "world's biggest salami" at the **North Beach Festival** (tel. 415/989–6426), the country's oldest urban street fair, held in mid-June. There's chalk street painting, small-press booksellers, and music (flamenco, jazz, and more).

Free Folk Festival has drawn such crowds that after 16 years at City College it has switched venues to Roosevelt Middle School (460 Arguello St, at Geary Blvd., San Francisco). Bring your guitar, harmonica, or fiddle to the workshops and impromptu jam sessions that spring up between concerts of folk, blues, and international music. It's a very loosely organized event, and participants change yearly; check newspaper entertainment listings for details.

On June 21, the longest day of the year, the streets vibrate with the sounds of more than 250 bands during the annual rendition of **Making Waves** (tel. 415/263–8760), when every kind of music—from local funk to zydeco to jazz to African indigenous sounds—entertains listeners at 25 downtown San Francisco stage sites.

Come see free music (classical, jazz, world music, and more) in a beautiful park setting at the **Stern Grove Music Festival** (tel. 415/252–6252), held throughout the summer on the first Sunday of every month, beginning the second weekend in June. Stern Grove is in the southwest corner of San Francisco, at 19th Street and Sloat Boulevard.

Known as San Francisco Pride for short (and formerly known as the Gay and Lesbian Freedom Day Parade), the **San Francisco Lesbian, Gay, Bisexual, Transgender Pride Celebration** parade (tel. 415/864–3733) traditionally attracts huge names in the gay community. Check local newspapers or call for location and date. June also brings the much-loved and internationally famous **International Lesbian and Gay Film Festival** (tel. 415/703–8650) (*see* Movie Houses *in* Chapter 6).

JULY • Summer heat keeps the festivals coming. In mid-July you can groove your way down Polk Street between Jackson and Bush streets during the festival of **Blues and Art on Polk** (tel. 415/249–4625).

Fourth of July Waterfront Festival (tel. 415/777–8498), the biggest Independence Day celebration in the Bay Area, takes place along the San Francisco waterfront (between Aquatic Park and Pier 39), with music in the afternoon and fireworks at night. The show is impressive even when the waterfront is fogged in.

In the 1940s, '50s, and '60s the Fillmore area was famous for its sizzling jazz and blues clubs. Old-time musicians (and younger ones, too) revive those heady days on the first weekend of every July with **Jazz and All That Art on Fillmore** (tel. 415/346–9162); on Fillmore Street between Post and Jackson streets, arts-and-crafts booths fill the sidewalks, and outdoor cafés serve everything from barbecued ribs to knishes.

Taking place during the last two weeks of July, the **Jewish Film Festival** (tel. 415/621–0556) is the largest of its kind in the world. Films are shown at theaters in Berkeley and San Francisco. Call for admission prices.

AUGUST • Oakland's large Chinatown celebrates its diversity on the fourth weekend in August during the **Oakland Chinatown Streetfest** (tel. 510/893–8979), with food and cultural activities representing all East Asian cultures.

SEPTEMBER • **The San Francisco Shakespeare Festival** (tel. 415/422–2222) brings free outdoor performances of a selected Shakespeare play to San Francisco's Golden Gate Park, beginning Labor Day weekend. In October the festival continues at Lakeside Park in Oakland and at St. James Park in San Jose. Shows take place at 1:30 PM weekends.

The San Francisco Opera kicks off the opera season with **Opera in the Park** (tel. 415/861–4008), a free concert in Golden Gate Park's Sharon Meadow on the Sunday after the first performance of the season, usually the week after Labor Day.

Even in San Francisco, the **Folsom Street Fair** (tel. 415/861–3247) has created controversy with its past displays of leather and bondage gear. People crowd the blocks of Folsom Street between 7th and 12th streets strutting their latest leather ware, usually the last or next-to-last Sunday in September.

Festival de las Americas (tel. 415/826–1401) celebrates the independence of Mexico and seven other Latin American countries. More than 80,000 people flock to 24th Street between Mission and Hampshire streets for this socially responsible, alcohol-free, family-oriented event that promotes pride in the Latino community. There are Latino musicians, ethnic food, and booths selling original crafts.

Big-name musicians like B. B. King and Robert Cray perform at the **San Francisco Blues Festival** (tel. 415/979–5588), the country's oldest, usually held the last weekend of the month at Justin Herman Plaza (Market St. at Embarcadero) and at Fort Mason's Great Meadow (Marina Blvd. and Laguna St.). Tickets average $20–$30 and advance purchase is recommended.

OCTOBER • The only celebration of its kind, the **Black Cowboys Parade** (tel. 510/531–7583) takes place the first Saturday in October and honors the role of minorities in the Old West.

On the first Sunday of the month, the **Castro Street Fair** (tel. 415/467–3354) brings out crafts vendors; booths run by community, health, and social organizations; and musical entertainment.

In mid-October San Francisco salutes its sailors with activities and booths on Fisherman's Wharf and a Blue Angels air show—all part of the annual **Fleet Week** (tel. 415/981–7437).

San Francisco's flamboyant **Halloween parade** (tel. 415/826–1401) has officially relocated to the Civic Center, but its soul remains in the Castro district. About 300,000 revelers attend each year.

San Francisco International Accordion Festival (tel. 415/775–6000) brings food, dancing, and booths to the Anchorage Shopping Center in Fisherman's Wharf on the third weekend in October. Perennial faves Zydeco Flames and Those Darn Accordions often compete in the "I'm San Francisco's Main Squeeze" contest, which chooses the accordionist with the wildest costume to be next year's poster child.

NOVEMBER • Bibliophiles eagerly await the **San Francisco Book Festival** (tel. 415/487–4550), held the first weekend in November at the Concourse exhibition center, at 8th and Brannan streets. More than 300 booths represent small, alternative presses as well as big publishing houses; many sell books at a discount. Some 250 authors also show up to read and sign their books; Isabel Allende, Tony Hillerman, and June Jordan are just a few who have appeared in recent years.

Día de los Muertos, or Day of the Dead, derived from Aztec rituals and the Catholic All Souls' Day, is celebrated in early November in San Francisco's Mission District with art exhibitions and a parade starting from the Mission Cultural Center (2868 Mission St., tel. 415/821–1155).

On the Sunday after Thanksgiving more than 13,000 people dressed like their favorite Gary Larson characters compete in the **Run to the Far Side** (tel. 415/759–2690), a 5-kilometer walk or 10-kilometer run through Golden Gate Park. The event benefits the California Academy of Sciences' environmental education programs.

DECEMBER • In celebration of the season, the San Francisco Ballet (tel. 415/865–2000) presents *The Nutcracker* every year. In Oakland the Mormon Temple (4766 Lincoln Ave., tel. 510/531–0704) holds a **tree-lighting ceremony** early in the month and offers musical entertainment during the evenings until Christmas Eve.

Celebration of Craftswomen (tel. 415/821–6480), held during the first two weekends of December at Fort Mason, features leather works, wearable art, and glassworks along with gourmet food and live entertainment.

EXPLORING THE BAY AREA

REVISED BY DENISE M. LETO, CHRIS BATY,

LISA HAMILTON, AND LOTUS ABRAMS

You'll never run out of opportunities for adventure in the Bay Area, no matter how long you stay. San Francisco is a densely populated cosmopolitan city, yet its historic Victorian homes, wide-open parks, and miles of waterfront render it anything but claustrophobic. The best way to explore is by walking its many distinct neighborhoods; along the way you'll encounter shops, parks, and cafés that invite you to stop and soak up the atmosphere. On days when you desire something more rugged, head for Marin County's stunning cliffs, forests, and beaches—an impressive backdrop to the multi-million-dollar homes that dot the landscape. The East Bay offers acres of hilly parks with incredible views of the city and the bay beyond. The East Bay's two major cities are Berkeley, known for its university, radical politics, and antic street scene; and Oakland, a sprawling, unpretentious city with a strong African-American identity. In the South Bay you'll find one of California's most renowned universities as well as Silicon Valley and the striking, windswept San Mateo County coast.

SAN FRANCISCO

San Francisco's eclectic history has left plenty for modern explorers to discover. In nooks and crannies all over the city, you'll find reminders of everything from the drinking and whoring of the gold prospectors to the living and loving of the country's largest lesbian and gay population. Weathered brick and iron warehouses of the Barbary Coast are now the sites of antiques shops in the Financial District, while huge Victorian mansions that survived the 1906 quake are still standing proud in the Mission. One minute you're marveling at the frenetic pace of Financial District workers, and the next you're strolling through Chinese herb shops and produce markets. You could down a cappuccino and biscotti at a noisy Italian café, and 10 minutes later be gazing at the Golden Gate Bridge from the water's edge. Bored? You should be ashamed of yourself.

You can spend countless days (and almost no money at all) just kicking around the city's hilly streets. Discover the latest artistic trend as you gallery-hop; get your exercise climbing Russian Hill's narrow, hidden stairway streets; gawk at the mansions that dominate the peaks of Pacific Heights and the Presidio; or get lost for a day in Golden Gate Park. When you tire, as you inevitably will on the dizzying hills

28

in some parts of the city, hop a bus for a higher-speed version of the San Francisco experience. You can get a Muni Street and Transit Map for $2.50 at most liquor and grocery stores. If you want enthusiastic locals to show you their fair city, tag along on one of San Francisco's quirky tours (*see box* Walk This Way *in* Chapter 1).

MAJOR SIGHTS

San Francisco's major sights truly merit that designation. Even the most jaded natives can't help but inhale a reverent breath at the sight of the majestic Golden Gate Bridge. The Alcatraz tour explores such a fascinating place—on such a genuinely stark, scary island—that for all the hype, it is utterly compelling. Coit Tower and Golden Gate Park will forever be places to get a feel for quintessential San Francisco. Even Fisherman's Wharf, despite its saccharin-sweet carnival atmosphere, never fails to attract hordes of people with its dazzling waterside location and nonstop activity.

GOLDEN GATE BRIDGE

The bridge to end all bridges has come to symbolize San Francisco more than any other monument. This masterpiece of design and engineering, which links San Francisco to its wealthy neighbor, Marin County, has endured wind, fog, a daily load of 100,000 cars, the ignominy of more than 1,000 suicides, and the weight of the more than 200,000 people who showed up to celebrate its 50th birthday in 1987. More than a mile long, the bridge is painted international orange for visibility in fog (so the seagulls don't crash into it). Engineer Joseph Strauss designed the bridge to withstand winds of more than 100 mi per hour and to swing nearly 27 ft at its center. The cables that support it are more than 3 ft in diameter, and the combined lengths of the individual strands would wrap around the earth three times.

To catch a glimpse of the bridge, you'll have to scale a hill or two or head to the waterfront near Fisherman's Wharf. Bus 28 will drop you at the toll plaza, at the northern tip of the Presidio (*see* Neighborhoods, *below*); the walk across and back takes about an hour, and the wind can be freezing. Bicycling across the bridge is a thrill; Lincoln Boulevard in the Presidio is a gorgeous way to get there (to reach Lincoln, take a gentle ride west down Lombard Street or have a screaming downhill adventure by approaching from the south on Presidio Boulevard; *see* San Francisco Biking in Chapter 8). The pedestrian walkway and the bicycle path are both open 5 AM–9 PM.

Below the bridge on the San Francisco side is historic **Fort Point** (tel. 415/556–1693). The massive fort, built between 1853 and 1861 by the U.S. Army Corps of Engineers, is an enduring symbol of the commercial and strategic military importance of San Francisco. Though it was designed to hold 500 soldiers and 126 cannons, it was never called on to fire a single shot. All the soldiers packed up and left around 1900, but the public can still drop by for guided tours, free movies on Fort Point and Golden Gate Bridge history, and "cannon drills" (where you do everything *but* fire the cannon), daily 10–5. From U.S. 101N take Lincoln Boulevard (the last San Francisco exit), then follow the signs. Admission is free.

ALCATRAZ ISLAND

Known as the Rock, Alcatraz Island served for 59 years as the nation's most notorious federal penitentiary, holding high-risk prisoners in its isolated maw. Al Capone, Robert "the Birdman" Stroud, and Machine Gun Kelly were among the more famous bad guys who got "Rock fever" gazing out day after day at the bittersweet sight of San Francisco.

Since the prison closed in 1963, people have been trying to get *onto* Alcatraz Island, not off it. In 1969 a group of Native Americans attempted to reclaim the land, saying that an 1868 federal treaty allowed Native Americans to use all federal territory that the government wasn't actively using. After almost two years of Indian occupation, the U.S. government forced them off, none too gently. The bloody incident is recounted in the island's small museum, and graffiti still reminds visitors that "this is Native American Land."

Today the island is part of the National Park System, and tourists visit the grounds in hordes—though even heavy weekend crowds don't alter the lonely, somber, abandoned feel of the place. Rangers on Alcatraz give a variety of free talks; subjects include escape attempts, the island's history as a 19th-century military fort, the Native American occupation, and Alcatraz's unique characteristics as part of an island chain in San Francisco Bay. Check for schedules at the ranger station at the ferry landing when you arrive or call the dock office at 415/705–1042 on the day of your visit.

SAN FRANCISCO

PACIFIC OCEAN

Golden Gate Bridge

Fort Point
National
Historic Site

Wave

101

Golden Gate
National
Recreation
Area

Palace of Fine Arts
and Exploratorium

1

The Presidio

W. Pacific Ave.

Lincoln Blvd

Presi

Baker
Beach

China
Beach

Lands
End

Lincoln
Park

Palace of
the Legion
of Honor

SEACLIFF

Lake St.

Clement St.

Arguello Blvd.

Geary Expres

Masonic

Point
Lobos

Cliff
House

43rd

34th
Ave.

Geary Blvd.

25th
Ave.

19th
Ave.

Park Presidio Blvd.

8th
Ave.

Balboa St.

Turk

Ave.

Fulton St.

RICHMOND

McLaren
Lodge

HAIG
ASHB

Kennedy Dr.

Martin   Luther

Middle Dr.

King

Jr.

Dr.

Stanyan St.

Clayton St.

COLE
VALLEY

Golden Gate Park

Lincoln Way

Judah St.

28th
Ave.

Lawton St.

1

Funston Ave.

7th Ave.

Noriega St.

Ortega St.

Quintara St.

19th
Ave.

14th
Ave.

Clarendon
Ave.

Tw
Pe

SUNSET

41st
Ave.

Sunset Blvd.

McCoppin
Square

Dewey Blvd.

Taraval St.

Larsen
Park

Portola
Dr.

Yerba Buena Ave.

Mt.
Davidson

Vicente St.

Stern Grove

Monterey Blvd.

Miramar
Ave.

Monte

Great
Highway

Ocean Beach

San Francisco
Zoo

Sloat Blvd

STONESTOWN

Ocean Ave.

Junipero Serra Blvd.

Plymouth Ave.

C
Cu

280

N

0   1 mile

0   1 km

Skyline Blvd.

Lake Merced Blvd

Harding
Park

Lake Merced

San Francisco
State Univ.

Font Blvd.

Holloway Ave.

Garfield St.

Fort
Funston

35

Brotherhood
Way

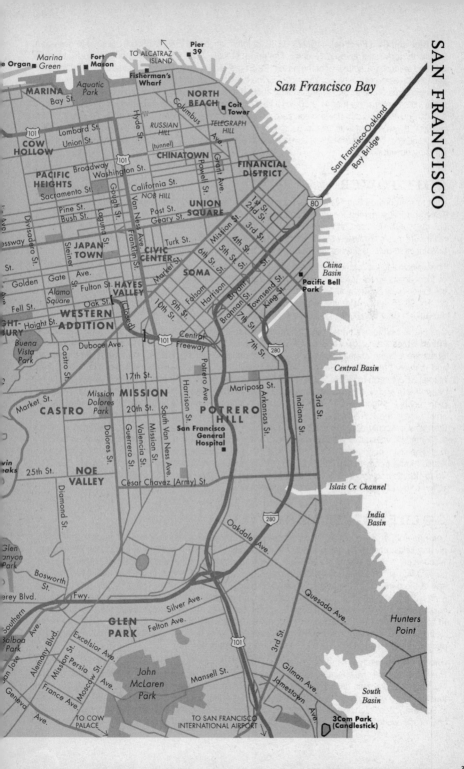

San Francisco Bay

TO ALCATRAZ ISLAND

Pier 39

e Organ Marina Green Fort Mason

Fisherman's Wharf

MARINA Bay St. Aquatic Park

NORTH BEACH Coit Tower

Columbus Ave.

COW HOLLOW Lombard St. Union St.

RUSSIAN HILL TELEGRAPH HILL

Hyde St.

(tunnel)

PACIFIC HEIGHTS Broadway Washington St. CHINATOWN

Van Ness Ave.

California St. NOB HILL

Howell St. Grant Ave.

FINANCIAL DISTRICT

San Francisco-Oakland Bay Bridge

80

Sacramento St.

Gough St.

Pine St. Bush St. Laguna St.

Post St. Geary St. UNION SQUARE

Divisadero St.

Steiner St.

JAPAN TOWN

Franklin St.

Turk St.

Mission St. 1st St. 2nd St. 3rd St.

4th St. 5th St. 6th St.

Gough St.

CIVIC CENTER

Market St.

SOMA

China Basin

Pacific Bell Park

essway

St.

Golden Gate Ave.

Alamo Square

Fulton St.

HAYES VALLEY

Folsom Harrison

Bryant

Brannan St. Townsend St. King St.

Fell St.

Oak St. (Closed)

10th St.

9th St.

7th St.

GHT- Haight St. WESTERN ADDITION
URY

101

Central Freeway

7th St.

280

Buena Vista Park

Duboce Ave.

Castro St.

17th St.

Central Basin

Market St.

CASTRO

Mission Dolores Park

MISSION 20th St.

Potrero Ave.

Harrison St.

Mariposa St.

Arkansas St.

Indiana St.

3rd St.

Dolores St.

Guerrero St.

Valencia St.

Mission St.

South Van Ness Ave.

POTRERO HILL

San Francisco General Hospital

vin 25th St.
eaks

NOE VALLEY

Diamond St.

César Chavez (Army) St.

Islais Cr. Channel

India Basin

Glen anyon Park

Bosworth St.

280

Oakdale Ave.

rey Blvd. Fwy.

Silver Ave.

Quesada Ave.

Hunters Point

Glen Park Felton Ave.

Southern
Ave.

Balboa Park

an Jose

Geneva Ave.

Alemany Blvd.

Excelsior Ave.

Mission St.

Persia Ave.

Moscow St.

France Ave.

John McLaren Park

Mansell St.

101

3rd St.

Gilman Ave.

Jamestown Ave.

South Basin

TO COW PALACE

TO SAN FRANCISCO INTERNATIONAL AIRPORT

3Com Park (Candlestick)

The **Blue and Gold Fleet** (tel. 415/773–1188 for information or 415/705–5555 for tickets) ferries you to the island from San Francisco's Pier 41. The price ($11.25, $18.75 for evening tours) includes the ferry ride and an audiocassette tour of the prison itself; tapes are available in several languages, and the average tour takes about 2½ hours. You can skip the cassette tour and pay only $7.75, but the tape, which features former inmates and guards talking about their experiences on Alcatraz, is one of the best parts of the visit. Ferries leave Pier 41 9:30–2:15 year-round (until 4:15 June–August; evening tours depart at 4:20 and 5:15). You can use a credit card to reserve tickets by phone (there's a $2 per ticket service charge). If you're buying tickets in person, go to the ferry ticket office (open 8:30–5) at Pier 41. You should reserve or purchase tickets *several* days in advance. Bus 32 will get you to Pier 41 from the Ferry Building downtown.

COIT TOWER

Built to memorialize San Francisco's volunteer firefighters, the 210-ft concrete observation tower atop Telegraph Hill is named for the colorful woman who willed the funds to build it, Lillie Hitchcock Coit (1843–1929). Heiress Coit was a cross-dresser (she could gain access to the city's more interesting realms in men's clothes) who literally chased fire engines around town. Most people agree that the building resembles a fire nozzle—supposedly, that's not intentional.

The walls inside the lobby are covered with Depression-era murals in the style of Diego Rivera, painted by local artists on the government dole. **City Guides** (tel. 415/557–4266) runs free descriptive tours of the tower every Saturday at 11, including the second-floor murals that are normally closed to the public. For $3.75 the elevator inside the tower will take you to the top for a drop-dead 360-degree view of the Golden Gate Bridge, the Bay Bridge, and Alcatraz.

One of the best (albeit tiring) ways to reach Coit Tower is via two old-fashioned stairways: The historic **Filbert Steps** are narrow wooden walkways that wind through gardens, while the concrete **Greenwich Stairs** are a prime vantage point for a full cityscape. It's best to tackle the Filbert Steps on the way up and marvel at magnificent views as you head down the Greenwich Stairs. To start, take Bus 42 from Market Street north to Filbert Street. At the base of the cliff, you will see a set of concrete steps; take a deep breath and start climbing. The concrete will eventually yield to a rickety wooden path. When the path meets Montgomery Street, look to your left and check out the building that was Lauren Bacall's apartment in the 1947 classic *Dark Passage*. Cross the street and continue up the steps to Coit Tower. Start your descent under the GREENWICH STREET sign near the parking lot. Brick steps will lead you back to Montgomery Street. Head south about half a block; on your left you'll find the second half of the stairway. The stairs bottom out at the site of a 1966 Janis Joplin concert hosted by a nearby drug halfway house (now a trendy health club). *Tel. 415/362–0808. From Market and 3rd Sts. downtown, Bus 30 or 45 to Washington Sq.; walk 2 blocks east on Union St., left on Kearny St. Or Bus 39 from Fisherman's Wharf to top of Telegraph Hill. Tower open daily 10–6.*

GOLDEN GATE PARK

The pride of San Francisco is Golden Gate Park: a thousand acres of manicured gardens, museums, playing fields, and bridle paths, not to mention a pair of Dutch windmills and a paddock full of bison. Wooded areas, wide swaths of open field, formal flower beds, and a zillion varieties of vegetation are all packed into an area that is 4 mi long and less than a mile wide. If you make it all the way to the west end of the park, you'll hit blustery Ocean Beach and the Pacific Ocean. The park's eastern boundary, lying close to Haight Street, has always been a natural hangout for the countercultural denizens of that neighborhood: Hippie historians should note that Ken Kesey and friends celebrated the first **Human Be-In** here on January 14, 1966. Fittingly, a devotional shrine was erected in tribute to Jerry Garcia after his death in 1995. The park has hosted rock concerts ranging from the Grateful Dead and Jefferson Airplane to Pearl Jam and the Beastie Boys' Tibetan Freedom benefit.

Once a lonely stretch of sand dunes, Golden Gate Park was designed in 1868 by William Hammond Hall, a 24-year-old civil engineer with no prior experience (his bid was lowest), and landscaped by John MacLaren. Its dramatic beauty debunks the claim of Frederick Law Olmsted—who designed the Stanford University campus and Manhattan's Central Park—that "beautiful trees could not be made to grow in San Francisco." Today blue-gum eucalyptus, Monterey pine, and Monterey cypress, not to mention one of the world's foremost horticulture displays, are scattered throughout the park. Bordered by

Stanyan Street, the Great Highway, Lincoln Way, and Fulton Street, Golden Gate Park is one of the largest urban parks in America.

Several places near the park rent bikes and in-line skates; **Park Cyclery** (1749 Waller St., at Stanyan St., tel. 415/221–3777) rents mountain bikes for $5 an hour or $25 a day (for skate rentals, *see* In-Line Skating *in* Chapter 8). For park information and maps, drop by the **McLaren Lodge** (John F. Kennedy Dr. near Stanyan St., tel. 415/831–2700) weekdays 8–5. A second visitor center is in the charming, historic **Beach Chalet** (415/751–2766), at the western edge of the park. The building's upper level houses the Beach Chalet Brewery and Restaurant (1000 Great Hwy., tel. 415/386–8439), where you can enjoy a fine microbrew as you gaze out to sea. Both the visitor center and brew pub opened in 1997 as part of a $6 million renovation of the park.

Strybing Arboretum and Botanical Gardens (tel. 415/661–1316), near the intersection of 9th Avenue and Lincoln Way, has a dazzling 70-acre display of plants, featuring some 5,000 specimens arranged by country of origin, genus, and fragrance. A $1 donation is suggested. Another star attraction is the **Japanese Tea Garden** (tel. 415/752–4227), originally built for the 1894 Mid-Winter Fair, the first world's fair held in San Francisco. During the week or on a rainy day, the garden is well worth the $3.50 admission (free before 9 and after 5); at other times crowds spoil any chance for serenity. The meticulously designed garden, open daily 8:30–6 (with shorter hours in winter), has an exquisite 18th-century Buddha and a scant number of koi in the fishponds—survivors of raids by local raccoons and hawks. The Hagiwara family took care of the garden until World War II, when they, along with other Japanese-Americans, were forced into internment camps. In 1994, on the garden's 100th anniversary, a cherry blossom tree was planted in their memory. While you're there, treat yourself to a pot of green tea and cookies.

On Sunday, John F. Kennedy Drive, the park's main thoroughfare, is closed to car traffic between Stanyan Street and 19th Avenue, and flocks of bicyclists, in-line skaters, and skateboarders take over.

The park's many free gardens include the **Shakespeare Garden,** which has every type of plant mentioned in Shakespeare's works (don't eat the nightshade) and quotations engraved in bronze; the 15-acre **National AIDS Memorial Grove** (tel. 415/750–8340), established in 1991, the only one of its kind in the country; and the **Rose Garden,** which explodes with color, especially in June. There's also the **Rhododendron Dell,** the **Fuchsia Garden,** and the **Queen Wilhelmina Tulip Garden,** with its two nearby Dutch windmills. A herd of **bison** lives in a large paddock near the park's northwest corner.

Park fixtures also include three world-class museums: the **Asian Art Museum;** the **M. H. de Young Memorial Museum,** notable for its collection of American art; and the **California Academy of Sciences** (*see* Museums, *below*). At the **Laserium** (at the California Academy of Sciences, tel. 415/750–7138), high-tech music and light shows are projected onto the planetarium's dome; Pink Floyd's *Dark Side of the Moon* is a favorite. Shows are held three or four times daily Thursday–Sunday. Admission is $7. To reach the park from downtown or the Civic Center, take Bus 5 or 71 or the N Judah streetcar.

FISHERMAN'S WHARF

Once the domain of Italian fishermen, the wharf is now San Francisco's prize tourist trap, whose sole purpose is to get you to spend money. You won't see many fishermen here unless you arrive in the misty early morning hours (around 5) to watch the fishing boats unload. Jefferson Street, the wharf's main drag, is packed with expensive seafood restaurants, tacky souvenir shops, and rip-off "museums" like the Wax Museum, Ripley's Believe It or Not!, the Guinness Museum of World Records, the Haunted Gold Mine, and the Medieval Dungeon (featuring graphic re-creations of torture devices from the Middle Ages). Each can be yours for the low admission price of $8–$12. The only thing that remains fairly authentic on the wharf (albeit rather pricey) is the array of seafood stands along Jefferson Street. If the weather's nice, buy clam chowder ($3–$4) or a half pound of shrimp ($7) from one of the sidewalk vendors and a loaf of sourdough bread ($2–$4) from **Boudin Bakery** (156 Jefferson St., tel. 415/928–1849) and eat on one of the piers, watching cruise ships and fishing boats glide in and out of the harbor. Then catch a ferry to Alcatraz (*see above*) or Angel Island (*see* Tiburon and Angel Island *in* Marin County, *below*) or walk over to Fort Mason (*see* The Presidio and Marina *in* Neighborhoods, *below*) to check out the museums.

GOLDEN GATE PARK

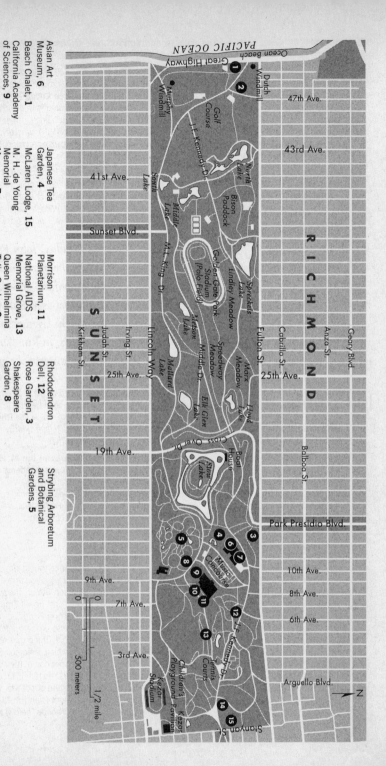

Three shopping complexes girdle the wharf: **Pier 39,** the **Cannery,** and **Ghirardelli Square.** Owned by the billionaire Bass brothers of Texas, Pier 39 (off Jefferson St., tel. 415/981–7437) is a bland imitation of a turn-of-the-century New England seaport village. A former Del Monte peach-canning factory, the **Cannery** (2801 Leavenworth St., between Beach and Jefferson Sts., tel. 415/771–3112) is now a gallery of chic boutiques. Chocolate is no longer made on-site at **Ghirardelli Square** (900 N. Point St., tel. 415/775–5500), but you can buy it here in bars or atop a huge, tasty ice cream sundae ($6). To reach Fisherman's Wharf, take Bus 32 from the Ferry Building downtown. Or fulfill your other tourist obligation by taking a cable car from Powell Street (*see* Bus Travel *in* Chapter 1) to the end of the line.

If you lack the stamina or credit rating to shop Fisherman's Wharf, for $6 you can set a course for the **USS *Pampanito* submarine** (Pier 45, tel. 415/775–1943), or visit the **Maritime Museum** (Beach St. at foot of Polk St., tel. 415/556–3002), housed in an Art Deco building that displays all sorts of artifacts from the maritime history of San Francisco. Admission to the museum is free, but for $4 you might have fun walking around on one of the old ships at the Hyde Street Pier, between the Cannery and Ghirardelli Square. Docked there are the ***Balclutha,*** a 100-year-old square-rigged ship; the ***Eureka,*** a restored turn-of-the century paddle-wheel ferry; and the ***C. A. Thayer,*** an equally venerable schooner. Comedian Jonathan Winters was once briefly institutionalized after he climbed the mast of the *Balclutha* and hung from it, shouting, "I am the man in the moon!"

At the other end of the wharf, **UnderWater World** (Beach St. just east of Pier 39, tel. 415/623–5300) is a 707,000-gallon "diver's-eye view" aquarium, where visitors listen to a taped 30-minute tour as they glide through a 300-ft transparent tunnel. Though the two main tanks are full of sharks, rays, anemones, and 10,000 types of fish, many visitors seem more amused by the scuba divers who scrub the tanks each morning. It's entertaining in a surreal sort of way, but the $12.95 admission price is mighty steep for an attraction that you can breeze through in under an hour.

A few years ago a swarm of sea lions took over several of the marina docks at Pier 39 and have refused to leave. The owners wanted them removed until they realized the barking sea mammals were attracting more tourists.

NEIGHBORHOODS

Though the city of San Francisco is a compact 49 sq mi, its neighborhoods guard their individuality like medieval fiefdoms. Each district is a distinct entity culturally, socially, and often politically, and they are all fascinating grounds for urban exploration. The best way to experience the city's neighborhoods is on foot: Plan your walk with a map or just start off in an interesting spot and surrender to the whims of the streets.

DOWNTOWN

Downtown is grand old San Francisco—that of tea dances and cocktail hours. Looking up at the beautiful architectural details, you might forget what century it is. Noteworthy architectural stops include the 1930 Art Deco **Shell Building** (100 Bush St., between Battery and Sansome Sts.) and the 1926 Romanesque château-style **Hunter-Dulin Building** (111 Sutter St., between Montgomery and Kearny Sts.). Today the downtown area has the major concentration of money-making businesses. It's typical cosmopolitan walking territory, with all the elements—both fascinating and horrifying—of urban American life.

UNION SQUARE • Union Square is the physical heart—though not the soul—of the city, especially for tourists who come to shop, browse the galleries, attend the theater, and then sleep in the finer hotels. The square, bordered by Powell, Post, Stockton, and Geary streets, was named in honor of pro-Union rallies held prior to the Civil War. Some San Franciscans will tell you the name more appropriately refers to the huge demonstrations held here in the 1930s by labor organizations, which at one point effectively shut down the city for a week.

Today Union Square consists of a park (where a few palm trees remind you that you're still in California) encircled by a ring—make that a solid-gold band—of the city's ritziest stores and boutiques, including Neiman Marcus, Saks Fifth Avenue, Chanel, Tiffany, Cartier, Hermès, Giorgio Armani, Gumps, Ralph Lauren, Macy's, Bulgari, Brooks Brothers, Coach, Williams-Sonoma, Versace, and NikeTown. Combined, Union Square merchants ring up an estimated $1 billion in sales annually. Even so, the park tends toward seediness at night; linger elsewhere.

① ②

CORN
HOLLOW

③ ④

Lombard St.

101

Octavia St.

Gough St.

Franklin St.

Van Ness Ave.

Polk St.

Larkin St.

Hyde St.

Leavenworth St.

Greenwi

Filbert S

Union St

Russell St.

Macondray Ln.

Green St.

RUSSIAN
HILL

Vallejo St.

Ina Coolbrith
Park

PACIFIC
HEIGHTS

Broadway

Broadway Tunnel

Pacific St.

Jackson St.

Taylor St.

Alta
Plaza

⑤ ⑥

Lafayette
Park

101

⑦

Washington St.

Clay St.

Sacramento St.

California St.

N
Hi

Leavenworth St.

Jones St.

②④

Pierce St.

Steiner St.

Fillmore St.

Webster St.

Buchanan St.

Laguna St.

⑧

Gough St.

Franklin St.

Van Ness Ave.

Polk St.

Larkin St.

Hyde St.

Pine St.

Bush St.

Sutter St.

Post St.

Geary St.

POLK
GULCH

JAPANTOWN

⑪
⑫

⑩ ⑨

Geary Expressway

O'Farrell St.

TENDERLOIN

Ellis St.

②③

Eddy St.

Turk St.

WESTERN
ADDITION

Golden Gate Ave.

McAllister St.

Market St.

⑬

Fulton St.

⑰

⑱

②⑳

⑯

CIVIC
CENTER

②① ②②

Grove St.

Civic Center
BART Station

ba

Alamo
Square

⑮

8th St.

7th St.

⑭

HAYES
VALLEY

Hayes St.

AMC Kabuki 8
theater, **11**

Ansel Adams
Center, **52**

Bank of America
World
Headquarters, **50**

Bella Union
Building, **38**

Belli Building, **46**

Cable Car
Museum, **25**

California Historical
Society Museum, **58**

Cartoon Art
Museum, **51**

Center for African
and African-American
Art and Culture, **13**

Center for the
Arts, **55**

Chinatown Gate, **43**

Chinese Historical
Society of
America, **29**

Chinese Telephone
Exchange, **39**

City Hall, **18**

City Lights
Bookstore, **36**

Civic Center Plaza, **20**

Coit Tower, **28**

Coleman House, **7**

Embarcadero
Center, **60**

Fairmont Hotel, **31**

Ferry Building, **61**

Glide Memorial
Methodist
Church, **23**

Golden Gate
Fortune Cookie
factory, **35**

Grace Cathedral, **24**

Haas-Lilienthal
House, **6**

Hallidie Plaza, **41**

Herbst Theatre, **17**

Hunter-Dulin
Building, **59**

Jackson Square
Historical
District, **45**

Japan Center, **9**

Jewish Museum, **63**

Justin Herman
Plaza, **62**

Kabuki Springs and
Spa, **12**

Kong Chow
Temple, **33**

KEY
- - - - - Cable Car
- Tourist Information

San Francisco Bay

N

0 _____ 1/2 mile

0 _____ 500 meters

Lombard St.

NORTH BEACH

TELEGRAPH HILL

Columbus Ave.

Grant Ave.

Mason St.

Powell St.

Stockton St.

Kearny St.

Waverly Pl.

CHINATOWN

FINANCIAL DISTRICT

Montgomery St.

Sansome St.

Battery St.

Front St.

Davis St.

Drumm St.

The Embarcadero

Halleck St.

Embarcadero BART Station

Montgomery St. BART Station

DOWNTOWN

Maiden Ln.

Union Square

Market St.

SOMA

New Montgomery St.

1st St.

2nd St.

3rd St.

Hawthorne St.

Fremont St.

Beale St.

Main St.

Spear St.

Steuart St.

The Embarcadero

Powell St. BART Station

Mission St.

4th St.

5th St.

6th St.

Howard St.

Moscone Center

Folsom St.

Harrison St.

Bryant St.

Brannan St.

Townsend St.

80

Little Fox Theatre, **37**	Pacific Heritage Museum, **48**
Lombard Street, **19**	Painted Ladies, **14**
Louise M. Davies Symphony Hall, **15**	Palace of the Fine Arts/ Exploratorium, **1**
Mark Hopkins Hotel, **30**	Peace Plaza, **10**
Mary Ellen Pleasant Memorial, **8**	Portsmouth Square, **44**
Minna Street Gallery, **57**	Rincon Center, **64**
North Beach Museum, **27**	St. Francis Hotel, **42**
Old Temple, **3**	San Francisco Shopping Centre, **40**

San Francisco Main Library, **21**	United Nations Plaza, **22**
San Francisco Museum of Modern Art, **56**	War Memorial Opera House, **16**
Shell Building, **65**	Washington Square, **26**
South Park, **67**	Wave Organ, **2**
Spreckels Mansion, **5**	Wedding Houses, **4**
Stanford Court Hotel, **32**	Wells Fargo History Museum, **49**
Tin How Temple, **34**	Yerba Buena Gardens, **54**
Transamerica Pyramid, **47**	Zeum, **53**
Transbay Terminal, **66**	

WELCOME ALL YE SINNERS

Ever been to church and come away humming and tapping your toes? Enjoy religion (with none of the guilt but possibly alongside Sharon Stone) at Glide Memorial United Methodist Church (330 Ellis St., at Taylor St., tel. 415/771–6300), presided over by a beaming Reverend Cecil Williams. Instead of organ music, a funky band and choir give parishioners reason to stand up and groove. Celebrations occur every Sunday morning at 9 and 11. It gets crowded and hot—arrive early. To get there, from the Powell Street BART/Muni station, walk one block on Powell Street, then go left on Ellis Street.

The message is in the music at St. John Coltrane's African Orthodox Church (351 Divisadero St., near Oak St., tel. 415/621–4054), where Sunday 11:45 AM services consist of a rousing three hours of the jazz great's sounds of salvation.

Heading south on Powell Street from Union Square, you'll come to the intersection of Market and Powell streets. Everyone passes through here: proselytizers, street musicians, artists, punks, young professionals, vendors, protesters, dogs, pigeons, and tourists in matching jogging suits. All converge around the **cable car turnaround,** the Powell Street BART station, and the **San Francisco Visitor Information Center** (*see* Visitor Information *in* Chapter 1), tucked below street level on **Hallidie Plaza.** Across Market Street from the cable car turnaround is the ritzy **San Francisco Shopping Centre** (*see* Chapter 3), which is built around a dizzying four-story atrium.

MAIDEN LANE • This short alley off the east side of Union Square was home to the "cribs" (brothels) that formed the center of a notoriously rowdy red-light district. Now it's a shopping arcade for the thick-walleted and the site of San Francisco's only Frank Lloyd Wright–designed building, **140 Maiden Lane,** which served as the prototype for the Guggenheim Museum in New York.

FINANCIAL DISTRICT

San Francisco is the financial capital of the West Coast. The center of the city's Financial District is **Montgomery Street,** the "Wall Street of the West," where the towers of wealth blot out the sun at street level. This part of town is built on landfill comprising the remains of hundreds of abandoned ships and docks; on the corner of Sacramento and Clay streets you'll find a plaque dedicated to the *Niantic*—a trading ship buried at this site. Nowadays it's a monument to the type A personality, where traffic lights stop vehicles in all four directions to allow harried office workers to cross diagonally and to let kamikaze bicycle messengers whiz by.

Begin your exploration at the glowering **Bank of America World Headquarters,** at the corner of California and Kearny streets. Its north plaza is graced with a black-granite shard of public art officially called *Transcendence,* but popularly known as "The Banker's Heart." In the elegant **Carnelian Room** (tel. 415/433–7500), on the building's 52nd floor, you can nurse a $6 cocktail and gaze in wonder at the city below. Bank of America's arch rival, Wells Fargo Bank, lures you in with the free **Wells Fargo History Museum** (420 Montgomery St., tel. 415/396–2619), detailing the history of California's oldest bank and celebrating the short-lived but picturesque Pony Express. The museum is open weekdays 9–5 (except for bank holidays).

TRANSAMERICA PYRAMID • The Pyramid (600 Montgomery St., between Clay and Washington Sts.) is *the* distinguishing feature of the San Francisco skyline. Despite Transamerica Corp.'s recent purchase by Aegon NV, a Dutch company, the pyramid retains its Transamerica name—a wise public relations choice by the new owners.

BARBARY COAST • In the 1850s San Francisco was home to the Barbary Coast, one of the most infamous red-light districts ever to exist. It was not uncommon to enter a bar; get drugged, clubbed, or fall through a trapdoor; and find yourself an involuntary sailor heading for Asia the next morning. The strip of Pacific Street between Sansome Street and Columbus Avenue, once called Terrific Pacific, was the heart of the action: Every building along this street was a saloon, a gambling hall, or a brothel, often featuring shows of women dancers engaged in acts of bestiality. To the chagrin of Bible-thumping reformers, many of these buildings survived the 1906 earthquake and fire. Today you can still visit the remains of the Barbary Coast by following the **Barbary Coast Trail,** a 3.8-mi path marked by bronze plaques that leads from the Old U.S. Mint (Fifth and Mission Sts.) to Aquatic Park. Along the way you'll pass through the **Jackson Square Historical District,** just north of the Financial District. One of the most notable structures in the area is the **Belli Building** (722 Montgomery St.), which once served as a musical saloon and was later the famed office of notorious San Francisco attorney Melvin Belli, the "King of Torts" (who represented the likes of the Rolling Stones, Mae West, and Jim Bakker and his then-wife, Tammy Fay). Belli, who died in July 1996, used to shoot cannons off the roof after winning big cases. Also worth a look are the nude nymphs carved on the entrance gateway to the **Bella Union** building (555 Pacific St.), as well as the **Little Fox Theatre** (535 Pacific St.), which was once a saloon and went on to illegally house a 60-ft distillery tank during Prohibition. Pick up the San Francisco Historical Society's *Official Guide to San Francisco's Barbary Coast* ($8.95) at bookstores throughout the city.

EMBARCADERO

The Embarcadero, Spanish for "wharf," looks more like a string of office buildings than anything vaguely maritime. One exception is the **Ferry Building,** at the end of Market Street. The 230-ft clock tower, modeled after Venice's Campanile, is an attractive landmark that can be seen along much of Market Street. Ferries still depart from here for Oakland, Sausalito, Larkspur, and Vallejo (*see* Ferry Travel *in* Chapter 1).

Embarcadero Center (tel. 800/733–6318) is a set of neatly stacked concrete buildings along Sacramento Street between Battery and Drumm streets. Its monolithic architectural style is no draw, but it *is* one of the few shopping malls that offer free parking on weekends for buying customers. The center is a conglomeration of four nearly identical towers housing offices, restaurants, boutiques that cater to the corporate crowd, and the **Embarcadero Center Cinema,** which features foreign and independent films (*see* Movie Houses *in* Chapter 6). Opened in 1996, the **Skydeck** (Embarcadero Center, 41st floor, tel. 888/737–5933) is an indoor-outdoor observation area ($7) with impressive views. Views from the fancy Equinox restaurant, at the **Hyatt Regency Hotel** (5 Embarcadero Center, tel. 415/788–1234), are dizzying (literally!): The rooftop bar revolves 360 degrees.

Shanghai Kelly was one of the nastiest bar owners along the Barbary Coast. He was famed for serving the occasionally deadly Mickey Finn: a whiskey, gin, brandy, and opium concoction named for the chemist who invented it.

JUSTIN HERMAN PLAZA • Between Embarcadero Center and the Ferry Building stretches Justin Herman Plaza, a favorite haunt of the office bag-lunch crowd and daredevil young skateboarders. Here, Jean Dubuffet's mammoth stainless-steel sculpture *La Chiffonière* poses like a Napoleonic Pillsbury Dough Boy. Nearby, Armand Vaillancourt's huge building-block fountain looks a little too much like prehistoric plumbing, but you can gambol among its girders even when the water is streaming through. Around the winter holidays, part of Justin Herman Plaza converts to an ice-skating rink. At other times of year it hosts free concerts, usually on a Wednesday or Friday at noon.

RINCON CENTER • Rincon Center, which houses shops, offices, and apartments, was formerly the city's main post office. The outside of the building is unassuming—you'll recognize it by the raised blue dolphins on its sides—but inside you'll find a recently restored 1940s lobby and a stately atrium into which a tall, shimmering column of water descends. The socialist-realist-type murals in the lobby depict the history of California, including the oppression of Native Americans and the exploitation of workers by capitalist overlords. *101 Spear St., at Mission St.*

CIVIC CENTER AREA

The Civic Center is the locus of San Francisco government and home of many of the city's cultural events, including dance and opera. The area immediately surrounding the center is also where a good percentage of San Francisco's homeless have camped since the 1940s. To reach the area, take BART to the Civic Center station or catch any of a thousand buses plying Market Street.

CITY HALL

The offices of San Francisco's mayor and board of supervisors are back in this building after a $300 million makeover following the 1989 Loma Prieta earthquake. Built in classic beaux arts style with a prominent bronze rotunda that can be seen blocks away, the newly reopened structure has received rave reviews, even from critics of San Francisco's flamboyant mayor, Willie Brown. City hall has a fascinating history: Joe DiMaggio and Marilyn Monroe got married here on January 15, 1954. In 1960 civil rights and freedom of speech protesters were washed down city hall's central stairway with giant fire hoses, while the hearings of the House Un-American Activities Committee went on inside—all depicted in the amusing government propaganda effort (now a cult film) *Operation Abolition.* Mayor George Moscone and Supervisor Harvey Milk were murdered here on November 27, 1978. And on February 14, 1991, scores of gay couples lined up to get "married" in celebration of the passage of San Francisco's Domestic Partners Act the previous November. *Between Van Ness Ave. and Grove, McAllister, and Polk Sts.*

Surrounding city hall are many of the city's cultural mainstays. On Van Ness Avenue the **Louise M. Davies Symphony Hall** and the more stately **War Memorial Opera House** offer San Franciscans their fill of high culture (*see* Classical Music *in* Chapter 6). You can catch a variety of cultural events, including concerts, readings, and lectures at **Herbst Theatre,** just north of the Opera House. Volunteers conduct 75-minute tours of the three buildings every Monday hourly from 10 to 2, leaving from the Grove Street entrance of Davies Symphony Hall. Tickets cost $5; call 415/552–8338 for information. The sparkling new **San Francisco Main Library** (Larkin St. at Grove St., tel. 415/557–4400) is one of the most technologically advanced in the country. It houses a fine collection of books, records, CDs, and San Francisco memorabilia, as well as 300 computer terminals, many with free Web access and CD-ROMs. In addition to books, you'll find a café, a rooftop garden, an incredible children's library, an excellent video library, an African-American center, the nation's first Gay and Lesbian Archive Center, an Asian-American center, and more, more, more! If you're walking around the area, head to Hayes Street between Franklin and Webster streets; dubbed **Hayes Valley,** this area is loaded with specialty shops, art galleries, cafés, and restaurants (*see* Chapters 4 and 5).

Just east of city hall is the sprawling **Civic Center Plaza,** which has seen its share of protest marches, political rallies (those during the Persian Gulf War drew crowds of more than 200,000), and riots. Continue east to the intersection of Market and 7th streets and then go left to find **United Nations Plaza,** commemorating the founding of the United Nations, in San Francisco in 1945. The plaza is presided over by a dramatic statue of Latin American revolutionary hero Simón Bolívar. It is also home to an excellent farmers' market (tel. 415/558–9455) on Sunday and Wednesday.

POLK GULCH

Once the gay heart of San Francisco, Polk Gulch (Polk Street between Geary and California streets) now takes second place to the even gayer Castro. The Gulch is part yuppie neighborhood, part urban blight: a good place to buy roast coffee, watch a drug bust, browse a bookstore, and get solicited for prostitution. There are more than a dozen small and special-interest bookstores here, including **Acorn Books** (*see* Books *in* Chapter 3). For coffee, try one of two **Royal Ground** locations (2216 Polk St., near Vallejo St., tel. 415/474–5957; 1605 Polk St., at Sacramento St., tel. 415/749–1731).

Once you get past the sleaze, Polk Street makes a pleasant 15-minute walk to Fisherman's Wharf. The street is lined with shops and cafés, including **Rainbow Café** (1406 Polk St., between Pine and California Sts., tel. 415/922–3286), a popular place to drink coffee and eat sandwiches. Bus 19 from the Civic Center BART station runs along Polk Street on its way to Ghirardelli Square at Fisherman's Wharf.

THE TENDERLOIN

The **Tenderloin** encompasses portions of O'Farrell, Geary, Post, and Sutter streets. For decades it's been considered a dangerous area: In the early days policemen got higher wages for working these streets, which enabled them to buy more tender cuts of meat—hence the name. The area still has the highest reported incidence of rape in the city; a particularly seedy triangle is formed by Larkin, Market, and Post streets. When the Tenderloin's call of cheap beer, live music, and inexpensive Vietnamese and Thai food beckons, you're best off visiting by cab.

CHINATOWN

The best way to experience San Francisco's Chinatown—possibly the most famous immigrant community in the world—is to arrive hungry and energetic. Skip the souvenir shops and instead wander the back alleys, soaking up the atmosphere and snacking on takeout bundles of dim sum. One of the largest Chinese populations outside Asia has made this district its home for 140 years. The original immigrants were refugees from the Opium Wars who came to San Francisco to seek their fortune during the gold rush; most ended up working on the railroad. To learn more about the history of Chinese immigration to San Francisco and the development of Chinatown, visit the **Chinese Historical Society of America** (*see* Museums, *below*).

If Chinatown's pagoda-heavy architecture looks contrived, that's because it is. In the late 1800s many right-wing groups blamed the shortage of jobs on the Chinese and wanted to bulldoze Chinatown. Indeed, in the wake of the destructive 1906 earthquake, it looked as if Chinatown wouldn't survive. But thanks to the persuasive powers of some local real estate barons, Chinatown was saved and rebuilt on the premise that it could attract tourists. Soon American and European architects were put to work constructing their stereotypes of Asian building styles into a Chinese theme park.

To reach Chinatown, take Bus 45 from Market and 3rd streets downtown. You'll know you're in the 16-block neighborhood when you see street signs in Chinese. The best way to enter is through the dragon-crowned **Chinatown Gate** (Grant Ave. at Bush St.); the sense of being in a different world is suddenly palpable. Or enter through **Portsmouth Square** (Washington and Kearny Sts.), where elderly Chinese men gather to gamble and shoot the breeze. If you are coming from the North Beach area, check out the **Imperial Tea Court** (1411 Powell St., at Broadway, tel. 415/788–6080), where you can relax and enjoy full tea service in an elegant Chinese tearoom.

During the late 1850s public hangings took place at Portsmouth Square (at the corner of Kearny and Clay streets), now part of Chinatown.

GRANT AVENUE

The main tourist thoroughfare in Chinatown, Grant Avenue, also reigns as the oldest street in San Francisco—dating to 1834. The Chinese characters above the Chinatown Gate read ALL UNDER HEAVEN IS GOOD FOR THE PEOPLE; decide if that's the case as you wander by gimmicky souvenir shops, restaurants, and flocks of wide-eyed visitors clutching $1.50 bamboo back-scratchers. Formerly known as Dupont Street, Grant Avenue once teemed with opium dens, bordellos, and gangs, especially in the sections near the Barbary Coast (*see* Financial District *above*). Today the real Chinatown can be better found by exploring the numerous small alleys that branch off of Washington, Clay, and Sacramento streets, where you're more likely to see locals shopping for groceries and carrying grandchildren down the street on their backs. The old **Chinese Telephone Exchange** building, now the Bank of Canton, stands at 743 Washington Street, at Grant Avenue. It's both architecturally and historically interesting: Operators here had to memorize the names of all their customers and speak English and five Chinese dialects.

STOCKTON STREET

The crowded shops and sidewalks of Stockton Street are the spitting image of the barter and trade district in Hong Kong. Between Sacramento and Green streets you'll find meat and produce shops letting it all hang out (even nonvegetarians might wince at the pigs hanging from hooks). The friendly staff at **Ellison Enterprises Co. USA Ltd.** (805 Stockton St., tel. 415/982–3886) will happily explain the secrets and powers of herbal medicine—and may show you a dried human placenta. Also worth seeing is the **Kong Chow Temple** (855 Stockton St., tel. 415/434–2513), a Taoist temple where you can light incense offerings to representations of 17 gods sitting on the altar.

WAVERLY PLACE

One of the most colorful streets in Chinatown is Waverly Place, off California and Clay streets, between Grant and Stockton streets. You may recognize the name from Amy Tan's *The Joy Luck Club*; it's also known as the "street of painted balconies." There are a number of Chinese temples along Waverly Place, including the **Tin How Temple** (125 Waverly Pl., top floor); founded in 1852, it's purportedly the oldest in the city. Don't miss nearby **Ross Alley,** between Grant and Stockton and Jackson and Washington streets, the home of the **Golden Gate Fortune Cookie factory** (56 Ross Alley, tel. 415/781–3956), where you can watch old women fold cookies—then pick up a bag (40 for $2). At the end of Ross Alley is **Jackson Street,** where you'll find several Chinese herbal medicine shops with drawers that contain medicines made from the therapeutic plants that line the walls.

THE ROOT OF THE PROBLEM

Chinese roots and herbs are widely believed to be highly effective in promoting good health. Some, like ginger and ginseng, are widely used in teas; you can pick these up in the many stores along Stockton and Washington streets. Besides tasting good, ginger prevents motion sickness and may also help prevent blood clots. Ginseng stimulates the immune system, helps defend the liver against toxins, and acts as a stimulant. Some people believe it also increases sexual potency. You be the judge.

NORTH BEACH

Walk north on Columbus Avenue from the Columbus and Broadway intersection (one of San Francisco's best-known red-light districts), and you'll find yourself in the heart of the legendary Italian district, where the beat movement was born. (Nowadays, North Beach is better known for its many trattorias, cafés, and delis.) Poets and writers including Jack Kerouac, Lawrence Ferlinghetti, and Allen Ginsberg came to North Beach around 1953 to write, play music, and generally promote a lifestyle that emphasized Eastern religions, free love, drugs, and crazy new means of artistic expression. Ferlinghetti's **City Lights Bookstore** (*see* Books *in* Chapter 3) continues to publish and sell works by little-known alternative authors, as well as the writings of the beats (who have been anthologized to high heaven and hardly qualify as alternative anymore). In the late 1980s Ferlinghetti led a movement to rename a number of small San Francisco streets after authors who had lived here; **Jack Kerouac Lane** is right next to the store, and in 1994 Ferlinghetti himself received the same honor: An alley off Union Street, near Stockton Street, was renamed **Via Ferlinghetti,** though the short dead-end street is barely longer than its new name.

Although the beats had their day in the 1950s and the number of Italian Americans living in North Beach is diminishing, the neighborhood remains one of San Francisco's most interesting. Many of North Beach's shops and watering holes look the same as they did during the bohemian era: At **Vesuvio** (*see* Chapter 6), a bar just across the alley from City Lights, the poets undoubtedly consumed more than one glass of red. **Caffè Trieste** (*see* Chapter 5) fueled the beats with their favorite legal amphetamine, espresso; the clientele, several decades later, still looks pretty beat.

A hefty walk up Russian Hill, **29 Russell Street** (between Larkin and Hyde streets and Union and Green streets) is where Kerouac crashed with Neal and Carolyn Cassady for a time in the early '50s. (His relationship with Neal is immortalized in his popular novel *On the Road,* though *The Subterraneans* better evokes Kerouac's North Beach days.) The **North Beach Museum,** on the mezzanine level of Bay View (1435 Stockton St., at Columbus Ave., tel. 415/391–6210), contains a handwritten manuscript of Ferlinghetti's "The Old Italians Dying," a poem about the old men of North Beach.

But real San Franciscans come to North Beach not for history but for food. Stop in at **Liguria Bakery** (1700 Stockton St., at Filbert St., tel. 415/421–3786) for focaccia right out of the oven. The **Molinari Delicatessen** (373 Columbus Ave., at Vallejo St., tel. 415/421–2337) has an extensive selection of salamis, olive oils, cheeses, pastas, wines, chocolates, and breads—perfect for a splendid picnic at **Washington Square** (*see* Parks, *below*). Bus 30 or 45 will get you to North Beach from Market and 3rd streets.

NOB HILL AND RUSSIAN HILL

The most elitist of San Francisco's districts is **Nob Hill** (between California, Powell, Broadway, and Leavenworth streets), the locus of San Francisco high society for more than a century. "Snob Hill," as it's called by some residents of the valley below, has great views that even the downtrodden will enjoy, though it's a strenuous walk to the top. North of Nob Hill lies **Russian Hill,** originally the burial ground for Russian seal hunters and traders, which today houses a combination of old Victorian homes, new high-rises, and more of San Francisco's moneyed class. On your way from Nob Hill to Russian Hill, check out the small **Cable Car Museum** (*see* Museums, *below*).

A steep walk (or a $2 cable car ride) up Powell Street from Union Square brings you to what once were the hilltop estates of the Big Four railroad kings: Leland Stanford, Mark Hopkins, Collis Huntington, and Charles Crocker. Now the city's most luxurious hotels are here, including the **Fairmont Hotel,** at California and Mason streets, and the **Stanford Court Hotel,** at California and Powell streets. Across California Street from the Fairmont is the plush Mark Hopkins Hotel, whose **Top of the Mark** (tel. 415/616–6916) is the perfect place for high tea (weekdays 3–5), cocktails (daily 5–midnight), and breathtaking views of the city. The mansion that belonged to silver magnate James Flood is one of the few that survived the 1906 quake; it now houses the **Pacific Union Club** (1000 California St.).

GRACE CATHEDRAL

A pseudo-Gothic structure that took 53 years to build, the cathedral is essentially a poured-concrete replica of an old European-style cathedral. The gilded bronze doors at the east entrance were taken from casts of Ghiberti's *Gates of Paradise* on the Baptistery in Florence. For a truly sublime experience, come for the singing of **vespers** every Sunday at 3:30 or Thursday at 5:15; an all-male choir will leave you feeling uplifted. If this doesn't do the trick, take a walk through the marble labyrinth to the right of the east entrance—it's a replica of France's Chartres Cathedral. Guided tours of the cathedral are free (donations accepted). *1100 California St., at Taylor St., tel. 415/749–6310. Guides available weekdays 1–3, Sat. 11:30–1:30, Sun. 12:30–2. From Embarcadero BART/Muni, Bus 1 west to corner of Sacramento and Jones Sts.*

Nob Hill derives its name from the term nabob, meaning "anyone of great worth or wealth."

LOMBARD STREET AND ENVIRONS

The most famous of Russian Hill's manicured streets is undoubtedly Lombard Street, a steep block of which is known as the **crookedest street in the world.** It descends the east side of Russian Hill in eight switchbacks between Hyde and Leavenworth streets.

Steep Russian Hill has a number of funky little stairways that wind through trees or lead to miniature parks. The steps at Lombard and Larkin streets eventually reach a small rest spot with an incredible view of the Golden Gate Bridge. On the east side of Russian Hill, the steps at Vallejo and Mason streets will transport you to **Ina Coolbrith Park,** which offers shady trees and views of Oakland and the Bay Bridge. When you reach Taylor Street, you can tackle an additional set of stairs across the street or visit **Macondray Lane.** To reach the lane, go right on Taylor Street and stroll two blocks to a set of wooden stairs between Green and Union streets (this is an official path, not someone's private entrance). These steps will bring you to a tiny cobblestone alley—Macondray Lane—the thinly veiled setting of Armistead Maupin's *Tales of the City.* Also look for the dark, wood-shingled houses designed by Willis Polk before the 1906 earthquake. One lies on the **1000 block of Green Street,** which also contains one of the city's two remaining eight-sided houses, built in the 1850s, as well as a firehouse dating from 1907. The more strenuous route from Coolbrith Park continues straight through the intersection of Taylor and Vallejo streets: The flower-lined path ends at **San Simone Park,** which has a prime view of Alcatraz and the East Bay. Coming down Vallejo Street, you will pass by a few side alleys; notable are **Florence Place** and the beautiful English cottages of **Russian Hill Place.**

THE PRESIDIO AND MARINA

Stretching over a gorgeous swath of waterfront between Fort Mason and the Presidio and bordered to the south by **Union Street,** the Marina provides a home—or rather, a series of multi-million-dollar Mediterranean-style homes—for San Francisco's young professionals. Ironically, all these folks with stable incomes live on decidedly unstable property: The Marina is built on landfill and is dangerously susceptible to the whims of Mother Earthquake. Recent college grads come to the Marina's main drag, **Chestnut Street,** from all over the city to chow down and drink up at innumerable restaurants and bars and to engage in mating rituals at singles bars. This is also the most convenient area to get a bite or a drink after visiting Fort Mason.

A well-stocked **Safeway** supermarket (15 Marina Blvd., between Laguna and Buchanan Sts., tel. 415/563–4946), right across the street from Fort Mason, provides cheap food for guests of the **Fort Mason International Hostel** (*see* Hostels *in* Chapter 7). This particular store is nicknamed Singles Safeway

THE $1 TOUR BUS

For a quick $1 tour of some of the city's most varied neighborhoods, hop aboard Muni's 30 Stockton bus. From the Montgomery Street BART station, the bus takes you through downtown and North Beach, then past the lavish Victorian mansions of Russian Hill. Next, you'll go through the Marina and Ghirardelli Square, and finally you'll wind right past the Palace of Fine Arts, the Exploratorium, and the eastern edge of the Presidio. On the return route, you'll go through the heart of Chinatown before ending up on Market Street, near the Powell Street BART station.

because of the "meat market" opportunities. If you're in a picnicking mood, **Marina Green,** directly west of Fort Mason, provides the necessary lawn as well as stunning views of the bay and the Marin Headlands.

FORT MASON

A series of warehouses built atop piers on the Marina's eastern border, Fort Mason was once an army command post. Now it's a nexus of artistic, cultural, and environmental organizations: The African-American, Mexican, and Italoamericano museums (*see* Museums, *below*) are all housed here, as is the Magic Theatre (*see* Theater *in* Chapter 6). Most days it's fairly quiet, so you can enjoy fantastic views of the bay in peace and solitude. Worth picking up is the Fort Mason monthly newsletter (available free at any of the museums), which details classes, lectures, concerts, and special exhibitions.

Tucked into one of the Fort Mason warehouses is the renowned vegetarian restaurant **Greens** (*see* Chapter 4). At the **Book Bay Bookstore** (Fort Mason Center, Bldg. C, tel. 415/771–1076), run by the Friends of the San Francisco Public Library, you can still get a book for 99¢. It's open daily 11–5. From Fisherman's Wharf Fort Mason is a 10-minute walk west: Follow Beach Street past the Municipal Pier and climb the forested hill past the AYH Hostel; as you descend on the other side, you'll see Fort Mason spread out along the waterfront. *Tel. 415/979–3010 for general information. Buses 22, 28, 30, 47, and 49.*

PALACE OF FINE ARTS

At the far western edge of the Marina is the Palace of Fine Arts, built to resemble a classic colonnaded Roman temple, with attractive landscaping and a pond out front. Several similar structures were erected for the 1915 Panama Pacific Expo, but this is the only one that remains. Adjacent you'll find the **Exploratorium** (*see* Museums, *below*), a hands-on museum devoted to making science interesting for common folk. *Baker and Beach Sts., tel. 415/563–6504. Buses 28, 30, and 43.*

THE PRESIDIO

The Presidio, a 1,480-acre chunk of prime waterfront land stretching from the west end of the Marina all the way to the Golden Gate Bridge, was originally a fort, founded by the Spanish in 1776. The flags of Mexico, the Bear Flag Republic, and the U.S. Army have all flown over the Presidio—one of the oldest military installations in the United States. On October 1, 1994, it became part of the National Park System, though the army will remain here in a reduced capacity for a while longer.

The ambitious plan for the Presidio is to turn it into the country's first self-sustaining national park by the year 2013, equal parts commerce and nature. A handful of nonprofit organizations have already moved into vacant army buildings, and George Lucas's Dreamworks has been chosen to develop part of the Presidio as a high-tech "campus." Residents are pleased because they're most worried about parking and traffic, and Lucas's development plan affects the area during the day only—but for now you can count on finding rolling hills crossed by plenty of trails (for specifics on hiking and biking, *see* Chapter 8); historic military buildings; and terrific views of the bay. A few paths lead through a man-made **forest** of 400,000 pine, cypress, and eucalyptus trees; these were planted in the 1880s by schoolchildren and soldiers to make the post seem larger. The **Officer's Club,** on Moraga Avenue, contains one adobe wall reputed to date from 1776. The free **Presidio Museum** has a collection relating to the Presidio's history, and at historic Fort Point (*see* Golden Gate Bridge, *above*), free guided tours give you an inside look at this 19th-century fort. *Funston Ave. at Lincoln Blvd., tel. 415/561–4331. Open Wed.–Sun. noon–4.*

The easiest way to get to the Presidio is to drive north toward the bay on Van Ness Avenue, turn left on Lombard Street, and then follow the signs. Otherwise, take Bus 38 from the Montgomery Street BART/Muni station to Geary Boulevard and Presidio Avenue, then switch to Bus 43, which travels into the Presidio.

UNION STREET

Union Street competes with Chestnut Street (*see above*) with its abundance of specialty boutiques and expensive coffee bars. The neighborhood around it is known as **Cow Hollow,** so named because it used to house a dairy-farming community. Its rows of sparkling refurbished Victorian houses are undoubtedly beautiful, but the area clobbers you over the cranium with quaintness.

Don't miss the **Wedding Houses** (1980 Union St., near Buchanan St.), two identical houses built side by side as wedding presents for two sisters who were marrying at the same time. The brides' father had the houses stationed next to each other so he could easily keep an eye on them. These days all he'd see are two stunning Victorians filled with upscale shops. **Carol Doda's Champagne and Lace Lingerie Boutique** (*see* Specialty Items *in* Chapter 3) is owned by the woman who led the movement to legalize topless dancing in the 1960s, when she became the first woman to bare her breasts as part of a nightclub show. A block north of Union Street, the Vedanta Society of Northern California's **Old Temple** (2963 Webster St., at Filbert St.) combines the best elements of Victorian architecture and the Taj Mahal's design. The Hindu temple (built in 1905) is closed to tourists. Bus 41 from the Embarcadero BART/Muni station runs along Union Street.

THE WAVE ORGAN

A visit to the wave organ, built by artists with help from the Exploratorium, is a unique and peaceful San Francisco experience. The funky sea-powered organ, decorated with recycled bits of marble and granite, consists of a set of pipes that run along the waterfront and extend into the bay. Take a seat at one of the stone benches, place your ear on one of the pipes, and listen to the soothing musical tones of lapping waves. Acoustics are best at high tide. To get to the wave organ from the Exploratorium, walk north on Baker Street across Marina Boulevard and walk right down the road past the St. Francis and Golden Gate Yacht clubs to the end of the jetty.

PACIFIC HEIGHTS

Pacific Heights is the posh neighborhood of Victorian mansions that rises up from Van Ness and over to the Presidio, between California and Union streets. The district's stately homes were fortunate to survive the great 1906 fire; houses east of Van Ness Avenue were utterly destroyed, and those along the avenue were dynamited to create a firebreak. **Upper Fillmore**—the stretch of Fillmore Street from Bush Street to Jackson Street—is a picturesque area in which to stroll, browse the neighborhood's ritzy boutiques, and have a cup of espresso. To get to Pacific Heights, take Bus 1 California from the Embarcadero BART/Muni station or Bus 22 Fillmore from the Marina.

HAAS-LILIENTHAL HOUSE

A good place to start your tour of Victorian Pacific Heights is at the Haas-Lilienthal House, the city's only Victorian mansion open to the public. The 1886 Queen Anne Victorian, considered modest in its day, is now the pride and joy of the **Foundation for San Francisco's Architectural Heritage,** headquartered here. You must join an hour-long docent-led tour ($5) to see the house's interior. Tours depart Wednesday 11–3 and Sunday noon–4 whenever a small group has gathered. Meet here at 12:30 on Sunday for a two-hour walking tour ($5) covering the surrounding blocks of Victorians and Edwardians—and learn once and for all that these terms refer to periods (1837–1901 and 1901–1910, respectively), not architectural styles. *2007 Franklin St., between Washington and Jackson Sts., tel. 415/441–3000.*

LAFAYETTE PARK

From the Haas-Lilienthal House, walk three blocks south to the corner of California Street to get to the **Coleman House** (1701 Franklin St.), which is now filled with law offices and closed to the nonlitigious public. This a Queen Anne tower house—you'll see the aforementioned tower prominently displayed on the corner. Turn right on California Street and right again on Octavia Street to reach **Lafayette Park.** Visited by dog walkers, picnickers, and sunbathers, the park's expansive lawns slope to a wooded crest, just as a well-behaved English-style garden should. On the north side of the park, behold the **Spreckels Mansion** (2080 Washington St.), an imposing 1913 French baroque structure now owned by author Danielle Steele and her husband. You can see the effects of San Francisco's moist and salty air on the ill-chosen Utah limestone, which has noticeably eroded. Blame architect George Applegarth, who also designed the California Palace of the Legion of Honor (*see* Museums, *below*).

JAPANTOWN

Modern Japantown, which spans the area north of Geary Expressway between Fillmore and Laguna streets, is dominated by the massive, somewhat depressing shopping complex called Nihonmachi, better known as **Japan Center.** The city's Japanese community was much larger prior to World War II, when California "relocated" Japanese-Americans into concentration camps. There are a number of good restaurants (*see* Chapter 4) here and some import shops.

Japan Center's **Peace Plaza** and five-story **Pagoda** were designed by architect Yoshiro Taniguchi as a gesture of goodwill from the people of Japan. The plaza is landscaped with traditional Japanese-style gardens and reflecting pools and is the site of many festivals throughout the year. The two-day **Nihonmachi Street Fair** (tel. 415/771–9861), held in early August, celebrates the contributions of Asian-Americans in the United States. The popular **Cherry Blossom Festival** (*see* When to Go *in* Chapter 1), held in late April, features *taiko* drumming, martial arts, food, music, dance, and a parade.

To relax after a tough day of sightseeing, try a Japanese steam bath at the **Kabuki Springs and Spa** (1750 Geary Expressway, tel. 415/922–6000), where you can use the steam room, sauna, and hot and cold baths for $10 ($15 after 5 PM and on weekends), no reservations necessary. A 25-minute shiatsu massage (with unlimited communal bath use) costs $40; appointments are recommended. The communal baths are reserved for women on Sunday, Wednesday, and Friday; men get to use it the rest of the week. Hours are daily 10–10. Also in the Japan Center, the **AMC Kabuki 8** theater (*see* Movie Houses *in* Chapter 6) shows first-run films in a high-tech complex. From the Montgomery Street BART/Muni station, Buses 2, 3, 4, and 38 will deposit you in Japantown.

RICHMOND DISTRICT

The Richmond District, north of Golden Gate Park, is a sprawling neighborhood of bland town houses. A bit of color comes from the large number of Southeast Asian and Chinese families who have moved here in recent years, escaping the cramped conditions of Chinatown. **Clement Street,** the main shopping boulevard, contain a dizzying array of produce markets, Chinese herb shops, and Asian restaurants, as well as a smattering of Irish pubs and a couple of good used-book stores. Bus 2 from the Montgomery Street BART/Muni station downtown will get you here.

Clement Street between Arguello Boulevard and 8th Avenue is a great place to refuel after a day at Ocean Beach or in Golden Gate Park. **Haig's Delicacies** (642 Clement St., at 8th Ave., tel. 415/752–6283) is a one-of-a-kind market and delicatessen, importing interesting food items from the Middle East, India, and Europe. **New May Wah Supermarket** (547 Clement St., no phone) has special ingredients (sauces, teas, noodles, and more) for Chinese, Vietnamese, Thai, and Japanese dishes. **Green Apple Books** (*see* Books *in* Chapter 3) has a huge selection of new and used books—you could lose yourself in this store for days.

HAIGHT-ASHBURY

East of Golden Gate Park sits the Haight-Ashbury district, a name that still strikes fear in the hearts of suburban parents everywhere. The Haight, nicknamed "Hashbury" by Hunter S. Thompson, began its career as a center for the counterculture in the late 1950s and early '60s, when some beat writers, several illustrious fathers of the drug culture, and bands like the Grateful Dead and Jefferson Airplane moved in. Attracted by the neighborhood's ensuing liberal atmosphere, several hundred thousand blissed-out teenagers soon converged on the Haight to spend their savings on acid, play music, and sing days-long renditions of "Uncle John's Band." But like the '60s themselves, Haight-Ashbury's atmosphere of excitement and idealism was pretty much washed up by the mid-1970s. Nowadays the Haight is more of a punk-rock haven where kids do things that frighten their formerly hippie parents.

Since the 1970s the stretch of **Haight Street** between Divisadero and Stanyan streets—often called the Upper Haight to distinguish it from the Lower Haight (*see below*)—has gone through various stages of increasing and decreasing seediness and gentrification. With no little irony, its countercultural spirit survives largely in terms of the goods you can buy: rock star T-shirts, bumper stickers, necklaces made with "healing crystals," and such. Neohippies still play guitar on the street corner, but the revolution is nowhere in sight. What *is* in sight is the gleaming Gap store now standing on the famed corner of Haight-Ashbury. The youthful slackers who live here now wear black, ride motorcycles, pierce body parts, and listen to dissonant music at bars like the **Thirsty Swede** (1821 Haight St., no phone) or to live jazz and swing at **The Deluxe** (*see* Bars *in* Chapter 6). The attraction is probably less the neighborhood's historical legacy than its bars, cafés, and breakfast joints, like the **Pork Store Café** (*see* Chapter 4).

As a tourist in Haight-Ashbury, you'll find there's little to do besides people-watching (while dodging panhandlers) and exploring the jewelry and secondhand clothing stores lining the blocks between Masonic and Clayton streets. For secondhand threads try **Aardvark's Odd Ark, Buffalo Exchange,** or **Wasteland** (*see* Secondhand and Vintage Clothing *in* Chapter 3). The Grateful Dead, Speed Racer, Alfred E. Newman, and Bob Marley are all represented on the walls of **Haight-Ashbury T-Shirts** (1500 Haight St., at Ashbury St., tel. 415/863–4639). Down the street, the **Haight-Ashbury Free Medical Clinic** (*see* Emergencies *in* Chapter 1) is one of the last vestiges of hippie idealism on the street; it's been offering free medical care ever since the '60s. When the weather is warm, head down the street to **Buena Vista Park** (*see* Parks, *below*). Buses 6, 7, 66, and 71 will get you to Haight-Ashbury from downtown's Market Street.

LOWER HAIGHT AND THE WESTERN ADDITION

The hip, alternative Haight of the '60s isn't dead; it's just relocated. Today's young urban nihilists congregate in the Lower Haight—between **Divisadero** and **Webster streets.** As in the Upper Haight, consumerism and counterculture go hand in hand here; the street is full of head shops, record stores, underground cafés, and nightclubs. This colorful haven of new subcultures is itself subverted, however, by the very real poverty of its neighboring district to the north, the Western Addition.

LOWER HAIGHT

Full of disaffected youths and battered Victorian houses, the Lower Haight is a new breeding ground for a community of angry youth, eccentrics of all ages, mental cases, and—perhaps an amalgam of all three—aspiring artists and writers. At night the street is loud with the din of '70s funk or '90s hip-hop blaring from the doorway of **Nickie's BBQ** (*see* Clubs *in* Chapter 6), which overflows with sweaty dancing youth of all races. If you're looking for a more laid-back scene, skirt the ornery drunks and drug dealers and head for **Mad Dog in the Fog,** an English-style pub (*see* Bars *in* Chapter 6). During daylight the **Horse Shoe** coffeehouse (*see* Chapter 5) is a meeting place for neopsychedelic artists and poetry-writing trust-fund kids, while **Café International** (508 Haight St., at Fillmore St., tel. 415/552–7390) plays those old Donovan songs you thought you'd finally escaped. Neobeatniks and punks brunch at **Kate's Kitchen** (*see* Chapter 4). **Naked Eye News and Video** (533 Haight St., between Fillmore and Steiner Sts., tel. 415/864–2985) stocks alternative comics and 'zines and avant-garde, foreign, and obscure videos.

WESTERN ADDITION

Best explored during daylight hours, the Western Addition is a community struggling with a legacy of poverty and discrimination. During World War II, African Americans migrated here in droves to fill vacated factory jobs; after the war most lost their jobs to returning white GIs, and the neighborhood became a nest of brothels and gambling joints. In the 1960s many older buildings were torn down as part of a city "urban renewal" program. Today the main commercial drag is Fillmore Street between Oak Street and the Geary Expressway. Among the highlights of the neighborhood is **Marcus Books** (*see* Books *in* Chapter 3), which sells an outstanding range of works on African-American literature and history. The **Center for African and African-American Art and Culture** (762 Fulton St., at Webster St., tel. 415/928–8546) has a modest library of books and magazines on African-American themes; Internet and computer databases; and an archive room full of rare pamphlets, magazines, and publications. Call for information on poetry workshops and other events. At the corner of **Octavia** and **Bush streets,** which is technically Japantown these days, a half dozen eucalyptus trees and a memorial plaque mark the former residence of Mary Ellen Pleasant (1816–1904), a heroine of the Western Addition. Rumored to be a madam, a murderer, a witch, or some combination thereof, Pleasant was most renowned for her business savvy—her profits financed the western leg of the Underground Railroad.

HOME SWEET HOME

Haight-Ashbury has had its share of famous (and infamous) residents. You probably won't run into Jimi today, but you can certainly check out the home where he once lived.

Janis Joplin: 112 Lyon St., between Page and Oak Sts.

The Grateful Dead: 710 Ashbury St., at Waller St.

The Manson Family: 636 Cole St., at Haight St.

Jefferson Airplane: 2400 Fulton St., at Willard St.

Sid Vicious: 26 Delmar St., at Frederick St.

Jimi Hendrix: 142 Central Ave., at Haight St.

Hunter S. Thompson: 318 Parnassus Ave., at Willard St.

PAINTED LADIES • The most famous row of houses in San Francisco is across from Alamo Square, a block west of Fillmore Street. Featured on hundreds of postcards and in the opening credits of several TV shows set in San Francisco, the Painted Ladies—six beautifully restored, brightly painted Victorians—sit side by side on a steep street with the downtown skyline looming majestically behind. To snap the obligatory picture, take Bus 6, 7, 66, or 71 from downtown Market Street to Haight and Steiner streets and walk north on Steiner to Hayes Street.

CASTRO DISTRICT

You'll know you're in the Castro when you see rainbow flags adorning businesses and homes and pink-triangle bumper stickers on cars. Since the early 1970s this neighborhood has been attracting gay men and women from around the world. Before the AIDS epidemic it was known as a spot for open revelry, with disco music pumping on Castro Street 24 hours a day. Today the community is less carefree than in the first years of open gay pride, but on weekends it still bustles with people socializing on the streets, in the bars, and at the gyms.

The heart of the district is **Castro Street** between Market and 19th streets. At the southwest corner of Market and Castro, where the K, L, and M Muni streetcar lines stop, is **Harvey Milk Plaza,** named in honor of California's first openly gay elected official. On November 27, 1978, Milk and then-mayor George Moscone were assassinated by Dan White, a disgruntled former supervisor. During his trial White claimed the high sugar content of his junk-food diet altered his mental state—the so-called Twinkie defense—and was convicted of voluntary manslaughter by reason of diminished capacity. The night of the verdict 40,000 San Franciscans gathered at the plaza and launched what have come to be known as the White Night riots, in which property was burned and destroyed. They then proceeded to city hall in a candlelight march; the procession is repeated every year on the anniversary of the event.

One block away, where 18th and Castro streets meet, you'll find the gayest four corners in the world: All of the shops, bars, and cafés cater to the gay community. On weekends people hand out advertisements for gay clubs, marches, lectures, and political causes. Travel agencies bill themselves as gay and lesbian vacation experts, and card shops have names such as **Does Your Mother Know. . .** (4079 18th St., tel. 415/864–3160) and stock coming-out and same-sex love cards. A block from the intersection is the **Castro Theatre** (*see* Movie Houses *in* Chapter 6), the grand Art Deco repertory house that hosts the much-loved International Lesbian and Gay Film Festival each summer.

Everywhere, the Castro abounds with unique shops and services. The offerings at **Man Line** (516 Castro St., tel. 415/863–7811) include Keith Haring earrings and rainbow-striped robes and flags. **Under One Roof** (*see* Specialty Items *in* Chapter 3) carries license plate holders marked with pink triangles, red-ribbon pins, and a good selection of soaps, lotions, books, and cards. It donates 100% of its profits to AIDS organizations. The renowned **A Different Light** (*see* Books *in* Chapter 3) stocks an extensive collection of lesbian, gay, and transsexual literature and serves as an unofficial information center for the gay and lesbian community.

The social hub of the neighborhood is east of Harvey Milk Plaza, at **Café Flore** (*see* Chapter 5), where heads turn and the gossip mills churn. Closer to Castro Street, **The Café** (*see* Bars *in* Chapter 6) is the only bar in the area where women are a majority of the clientele, although even the Café has shifted toward a more male crowd in recent years. At the intersection of Castro and Market streets, **Twin Peaks** (*see* Bars *in* Chapter 6) has the distinction of being the first gay bar in the city with clear glass windows.

NAMES PROJECT FOUNDATION

For a sobering reminder of the continuing crisis facing the gay community, drop by the NAMES Project Foundation's **Visitor Center and Panelmaking Workshop,** where panels from the now-famous *NAMES Quilt*—a tribute to many who have died of AIDS—are displayed. The project started in 1987 when gay rights activist Cleve Jones organized a meeting with several others who had lost friends or lovers to AIDS, hoping they could create a memorial. They decided on a quilt, each panel to be created by loved ones of individuals who have succumbed to the disease. The idea caught on, and people from all over the country sent in quilt panels. To date, the entire quilt (more than 40,000 panels) has been displayed in front of the White House four times. There are always some panels on display in the San Francisco office, as well as in other offices all over the world. For those who are interested in creating a panel, the foundation provides sewing machines, fabric, and support at their weekly quilting bee, on Wednesday 7 PM–10 PM. *2362A Market St., at Castro St., tel. 415/863–1966. Visitor center open daily noon–5.*

You can watch a nonmainstream film, admire the Art Deco architecture and fabulous ceiling decorations, and listen to a live organist—all at the beloved Castro Theatre.

TWIN PEAKS

When the Spanish came to this area in the 18th century, they named the pair of peaks looming over the bay *Los Pechos de la Choca* (the Breasts of the Indian Maiden). The name has changed, but the Twin Peaks remain spectacular: From here you can see both the bay and the ocean and everything in between. To reach Twin Peaks, take Bus 37 west from Market and Castro streets. Bring a picnic and allow at least 30 minutes to walk up and around.

One of San Francisco's most beautiful staircases, **Pemberton Place,** is worth a visit if you're in the Twin Peaks area. Take Bus 33 to Corbett Avenue and start climbing the stairs off Clayton Street. You will be rewarded with incredible views—and a workout to boot!

NOE VALLEY

Lying one major hill away from the hectic Mission and Castro districts, Noe Valley seems like a sedate older sister, one who traded the glitz and glamour and hard edges of city life for a more settled arrangement. It's a sunny, neighborly venue for eco-conscious types, their babies, and their dogs. Decades ago this was strictly an enclave of Irish and German immigrants; these days you can still find grandmotherly types gossiping in German on Noe Valley's street corners. **Lehr's German Specialties** (1581 Church St., at 28th St., tel. 415/282–6803) stocks Old Country favorites, from bottled bitters to Bavarian tunes. **Speckmann's** (1550 Church St., between 27th and 28th Sts., tel. 415/282–6850) serves up delicious, embarrassingly outsized platefuls of kraut, wurst, and goulash. Their adjacent deli stocks your favorite German specialties.

Noe Valley's main drag, **24th Street,** is a comfortable mixture of old-timey restaurants and trendy new clothing stores, of hardware stores and chic cafés. The blocks surrounding its intersection with **Noe Street** are best for exploring. **Global Exchange** (*see* Charitable Causes *in* Chapter 3) satisfies the neighborhood's social conscience: It's an international organization that promotes exchange between the United States and developing countries. At the end of the day grab a cup of espresso at **Tully's** (3966 24th St., near Noe St., tel. 415/550–7416), relax on one of the benches outside, and contemplate which Brie you're going to bring home from the **24th Street Cheese Company** (3893 24th St., at Sanchez St., tel. 415/821–6658).

GAY AND LESBIAN SAN FRANCISCO

San Francisco promotes itself as not only a gay city but the gayest in the world. Some neighborhood populations are as much as 95% gay; it is possible here for lesbians and gay men to go about their lives dealing almost exclusively with other gays and lesbians, both in business and in pleasure. And although gay bashing is still a reality, at least here many such cases are fully prosecuted.

San Francisco's most concentrated gay neighborhood is the Castro District, followed closely by Polk Gulch. Although there isn't a lesbian neighborhood per se, many young lesbians gravitate to the Mission. Bernal Heights attracts slightly older gay women, while the more upwardly mobile lesbian set heads to Noe Valley. Valencia Street in the Mission is home to the greatest concentration of women-oriented shops, though it is not nearly the lesbian enclave it was in the 1980s.

Until the early 1970s the Castro was a neighborhood of middle-class heterosexual families. When the countercultural fervor in nearby Haight-Ashbury came too close for comfort, whole blocks of families fled for more suburban digs. Houses stood vacant, rents plummeted, and young single men moved in. The first gay bars had opened on Castro Street by 1967, and in the '70s the scene exploded. Lured by national publicity, gay men and lesbians from all over the country migrated to the Castro and Polk Street, and the community became a serious force in city politics. Many gays and lesbians hold public office, ranging from sitting on the Board of Supervisors to being Police Commission members to being judges on the Municipal Court.

MISSION DISTRICT

The Mission District, named after the historic Mission Dolores (*see below*) and stretching south along Mission Street from Market Street to César Chavez (Army) Street, is blessed with an unbelievable climate: Although the city's other districts are shrouded in fog, the Mission is usually basking in sun. For centuries it was considered San Francisco's prime real estate, first by Ohlone Native Americans and then by Spanish missionaries. Over the years various populations, primarily European, have given way to immigrants from Central and South America, though the neighborhood also currently includes a significant contingent of artists and radicals of all ethnicities. Today the Mission is the front line of a battle over gentrification, with low-income-housing advocates cursing young hipsters who move into the neighborhood for its alternative cachet, causing rents to rise. In all, the Mission is a colorful, friendly place, but it can also be dangerous. Be particularly careful on Mission Street between 14th and 20th streets, 24th Street near Treat Avenue, and on South Van Ness Avenue. Most women won't feel comfortable walking alone here at night, and when you actually find a parking space, you might think twice about leaving your car. Luckily, public transportation is a snap: Two BART stations (one at Mission and 16th streets, the other at Mission and 24th streets) put you right in the heart of things.

The Mission is the place to go for cheap food, especially huge burritos and succulent tacos made fresh in the numerous storefront *taquerías.* The area is also full of specialty bookstores (*see* Books *in* Chapter 3), inexpensive alternative theater companies, and an increasing variety of bars, which often have live music, poetry readings, and dance spaces. The architecture is worth noting, too, since many of the Mission's large Victorians survived the 1906 quake. For a listing of neighborhood culture stops, pick up *A Booklover's Guide to the Mission,* a free fold-out map available at most bookstores in the area.

The Mission's art scene is concentrated in the northern half of the neighborhood. A notable collection of cafés, bars, thrift shops, and cheap restaurants are gathered at the intersection of **16th** and **Valencia streets** (*see below*), which is also the site of an independent movie theater, the **Roxie Cinema** (*see* Movie Houses *in* Chapter 6). A few blocks north, **Red Dora's Bearded Lady** (*see* Chapter 5), a lesbian-owned café, is the only full-time lesbian-oriented space around. The southern half of the Mission is densely Mexican and Latin American, especially **24th Street** between Mission and Potrero streets. Here you'll find produce stands, *dulcerías* (sweets shops), and *panaderías* (bakeries) like **La Mexicana Bakery** (2804 24th St., at York St., tel. 415/648–2633). The **St. Francis Soda Fountain and Candy Store** (*see box* Sweet Treats *in* Chapter 4) has been serving homemade ice cream since 1918.

VALENCIA STREET

A good place to discover the offbeat side of the Mission is on Valencia Street (a block west of Mission Street) between 16th and 24th streets. The shops here are unusual, to say the least: **Botanica Yoruba** (998 Valencia St., at 21st St., tel. 415/826–4967) has incense, candles, herbs, and oils, as well as hour-long *limpieza* (spiritual cleansing) sessions, performed by a member of the Santeria religion (reservations required). For leftist books, try **Modern Times** (*see* Books *in* Chapter 3); and for avant-garde videos, head to **Leather Tongue** (*see* Specialty Shops *in* Chapter 3).

Neighborhood landmarks include the **Women's Building** (3543 18th St., between Valencia and Guerrero Sts., tel. 415/431–1180), a meeting place for progressive and radical political groups. Note the mural *Women's Wisdom through Time,* completed in 1995 with the help of more than 500 artists. You'll see Audre Lorde, Georgia O'Keeffe, and Rigoberta Menchú among many other women's names woven into the fabric of the mural (*see box* Murals with a Mission, *below*). The 1906 **Levi Strauss factory** (250 Valencia St., near 14th St., tel. 415/565–9159), the oldest jeans-making facility in the West, conducts free, 1½-hour tours every Tuesday and Wednesday at 9, 11, and 1:30. Reservations are required.

DOLORES STREET AND THE MISSION DOLORES

West of Valencia Street, the Mission becomes green, hilly, and residential. Dolores Street, its median, is graced with a row of stately old palm trees and marks the district's western border. Although many gay men live just west of here, in the Castro, Dolores Street and the surrounding residential area are quietly, though not exclusively, lesbian. **Mission Dolores Park** (*see* Parks, *below*) is a favorite with locals on warm, sunny days—if you stop by, be sure to look for the **gold fire hydrant** at the park's southwest corner (20th and Church streets). When all the other hydrants went dry during the firestorm that followed the 1906 earthquake, this one kept pumping.

Though it's made of humble adobe, **Mission Dolores,** the oldest building in San Francisco, has survived some powerful earthquakes and fires. It was commissioned by Junípero Serra to honor San Francisco de Asís (St. Francis of Assisi) and completed in 1791. The Spanish nicknamed it Dolores after a nearby stream, *Arroyo de Nuestra Señora de los Dolores* (Stream of Our Lady of the Sorrows), and the name stuck long after the river dried up and disappeared. Architecturally, Mission Dolores is the simplest of all the California missions—it's also seen the fewest modifications over the centuries. Look up at the ceiling and you'll see traditional Native American designs, hand-painted by local Costanoan Indians. The mission bells still ring on holy days, and the cemetery next door is the permanent home of a few early rancheros, including San Francisco's first mayor, Don Francisco de Haro. The small admission fee gives you access to the mission, the cemetery, and a small display of artifacts; another option is the worthwhile 45-minute tour ($5). *16th and Dolores Sts., tel. 415/621–8203. Admission $2. Open daily 9–4:30.*

POTRERO HILL

Just east of the Mission and South of SoMa, Potrero Hill is a sunny, quiet, and untouristed community where you can feast your eyes on spectacular views of the Financial District skyline and the East Bay. The main strip of Goat Hill, as it's also known, is along 18th Street between Arkansas and Connecticut streets, where you'll find an assortment of mellow restaurants, cafés, and a bookstore, as well as the

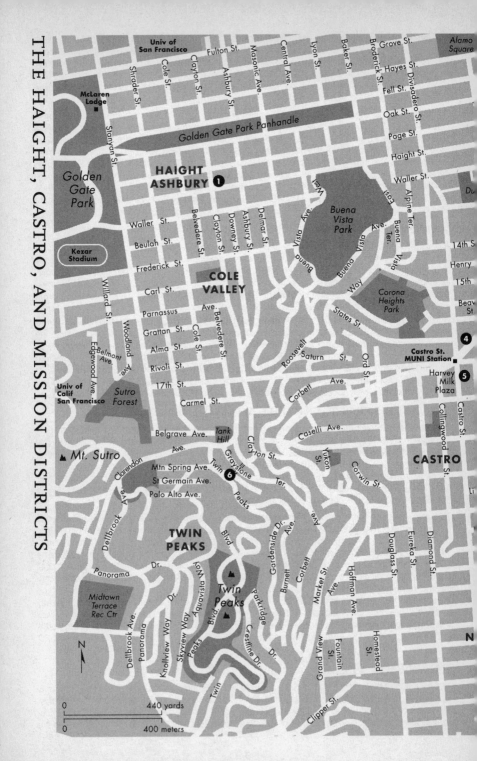

Univ of
San Francisco

Fulton St.

Grove St.

Alamo
Square

McLaren
Lodge

Cole St.

Clayton St.

Ashbury St.

Masonic Ave.

Central Ave.

Lyon St.

Baker St.

Broderick St.

Hayes St.

Divisadero St.

Fell St.

Shrader St.

Stanyan St.

Golden Gate Park Panhandle

Oak St.

Page St.

Haight St.

HAIGHT
ASHBURY ❶

Waller St.

Du

Golden
Gate
Park

Waller St.

Beulah St.

Belvedere St.

Clayton St.

Downey St.

Ashbury St.

Delmar St.

West

Buena
Vista
Park

Buena Vista Ave.

Alpine Ter.

Buena Vista Ter.

Buena Vista

14th S

Kezar
Stadium

Frederick St.

buena

Henry

15th

COLE
VALLEY

Way

Corona
Heights
Park

Beav
St

Carl St.

Willard St.

Parnassus

Ave.

Belvedere St.

States St.

❹

Grattan St.

Cole St.

Roosevelt

Saturn

St.

Ord St.

Castro St.
MUNI Station ■

Univ of
Calif
San Francisco

Woodland

Ave.

Alma St.

Edgewood Ave.

Belmont Ave.

Rivoli St.

17th St.

Corbett

Ave.

Harvey
Milk
Plaza

❺

Castro St.

Collingwood St.

Sutro
Forest

Carmel St.

Caselli Ave.

Li

▲ Mt. Sutro

Belgrave Ave.

Ave.

Tank
Hill

Clayton St.

Graystone

Yukon St.

Corwin St.

CASTRO

Clarendon Ave.

Mtn Spring Ave.

St Germain Ave.

Palo Alto Ave.

Twin

Peaks

Ter.

❻

Dellbrook Ave.

TWIN
PEAKS

Dr.

Blvd.

Gardenside Dr.

Ave.

Corbett

Ave.

Douglass St.

Eureka St.

Diamond St.

Panorama

Midtown
Terrace
Rec Ctr

Dr.

Mt. Olympus Way

Twin
Peaks

Peaks Blvd.

Parkridge Dr.

Burnett

Market St.

Hoffman Ave.

Grand View

Fountain St.

Homestead St.

N

Dellbrook Ave.

Panorama

Knollview Way

Skyview Way

Peaks

Crestline Dr.

Clipper St.

N

0 ____ 440 yards

0 ____ 400 meters

Café Flore, **3**
Castro Theatre, **5**
Four Walls, **9**
Gold fire hydrant, **13**
Haight-Ashbury Free Medical Clinic, **1**
The Lab, **11**
Levi Strauss factory, **8**
Mission Cultural Center, **15**
Mission Dolores, **7**
NAMES Project, **4**
Painted Ladies, **2**
Pemberton Place stairway, **6**
Precita Eyes Mural Arts Center, **14**
Roxie Cinema, **10**
Women's Building, **12**

WESTERN ADDITION
LOWER HAIGHT
Van Ness MUNI Station
Church St. MUNI Station
MISSION
Mission Dolores Park
16th St./Mission BART Station
24th St./Mission BART Station
VALLEY
TO POTRERO HILL
[Closed]
101

10th St.
11th St.
12th St.
14th St.
15th St.
16th St.
17th St.
18th St.
19th St.
20th St.
21st St.
22nd St.
23rd St.
24th St.
25th St.
26th St.
27th St.
Jersey St.
Clipper St.
César Chavez (Army) St.

Steiner St.
Fillmore St.
Webster St.
Buchanan St.
Laguna St.
Gough St.
Octavia St.
Brady St.
South Van Ness Ave.
Howard St.
Mission St.
Hermann St.
Duboce Ave.
Market St.
Clinton Park
Brosnan St.
Caledonia St.
Minna St.
Natoma St.
Shotwell St.
Landers St.
Dolores St.
Guerrero St.
Ramona Ave.
Albion St.
Valencia St.
Sharon St.
Prosper St.
Pond St.
Noe St.
Chula Ln.
Sycamore St.
Lexington St.
San Carlos St.
Capp St.
Oakwood St.
Lapidge St.
Linda St.
Bartlett St.
Chattanooga St.
Church St.
Fair Oaks St.
Vicksburg St.
Sanchez St.
Osage Al.
Lilac St.

Pemberton
Pond St.
Prosper St.

53

MURALS WITH A MISSION

Following in the tradition of Mexican muralist Diego Rivera (1886–1957), various San Francisco artists have been painting huge, vibrant works on walls all over the city since the 1970s—especially in the Mission District. Pick up a "Mission Mural Walk" map ($1.50 donation) at the Precita Eyes Mural Arts Center (2981 24th St., at Harrison St., tel. 415/285–2287), or sign up for one of their mural walks ($7), Saturday at 1:30. From the 24th Street BART station, take Bus 48 to Harrison.

Daily Scoop (1401 18th St., at Missouri St., tel. 415/824–3975), an old-fashioned ice cream parlor. Come on a Monday evening, and your trek will be rewarded with pizza galore at **Goat Hill Pizza** (300 Connecticut St., at 18th St., tel. 415/641–1440). The waitstaff circles around the restaurant with different slices, and $8.50 buys you all you can stuff in your mouth—plus a salad. There's live piano Thursday and Friday. At **Bottom of the Hill** (*see* Live Music *in* Chapter 6), you can enjoy a great selection of local bands and occasional surprise visits by big-timers. And finally, don't tell Lombard Street enthusiasts (*see* Nob Hill and Russian Hill, *above*), but **Vermont Street,** at 20th Street, is *more* crooked—and without a tourist in sight. To get to Potrero Hill, take Bus 9 south from Civic Center to 16th Street and Potrero Avenue and then transfer to Bus 22 heading east.

SOUTH OF MARKET

Until recently SoMa—the area bordered by Mission Street, Townsend Street, the Embarcadero, and 12th Street—was merely a flat, nondescript stretch of abandoned factories. Only since the 1980s has the region come alive, filling those rows of empty warehouses with new-media start-ups, art galleries, alternative theaters, and dusk-to-dawn nightclubs. The SoMa nightlife scene centers around **Folsom Street,** a heathen's haven of dance clubs (*see* Chapter 6). SoMa is also home to the city's outlet stores and bargain warehouses (*see* Chapter 3). Closer to the water it's strictly a suits-and-heels crowd, but sort-of-hip, sort-of-yuppie cafés and restaurants have sprung up to serve the on-line professionals around surprisingly green **South Park** (*see* Parks, *below*).

The Yerba Buena Center for the Arts and the San Francisco Museum of Modern Art (*see* Museums, *below*) are the stars of the SoMa arts scene. Smaller, edgier galleries are relocating to the neighborhood as fast as they can, using light from the big names to draw attention to themselves; there are dozens of warehouse-cum-gallery spaces within a three-block radius of SFMOMA. One such venture, **Minna Street Gallery** (111 Minna St., between 2nd and 3rd Sts., tel. 415/974–1719), is a favorite after-work stop for new-media types. In addition to art, the gallery features funky music and happy hour Tuesday through Friday from 4 to 7.

YERBA BUENA GARDENS

This 8½-acre arts and performance space opened to much fanfare in 1993, after more than 30 years of planning and bureaucratic disputes. On the east side of the garden complex, the **Center for the Arts** houses galleries (*see* Museums, *below*) and a theater (*see* Multimedia Performance Spaces *in* Chapter 6) whose purpose is to celebrate the multicultural nature of the Bay Area. However, critics point out that the multicultural emphasis may be to the exclusion of mainstream arts. Others smirk at the money spent building the center: a whopping $41 million. *Mission St. at 3rd St., tel. 415/978–2787.*

Yerba Buena isn't just about high-concept art: Its manicured lawns provide a down-to-earth respite from the frenzy of downtown—just a couple of blocks southeast of the Montgomery Street BART station. Walk along the grassy, spacious esplanade to find the Martin Luther King Jr. Memorial: 12 glass panels, all behind a shimmering waterfall, engraved with quotes from Dr. King in English and in the languages of each of San Francisco's sister cities.

Metreon, Sony's brand-new $85 million entertainment mall at Yerba Buena Gardens, includes a 15-screen movie theater (offering full meals served on trays), an IMAX theater, a chichi restaurant and "Taste of San Francisco" food court, stores designed to sell you products by a few select brands, and interactive, imagination-teasing games for the kids. The city hopes that the 350,000-square-ft commercial theme park will mark the final step in SoMa's transition from gritty 'hood to upscale paradise. Then again, the city is also assuming the convention-size crowd expected to descend upon the center every day will take public transit (Metreon has no parking structure). Locals are gearing up for serious gridlock as would-be visitors try to snatch one of the few parking spots in the already-congested area. *Fourth and Mission Sts., South of Market, tel. 415/369–6000.*

The **San Francisco Museum of Modern Art** (*see* Museums, *below*), the **California Historical Society Museum** (678 Mission St., at 3rd St., tel. 415/357–1848), with an admission of $2, and the **Cartoon Art Museum** (*see* Museums, *below*) are all new neighbors of Yerba Buena Gardens. The **Mexican Museum** (*see* Museums, *below*), now in cramped quarters at Fort Mason, will make its new home here in late 2000.

PARKS

Along with Golden Gate Park (*see* Major Sights, *above*), the city has an abundance of smaller strips of greenery where you can cavort or sprawl on a blanket with the Sunday paper.

Folsom Street is the center of the hypermacho leather-oriented gay circuit. At no time is this more obvious than during September's Folsom Street Fair (tel. 415/861–3247), when studded bikers, cowboys, and construction workers choke the strip.

BUENA VISTA

They named this Buena Vista (good view) for a reason: It's set on a steep hill covered with cypress and eucalyptus, and from the summit, the views of the Golden Gate Bridge, the ocean, the Bay Bridge, and downtown create a mystical backdrop. The park has a reputation for being dangerous at night, but in the daytime it's a largely undiscovered escape from the asphalt chaos below. Entrance to the park is at the intersection of Haight and Lyon streets; from Market Street downtown, take Bus 6, 7, 66, or 71.

GLEN CANYON

Glen Canyon Park is hidden in part of the southwest corner of the city that isn't crawling with tourists; a visit is a total escape from urban life. Eucalyptus trees and a few climbing boulders loom above you, and grass-covered slopes lead down to a shady path, equal parts poison oak and soothing stream. Take BART to the Glen Park station, then walk about five blocks uphill (west) on Bosworth Street.

MISSION DOLORES PARK

In a sunny residential area between the Mission and Castro, beautiful Dolores Park attracts picnickers, dogs and dog owners, and families of all sorts. On warm days there's usually a contingent of sunbathing men wearing Speedos—they are Castro residents who've dubbed the park "Castro Beach." The park, set on a gently sloping hill, has tennis courts, a basketball court, a playground, and wide expanses of grass, not to mention spectacular views of the city and the Bay Bridge. The thoroughfare down the park's center is where prostitutes transact business: Avoid this area at night. On July 4 weekend and Labor Day, the San Francisco Mime Troupe (*see* Theater *in* Chapter 6) gives free performances here. The park is between Dolores, Church, 18th, and 20th streets. From downtown take the J Church streetcar to 18th Street.

SAN FRANCISCO ZOO

Northern California's largest zoological park is home to 1,000 species of birds and animals, more than 120 of which have been designated endangered. In recent years zoo caretakers have gone to great lengths to create natural environments for their charges: **Gorilla World,** a $2 million exhibit, is one of the largest and most natural gorilla habitats of any zoo in the world. Nearby, the $5 million **Primate Discovery Center** is home to 14 endangered species of monkeys. The **Feline Conservation Center** was designed with rare ocelots and jaguars in mind, while the **South American Gateway** exhibit contains 7 lush acres of rain forest that tapirs and howler monkeys call home. Other enclosures worth a look include Koala Crossing, Otter River, the Lion House, and the Australian Walkabout. And don't forget to

GREAT VIEWS

Baker Beach. The bridge looms to your right, the ocean extends to your left, and the Marin Headlands rise before you.

Treasure Island. See the familiar San Francisco skyline from a different angle. By car, take the Treasure Island exit from the Bay Bridge and park at the water's edge.

Upper Market Street. Where Portola Street ends and Market Street begins, near Twin Peaks, you'll find a view of the city and the East Bay.

Tank Hill. Drive south on Stanyan Street to Belgrave Avenue, turn left, and continue to the road's end. A footpath leads to a high, craggy overlook.

say hello to **Prince Charles,** a rare white tiger (the first of its kind to be exhibited in the West). A children's zoo houses 300 cuddly mammals, and there's also a 1921 carousel ($1). Feeding time for the big cats is 2 Tuesday–Sunday; feeding time for the penguins is 3 daily. *Sloat Blvd. at 45th Ave., tel. 415/ 753–7080. From any downtown Muni station, take L Taraval streetcar to last stop (45th Ave. and Wawona St.), then walk 1 block south. Admission $9; free 1st Wed. of month. Open daily 10–5.*

SOUTH PARK

Set in the middle of the warehouse-laden and utterly ungreen SoMa District is a welcome surprise: South Park, a tree-filled square that looks like it was airlifted in from Paris. With a playground, several cafés and restaurants, and dozens of inviting benches, it's an old-fashioned antidote for postmodern angst. South Park, playground of the new-media types who spend their days in Multimedia Gulch—the first cousin of Silicon Valley—has plenty of harried graphic artists, writers, architects, and attorneys guiltily gulping a midmorning latte. *South Park Ave. off 2nd and 3rd Sts., between Bryant and Brannan Sts.*

SUTRO FOREST

Sutro Forest is that big patch of trees, visible from almost anywhere in the city, that *isn't* Golden Gate Park. This wild, dense forest is just off Stanyan Street, above the more famous Golden Gate Park and behind the UCSF Medical Center (in fact, most hiking trails lead to UCSF residence halls). Take the N Judah streetcar to Willard Street, head south on Willard, right on Belmont Avenue, and left on Edgewood Avenue.

WASHINGTON SQUARE

This tiny urban park at the north end of North Beach is a perfect example of the blending of cultures within San Francisco. Old Italian men chew on long-dead cigars as the bells of a Romanesque church ring the hour. Early mornings, Chinese women engage in the graceful movements of tai chi, surrounded by lingering wisps of fog. Grab an Italian-style picnic at one of the nearby markets and watch the show. From Market Street (at Kearny Street), Bus 15 or 30 will bring you to the intersection of Powell and Union streets, the heart of Washington Square.

BEACHES

Step off the bus at Ocean Beach in your bikini and flip-flops, and you might be in for a shock. San Francisco's beaches are not the kind of sunny, sandy expanses you see on *Baywatch;* locals prefer to use city beaches for activities like meditating, kite flying, and exercising their dogs. At **Fort Funston,** San Francisco's southernmost beach, watch hang gliders soar overhead, then take a 7-mi stroll north to Ocean Beach (*see below*). From the Balboa Park BART station, take Bus 88 west.

BAKER BEACH

One end of Baker Beach sees families, tourists, anglers, and wealthy homeowners walking their dogs, while the other end sees a lot of skin as one of the city's most popular nude beaches. Beautiful views of the Marin Headlands, the Golden Gate Bridge, and the bay make this a great place to sunbathe. From Clay and Drumm streets (near Embarcadero Center), take Bus 1 to 25th Avenue in the Richmond, then transfer to Bus 29 heading north into the Presidio.

CHINA BEACH

Named after a Chinese fisherman who camped here in the 1870s, China Beach (also known as Phelan Beach) is one of the city's safest swimming beaches *and* the most convenient, with its free changing rooms and showers. (Watch out for the occasional deadly rip currents.) The beach is tucked between Lands End and the Presidio, just off Seacliff Avenue (home to actor Robin Williams and many other multimillionaires). Take Bus 1 from Clay and Drumm streets (near Embarcadero Center) to 30th Avenue in Richmond, then walk north.

LANDS END

The mile-long Lands End loop trail is popular with mountain bikers, hikers, and picnickers—largely because of its amazing views of the Golden Gate Bridge, the ocean, and the Marin Headlands. Lands End Beach, just off the main trail, is a nude beach that's no longer exclusively gay. It's rocky and unsafe for swimming—but at least there's sand. From downtown go west on Geary Street (which becomes Point Lobos Ave.), turn right on Merrie into the Sutro Baths (*see* Ocean Beach, *below*) main parking lot, and look for trail signs. Or take Bus 38 west from Union Square.

OCEAN BEACH

This is the surfers' beach, the family beach, the walkers' beach. It's also the tourists' beach: The **Cliff House** (1090 Point Lobos Ave., tel. 415/386–3330) is a historic landmark restaurant; on its lower level is a National Park Service office (tel. 415/556–8642), open daily 10–5. Next door is the offbeat Musée Mécanique (*see* Museums, *below*). Just west of the Cliff House lie the ruins of the **Sutro Baths,** a huge complex of fresh and saltwater pools modeled after ancient Roman baths. Opened in 1896, the baths had five saltwater tanks and one freshwater tank, as well as restaurants, art exhibits, and an amphitheater. Alas, the baths fell victim to budget problems and were torn down in 1966. Offshore, look for **Seal Rock,** so named because seals used to sun themselves here—before they relocated to cozier digs by Fisherman's Wharf. Take the N Judah streetcar from any downtown underground Muni station to reach Ocean Beach.

MUSEUMS

San Francisco has its share of large, world-class institutions of art—like the Museum of Modern Art and the renovated California Palace of the Legion of Honor—and a bevy of smaller, avant-garde spaces complement the city's eclectic cultural landscape with offerings ranging from the funky to the downright odd.

AFRICAN-AMERICAN MUSEUM

A contemporary art gallery displays works by African and African-American artists, and an intriguing gift shop sells jewelry and artifacts. There's also a historical archive and research library. Call for information on lectures and performing arts classes. The Center for African and African-American Art and Culture (*see* Western Addition, *above*) is an affiliate of the museum. *Fort Mason Center, Bldg. C, tel. 415/441–0640. Admission $3. Open Wed.–Sun. noon–5.*

ANSEL ADAMS CENTER

If you're even remotely interested in serious photography, this is a place you shouldn't miss. The largest repository of art photography on the West Coast, the center has three rotating exhibits, one of which is devoted to Adams's work (despite the name, there aren't that many works by Adams); the other exhibits range from traditional portraiture to computer-altered images (the center's 1993 Annie Leibovitz retrospective put it on the pop-culture map). For serious photographers there are educational programs and competitions. The bookstore alone is worth a trip. *250 4th St., between Howard and Folsom Sts., tel. 415/495–7000. Admission $5. Open daily 11–5 (until 8 on 1st Thurs. of month).*

ASIAN ART MUSEUM

Housed in the same building as the M. H. de Young (*see below*), this is the West Coast's largest Asian museum. The first floor is devoted to Chinese and Korean art; the second floor holds treasures from Southeast Asia, India and the Himalayas, Japan, and Persia. The collection of more than 12,000 pieces from 40 Asian countries is rotated periodically, so everything comes out of storage once in a while. Highlights of the permanent collection include the oldest known Buddha image (AD 338) and superb carved jade and ancient Chinese ceramics (all on permanent exhibit). *John F. Kennedy and Tea Garden Drs., Golden Gate Park, tel. 415/379–8801. Admission $7, includes adjacent M.H. de Young; free 1st Wed. of month. Open Tues.–Sun. 9:30–5 (until 8:45 on 1st Wed. of month).*

CABLE CAR MUSEUM

Between Nob Hill and Russian Hill is this small museum chockablock with photographs, scale models, vintage cars, and other memorabilia devoted to the cable car's history, from their start in 1874 to the present. From the adjacent overlook or from an underground room you can gander at the brawny cables that haul the cars up and down the city's hills. *1201 Mason St., at Washington St., tel. 415/474–1887. Admission free. Open daily 10–5 (Apr.–Oct. until 6).*

CALIFORNIA ACADEMY OF SCIENCES

This huge natural history complex is subdivided into blockbuster sights, including the **Morrison Planetarium,** the **Steinhart Aquarium,** and the **Natural History Museum.** Wander the complex's labyrinthine corridors until you find the aquarium's **Fish Roundabout,** which places you in an underwater world of 14,500 different creatures. The living coral reef, with its fish, giant clams, and tropical sharks, is one of the academy's most fascinating sights. The Space and Earth Hall has an Earthquake Room, where you can experience the vibrations of an 8.0-magnitude quake. Also worth visiting are the Life through Time Hall, which chronicles evolution from the dinosaurs through early mammals, and the Birds of a Feather exhibit, which explores the languages, physical features, and learning habits of birds. To see the *Sky Show* on the 65-ft dome at the Morrison Planetarium, you'll need to pay a separate admission fee ($2.50). For information on **Laserium** shows ($7) at the academy, *see* Golden Gate Park *in* Major Sights, *above. Between John F. Kennedy and Martin Luther King Jr. Drs., Golden Gate Park, tel. 415/750–7145. Admissions: Natural History Museum and Steinhart Aquarium $8.50, Morrison Planetarium $2.50; all exhibits (except Laserium) free 1st Wed. of month. Open daily 10–5 (June–Sept. 9–6).*

CALIFORNIA PALACE OF THE LEGION OF HONOR

This landmark building now has an underground gallery complex and a full-service restaurant overlooking the Pacific Ocean. On display are San Francisco's European fine arts; though the collection isn't stunning, it does include some fine pieces from the late 19th century. Among them are several Rodin sculptures, including a cast of *The Thinker,* and one of Monet's *Water Lilies. Lincoln Park, Richmond District, tel. 415/750–3600. From Union Square, Bus 38 Geary west to 33rd Ave., then transfer to Bus 18 north; park entrance at 34th Ave. and Clement St. Admission $7; free 2nd Wed. of month. Open Tues.–Sun. 9:30–5.*

CARTOON ART MUSEUM

This tiny gem, near Yerba Buena Gardens, is the only museum on the West Coast devoted to the funnies. Its 10,000-piece collection includes everything from political cartoons of the 1700s to the *Far Side* and *New Yorker* cartoons. You'll find special exhibitions in the main rooms, plus an interactive CD-ROM room, a children's gallery, and a gift shop overflowing with your favorite comic books. *814 Mission St., between 4th and 5th Sts., tel. 415/227–8666. Admission $5; 1st Wed. of month pay what you wish. Open Wed.–Fri. 11–5, Sat. 10–5, Sun. 1–5.*

CENTER FOR THE ARTS

Part of Yerba Buena Gardens (*see* South of Market, *above*), this cultural complex houses three spacious galleries in its Visual Arts Building, plus a media screening room for video and film and a multiuse forum. Exhibits focus on contemporary works, usually of emerging local and regional artists. The center's goal is to reflect San Francisco's multicultural community in a welcoming, unpretentious, and appealing space to as large a community as possible. *701 Mission St., at 3rd St., tel. 415/978–2787. Admission $5; free 1st Thurs. of month 5 PM–8 PM. Open Tues.–Sun. 11–6 (until 8 Thurs. and Fri.).*

CHINESE HISTORICAL SOCIETY OF AMERICA

This nonprofit organization houses a modest museum in its fourth-floor headquarters. Historical photos and graphics accompanied by moving explanations trace the experiences of Chinese-Americans from the 1850s to the present. Among other artifacts the small museum contains opium pipes, a *queue* (the long braid men wore as a symbol of allegiance to the Manchu emperor of China before the 1911 Revolution), an altar built in the 1880s, and a parade dragon's head from 1909. *644 Broadway, 4th Fl., between Stockton St. and Grant Ave., tel. 415/391–1188. Admission free, donations accepted. Open Mon. 1–4, Tues.–Fri. 10:30–4.*

EXPLORATORIUM

The Exploratorium is a cavernous warehouse with more than 650 hands-on exhibits, many computer-assisted, about science and technology. It's a fun place for children—and grown-ups—to overcome their fear of science. Advance reservations ($12, includes Exploratorium admission) are required for the enormously popular **Tactile Dome,** a series of small rooms, each with a different texture, through which you walk, crawl, and slither in total darkness. Adjacent to the Exploratorium is the **Palace of Fine Arts** (*see* The Presidio and Marina, *above*). *3601 Lyon St., between Marina Blvd. and Lombard St., tel. 415/563–7337 or 415/561–0360 for recorded information. Admission $9; free 1st Wed. of month. Open Sept.–May, Tues.–Sun. 10–5 (Wed. until 9); Memorial Day–Labor Day, daily 10–6 (Wed. until 9).*

Save $1 on admission at the Asian Art Museum, California Academy of Sciences, or M. H. de Young Museum by presenting a valid Muni pass or transfer ticket. . . . Here's to public transportation!

JEWISH MUSEUM

Here you'll find works by Jewish artists—contemporary ones as well as old masters—and revolving exhibits that trace important moments in Jewish history. *121 Steuart St., between Mission and Howard Sts., tel. 415/543–8880. Admission $5; free 1st Mon. of month. Open Sun. 11–6, Mon.–Wed. noon–6, Thurs. noon–8.*

MEXICAN MUSEUM

It has long been the bittersweet curse of the Mexican Museum to have an enormous permanent collection (including works by Rodolfo Morales and Diego Rivera), a strong reputation as a national center for Mexican and Chicano culture, and only a few tiny rooms to move around in. Fortunately, the museum will relocate to more spacious quarters at Yerba Buena Gardens (*see* South of Market, *above*) in late 2000. Meanwhile, come and enjoy the few pieces on display, usually focusing on 20th-century artists. *Fort Mason Center, Bldg. D, tel. 415/441–0404. Admission $4; free 1st Wed. of month. Open Wed.–Sun. 11–5 (until 7 on 1st Wed. of month).*

M. H. DE YOUNG MEMORIAL MUSEUM

The de Young is best known for its substantial survey collection of American art, which includes paintings, sculpture, decorative arts, textiles, and furniture dating to 1670. There are works by Sargent, Whistler, Church, and Wood; look for George Caleb Bingham's *Boatmen on the Missouri* and Georgia O'Keeffe's *Petunias.* The de Young also houses impressive collections of art from Africa, Oceania, and the Americas. There are docent-led tours on the hour; call for information on lectures and other events (tel. 415/750–3636). *Golden Gate Park, between John F. Kennedy Dr. and 8th Ave., tel. 415/750–3600. Admission $7, includes adjacent Asian Art Museum; free 1st Wed. of month. Open Tues.–Sun. 9:30–5 (until 8:45 on 1st Wed. of month).*

MUSÉE MÉCANIQUE

This quirky museum is at the end of Geary Boulevard downstairs from the Cliff House (*see* Ocean Beach, *above*). It's stuffed with coin-operated antique carnival attractions like player pianos, marionettes, and a truly frightening mechanical laughing lady. Don't miss the miniature amusement park—complete with a Ferris wheel—built out of toothpicks by San Quentin inmates. *1090 Point Lobos Ave., tel. 415/386–1170. Admission free. Open Oct.–Apr., weekdays 11–7, weekends 10–7; May–Sept., daily 10–8.*

MUSEO ITALOAMERICANO

If this modest collection of 20th-century Italian and Italian-American art seems out of place at Fort Mason, consider that it was founded two decades ago in North Beach. Though throngs of Italian Americans do not seem to be pouring in, the museum has stuck to its mission to research, collect, and display new works by Italians and Italian Americans in an effort to restore appreciation of contemporary Italian art and culture. The most important work of the rotating permanent collection is Arnaldo Pomodoro's 1961 bronze sculpture *Tavola della Memoria* (Table of Memory). *Fort Mason Center, Bldg. C, tel. 415/673–2200. Admission $2; free 1st Wed. of month. Open Wed.–Sun. noon–5 (until 7 on 1st Wed. of month).*

PACIFIC HERITAGE MUSEUM

On display are rare works from private collections representing China, Taiwan, Japan, Thailand, and many other Asian nations. Past exhibitions have featured Chinese classical furniture, paintings, vases, and ceramics. Call for the latest exhibition information. *608 Commercial St., at Montgomery St., tel. 415/399–1124. Admission free. Open Tues.–Sat. 10–4.*

SAN FRANCISCO MUSEUM OF MODERN ART

Designed by Swiss architect Mario Botta, the new brick-and-stone home of the SFMOMA is dominated by a huge cylindrical skylight trimmed with black and white stripes of stone. The interior is just as impressive: The stately entrance hall and galleries provide a sleek setting for the museum's sprawling exhibits. The space doubles that of the museum's prior home at the War Memorial Veterans Building, where it opened in 1935 as the West Coast's first museum devoted to 20th-century art. The permanent collection includes works by Jackson Pollock, Jasper Johns, Frida Kahlo, Henri Matisse, and Frank Stella, as well as a healthy representation of contemporary photography and Bay Area figurative movement works. *151 3rd St., near Howard St., tel. 415/357–4000. Admission $8; free 1st Tues. of month, ½ price Thurs. 6–9. Open Mon.–Tues. 11–6, Thurs. 11–9, Fri.–Sun. 11–6.*

ZEUM

On the rooftop at Yerba Buena Gardens, this spanking-new youth-oriented space is designed with creative kids in mind: Five environments offer children hands-on experience in arts and new media, from television production to the performing arts. Kids of all ages will appreciate the gorgeous carousel. *221 Fourth St., at Howard St., tel. 415/777–2800. Admission $7. Open Wed.–Fri. noon–6, weekends 11–5.*

GALLERIES

The best time to wade into the gallery world is the first Thursday evening of each month, when many art houses host receptions with free drinks and snacks and occasionally some interesting new art. It's a great and fairly casual scene. For current happenings keep an eye on publications like the *San Francisco Arts Monthly* and *San Francisco Gallery Guide,* both available at galleries throughout town.

DOWNTOWN

No fewer than 30 galleries, most relatively mainstream and high-end, are in this area, a stone's throw from ritzy Union Square. The thickest concentrations are along the first three blocks of Grant Avenue, the 100 block of Geary, the 100 and 200 blocks of Post, and the 200 block of Sutter. At **49 Geary Street,** each of the second through fifth floors claims a separate swank gallery. On the fifth floor the **Robert Koch** gallery (tel. 415/421–0122) explores traditional and experimental photography; other floors focus on painting or multimedia art. All galleries within the building are open at least Tuesday–Saturday 11–5.

MISSION DISTRICT

The Mission is the undisputed center of the city's Latino arts scene; it's also the place for experimental art by up-and-coming female artists. **Galeria de la Raza** (2857 24th St., at Bryant St., tel. 415/826–8009), founded in 1970 by members of the Chicano Arts Movement, was the first Mexican museum in the United States; it remains an influential cultural resource, with its exhibits of local Latin American art and community arts programs. The **Women's Building** (*see* Mission District, *above*) occasionally hosts visual arts installments by San Francisco women. Check out local and traveling artists and performances at the following up-and-coming Mission galleries: **Southern Exposure** (401 Alabama St., at 17th St., tel. 415/863–2141); **Four Walls** (3160-A 16th St., between Valencia and Guerrero Sts., entrance on Albion St., tel. 415/626–8515); and the **Lab** (2948 16th St., at Capp St., tel. 415/864–8855).

Mission Cultural Center. This Mission District landmark has gallery space as well as classrooms, dance spaces, painting studios, and a theater, all devoted to promoting the Latino arts community. Current budget woes are keeping performance arts to a minimum, but visual arts exhibits continue, often featuring neighborhood artists, and the center is a great place to find out what's going on in the neighborhood. Call or stop by for a complete rundown of events, including exhibits, performances, lectures, and classes. *2868 Mission St., between 24th and 25th Sts., tel. 415/821–1155. Donation requested. Open Tues.–Sat. 10–4.*

SOUTH OF MARKET

In SoMa plain old paintings won't draw a crowd anymore; everyone who's anyone is jumping on the mixed-media and multimedia bandwagons. Two galleries that are old hands at the multimedia game are **SOMAR** (934 Brannan St., at 8th St., tel. 415/552–2131), which is known more for its theater than its visual arts, and **New Langton Arts** (1246 Folsom St., between 8th and 9th Sts., tel. 415/626–5416), the granddaddy of the city's mixed-media centers.

By day the endearingly awkward **Gallery 111** (111 Minna St., between New Montgomery and 2nd Sts., tel. 415/974–1719) is a gallery showcasing contemporary California artists; at night it's a performance space, with musical and multimedia events. Drink specials during happy hour (Tues.–Fri. 4–7) bring a sociable crowd. **Omni Circus** (550 Natoma St., tel. 415/621–4068) offers unusual performances, often involving music and robots. **SF Camera Work** (115 Natoma St., between New Montgomery and 2nd Sts., tel. 415/764–1001) is a good photography gallery with strong alternative shows in an airy warehouse space.

EAST BAY

The funk and soul of San Francisco extend beyond the city limits: Only a bridge away are Berkeley and Oakland, each with its own flavor and its own set of unmatchable attractions. Sample the hip-hop beat of Oaktown (as it's called), join in Berkeley's hippie parade . . . Whether you're looking for a New Age healing session or a good blues band, odds are good that you'll find it somewhere in the East Bay.

BERKELEY

Berkeley and the University of California campus there may not be synonymous, but they're so interdependent it's difficult to tell where one stops and the other begins. You won't find many backpack-toting students in the upscale neighborhoods that buffer the north and east sides of campus, but for the most part Berkeley is a student town, dominated by the massive UC campus and its 30,000 undergraduate and post-graduate enrollees. Because of its offbeat, countercultural reputation, the university attracts every sort of person imaginable—from artists, anarchists, and hypergenius intellectuals to superjocks and fashion slaves, not to mention the stubbornly apathetic and the piously ideological. Recent campus celebrities have included former math professor Theodore Kaczynski (the Unabomber) and the former student known as the Naked Guy (expelled for attending classes in the nude). But anyone who has watched the documentary *Berkeley in the Sixties* might be surprised to find out that the city isn't what it used to be. Berkeley *is* still a breeding ground for alternative social trends both important and inane, for posers and protesters. But ever since the 1994 election of a more conservative mayor, Shirley Dean, there has been a reaction by some Berkeley residents against the city's free-for-all reputation. Those who continue their love affair with the '60s still influence the city, but others want to drag Berkeley kicking and screaming into the new millennium.

Berkeley's University of California **campus** is surprisingly beautiful, with walking paths, a creek, and eucalyptus and redwood groves. Southside, or the area south of campus, is dominated by chaotic **Telegraph Avenue,** and just east of it, **College Avenue** is the heart of the Elmwood District, lined with boutiques and cafés with a bohemian flair. North Berkeley, a more sedate and residential area, is where you'll find the **Gourmet Ghetto,** home of the famed restaurant Café at Chez Panisse (*see* Chapter 4) and a number of excellent organic food markets. The Berkeley Hills, rising north and east of campus, shelter the huge **Tilden Regional Park** and acres of densely forested slopes. Farther west, around **University** and **San Pablo avenues,** you'll find working-class Berkeley, a gritty neighborhood that is also among the city's most ethnically diverse. No matter what part of town you're in, you're never far from movie houses, bookstores, restaurants, and cafés geared toward counterculture tastes and student budgets.

WORTH SEEING

TELEGRAPH AVENUE

The first five blocks of this congested and colorful avenue—which begins at the campus and runs south into Oakland—form the spiritual heart of Berkeley. It's a jumble of cafés, bookstores, used-clothing stores, and cheap restaurants populated by harried students, long-haired hippies, homeless people and street entertainers, metaphysical warriors, street vendors, and wide-eyed tourists. Telegraph today is a unique fusion of '60s and millennial counterculture, and the two elements blend nicely. This is especially evident on Sunday between 11 and 3, when a diverse group including students, hippies, former hippies, and yuppies with a penchant for organic produce gather on Telegraph around Haste Street for the weekly farmers' market. Most Fridays a Peruvian band sets up on the corner of Telegraph and Bancroft avenues, while other afternoons bring folks hammering on dulcimers, drumming on buckets, and strumming on acoustic guitars. The first or second Sunday in May, Telegraph hosts a **world music festival,** which has drawn such international acts as the West African Highife Band and Ali Kahn. Call the Telegraph Area Association (tel. 510/649–9500) for news of upcoming events.

Shops along Telegraph come and go, but neighborhood landmarks include **Amoeba** and **Rasputin Music,** both of which feature a huge selection of vinyl, tapes, and CDs (*see* Records, Tapes, and CDs *in* Chapter 3). Book lovers should check out **Cody's** and **Moe's** (*see* Books *in* Chapter 3). The former hosts regular readings and has probably the largest selection of new books, magazines, and 'zines in the area, while the latter specializes in used and rare books. For candles, incense, black-light posters, hookahs, and decorative pipes (for tobacco, of course), stop by Southside's infamous **Annapurna** (2416 Telegraph Ave., between Haste and Channing Sts., tel. 510/841–6187). One block south, **Mediterraneum Caffè** (*see* Chapter 5), alleged to once have been the workplace of beat poet Allen Ginsberg, opened in 1957 and was immortalized by an anxious Dustin Hoffman in the film *The Graduate.*

PEOPLE'S PARK

In 1969 the now-defunct *Berkeley Barb* urged people to "bring shovels, hoses, flowers, soil, colorful smiles, laughter, and lots of sweat" to convert a 2.8-acre vacant lot owned by the university into a park for the people. Thousands of people showed up at the newly green space, and People's Park was born. Conflict began when the university decided to build a dormitory on the spot. Protests ensued, ending in a 17-day occupation of Berkeley by the National Guard (ordered by then-governor Ronald Reagan), thousands of arrests, one death, and the dropping of tear gas on Sproul Plaza. Over the years the park has decayed as activists and university officials continue to struggle over its future. The conflict escalated further in 1999, when the UC Chancellor re-raised the prospect of dorms on the site. The anniversary of People's Park is celebrated on the last Sunday in April, with music, arts and crafts, and food. **People's Park Annex** (Telegraph Ave. at Dwight Way) is another vacant, fenced-in lot with witty graffiti and art displays made out of recycled material. *Between Haste St. and Dwight Way, just east of Telegraph Ave.*

UNIVERSITY OF CALIFORNIA CAMPUS

Established in 1868 as the first branch of the statewide University of California system, the UC Berkeley campus retains some of the beauty and gentility of its early years, particularly in the old brick and stone buildings scattered about campus. On a walk through campus you'll find peaceful glades and imposing academic buildings in the architectural style known as brutalism, as well as battalions of musicians, zealots, and students "on their way to class" (i.e., napping in the sun). Free student-led tours of campus leave from the **visitor center** (University Hall, Room 101, 2200 University Ave., at Oxford St., on the west side of campus, tel. 510/642–5215) weekdays at 10, and Sunday at 1. Saturday tours depart at 10 from the Campanile. The visitor center can also outfit you with a map or brochure outlining a self-guided walking tour.

SPROUL PLAZA • UC Berkeley's Sproul Plaza, just north of the Telegraph and Bancroft intersection, is where the Free Speech Movement began in 1964. Look inside imposing **Sproul Hall** for a display of photographs from this first demonstration in which 3,000 students surrounded a police car containing a UC Berkeley student arrested for distributing political flyers. Both the man and the car were released after 32 hours, but the students famously continued to battle university head Clark Kerr. Today Sproul Plaza is a source of endless entertainment for locals and tourists, where some of Berkeley's most famous loonies congregate: Look out for the Hate Man (the man in a bra, high heels, long skirt, and lipstick), who professes hatred for everything. **Lower Sproul Plaza,** just west of Sproul Plaza, is the site of occasional free noon concerts during the school year on Wednesday (usually rock) and Thursday (usually the Cal jazz band). Nearby **Zellerbach Hall** (*see* Classical Music *in* Chapter 6) hosts professional theater and concerts; check the box office for upcoming events.

SATHER GATE AND DOE LIBRARY • North of Sproul Plaza, pass through Sather Gate, the main entrance to campus until expansion in the 1960s. The second building on your right, Doe Library, is worth a look for its cavernous and beautiful reference room, and the cozy oak-paneled **Morrison Reading Room** (open weekdays 9–5 during school year, noon–5 in summer). Though the reading room is technically only open to students, in practice anyone with a photo ID is welcome to peruse their selection of international newspapers and magazines, listen to its collection of compact discs and records with headphones, or just kick back in a cushy leather easy chair.

The Doe Library building also contains the **Bancroft Library** (accessible from the east side of the building), which houses a vast collection of historical documents, rare books, and old photographs. Anyone with a photo ID can gain access to the huge, noncirculating collection. On permanent display in the administrative office is a gold nugget purported to have started the California gold rush when it was discovered on January 24, 1848, at Sutter's Mill.

CAMPANILE AND AROUND • Directly east of Bancroft Library is **Sather Tower** (more commonly known as the Campanile), a 307-ft clock tower modeled after the one in Venice's Piazza San Marco. The carillon is played daily (except during final exams), weekdays at 7:50, noon, and 6; Saturday at noon and 6; and Sunday at 2 for an extended 45 minutes. At the top of the Campanile is an observation deck, open Monday–Saturday 10–3:30 and Sunday 10–1:45 and accessible by elevator ($1); the view of the bay is spectacular. Southwest of the Campanile, the redbrick South Hall is the only one of the original university buildings still standing. Or walk northeast from the clock tower to check out the **Hearst Mining Building,** a masterpiece of beaux arts architecture designed by John Galen Howard.

> *If you're lucky you may cross paths with the Bubble Lady (poet and bubble maker Julia Vinograd), Rare (a lunatic and sports-trivia fiend), Pink Man (hot-pink-unitard-wearing unicyclist), or any of the other wacky denizens who give Berkeley its odd appeal.*

UNIVERSITY AVENUE AND ENVIRONS

University Avenue stretches from I–80 along the bay to the UC campus in the Berkeley foothills. It teems with cheap ethnic restaurants, cafés, and offbeat clothing stores—as well as car-repair shops and seedy motels. The area can be dangerous at night, and most things worth seeing are too few and far between to be conducive to exploration on foot. Near the university campus, the **UC Theatre** (*see* Movie Houses *in* Chapter 6) shows a diverse range of classics, along with Saturday midnight performances of *The Rocky Horror Picture Show.* A few miles west of campus, University Avenue intersects **San Pablo Avenue,** which recently has been colonized by a smattering of funky shops, bars, and cafés. Within a few blocks of each other, you'll find the ultracasual pub the **Albatross,** the folk music club **Freight and Salvage,** and the world-music emporium **Ashkenaz** (for more on Berkeley nightlife, *see* Chapter 6).

Upscale shops abound on **4th Street,** in a former warehouse district near the bay just north of University Avenue. The street is a fine place to browse for overpriced goodies like sleigh beds, hummingbird feeders, and organic cotton bathrobes; for real bargains head to the **Crate and Barrel Outlet Store** (1785 4th St., between Virginia St. and Hearst Ave., tel. 510/528–5500). **Vivarium** (1827 5th St., at Hearst St., tel. 510/841–1400) stocks exotic pets like pythons, giant tortoises, and iguanas. **Takara Sake** (708 Addison St., at 4th St., tel. 510/540–8250), one of only three makers of sake (Japanese rice wine) in the United States, offers a video and free samples of their product daily noon–6. From here it's a short drive to the **Berkeley Marina** (*see* Parks and Gardens, *below*).

COLLEGE AVENUE/ELMWOOD DISTRICT

The heart of the Elmwood District is the intersection of College Avenue (which runs south from campus) and Ashby Avenue. This neighborhood has some well-preserved examples of California Craftsman homes, as well as a plethora of upscale cafés, specialty stores, and gourmet restaurants, including **Nabolom Bakery** (2708 Russell St., at College Ave., tel. 510/845–2253), a co-op that produces great breads and the world's best chocolate croissant. Hotshot composer John Adams has been known to quaff caffeine at stylish **Espresso Roma** (*see* Chapter 5), while just about everyone in the neighborhood goes to **Slash** (*see* Chapter 3) to buy fashionably pre-owned Levi's jeans.

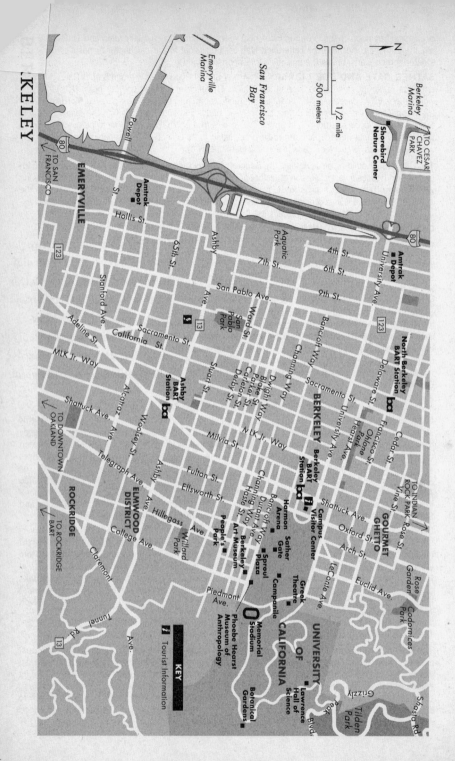

BERKELEY

EMERYVILLE

ROCKRIDGE

ELMWOOD DISTRICT

BERKELEY

GOURMET GHETTO

UNIVERSITY OF CALIFORNIA

N

0   0
500 meters   1/2 mile

San Francisco Bay

Emeryville Marina

Berkeley Marina

TO CESAR CHAVEZ PARK

Shorebird Nature Center

Aquatic Park

Amtrak Depot

North Berkeley BART Station

Ashby BART Station

Berkeley BART Station

Campus Visitor Center

People's Park

Art Museum

Harmon Arena

Sather Gate

Greek Theatre

Sproul Plaza

Campanile

Memorial Stadium

Phoebe Hearst Museum of Anthropology

Lawrence Hall of Science

Botanical Gardens

San Pablo Park

Willard Park

Rose Garden

Codornices Park

Tilden Park

Grizzly Peak

80

123

13

TO SAN FRANCISCO

TO DOWNTOWN OAKLAND

TO ROCKRIDGE BART

TO INDIAN ROCK PARK

Powell St.

Hollis St.

65th St.

Ashby Ave.

7th St.

4th St.

6th St.

9th St.

University Ave.

San Pablo Ave.

Sacramento St.

Stanford Ave.

Adeline St.

California St.

MLK Jr. Way

Alcatraz Ave.

Woolsey St.

Telegraph Ave.

Ashby Ave.

Hillegass Ave.

College Ave.

Claremont Ave.

Tunnel Rd.

Piedmont Ave.

Fulton St.

Ellsworth St.

Milvia St.

N LK Jr. Way

Shattuck Ave.

Ward St.

Stuart St.

Derby St.

Carleton St.

Parker St.

Blake St.

Dwight Way

Channing Way

Bancroft Way

Sacramento St.

Channing Way

Dana Ave.

Bancroft Way

Durant Ave.

Haste St.

Channing Way

Delaware St.

Francisco St.

Ohlone Park

Hearst Ave.

Cedar St.

Vine St.

Rose St.

Garden Circle

Oxford St.

Arch St.

Le Conte Ave.

Euclid Ave.

Gayley Rd.

Centennial Dr.

Shasta Rd.

KEY

i Tourist Information

NORTH BERKELEY

Grad students, professors, and folks with steady jobs frequent Northside, lending it a calmer atmosphere than you'll find on the campus's Southside. Homes in the hilly neighborhoods here date from the 1920s and are in a variety of architectural styles. The area's crowning glory is the so-called **Gourmet Ghetto** (Shattuck Ave. and Vine St.), lined with dozens of tantalizing restaurants, including **Café at Chez Panisse** (*see* Chapter 4), as well as specialty stores, clothing boutiques, and bookstores. Of note are **Black Oak Books** (*see* Books *in* Chapter 3) and the original **Peet's Coffee & Tea** (2124 Vine St., at Walnut St., tel. 510/841–0564), now part of a caffeine empire. Cafés and restaurants also line a block-long section of **Euclid Street,** where it dead-ends at the campus. Continue north on Euclid to reach the Berkeley Rose Garden (*see below*).

Shattuck Avenue becomes **Solano Avenue** about 2 mi north of University Avenue. The small shopping district here is worth a trip simply because of **Zachary's Chicago Pizza Inc.** (*see* Chapter 4), which sells heavenly Chicago-style pies ($11 and up).

PARKS AND GARDENS

TILDEN REGIONAL PARK

Tilden Park's more than 2,000 acres of forests and grasslands are a wonderful escape from the gridlocked lowlands. Follow the signs to **Inspiration Point** for a view of reservoirs and of rolling hills where cows laze. There are plenty of picnic spots (call 510/636–1684 to reserve a group picnic area) and miles of hiking and biking trails (*see* Chapter 8).

The Berkeleyan, a campus newspaper published every Wednesday, has a long list of free events and lectures—everything from "Double-Strand Break Repair and the Specific Cloning of Human DNA in Yeast" to "Spatialization of Violence."

Tilden Nature Area Environmental Education Center (EEC; tel. 510/525–2233), at the north end of the park, sponsors a number of naturalist-led programs throughout the year. Independent types can borrow or buy a self-guided trail booklet ($2) at the center, which is open Tuesday–Sunday 10–5. For a nice, easy walk (about a mile), take the **Jewel Lake Trail** loop from the EEC office, and look out for the salamanders. To make friends with domestic animals, detour to the nearby **Little Farm.**

Other destinations in the park include **Lake Anza** (tel. 510/848–3028), which is open for swimming late March to mid-October, daily 11–6; pony rides ($2.50); a vintage carousel ($1); a botanical garden of California plants, open daily 8:30–5, with no admission charge; the 18-hole **Tilden Park Golf Course** (tel. 510/848–7373 for reservations); and a miniature steam train ($1.50). Rides operate on weekends and holidays when school is in session and daily during spring and summer vacations; call 510/843–2137 for specific hours.

To reach Tilden Park from the Berkeley BART station, take Bus 8, 65, or 67. If you're driving, take University Avenue east from I–80 to Oxford Street, go left on Oxford, right on Rose, and left on Spruce to the top of the hill, cross Grizzly Peak Boulevard, make an immediate left on Canon Drive, and follow the signs. The park is open 5 AM–10 PM.

BERKELEY MARINA

Warm days were meant to be spent at the Berkeley Marina, at the end of University Avenue approximately half a mile west of I–80. Head for the ¾-mi pier jutting out into the bay to enjoy the unbeatable views of the Golden Gate Bridge and Alcatraz Island. Winds along the bay can be quite chilly, which makes nearby **César E. Chávez Park** (formerly North Waterfront Park) a perfect retreat. The hilly 92-acre park is Berkeley's only open space without a leash law for dogs and is also one of the most popular kite-flying areas in the Bay Area.

The **Shorebird Nature Center** (160 University Ave., tel. 510/644–8623) offers visitors a glimpse of bay marine life in its 100-gallon saltwater aquarium and runs all sorts of educational and environmental programs. For information on renting boats or hooking up with one of the sailing clubs stationed at the marina, stop by the **Marina Office** (201 University Ave., tel. 510/644–6376). To get to the marina, drive west on University Avenue across I–80 or take Bus 51M from the Berkeley BART station.

BERKELEY ROSE GARDEN/CODORNICES PARK

Built during the Depression, the rose garden is an attractive spot for a picnic or to watch the sunset. It has a multilevel rose garden, an amphitheater with roses and more roses, and a panoramic view of the bay. It's north of campus on Euclid Avenue, between Bayview Place and Eunice Street. Across the street is Codornices Park, where you'll find basketball courts, a baseball diamond, swings, grass and sand, and picnic areas. Hiking paths lead up the hill from Codornices Park, along Codornices Creek. To reach the rose garden and the park, walk north from campus on Euclid Street for 20 minutes or take Bus 65 from the Berkeley BART station.

U.C. BOTANICAL GARDEN

Nestled in the hills east of Strawberry Canyon, the garden is a valuable research and education center with a diverse collection of plants—more than 10,000 neatly labeled species from around the world. In addition to regional areas with habitats ranging from South African deserts to Himalayan forests, there are also specialized plots, like the Chinese Medicinal Herb Garden and the Garden of Economic Plants, as well as three indoor exhibits and a slew of paths to explore. Relax on a rock along Strawberry Creek in the shady Asian Garden, on a bench near the sunny Cactus Garden, or uphill, where there's a lovely green-framed view of the bay. The garden is especially colorful in spring when the extensive rhododendron collection is in full bloom. Check the visitor center for bulletins on various plant seminars and public education programs, then take home some plants, for sale at bargain prices. *200 Centennial Dr., tel. 510/642–3343. From the Berkeley BART station, take Bus 8 or take Hill Service Shuttle (50¢) from Hearst Mining Circle, on campus. Admission $3; free Thurs. Open daily 9–4:45; tours weekends at 1:30.*

BERKELEY HILLS FIRE TRAIL

One of Berkeley's best semiurban hiking trails begins at a small dirt parking area just uphill from the Strawberry Canyon Recreational Facility, on Centennial Drive (and just downhill from the UC Botanical Garden). Peppy joggers, thoughtful ramblers, and dog walkers come to enjoy this wide dirt path; though sometimes crowded, it's a wonderful and accessible escape for nature seekers. The path climbs steeply at first, then levels off to meander along the hillside, with stellar views of Berkeley and the bay. *Off Centennial Dr. Follow directions to UC Botanical Garden* (see above).

INDIAN ROCK PARK

Head north on Shattuck Avenue to reach Indian Rock Avenue, where you'll see clumps of volcanic-rock outcroppings jutting from the hillside. As there was no way for developers to sandblast the stone, the city eventually set it aside as a park. The view of Solano Avenue far below, Albany Hill in the distance, and the Marin Headlands is humbling. Rock climbers both awkward and nimble converge here to practice their sport on the north side of the boulder, making it a great place to find climbing buddies. Steps are available for those who would prefer to saunter up the rock. The park is open from dawn to dusk.

MUSEUMS

LAWRENCE HALL OF SCIENCE

Perched on a cliff overlooking the East Bay, the museum is a memorial to Ernest O. Lawrence, UC Berkeley's first Nobel laureate, who helped design the atomic bomb. The exhibits here are mostly hands-on and geared toward children, with an emphasis on the life sciences. On weekends and daily during summer, you can catch films, lectures, laboratory demonstrations, and planetarium shows. On the hillside outside the museum's rear patio, look for a set of 36 long, slender pipes sticking out of the ground, part of a wind organ. If you walk among them when the wind is blowing, you'll hear their music; you can play with the tones by turning one of six moveable pipes. On clear Saturday nights employees and local amateur astronomers break out their telescopes from about 8 to 11 to give interested visitors a free peek at the moon, planets, star clusters, galaxies, and whatever else the universe has on tap that night. Call the hall for details. *Centennial Dr. near Grizzly Peak Blvd., tel. 510/642–5132. Drive east on Hearst Ave., which borders campus on the north, and follow signs; or Bus 8, 65, or 67 from Berkeley BART station (ask driver for a transfer, 25¢, redeemable for $1 off museum admission); or Hill Service Shuttle (50¢) from Hearst Mining Circle, on campus. Admission $6, free Thurs.; planetarium show an additional $2. Open daily 10–5.*

PHOEBE HEARST MUSEUM OF ANTHROPOLOGY

Perhaps a yawner for those without a passion for cultural anthropology, the Phoebe Hearst Museum features rotating exhibits that cover everything from ancient America to neolithic China. Also on display are artifacts used by Ishi, the last survivor of California's Yahi tribe, who was brought to live on the UC campus in 1911 after gold miners slaughtered the rest of his tribe. Frequent talks by artists, anthropologists, and other scholars shed light on the artifacts on display; call for a schedule. *Kroeber Hall, Room 103, UC Berkeley campus, tel. 510/642–3681. Admission $2; free Thurs. Open Wed.–Sun. 10–4:30 (Thurs. until 9 during school year).*

BERKELEY ART MUSEUM

The BAM houses the largest university-owned art collection in the country. Though the low concrete building may not look like much from the street, the galleries inside are surprisingly airy. Displays may include anything from a 16th-century altar panel to a passel of Bibles made of sugar candy by a Berkeley MFA candidate. One of the most impressive permanent installations is a room full of violently colorful paintings by the abstract expressionist Hans Hofmann. On the ground floor of the museum is the **Pacific Film Archive** (*see* Movie Houses *in* Chapter 6). Pick up a schedule of upcoming exhibits and movies at the museum entrance. A sculpture garden to the rear of the museum is pleasant during summer. *2626 Bancroft Way, tel. 510/642–0808. Admission $6; free Thurs. 11–noon and 5–9. Open Wed.–Sun. 11–5 (Thurs. until 9).*

The Berkeley History Center and Museum (1830 Center St., tel. 510/848–0181) has changing exhibits on topics of community interest such as the Berkeley literary scene. It's open Thursday–Saturday 1–4; admission is free.

OAKLAND

Voted All-American City in 1993, predominantly working-class Oakland is a typical example of American cities built after 1850—a diverse cultural landscape, a struggling downtown, some great architecture, some crime-ridden areas, and high hopes for community renewal. It doesn't have the same dazzling effect on visitors as San Francisco, so if you're looking for glitz, you might want to save the $2 BART fare and use it for another cable car ride through Union Square. But it does have its own special flair as home to the West Coast blues; the Oaktown school of rap (heard in the music of local-artists-made-good Digital Underground, Tony! Toni! Toné!, Mystik Journeymen, Living Legends, and the late Tupac Shakur); and a vibrant art scene from the many artists who live in the city's plentiful, low-rent warehouse spaces.

Oakland was founded in the mid-1800s by three unsuccessful gold miners who leveled the area's oak groves and set up a town. Oakland prospered thanks to a thriving port, profitable manufacturing industries, and the arrival of the railroad. By the early 1890s the city was home to a large number of businesses, an electric streetcar system, and an ever-swelling population lured from around the country by job prospects and cheap housing. Wealthy families crossed the bay to escape San Francisco's urban blight, and still others migrated after damage wrought by the 1906 earthquake. Encouraged by this rapid growth, a group of powerful citizens spearheaded a beautification plan with the hope of changing Oakland's image from a suburb of San Francisco into a thriving metropolis in its own right. These boom days saw a flurry of new buildings downtown (many of which are now empty); a bigger, better city hall (once the tallest building west of Chicago); and the creation of Lake Merritt Park. Unfortunately, the growing downtown was shattered by the Depression, the flight of wealthy citizens to the hills, and a poor development plan. Today Oakland is a mosaic of its past: the city's hillside homes continue to serve affluent types seeking a warmer and more spacious alternative to San Francisco, while a constant flow of new residents—many from Central America and Asia—ensures continued diversity, vitality, and growing pains. Many neighborhoods to the west and south of downtown remain run-down and unsafe, but a renovated downtown area and the thriving Jack London Square have injected new life into the city. The national visibility from the 1998 election of former California governor Jerry Brown to Oakland mayor further invigorated the city's rising spirits.

Despite economic disparities between its separate parts, Oakland is held together by a strong sense of community. Everyday life here centers around the neighborhood, with a main business strip attracting both shoppers and socializers. The neighborhoods around **Grand, College,** and **Piedmont avenues** are lined with cafés, reasonably priced and upscale restaurants, bookstores, and boutiques. Wander

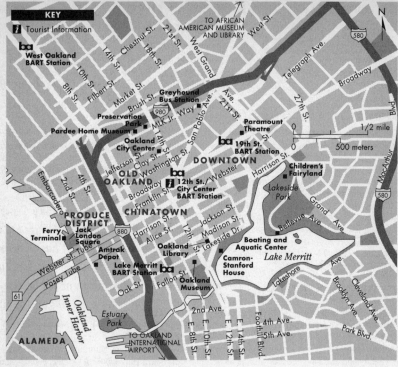

KEY

i Tourist Information

ba West Oakland
BART Station

through **Chinatown** for lively restaurants and markets selling produce, pungent spices, and meats. Check out the downtown revitalization efforts around **Jack London Square** and **City Center,** or if the city is fraying your nerves, head for the parks in the hills to the east (*see* Chapter 8). Though some residential areas in these hills were devastated by a fire in October 1991, most of the multi-million-dollar homes have been rebuilt in a variety of interesting architectural styles. You'll need a car or bike to explore Oakland's hills, but most everything else is within reach of a BART station.

WORTH SEEING

DOWNTOWN

Downtown Oakland, occupying 10th through 20th streets along Broadway, is an odd conglomeration of Art Deco, beaux arts, and Victorian buildings in various states of repair, interspersed with shiny office complexes and the grimy concrete facades of abandoned businesses. Though it's not a place you should visit alone at night, it's definitely worth a trip during the day to see some surprisingly impressive late-19th- and early 20th-century architecture. One of the most impressive Art Deco buildings in the Bay Area is the 1931 **Paramount Theatre** (*see* Movies Houses *in* Chapter 6), home to the Oakland Symphony and the Oakland Ballet. Two-hour tours ($1) of the historic building are held at 10 on the first and third Saturday of the month; no reservations are required. Next to the Paramount is the emerald green Art Deco I. Magnin Building; as if symbolizing downtown's problems, it now stands empty. Though many downtown businesses have moved, the **De Lauer Super Newsstand** (1310 Broadway Ave., at 14th St., tel. 510/451–6157) has been selling "your hometown newspaper" for years, as well as maps, paperbacks, foreign-language and domestic newspapers, and an overwhelming number of magazines; it's open 24 hours.

Farther south, the new federal building at **Oakland City Center** (between Clay, Jefferson, 12th, and 14th Sts.) has a 70-ft-high glass rotunda and a courtyard full of funky modern sculptures. During business hours you can enter the Center—which houses the IRS as well as the Bureau of Alcohol, Tobacco, and

Firearms—to visit the two-tiered glass-enclosed walkway that connects the building's two towers. Security tightened in the wake of the 1995 Oklahoma City bombing, so be prepared to show picture ID.

Old Oakland, between 8th and 10th streets just west of Broadway, is a slice of the city from the days when houses were Victorian and sidewalks were made of hand-placed red bricks. This was a bustling business district during the 1870s, and slowly it's beginning to regain some of the old buzz and hum. Area anchors include **Café 817** (817 Washington St., at 9th St., tel. 510/271–7965), the 101-year-old delicacy-filled **Ratto's International Market and Café** (821 Washington, near Broadway, tel. 510/832–6503), and the **Pacific Coast Brewing Company** (*see* Bars *in* Chapter 6), which makes its own delicious brews. **Pro Arts Gallery** (461 9th St., at Broadway, tel. 510/763–4361) hangs work by artists in the neighborhood. Gallery staff can also provide information about **East Bay Open Studios,** in which artists' work spaces are opened to the public for two weekends in June.

PRESERVATION PARK • In the shadow of Oakland City Center (*see above*), Preservation Park is a re-creation of an idyllic 19th-century Oakland neighborhood, complete with decorative wrought-iron fences and period street lamps. Forty years of architectural history can be seen in the 16 restored houses here (five are in their original location; the others were condemned houses that were transplanted here), including Queen Anne and Italianate cottages, as well as colonial revival and Craftsman homes. The buildings are private office spaces and aren't open to visitors, but you can stroll the grounds.

LAKE MERRITT

Lake Merritt was built in the early 1900s as part of a city beautification program. Formerly swamp, it is now a 155-acre oasis in the middle of urban Oakland. By day the 3½-mi paved path around the lake is filled with sun seekers, joggers, business types on lunch break, and old men feeding the ducks. The 1876 **Camron-Stanford House** (1418 Lakeside Dr., near 14th St., tel. 510/444–1867), near the southwestern edge of the lake, is the only remaining Victorian building in this formerly bourgeois neighborhood. Tours ($4) of the meticulously refurbished interior are offered Wednesday 11–4 and Sunday 1–5. **Lakeside Park** (tel. 510/238–3091), on the north shore, has picnic facilities, Japanese and herb gardens, the oldest urban bird sanctuary in the United States (1879), and frequent music events. Nearby, the **Boating and Aquatic Center** (568 Bellevue Ave., tel. 510/444–3807) rents rowboats, paddleboats, kayaks, and sailboats for $6–$12 an hour, plus deposit. It's open year-round; call for hours. The **Children's Fairyland** (Grand and Bellevue Aves., tel. 510/238–6876) is a storybook theme park with rides, puppet shows, strange mushroom-, whale-, and shoe-shape buildings, and other miniature delights. Walt Disney reputedly visited Fairyland to gather ideas for his own theme parks. Admission to Fairyland is $5 for adults, who are allowed inside only if they bring a child.

A much-loved feature of downtown Oakland's skyline is the Tribune Tower; built in 1923, it was the city's first landmark building. The Oakland Tribune's commitment to move its offices back into the tower in 2000, after an eight-year absence, was a big boost to downtown revival.

Grand Avenue, which begins at the north tip of the lake, is also a good place for a stroll, with a number of reasonably good ethnic restaurants and cafés, including the **Grand Bakery** (3264 Grand Ave., tel. 510/465–1110), which makes great breads, pastries, and kosher treats, and the **Coffee Mill** (3363 Grand Ave., tel. 510/465–4224), which claims to be Oakland's oldest coffeehouse. Across the street is **Walden Pond** (3316 Grand Ave., tel. 510/832–4438), a cozy bookstore with frequent poetry readings. On your way back to the lake, peek inside the **Grand Lake Theatre** (*see* Movie Houses *in* Chapter 6), an Art Deco movie palace where an enormous chandelier and grand staircase remain from the 1920s. The theater now shows first-run movies on four screens. For information on local summer events like the **Festival at the Lake** and the **Juneteenth Festival,** *see* Festivals *in* Chapter 1. To reach the south end of the park, walk three blocks northeast from the Lake Merritt BART station. To reach the north end of the lake and Grand Avenue, take BART to 19th Street and walk east.

JACK LONDON SQUARE

Although born in San Francisco, Jack London spent his early years in Oakland before shipping out on the adventures that inspired *The Call of the Wild, The Sea Wolf,* and *The Cruise of the Snark.* In an effort to cash in on this legacy, Oakland created Jack London Square on the waterfront west of downtown, at the foot of Broadway. Though several years ago the project resembled a ghost town with more FOR LEASE signs than tenants, the buildings are now filled by boutiques, pricey eateries, a massive Barnes and Noble bookstore, and the **Jack London Cinema** (100 Washington St., tel. 510/433–1320), which fea-

MARCHING TO A DIFFERENT BEAT

Oakland has a legacy of revolutionary politics. In the 1960s the militant Black Panther Party began here. In the 1970s the city was headquarters for the Symbionese Liberation Army, which kidnapped Patty Hearst and demanded as part of her ransom that food be distributed to Oakland's poor. Most recently, the Oakland school board set off national controversy by recognizing Ebonics (black English) as a distinct language. Even the city's most famous literary figure, Jack London, was an ardent socialist who wanted California to secede from the United States.

tures first-run films. The 1997 relocation of the enormously popular Berkeley jazz club **Yoshi's** (*see* Live Music *in* Chapter 6) has been a boon to the area; these days weekends at the square can be downright bustling. There's a swell Sunday Farmers' Market (10–2), often in conjunction with free live theater and concert events on the square.

Somewhat scant remnants of the square's namesake include **Heinold's First and Last Chance Saloon** (56 Jack London Sq., tel. 510/839–6761), the former hangout of Jack London, as well as Robert Louis Stevenson and Joaquin Miller. The proprietors will proudly tell you about the memorabilia on the walls and the crazily sloping floor (a result of the 1906 earthquake). Next door you can look through the window of a reassembled (and often litter-strewn) cabin in which Jack once spent a winter (the cabin was transplanted here from Alaska). Also near the saloon is the tiny **Jack London Museum** (30 Jack London Sq., Suite 104, tel. 510/451–8218), open weekends 10:30–6, displaying a small collection of London-related artifacts ($1 donation requested).

MUSEUMS

Oakland has a number of excellent museums, including the **Ebony Museum of Art** (30 Jack London Sq., Suite 208–209, tel. 510/763–0745), with work by African and African-American artists. It's open Tuesday–Saturday 11–6, Sunday noon–5, and admission is free. The **Creative Growth Art Center** (355 24th St., at Valdez St., tel. 510/836–2340), also free, displays arts and crafts by artists with disabilities. It's open weekdays 10–4, but closes one week out of every six for installation, so call ahead.

AFRICAN AMERICAN MUSEUM AND LIBRARY

This branch of the Oakland public library focuses on the history of people of African descent in North America, with a special emphasis on Oakland and the Bay Area. The collection includes original manuscripts, photos, journals, audiotapes, and photographs of Bay Area residents, as well as special exhibits and a reference library for those interested in learning more about the history of black Americans. At press time, the facility was closed to the public with tentative plans for a summer 2000 reopening; call to confirm that it's open before visiting. *5606 San Pablo Ave., at 56th St., tel. 510/597–5053. From downtown, Bus 72 north on Broadway. Admission free.*

OAKLAND MUSEUM

This well-designed building, a few blocks from Lake Merritt, houses collections on the environment, history, and art of California. On the ground floor is the **Gallery of Natural Sciences,** where a simulated walk takes you through the state's eight biotic zones, with their various plants and animals. If the stuffed animals don't intrigue you, perhaps the quotes by eminent scientists and writers hanging overhead will. The **Cowell Hall of California History,** on the second floor, puts today's multicultural population in context, with documents on the rise and fall of the Ohlone Native American people (the region's first inhabitants), the Spanish settlers, the suburban California dreamers, and the 1967 "Summer of Love," and tackles present-day issues of urban violence. The third-floor **Gallery of California Art** showcases paintings, sculpture, crafts, and installations by international and local artists; the art of the gold rush and the clothing of Chinese-American women are among the current (and past) exhibits. Spend some time walking around the museum's terraced gardens and the nearby **Sculpture Court** (1111 Broadway, at Oakland City Center) for a look at some surprisingly beautiful assemblages. *1000 Oak St., at 10th St., 1 block east of Lake Merritt BART, tel. 510/238–2200. Admission $6, free Sun. 4–7. Open Wed.–Sat. 10–5, Sun. noon–7.*

MARIN COUNTY

In Marin County, movie stars mingle with corporate moguls in Tiburon while homesteaders and members of the Grateful Dead hide in the hills of Fairfax and Bolinas. Yet from the urban capital, San Rafael, to coastal Dogtown (population 10), every community is connected by the county's pervasive natural beauty and the civic pride that radiates from it.

Because 42% of land in the county is public, there is always somewhere new and uncrowded to explore. The stunning ocean views of western Marin give way to thick redwood forests of **Mt. Tamalpais** (*see below*). On the steep east side of the mountain are perched small, woodsy towns, including **Mill Valley.** You could spend a lifetime describing the pleasures of hiking in **Muir Woods** and the **Point Reyes National Seashore,** and it's hard to act blasé about the view from **Coastal Highway 1,** no matter how many times you've driven that road.

Even the most bucolic corners of Marin County are little more than two hours from San Francisco (except during rush hour, when it can take nearly an hour just to cross the bridge). It's possible to bike across the Golden Gate Bridge from San Francisco, then take a ferry (*see* Ferry Travel *in* Chapter 1) back from Sausalito or Tiburon. A final note: If you opt for public transportation in this area, be forewarned that service is infrequent and travel times long.

MARIN HEADLANDS

For a quick taste of Marin County's natural beauty, cross the Golden Gate Bridge, exit at Alexander Avenue, and drive up Conzelman Road to the Marin Headlands. This undeveloped 1,000-acre area consists of several small but steep bluffs overlooking San Francisco Bay and the Pacific Ocean. Thick fog often whips across the headlands, obscuring everything but the top of the towers of the Golden Gate Bridge; on a sunny day, however, the views of downtown San Francisco, the East Bay, and Point Reyes to the north are stunning. Hundreds of hiking and biking trails meander along the wind-carved hills and cliffs (*see* Chapter 8).

The headlands were used as a military camp in the late 19th century, and during World War II emplacements were dug for huge naval guns to protect the approaches to the bay. The guns are long gone, but several overgrown concrete batteries still stand watch along the coast. One of the most impressive, Battery Wallace, is off Conzelman Road before you reach the Point Bonita Lighthouse. The two forbidding concrete structures you see today, once the site of 12-inch guns aimed 17 mi out to sea, are only part of the structure: They are connected by an inaccessible series of underground rooms used to hold troops and supplies.

From the Battery Wallace parking lot, follow the 1-mi trail and creaky suspension bridge to the **Point Bonita Lighthouse** for a unique view of San Francisco to the southeast and the wild coast to the north. Pick your day wisely, though; the fog here can get so thick the Coast Guard used to sound a cannon every half hour to alert sailors who couldn't see the lighthouse. *Open Sat.–Mon. 12:30–3:30 (weather permitting).*

Stop by the **Marin Headlands Visitor Center** (Field and Bunker Rds., tel. 415/331–1540) to pick up the free "Park Events" brochure or the almost indispensable "Marin Headlands Map and Guide to Sights, Trails, and Wildlife" ($1.50).

About a mile past the visitor center (follow signs from Bunker Rd.) is the **Marine Mammal Center.** The center rescues and rehabilitates suffering marine mammals, including sea lions, dolphins, and whales. One of the more famous rescuees was Humphrey, an endangered humpback who was stuck in the mud for three days. More than 600 volunteers help operate the center alongside veterinary and medical staff.

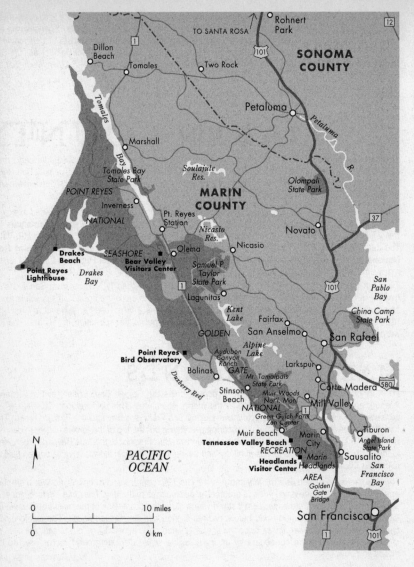

TO SANTA ROSA

Rohnert Park

12

SONOMA COUNTY

Dillon Beach

Tomales

Two Rock

101

Petaluma

Petaluma R.

Marshall

Tomales Bay State Park

Soulajule Res.

MARIN COUNTY

Olompali State Park

37

POINT REYES

Inverness

NATIONAL

Pt. Reyes Station

Nicasio Res.

Novato

Nicasio

San Pablo Bay

Drakes Beach

SEASHORE

Olema

Bear Valley Visitors Center

Samuel P. Taylor State Park

101

China Camp State Park

Point Reyes Lighthouse

Drakes Bay

Lagunitas

Kent Lake

Fairfax

San Anselmo

San Rafael

GOLDEN

Point Reyes Bird Observatory

Alpine Lake

Audubon Canyon Ranch

Larkspur

580

Bolinas

GATE

Mt. Tamalpais State Park

Corte Madera

Duxberry Reef

Stinson Beach

Muir Woods Nat'l Mon.

Mill Valley

NATIONAL

Green Gulch Farm Zen Center

Muir Beach

Tennessee Valley Beach

Marin City

RECREATION

Tiburon

Angel Island State Park

Sausalito

PACIFIC OCEAN

N

Headlands Visitor Center

Marin Headlands

AREA

Golden Gate Bridge

San Francisco Bay

0 ——— 10 miles
0 ——— 6 km

San Francisco

1   101

Visitors are welcome year-round, but call first to find out which animals are in residence. *Tel. 415/289–7325. $1 donation suggested. Open daily 10–4.*

SAUSALITO

Only a few miles north of San Francisco is Sausalito, which flourished during the 1880s and '90s as a whaling town infamous for its unruly saloons, gambling dens, and bordellos. Even after the town became suburbanized in the 1940s, it continued to attract an offbeat and raffish element, becoming by midcentury a well-known artists' colony. Over the last several decades, however, Sausalito's wharf rats have been replaced by lawyers and investment bankers escaping the San Francisco rat race. Today this is a wealthy resort town, popular with yachters and tourists. Parking is next to impossible, and shops and restaurants are shockingly expensive. Still, if you can arrange to arrive by bike or by ferry, the views of the bay make Sausalito a worthwhile excursion.

Bridgeway is Sausalito's main thoroughfare, bordered on one side by waterfront restaurants and the bay, on the other by shops hawking pricey antiques or tacky pelican paperweights. At the south end of Bridgeway is the Sausalito Ferry Terminal, where the commuter ferry from San Francisco docks (*see* Ferry Travel *in* Chapter 1). Farther south on Bridgeway is Sausalito's oldest restaurant, built in 1893 and originally known as Valhalla. It was used as a backdrop in the classic Orson Welles film *The Lady from Shanghai*; today it's the **Sausalito Chart House Restaurant** (201 Bridgeway, tel. 415/332–0804), part of an upscale seafood-and-steak chain, with one of the best views in town.

To find the local heart of Sausalito, head one block up from Bridgeway at San Carlos Avenue to **Caledonia Street.** While the Thai, Indian, and sushi restaurants here don't have views of the ocean, they also don't have chilly shore winds or touristy pricetags. Try **Sartaj India Café** (43 Caledonia St., tel. 415/332–7103) for cheap, homemade curries and chai made fresh 20 times daily. Another good bet is **Sausalito Gourmet Delicatessen** (209 Caledonia St., tel. 415/332–4880), where you can buy substantial $5 sandwiches and wash them down with wine, beer, and sodas from the cooler's extensive offerings. Eat by the fountain in the sunny back courtyard or brown bag your lunch across Bridgeway to grassy **Earl F. Dunphy Park** and watch yachts glide by in the harbor.

Salty dogs can get out on the water themselves by renting sailboats at **Cass' Marina** (1702 Bridgeway at Napa, tel. 415/332–6789). Six-person, 22-ft boats start at $100 for a half day, and cruising boats for longer trips start at $210 a day.

TIBURON AND ANGEL ISLAND

Some folks come to Tiburon with picnic baskets in hand and set out their spread on the harbor-front lawns. Others dock their boats at the harbor and head to one of the many waterside restaurants. Do both these things, and you'll have just about exhausted the possibilities of this tiny, peninsula-tip town north of Sausalito. The atmosphere is relaxed, and the views of Angel Island and San Francisco are superb, but since it's really no more that a cluster of waterfront gift shops and pricey boutiques, it can quickly become cloying. Escape uphill to **Old St. Hilary's Landmark and Wildflower Preserve,** which protects both a simple 1888 Carpenter Gothic church (now a historical and botanical museum) and the windswept field of rare black-jewel wildflowers in which it stands. The flowers bloom in May and June. *At top of Esperanza St., tel. 415/435–2567. Admission free. Open Apr.–Oct., Wed. and Sun. 1–4.*

Most of Tiburon's restaurants and boutiques are on Main Street or on tree-lined **Ark Row,** which veers west at the end of Main Street. For less expensive delis and grocery stores, try Tiburon Boulevard, a few blocks up from the waterfront. **Windsor Vineyards** (72 Main St., tel. 415/435–3113) gives out samples of their 30 or so red, blush, white, sparkling, and dessert wines, all grown in Sonoma County. Bottles run $8–$25, and personalized labels are free.

From Tiburon take the 15-minute ferry ride to **Angel Island,** a 750-acre state park where you can explore sandy beaches and old military installations. **Ayala Cove,** the area around the ferry landing, is congested with picnickers taking advantage of tables and barbecue grills (bring your own charcoal, as wood gathering is not allowed). The **Ayala Cove Visitor Center** (tel. 415/435–1915) distributes a brochure that details the history and geography of the island ($2). Nearby you can rent day-use lockers (50¢).

The 5-mi perimeter road that rings the island offers access to plenty of scenic and historic sites (*see* Hiking and Biking on Angel Island *in* Chapter 8), as well as plenty of tourists. To escape the crowds, tote your picnic fixings about a mile from Ayala Cove to **Camp Reynolds,** which functioned as an army camp from the Civil War to World War II. Plenty of people linger at the Commanding Officer's House along the road, but about a quarter mile past the old army barracks, at the water's edge, you'll find some isolated picnic tables and an outstanding close-up view of the Golden Gate Bridge. You can also camp on the island (*see* Chapter 7).

On the other side of the island is an **immigration station** once known as "the Ellis Island of the West," where immigrants (mostly Asian) were detained when trying to enter the United States between 1910 and 1940. A few poems written by despairing detainees are still etched into the walls.

COMING AND GOING

To get to Tiburon, exit U.S. 101 at Tiburon Boulevard and drive 3 mi to the tip of the peninsula, where Main Street curves to the right. The **Tiburon–Angel Island Ferry** (tel. 415/435–2131) leaves for Angel Island from Tiburon's Main Street Pier (21 Main St.) every hour from 10 to five on weekends year-round, and at 10, 11, 1, and 3 on spring and summer weekdays (schedules are subject to change; call ahead). Boats depart from Angel Island 20 minutes after they dock. Round-trip fares, which include entry fees for the island state park, are $7, plus $1 for bicycles. Cars are not allowed. Ferries also leave from Fisherman's Wharf in San Francisco (*see* Ferry Travel *in* Chapter 1). For information on bike rental on the island, *see* Hiking and Biking *in* Chapter 8.

MILL VALLEY

Nestled among California redwoods on the eastern flank of Mt. Tamalpais, Mill Valley is a community of millionaires and mountain bikers, where people have paid enormous sums of money for their solitude. Sneak up on them by taking the East Blithedale exit from U.S. 101.

On weekends all the action is on the plaza at the corner of Miller and Throckmorton avenues; here people play Hacky Sack and drink coffee bought at one of the three nearby coffeehouses. The best of the lot is the **Depot Bookstore & Café** (87 Throckmorton Ave., at Miller St., tel. 415/383–2665), a favorite of mountain bikers after a run down Mt. Tam (as the locals call it). Another Mill Valley institution is **Village Music** (9 E. Blithedale Ave., at Throckmorton Ave., tel. 415/388–7400), where the collection is almost exclusively vinyl. The store has become a landmark on the international music map, attracting big-name customers like Mick Jagger. Tucked into the redwoods at the western edge of town, the **Mill Valley Public Library** (375 Throckmorton Ave., tel. 415/389–4292) is a friendly place to relax in front of a cozy hearth and two-story views of the forest. Book sales held on the third Saturday of each month support the library and offer an eclectic selection of rare volumes and dog-eared paperbacks.

If you've come to enjoy more pastoral pursuits, take a "walk around the block," Mill Valley–style: The short **Three Wells** and **Cascade Falls** walks follow a gentle uphill route through the redwoods, along a creek, and past a few frigid swimming holes to a small waterfall. To get here, walk or drive up Throckmorton and turn left on Cascade Drive until you see the THREE WELLS sign nailed to a tree. Follow the path starting at the sign for about a quarter mile, cross the street, and continue uphill at the CASCADES FALLS sign.

Cyclists will enjoy a favorite local ride over the bay tree–covered hill to **Corte Madera** and **Larkspur.** Follow East Blithedale Avenue to Camino Alto and head north 2 mi along the winding road until it turns into Magnolia Avenue. Corte Madera offers a few quaint stores and eateries, but it's worth it to continue another mile to **Left Bank** (507 Magnolia Ave., Larkspur, tel. 415/927–3331), a Parisian-style café with a handsome and relaxed clientele.

SAN RAFAEL

Unassuming San Rafael, set between the foot of Mt. Tamalpais and San Rafael Hill, would attract more day-trippers from foggy San Francisco if people realized it's almost always warmer here than elsewhere in the Bay Area. In fact, that's exactly why the town was founded in the first place: In 1817, when Native Americans at San Francisco's Mission Dolores started dying at an alarming rate, missionaries built a hospital here so the sick could receive care in a more hospitable climate. The original buildings of the Mission San Rafael Archangel were torn down in the 1870s, but a replica of the **chapel** (corner of 5th and A Sts.), built of stuccoed concrete instead of the original adobe, now sits next to a gift shop selling Catholic kitsch. A block away from the chapel, **4th Street** is the town's main drag, lined with used bookstores, a large contingent of department stores, and some good cafés and clubs, including **New George's** (842 4th St., at Cijos St., tel. 415/457–1515) and **Broken Drum Brewery & Wood Grill** (1132 4th St., tel. 415/456–4677). New George's has been voted "best nightlife in Marin" for its impressive calendar of live jazz, R&B, and acoustic entertainment. The Broken Drum's action happens on two levels: diners and dancers sip microbrews in the café, while owner Noah Berry brews the drinks and DJ's spin triphop and blues on the balcony. San Rafael's **Farmers' Market** (4th and B Sts., tel. 415/457–2266) takes place April–October, Thursday 6 PM–9 PM. The market is more like a weekly block party than a simple produce sale; locals come in droves to buy handicrafts, listen to live music, and let the kids take pony rides. The **Falkirk Cultural Center** (1408 Mission Ave., at E St., tel. 415/485–3328) is an

11-acre estate with picnic-perfect lawns and a Queen Anne–style Victorian mansion built in 1888. Its second floor houses an elegant gallery showcasing both local artists and national exhibitions. The center is open Tuesday–Friday 10–5, Thursday 10–9, and Saturday 10–1.

North of downtown—take the North San Pedro Road exit off U.S. 101—is the **Marin Civic Center** (3501 Civic Center Dr.; tel. 415/499–7407), a collection of massive, freestanding concrete structures designed by Frank Lloyd Wright. Concerned with preserving the site's natural contours, Wright lined the eaves with blue curves that mimic the rolls of Mt. Tam. The inside of the main building has been called one of the most functional and offbeat office spaces ever conceived. Docents offer guided tours Wednesday at 10:30 AM. For information on dance and drama performances in the adjoining theater, call the Marin Center box office (tel. 415/472–3500).

Four miles east of San Rafael on North San Pedro Road is **China Camp State Park,** a pristine 1,600-acre wilderness area. Remnants of an old Chinese fishing village are still visible, and the oak knolls and saltwater marshes are great for hiking and camping (*see* Chapter 7). Park ($3) at China Camp Point for the 5-mi hike along the well-marked **Shoreline Trail.** The steeper **Bay View Trail** is a favorite of park rangers (it's also much less crowded). Pick up a trail map from the **ranger station** (tel. 415/456–0766), about a mile from the park entrance on North San Pedro Road. All areas are open 8 AM to sunset.

MUIR WOODS AND MT. TAMALPAIS

MUIR WOODS NATIONAL MONUMENT

During the Great Depression, a local grocer graciously honored his customers' credit, preventing countless Sausalito residents from going hungry. Today, where Bridgeway meets the bay, the eponymous Yee Tock Chee Park stands as a monument to him.

If you judge only by the crowded parking lot and tacky gift shop, the Muir Woods National Monument looks like just another overtouristed attraction to be avoided. This 550-acre park, however, contains one of the most impressive groves of coastal redwoods in the world, some more than 250 ft tall and over 800 years old. It's crowded, to be sure, but you can find rugged, unpopulated trails that meander along cool, fern-filled ridges high above the clogged canyon. The **Ocean View Trail,** one of the best for beating the crowds, ascends for 1⅓ mi before connecting with the **Lost Trail,** which descends through forests of Douglas fir before returning to the redwood groves. The Lost Trail hooks up with the **Fern Creek Trail,** which takes you back to the parking lot. The moderate hike is 3 mi round-trip and passes some of the park's most impressive stands of redwoods. (For more trail tips, *see* Hiking and Biking *in* Chapter 8.)

Neither picnicking nor camping is allowed in the park, but snacks are available at the gift shop, along with every type of redwood souvenir imaginable. The **visitor center** (tel. 415/388–2596) organizes free nature walks through the woods; call for the current schedule. From U.S. 101 take the Stinson Beach/Highway 1 exit and follow the signs. The monument is open daily 8 AM–sunset; admission is $2, and parking is free, though on sunny weekends Muir Woods is so crowded you may have to park a mile or more from the lot.

MUIR BEACH

If you continue on Highway 1 instead of following the turnoff to Muir Woods, you'll come to **Muir Beach,** a quiet strip of sand punctuated by hundreds of tidal pools. The strikingly scenic beach, the site of the first coastal settlement north of San Francisco, attracts folks looking to relax—not the Budweiser-and-volleyball crowd you'll find at Stinson Beach (*see below*), 6 mi farther north.

If you really want to get a feel for Marin's landscape, park your car at Muir Beach and hike the **Coastal Trail** (*see* Hiking and Biking *in* Chapter 8), which leads up a steep hill overlooking the ocean and then winds through a series of deserted coves and valleys. Return the same way and reward yourself with a pint of Guinness in front of the fire at the **Pelican Inn** (10 Pacific Way, at Hwy. 1, tel. 415/383–6000). You can eat lunch here for less than $10; the adjoining pub has a dartboard and a healthy sampling of British ales and bitters. Ask the innkeeper about renting horses from the nearby stables.

Less than a mile south of Stinson Beach, the **Green Gulch Farm Zen Center** (1601 Shoreline Hwy., tel. 415/383–3134) offers seven-week Zen training sessions, with everything from walking meditation to

Japanese tea ceremonies—as well as less intensive programs for visitors. On Sunday you can sign up for instruction, meditation, a lecture, tea, a discussion period, and optional lunch ($7 for the lunch, donations appreciated for the instruction); you may also wander the idyllic grounds and gardens any day of the week. Expect to pay a $5 parking fee on Sunday between 8:45 AM and 10:30 AM unless you have three or more people in your car. Another option is to carpool, as many people do, from the Manzanita Parking Lot (Shoreline Hwy., at U.S. 101, Mill Valley); look for someone holding a GREEN GULCH CARPOOL-ING sign.

MT. TAMALPAIS STATE PARK

There are several theories about the origin of the name *Tamalpais,* but it's most commonly believed to be a combination of the Miwok words *tammal* (bay country) and *plis* (mountain). Begin your exploration of Mt. Tamalpais State Park at the **Pantoll ranger station** (tel. 415/388–2070), where you can pick up one of several topographical maps ($1–$7) describing all the trails and roads. If you're going mountain biking, take care to distinguish the fire trails (where biking is allowed) from the walking trails (where biking nets you a steep fine). One strenuous and popular hike, the 2-mi **Steep Ravine Trail** (*see* Hiking and Biking *in* Chapter 8), starts from the Pantoll station and takes you down a series of ladders to the Steep Ravine cabins (*see* Chapter 7). Parking is $5 in the Pantoll parking lot, but you can park for free anywhere along the road. The place is packed on weekends, so you'll have trouble parking if you arrive after noon.

The **summit** of Mt. Tam can be reached by car (look for the turnoff opposite the Pantoll station), and the gates are open dawn to dusk. Unfortunately, the military owned the summit until recently and left the kind of squat buildings and strange towers that only the military seems to build. Also near the summit is the open-air **Mountain Theater,** where for three consecutive summer weekends, a play or musical is produced. For performance and ticket information ($16–$20) contact the Mountain Play Association (tel. 415/383–1100). Plays do sell out, so it's wise to purchase tickets well in advance.

STINSON BEACH

Six treacherous miles north of Muir Beach on Highway 1 lies Stinson Beach, one of northern California's most popular coastal towns. It's loaded with weather-beaten wooden houses and neighborly general stores, and its 3-mi beach—the longest in Marin County—has a beach-bum appeal that's hard to find north of Santa Cruz. Despite Stinson's isolated location, chilly waters, and lurking sharks, hordes of surfers and sun worshipers descend on this town of 1,200 every spring and summer weekend. Even if you're not planning to surf or swim, the 20-minute (10-mi) drive from Muir Woods to Stinson, past towering cliffs and jagged granite peaks, is incredible. For groceries, stop by **Beckers by the Beach** (101 Calle del Mar, tel. 415/868–1923), next to the stop sign on Highway 1. Traffic can be a problem on summer weekends, but there are plenty of scenic overlooks along the way to cushion the blow of bumper-to-bumper traffic. Bus service from San Francisco to Stinson Beach operates on weekends and holidays only: From the Transbay Terminal (1st and Mission Sts.), take Golden Gate Transit Bus 20 to Marin City, then transfer to Bus 63. For information on surfboard rentals, *see* Water Sports *in* Chapter 8.

Along Bolinas Lagoon, just north of Stinson on Highway 1, you'll find **Audubon Canyon Ranch** (tel. 415/868–9244), a 1,000-acre nesting ground for blue herons, snowy egrets, and other shore birds. The sanctuary and its hiking trails are open to the public March 11–July 16, weekends 10–4 (additional hours Tuesday–Thursday 2–4 by appointment only). There's a small museum ($5 donation suggested) with geological and natural history displays, a bookstore, a gift shop, and a picnic area.

For an encounter with a different sort of wildlife, walk down to **Red Rocks Beach,** where during extremely low tides, caves containing hot springs are revealed—as well as the bare buns of bathers. Even when the caves are concealed by water, the beach is peopled by nudists: Leave your inhibitions in the car. To get here, drive ¾ mi south of Stinson Beach and park in the big gravel lot you'll see on the right. A path leads down to the beach.

BOLINAS

A few miles north of Audubon Canyon Ranch (*see above*) lies Bolinas, a town dedicated to discouraging tourism: Locals are perpetually taking down the sign marking the Bolinas/Olema Road (it's the first left after you curve around the lagoon to your left). If you breeze into town to wander Main Street and do some shopping, you'll feel tolerated at best. The **Fourth of July** brings out the town's friendliest faces; past festivities have included outrageous parades and a tug-of-war with Stinson Beach (the loser ended up in the muddy mouth of the estuary between the two towns).

Though the Bolinas of the new millennium looks much like any of Marin's wealthy towns, you'll still find a few bearded radicals hanging out on street corners, strumming their guitars or fixing their VW microbuses, and a handful of '60s-style establishments. The **Bolinas People's Store** (14 Wharf Rd., at Brighton Ave., tel. 415/868–1433) is famous for its fresh, high-quality local produce, grown by the same sweaty hippies who once gave Bolinas so much of its character. For a bite to eat, go next door to the **Bolinas Bay Bakery and Café** (20 Wharf Rd., tel. 415/868–0211), stocked with freshly baked goods, pasta salads, and pizzas. The only nightlife in town is **Smiley's Schooner Saloon** (41 Wharf Rd., at Brighton Ave., tel. 415/868–1311), which at 150 years of age is ostensibly the oldest continually operated saloon in California. Huddled around the pool table and jukebox are an odd combination of suit-and-tie professionals and tie-dyed hippies.

A worthwhile detour is the **Point Reyes Bird Observatory** (tel. 415/868–0655), which harbors 225 species of birds. From the second stop sign on Bolinas/Olema Road, take Mesa Road 4½ mi north. It's open year-round dawn to dusk, and admission is free (donations requested). On your way you'll pass a turnoff for **Duxberry Reef,** a peaceful breaker that's dotted with hundreds of tidal pools. To reach the reef from Mesa Road, go left on Overlook Drive and right on Ocean Park Way. For hikes in this area, *see* Chapter 8.

With its lush grazing land and rambling farms, Point Reyes—a hammerhead-shape peninsula that juts 10 mi into the ocean—could easily pass for western Ireland, minus the pubs.

POINT REYES NATIONAL SEASHORE

Explore the Point Reyes National Seashore—a 66,500-acre mosaic of marshes, ferocious cliffs, and undisturbed beaches—and you'll feel a lot farther than 40 mi away from San Francisco. And with good reason: Point Reyes is on the Pacific tectonic plate, while most of the rest of California is on the North American plate. As a result, its bedrock, plants, and the terrain are all very different from the rest of the Bay Area. Even though it's isolated, Point Reyes is a manageable day trip from San Francisco, a drive of about 90 minutes each way. There are hundreds of hiking trails and biking routes on the peninsula (*see* Chapter 8), along with four backpackers-only campgrounds and an excellent hostel (*see* Chapter 7), should you want to spend the night.

Twelve miles north of Bolinas on Highway 1, past the block-long town of Olema, look for a sign marking the turnoff for Point Reyes and the **Bear Valley Visitor Information Center** (Bear Valley Rd., tel. 415/663–1092), open weekdays 9–5, weekends 8–5. Here you can see a short orientation film, sign up for ranger-led hikes, explore a small museum of cultural and natural history, or pick up trail maps and camping permits. A short walk away, look for the replica of a typical Miwok village, built on the ruins of a 400-year-old Native American farming settlement. Also nearby is the **Bear Valley Trail,** a lightly traveled 4-mi hike that wanders through the woods and down to a secluded beach with a view of the peninsula.

Two miles farther down Bear Valley Road (which turns into Sir Francis Drake Boulevard), you'll pass through the quiet town of **Inverness.** Coming across this town's Czech architecture (it's full of oddly colored, intricately carved wooden houses) can be disorienting after miles of empty coastline, but the town's Eastern European flavor is genuine. In 1935, after a freighter ran aground in San Francisco Bay, a number of its Czech deckhands jumped ship and settled here. Since then dozens of Czech families have immigrated to Inverness, bringing their culture, language, and cuisine.

Continue west through Inverness on Sir Francis Drake Boulevard, then take Drakes Beach Road to a massive stretch of white sand fittingly called **Drakes Beach**—supposedly Sir Francis himself landed here on his world tour. It's often windy and too rough for swimming (unless you're a great white shark—they love it here), but the beach is terrific for sunning.

A quarter mile north of Drakes Beach, a sign directs you to the **Point Reyes Lighthouse,** 6 mi to the west. The 300 stairs down to the lighthouse are open whenever a ranger is there, usually Thursday–Monday 10–4:30 barring storms or heavy winds; admission is free. The **Visitors Center** (tel. 415/669–

1534) is open Thursday–Monday 10–5. Admission is free. From the parking lot a steep trail leads down to the lighthouse, and a dozen or so trails are carved into the surrounding cliffs. The ¾-mi hike to **Chimney Rock** is one of the most scenic; look for the trailhead in the parking lot. On clear days you can see San Francisco, but usually thick fog provides little visibility. From mid-December to April, and especially in January and March, this is a great place to look for the gray whales on their 12,000-mi round-trip migration along the Pacific coast.

To reach Point Reyes from San Francisco, cross the Golden Gate Bridge on U.S. 101. If speed is more important than scenery, exit at Sir Francis Drake Boulevard and follow it 21 mi to the coast. Eventually you'll end up 2 mi north of Olema on Highway 1. Otherwise, take the Stinson Beach/Highway 1 exit and enjoy the 30-mi curvy, scenic drive along the coast. Bus service from San Francisco to Point Reyes operates on weekends and holidays only: From the Transbay Terminal (1st and Mission Sts.) take any Golden Gate Transit bus to the San Rafael Transit Center (Bus 80 is the most direct), then transfer to Bus 65.

Amidst the group of new restaurants that arise around Point Reyes every season, the **Gray Whale Inn** (12781 Sir Francis Drake Blvd., Inverness, tel. 415/669–1244) remains the best place to munch home-style pizza, sandwiches, and pastries and watch day fade into night from the sunny patio. The **Bovine Bakery** (11315 Hwy. 1, 2 mi north of Olema, tel. 415/663–9420) has excellent, reasonably priced sandwiches, pastries, and breads for picnickers. If you drive on to Point Reyes Station, **Tomales Bay Foods** (80 4th St., Point Reyes Station, tel. 415/663–9335) is another stop for goodies-to–go. The rustic barn-style building encloses a local-vegetable stand, a creamery with herbed goat cheeses, and a deli boasting homemade sausage and exotic salads made to order.

SOUTH BAY

Heading south on U.S. 101 brings a change of both scenery and pace. As the cosmopolitan frenzy of San Francisco fades, you sense the quiet blandness of industrial parks, shopping malls, and tract housing. To its credit, the South Bay has its own interesting, amusing, or just plain weird attractions that San Francisco snobs thoroughly underrate (or don't know about). The cities that stretch south from San Francisco to San Jose lie on what locals refer to as the **Peninsula,** a finger of land wedged between the San Francisco Bay on the east and the Pacific Ocean on the west; a number of cities, including Palo Alto, make for easy day trips from San Francisco. Geographically near but seemingly worlds away from the urban commotion of the San Jose area and the Peninsula, the secluded **San Mateo County coast** is a long stretch of windswept coastline punctuated by quiet coastal communities.

PALO ALTO

Palo Alto, about 30 mi south of San Francisco, is mostly known as the home of **Stanford University,** and it's certainly worth the drive just to check out the beautiful 8,200-acre campus designed by Frederick Law Olmsted, landscape designer, and Charles Allerton Coolidge, architect. And, contrary to popular Bay Area opinion (held particularly by UC Berkeley students, Stanford's arch rivals), the town of Palo Alto itself has some cultural attractions that are also worth a look, as well as a downtown area with a few good cafés and restaurants. Off U.S. 101, **University Avenue,** between Middlefield Road and High Street, is Palo Alto's main drag; west of El Camino Real it metamorphoses into **Palm Drive,** Stanford's entrance and main thoroughfare. University Avenue travels through Palo Alto's oldest and wealthiest neighborhood—be sure to notice the mansions. In the downtown area University Avenue and its side streets are loaded with restaurants, cafés, galleries, boutiques, and bookstores. All are rather upscale for a student shopping district, but the streets are pleasantly punctuated by plazas with benches and plants.

STANFORD UNIVERSITY

Sometimes called the Ivy League university of the West Coast, Stanford opened its doors to scholars in October 1891. The land it occupies was once a stud farm, hence the school's popular nickname, the Farm. Today its mustard-color buildings combine Romanesque and Spanish-mission styles to achieve a look that's described alternately as Western Ivy League and Giant Taco Bell.

From downtown enter the campus along the aptly named Palm Drive, which will take you to the **quad,** the heart of campus and a popular hangout. At the **visitor center** (tel. 650/723–2560) in Memorial Hall you can pick up free maps or take an hour-long guided walking tour (departures at 11 and 3:15 daily). Standing in the center of the quad is the stately Romanesque **Memorial Church,** best known for its Venetian mosaic. Organ recitals take place in the church; ask at the visitor center for a schedule. Near the entrance to the quad, the grassy **Memorial Court** has a couple of Auguste Rodin statues including *The Burghers of Calais,* depicting 14th-century French martyrs at the moment of painful departure from their families and other citizens. A less traditional New Guinean **sculpture garden,** installed in 1995, can be found near the intersection of Lomita Drive and St. Theresa Street. Just to the south of the quad, the 280-ft **Hoover Tower** thrusts mightily into the sky. It's home to the famed Hoover Institution for the Study of War, Revolution, and Peace. To get the classic view of campus and parts of Palo Alto, pay $2 to climb to the tower's observation deck; it's open daily 10–4:30 when classes are in session.

After 10 years of closure due to damage from the Loma Prieta earthquake, the Stanford Museum of Art has reopened, with expanded space and a new name: **The Iris & B. Gerald Cantor Center for Visual Arts.** The museum's collection includes a Ming Dynasty bronze Buddha, African masks and carved figurines from the 18th and 19th centuries, and works by Georgia O'Keeffe, Frank Lloyd Wright, and Willem de Kooning. The **Rodin Sculpture Garden,** in a small area outside the museum, features 20 or so works by French sculptor Auguste Rodin (1840–1917). Most pieces depict nudes in various stages of introspection, ecstasy, or anguish. Check out the particularly intense *Gates of Hell*—the subject of innumerable art history lectures and descriptive tours (held Sat. 11 AM, Sun. 3 PM; call for details). *Museum Way and Lomita Dr., tel. 650/723–4177. From Palm Dr. turn right on Museum Way, 1 block past Campus Dr. Admission free. Open Wed.–Sun. 11–5, Thurs. until 8.*

The huge, sprawling campus is best explored by bike (the cycling is even better in the foothills west of the university). For rentals, try **Campus Bike Shop** (551 Salvatierra La., on campus, tel. 650/325–2945), which can get you rolling on a mountain bike for $10 a day or a three-speed for $8. Either kind of bike requires a cash, check, or credit card deposit.

STANFORD LINEAR ACCELERATOR

Even if you're only vaguely interested in science, make the trek up Sand Hill Road (west from campus toward I–280) to see this masterpiece of modern ingenuity. The 2-mi-long atom smasher is truly amazing—thousands of house-size machines, dials, and diodes, as well as scientists who get excited when you mention n-orbits and electrons. Reserve space for the free two-hour tour, generally held twice a week, which includes a slide show and lecture (days and times vary); it's geared toward lay people and is extremely interesting. The accelerator is only open to the public during tour times, but a new visitor center, with information on the facility's research efforts, is open weekdays 8–5. *2575 Sand Hill Rd., Menlo Park, tel. 650/926–2204. From I–280, exit east at Sand Hill Rd.*

NEAR PALO ALTO

FILOLI

Once the set for the TV series *Dynasty,* this country estate in Woodside (just west of Palo Alto) is one of the last of its kind in California to remain intact and in its original setting. The Georgian Revival mansion, with its Flemish bond brick exterior, Spanish tile roof, and marble fireplace facades, was built between 1915 and 1917 for William B. Bourn II, the owner of a lucrative gold mine in Grass Valley. The estate's garden, actually a series of separate "garden rooms," is equally magnificent. Particularly interesting is the Walled Garden, entirely enclosed by brick walls with an Italian Renaissance–style pavilion in the center. *Cañada Rd., near Edgewood Rd., Woodside, tel. 650/364–2880. From I–280, exit Edgewood Rd. west, then make a right on Cañada Rd. Admission $10. Open Tues.–Sat. 10–2 for docent-led and self-guided tours. Reservations necessary for guided tours.*

NASA AMES RESEARCH CENTER

For a true technological trip, visit this 140-acre research center devoted to the design of all types of flying machines, at Moffett Field in Mountain View (about 5 mi southeast of Palo Alto). Though the research facility is normally closed to the general public, you can check out the aviation and space-flight paraphernalia at the **NASA Visitors Center Museum,** which is open weekdays 8–4:30. Better yet, call two weeks ahead and sign up for an escorted tour of the main plant. Depending on what's available that day, the free two-hour tour may take you around flight simulators, design centers, retired research crafts, or construction hangars. *Tel. 650/604–6274. From U.S. 101, exit at Moffett Field, left on Moffett Blvd. at main gate, and head toward space shuttle.*

SAN JOSE

Too sprawling to have cultivated any sort of cohesive identity, northern California's largest city wallows in misunderstanding. To many, San Jose is another faceless component of **Silicon Valley**—the conceptual land of whirring computer chips and complex equations. In reality, San Jose is part high-tech wonderland and part minimall suburbia. It's encircled by mountain ranges, buffered by city parks and gardens, and home to museums, symphonies, and wineries as well as industrial parks, computer companies, and corporate headquarters.

The new billion-dollar **downtown** is a good place to start exploring. Hop on the **light rail** (tel. 408/321–2300) that connects San Jose State University on one end with the Center for Performing Arts on the other (fare is $1.10); its numerous stops should give you a good overview of the city center, which is architecturally interesting in its attempt to meld existing Old West themes with modern styles and materials (note the traditional small-town clock tower built from marble and stainless steel). Around the intersection of Market and San Carlos streets you'll find a number of pedestrian plazas and a host of museums, including the **San Jose Museum of Art** (110 S. Market St., tel. 408/294–2787), with its numerous paintings, photographs, and large-scale multimedia exhibits by local and nationally recognized artists. Admission is $7. The ornate, Renaissance-style **Cathedral Basilica of St. Joseph** (90 S. Market St., tel. 408/283–8100), built in 1877, is another nearby attraction worth visiting; its Odell pipe organ, which was built and installed in the church in 1886, is the only instrument of this type in its original condition on the West Coast. It operates almost entirely mechanically, without electricity. The **Plaza de Cesar Chavez** (S. Market St., in front of Fairmont Hotel), a pleasant grassy strip, runs for two blocks tying the whole area together. The fountain is great for splashing around (the water shoots straight up out of grates in the ground).

Though it's known more for its corporate image than anything else, San Jose is becoming increasingly recognized for its cultural diversity. You can get the full flavor in July, when the two-day **San Jose America Festival** (tel. 408/294–2100, ext. 444) brings live entertainment and crafts booths to town. Other festivals to look for: June's **Juneteenth Festival** (tel. 408/292–3157) showcases the achievements of African-Americans through lecture, cinema, art, and cultural foods. For some hip action (literally) catch the **Tahiti Fête** (tel. 408/486–9177), a three-day dance competition in July that brings together Tahitian dance groups (*halaus*) from all over the Bay Area and even draws dancers from as far as Hawaii. August nights heat up (as if it weren't already scorching) when the **San Jose Jazz Festival** (tel. 831/457–1141) rolls into town.

CHILDREN'S DISCOVERY MUSEUM

Inside this brilliant purple building you'll find interactive science, humanities, and arts exhibits geared toward kids. Young visitors can fashion art from recycled materials; create their own plays, costumes, and set designs in a realistic theater; learn how electricity is generated through using a "people-powered" generator; or explore the physics of bubbles. *180 Woz Way, at Auzerais St., tel. 408/298-5437. From the convention center on Almaden Blvd. go south and turn right on Woz Way. Admission $6. Open Tues.–Sat. 10–5, Sun. noon–5.*

GUADALUPE RIVER PARK AND GARDENS

This ever-expanding 3-mi-long stretch of green follows the river's course and runs by many of the city's attractions. The **Discovery Meadow** area, next to the Children's Discovery Museum, has some bronze animal sculptures that kids love to climb on and is the site of many of the park's festivals. The **Arena Green** area, across from the San Jose Arena, is a popular pregame picnic spot with grills, picnic tables, and a new carousel. The 4-acre **Heritage Rose Garden** at Spring and Taylor streets has 3,500 rosebushes that should be blooming mid-April through October. Behind it is the young, 4-acre **Historic Orchard,** filled with apricot, cherry, and pear trees that recapture a time when Santa Clara Valley was known as "the valley of heart's delight," for its numerous fruit trees. *Park runs along Guadalupe River and Guadalupe Parkway between I-280 and I-880, tel. 408/277-2757.*

PERALTA ADOBE AND FALLON HOUSE

You can visit both of these well-preserved historic buildings for one admission price. The Peralta Adobe, built in 1797, is the last remaining adobe structure left from the original settlement of San Jose, called El Pueblo de San José. The two-room home is furnished to show both the early Spanish colonial period and the later Mexican territorial period. The more ornate Fallon House, a 15-room Victorian mansion across the street, was built in 1855 by San Jose's seventh mayor. The period-decorated rooms and small formal gardens can be visited on a 90-minute tour that includes the Peralta Adobe. *Peralta Adobe: 184 W. St. John St.; Fallon House: 175 W. St. John St.; both at San Pedro St., tel. 408/993–8182. Admission $6 for both. Guided tours Tues.–Sun. noon–5.*

ROSICRUCIAN EGYPTIAN MUSEUM AND PLANETARIUM

This museum houses one of the most impressive collections of Egyptian, Assyrian, and Babylonian artifacts west of the Nile. Standouts are the animal and human mummies, the underground tomb, and the decorative wall reliefs. Sign up for a guided tour of the walk-through replica of a pyramid tomb or catch a planetarium show. *1342 Naglee Ave., at Park Ave., tel. 408/947–3636. Get off I–880 at Alameda East exit, turn right at Naglee Ave. Admission $7. Open daily 9–5 (last entry at 4:30).*

SAN JOSE HISTORICAL MUSEUM

You can hop a historic trolley, experience a Chinese temple, observe letterpress printing, and buy ice cream at an old-fashioned ice cream parlor at this outdoor "museum" in Kelly Park. The 25-acre museum emphasizes the history of San Jose and Santa Clara Valley, with 28 historic and reconstructed buildings, Native American artifacts, and historic photographs and documents. *1600 Senter Rd., at Phelan Ave., tel. 408/287–2290. From downtown, take Market St. (becomes First St.) south, turn left on Keyes St., turn right on Senter Rd. Admission $6. Open Tues.–Sun. 12–5.*

TECH MUSEUM OF INNOVATION

The Tech unveiled its new, larger location, designed by acclaimed architect Ricardo Legorreta, in the fall of 1998. The $96-million-dollar facility, financed in part by Silicon Graphics, Adobe, Compaq, Intel, and Microsoft, presents the high-tech world in understandable terms, with hands-on exhibits on multimedia, biotechnology, robotics, and space exploration. Also new is the Hackworth IMAX Dome Theater under the bright blue dome. *201 S. Market St., across from the Plaza de Cesar Chavez, tel. 408/795–6100. Admission $8 museum or IMAX theater, or $13.50 for both. Open daily 10–5 (to 6 PM Memorial Day through Labor Day,) to 8 PM the 3rd Thurs. of each month.*

The student population of San Jose State has gradually encouraged the growth of a trendier side of downtown, which has become known as **SoFA** (South of First Area)—a small section roughly between East Carlos and West Reed streets. Make a beeline here if you find yourself in San Jose after dark (*see* South Bay *in* Chapter 6).

NEAR SAN JOSE

GARBAGE MUSEUM

Californians generate more garbage per capita than any other group of people in the world, and this museum gives you some dramatic ways to feel guilty about it. The massive 100-ft Wall of Garbage exhibit represents merely one second's worth of what the country is continually throwing out. Here's your chance to play "Zap the Scrap": Choose any item on the wall of garbage and find out whether it's recyclable. *1601 Dixon Landing Rd., Milpitas, tel. 408/262–1401. Take Dixon Landing exit off I–880, 5 mi north of San Jose. Admission free. Open Tues.–Fri. 9–5, Sat. 7:30–4.*

GREAT AMERICA

Favorite rides here include the occasionally drenching water ride called **Logger's Run,** the **Vortex,** a stand-up roller-coaster that cost a whopping $5 million to build, and the **Drop Zone Stunt Tower**—the world's tallest free fall, at 22 stories. Then newest addition to the park is **KidZville,** a whole area devoted to children, with more than a dozen rides and attractions in four different "neighborhoods." If you'd rather not eat amusement park food, bring your own, leave it in a locker near the front gate, and eat in the picnic area outside. *Great America Pkwy., Santa Clara, tel. 408/988–1776. Take Great America Pkwy. exit off U.S 101, about 10 mi north of San Jose. Admission $32.99, parking $6. Open spring and fall, weekends only; summer, daily. Park opens at 10, and closing times vary with the season.*

WINCHESTER MYSTERY HOUSE

The continuous construction of this 160-room Victorian mansion occupied the last 38 years of Sarah Winchester's life. Apparently Mrs. Winchester was told by a fortune-teller to begin nonstop construction to placate the ghosts of those killed by Winchester guns; according to the seer, if she followed through with the project, she would have eternal life. (Luckily, her $20 million inheritance was enough to fund her venture!) The end result was a floor plan so bizarre and complex that she and her servants used maps to get around.

DYING TO GET TO COLMA

Along I–280 (southbound, en route to Palo Alto) lies Colma, a modern-day necropolis. In 1914 San Francisco's mayor ordered most city cemeteries to relocate their occupants to Colma; since then no new cemeteries have been created within San Francisco's city limits. The Colma town hall (1198 El Camino Real, at Serramonte Blvd., tel. 650/997–8300) provides a self-guided tour of the city's cemeteries ($2.50), including Pet's Rest, where Tina Turner's poodle was put out to pasture. Look for the graves of Dodge City's Wyatt Earp, baseball legend Lefty O'Doul, and blue-jeans king Levi Strauss.

On March 5, 1996, the San Jose City Council designated the Winchester Mansion a city landmark. General building manager Keith Kittle was quoted in the *San Francisco Chronicle* as saying, "I think Sarah Winchester would be proud. We're going to have a seance and talk to her and see." It's one of the most unusual attractions in the area, so try to stomach the high price. *525 S. Winchester Blvd., tel. 408/247–2101. From I–280, take Stevens Creek exit to Winchester Blvd. Admission $13.95. Open daily 9–5.*

SAN MATEO COUNTY COAST

PACIFICA AND MONTARA

Highway 1 and the secluded San Mateo County coast consist of more than 75 mi of winding shoreline and gently undulating hills that seem a world away from the overdeveloped inland communities. Along the highway are long, sandy beaches frequently devoid of any life aside from the local sea lions, surfers, and gulls; small towns just beginning to awaken to their potential as tourist destinations; and redwood groves filled with great hiking trails. At the north end of the coast, about 20 minutes south of San Francisco along Highway 1, Pacifica and Montara are sleepy seaside towns that offer an easy escape from urban chaos.

The "historic" section of Pacifica, on the northernmost outskirts of town, is full of unpretentious bungalow-style homes that once served as weekend retreats for wealthy San Franciscans but today house a majority of the town's locals. In this area you can visit the **Sanchez Adobe** (1000 Linda Mar Blvd. off Hwy. 1, tel. 650/359–1462), a historic building that traces various periods in California history through its varied past functions as a mission farm, a cattle ranch, a speakeasy, and the residence of Francisco Sanchez, a Mexican land-grant holder whose property included nearly all of what is now Pacifica. The town's small commercial district, to the south, is an eclectic combination of old mom-and-pop stores and upscale specialty shops, the latter suggesting the town is growing a little weary of its backwater authenticity and wants to start attracting some yuppie weekend tourists. Linking past and present are the recently renovated paved promenade and old fishing pier. Come here to smell the saltwater, feed the pigeons, and watch fishermen ply their trade; the pier also affords brilliant views of San Francisco and Marin County.

In addition to some fine hiking trails (*see* Chapter 8), Pacifica harbors a number of dark-sand beaches. About 2 mi south of old Pacifica, **Rockaway Beach** consists of two large dollops of sand on either end of a gorgeous cove—just large enough for half a dozen sunbathers and a handful of surfers and fishermen (swimming is not advised here as the waves are rough). Immediately south of Rockaway you'll come to the more popular **Pacifica State Beach,** a longer stretch of sand favored by surfers and a fair number of local sun worshipers.

Just a few miles farther south of San Francisco, Montara consists almost entirely of beach—its commercial district is virtually nonexistent. **Montara State Beach,** in the north end of town, is a wide, picturesque stretch of sand, less crowded than Pacifica's beaches. It's a good place to catch some rays, play Frisbee, have a picnic, or walk along the beach. Half a mile farther north, **Gray Whale Cove State Beach** (tel. 650/728–5336) is an American anomaly: a government-supported clothing-optional beach. Entrance to the spectacular, secluded cove is $6.50 weekdays, and $7.50 weekends. Immediately south of Montara, in Moss Beach, the rich tide pools of the **James V. Fitzgerald Marine Reserve** (tel. 650/728–3584) stretch along the coast for 4 mi. Go at low tide (call ahead to find out when) to check out abalone, barnacles, kelp, shells, and maybe an octopus or two; but remember, this is a reserve, so look but don't touch. Pick up a tidal timetable at the Point Montara Lighthouse Hostel (*see* Chapter 7); from there you can reach the reserve by taking Highway 1 south to California Avenue and turning right. The beaches and reserve are open from dawn to dusk.

For a meal in Pacifica, head straight to Francisco Boulevard, paralleling Highway 1 to the west. Here you'll find **Pacifica Thai Cuisine** (1966 Francisco Blvd., tel. 650/355–1678)—good for traditional specialties like chicken curry in coconut milk ($7)—and the oddly named **Pacifica Harry** (1780 Francisco Blvd., tel. 650/738–8300), an upscale Chinese restaurant with enticing entrées like cashew-nut shrimp. Both restaurants have vegetarian options. In Montara, **A Coastal Affair** (Hwy. 1 at 8th St., tel. 650/728–5229), ⅓ mi north of the Point Montara Lighthouse Hostel (*see* Chapter 7), is a combination craft gallery and café, with excellent espresso and freshly made sandwiches. Half a mile south of the hostel, in Moss Beach, **El Gran Amigo** (2448 Hwy. 1, at Virginia Ave., tel. 650/728–3815) serves up a wide variety of authentic Mexican specialties including enchiladas and nachos. Across the street, **Coastside Market** (501 Virginia Ave., tel. 650/728–3142) is an amply stocked spot to buy picnic supplies.

Get to Pacifica and Montara via public transportation by taking BART to the Daly City or Colma station. From Daly City take SamTrans Bus 1L, and from Colma take Bus 1C. Both bus lines will take you down Highway 1. Fares are $1.10.

HALF MOON BAY

Twenty-eight miles south of San Francisco, Half Moon Bay is the closest thing to a major town along the San Mateo County coast. In the late 1800s this was a sleepy agricultural hamlet called Spanish Town—until Prohibition paved the way for Canadian bootleggers to seek refuge (and a good time) in the town's then-untrafficked streets. The festive spirit still lives on: These days Half Moon Bay hosts a variety of festivals and events and is famous for growing pumpkins, Christmas trees, and flowers. It's also a mecca for surfers, with its immense waves (*see* Water Sports *in* Chapter 8). The revitalized downtown area centers around **Main Street,** which parallels Highway 1; the cozy street is cluttered with crafts stores, produce markets, gardens, cafés, and straightforward burger joints. If lolling on the beach is more your speed, follow Kelly Avenue west from Highway 1 to the popular **Half Moon Bay State Beach,** actually a series of beaches covering more than 2 mi. To avoid the $5 parking fee, walk from downtown. Before too long it will get a little chilly as you near the water, a perfect excuse to trek 2 mi inland along Highway 92 and sample—for free—the local wines at **Obester Winery** (12341 State Hwy. 92, tel. 650/726–9463), open daily 10–5.

Half Moon Bay hosts literally dozens of annual festivals, any of which you could plan a visit around. The largest and most popular is the **Art and Pumpkin Festival,** held the weekend after Columbus Day. The high-spirited fall celebration includes live music, local foods, crafts, vendors, a children's parade, and outrageous pie-eating and pumpkin-carving contests. Also popular is the aptly named **Coastal Flower Market,** which takes place on the third Saturday of each month from May through September. Another annual event is the **Fourth of July** parade down Main St. and fireworks display on the beach, which draws people from all over the Bay Area. For more information on any of these festivals, contact the **Half Moon Bay Chamber of Commerce** (520 Kelly Ave., at Hwy. 1, tel. 650/726–8380). Traffic can be overwhelming during the festivals; avoid gridlock headaches by visiting on a weekday when activity is more subdued. Better yet, leave your car behind and take SamTrans Bus 1L from the Daly City BART station (Bus 1C from Colma BART).

For a meal, Half Moon Bay offers everything from health food markets to overpriced seafood restaurants. The best of the former is **Healing Moon Natural Foods Market** (523 Main St., tel. 650/726–7881); if you're not looking for groceries, serve yourself a cup of soup and eat it on the peaceful outdoor patio. At **La Di Da** (500C Purissima St., tel. 650/726–1663) you can sip a cherry mocha while admiring monthly changing art exhibits—or listening to live music on weekends. At the **Half Moon Bay Bakery** (514 Main St., tel. 650/726–4841) watch piping hot muffins emerge from a 19th-century brick oven. You'll find reasonably priced seafood—a rarity in this area—at the **Flying Fish Grill** (99 Hwy. 92, at Main St., tel. 650/712–1125), closed Monday.

THE MERRY PRANKSTERS

In the early 1960s La Honda was home to one of the hippie era's most renowned groups of psychedelic crazies, the Merry Pranksters. Led by Ken Kesey, author of "One Flew Over the Cuckoo's Nest," the pranksters spent several years on a La Honda farm exploring "states of nonordinary reality"— dropping acid and smoking dope. When La Honda became too limiting, they outfitted an old school bus with Day-Glo paintings and filming and recording equipment and set off to travel across the country, a journey made famous by Tom Wolfe in his popular chronicle "The Electric Kool-Aid Acid Test."

SAN GREGORIO TO AÑO NUEVO

Day-trippers seeking sand, sea, and forest in quiet solitude are likely to find it along the desolate stretch of coastline south of Half Moon Bay. With the exception of Año Nuevo State Reserve during the elephant seals' mating season, this area is nearly deserted year-round. Though the beaches are usually cold and the choice of affordable food and lodging limited, the area is rich with natural assets: tide pools at Pescadero State Beach, the sky-high trees lining Highway 84 through La Honda—and the cliff-hugging Pigeon Point Lighthouse Youth Hostel (*see* Chapter 7) is nothing short of spectacular.

SAN GREGORIO

Although not much of a destination in itself, San Gregorio is a worthwhile stop if you're traveling up or down the coast between Santa Cruz and Half Moon Bay. Half the fun is the drive in from the coast to this hitching-post of a town, at the junction of Highways 1 and 84—even if you don't come by the spectacular coast road. **Highway 84,** the east–west road running to San Gregorio from I–280 (also known as La Honda Road), is not for the car-sickness-prone; but if you can take it, the highway is so thick with redwoods you'll barely believe it's daytime. Best of all, the road spits you out at the isolated **San Gregorio State Beach,** where you can lie back and soak up some rays or, more likely, throw on a sweater and battle the wind as the fog comes rolling in. If you get too cold, the bluff north of the parking lot is a good place for a brisk, blood-warming walk.

Don't miss the **San Gregorio General Store** (Stage Rd., tel. 650/726–0565), open daily 9–6, Friday until 7, a mile east of Highway 1 on Highway 84. This eclectic Old West–style store, which has served the ranching and farming community since 1889, sells everything from used books and stuffed animals to cast-iron pots and antiques (it also doubles as the town saloon and community center). Weekends bring live bands playing bluegrass and Grateful Dead covers; locals, bicyclists, and tourists gather round to stomp their heels and drink local brews.

LA HONDA

For an interesting contrast to coastal scenery, head inland about 11 mi east of Highway 1 to the densely forested community of La Honda—a town that seems almost lost in the shadows of countless giant redwoods. If you don't have time for the trip north to California's redwood country, this is a surprisingly good substitute. Before you head out into the wilds, stop at the **Pioneer Market** (La Honda Center, tel. 650/747–0551), where you can stock up on camping supplies and sandwiches. Later you can stop in for a drink at **Apple Jack's Tavern** (8790 La Honda Rd., tel. 650/747–0331), a scruffy bar, open weekdays noon–2 AM and weekends 10 AM–2 AM, where men drink their whiskey straight up, the women are loud and boisterous, and a brawl seems ready to erupt any minute.

Ringing the tiny town are four state and county parks whose forested hills provide excellent terrain for hiking and biking (*see* Chapter 8). Take Highway 84 about a mile west of La Honda, make a left on Alpine Road, and 4½ mi later you'll come to the parking lot of **Pescadero Creek County Park** (tel. 650/

879–0238), a secluded expanse of fir- and pine-covered hills crisscrossed by a series of gentle streams. From the parking lot follow the **Tarwater Trail Loop** in either direction for a moderate hike of about 2 mi, which will take you from a ridge with ocean views down through the scrub and into the redwoods. For yet another encounter with towering redwoods, Douglas fir, and pine trees, drive a bit farther along Alpine Road and you'll reach the turnoff for **Portola Redwood State Park** (Portola State Park Rd., tel. 650/948–9098), 2,900 acres of even more remote and scenic forest—the only drawback is the $6 parking fee. Just past the entrance to the park, the visitor center sells trail maps ($1) and wood ($5) for camping (*see* South Bay *in* Chapter 7). For information on hikes here, *see* Chapter 8.

Two more woodsy parks lie on Pescadero Road, which meets up with Alpine Road a mile south of Highway 84. The first is **Sam McDonald County Park** (for information call Memorial County Park, tel. 650/879–0238), a small, almost deserted redwood forest good for short hikes and complete solitude. A bit farther along Pescadero Road you'll come to **Memorial County Park** (tel. 650/879–0238), the most developed of the four parks—with a freshwater swimming hole, picnic areas, fire roads popular with mountain bikers, and a number of short- and medium-length hiking trails through the redwoods (*see* Hiking and Biking *in* Chapter 8). Parking is $4.

PESCADERO

In the flatlands 1 mi inland from the coast on Pescadero Road is the small fishing village of Pescadero. More than 100 years ago all the wooden buildings here were painted white with paint that washed up when the clipper ship *Carrier Pigeon* crashed into the rocks off Pigeon Point, a few miles south of town. Today the bakery, general store, bank, local post office, and other shops that populate Pescadero still retain their whitewashed uniformity, giving this town a calming, subdued ambience.

After you've rambled around the three blocks that make up Pescadero's commercial district, head to **Duarte's Tavern** (202 Stage Rd., at Pescadero Rd., tel. 650/879–0464), open 7 AM–9 PM daily, a combination bar and restaurant. Duarte's has been run by four generations of Duartes since 1894, and they're in no big hurry to serve you before the next generation takes over. The homey restaurant serves everything from peanut butter and jelly sandwiches to lamb chops, but it's most famous for its cream of artichoke soup, made with local produce, as well as fresh seafood plates and homemade pies.

On the coast just west of town, you'll find **Pescadero State Beach**, a long, sandy expanse rich with tide pools. Just north of the beach, the **Pescadero Marsh Reserve** (tel. 650/879–2170) is a protected area favored by ornithologists. Free guided walks leave from the parking lot just south of Pescadero Creek Bridge on Saturday at 10:30 and Sunday at 1 year-round, weather permitting. If you prefer to take to the hills, **Butano State Park** (tel. 650/879–2040), 5 mi south of Pescadero on Cloverdale Road, has 30 mi of trails on 3,200 acres (*see* Chapter 8). You can reach the park from Gazos Creek Road, off Highway 1 near Año Nuevo State Reserve (*see below*), or take Pescadero Road a couple miles east from town and head south on Cloverdale; there's a $5 parking fee.

AÑO NUEVO STATE RESERVE

Named by explorer Sebastian Viscaino on New Year's Day 1603, the Punta del Año Nuevo is one of the few places in the world where you can safely view live elephant seals up close (if you're here between December and March, you even get to watch them do the wild thing). During mating season you'll need to make reservations up to eight weeks in advance through California State Parks (tel. 800/444–4445), and you can only visit the reserve on one of the 2½-hour guided walks ($4, plus a $5 parking fee). If you're lucky, you may catch sight of migrating gray whales at the same time. Sea lions, sea otters, and harbor seals have also been known to make appearances, mostly off the coast and on Año Nuevo Island, inhabited only by seals and birds.

Though not as thrilling as the fighting and preening of mating season, the elephant seals come ashore from April through September to shed their old, furry brown skin for a sleek new one; the yearlings stick around until November, gaining strength for the upcoming months spent entirely in the water. At these times you can gain access to the reserve by obtaining a free permit from the visitor center (tel. 650/879–2025), open April through September, daily 8–6, October through November, daily 8–4. To avoid the $5 parking fee, continue about a half mile south past the main reserve entrance and park on the west side of Highway 1 (where you'll also find an alternate trail to the reserve). The path to the elephant seals' beach from the main parking lot is 1½ mi long; and if you come in spring, you'll be treated to the sight of thousands of colorful wildflowers along the trail. The reserve, about 40 mi south of San Francisco, can be reached on SamTrans Bus 96C (*see* Bus Travel *in* Chapter 1).

SHOPPING

REVISED BY DENISE M. LETO

I n the Bay Area, your challenge won't be finding something to buy, but deciding how much you're willing to spend. **Chinatown** has tons of inexpensive electronic goods and silk items; the **Castro** abounds with places catering to gay lifestyles; and the **South of Market** area has bargain warehouses that stock slightly flawed brand-name threads at good prices. **North Beach** has unique (and often expensive) specialty stores, mostly boutiques selling fabulous women's fashions. Tony **Union Street,** at the foot of Pacific Heights, is off-limits to budget travelers—though the shops full of beautiful clothing and antiques make for pleasant window-shopping. On trendy **Haight Street** neohippies will find wall-to-wall sellers of secondhand and vintage clothing, alternative music shops, tie-dye boutiques, costume jewelry shops, and radical bookstores—all selling their wares at a premium. A cheaper option is the **Mission District,** rife with warehouses for secondhand clothing, books, and furniture, with *botanicas* and magic shops for those who want to flirt with the occult.

Downtown San Francisco is a shopper's paradise. The **Embarcadero Center** (Clay and Sacramento Sts. between Drumm and Battery Sts., tel. 800/733–6318) is a three-square-block complex with 175 chichi shops catering to harried Financial District types on their lunch breaks. **San Francisco Shopping Centre** (865 Market St., between 4th and 5th Sts.) houses a Nordstrom department store and dozens of other upscale shops, built around a dizzying four-story atrium. The city's ritziest emporiums (*see* Department Stores, *below*) are clustered around **Union Square** and adjacent **Post Street.** On Post alone you'll find Giorgio Armani, Ralph Lauren, Bulgari, Brooks Brothers, Coach, Williams-Sonoma, Versace, Cartier, Gump's, Eddie Bauer, and a three-story NikeTown shrine to sports. This is first-class shopping at its finest.

In the East Bay, Oakland's few viable shopping districts, like **Piedmont Avenue** and **Rockridge** (College Ave. between Alcatraz Ave. and Broadway), are chock-full of boutiques and antiques stores. Head to **Berkeley** if you're looking for political consumerism, eco-friendly products, abundant bookstores, or used clothing to fit cheapskate student budgets. **Telegraph Avenue,** next to the UC Berkeley campus, is a rollicking seven-day street fair, with stands selling tie-dye clothing, cheap silver jewelry, handmade pottery, and New Age crystals.

NEW CLOTHES

Bay Area clothing stores stock everything from Armani suits to vinyl pants. The trick is knowing where to look and when to buy. Almost all clothing stores slash prices by 30%–50% January–February and July–August to make way for next season's fashions. Year-round, discount outlets like **Loehmann's** (*see below*) offer amazing bargains—if you have the stamina to paw through racks of flowered dresses in search of a Calvin Klein. This section steers you toward some of the cheaper clothing stores, as well as some of the most cutting edge. If you're looking for mainstream, stick with the department stores—or the Gap(s).

SAN FRANCISCO

Behind the Post Office. Come here for the latest and greatest hip-hop gear, including in-your-face T-shirts, skate-girl dresses, and "phat" baggy pants. *1510 Haight St., at Ashbury St., Haight-Ashbury, tel. 415/861–2507.*

Betsey Johnson. Postmodern designer-goddess Betsey Johnson brings you outrageous women's fashions in a campy neon-lighted shop. The often silly clothes aren't cheap, but half-off sales are frequent. *2031 Fillmore St., between Pine and California Sts., Pacific Heights, tel. 415/567–2726; 160 Geary St., between Stockton St. and Grant Ave., Union Square, tel. 415/398–2516.*

Esprit Factory Outlet. In-season clothing from Esprit women's and children's lines, as well as shoes and accessories, are sold with deep discounts at this enormous, airy outlet store. For best results check the bins in the back. *499 Illinois St., at 16th St., China Basin, tel. 415/957–2550.*

Jeremy's. Spruce up your wardrobe with big-name seconds and samples of a practical (yet stylish) nature at markdown prices. *2 South Park, on Second St. between Bryant and Brannan Sts., South of Market, tel. 415/882–4929; 2967 College Ave., at Ashby Ave., Berkeley, tel. 510/849–0701.*

Joshua Simon. This personalized shop stocks unusual women's garments: flowing pants, romantic dresses, woven vests, hand-painted shirts. Many items are by local designers. *3915 24th St., near Sanchez St., Noe Valley, tel. 415/821–1068.*

Loehmann's. Some of the city's best-dressed women swear by this discount store, which stocks labels like Karl Lagerfeld and Krizia at drastically reduced prices. *222 Sutter St., Union Square, tel. 415/982–3215.*

Na Na. The San Francisco branch of this national chain sells clothes and shoes to ultrahip Gen-Xers. The sales rack (up to 50% off) guarantees you won't go broke looking cool. *2276 Market St., near Noe St., Castro District, tel. 415/861–6262.*

North Beach Leather. Though it's not in North Beach anymore, this ritzy shop offers rack upon rack of high-quality leather jackets, coats, pants, and accessories for men and women. Prices reflect the upscale Union Square neighborhood, but there are good bargains at the occasional sales. *224 Grant Ave., Union Square, 415/362–8300.*

Rolo. This San Francisco minichain is wildly popular with club goers. The store on Market is heavy on flamboyant, expensive menswear; the Howard Street store is a discount outlet featuring a flashy women's selection; Castro Street caters to style-conscious men; and the downtown branch targets the more conservative crowd. *1301 Howard St., at 9th St., South of Market, tel. 415/861–1999; 2351 Market St., Castro District, tel. 415/431–4545; 450 Castro St., Castro District, tel. 415/626–7171; 25 Stockton St., at Market St., Union Square, tel. 415/989–7656.*

Shoe Biz. The latest European styles are here, in neon pink glitter or on 4-inch platforms. Check the sale corner for high-quality shoes at fantastic discounts. Shoe Biz 2 (1553 Haight St., tel. 415/861–9399) stocks more comfort-oriented shoes and domestic brands. *1446 Haight St., at Masonic Ave., Haight-Ashbury, tel. 415/864–0990.*

Yerba Buena Square. The square is a collection of seven shops selling discount apparel, shoes, and toys. Spend a few hours weeding through the racks, and you'll find gems by Armani, Calvin Klein, and Dior. *899 Howard St., at 5th St., South of Market, tel. 415/543–1275.*

EAST BAY

Earthly Goods. Former flower children driving SUVs get outfitted at this wood-floored, loftlike space in the heart of Berkeley's gourmet ghetto. The shop specializes in flowing skirts and dresses as well as elegant, casual businesswear for women. Accessories and shoes, starting on the classic side and moving toward trendy, round out the offerings. *2100 Vine St., at Shattuck Ave., Berkeley, tel. 510/845–4564.*

Futura. A whimsical blend of new and used clothes for men and women includes vintage jackets, bowling shirts, baby Ts, and baggy pants. *2350 Telegraph Ave., near Durant Ave., Berkeley, tel. 510/883–9050.*

The Walk Shop. The classy-but-comfortable store matches most of its offerings—walking shoes in every style for men and women by such designers as Joseph Seibel, Mephisto, and Ecco. The philosophy seems to be that if you spend your whole life walking, you won't mind parting with a few hundred clams to get the best. *2120 Vine St., near Shattuck Ave., Berkeley, tel. 510/849–3628.*

SECONDHAND AND VINTAGE CLOTHING

The cheapest clothes in the Bay Area are someone else's castoffs, though many secondhand shops carry expensive vintage fashions as well. The big-name stores **Buffalo Exchange** (1555 Haight St., Haight-Ashbury, tel. 415/431–7733; 1800 Polk St., tel. 415/346–5726; 2512 Telegraph Ave., Berkeley, tel. 510/644–9202; 3333 Lake Shore Ave., Oakland, tel. 510/452–4464) and **Wasteland** (*see below*) are dependable sources for flannel, polyester shirts, and basic black dresses, often with inflated prices. For a better selection at cheaper prices, try the smaller shops in the **Mission** and **Haight** districts or in the East Bay along **College Avenue** in Rockridge and **Telegraph Avenue** near the UC Berkeley campus.

Looking for a vintage silk Chanel suit or a 1930s beaded satin gown? Head to **Divisadero Street** (between Pine and Bush Sts.) or **Fillmore Street** (between Bush and Sacramento Sts.), where ritzy vintage shops and high-end secondhand stores carry designer labels tossed aside by wealthy Pacific Heights matrons. The stretch of Hayes Street between Franklin and Buchanan streets, known as **Hayes Valley,** is another happy hunting ground.

SAN FRANCISCO

Aardvark's Odd Ark. Aardvark's enthralls thrift store shoppers with a wide selection of used clothing: men's basics, cotton dress shirts, hats, and vintage Levi's. *1501 Haight St., at Ashbury St., Haight-Ashbury, tel. 415/621–3141.*

American Rag. There's old and new stocked here, and precious little is cheap. But they do have the best selection of black vintage dresses in San Francisco, plus racks of stylish suits and classy jackets. *1305 Van Ness Ave., between Sutter and Bush Sts., Polk Gulch, tel. 415/474–5214.*

Clothes Contact. You really can't go wrong, as just about everything here—used, vintage, old jeans, jackets—is $8 per pound. On the occasional bargain days the price is reduced to $4. *473 Valencia St., near 16th St., Mission District, tel. 415/621–3212.*

Crossroads Trading Co. The Fillmore store tends to carry early '80s wear, while the other three branches are better for jeans (under $25) and unusual vintage dresses. *2231 Market St., between Sanchez and Noe Sts., Castro District, tel. 415/626–8989; 1901 Fillmore St., at Bush St., Japantown, tel. 415/775–8885; 2338 Shattuck Ave., Berkeley, tel. 510/843–7600; 5636 College Ave., near Keith St., Oakland, tel. 510/420–1952.*

Departures from the Past. It's exclusively vintage clothing here, including costumes, formal attire, and some casual wear. Tuxedos sell for $100–$160 or rent for $50–$75 per night. A partner store, **Costumes on Haight** (735 Haight St., tel. 415/621–1356), rents costumes and has some vintage items for sale. *2028 Fillmore St., between California and Pine Sts., Japantown, tel. 415/885–3377.*

560 Hayes Vintage Boutique. Vintage, one of a cluster of boutiques in Hayes Valley, stocks an assortment of used clothing, mostly women's. You'll find pants, coats, and dresses that reek deliciously of the '70s. *560 Hayes St., between Laguna and Octavia Sts., Hayes Valley, tel. 415/861–7993.*

Martini Mercantile Co. Swinging cats and kittens know that of all the city's vintage stores, this is the place to find well-organized and well-maintained threads from the 1930s through the 1960s, with the

emphasis on rat-pack lounge wear. The store at Cole Street stocks the more upscale se.
the shop at Ashbury is the address for hats. *1736 Haight St., at Cole St., Haight-Ashbury, te.*
1942; 1519 Haight St., at Ashbury St., Haight-Ashbury, tel. 415/552–1940.

Wasteland. Wasteland brings you trendy and outrageous treasures, like bell-bottoms, as well as vi.
gowns, suits, and costume jewelry. It's one of the city's most popular—but priciest—secondhand stor
1660 Haight St., between Belvedere and Clayton Sts., Haight-Ashbury, tel. 415/863–3150.

Worn Out West. Budget-conscious cowboys come here for secondhand Western wear and leather
goods. *582 Castro St., between 18th and 19th Sts., Castro District, tel. 415/431–6020.*

EAST BAY

Madame Butterfly. Vintage hats and gloves, summer dresses, and a small selection of men's jackets go
for $15–$40. Fancy dresses cost $30–$80. *5474 College Ave., at Taft St., Oakland, tel. 510/653–1525.*

Mars Mercantile. The most reliable used- and vintage-clothing store on Telegraph Avenue has racks of
vintage dresses, acrylic men's shirts, genuine leather jackets, and '50s-era jeans ($300!). *2398 Tele-
graph Ave., at Channing Way, Berkeley, tel. 510/843–6711.*

Rockridge Rags. Here racks of secondhand clothing are conveniently arranged by size and often include upscale items
like Anne Klein suits or Polo chinos—at bargain basement
prices. *5711 College Ave., near Rockridge BART, Oakland, tel.
510/655–2289.*

Slash. This tiny shop deals exclusively in used denim and cor-
duroy, including Levi's ($15–$30) and overalls ($20). Owners
Carla Bell and Ocean Edgars are always happy to help you
rummage for the perfect pair of 5-0-whatevers. *2840 College
Ave., at Russell St., Berkeley, tel. 510/841–7803.*

*If outlet malls are your gig, the
peninsula is the place to go. Worth
checking out are the Metro 280
Center (Colby Blvd. at I–280 in
Colma) and Marina Square
(Marina Blvd. at I–880 in San
Leandro).*

BOOKS

For some a trip to the Bay Area is not complete without an evening spent browsing the shelves at **City
Lights** (*see below*), San Francisco's most famous bookshop. However, the city has more than 200 other
bookstores—new and used, tiny and huge, nonprofit and corporate—for every language, political bent,
and cultural interest. The best browsing grounds are around the **Upper Haight,** in **Polk Gulch** (Polk
Street between Ellis and Union Sts.), and in the **Mission District,** particularly along Valencia Street.

East Bay intellectuals don't have to trek to San Francisco to look for quality new and used books. With
a huge university in its midst and more ambitious scholars per square mile than anywhere outside the
Académie Française, you'll find enough bookstores here to keep you occupied for a year. **Telegraph
Avenue,** in Berkeley, has the highest concentration of bookstores.

SAN FRANCISCO

Abandoned Planet Bookstore (518 Valencia St., near 16th St., The Mission, tel. 415/861–4695) has
music, theater, and art history books at rock-bottom prices. It's a homey place, with an old piano in one
corner and a pair of pet cats. **Dog Eared Books** (900 Valencia St., at 20th St., the Mission, tel. 415/282–
1901) is another favorite.

Acorn Books. Customers in search of an antiquarian, out-of-print, or used book know that the dedicated
staff at Acorn would scour the earth to find it—although the well-stocked store probably already has it
somewhere on the shelves. Acorn is one of a dozen bookstores in Polk Gulch. *1436 Polk St., between
Pine and California Sts., Polk Gulch, tel. 415/563–1736.*

Adobe Book Shop. Adobe specializes in used and rare books (particularly art and modern philosophy);
it's probably the cheapest in the city for those categories. The staff is erudite and affable. *3166 16th St.,
between Valencia and Guerrero Sts., Mission District, tel. 415/864–3936.*

Collective. For more than 20 years budding anarchists have come here for their
ʳground magazines, controversial political tracts, and all-around subversive mate-
ʳnear Masonic Ave., Haight-Ashbury, tel. 415/431–8355.

most famous bookstore, opened in 1955 by poet Lawrence Ferlinghetti, is *the*
ʳe—much of it published under the store's own imprint. The upstairs room is
ᵗ literature, and a few used books; a "little press" alcove contains local journals
ˡonfiction downstairs. *261 Columbus Ave., at Broadway, North Beach, tel. 415/*

⬧⬧⬧ᵗ Light. This renowned Castro bookstore stocks an extensive collection of lesbian, gay, and
transgender literature; T-shirts and knicknacks; and "queerzines" (*see* Gay & Lesbian Travel *in* Chapter
1) to suit every taste. Book signings and readings take place weekly. *489 Castro St., near 18th St., Castro District, tel. 415/431–0891.* ·

Eastwind Books and Arts, Inc. Eastwind deals exclusively in new books on Asian-American themes,
and on Asia itself—particularly China. There are both Chinese- and English-language sections. *1435
Stockton St., 2nd floor, at Columbus Ave., Chinatown, tel. 415/772–5899.*

European Book Company. Come here for new French-, German-, and Spanish-language books, magazines, and newspapers, as well as foreign-language dictionaries and travel guides. *925 Larkin St.,
between Post and Geary Sts., the Tenderloin, tel. 415/474–0626.*

Green Apple Books and Music. Consistently voted the Bay Area's best used-book store by *SF Bay
Guardian* readers, this ramshackle institution is not for neat freaks. New, used, and rare books are jum-
bled together in a space reminiscent of grandma's attic—ask for help from the knowledgeable and
friendly staff. A fiction and music annex is two doors down at 520 Clement Street (same tel.). *506
Clement St., between 6th and 7th Aves., Richmond District, tel. 415/387–2272.*

Marcus Books. Marcus specializes in books by and about African-Americans: fiction, history, religion,
art, children's literature, and more. Readings are held twice a week. *1712 Fillmore St., near Post St.,
Western Addition, San Francisco, tel. 415/346–4222; 3900 Martin Luther King Jr. Way, between 39th
and 40th Sts., Oakland, tel. 510/652–2344.*

Modern Times. The collectively run Modern Times carries underground papers and 'zines and hosts
readings and forums with a politically progressive, multicultural focus. It's best for Spanish-language
titles, art, current affairs, gay and lesbian issues, and cultural theory. *888 Valencia St., between 19th
and 20th Sts., Mission District, tel. 415/282–9246.*

San Francisco Mystery Bookstore. This shop stocks everything imaginable, new and used, for the arm-
chair Sherlock Holmes. *4175 24th St., between Castro and Diamond Sts., Noe Valley, tel. 415/282–7444.*

Sierra Club Bookstore. Come here for new books on all aspects of environmentalism, including political
tomes and nature poetry. In addition, there are environment-themed children's books, practical guides
for hiking and camping, and topographical maps. A bulletin board lists area hikes, meetings, and
events. *6014 College Ave., Oakland, tel. 510/658–7470; mail order: tel. 415/977–5600.*

William Stout Architectural Books. Books and periodicals on architecture and design are what you'll
find here, including an impressive out-of-print collection. The store also features a fine section devoted
solely to the architecture of San Francisco. *804 Montgomery St., between Jackson and Pacific Sts.,
Financial District, tel. 415/391–6757.*

EAST BAY

Black Oak Books. This well-stocked north Berkeley shop is popular with UC professors for its rare books,
or maybe it's the collection of cheap paperback fiction ($1 and up). Weekly author readings and book sign-
ings include occasional big-name writers. *1491 Shattuck Ave., at Vine St., Berkeley, tel. 510/486–0698.*

Cody's. A Berkeley institution if there ever was one, Cody's stocks every imaginable genre, from poetry
and philosophy to self-defense and women's studies. It also has an impressive newsstand, a cheery children's room, and an extensive selection of foreign-language books. Readings by local and nationally
known authors are always crowded; arrive early if you want a shot at a seat. *2454 Telegraph Ave., at
Haste St., Berkeley, tel. 510/845–7852; 1730 4th St., at Virginia St., Berkeley, tel. 510/559–9500.*

Diesel—A Bookstore. In Rockridge near the College of Arts and Crafts, Diesel has an excellent collection of fiction, history, political, and art books. Weekly readings and book signings run the gamut from local history to poetry. *5433 College Ave., at Kales St., Oakland, tel. 510/653–9965.*

Gaia Books, Music, and Crafts. Books on spirituality, ecology, holistic health, and sexuality fill this bright, airy space. Readings and lectures are held regularly. *1400 Shattuck Ave., at Rose St., Berkeley, tel. 510/548–4172.*

Moe's. The gruff, cigar-chomping Moe Moskowitz may have passed on, but his bookstore continues to thrive. The shop has five floors of new, used, and antique books, with a strong emphasis on the used and antique. *2476 Telegraph Ave., between Haste St. and Dwight Way, Berkeley, tel. 510/849–2087.*

Shambhala Booksellers. Shambhala stocks new and used books on Eastern religions, alternative medicine, mysticism, psychology, and theology. *2482 Telegraph Ave., between Haste St. and Dwight Way, Berkeley, tel. 510/848–8443.*

University Press Books. Here you'll find titles from more than 100 university presses, representing all disciplines. Pick up the latest treatise on cultural theory and read it next door at the Musical Offering café (*see* Records, Tapes, and CDs, *below*). *2430 Bancroft Way, near Telegraph Ave., Berkeley, tel. 510/548–0585.*

DEPARTMENT STORES

City Lights, the legendary home of the beat generation, was once charged with obscenity for selling Allen Ginsberg's poem "Howl."

To the die-hard shopper there's nothing more pleasurable than an afternoon spent drifting through the perfumed halls of San Francisco's venerable department stores, all grouped conveniently within walking distance of Union Square.

Macy's. Recently revamped, Macy's on Union Square is more fabulous than ever. One huge store bordering the square houses the women's and children's departments; dream of a gourmet kitchen downstairs in the Cellar, paradise for foodies. Across the street in its very own building on Stockton is Macy's for Men. *Stockton and O'Farrell Sts., Union Square, tel. 415/397–3333; Market and Fifth Sts., Union Square, tel. 415/296–4061.*

Neiman-Marcus. A lovely atrium at the entrance topped with a stained-glass window welcomes shoppers to this swank emporium. The jewelry and makeup counters are favorite destinations of Nob Hill matriarchs and trust-fund kids. *150 Stockton St., at Geary St., Union Square, tel. 415/362–3900.*

Nordstrom. This high-end department store sprawls over four sprial escalator–connected floors of the San Francisco Centre mall, selling major brand-name men's, women's, and children's wear, all at a premium. The women's and men's shoe departments are especially good. *865 Market St., at 5th St., Union Square, tel. 415/243–8500.*

Saks Fifth Avenue. Saks exudes old-money elegance and reserve. The store caters mostly to women, and conservative women at that; a small men's section (equally staid) is also available. For all but a loyal handful of wealthy shoppers, prices are prohibitively high. *384 Post St., at Powell St., Union Square, tel. 415/986–4300.*

FLEA MARKETS

Bay Area flea markets often swallow up entire fairgrounds, parking lots, or football fields, all full of good deals on antique furniture, clothes, toys, books, bikes . . . anything remotely old, quirky, or dusty. In all cases, you'll find the best selection if you arrive just after dawn, but prices are lower late in the day, when vendors are tired and anxious to avoid reloading their trucks. For complete, up-to-date listings, pick up a copy of the free *Classified Flea Market,* available at most newsstands and convenience stores. On summer weekends Noe Valley, particularly Church Street between 19th and 27th streets, is garage-sale paradise. So, too, are Dolores and Guerrero streets between 16th and 24th, and 18th Street between Church and Castro.

SAN FRANCISCO

Alemany Flea Market. This flea market is a fairly mellow affair with prices on the high end. Funky knick-knacks are plentiful; you'll also find small selections of clothing, household appliances, furniture, and some antiques and collectibles. *100 Alemany Blvd., at Crescent Ave., Bernal Heights, tel. 415/647–2043. From I–280, take Alemany Blvd. exit; market is under exit ramp at the Hwy. 101 and I–280 interchange. Open Sun. 8–3.*

Geneva Swap Meet. Get down and dirty at this anything-sells market, held in the parking lot of the Geneva drive-in theater, next to the Cow Palace. New things like T-shirts and polyester underwear can be found near the entrance; the real finds lurk in the stalls at the back. *607 Carter St., at Geneva Ave., Daly City. From I–280 or Hwy. 101, take Cow Palace exit and follow signs on Geneva Ave. Open weekends 7–4.*

Pier 29 Antique and Collectible Market. A cut above the city's other flea markets, Pier 29 has dozens of indoor booths selling antique furniture, rare books, vintage clothing, kitchenware, costume jewelry, and other collectibles. Unlike other markets, it charges admission: $2, or $10 before 9:30 AM. *Pier 29, The Embarcadero, between Sansome and Battery Sts., no phone. Open Sun. 7–5.*

San Francisco Flea Market. Vendors at this parking lot hawk mostly junk, like plastic toys, Chinese-made batteries, and used clothes that were never in fashion. But if you're in the market for new or used kitchen appliances, clock radios, and other small electronics, it's worth a look. *1651 Mission St., between S. Van Ness Ave. and 12th St., South of Market, tel. 415/646–0544. Open weekends 6–4:30.*

EAST AND SOUTH BAY

Berkeley Flea Market. Vendors of used furniture and clothing always have some funky desks or a good vintage coat they're willing to lower the price on, as well as "manly man" tools, kitchen appliances, African jewelry, used bikes, and secondhand (or thirdhand) books. To top it off, there's fresh produce from local farmers. *Ashby BART station, corner Ashby Ave. and MLK Jr. Way, Berkeley, tel. 510/644–0744. Open weekends 6:30–6:30.*

Coliseum Swap Meet. This vast flea market sprawls across the drive-in movie theater parking lot, next to the Oakland Coliseum. You'll find furniture, clothing, electronic goods, and more. *5401 Coliseum Way, tel. 510/534–0325. I–880 and Coliseum Way, near Coliseum BART station. Open weekends 8–4.*

NorCal Swap Meet. Larger than the Berkeley but smaller than the Coliseum, this market at Laney College, in Oakland, is especially good for wacky, off-the-wall items and lots of fresh produce. Although there are plenty of organized stands, the best finds require digging through the vendors' piles. *7th and Fallon Sts., near Lake Merritt BART station, tel. 510/769–7266. Open weekends 7–4.*

San Jose Flea Market. One of the world's largest, this market-to-end-all-markets houses around 2,600 vendors on a 120-acre selling area. Everything from furniture to car parts to clothes to farm-fresh produce is up for grabs. *1590 Berryessa Rd., tel. 408/453–1110. 13th St. exit from U.S. 101; or from College Park CalTrain station, Bus 36 toward East San Jose. Open Wed.–Sun. 7–5:30.*

RECORDS, TAPES, AND CDS

You can find virtually any new CD at the gargantuan **Virgin Megastore** (2 Stockton St., at Market St., tel. 415/397–4525), but your friendly neighborhood store is bound to be cheaper, with more used goods and vinyl. Most places guarantee their records against scratches; check to make sure. The **Upper Haight** is a good place to look for obscure titles and classic punk, while the **Mission District** is great for Latin music. And Berkeley's **Telegraph Avenue** boasts no fewer than four mammoth record stores within five blocks of the UC campus.

For Middle Eastern music, try **Samiramis Imports** (2990 Mission St., tel. 415/824–6555). If it's gospel you're craving, make a trip to **Reid's** (3101 Sacramento St., at Prince St., Berkeley, tel. 510/843–7282).

SAN FRANCISCO

Amoeba. Berkeley's best music store (*see below*) finally made it across the bay in 1997 and now reigns as the ultimate shopping destination for music lovers in the city as well. The massive, warehouselike space at the end of Haight-Ashbury contains an unusually large variety of CDs and records, from indie to European jazz, and an enormous selection of used CDs. The store frequently hosts live bands and is a good source of information on the local music scene. *1855 Haight St., near Stanyan St., Haight-Ashbury, tel. 415/831–1200.*

Groove Merchant. Groove Merchant was opened by the same folks who run the highly recommended Luv 'n Haight and Ubiquity labels, both of which spotlight the local acid jazz scene. The store has plenty of great finds for the collector, DJ, or serious amateur. *687 Haight St., between Pierce and Steiner Sts., Lower Haight, tel. 415/252–5766.*

Reckless Records. A reliable source for used cassettes and CDs, Reckless also carries new music, T-shirts, posters, and used videos. They specialize in independent and mainstream rock, hip-hop, and soul. *1401 Haight St., at Masonic Ave., Haight-Ashbury, tel. 415/431–3434.*

Recycled Records. Vinyl junkies will find their fix among the great selection of mostly used records. The collection focuses on rock, but other genres are well represented. *1377 Haight St., at Masonic Ave., Haight-Ashbury, tel. 415/626–4075.*

Reggae Runnins Village Store. This reggae wonderland carries records, tapes, videos, T-shirts, jewelry, and other paraphernalia in red, gold, black, and green. *505 Divisadero St., between Fell and Hayes Sts., Lower Haight, tel. 415/922–2442.*

Ritmo Latino. This colorful, Carnaval-esque store sells an enormous variety of Latin music: *ranchero,* mariachi, salsa, Tex-Mex, merengue, *norteño,* and more. You can use the listening stations to sample CDs before buying. *2401 Mission St., at 20th St., Mission District, tel. 415/824–8556.*

Star Classics. Star stocks classical, jazz, cabaret, and New Age CDs and cassettes (new, not used). The adjoining Star Classics Recital Hall hosts vocal and musical performances every week; Friday usually features classical and Sunday brings jazz or cabaret. *425 Hayes St., at Gough St., Hayes Valley, tel. 415/552–1110.*

Street Light Records. Because they buy and sell at great prices to a diverse clientele, Street Light's selection of records, tapes, and CDs is usually offbeat and always fresh. The Noe Valley store is smaller but has a better selection of vinyl. *3979 24th St., between Noe and Sanchez Sts., Noe Valley, tel. 415/282–3550; 2350 Market St., near Castro St., Castro District, tel. 415/282–8000.*

EAST BAY

Amoeba. The Bay Area's widest and choicest selection of new and used 7-inch records—and used CDs—includes jazz, international, indie, hip-hop, import rock, and more. The experienced staff will show you the newest artists and dig out their rarest records. *2455 Telegraph Ave., at Haste St., Berkeley, tel. 510/549–1125.*

Groove Yard. Venture out to this cozy shop, halfway between Berkeley and downtown Oakland, for acid jazz, funk, blues, Latin and Brazilian discs, and plenty of used jazz and soul records. *4770 Telegraph Ave., at 48th St., Oakland, tel. 510/655–8400.*

Hear Music. A walk through this stylish wood- and iron beam–accented store is more guided musical exploration than random browse. Headphones line the sections, arranged by genre and historical period, encouraging shoppers to listen to something new, and recommendations are happily given. Jazz, blues, and world music are especially well represented. *1809 Fourth St., near Hearst St., Berkeley, tel. 510/204–9595.*

Mod Lang. At Mod Lang shipments of ambient, indie, and psychedelic '60s music arrive from the United Kingdom every week—and sell at amazingly low prices. *2136 University Ave., near Shattuck Ave., Berkeley, tel. 510/486–1880.*

Musical Offering. Browse bins of new classical CDs with Berkeley professors and black-clad philosophy grad students at this music store across the street from the UC Berkeley campus, then grab a cup of coffee or a sandwich at the store's café and stick around to soak up the highbrow intellectual atmosphere. *2430 Bancroft Way, near Dana St., Berkeley, tel. 510/849–0211.*

Rasputin Music. Rasputin had the lock on Telegraph Avenue cool until Amoeba showed up in 1990. Still, Rasputin has miles of new and used CDs (at higher prices than Amoeba) and regularly hosts live performances. *2403 Telegraph Ave., at Channing Way, Berkeley, tel. 510/848–9005.*

Saturn Records. The wall-to-wall racks here contain excellent and extensive selections of rock, jazz, blues, oldies, show tunes, and soundtracks in hard-to-find vinyl and on new or used CDs. *5488 College Ave., at Lawton St., Oakland, tel. 510/654–0335.*

SPECIALTY ITEMS

If you're looking for a gift, souvenir, or shopping experience unique to the Bay Area, poke your head into one of the city's many New Age or herbal medicine shops, make a purchase at a store that donates its proceeds to charity, or patronize a purveyor of alternative or avant-garde posters, toys, or videos.

ART AND PHOTOGRAPHY

Adolph Gasser. Your best source for photography and video equipment, Gasser has the largest inventory of such items in northern California. *181 2nd St., between Howard and Mission Sts., South of Market, tel. 415/495–3852; 5733 Geary Blvd., Richmond District, tel. 415/751–0145.*

Amsterdam Art. A favorite of local artists for years, Amsterdam Art stocks supplies for painting, printmaking, and ceramics, a full selection of frames, and more. The staff is always helpful. *5424 Geary Blvd., Richmond District, San Francisco, tel. 415/751–6248; 1013 University Ave., near San Pablo Ave., Berkeley, tel. 510/649–4800.*

Art Rock Gallery. Handmade silk-screened posters—many in an artsy vintage style—range from $20 up to $2,000. The gallery frequently holds exhibitions of rare and classic posters. *1155 Mission St., between 7th and 8th Sts., South of Market, tel. 415/255–7390.*

Looking Glass. This small store sells tripods, paper, film, books, and other photographic supplies. *2848 Telegraph Ave., at Oregon St., Berkeley, tel. 510/548–6888.*

BEAUTY

The Beauty Store. These San Francisco shops focus on educating shoppers about beauty and skin care; the staff is happy to help you select products just right for your skin tone and texture. They carry traditional brands like Vidal Sassoon and Aveda as well as products for their culturally diverse clientele. *2124 Fillmore St., Pacific Heights, tel. 415/346–2511; 3600 16th St., Castro District, tel. 415/861–2019; 1560 Haight St., Haight-Ashbury, tel. 415/552–9696.*

Body Time. Founded in Berkeley in 1970, Body Time foregoes expensive packaging in favor of high-quality all-natural ingredients in its own line of scents, skin-care products, and aromatherapy products. You can combine sustainably harvested essential oils to create your own personal fragrances; bring back the empty bottle and refill it at a discount—another way the store demonstrates its commitment to the environment. *2072 Union St., Cow Hollow, tel. 415/922–4076; 1932 Fillmore St., Japantown, tel. 415/771–2431; 1465 Haight St., Haight-Ashbury, tel. 415/551–1070; 2509 Telegraph Ave., Berkeley, tel. 510/548–3686.*

Sephora. Union Square is the perfect location for this swank beauty shop, where products are arranged by function instead of by brand. A red carpet leads you through the store's three categories: fragrance, color, and well-being. Those with a penchant for perfumes and powders will enjoy a romp through this ritzy beauty fest. *1 Stockton St., at Market St., Union Square, tel. 415/392-1545.*

CHARITABLE CAUSES

Global Exchange Fair Trade Center. With a mission to foster economic self-sufficiency for Third World communities, this nonprofit shop specializes in handmade crafts, from African jewelry to Guatemalan backpacks. Call for information about lectures and seminars. *4018 24th St., between Noe and Castro Sts., Noe Valley, tel. 415/648–8068; 2840 College Ave., at Russell St., Berkeley, tel. 510/548–0370.*

Planet Weavers Treasure Store. Indulge your socially conscious side at this UNICEF-run store, stocked with handcrafted gifts, toys, and an international selection of musical instruments, from bongos to Australian didgeridoos. A portion of the proceeds goes to the UN Children's Fund. *1573 Haight St., between Ashbury and Clayton Sts., Haight-Ashbury, tel. 415/864–4415.*

Under One Roof. Affiliated with the NAMES Project (*see* Castro District *in* Chapter 2), this shop sells goods gathered from many AIDS organizations—gay pride T-shirts, greeting cards, and more. *549 Castro St., between 18th and 19th Sts., Castro District, tel. 415/252–9430.*

EROTICA

Carol Doda's Champagne and Lace Lingerie Boutique. Let the legendary and alluring Carol Doda, who led the effort to legalize topless dancing in the 1960s, help you find just the right bra, teddy, bustier, corset, garter belt, slinky dress, or bikini. *1850 Union St., No. 1, at Laguna St., Cow Hollow, tel. 415/776–6900.*

Good Vibrations. This self-described "clean, well-lighted place to shop for sex toys, books, and videos" is a friendly woman-owned-and-operated enterprise. If you think all sex shops are sleazy, you haven't been here. *1210 Valencia St., at 23rd St., Mission District, tel. 415/974–8980; 2504 San Pablo Ave., at Dwight Way, Berkeley, tel. 510/841–8987.*

FOOD

Imperial Tea Court. Stop in at this lovely, old-world Chinese tea shop for a cup of traditionally prepared tea, from such exotic choices as green peony and monkey-picked tikuanyin to more familiar teas like oolong and Darjeeling. Teas can be enjoyed at the shop's tables or brought home in bulk. Gorgeous Chinese earthenware teapots and services tempt the tea lover and beautify the shop, as do the gilded birdcages hanging from the ceiling. *1411 Powell St., at Broadway, Chinatown, tel. 415/788–6080.*

Joseph Schmidt Confections. Even for nonchocoholics, it's worth going out of the way to visit this small shop in the Castro. The seasonal edible art—from pastel-color Easter tulips to life-size chocolate turkeys—sculpted by the city's übergourmet chocolatier may look too good to eat, but don't let that stop you from indulging! Schmidt ships around the world. *3489 16th St., at Sanchez St., Castro District, tel. 415/861–8682.*

Ratto's International Market. Bins overflowing with dry beans, brightly labeled canned goods from the home country, and a mouthwatering cheese counter make this gourmet Italian shop in old Oakland worth a trip. But this isn't a haven for food snobs: Ratto's maintains its down-to-earth atmosphere and friendly service, and prices are set with the housewife, not the yuppie, in mind. Head next door to the attached café for simple, tasty fare. *827 Washington St., at 9th St., Oakland, tel. 510/832–6503.*

RoCocoa Faerie Queene Chocolates. This very pink gourmet chocolate shop falls under the "only in the Castro" category; the tiny space is almost too small to contain the fabulous flamboyance of the service. Handmade chocolates and Belgian imports with names like Oscar Wilde Cherry and Queen O' Denial are available. If nothing else, stop in at least for a sample of Faerie Fudge and a gander at this uniquely San Francisco shop. *415 Castro St., at 17th and Market Sts., Castro District, tel. 415/252–5814.*

Superior Trading Co. This jumble of a shop amid Chinatown's dizzying bustle dispenses herbs and roots for every deficiency and ailment and provides a glimpse into the mysterious millennia-old Chinese tradition of healing. Peruse the counter and barrels, and eventually resort to assistance from the staff to help decipher the labels. *837 Washington St., between Grant Ave. and Stockton St., Chinatown, tel. 415/982–8722.*

Wine House Limited. This homey, unassuming SoMa shop overflows with open wine crates featuring an excellent selection of premium Bordeaux, Burgundy, and Rhone wines as well as a smaller but well-chosen range of California wines, all at terrific prices. The friendly and knowledgeable staff gladly guides the novice and the connoisseur. *535 Bryant St., between 3rd and 4th Sts., South of Market, tel. 415/495–8486.*

GAMES AND TOYS

FAO Schwarz Fifth Avenue. At the lavish San Francisco branch of this famed toy store, you'll find dancing bears, singing dolls, motorized cars, and toys galore. *48 Stockton St., at O'Farrell St., Union Square, tel. 415/394–8700.*

Gamescape. They've got a splendid selection of new and used board, computer, and role-playing games, from old favorites like Monopoly to the latest high-tech offerings from Nintendo. *333 Divisadero St., between Page and Oak Sts., Lower Haight, tel. 415/621–4263.*

Kitty Katty's Roadside Shack. The kooky shop of underground cartoonist Flower Frankenstein is your source for unique gifts like the Betsy Beatnik existentialist poet doll or the Miss PMS Fun Action Toy. *3804 17th St., at Sanchez St., Castro District, tel. 415/864–6543.*

Uncle Mame. Stuffed with retro kitch, from *Mod Squad* lunch boxes to candy from the 1950s, this temple to all things pop culture is prime browsing territory. Moveable action figures and greeting cards run the gamut from offbeat to off color—there's something for everyone. You'll walk out with at least an Abba

Zabba candy bar or a Wonder Woman key chain. *2241 Market St., between Noe and Sanchez Sts., Castro District, tel. 415/626–1953.*

HANDICRAFTS

African Outlet. Handmade goods from all over Africa include Zulu spears and shields, Berber and Tuareg jewelry, cowrie-shell necklaces, brilliant West African textiles, and plenty of other artifacts and accessories. *524 Octavia St., between Hayes and Grove Sts., Hayes Valley, tel. 415/864–3576.*

Asakichi. When you're exploring Japantown, stop by this tiny shop for wind chimes, teapots, handmade chopsticks, simple Japanese furniture, and other delights. *Japan Center, on the bridge between Kinokuniya and Kintetsu Bldgs., Japantown, tel. 415/921–3821.*

F. Dorian. F. Dorian specializes in cards, jewelry, and crafts from Mexico, Peru, Indonesia, the Philippines, Sri Lanka, and Japan, as well as works by local craftspeople. *388 Hayes St., at Gough St., Hayes Valley, tel. 415/861–3191.*

Worldware. Recycling is art at Worldware: Picture frames and candlesticks are made from aluminum cans; purses and wallets are cut from discarded inner tubes. The owner, Shari Sant, also designs her own line of clothing made from organic hemp, wool, and cotton. *336 Hayes St., between Franklin and Gough Sts., Hayes Valley, tel. 415/487–9030.*

JEWELRY

Body Manipulations. The ultraprofessional and hygiene-conscious staff does piercings, scarification, even branding. Stop in just for a peek at the jewelry cases and you're sure to walk out with at least some new ideas. *16th St., near Guerrero St., Mission District, tel. 415/621–04058.*

Gallery of Jewels. Gallery of Jewels stocks rhinestone, glass, and silver jewelry crafted by local artisans. The styles are eclectic, and the prices are well below Tiffany & Co.'s. *4089 24th St., at Castro St., Noe Valley, tel. 415/285–0626.*

Gargoyle Beads. Why buy jewelry when you can make your own from Gargoyle's exotic beads, seeds, and polished stones? *1324 Haight St., at Central St., Haight-Ashbury, tel. 415/552–4274.*

Gotham. Run by the granddaddies of the city's piercing scene, Gotham is a no-attitude joint that emphasizes education and cleanliness. This is the place to get all your questions answered by an extremely knowledgeable staff; don't miss the photo book. *3991 17th St., at Market and Castro Sts., Castro District, tel. 415/701–1970.*

Zeitgeist Timepieces & Jewelry. The owners repair and restore clocks, jewelry, and fine watches. They also sell beautiful vintage wrist and pocket watches from the likes of Grüen and Bulova. *437B Hayes St., at Gough St., Hayes Valley, tel. 415/864–0185.*

NEW AGE AND HERBAL MEDICINE

Lady Luck Candle Shop. The friendly proprietor of this tiny shop can convince even the most bitter cynic to buy a hope candle. The wide selection of incense, devotional candles, and love potions will thrill your favorite mystic. *311 Valencia St., between 14th and 15th Sts., Mission District, tel. 415/621–0358.*

Lhasa Karnak Herb Co. This place is an excellent source for herbs and herbal information. *2513 Telegraph Ave., at Dwight Way, Berkeley, tel. 510/548–0380; 1938 Shattuck Ave., Berkeley, tel. 510/548–0372.*

ONE-OF-A-KINDS

Binky's. Relive your lost childhood at Binky's: They've got everyone's favorites from the '60s and '70s, like the *Charlie's Angels* board game, the Bionic Woman lunch box, and plenty of Barbies. *1009 Guerrero St., at 22nd St., Noe Valley, tel. 415/267–3903.*

Capezio. At San Francisco's best costume shop you'll find fake hands, clown ruffles, vampire teeth, ball gowns, sinister capes, and other miscellany. *180 Sutter St., 2nd floor, at Kearny St., Financial District, tel. 415/421–5657.*

Dudley Perkins Harley-Davidson. This is the oldest Harley-Davidson dealership in the world, selling new and vintage Harley motorcycles and clothes for hog-riding. The smaller **Dudley Perkins Gift Shop** (2595 Taylor St., at N. Point St., tel. 415/776–7779), on Fisherman's Wharf, stocks a mind-boggling array of Harley-Davidson T-shirts, caps, key chains, and tool kits. *66 Page St., between Franklin and Gough Sts., Civic Center, tel. 415/703–9494.*

Red Desert. Hundreds of species of cacti are for sale here, big and small, rare and common, for indoors or out. *1632 Market St., at Franklin St., Civic Center, tel. 415/552–2800.*

Urban Ore. You could outfit your entire house here, with everything used you can imagine, from antique furniture to small-enough-to-fit-in-your-luggage knickknacks to coat racks to sinks and lumber. Don't be put off by the junkyard feel of the place; it's full of great bargains. *7th St., at Gilman St., Berkeley, tel. 510/559–4450.*

Used Rubber USA. This is the ultimate in recycling—address books, wallets, journals, and satchels are all made of 100% postconsumer rubber: tires. The prices may not be a steal, but this stuff is guaranteed to last forever. Bicycle chain picture frames, glass bottle drinking glasses, and cuff links made of old-fashioned typewriter keys are just a few of the other quirky items that fill this ecoconscious shop. *597 Haight St., at Steiner St., Lower Haight, 415/626–7855.*

PAPER, CARDS, AND STATIONERY

Flax. A huge haven for artistic do-it-yourselfers, Flax offers handmade papers, cards, and journals, and, in case you're inspired, the materials to make your own. It's easy to get lost among this warehouse's one-of-a-kind picture frames and tchotchkes; the generous kids' section could keep little ones interested for hours. *1699 Market St., at Valencia St., Mid-Market, tel. 415/552–2355.*

Kozo Bookbinding. For beautiful Japanese stationery, blank books, and other exotic paper goods, come here. The poster-size silk-screened wall hangings range from $4 for a basic print to $40 for an elaborate design on handmade paper. *1969A Union St., between Buchanan and Laguna Sts., Cow Hollow, tel. 415/351–2114.*

Quantity Postcards. A wide and whimsical selection of postcards includes old snapshots of San Francisco, bits of Americana, and images from the '50s. Quantity is also the exclusive distributor of posters by Frank Kozik, whose psychedelic art has advertised bands like Green Day, among others. *1441 Grant Ave., between Green and Union Sts., North Beach, tel. 415/986–8866.*

VIDEO

Leather Tongue. This Mission institution sells and rents cult films, film noir, sci-fi, and more, but its greatest claim to fame is an extensive collection of films by local and independent filmmakers. *714 Valencia St., at 18th St., Mission District, tel. 415/552–2900.*

Le Video. Le Video, one of the best video stores on the West Coast, boasts an exhaustive collection of more than 45,000 titles spread among all genres. The smaller Vault stocks alternative cinema. *1231 9th Ave., at Lincoln Ave., Sunset District, tel. 415/566–3606. Le Video Vault: 1239 9th Ave., same phone.*

Movie Image. Film buffs will appreciate the great selection of film noir and American classics here, as well as the foreign and independent sections. The racks at the center of the store are arranged alphabetically according to director. *64 Shattuck Sq., near University Ave., Berkeley, tel. 510/649–0296.*

FOOD

REVISED BY SHARON SILVA AND LOTUS ABRAMS

Waves of Asian and Central American immigrants have made San Francisco a flavorful and festive hotbed of cheap taquerías, backstreet Chinese holes-in-the-wall, gracious Thai and Vietnamese establishments, reasonably priced sushi houses, and Korean barbecue joints. Oakland is known for Southern-style eats and its less touristy version of Chinatown; and Berkeley has its Gourmet Ghetto, with everything a foodie could want. Marin County and the South Bay, though generally more expensive, both have their share of worthwhile restaurants, with Marin County's known for their waterfront views.

For serious food mavens, a trip to Alice Waters's legendary Chez Panisse (*see below*) is a must: It's the birthplace of the seasonal, Mediterranean-inspired style known as California cuisine. You can sample great versions of this now common fare at hundreds of excellent sit-down restaurants throughout the Bay Area where entrées cost less than $10–$15. In addition, we've included a handful of the city's most cutting-edge restaurants, where entrées cost up to $20—but at any of these places you can get away with ordering appetizers for dinner or splitting a main course. Our price categories refer to the cost of the majority of main courses at the establishment being reviewed. Unless otherwise noted, the restaurants in this chapter accept one or more major credit cards.

SAN FRANCISCO

CASTRO/NOE VALLEY

The Castro District teems with lively restaurants, many with outdoor patios. Brunch is an institution here: Mimosas and espressos flow freely on weekend mornings, and the crowd is always jovial and loud. Follow the sunglasses-wearing masses to the two hottest brunch spots, **Café Flore** (*see* Chapter 5) and the **Patio Café** (*see below*), and brace yourself for a long afternoon of Bloody Marys. The after-hours eating scene around **Castro Street** is just as vibrant—you don't have to look too far for a casual dinner spot, even late into the night (*see box* Late-Night Eats, *below*). But if you really want to impress someone, the supertrendy **2223 Market** (2223 Market, at Noe St., tel. 415/431–0692) is considered the best restaurant in the neighborhood. The cuisine is all Californian, and entrées cost under $20 each.

Just over the hill from the Castro, around 24th Street, **Noe Valley** is a placid oasis awash in young liberal professionals, including a sizable lesbian contingent. It's a popular destination on sunny weekend mornings for a lazy brunch and a bit of window-shopping with the dog or the stroller. At night Noe gets fairly quiet, as it's mostly residential.

UNDER $5

Hot 'n' Hunky. This pink, perky little restaurant with a preponderance of Marilyn Monroe posters on the walls is a Castro institution for thick, juicy burgers. With names like the Macho Man, I Wanna Hold Your Ham, and Ms. Piggy, the burgers here make ordering half the fun. *4039 18th St., near Castro St., tel. 415/621–6365. Cash only.*

Marcello's. Right across the street from the Castro Theatre (*see* Movie Houses *in* Chapter 6), this place is very convenient when it's almost showtime, or for a post-theater snack (they're open late on weekends). They sell respectable pizza—by the slice or the pie—in a wide range of combinations, like ham and pineapple or spinach with black olives and feta. *420 Castro St., near Market St., tel. 415/863–3900. Cash only.*

Tom Peasant Pies. Tom serves only one thing—pies. Not big, meaty pies, but butter-and-cholesterol-free, fresh-outta-the-oven pies for less than $3. One fits neatly into the palm of your hand, and two will easily satisfy your hunger. Start with spinach and jack cheese or clam and spicy tomato sauce and finish with cherry–Anjou pear. Come early, as the doors close at 7 PM. *4108 24th St., at Castro St., tel. 415/642–1316; 4117 18th St., at Castro St., tel. 415/621–3632. Cash only.*

UNDER $10

Chow. Homespun standards like spaghetti and meatballs, thick, juicy burgers, and roasted chicken and mashed potatoes are offered alongside more au courant fare—iron-platter-roasted mussels, Caesar salad, noodles with peanut sauce—at

Waiters on Wheels (tel. 415/252–1470) and Dine-One-One (tel. 415/771–3463) deliver anything from burgers to Italian to Cajun to Japanese from San Francisco restaurants for a $7-per-stop fee. Pick up a free delivery guide at a newspaper stand.

this unpretentious, yet utterly hip neighborhood spot. The no-reservations policy guarantees a wait, but the comfort-food seekers don't seem to mind. A second location, **Park Chow**, is a little less crowded and serves the same satisfying dishes, including a banana butterscotch cream pie that wins a thumbs-up from even the fussiest sweet tooth. *215 Church St., near Market St., tel. 552–2469; 1240 9th Ave., near Lincoln Way, tel. 415/665–9912.*

Firewood Cafe. The formula is a familiar one: roasted chicken, pizzas baked in a wood-fired oven, bountiful salads. But the good food, handsome space, and reasonable prices make the difference. A moist, crispy-skinned half chicken with salad and a mound of roasted potatoes costs only $7.50. The thin-crusted pizzas, including an excellent one with fresh mozzarella, prosciutto, and arugula, and the big Caesar salad are good choices. A long table for shared seating makes solo diners feel part of the whirl. *4248 18th St., between Collingwood and Diamond Sts., tel. 415/252–0999.*

Fuzio. San Francisco has gone noodle crazy, and this hugely popular penny-wise outpost is helping to fuel the mania. The dishes, mostly Italian in spirit but with a strong Asian accent, run the gamut from linguine with fried calamari to pad Thai. Neighborhood residents and visitors fill the banquettes and counter seats at lunch and dinner, all of them happy to be dining on plates of noodles that never cruise over $6.75. *469 Castro St., near 18th St., tel. 415/863–1400.*

La Méditerranée. This small, personable restaurant on the edge of the Castro District serves great Mediterranean food, including dolmas, salads, hummus, *baba ghanoush*, and the like. If you can't decide, get the Middle Eastern combination plate (vegetarian or not): two phyllo pastries, a Levant sandwich, a kabob, and salad for $7.50. *288 Noe St., at Market St., tel. 415/431–7210; other locations: 2210 Fillmore St., at Sacramento St., tel. 415/921–2956; 2936 College Ave., at Ashby Ave., Berkeley, tel. 510/540–7773. Closed Mon.*

Miss Millie's. The carved-wood booths, frilly curtains, and antique fixtures will get you in the mood for homemade jams, scones, and cinnamon rolls. Indeed, breakfast is when you want to be at Miss Millie's. Try the lemon-ricotta pancakes in blueberry syrup or a fluffy omelet filled with oven-roasted tomatoes, basil, and feta cheese. *4123 24th St., at Castro St., tel. 415/285–5598. No dinner Sun.–Tues.*

LATE-NIGHT EATS

Most of the city's restaurants close by 11 PM, even on weekends. But if you just danced up an appetite, you indeed can find a few places serving omelets and burgers, or even pot stickers, into the wee hours.

Bagdad Cafe. This 24-hour restaurant in the Castro—where people-watching is a high art—is as famous for its expansive street-level windows as for its home-style breakfasts. 2295 Market St., at 16th St., tel. 415/621–4434.

El Farolito. Stagger in here for a burrito as late as 2:45 AM (until 3:45 AM Friday and Saturday). At this hour you probably won't notice the grimy cafeteria-style atmosphere. 2777 Mission St., between 23rd and 24th Sts., tel. 415/824–7877.

Grubstake. Housed in a converted railroad car, this diner fits right in to the grungy late-night Polk Gulch scene. 1525 Pine St., between Polk St. and Van Ness Ave., tel. 415/673–8268.

Orphan Andy's. This all-hours Castro hangout has red-vinyl booths, a lunch counter, and a jukebox—bring a date. 3991A 17th St., at Market and Castro Sts., tel. 415/864–9795.

Pinecrest. A real, live retro diner—complete with a long Formica counter and old vinyl booths—Pinecrest serves juicy charbroiled half-pounders to late-night downtowners. 401 Geary St., at Mason St., tel. 415/885–6407.

Silver. Reputedly popular with Chinatown gangsters, Silver serves Chinese cuisine around the clock in a glaring fluorescent setting. 737 Washington St., at Grant Ave., tel. 415/433–8888.

Sparky's. The menu might remind you of Denny's, but Sparky's serves a much trendier post-club clientele. 242 Church St., near Market St., tel. 415/626–8666.

No-Name (Nippon) Sushi. Everybody calls this small wood-paneled restaurant on Church Street No-Name Sushi, even though the proprietors did eventually put up a tiny sign in the window officially dubbing it NIPPON. Name or no name, locals know they'll get huge sushi combos at prices that are hard to believe—$7–$10. (If you're a sushi snob, you'll know that such low prices do come at the price of freshness.) No alcohol is served, but most people bring theirs in a bag. 314 Church St., at 15th St., no phone. Cash only. Closed Sun.

Pasta Pomodoro. At this bustling Castro hangout you can eat a supercheap plate of pasta and do a bit of cruising on the side. It's always full of people, but the waiting list moves fast. Try the polenta with fontina cheese, the penne puttanesca, or dig into a caprese sandwich built with fresh mozzarella, tomatoes, basil, and olive puree. Branches around town are equally popular. 2304 Market St., at 16th St., tel. 415/558–8123; other locations: 2027 Chestnut St., near Fillmore St., tel. 415/474–3400; 655 Union St., near Columbus St., tel. 415/399–0300; 816 Irving St., at 9th Ave., tel. 415/566–0900; 598 Haight St., at Steiner St., tel. 415/436–9800; 3611 California St., near Spruce St., 415/831–0900; 4000 24th St. at Noe, tel. 415/920–9904; 1865 Post St., near Fillmore St., tel. 415/674–1826.

Patio Café. The Castro's premier brunch spot operates out of an enormous converted greenhouse, complete with fake parrots perched among the foliage. Feast on eggs or omelets with home fries or on sinful cheese blintzes with cherry sauce—and don't forget the requisite Bloody Mary (or two or three). Later in the day, come for sandwiches, burgers, and pastas or for a more formal dinner. *531 Castro St., between 18th and 19th Sts., tel. 415/621–4640.*

Thai House on Noe. The elegant dining room makes this Duboce Triangle restaurant a popular choice for an intimate dinner. Try the duck on a bed of spinach with hot chili sauce or seafood soup with or without coconut milk. If you get stuck waiting for a table, pass time with a stroll down Henry and Noe streets—both are lined with some of the most colorful Victorians in the city. **Thai House II,** under the same management and located right around the corner on Market Street, has more room. *151 Noe St., at Henry St., tel. 415/863–0374. Thai House II: 2200 Market St., at Sanchez St., tel. 415/864–5006.*

UNDER $15

Tin-Pan. There are Asian noodles for everyone here: fat wheat noodles tossed with Mongolian lamb and crisp long beans, the familiar pad Thai, thin rice noodles with crunchy nuggets of sesame chicken, flat rice noodles mixed with beef. Some of the sauces are harsh and murky, but that doesn't keep the crowds away, who line up (no reservations taken) not only for the noodles, but for such dishes as batter-fried squid, five-spice barbecued pork ribs, shrimp-filled pot stickers, and chocolate-filled fried dessert wontons. A congenial bar scene adds to the operation's easygoing panache. *2251 Market St., between Sanchez and 16th St., tel. 415/864–0733. No lunch.*

UNDER $20

Firefly. Firefly's homey atmosphere captures Noe Valley's small-town charm. The menu changes weekly and incorporates global influences in typical California fashion—you might order Mediterranean or Southeast Asian or American home cooking (or a variation on the above) on any given night. Innovative appetizers steal the show here: Try Thai salmon cakes or shrimp and scallop pot stickers. The seasonal fruit shortcakes and rich brownie sundae are divine. Order carefully, though, as the bill can soar. *4288 24th St., at Douglass St., tel. 415/821–7652. Reservations recommended. No lunch.*

CHINATOWN

Finding something to eat in Chinatown is a cinch. Finding something *good* to eat is much trickier. Your best bet is to wander through the heart of Chinatown—**Washington, Clay,** and **Sacramento streets** between Mason and Kearny streets—until you find a restaurant that has the four elements that spell success: small, spare, cheap, and packed with locals. **Stockton Street** is the main market street, where you can load up on chow fun noodles, gingerroot, and live turtles. If you're wondering about the mysteries of dim sum, *see box, above.*

UNDER $5

Golden Flower. Nearly everyone who eats in this modest Vietnamese restaurant orders a big bowl of *pho,* fragrant rice noodle and beef soup. You can also order fresh or deep-fried rice-paper rolls stuffed with shrimp, pork, and vegetables, or tender, tasty barbecued meat on a bed of noodles. *667 Jackson St., between Grant Ave. and Kearny St., tel. 415/433–6469; 1936 Irving St., between 20th and 21st Aves., tel. 415/566–2892.*

Kowloon. This is the only place in the city with strictly vegetarian dim sum—hence its popularity with tree huggers and Buddhists. A cabbage-stuffed pot sticker or a crispy mushroom-potato cake sells for only about 60¢. If you'd rather go for a rice dish (brown rice optional), choose from a huge list that includes such exotica as vegetarian "duck gizzards" or vegetarian "eel." *909 Grant Ave., near Washington St., tel. 415/362–9888.*

Lucky Creation. From the green sign to the green menus, this small restaurant in the heart of Chinatown declares loud and clear its aim to please the vegetarian palate, and the prices are sure to please even the thinnest wallets. Try spicy bean cake over rice or braised eggplant in a clay pot. *854 Washington St., between Grant Ave. and Stockton St., tel. 415/989–0818. Cash only. Closed Wed.*

UNDER $10

House of Nanking. This legendary Chinatown hole-in-the-wall serves Shanghai home cooking at righteously low prices. You'll be crammed into tiny tables with total strangers, and the no-nonsense waiters

A CANTONESE BREAKFAST

Dim sum, the common morning and midday fare of the Cantonese, is traditionally served in large dining rooms by waiters pushing carts loaded with small plates and bamboo baskets holding savory pastries and dumplings. After choosing some items, dip your selections in tiny saucers of soy before popping them in your mouth. Options might include flaky taro cakes, sticky rice (steamed in bamboo leaves with meat and spices), shrimp and pork dumplings, steamed buns filled with barbecued pork or ginger chicken, and large rice noodles rolled around shrimp. You pay by the plate or basket at the end of your meal (the cart pushers stamp your bill every time you choose something).

will keep you on your toes, but all that only adds to the experience. Ask for the delicious shrimp cakes in peanut sauce—they're not on the menu—and the Nanking chicken. The dishes have been adapted to meet non-Chinese taste, and that keeps the tourists and non-Asian locales lining up at the door. *919 Kearny St., between Jackson and Columbus Sts., tel. 415/421–1429. Cash only.*

Yuet Lee. This ambience-free joint on the congested corner of Broadway and Stockton serves Cantonese cuisine and lots of exotic seafood. Share a huge platter of New Zealand mussels with black bean sauce, or head for the land and try the home-style beef stew in a clay pot. The kitchen hums until 3 AM. *1300 Stockton St., at Broadway, tel. 415/982–6020. Cash only. Closed Tues.*

UNDER $15

R&G Lounge. No one is going to accuse this upscale, somewhat sterile restaurant of being too festive, but it's worth the minisplurge for superfresh Cantonese dishes such as clams with spicy black bean sauce or meaty shiitake mushrooms with tender greens. When money is no object, order the house special, salt-and-pepper crab; its price varies according to the size of the fisherman's catch. Lunch prices—around $5 a rice plate—are easier to swallow. *631B Kearny St., between Sacramento and Clay Sts., tel. 415/982–7877.*

THE CIVIC CENTER AREA

The Civic Center area comprises a few low-lying neighborhoods that aren't exactly what you'd call classy, except, of course, for the area immediately surrounding the War Memorial Opera House and the Davies Symphony Hall (*see* Chapter 6). **Hayes Valley,** to the west of the **Civic Center,** along Hayes and Grove streets between Franklin and Laguna streets, is a good example of galloping gentrification, with wine bars and chichi restaurants sprouting up beside fledgling art galleries and secondhand stores. Running north of Civic Center on Polk Street, **Polk Gulch** gets some of the runoff from the drug and male-prostitution trade in the nearby Tenderloin. But a bunch of movie theaters, laid-back cafés, and terrific international and ethnic dives might convince you of the Gulch's seedy charm. Stretching northeast of downtown toward downtown, the **Tenderloin** is definitely *not* where you want to take Grandma to dinner. Although there are a few authentic Vietnamese outposts in the area, the blocks surrounding Larkin, Market, O'Farrell, and Mason streets are sketchy after dark: Either stick to lunch or take a cab.

UNDER $5

Café at the Main Library. After you've finished surfing the net on one of the Main Library's glitzy color monitors, stop in at this sleek, light-wood café for a hearty sandwich of pesto and smoked turkey on five-grain bread. *Grove and Larkin Sts., tel. 415/557–4400. Closing hrs vary daily.*

Main Squeeze. This space-age juice bar on Polk Street is full of industrial materials molded into post-modern pieces of fruit. Drink your fill of healthy juices and smoothies or try their vegetarian and vegan lunch and breakfast items. *1515 Polk St., at California St., tel. 415/567–1515. Cash only.*

Moishe's Pippic. Relocated East Coasters will want to head to this Hayes Valley Jewish deli to satisfy their corned beef pangs. Or their cravings for kosher salami, hot dogs, pastrami, chopped liver, bagels and lox, matzo ball soup, poppy-seed buns, knishes . . . it's a big Bronx cheer to obsessively healthy California cuisine. *425A Hayes St., at Gough St., tel. 415/431–2440. Cash only. Closed Sun. No dinner.*

Saigon Sandwiches. Small and utilitarian, this lunch-hour favorite builds the traditional sandwiches of Vietnam: a split length of baguette packed with lightly pickled vegetables, cilantro, a few chili slices, some "secret sauce," and your protein of choice, from roast pork to meatballs to pâté. Accompany your Asian Dagwood with one of the house's coconut-based drinks-cum-desserts. *560 Larkin St., between Turk and Eddy Sts., tel. 415/474–5698. Cash only. No dinner.*

UNDER $10

Ananda Fuara. Escape from grimy Market Street into this soothing vegetarian restaurant with sky-blue walls and draped ivy plants. Servers sway by the tables in flowing saris, bringing sandwiches and entrées like curry with rice and chutney. The massive Brahma burrito will fill you up for the rest of the day. *1298 Market St., at 9th St., tel. 415/621–1994. Cash only. No dinner Wed., Sun.*

If your wallet's feeling light, a number of bakery/cafés around Chinatown and the Richmond District sell dim sum to go at about $1 for three items.

Cordon Bleu. If you're on your way to the Lumière Theater (*see* Chapter 6), stop right next door at this tiny Vietnamese counter for a satisfying meal prepared before your eyes. The two women who own the place only make a few things—kebabs, rice with a rich meat sauce, crispy imperial rolls, and five-spice roast chicken—but they're all dangerously addictive. Special Number 5 includes all of the above and can easily satisfy two carnivores. Lunch specials go for $3.50. *1574 California St., between Polk and Larkin Sts., tel. 415/673–5637. Cash only. Closed Mon.*

Mad Magda's Russian Tea Room & Mystic Cafe. Hand-painted floors and a tarot reader seated in the front window set the mood for this funky joint amid the growing Hayes Valley glitter. Piroshkis (baked dough concealing savory fillings) have unusual fillings like roast beef and capers or smoked chicken and pears. The not-so-unusual sandwiches have playful names, like the Stalin (smoked turkey and cheddar) and the Khrushchev (ham and cheese). *579 Hayes St., between Octavia and Laguna Sts., tel. 415/864–7654. Cash only.*

Racha Café. Industrial meets tropical at this Thai outpost on the edge of the Tenderloin. Though the neighborhood is iffy (make sure you come via Polk Street at night), the wide range of vegetarian, seafood, and meat entrées is excellent, and the coconut milk–based soups (with chicken, seafood, or vegetables) are out of this world. *771 Ellis St., between Polk and Larkin Sts., tel. 415/885–0725.*

Swan Oyster Depot. Politicians from nearby City Hall can open their mouths wider than this tiny fish-market eatery, which consists of nothing more than one long counter and some of the best seafood in town. Settle down to a bowl of clam chowder, thick sourdough bread, and an Anchor Steam beer. You might be lucky enough to spot the mayor downing a crab cocktail on the bar stool next to you. *1517 Polk St., between California and Sacramento Sts., tel. 415/673–1101. Cash only. Closed Sun.*

Vicolo Pizzeria. A crisp cornmeal crust and a treasure trove of fresh gourmet toppings have put this cathedral-ceilinged spot on nearly every pizza lover's map. The choices, by the slice or the pie, hop from spicy andouille to eggplant and blue cheese to fennel with mozzarella and red onions. Calzone and healthy salads are also available. The drill is simple: order at the counter, grab a table, and your meal is delivered. *201 Ivy St., at Franklin, 415/863–2382.*

UNDER $15

Suppenküche. In the Asian- and Mediterranean-oriented Bay Area dining scene, this Hayes Valley restaurant with a lively atmosphere and authentic but dignified German cuisine stands out as a novelty. Get ready to feast on venison sautéed in red wine sauce with red cabbage and noodles or farmers' sausage with sauerkraut and mashed potatoes. The weekend brunch packs a crowd. *601 Hayes St., at Laguna St., tel. 415/252–9289. No lunch weekdays.*

UNDER $20

Carta. The menu changes monthly to feature cuisines from around the world. One month might focus on Provence, with such offerings as salt cod beignets and bouillabaisse, while the next month might serve a selection of South American dishes, including empanadas (savory turnovers) and *feijoada* (Brazilian black beans and meats). Following that, there could be Russian or Scandinavian, Southeast Asian or Tuscan, all of them expertly turned out by a talented kitchen crew. A recent expansion has brought the addition of a comfortable cocktail lounge and a private dining room. *1772 Market St., between Gough and Octavia Sts., tel. 415/863–3516.*

Zuni Café. An established temple of Mediterranean cuisine, Zuni is an upscale restaurant with an affordable menu if you shop the list wisely. Arguably the best chicken in town is chef Judy Rodgers's whole roast bird with Tuscan bread salad for two for $32. House-cured anchovies with Parmesan or pureed asparagus soup with lemon oil is a good way to start. And don't miss the espresso granita with whipped cream. *1658 Market St., between Gough and Franklin Sts., tel. 415/552–2522. Closed Mon.*

DOWNTOWN/EMBARCADERO

Downtown abounds with both old, classic restaurants that evoke San Francisco's golden years and trendy, new let's-do-lunch-and-expense-it bistros; both take advantage of the high-rolling Financial District's need to dispose of income. Except for a few options below, it's difficult to find a decent *and* inexpensive sit-down restaurant in this area—but it's usually worth it when you decide to go for it, especially in the "French Quarter," home to the popular Cafés **Claude** and **Bastille** (*see below*). On the other end of the fiscal spectrum, it's not so hard to find healthy soup-and-salad buffets catering to working stiffs on the go. Where downtown flows into the **Embarcadero,** stop by the bakery at **Il Fornaio** (1265 Battery St., at Greenwich St., tel. 415/986–0100) for a *panino* picnic on the pier.

UNDER $5

Specialty's. These six tiny take-out stands bake some 12 kinds of bread, including potato-cheese and carrot-curry varieties, with which they make some three dozen different fresh sandwiches. They also have daily soup specials such as corn chowder and cream of asparagus and insanely rich sweets. If you don't feel like eating on the sidewalk, take your lunch over to the rooftop garden at Crocker Galleria, at the corner of Kearny and Post streets. *312 Kearny St., between Bush and Pine Sts.; 22 Battery St., between Market and Bush Sts.; 150 Spear St., between Mission and Howard Sts.; 1 Post St., at Market St.; 101 New Montgomery St., at Mission St.; 369 Pine St., between Montgomery and Sansome Sts.; tel. 415/896–2253 for daily specials or 415/512–9550 for phone orders. Cash only. No dinner.*

UNDER $10

Shalimar. If you hunger for simple yet satisfying Indian cooking, for seekh kebab (sausage) and lamb curry, fragrant dal and big, blistered nan, this utterly plain-jane, self-serve operation is a godsend. After ordering at the counter, you take a seat among the crowd of Indian families and other Indian food fanciers who regularly fill the dining area. The wait can be long, so don't plan a quick exit. *532 Jones St., between Geary and O'Farrell Sts., tel. 415/928–0333. Cash only.*

UNDER $15

Café Bastille. Nibble on neat little French first courses like onion soup, pâté, or baked goat cheese on eggplant in a casual Gallic atmosphere. Ratatouille-filled crepes, roast chicken and potatoes, or *steak frites* make nice mains. Filled with Financial District workers and bohemians with a few bucks to blow, the café gets pretty fun and friendly, especially Thursday and Friday nights, when there's live jazz. *22 Belden Pl., between Pine and Bush Sts. and Kearny and Montgomery Sts., tel. 415/986–5673. Closed Sun.*

Café Claude. Live jazz accompanies your meal most nights at this youthful but bourgeois French bistro in an alley near Chinatown's gates. With a more relaxed atmosphere than Café Bastille (*see above*), it's a great place to while away a lazy afternoon or evening with a few glasses of wine and a plate of rich pâté, a dish of cassoulet, or a *croque-monsieur*. On warm nights, snag one of the outdoor tables for a Paris-in-San Francisco experience. *7 Claude La., off Bush St. between Grant and Kearny Sts., tel. 415/392–3515. Closed Sun.*

Caffe Macaroni. This place is tiny and usually packed elbow to elbow, so to speak—though there's an additional room upstairs—but it's worth squeezing in for some of the city's most affordable, authentic southern Italian food, served with a Neapolitan flair. An antipasto plate of marinated vegetables will whet at least three people's appetites, and the pasta dishes, such as gnocchi with Gorgonzola sauce, are generally good choices. Look for specials like squid-ink fettuccine heaped with fresh mussels, clams, calamari, and crab legs. *59 Columbus Ave., at Jackson St., tel. 415/956–9737. Cash only. Closed Sun.*

Yank Sing. With locations in the Financial District and South of Market, Yank Sing has great dim sum in a tasteful, modern setting. A meal should cost $10–$15, but watch out: Let your appetite run away with you, and next thing you know, stacks of plates are sliding off the table, and the waiter is handing you a bill the size of Beijing. *427 Battery St., at Clay St., tel. 415/362–1640; 49 Stevenson Pl., between 1st and 2nd Sts., tel. 415/541–4949. Closed Sat.*

FISHERMAN'S WHARF

Steer clear of the mediocre, high-priced seafood restaurants that crowd the wharf: The best dining experience you could have here would involve a loaf of sourdough, some cracked crab, a bottle of wine, and a seat on the pier. The corner of **Jefferson** and **Taylor streets** is jam-packed with street stands that hawk all sorts of seafood goodies, including shrimp or crab cups and thick clam chowder in a bread bowl. The only authentically rustic place to sit down and eat in the area is **Eagle Café** (Pier 39, upper level, tel. 415/433–3689), where windows and patio tables offer a view of the waterfront and Alcatraz (although the authenticity goes only so deep, since the Eagle was moved here lock, stock, and countertop from another location). Or grab an Irish coffee at the old-fashioned **Buena Vista Café** (2765 Hyde St., tel. 415/474–5044), purportedly where the drink was introduced in America. And, of course, there's always **Ben and Jerry's** ice cream—it's near the Red and White Fleet's ticket booth.

THE HAIGHT

The Haight (both its lower and upper sections) is renowned for its breakfast spots, including the **Pork Store Café,** the **Crescent City Café,** and **Kate's Kitchen** (*see below*). These are frequented by ragged-looking youths who suck up coffee as if it's the primal life force. For dinner, the Haight has a few trendy hot spots among the pizza, falafel, and burrito joints.

UNDER $5

Rosamunde. Sausages—knockwurst, smoked lamb, Italian fennel, bratwurst, chicken, and more—are grilled to order and tucked into French rolls at this tidy Lower Haight operation. House-made mustard, curry ketchup, and pepper relish are on hand for dressing up the simple but simply wonderful fare. *545 Haight St., between Fillmore and Steiner Sts., 415/437–6851. Cash only.*

Taqueria El Balazo. This isn't the Mission, but that's precisely Balazo's appeal: irresistible New Age Cal-Mex food. Choose from three kinds of veggie burritos, all stuffed with saffron rice, beans, Mexican goat cheese, and vegetables sautéed on a vegetarian grill—or dig into the burrito Vallarta, with sautéed rock prawns and tender nopal cacti. Deadheads will find burritos named for their heroes, and the kitchen turns out huge dinner platters meant to be shared (about $5). In the back room you will sometimes be treated to live flamenco guitar. *1654 Haight St., between Belvedere and Clayton Sts., tel. 415/864– 8608; 54 Mint St., off Mission St. between 5th and 6th Sts., tel. 415/882–9575. Cash only.*

UNDER $10

Crescent City Café. At this New Orleans–style café with six small tables and maybe a dozen counter seats, weekend brunch brings crowds in search of andouille sausage hash, or eggs Creole (like eggs Benedict except with avocado and Creole sauce). Thursday night there's a terrific barbecued ribs special ($9.50). Red beans and rice and delectable corn bread are standard nightly issue. *1418 Haight St., at Masonic St., tel. 415/863–1374.*

Kan Zaman. Patrons pack this trendy Mediterranean restaurant to listen to hypnotic Middle Eastern music and indulge in hummus, *baba ghanoush,* and spinach pies. On Friday, Saturday, and Sunday nights the Fat Chance Belly Dancers strut their stuff. *1793 Haight St., at Shrader St., tel. 415/751– 9656. Cash only.*

Kate's Kitchen. This wholesome breakfast spot is no secret: The line stretches out the door, especially on weekends. Once you make it in, chummy servers bring you classics like buttermilk-cornmeal pancakes, hush puppies with honey butter, and red flannel hash with two eggs on top. *471 Haight St., between Fillmore and Webster Sts., tel. 415/626–3984. Cash only.*

Massawa. Come to this Ethiopian restaurant if you like trying unusual spices and eating with your hands. Dinner platters are filled with tender lamb or beef or vegetarian plates, along with side portions of lentils, greens, or yellow split-pea paste. Everything comes with *injera*, a flat, spongy bread used instead of utensils to scoop up food. *1538 Haight St., between Ashbury and Clayton Sts., tel. 415/621–4129.*

Pork Store Café. Mounds of grits, big, fluffy omelets, and plate-size pancakes (try a chocolate short stack) are all slapped together on the same griddle. The café serves lunch, too, including comfort-food entrées like pork chops and applesauce with mashed potatoes, spinach, and biscuits. Check out the collection of posters from Haight-Ashbury street fairs past—they're almost as entertaining as the stream of locals strutting by. *1451 Haight St., between Ashbury St. and Masonic Ave., tel. 415/864–6981. No dinner.*

Spaghetti Western. The pierced-and-tattooed set hangs out at this chaotic Lower Haight spot, where Western-style breakfasts include corn bread, black beans, and assorted *huevos* (eggs). Gorge yourself on Spuds O'Rama, a huge mound of home-fried potatoes topped with cheese and sour cream, or the thick sourdough French toast blanketed with bananas and strawberries. *576 Haight St., near Steiner St., tel. 415/864–8461. No dinner.*

Squat and Gobble Café. Lower Haight types come to this sprawling café with the Sunday paper, a pack of Marlboro reds, and nothing else to do all day (so it seems). Try the massive Lower Haight omelet, with fresh veggies, pesto, and cheese, or any number of inventive crêpes, including the Zorba the Greek, with feta, olives, artichokes, spinach, and cheddar. There's also a decent selection of salads and sandwiches. *237 Fillmore St., between Haight and Waller Sts., tel. 415/487–0551; 1428 Haight St., between Ashbury and Masonic Sts., tel. 415/864–8484.*

Thep Phanom. This comfortably stylish spot regularly turns up on critics' lists as one of the city's best Thai restaurants. The authentically hot, colorful curries are undoubtedly one reason why, and the attentive but not hovering service is another. You can easily make a meal of the excellent appetizers and salads: fish cakes, minced duck salad, squid spiked with lime, and green papaya salad are standouts. *400 Waller St., at Fillmore St., tel. 415/431–2526. No lunch.*

UNDER $15

Cha Cha Cha. Though you may wait up to two hours for a table under the watchful eyes of the pseudo-Catholic icons that hang on the wall, you might not mind when you finally taste the tapas that make Cha Cha Cha such a hit. Try fried plantains with black beans and sour cream, tuna with mango salsa, pork quesadillas, or shrimp sautéed in Cajun spices; any one of them is great with the house-made sangria. To avoid the crowds, come for a late lunch. A second location in the Mission, **Cha Cha Cha at the Original McCarthy's,** is filled with martini-drinking hipsters listening to live music and eating the same irresistible plates. *1801 Haight St., at Shrader St., tel. 415/386–7670; 2327 Mission St., between 19th and 20th Sts., tel. 415/648–0504. No lunch in Mission location.*

Indian Oven. The seductive aroma from a fired-up tandoor oven drifts out of this favorite Lower Haight restaurant, pulling in folks who crave the food of the subcontinent. The tandoori chicken and lamb are superb, as are the *saag paneer* (spinach and cheese), *began bhartha* (roasted eggplant), and the various breads, from nan to kulcha. Cool down the heat with a tall Indian beer or freshly made lemonade. *233 Fillmore, between Waller and Haight Sts., tel. 415/626–1628. No lunch.*

JAPANTOWN

In the **Japan Center** (1737 Post St., between Geary and Fillmore Sts.), the veritable essence of Japantown, a bunch of decent restaurants—spanning a wide range of price categories—display their edibles with shiny photos or shellacked plastic miniatures. If nothing piques your interest, explore the surrounding streets, especially **Buchanan** and **Webster streets** to the north of the center, for even more possibilities. The cheapest option of all is to visit the Japanese market **Maruwa,** on the corner of Post and Webster streets. Along with fruits and vegetables and all manner of Japanese products, the delicatessen section has ready-to-eat sushi, rice and noodle dishes, and other bites. Afterward, catch a flick at the multiscreen AMC Kabuki 8 (*see* Movie Houses *in* Chapter 6), in the same complex as the center.

UNDER $10

Isobune. Patrons at this gimmicky but fun sushi restaurant pack in around a large table elbow to elbow and fish their sushi off little boats that bob about in the water in front of them. It may not be the best sushi you'll ever eat, but it's good enough for the price: $1.50–$3 for two pieces. *Japan Center, 1737 Post St., tel. 415/563–1030; 5897 College Ave., at Chabot St., Oakland, tel. 510/601–1424.*

Mifune. A steady stream of Asian and American patrons slurp up cheap, tasty *udon* (thick white noodles), *soba* (thin buckwheat noodles), and *donburi* (rice) dishes in the simple Mifune dining room. The house-made noodles come with various meats and vegetables; there's even one with jumbo shrimp. *Japan Center, 1737 Post St., tel. 415/922–0337.*

UNDER $15

Izumiya. Ignore the requisite plastic sushi prototypes in the window and the cheesy decor—this place is almost always packed with a young crowd, giving it a kind of Japanese Mel's Diner atmosphere. The house special, steamed orange roughy ($10.50, including salad, soup, and rice), is special for a reason, and the appetizers, such as clams steamed in sake, are equally fantastic. *Okonomoyaki,* a kind of Japanese pancake loaded with vegetables and meat, is a draw. Skip the sushi; it's not memorable. *Japan Center, 1581 Webster St., tel. 415/441–6867. Closed Mon.*

Sanppo. This old-timer, which stands just across Post Street from the Japan Center, offers the full range of Japanese fare, from noodles and *donburi* to teriyaki, tempura, *nabemono, yakitori,* and sushi, and does most of it very well. The dining room is nicely decorated with plants and screens, and the staff is friendly if not always efficient. *1702 Post St., 415/346–3486. No lunch Sun.*

MARINA DISTRICT/COW HOLLOW

The Marina has recently been flooded with scores of new culinary hotspots. A 20-minute walk west of Fisherman's Wharf will bring you to **Chestnut** and **Union streets,** the heart of this not-exactly-budget district, where grills, sushi spots, and California-cuisine eateries are a dime a dozen.

UNDER $10

Hahn's Hibachi. This tiny restaurant, little more than a take-out counter, dishes up healthy portions of Korean-barbecued chicken, beef, or pork with rice and kimchi. So many people order takeout that there's rarely a wait for the five or so tables. A more commodious Hahn's feeds Noe Valley residents. *3318 Steiner St., between Chestnut and Lombard Sts., tel. 415/931–6284; 1710 Polk St., at Clay St., tel. 415/776–1095; 1305 Castro St., at 24th St., tel. 415/642–8151. Cash only at Steiner and Polk outlets. Steiner closed Sun.*

Pluto's. A wall covered with adjectives describing food is part of Pluto's decor, but you won't need this to make you hungry after waiting in line with the young Marina folks who come here in droves. The generous portions of American comfort food include herb-roasted Sonoma turkey with the smashed spuds of the day, as well as hefty salads and sandwiches. Breakfast is served on weekends. *3258 Scott St., at Chestnut St., tel. 415/775–8867.*

Rosti. *Pollo al mattone,* grilled chicken under a brick, is the specialty here, served with vegetables, potatoes, and bread—a great deal for well under ten bucks. There are salads, too, and various antipasti, pizzas, and pastas. Tile floors, brick walls, and an open kitchen add to the practical Italian-inspired charm of the place. *2060 Chestnut St., between Fillmore and Steiner Sts., tel. 415/929–9300 .*

MISSION DISTRICT

Here you can wander from taquería to café to bookstore to taquería again in a salsa-and-*cerveza*-induced state of bliss. To add to the zillions of Mexican and Central American eateries that already crowd the neighborhood, a smattering of trendy restaurants has sprouted up in recent years, especially along **16th** and **Valencia streets**—without a doubt the favorite area in town for young hipsters to wine and dine. The Mission's restaurants are accessible from either the 16th Street/Mission or the 24th Street/Mission BART station.

UNDER $5

El Toro. This lively, gringo-frequented taquería presents many choices: Spanish or vegetarian rice, four kinds of salsa, four types of tortilla (white, wheat, red chili, or green chili), and no fewer than 10 types of protein, including *lengua* (beef tongue) and tofu *ranchero.* You'll have plenty of time to make up your mind, since the line often snakes out the door. *598 Valencia St., at 17th St., tel. 415/431–3351. Cash only.*

El Trébol. What El Trébol lacks in decor it quickly makes up for with incredibly cheap Central American fare and an animated, Spanish-speaking clientele. Specialties include *salpicón* (chopped beef), *chan-*

FARMERS' MARKETS

Stock up on seasonal and organic produce at the city's farmers' markets, held year-round. The Ferry Plaza Market, at the foot of Green Street on the Embarcadero (Sat. 8–1:30 year-round; Tues. 11–3 and Sun. 10–2 spring through fall), has free samples of home-grown fruits, homemade cheeses, and other irresistible artisanal items; it's also one of the best places in the city to get shellfish straight out of Tomales Bay. Other farmers' markets take place at the United Nations Plaza, Wednesday and Sunday 8–5, and at 100 Alemany Boulevard (tel. 415/647–9423), near Crescent Avenue in Bernal Heights, Saturday from dawn to dusk (although little is left near dusk) and Thursday in summer from 3 to 8.

Every Friday from 8 to 2 you can buy from East Bay farmers and bakers at the Old Oakland Certified Farmers' Market (Broadway and 9th St., tel. 510/452–3276). Oakland's other farmers' market is at Jack London Square (Broadway and Embarcadero), Sunday 10–2. You can also stock up on farm-fresh products at one of Berkeley's farmers' markets, sponsored by the Ecology Center (tel. 510/548–3333), every Saturday 10–2 on Center Street at Martin Luther King Jr. Way; Sunday 11–3 on Haste Street at Telegraph Avenue (from May through November); and Tuesday 2–7 on Derby Street at Martin Luther King Jr. Way.

cho con yuca (fried pork with cassava), and *pollo encebollado* (chicken with onions). Most entrées come with beans, rice, and tortillas. *3324 24th St., at Mission St., tel. 415/285–6298. Closed Sun.*

La Cumbre. Large, colorful Mexican paintings line the walls, and the requisite Virgin Mary statue guards the front door of this bustling taquería. If you like beef tongue, this is place to pack it into a taco or burrito. Or try *carne asada*, and throw your cholesterol cares to the wind. Meat and veggie dinner platters, which include beans and rice, will fuel you through the night and most of the next day. *515 Valencia St., between 16th and 17th Sts., tel. 415/863–8205.*

La Taquería. Grab a seat on the sunny outdoor patio for a front-row view of the bustling Mission. Inside counter workers chop and fold quickly and furiously to keep up with a seemingly endless line of hungry neighborhood families, local laborers, and visiting hipsters. The tacos and burritos are first-rate, and the house-made salsas add the perfect punctuation. The always-fed jukebox will keep your toes tapping. *2889 Mission St., between 24th and 25th Sts., tel. 415/285–7117. Cash only.*

Pancho Villa. This always-packed taquería, a brother of El Toro (*see above*), is a step above the myriad others, with a full range of seafood dinners such as savory garlic prawns, as well as the requisite burrito selections. The eclectic, ever-changing artwork is fun to peruse, and itinerant mariachi bands often stop in on weekends to play a few selections. *3071 16th St., between Mission and Valencia Sts., tel. 415/864–8840.*

Truly Mediterranean. This tiny take-out counter, tucked right next door to the popular Roxie movie house (*see* Chapter 6), serves all your basic Mediterranean salads and pita sandwiches; but their falafel deluxe (with eggplant and potatoes) and *shawerma* compete with neighboring taquerías when it comes to a cheap, filling, and tasty meal to go. *3109 16th St., between Valencia and Guerrero Sts., tel. 415/252–7482. Cash only.*

UNDER $10

La Rondalla. A strolling mariachi band follows iron-haired waitresses in a room decorated with Christmas ornaments year-round, a scene played and replayed since La Rondalla opened in 1951. The Mexican food is decent and reasonably priced, but the real draws here are the margaritas, the crazy atmosphere, and the late hours (until 3:30 AM). *901 Valencia St., at 20th St., tel. 415/647–7474. Cash only. Closed Mon.*

Nicaragua. The plate of fried plantains with *crema* (the Nicaraguan equivalent of French crème fraîche) and fried cheese is as flavorful (and fattening) as it gets; featherlight *yoltamál* (cornmeal) is another favorite. The restaurant is a classic dive, with plastic tablecloths and cheesy pictures of Nicaragua on the walls. The area is seedy, so be careful at night. *3015 Mission St., between 26th and César Chávez (Army) Sts., tel. 415/826–3672. Cash only.*

Panchita's. You could walk down 16th Street a hundred times without noticing this basic but fantastic El Salvadoran–Mexican restaurant where a jukebox plays mariachi tunes. For breakfast there's *huevos rancheros* (eggs with tortillas, cheese, and salsa), for dinner *carne desilachada* (shredded beef with egg, tomatoes, peppers, beans, and rice). Or order a pair of *pupusas* (a cornmeal round stuffed with cheese) with some *platanos con crema* (fried plantains with refried beans and cream) on the side. *3091 16th St., at Valencia St., tel. 415/431–4232.*

UNDER $15

Amira. This is the place to lie back on low couches with velveteen cushions, order *meze* (appetizers) and wine, and admire belly dancers. It's also the place to indulge: Start off with the chef's intense walnut-garlic dip, then move on to Libyan chicken or Moroccan couscous. Belly dancers perform nightly, with live Near Eastern music on Wednesday, Friday, and Saturday, when reservations are advised and there's a $1 cover. *590 Valencia St., between 16th and 17th Sts., tel. 415/621–6213. Closed Mon. No lunch.*

If you're looking to celebrate, head to one of the Mission's many Mediterranean or Spanish tapas restaurants, where live music keeps things animated, red wine flows freely, and plates are meant to be shared and lingered over.

Esperpento. Lines snake out the door at this great tapas joint—especially on weekends. Feast on clams with white beans, *calamares en su tinta* (squid in their own ink), mussels in a peppery vinaigrette, or fish with garlic mayonnaise. If you want to dispense with the small plates, order one of the huge paellas strewn with all kinds of shellfish, sausage, and fowl. The sangria is tastier and cheaper than at most tapas joints, and the room is lively and fun, with colorful Miró-esque touches. *3295 22nd St., between Valencia and Mission Sts., tel. 415/282–8867. Cash only.*

Scenic India. Tasty *shaag bhajee* (spinach with tomato and onion), chicken tandoori (half chicken baked in a clay oven), and other traditional Indian specialties are all served with delicious breads. Though service is slow there's never a wait for a table (a major plus in this neighborhood). *532 Valencia St., between 16th and 17th Sts., tel. 415/621–7226. No lunch.*

Slanted Door. Compared with all the party-oriented restaurants surrounding it, this place is decidedly subdued—but still wildly trendy. The regularly changing menu includes vegetarian spring rolls, spicy stir-fried squid infused with red chilies and garlic, moist five-spice chicken, and shrimp with glass noodles. Wash your meal down with a pot of exotic tea or a microbrew. *584 Valencia St., at 17th St., tel. 415/861–8032. Closed Mon.*

Ti Couz. An impatient crowd hangs around the bar sipping cider out of *bols,* waiting to get a taste of the succulent, piping-hot crêpes whipped up in the style of Breton crêperies in western France. Dinner crepes come with savory fillings like ratatouille, smoked salmon, or mushrooms; dessert crêpes are filled with Nutella and banana or fragrant poached pears. *3108 16th St., at Valencia St., tel. 415/252–7373.*

Timo's. Visit this dimly lighted, cozy restaurant with a group of friends, and you can sample widely from its huge selection of South American–, Spanish-, and Mediterranean-style tapas: delicate salads, roasted potatoes with garlic mayonnaise, grilled prawns, quail, and salt-cod potato cake with mint salsa, and more. *842 Valencia St., between 19th and 20th Sts., tel. 415/647—0558.*

Vineria. Sleek yet inviting, this charming spot serves authentic Italian plates at pocketbook-friendly prices. Among the antipasti are tiny white onions marinated in balsamic vinegar and grilled prosciutto-wrapped radicchio wedges. Pastas include light, tender gnocchi and pumpkin-stuffed ravioli, and pork cooked in milk is a superb main dish. The wine list is all Italian and smartly chosen. *3228 16th St., between Guerrero and Dolores Sts., 415/552–3889. Closed Mon. and Tues. No lunch.*

NORTH BEACH/RUSSIAN HILL

The old-time Italian neighborhood of North Beach has the highest concentration of restaurants (and lowest concentration of parking) in the city. **Columbus Avenue** and **Grant Avenue** north of Columbus are lined with reasonably priced eateries with everything from old-fashioned "American-style" Italian food to trendy neo-Italian cuisine.

UNDER $5

Golden Boy Pizza. Young North Beach residents fill up the bar stools at this tiny dive to get fat, greasy slices. Check out what's available in the window—pesto vegetarian and clam garlic are good bets. The purple-coiffed people behind the bar might even smile at you as they warm up your square. *542 Green St., between Grant Ave. and Stockton St., tel. 415/982–9738. Cash only.*

San Francisco Art Institute Café. With the kind of view for which you normally have to pay through the nose, this unpretentious café on the rooftop of an art school a couple of steep blocks up Russian Hill from North Beach has a reassuring sign that promises PSEUDO BOHEMIANS WELCOME—and the prices reflect that claim. There's a nice selection of burgers (some vegetarian), thick sandwiches on good bread, healthy salads, a couple of hot dishes on the daily specials menu, and irresistible baked goods, including hubcap-size scones. *800 Chestnut St., between Leavenworth and Jones Sts., tel. 415/749–4567. Cash only. Closed Sun. No dinner Sat. Hrs vary with the school terms.*

UNDER $10

Bocce Café. The choose-your-own-adventure menu might not blow you away, but Bocce continues to pack 'em in with its reasonable prices, jovial atmosphere, and cozy decor. Sit back on cushions and admire the high ceilings and ornate mirrors while you feast on one of five pastas with 15 different sauces—including clams, pesto, and sautéed eggplant. On warm Friday and Saturday evenings you can eat in the garden to the strains of live jazz. *478 Green St., at Grant Ave., tel. 415/981–2044. Closed Sun.*

Il Pollaio. This small Italian kitchen serves up tasty grilled chicken, and lots of it, in a homey atmosphere that attracts Italian old-timers year after year. A fantastic half chicken with salad, crusty bread, and wine costs less than $10. Desserts run from flan and cheesecake to chocolate mousse. *555 Columbus Ave., between Union and Green Sts., tel. 415/362–7727. Closed Sun.*

L'Osteria del Forno. Two Italian women have created an affordable menu and a chic-but-casual atmosphere for their tiny Italian restaurant. Focaccia sandwiches and thin-crust pizza are deliciously authentic, especially the pizza *bianca* with white cheese and wild mushrooms. There are usually one or two homemade pastas available daily—look for the spinach- or pumpkin-filled ravioli. A popular dinner house run by the same women (*see* Vineria, *above*) keeps Mission eaters happy. *519 Columbus Ave., at Green St., tel. 415/982–1124. Cash only. Closed Tues.*

North Beach Pizza. On weekends you'll have to stand on the street and be tortured by the smell of garlic while you wait for a table. Once inside, you can sink your teeth into thick-crust pizzas heaped with pepperoni, spinach, pesto, feta, and mushrooms. Pizzas come by the pie only—sorry, no slices. *1499 Grant Ave., at Union St., tel. 415/433–2444; 1310 Grant Ave., at Vallejo St., tel. 415/433–2444; 800 Stanyan St., at Beulah St. (take-out only), tel. 415/751–2300; 4787 Mission St., at Ocean Ave., tel. 415/586–1400; 3054 Taraval St., at 41st Ave. (take-out only), tel. 415/242–9100; 1598 University Ave., at California St., Berkeley, tel. 510/849–9800.*

UNDER $15

Capp's Corner. Italian family-style dining is alive and well at this venerable North Beach establishment. A five-course meal, including soup, salad, pasta, main course, and spumoni for dessert, comes in under $15. The choices range from osso buco (veal shank) to calamari steak, roast lamb to roast pork, and the friendly saloonlike interior guarantees a no-pretension, old-fashioned meal. 1600 Powell St., at Green St., tel. 415/989–2589.

Ristorante Ideale. This is like a true Roman restaurant—the waiters are distracted but warmhearted, the antipasti are top-notch, and the atmosphere is refined but relaxed. You can stick to the antipasti menu and sample delectable *cozze con fagioli* (steamed mussels with garlic and fava beans), or you can go for a perfectly al dente pasta dish, like *pappardelle all'agnello* (homemade wide noodles with lamb-tomato sauce). In true Roman style, waiters here will let you linger for hours. *1309 Grant St., between Green and Vallejo Sts., tel. 415/391–4129. Closed Mon.*

Zarzuelā. Though this warm, rustic Spanish restaurant is always bustling, it doesn't have the "PAR-dee!" feel of tapas joints in the Mission, befitting its Russian Hill setting. Sample small but satisfying plates of mushrooms in garlic sauce, tortilla *española,* or steamed mussels. There's also a couple of heavenly saffron-rich paellas for those who want to go beyond tapas. *2000 Hyde St., at Union St., tel. 415/346–0800. Closed Sun. and Mon. No lunch.*

UNDER $20

Rose Pistola. Every food lover's itinerary includes this North Beach hotspot. The menu, inspired by the tables of Liguria, lists various antipasti—fava beans with pecorino cheese, tiny octopus with potatoes and green beans, roasted peppers, grilled sardines, prosciutto-and-arugula-topped crostini—pizzas from a wood-burning oven, and hearty main courses that can easily be shared, including a superb cioppino. Reservations are hard to come by, but a number of tables are kept for walk-ins. *532 Columbus Ave., between Union and Green Sts., tel. 415/399–0499.*

RICHMOND AND SUNSET DISTRICTS

From the way San Franciscans talk, you'd think the Richmond and Sunset districts were in another county. In fact, these districts flanking Golden Gate Park are only a few minutes from the Haight and Japantown by car or just three or four more stops on the MUNI. In the Richmond District, Vietnamese, Chinese, Burmese, and Japanese places solidly line **Clement** and **Geary streets** between Arguello Boulevard and 11th Avenue and between 20th and 25th avenues, where you'll also find produce markets brimming with items unfamiliar to a Western eye. On the other side of the park, in the Sunset, **Irving Street** between 5th and 25th avenues yields numerous Chinese, Thai, and Vietnamese restaurants.

Intimate restaurants, sidewalk cafés, and dimly lighted bars make North Beach a prime destination for a romantic tête-à-tête. If dinner and drinks don't do the trick, hike up to Coit Tower for a view that will leave your date swooning.

UNDER $10

King of Thai Noodle House. If you shut out Clement Street, you can dream you are in Southeast Asia as you work your way through a bowl of duck noodle soup at this small, funky establishment. The price for a plate of rice noodles tangled around pork, long beans, and fragrant basil barely cruises beyond the $5 mark, and some of the soup noodles rest below it. The restaurant stays open until 1:30 AM, making it a good place for a late-night Asian food fix. The owner's brother has a larger, slightly pricier Thai place, King of Thai Kitchen, up the block that offers a fuller range of dishes. *639 Clement St., between 7th and 8th Aves., tel. 415/752–5198; cash only; King of Thai Kitchen: 346 Clement St., between 4th and 5th Aves., tel. 415/831–9953.*

River Side Seafood Restaurant. There are a slew of Chinese restaurants in the Sunset, most of them catering to large groups of eight or 10—commonly multigenerational Chinese families—who love good food and good value. River Side offers both. Everything, from the Peking duck, its crisp skin a wonderful marriage of texture and flavor, to thick chunks of black cod speckled with chilies, to Dungeness crab pulled kicking from a tank just before it's stir-fried with scallions and ginger, is done well here. *1201 Vicente St., at 23rd Ave., tel. 415/759–8828.*

Ton Kiang. Dim sum connoisseurs regularly head to this Richmond outpost for satisfying rice-noodle rolls, stuffed bean curd sheets, pea sprout–stuffed dumplings, black bean spareribs, and countless other superb midday delicacies. At dinner Hakka (southern Chinese) specialties move front and center: salt-baked chicken, wine-flavored meats and seafood, and braised, stuffed bean curd crowned with slivered vegetables. *5821 Geary Blvd., between 22nd and 23rd Aves., tel. 415/387–8273.*

UNDER $15

Brother's Restaurant. There's authentic Korean barbecue—lots of it—at this minimalist Richmond joint. Each table comes with its own piping-hot wood-charcoal grill, which you use to sear your marinated short ribs, chicken, or shrimp. Once you've ordered your meat, servers will bring you never-ending bowls of kimchi, assorted pickled vegetables, seaweed wraps, and rice—until you cry for mercy. There are two

SWEET TREATS

Bombay Ice Creamery. When exotic is what you crave, head here for flavors to make you dream of the subcontinent: cardamom, rose petal, saffron and pistachio, mango. 552 Valencia St., between 16th and 17th Sts., tel. 415/431–1103.

Just Desserts. Since 1974 it's been a favorite. Look for 10 branches throughout the Bay Area; the main location, on Church Street in San Francisco, has a secluded outdoor courtyard. 248 Church St., at Market St., tel. 415/626–5774.

Lovejoy's Antiques and Tea Room. This Noe Valley shop serves English high tea, with scones, finger sandwiches, and crumpets. 1195 Church St., at 24th St., tel. 415/648–5895.

Mitchell's Ice Cream. This family-owned shop in the Mission serves unusual homemade ice creams—try avocado or yam. 688 San Jose Ave., at 29th St., tel. 415/648–2300.

St. Francis Soda Fountain and Candy Store. In the Mission since 1918, St. Francis still makes its own ice cream, syrups, and candy. Order a phosphate and wax nostalgic. 2801 24th St., at York St., tel. 415/826–4200.

Swensen's. Climb to the top of Russian Hill, and you'll find the original Swensen's ice cream parlor. You might need a chocolate double dip (if not a respirator) to get going again. 1999 Hyde St., at Union St., tel. 415/775–6818.

Toy Boat. Come here for a scoop and marvel for hours at the hundreds of toys lining the walls. 401 Clement St., at 5th Ave., tel. 415/751–7505.

locations only a block from each other; the one between 5th and 6th is more lively. *4128 Geary Blvd., between 5th and 6th Aves., tel. 415/387–7991; 4014 Geary Blvd., near 4th Ave., tel. 415/668–2028.*

Ebisu. This Inner Sunset sushi bar is one of the city's best—there's always a line out the door. The sushi specials, which include miso soup and tea, are a good way to sample a selection. Try the delicate *hirame* (halibut) or the slippery, pearly white *kaibashira* (scallops), and always ask the sushi masters which fish is on special. Across the street, the same owner has opened Hotei, which features Japanese noodle soups, panfried noodles, and various snacks and salads. Neither place takes reservations. *1283 9th Ave., between Irving St. and Lincoln Way, tel. 415/566–1770, no lunch Sat., closed Sun; Hotei: 1290 9th Ave., tel. 415/753–6045, closed Tues.*

P.J.'s Oyster Bed. Sharing a meal is the best policy at this happening Cajun restaurant; with an appetizer thrown in, most entrées will successfully fill two big eaters. The best dishes are superfresh oysters, gigantic bowls of tasty, traditional gumbo, and the enormous shellfish roast, full of spicy crawdads and other bivalves. If there's a wait, put your name on the list and cross the street to Yancy's, a cavernous dive bar that's connected to the restaurant via an intercom. *737 Irving, at 9th Ave., tel. 415/566–7775.*

SOUTH OF MARKET

Not long ago, the South of Market area, nicknamed SoMa, was mostly warehouses, with some small businesses and a few residential pockets dotting the landscape. Today, with a boomlet of multimedia companies putting down roots, the neighborhood boasts many attractive and friendly restaurants. Wander along **Folsom Street** between 7th and 12th streets or along **11th** and **9th streets** between Howard and Harrison streets, and you'll have the SoMa eating scene in the palm of your hand. Oddly, there are few late-night eating spots to satiate clubbers' cravings. Besides **Hamburger Mary's** and **Club Za Pizza** (*see below*), you can try **20 Tank Brewery** (*see* Bars *in* Chapter 6), which serves sandwiches, nachos, and other munchies most nights until 1 AM and beer until 1:30 AM.

UNDER $5

Club Za Pizza. Next to the DNA Lounge (*see* Clubs *in* Chapter 6), Club Za is a convenient stop for a $3 "zlice." Fancifully named pies range from their Vegan Friendly (with cilantro pesto and lots of veggies) to Vegan Nightmare (with extra cheese and lots of meats); but the Potesto (with pesto, cheese, and potatoes) is king. Za is also popular with the lunchtime SoMa multimedia crowd, to whom it serves great "zalads" and "zoups." *371 11th St., between Folsom and Harrison Sts., tel. 415/552–5599; Little Za (take-out only), 2162 Polk St., between Vallejo St. and Broadway, tel. 415/563–8515. Za Gourmet Pizza: 1919 Hyde St., between Green and Union Sts., tel. 415/771–3100.*

UNDER $10

Hamburger Mary's. The messy hamburgers and cluttered decor go together wonderfully. Come by at 1 AM to hang out with SoMa clubbers in various states of inebriation. Vegetarians can feast on the tofu burger or the Meatless Meaty, a hot sandwich of mushrooms, cream cheese, and olives. *1582 Folsom St., at 12th St., tel. 415/626–5767.*

Manora's Thai Cuisine. Trendier than most Thai restaurants in the city, this place attracts big crowds—but the fresh, attractive dishes are worth the wait. Try garlic quail or spicy Japanese eggplant with prawns, chicken, and pork. *1600 Folsom St., at 12th St., tel. 415/861–6224. No lunch weekends.*

UNDER $15

South Park Café. Pretend you're Hemingway, Gertrude Stein, or Henry Miller in glorious Parisian exile while you sup on *boudin noir* (blood sausage) and *frites*. This French bistro opens at 7:30 AM weekdays with fresh croissants and coffee and stays open for country-cooked lunches and dinners. *108 South Park Ave., between 2nd and 3rd and Bryant and Brannan Sts., tel. 415/495–7275. Closed Sun.*

UNDER $20

LuLu. A meal at this innovative restaurant is worth the money. The menu marries the food of the French and Ligurian rivieras and the dishes are served family style, which means you can try a variety of things and not break the bank. Roasted meat entrées and grilled vegetables are the specialty: Watch the "designated roasters" at the wood-fired oven with their official-looking walkie-talkies. Pastas, such as butternut squash gnocchi in sage and olive oil, are fantastically rustic, and thin-crust pizzas taste as amazing as they look. *816 Folsom St., at 4th St. tel. 415/495–5775.*

EAST BAY

Sure, San Francisco has enough restaurants to keep a gourmand feasting for years, but the East Bay outdoes San Francisco in some types of cuisine. Not only is it the home of "California cuisine," it's also the best place to find an Ethiopian meal, or to pick up a barbecued rib dinner. Oakland's Chinatown rivals San Francisco's in authenticity, and Berkeley has a classier breakfast scene than the Haight for about the same price.

BERKELEY

California cuisine, that designer fuel for the yuppie generation, got its start in Berkeley, and locals take their food very seriously. The area around Shattuck Avenue at Vine Street has become known as the **Gourmet Ghetto** and is home to a number of high-quality restaurants, including the famed **Chez Panisse** (*see below*). On **Telegraph Avenue** between Dwight Way and the UC Berkeley campus, you'll find the city's cheapest restaurants, serving fast food with a Berkeley twist: Heaping green salads and gourmet sandwiches are far more common than burgers. West of campus along **University Avenue,** there's a string of mostly Asian and Indian restaurants. Both **College Avenue** (running south from campus into Oakland) and **Solano Avenue** (just north of Berkeley in Albany) are lined with cafés, sandwich shops, and upscale restaurants that cater to the neighborhood's students and professors.

UNDER $5

Telegraph Avenue near the Berkeley campus is full of cheap eats. At Telegraph and Bancroft Way a cluster of food carts sells everything from burritos and smoothies to Japanese food, falafel sandwiches, and wonderfully stuffed potatoes—try the spud with pesto and mozzarella from Berkeley's Best. The ever-popular **Noah's Bagels** (2344 Telegraph Ave., tel. 510/849–9951; 1883 Solano Ave., tel. 510/525–4447; 3170 College Ave., Oakland, tel. 510/654–0941) spreads flavored cream-cheese schmears on chewy New York–style bagels. **Smart Alec's** (2355 Telegraph Ave., tel. 510/704–4000) is a vegan fast-food joint where you can get a veggie burger, air-baked fries, and soda for less than $5. For pizza along with an "eat-it-or-screw-you" attitude, stop by **Blondie's** (2340 Telegraph Ave., near Durant Ave., tel. 510/548–1129), popular with street freaks and bleary-eyed students in need of a pepperoni fix, until 1 AM (2 AM Friday and Saturday); a big, floppy, tasty slice and a beverage chaser is usually yours for less than $3. **Bongo Burger** (2505 Dwight Way, at Telegraph Ave., tel. 510/540–9147; 1839 Euclid Ave., tel. 510/540–9573; 2154 Center St., tel. 510/540–9014) serves some of the cheapest meals in town—two eggs, home fries, and toast; a Polish dog; and a falafel sandwich each cost about $3. The Persian burger (charcoal-grilled ground lamb on a roll with plenty of trimmings) is recommended. A few blocks south of campus at Dwight Way, **Ann's Soup Kitchen and Restaurant** (2498 Telegraph Ave., tel. 510/548–8885) dishes out exceptionally cheap breakfasts, homemade soups, and sandwiches.

Café Intermezzo. This Berkeley institution, with a harried, occasionally rude staff, indisputably serves the biggest salads around. The Veggie Delight is a family-size mound of greens topped with kidney and garbanzo beans, hard-boiled egg, sprouts, avocado pieces, and croutons. Salads are served with your choice of homemade dressings and include a bookend-size slab of homemade honey-wheat bread. The sandwiches are equally generous and built on the same sturdy bread. *2442 Telegraph Ave., at Haste St., tel. 510/849–4592.*

Crêpes-a-Go-Go. Slimane Djili, the owner of this small café, used to sell crêpes on the streets of Paris. Now, bless him, he's settled on busy University Avenue, offering sweet and savory crêpes filled with Nutella and banana or spinach, green onions, and cheese. One is filling; with two you'll be staggering out the door. *2125 University Ave., at Shattuck Ave., tel. 510/841–7722. Cash only.*

Juice Bar Collective. Smack in the middle of the Gourmet Ghetto, the tiny Juice Bar offers fresh and organic sandwiches and hot dishes like spinach lasagna and various pizzas in addition to their namesake smoothies. Try the Sunset, made with bananas, orange juice, and yogurt, while you sit at one of the few alfresco tables. *2114 Vine St., tel. 510/548–8473. Cash only. Closed Sun.*

UNDER $10

Berkeley Thai House. Locals and students in the know come to this restaurant near the Berkeley campus to wolf down pad Thai and other reasonably priced lunch specials. For dinner try the *mus-a-mun* curry (beef with red curry, peanuts, potatoes, carrots, and coconut milk) or the basil tofu. On a sunny day dine on the peaceful patio, sheltered from the street by tall bushes. *2511 Channing Way, at Telegraph Ave., tel. 510/843–7352. Closed Sun. lunch.*

Bette's Oceanview Diner. This bright, crowded '50s-style diner, on the happening stretch of 4th Street near I–80, redefines American diner food: Instead of grilled American cheese and white bread, try jack and cheddar on sourdough. The buttermilk pancakes are legendary, as are the home-baked pies. The wait can stretch to 45 minutes, so if you're in a hurry, grab a cup of strong coffee and a heavenly scone or get a take-out salad or sandwich from **Bette's To Go**, next door, and head for the Marina. *1807A 4th St., near University Ave., tel. 510/644–3230. No dinner.*

Blue Nile. This is one of Berkeley's best Ethiopian restaurants, serving everything from thick split-pea stew and pepper-cooked beef to *tej* (honey wine) and freshly blended fruit shakes. The food is served family style, and you use *injera* bread instead of silverware to scoop it up. *2525 Telegraph Ave., between Dwight Way and Parker St., tel. 510/540–6777. No lunch Sun.*

Breads of India. Not surprisingly, Indian breads are the specialty here, and types offered—nan, paratha, roti topped and flavored in various ways—vary daily. So do the curries and vindaloos. The line for the seven tables in this modest spot starts forming before the doors open for both lunch and dinner, with anxious diners busying themselves peering through the curtained windows. Small parties and singles are expected to share tables. *2448 Sacramento, near Dwight Way, tel. 510/848–7684. No lunch Sun. Cash only.*

Brick Hut Café. A collective owned and operated by women, this mom-and-mom café is one of the best breakfast joints around. It's also a hot lesbian pickup spot on an increasingly womanish stretch of San

Pablo Avenue. The pesto eggs are a house favorite; there are also respectable blueberry p̲
real maple syrup and well-prepared salads, burgers, and sandwiches. The high ceilings, expo̲
walls, polished wooden floors, and friendly waitstaff create an atmosphere conducive to postme̲
gering. *2512 San Pablo Ave., at Dwight Way, tel. 510/486–1124. No dinner.*

Cha Am. This place feels pleasantly removed from Shattuck Avenue, even though its greenhouselike
window seats overlook the street. Try the magical *tom ka gai* (chicken and coconut soup) or the mixed
seafood plate with chili, garlic, and vegetables. Although the food is usually more Berkeley than Thai,
the steady clientele clearly doesn't mind. *1543 Shattuck Ave., at Cedar St., tel. 510/848–9664. No
lunch Sun.*

Chester's Café. Looking out over the bay from Chester's sunny upstairs deck is one of the best ways to
start a lazy weekend morning. The friendly staff will bring you mug after mug of hot coffee and weekend
brunch specials like eggs Juneau (poached eggs and smoked salmon on an English muffin topped with
Hollandaise sauce). *1508B Walnut Ave., at Vine St., tel. 510/849–9995. No dinner.*

Homemade Café. You'll probably have to wait for a table (at least on weekends), so grab a cup of coffee and a menu, park yourself on the sidewalk, and start deliberating. Will it be a whole-wheat buttermilk waffle with homemade blueberry sauce? Matzo *brei* (matzo with scrambled eggs and cheese)? Or
their famous Home-Fry Heaven (home fries with cheese, salsa, sour cream, and guacamole or pesto)?
2454 Sacramento St., at Dwight Way, tel. 510/845–1940. Cash only. No dinner.

Juan's Place. Surrounded by steel factories and warehouses, this traditional Mexican restaurant has the
feel of an old cantina, complete with piñatas, mirrored beer ads, and cheesy portraits of matadors—the
perfect setting in which to indulge in large portions of tacos, burritos, and tamales. Try the crab enchi-
lada with red sauce and cheese, and wash it down with a wine margarita from the adjoining bar. *941
Carleton St., at 9th St., tel. 510/845–6904.*

Long Life Vegi House. Load up on healthy Chinese food at this longtime favorite just west of campus. If
you're feeling adventurous, try vegetarian "pork" or "chicken," made with wheat gluten and soy protein.
Otherwise, stick to standard vegetarian and seafood dishes like cold *tan tan* noodles with peanut sauce
or prawns and string beans in black bean sauce. Lunch specials, at less than the cost of a bargain matinee, include soup, a spring roll, and an entrée over surprisingly tasty rice. *2129 University Ave., near
Shattuck Ave., tel. 510/845–6072.*

Rick and Ann's. Join East Bay locals in bicycle shorts (babies and dogs in tow) as you wait for the best
breakfast in town—and in Berkeley, that's really saying something. Try the Down South, a combination
of two cornmeal pancakes, two spicy turkey sausages, and two fluffy scrambled eggs with cheese. The
special omelets and scrambles are also delicious, as is the challah French toast. Breakfast is the draw
here, but the dinner menu has the same straightforward appeal. *2922 Domingo St., near Ashby St.,
across from Claremont Resort, tel. 510/649–8538.*

Saul's. This Gourmet Ghetto nosherie is the closest thing to a New York deli in the East Bay. Shelves of
Manischewitz products line the entryway, and a glass deli counter displays bowls of chopped liver,
sauerkraut, and whole smoked fish. There are sandwiches stuffed with pastrami, corned beef, brisket,
and tongue and Eastern European specialties like knishes, potato latkes, and matzo ball soup. Saul's
gets noisy and crowded during peak hours; avoid the lunch-hour wait by getting your food to go. *1475
Shattuck Ave., at Vine St., tel. 510/848–3354.*

UNDER $15

Pasand Madras Cuisine. If you feel like filling up at this southern Indian restaurant, get a complete *thali*
dinner, including lentil curry, lentil vegetable soup, spicy tamarind soup, yogurt with vegetables, a selection of Indian flat breads, rice pilaf, sweet mango chutney, and a dessert surprise—all for about $15. If
you are in the mood for something more modest, order the *dosa*, a rolled crepe nearly the length of a
baseball bat filled with spiced potatoes. A raised seating area lets you watch cross-legged sitar and tabla
players who whip up a musical frenzy during dinner. *2286 Shattuck Ave., at Bancroft Way, tel. 510/549–
2559.*

UNDER $20

Café at Chez Panisse. Though the ground floor of Alice Waters's mecca for foodies is a big-deal affair
(the multicourse dinner menu will set you back $35–$65), you can sample the same artful presentations of local ingredients in the café upstairs for half the price. Reservations are taken for the same day
only, so call in the morning and be ready to hit redial. The *pollo al mattone* (chicken grilled under a

turns up often. Simple salads and first courses such as blood oranges and olives,
⟨...⟩a and Parmesan, or squid with favas beans are memorable. *1517 Shattuck Ave.,*
⟨...⟩*0/548–5049. Closed Sun.*

⟨...⟩declare this lively spot the East Bay's best Japanese restaurant. Try the vegetable
⟨...⟩n varieties of *robata* (grilled skewered meats or vegetables), or *soba* noodles—and
⟨...⟩elf. There's also a great selection of sushi, or full dinners served with good-for-the-soul
⟨...⟩anese salad, and rice, all for about $16. Some nights the line for a table spills around the
⟨...⟩ervations are accepted), but there's usually room at the sushi bar. *2100 Ward St., at Shat-*
tuck Ave., ⟨...⟩ *510/549–3486. No lunch Sat.–Mon.*

Mazzini. Stylish and authentic, this Tuscan trattoria, complete with marble tabletops and tile floors,
serves some memorable dishes, including a *fritto misto* of fennel and mushrooms, a simple, yet simply
divine *bresaola* (air-cured beef) with arugula, a New York steak dusted with Parmesan shards, a thin,
crisp pizza with Gorgonzola, and a lovely apple tart. A first-class list of reasonably priced Italian wines
provides plenty of opportunity for fine sipping. *2826 Telegraph Ave., between Oregon and Stuart Sts.,*
tel. 510/848–5599.

MARKETS AND SPECIALTY STORES

Newly housed in what once was home to a Safeway (after moving a block from its original location in a
former bowling alley), **Berkeley Bowl Marketplace** (2020 Oregon St, near Shattuck, tel. 510/843–6929)
represents alternative and cooperative grocery shopping at its finest. Try **Trader Joe's** (5796 Christie
Ave., at Powell St., tel. 510/658–8091) for inexpensive international gourmet food and reasonably
priced wine and beer (the San Francisco branches are at 559 9th St. and 3 Masonic Ave.). **Seabreeze
Market** (585 University Ave., at the entrance to the Berkeley Marina, tel. 510/486–8119) sells fresh
shellfish, fruits, and vegetables, as well as sandwiches to go. **Whole Foods** (3000 Telegraph Ave., at
Ashby Ave., tel. 510/649–1333) is a health food supermarket with a deli, a bakery, an organic salad bar,
and even a massage chair.

The collectively owned **Cheese Board** (1504 Shattuck Ave., between Cedar and Vine Sts., tel. 510/549–
3183) has an incredible selection of cheeses and freshly baked breads. A few doors down, their offshoot
Cheese Board Pizza Collective (1512 Shattuck Ave., tel. 510/549–3055) has ridiculously short open
hours (Tues.–Thurs. 11:30–2, Mon. and Fri. 4:30–6:30, Sat. noon–3) but pizza that would wow the most
finicky of pizza connoisseurs. They make just one kind of vegetarian pizza each day, with toppings like
eggplant, red peppers, pesto, and feta cheese.

For freshly baked loaves, such as seeded baguettes or potato-rosemary bread, stop by the retail outlets
of **Semifreddi's** (372 Colusa Ave., Kensington, tel. 510/596–9935) and **Acme** (1601 San Pablo Ave., tel.
510/524–1327; 2730 9th St., tel. 510/843–2978). Both supply many Bay Area markets with fresh
bread daily.

OAKLAND

You'll find Southern-style barbecue shacks, El Salvadoran holes-in-the-wall, and plenty of other ethnic
eateries in Oakland. **Chinatown,** though less colorful than its counterpart across the bay, has increasing
numbers of Southeast Asian restaurants and markets alongside the older and more established Chinese
ones. You'll find them in the area bounded by 7th, 10th, Broadway, and Alice streets downtown. The
Fruitvale district, encompassing the neighborhoods around the Fruitvale BART station, has dozens of
cheap Mexican and Central American restaurants. It is safest, however, to restrict your visits here to
main streets and daylight hours. Join the young professionals on **College Avenue** or **Piedmont Avenue,**
where you'll find a wide selection of familiar delis, burger joints, gringo burrito shops, and upscale
bistros. From downtown Oakland take Bus 59 or 59A to Piedmont Avenue; for College Avenue take
BART to Rockridge.

UNDER $5

Taquería Morelia. Here are some of the best quesadillas around, complete with chopped tomatoes and
cilantro. Locals of all ages flow between the restaurant and the adjacent dive bar, Talk of the Town, while
carrying cheap beer and plastic baskets of tacos and burritos. *4491 E. 14th St., near High St., tel. 510/*
535–6030.

UNDER $10

Asmara Restaurant. Colorful baskets and rugs suspended from the ceiling cheer up the interior of this East African restaurant in north Oakland. Sample your choice of three meat or vegetarian items in the combination platter. In keeping with Ethiopian tradition, food is served family style with *injera* bread and a notable lack of utensils—wash your hands well before starting. *5020 Telegraph Ave., near 51st St., tel. 510/547–5100. No lunch Tues.*

Barney's Gourmet Hamburger. Sample one (or several) of 20 kinds of burgers, among them the Greek, Canadian, Russian, and Western—or load up on your spinach with the Popeye burger. For those who like their burgers meatless, there are tofu and garden burgers, too. *5819 College Ave., near Chabot Ave., tel. 510/601–0444; 4162 Piedmont Ave., Oakland, tel. 510/655–7180; 1591 Solano Ave., Albany, tel. 510/526–8185; 4138 24th St., between Castro and Diamond Sts., San Francisco, tel. 415/282–7770; 3344 Steiner St., at Lombard St., San Francisco, tel. 415/563–0307.*

Cactus Taquería. This festive cafeteria-style Mexican restaurant in Rockridge has a dizzying array of fillings for burritos, tacos, *tortas*, and quesadillas. Try the excellently spiced vegetables, shrimp, *carne asada*, red or green chicken *mole*, or anything else; you can't go wrong here. *5525 College Ave., tel. 510/547–1305; 1881 Solano Ave., Berkeley, tel. 510/528–1881.*

Chef Edwards Barbeque. The brisket and pork are cooked over mesquite and then tucked into a sandwich or eaten with a fork and knife. The ribs, smeared with a spicy red sauce, are soulful and filling, and the corn bread is divine. The place is no bigger than a shoe box, but its counter is a great place to eat the kind of barbecue that Southerners appreciate. Don't wait too long: the Chef closes at 6 PM on weekdays and 8 PM on weekends. *1998 San Pablo Ave., at Telegraph Ave., tel. 510/834–9516.*

Lois the Pie Queen. Despite the name, most people come here for breakfast rather than dessert. A family-run diner with vinyl swivel chairs, checkered tablecloths, and root beer floats, Lois has all the breakfast favorites as well as excellent burgers and fries. For traditionalists there's the two-egg breakfast with homemade biscuits and grits, or try the Reggie Jackson Special (pork chops, eggs, hash browns or grits, and coffee or tea). Don't forget the pies that made Lois a monarch. *851 60th St., at Adeline St., tel. 510/658–5616. Cash only. No dinner.*

Los Cocos. Fruitvale's best (not to mention only) El Salvadoran restaurant is famous for its fried bananas and pupusas. It may not look like much from the outside (or the inside), but the food is excellent and cheap. *1449 Fruitvale Ave., at 14th St., tel. 510/536–3079. Closed Mon.*

Mama's Royal Café. Although you can get lunch here after 11:30, breakfast is the reason to come: It's served until closing. More than two dozen different omelets all come with home-style potatoes, fruit, and a muffin. On weekend mornings, bring the paper and be prepared for a wait. *4012 Broadway, at 40th St., tel. 510/547–7600. Cash only. No dinner.*

Mexicali Rose. The massive portions at this lively place are served on sizzling hot platters (not plates—*platters*). The bilingual menu is heavy on meat dishes, though there are some vegetarian items. Two people could easily split the Mexicali Rose combo ($9.95): taco, stuffed chili pepper, green enchilada, guacamole salad, rice, beans, and a drink (whew!). Right across from the Oakland jail, Mexicali serves regular patrons that include both recently released jailbirds and their arresting officers. *701 Clay St., at 7th St., tel. 510/451–2450. 6 blocks southwest of 12th St. BART.*

Nan Yang. Step into this airy restaurant in Rockridge for delicious Burmese food. Especially tasty dishes are the ginger salad, garlic noodles with spring or curry vegetables, and curried tofu with shrimp. Service is friendly, and there is an extensive vegetarian menu. *6048 College Ave., at Claremont Ave., tel. 510/655–3298. Closed Mon.*

Phở Lâm Viên. This Vietnamese restaurant in Oakland's Chinatown is worth a trip for those with a sense of culinary adventure. Ignore the piped-in Muzak and focus on pork with fish sauce, spicy lemongrass gluten, and all sorts of *phở* (noodle soups), *bún* (thin rice noodles), and rice dishes. This restaurant is the real McCoy. *930 Webster St., between 10th and 11th Sts., tel. 510/763–1484. Closed Tues.*

Vi's. Big bowls of rice noodle and beef soup, mainstays of the Vietnamese diet, are the most popular items at this Chinatown favorite, but five-spice chicken, deep-fried spring rolls filled with pork, noodles, and aromatic herbs, and lime-and-fish-sauce-spiked salads of shrimp and pork are also delicious. Rice plates and noodle concoctions are particularly sound pennywise choices. *724 Webster St., between 7th and 8th Sts., tel. 510/835–8375.*

Zachary's Chicago Pizza Inc. The stuffed pizza here comes surrounded by a wall of chewy crust and topped with a layer of oozing mozzarella and stewed tomatoes. A wildly popular stop for more than a dozen years, Zachary's typically has a line snaking around the corner, so be prepared to wait. At lunchtime get a slice to go. *5801 College Ave., tel. 510/655–6385; 1853 Solano Ave., Berkeley, tel. 510/525–5950.*

UNDER $15

Le Cheval I. This gleaming restaurant in downtown Oakland serves delicious Vietnamese food with a French twist. Try the exotically named firepot, with prawns, calamari, clams, fish balls, and vegetables. Singapore noodles, marinated beef, and a variety of fish dishes are generously proportioned and uniquely spiced. A recommended appetizer is the shrimp or tofu imperial rolls served with an addictive peanut sauce. *1007 Clay St., at 10th St., tel. 510/763–8957; Kaiser Center, 344 20th St., tel. 510/763–8953. No lunch Sun. at Clay St.; no dinner weekends at Kaiser.*

UNDER $20

Bay Wolf. At this elegant Oakland outpost you can sample Californian cuisine at its finest: grilled duck with ginger-peach chutney, for example, or smoked trout salad with arugula, pickled beets, and dill crème fraîche. The seasonal menu mixes Provençal, northern Italian, and Californian influences. When it's warm enough, you can dine on the outdoor patio. *3853 Piedmont Ave., between 40th St. and MacArthur Blvd., tel. 510/655–6004. No lunch weekends.*

Kincaid's Bayhouse. On the waterfront at Jack London Square, this spiffy restaurant spit-roasts, sear-grills, and hardwood-broils steaks and seafood. Savor the renowned crab cakes or the Fireworks, prawns with a spicy tartar sauce. During happy hour (weekdays 4:30–6:30) you can hang out at the bar watching sailboats breeze into the harbor. *1 Franklin St., in Jack London Sq., tel. 510/835–8600.*

Oliveto's. This upstairs dining room houses the most celebrated restaurant in Oakland, but watch yourself, or you'll need a bank loan to cover the bill. Everything that chef Paul Bertolli creates is lovely, from a perfectly grilled quail resting atop a bed of tender, young salad greens to a plate of heirloom tomatoes to skate wings drizzled with brown butter. For a more casual taste of Oliveto's, take a table downstairs in the café and enjoy some simpler, less costly fare. *5655 College Ave., at Shafter St., tel. 510/547–5356. No lunch Sat. and Sun.*

MARKETS AND SPECIALTY STORES

In Oakland's Rockridge District, **Market Hall** (5565 College Ave., at Shafer St.) is a one-stop gourmet haven. Sip a nonfat decaf mocha from **Peaberry's Coffee and Tea** between bites of delicious pastry from **Grace Bakery.** Sample free olives and cheese at the **Pasta Shop.** With meat, poultry, fish, and fine wine from **Enzo's,** you can make your own feast.

Downtown Oakland has a huge variety of ethnic markets. Look for Chinese and Southeast Asian groceries in Chinatown. On the other side of Broadway, **Mi Rancho Tortilla Factory** (464 7th St., at Broadway, tel. 510/451–2393) sells the fixings for burritos and tacos. **Housewives Marketplace** (9th and Clay Sts., tel. 510/444–4396) is a warehouse full of specialty stands with a Southern flair. Here locals stock up on fresh produce and smoked meats such as ham hocks, as well as dry goods such as beans, roasted peanuts, and mix for Cajun jambalaya. **G. B. Ratto & Company** (821 Washington St., between 8th and 9th Sts., tel. 510/832–6503) is your source for delicacies like buffalo-milk mozzarella, many varieties of olive oil, and salted anchovies. They also prepare sandwiches (about $4) and have everything you need for a gourmet picnic.

MARIN COUNTY

In this land of the rich and established, you'll have to look hard for budget eats. If you're not in the mood to splurge, your best bet is to pack a picnic and dine in the open, far from the din of well-heeled civilization. For Marin County picnic supplies, and for restaurants on the Marin coast, including Muir Woods and Mt. Tamalpais, Stinson Beach, Bolinas, and Point Reyes, *see* Marin County *in* Chapter 2.

SAUSALITO

Restaurants and cafés line **Bridgeway,** Sausalito's main street, but they're generally overpriced and crowded with sightseers. Expect to pay at least $15–$20 for seafood on the waterfront. If you head one block inland to **Caledonia Street,** you'll find much better bargains and a calmer atmosphere. The grassy areas between Bridgeway and the bay make nice picnic spots.

UNDER $10

Hamburgers. If you're lucky enough to see a few locals in Sausalito, it'll be in the line outside this hole-in-the-wall. As the name suggests, all they do here are a few variations on the hamburger-and-fries theme. Most people take their food to one of the benches in the park rather than eat in the steamy restaurant. If neither option appeals, head to Paterson's Bar next door, where they'll serve you the same burger for about a buck more. *737 Bridgeway, tel. 415/332–9471. No dinner.*

Lighthouse Coffee Shop. Beginning at the crack of dawn, this no-frills eatery serves huge fruit pancakes and other breakfast and lunch specials. Hearty Danish food is the specialty: Try the meatballs with potato salad or the Copenhagen burger with horseradish, pickles, capers, onion, and egg yolk. *1311 Bridgeway, tel. 415/331–3034. No dinner.*

UNDER $15

Arawan. Once you've eaten at this unremarkable-looking place, you'll see why loyal Thai-food devotees patronize it regularly. Though the lunch specials are standard, the kitchen pulls out all the stops at dinner, with such savory plates as squid fried with garlic and pepper and chicken with basil leaves and chili. *47 Caledonia St., 1 block inland from Bridgeway, tel. 415/332–0882. No lunch weekends.*

After dark a rowdy over-30 crowd congregates at Sausalito's No Name Bar (757 Bridgeway, tel. 415/332–1392) to enjoy free live jazz, blues, or Dixieland music Wednesday–Sunday.

TIBURON

With some exceptions, Tiburon's restaurants—found mostly on **Main Street**—are more notable for their views than for their food. Most have decks hanging out over the bay, but you'll pay for the privilege of gazing at the San Francisco skyline or at Angel Island. If you're short on cash, pack a picnic, take a ferry over from San Francisco (*see* Ferry Travel *in* Chapter 1), and eat on the grass at the tip of the peninsula.

UNDER $10

Sweden House Café. The Swedish chef at this Tiburon café serves up fresh and unusual breakfast and lunch specials on a peaceful wooden deck jutting out over the water. Regulars order the Swedish pancakes with lingonberries and sour cream. For lunch there are salads and open-faced sandwiches—and decadent desserts. *35 Main St., tel. 415/435–9767. No dinner.*

UNDER $15

Sam's Anchor Café. One of the cheaper waterfront restaurants, Sam's is known across the Bay as *the* place to hang out on the deck sipping Famous Ramos gin fizzes and Bloody Marys. Even on wet and windy days, diehards and docked yachters take brunch (served on weekends until 2 PM) or dinner outside. Hearty breakfast dishes include the Hangtown Fry omelet, with oysters, bacon, scallions, and cheese. *27 Main St., tel. 415/435–4527.*

UNDER $20

Guaymas. Next to the Tiburon ferry landing you'll find some of the best, most innovative Mexican food in the Bay Area. After polishing off a basket of steaming, fresh corn tortillas and three salsas, you could easily make a meal of appetizers—*chalupas* (tortilla pockets with chicken breast, cheese, and jalapeños) and *cazuelitas* (potato and corn tortillas with baked zucchini and cheese)—but entrées are equally tempting. Sit outside on the heated deck or enjoy the colorful adobe-style dining room. *5 Main St., tel. 415/435–6300.*

MILL VALLEY

You'll pass through Mill Valley on your way to Muir Woods, Mt. Tamalpais, Stinson Beach, or Point Reyes. If you're eager to push on to the coast, grab a quick slice at **Stefano's Pizza** (8 E. Blithedale Ave., at Throckmorton Ave., tel. 415/383–9666).

UNDER $10

Joe's Taco Lounge. The colorful walls lined with hot-sauce bottles and religious memorabilia from Mexico make for a festive dining atmosphere at Joe's. Settle in with the locals to enjoy excellent burritos, both meat and vegetarian, pasilla peppers stuffed with corn bread and cheese, or a pair of fish tacos. *382 Miller Ave., at La Goma Ave., tel. 415/383–8164.*

Mama's Royal Café. Full of thrift-store artifacts, board games, and psychedelic murals, this funky café serves unbeatable huevos rancheros and omelets, as well as various lunch and dinner items. You can grab a board game and play a round of Battleship while you wait for your food to arrive. There's live rock and jazz Tuesday through Saturday 6 PM–10 PM. *393 Miller Ave., at La Goma Ave., tel. 415/388–3261.*

SAN RAFAEL

Compared to most of Marin County, San Rafael has a down-to-earth restaurant scene, with lots of cafés, Mexican joints, and other ethnic eateries lining **4th Street** downtown.

UNDER $10

Royal Thai. You'd hardly expect to find great Thai food in a leafy courtyard called the French Quarter in San Rafael. Nonetheless, Bay Area folks rave about this restaurant, started by a couple who defected from the kitchen of a popular San Francisco Thai restaurant. The friendly staff serves no-frills seafood and curry dishes and a terrific pad Thai in a restored Victorian house. *610 3rd St., between Hetherton and Irwin Sts., tel. 415/485–1074. No lunch weekends.*

San Rafael Station Café. This breakfast and lunch spot has a neighborhood feel—pictures of people's pooches line the mirror behind the counter, and locals hang out on weekends reading the paper and ingesting phenomenal amounts of cholesterol. There are omelets of every persuasion and a variety of sandwiches. *1013 B St., between 4th and 5th Sts., tel. 415/456–0191. No dinner.*

UNDER $20

Kasbah. Moroccan food is an aromatic array of seductive dishes, and the chef at Kasbah is an expert at producing them. Main dishes include lovely lamb and rabbit *tagines* (braises) and tender lamb kabobs served with couscous. A fragrant lentil soup, an assortment of five salads accompanied with chewy Moroccan bread, and *bastilla*, chicken, nuts, and eggs tucked into a phyllo package, precede the main courses, and a sweet mint tea and house-baked cookies follow them. Alas, the full dinner comes in at slightly over $20, but the value makes its inclusion here a must. *200 Merrydale Rd., at Willow Rd., tel. 415/472–6666. Closed Mon. No lunch.*

SOUTH BAY

PALO ALTO

Running west from U.S. 101 into the Stanford University campus is University Avenue, packed with California-casual restaurants, most with mediocre food. At **Mr. Chau** (3781 El Camino Real, at Curtner Ave., tel. 650/856–8938), open daily until 9, $4 goes a long way for buffet-style Chinese food. Another option is California Avenue, east of Stanford, where you'll find **Printer's Inc.** (310 California Ave., at Birch St., tel. 650/327–6500) a café-bookstore serving sandwiches and salads for less than $8.

UNDER $10

Jing Jing. This popular Chinese restaurant near the Stanford campus is *the* place for spicy food. Lunchtime brings a steady stream of students and professors for the $5–$6 lunch specials (11:30–2)—expect a wait. *443 Emerson St., off University Ave., tel. 650/328–6885.*

Mango Café. Come to this splashy neo-Jamaican outpost for Caribbean dishes such as hot curried goat with vegetables or jerk joints—a spicy chicken dish. Fruit-juice smoothies, served in glasses the size of fishbowls, come in a wide range of exotic flavors. *435 Hamilton Ave., at Cowper St., tel. 650/325–3229. From U.S. 101, take University Ave. exit west (toward Stanford), left on Cowper St.*

Miyake. Despite the din of sake-drinking college students and waiters yelling greetings to customers across the restaurant, you get surprisingly good sushi at a truly reasonable price—about $1–$2 per piece. For just a bit more you can order specialties like the *tazana* roll (yellowtail, wild carrots, sprouts, and flying fish roe). There's almost always a wait, so consider squeezing in at the sushi bar. *140 University Ave., tel. 650/323-9449.*

Oasis Beer Garden. This grubby but immensely popular college hangout near the Palo Alto–Menlo Park border serves tasty burgers and sandwiches; vegetarians will have to stick to pizza. You can play pinball, watch sports on TV, or soak up sun at one of the outdoor tables. *241 El Camino Real, Menlo Park, tel. 650/326-8896. Just north of Stanford campus at Cambridge St.*

Peninsula Fountain & Grill. American comfort food and a homey atmosphere await you at this diner that opened in 1923. The decor looks much as you would imagine it did in that year: Red vinyl booths each have their own hat stands, and the black and white checkerboard flooring is polished like new. You can have favorites like turkey potpie, hamburgers, or baked macaroni and cheese, but this restaurant is best known for its fountain drinks made with ice cream from the nearby Peninsula Creamery. *566 Emerson St., at Hamilton Ave., tel. 650/323-3131. From University Ave. heading west, turn left on Emerson St.*

Zao Noodle Bar. As expected, noodles are the specialty in this modern skylit restaurant with bare concrete walls. They're prepared with a variety of Asian flavors in dishes like green curry-coconut prawns with ramen noodles and Vietnamese rice noodle salad with crunchy bean sprouts and soy-lime dressing, all arriving at your table in huge ceramic bowls. Lunch is always busy, but if you can't get a table try to grab a seat at the bar and watch the cooks transform the simple noodle into a flavorful work of art. *261 University Ave., at Ramona St., tel. 650/328-1988.*

UNDER $15

The Good Earth. Before wheat-grass blends and ginseng shots, there was the Good Earth, where generous portions of salads, sandwiches, and soups are served in a casual, down-to-earth atmosphere. Expect a wait on weekend mornings. *185 University Ave., tel. 650/321-9449.*

Nola. With its kitschy folk art, Mardi Gras beads, and outdoor courtyard festooned with strings of lights, this local hot spot could be mistaken for a restaurant in New Orleans—until you see all the Silicon Valley types crowded around the bar. Be prepared for the party atmosphere and fanciful dishes melding Cajun, Creole, Caribbean, and Southwest flavors, like jambalaya with voodoo rice, grilled jerk chicken skewers, and the more unusual bayou dumplings, made with alligator and crawfish. Top it off with a powerful New Orleans–style hurricane and pecan pie with boozy sauce for dessert. *535 Ramona St., at University Ave., tel. 650/328-2722.*

SAN JOSE

The Bay Area's biggest city has its fair share of good ethnic food—especially Vietnamese—though it's too far from San Francisco to warrant a special trip. (Chez Sovan is the one exception; *see below*). If you find yourself in San Jose and need a good, cheap meal, try **Taco Al Pastor** (400 S. Bascom Ave., at San Carlos St., tel. 408/275-1619), which has been serving excellent Mexican food for more than 15 years. You'll find the best grub in the downtown area between Santa Clara and San Salvador streets (which run east–west) and Almaden and 3rd streets (running north–south). The **Flying Pig Pub** (78 S. First St., between San Carlos and San Fernando Sts., tel. 408/298-6710) is recommended for its variety of finger foods (crab cakes and pig skins) and salads for under $7.

UNDER $5

Peggy Sue's. This '50s-style eatery filled with Elvis and Marilyn memorabilia has been serving burgers since 1958. You have 19 different hamburger or, in a concession to modern times, veggie burger options, from the classic cheeseburger to more creative choices like the Karate Burger, with mushrooms and teriyaki sauce. Don't forget fries and a milkshake. *29 N. San Pedro St., at Santa Clara St., tel. 408/298-6750*

UNDER $10

Aqui. Don't be deterred by Aqui's strip-mall exterior—the food is anything but ordinary Mexican. Tasty dishes include burritos with grilled ahi and wasabi vinaigrette, or teriyaki steak and grilled onions. The restaurant, located in San Jose's burgeoning Willow Glen neighborhood south of downtown, offers outdoor patio seating in the back. *1145 Lincoln Ave., at Willow St., tel. 408/995-0381. From downtown, head south on First St. and turn right on Willow St. for about 3 mi to Lincoln Ave.*

Chez Sovan. Carloads of Bay Area residents regularly make the 45-minute trek to San Jose for Chez Sovan's incredible Cambodian cuisine. The owners opened a second Chez Sovan just south of San Jose in Campbell, and now the original location serves lunch only. The food—including a selection of ginger-cooked meats and vegetables, coconut and leek soups, and other traditional Cambodian specials—is well worth the journey. *923 Oakland Rd., tel. 408/287–7619. 1 block north of Hedding, where 13th St. becomes Oakland Rd. Closed weekends. No dinner. Other location: 2425 S. Bascom Ave., Campbell, tel. 408/371–7711.*

White Lotus. This Southeast Asian–influenced vegetarian restaurant may be slightly worn in appearance, but the food is delicious. You can choose from familiar-sounding dishes like chow mein or spicy garlic eggplant, or opt for something more adventurous, like lotus root salad or "pork" (made from gluten) with lemongrass. Deserts like lychee fruit or steamed plantain with coconut milk are also interesting. *80 N. Market St., at E. Santa Clara St., tel. 408/977–0540.*

UNDER $15

Bella Mia. Locals love this restaurant for its elegant atmosphere—high ceilings and dark wood furnishings—and its tasty yet affordable Italian cuisine. The restaurant serves pastas like salmon ravioli and pasta carbonara, flatbread pizzas, and wood-grilled meats. The brick-walled outdoor patio, with its lush greenery, gurgling fountain, and outdoor heating, is pleasant year-round. Reservations are recommended. *58 S. First St., at San Fernando St., tel. 408/280–1993.*

REFERENCE LISTINGS
BY CUISINE

AMERICAN

Under $5

Ann's Soup Kitchen and Restaurant *(Berkeley)*

Café at the Main Library *(Civic Center)*

Café Intermezzo *(Berkeley)*

Moishe's Pippic *(Civic Center)*

New Dawn *(Mission)*

Noah's Bagels *(Berkeley)*

Peggy Sue's *(San Jose)*

Rosamunde *(The Haight)*

San Francisco Art Institute Café *(North Beach/Russian Hill)*

Specialty's *(Downtown)*

Tom Peasant Pies *(Castro/Noe Valley)*

Under $10

Bagdad Cafe *(Castro/Noe Valley)*

Bette's Oceanview Diner *(Berkeley)*

Brick Hut Café *(Berkeley)*

Buena Vista Café *(Fisherman's Wharf)*

Chef Edwards Barbeque *(Oakland)*

Chester's Café *(Berkeley)*

Crescent City Café *(The Haight)*

Eagle Café *(Fisherman's Wharf)*

Flying Pig Pub *(San Jose)*

Grubstake *(Civic Center)*

Homemade Café *(Berkeley)*

Kate's Kitchen *(The Haight)*

Lois the Pie Queen *(Oakland)*

Mama's Royal Café *(Mill Valley)*

Mama's Royal Café *(Oakland)*

Miss Millie's *(Castro/Noe Valley)*

Orphan Andy's *(Castro/Noe Valley)*

Patio Café *(Castro/Noe Valley)*

Peninsula Fountain & Grill *(Palo Alto)*

Pinecrest *(Downtown)*

Pork Store Café *(The Haight)*

Rick and Ann's *(Berkeley)*

San Rafael Station Café *(San Rafael)*

Saul's *(Berkeley)*

Spaghetti Western *(The Haight)*

Sparky's *(Castro/Noe Valley)*

Squat and Gobble Café *(The Haight)*

Under $15

Sam's Anchor Café *(Tiburon)*

The Good Earth *(Palo Alto)*

BURGERS

Under $5

Hot 'n' Hunky *(Castro/Noe Valley)*

Under $10

Barney's Gourmet Hamburger *(Oakland)*

Hamburger Mary's *(SoMa)*

Hamburgers *(Sausalito)*

Oasis Beer Garden *(Palo Alto)*

CALIFORNIA

Under $5

Juice Bar Collective *(Berkeley)*

Main Squeeze *(Civic Center)*

Under $10

Pluto's *(Marina)*

Under $20

Bay Wolf *(Oakland)*

Café at Chez Panisse *(Berkeley)*

Firefly *(Castro/Noe Valley)*

Lulu *(SoMa)*

2223 Market *(Castro)*

CHINESE

Under $5

Kowloon *(Chinatown)*

Lucky Creation *(Chinatown)*

Under $10

Jing Jing *(Palo Alto)*

House of Nanking *(Chinatown)*

Long Life Vegi House *(Berkeley)*

River Side Seafood Restaurant *(Richmond/Sunset)*

Silver *(Chinatown)*

Ton Kiang *(Richmond)*

Yuet Lee *(Chinatown)*

Under $15

R&G Lounge *(Chinatown)*

Yank Sing *(Downtown)*

ETHIOPIAN

Under $10

Asmara *(Oakland)*

Blue Nile *(Berkeley)*

Massawa *(The Haight)*

FRENCH

Under $5

Crêpes-a-Go-Go *(Berkeley)*

Under $15

Café Bastille *(Downtown)*

Café Claude *(Downtown)*

South Park Café *(SoMa)*

Ti Couz *(Mission)*

Under $20

Bay Wolf *(Oakland)*

INDIAN

Under $10

Ananda Fuara *(Civic Center)*

Breads of India *(Berkeley)*

Shalimar *(Downtown/Embarcadero)*

Under $15

Indian Oven *(The Haight)*

Pasand Madras Cuisine *(Berkeley)*

Scenic India *(Mission)*

ITALIAN

Under $10

Bocce Café *(North Beach/Russian Hill)*

Chow *(Castro/Noe Valley)*

Firewood Cafe *(Castro/Noe Valley)*

Fuzio *(Castro/Noe Valley)*

Il Pollaio *(North Beach/Russian Hill)*

L'Osteria del Forno *(North Beach/Russian Hill)*

Pasta Pomodoro *(Castro/Noe Valley)*

Rosti (Marina District/Cow Hollow)

Vicolo Pizzeria *(Civic Center)*

Under $15

Caffe Macaroni *(Downtown)*

Capp's Corner *(North Beach/Russian Hill)*

Il Fornaio *(Downtown)*

Ristorante Ideale *(North Beach/Russian Hill)*

Vineria *(Mission)*

Under $20

Mazzini *(Berkeley)*

Oliveto *(Oakland)*

Rose Pistola *(North Beach/Russian Hill)*

JAPANESE

Under $10

Isobune *(Japantown)*

Mifune *(Japantown)*

Miyake *(Palo Alto)*

No-Name (Nippon) Sushi *(Castro/Noe Valley)*

Under $15

Ebisu *(Richmond/Sunset)*

Izumiya *(Japantown)*

Sanppo *(Japantown)*

Under $20

Kirala *(Berkeley)*

MEDITERRANEAN AND MIDDLE EASTERN

Under $5

Bongo Burger *(Berkeley)*

Truly Mediterranean *(Mission)*

Under $10

Kan Zaman *(The Haight)*

La Méditerranée *(Castro/Noe Valley)*

Under $15

Amira *(Mission)*

Under $20

Zuni Café *(Civic Center)*

MEXICAN AND CENTRAL AMERICAN

Under $5

El Farolito *(Mission)*

Joe's Taco Lounge *(Mill Valley)*

El Toro *(Mission)*

El Trébol *(Mission)*

La Cumbre *(Mission)*

La Taquería *(Mission)*

Pancho Villa *(Mission)*

Taqueria El Balazo *(The Haight)*

Taquería Morelia *(Oakland)*

Under $10

Cactus Taquería *(Oakland)*

Juan's Place *(Berkeley)*

La Rondalla *(Mission)*

Los Cocos *(Oakland)*

Mexicali Rose *(Oakland)*

Nicaragua *(Mission)*

Panchita's *(Mission)*

Taco Al Pastor *(San Jose)*

Under $20

Guaymas *(Tiburon)*

PIZZA

Under $5

Blondie's *(Berkeley)*

Club Za Pizza *(SoMa)*

Golden Boy Pizza *(North Beach/Russian Hill)*

Marcello's *(Castro/Noe Valley)*

Stefano's Pizza *(Mill Valley)*

Under $10

North Beach Pizza *(North Beach/Russian Hill)*

Vicolo Pizzeria *(Civic Center)*

Zachary's Chicago Pizza Inc. *(Oakland)*

SEAFOOD

Under $10

River Side Seafood Restaurant *(Richmond/Sunset)*

Swan Oyster Depot *(Civic Center)*

Under $15

P.J.'s Oyster Bed *(Richmond/Sunset)*

R&G Lounge *(Chinatown)*

Under $20

Kincaid's Bayhouse *(Oakland)*

SPANISH AND CARIBBEAN

Under $10

Mango Café *(Palo Alto)*

Under $15

Cha Cha Cha *(The Haight)*

Esperpento *(Mission)*

Timo's *(Mission)*

Zarzuela *(North Beach/Russian Hill)*

THAI

Under $10

Berkeley Thai House *(Berkeley)*

Cha Am *(Berkeley)*

King of Thailand Noodle House *(Richmond/Sunset)*

Manora's Thai Cuisine *(SoMa)*

Racha Café *(Civic Center)*

Royal Thai *(San Rafael)*

Thep Phanom *(The Haight)*

Under $15
Arawan *(Sausalito)*
Thai House on Noe *(Castro/Noe Valley)*

VIETNAMESE AND CAMBODIAN
Under $5
Saigon Sandwiches *(Civic Center)*
Under $10
Chez Sovan *(San Jose)*
Cordon Bleu *(Civic Center)*
Golden Flower *(Chinatown)*
Phó' Lâm Viên *(Oakland)*
Vi's *(Oakland)*
Zao Noodle Bar *(Palo Alto)*
Under $15
Le Cheval I *(Oakland)*
Slanted Door *(Mission)*

OTHER
Under $10
Hahn's Hibachi *(Korean; Marina)*
Lighthouse Coffee Shop *(Danish; Sausalito)*
Mad Magda's Russian Tea Room & Mystic Cafe *(Russian; Civic Center)*
Nan Yang *(Burmese; Oakland)*
Sweden House Café *(Swedish; Tiburon)*
Under $15
Brother's Restaurant *(Korean; Richmond/Sunset)*
Suppenküche *(German; Civic Center)*
Tin-Pan *(Asian Noodles; Castro/Noe Valley)*
Under $20
Carta *(World Cuisine; Civic Center)*
Kasbah *(Moroccan; San Rafael)*

SPECIAL FEATURES

BREAKFAST/BRUNCH
Under $5
Ann's Soup Kitchen and Restaurant *(Berkeley)*
New Dawn *(Mission)*
Under $10
Bette's Oceanview Diner *(Berkeley)*
Brick Hut Café *(Berkeley)*
Chester's Café *(Berkeley)*
Crescent City Café *(The Haight)*
Homemade Café *(Berkeley)*
Kate's Kitchen *(The Haight)*
Lighthouse Coffee Shop *(Sausalito)*
Lois the Pie Queen *(Oakland)*
Mama's Royal Café *(Mill Valley)*
Mama's Royal Café *(Oakland)*
Miss Millie's *(Castro/Noe Valley)*
Patio Café *(Castro/Noe Valley)*
Peninsula Fountain & Grill *(Palo Alto)*
Pork Store Café *(The Haight)*
Rick and Ann's *(Berkeley)*
San Rafael Station Café *(San Rafael)*
Spaghetti Western *(The Haight)*
Squat and Gobble Café *(The Haight)*
Sweden House Café *(Tiburon)*
Under $15
Bella Mia *(San Jose)*
Sam's Anchor Café *(Tiburon)*
The Good Earth *(Palo Alto)*

DINNER AND ENTERTAINMENT
Under $5
Taqueria El Balazo *(The Haight)*

Under $10
Bocce Café *(North Beach/Russian Hill)*
Kan Zaman *(The Haight)*
La Rondalla *(Mission)*
Mama's Royal Café *(Mill Valley)*
Under $15
Amira *(Mission)*
Café Bastille *(Downtown)*
Café Claude *(Downtown)*
Pasand Madras Cuisine *(Berkeley)*

LATE-NIGHT EATS (AFTER 1 AM)
Under $5
Blondie's *(Berkeley)*
Club Za Pizza *(SoMa)*
El Farolito *(Mission)*
Hot 'n' Hunky *(Castro/Noe Valley)*
Marcello's *(Castro/Noe Valley)*
Under $10
Bagdad Cafe *(Castro/Noe Valley)*
Buena Vista Café *(Fisherman's Wharf)*
Grubstake *(Civic Center)*
Hamburger Mary's *(SoMa)*
Kan Zaman *(The Haight)*
King of Thailand Noodle House *(Richmond/Sunset)*
Mexicali Rose *(Oakland)*
North Beach Pizza *(North Beach/Russian Hill)*
Oasis Beer Garden *(Palo Alto)*
Orphan Andy's *(Castro/Noe Valley)*
Panchita's *(Mission)*
Pinecrest *(Downtown)*
La Rondalla *(Mission)*
Silver *(Chinatown)*
Sparky's *(Castro/Noe Valley)*

OUTDOOR EATING

Under $5

Juice Bar Collective *(Berkeley)*

La Taquería *(Mission)*

Under $10

Aqui *(San Jose)*

Berkeley Thai House *(Berkeley)*

Bocce Café *(North Beach/Russian Hill)*

Chester's Café *(Berkeley)*

Oasis Beer Garden *(Palo Alto)*

Sweden House Café *(Tiburon)*

Under $15

Bella Mia *(San Jose)*

Café Bastille *(Downtown)*

Café Claude *(Downtown)*

Nola *(Palo Alto)*

Sam's Anchor Café *(Tiburon)*

Under $20

Guaymas *(Tiburon)*

Bay Wolf *(Oakland)*

VEGETARIAN

Under $5

Cheese Board Pizza Collective *(Berkeley)*

Juice Bar Collective *(Berkeley)*

Kowloon *(Chinatown)*

Lucky Creation *(Chinatown)*

Main Squeeze *(Civic Center)*

Smart Alec's *(Berkeley)*

Under $10

Ananda Fuara *(Civic Center)*

Long Life Vegi House *(Berkeley)*

White Lotus *(San Jose)*

CAFÉ CULTURE

REVISED BY CHRIS BATY

O n Friday night Bay Area cafés are often as crowded as the local bars. More than mere filling stations, they are where locals come to meet friends, gossip, discuss Descartes, read pulp fiction, pen poetry, or polish dissertations. In particularly café-dependent societies like Berkeley and San Francisco, coffeehouses do more than just grind and brew coffee beans: Neighborhood artists display their works; bands ply their trade; and open-mike poetry readings take place nightly. For up-to-date information on what's happening, check the "Calendar" section of the *Bay Guardian* or any free weekly.

Though you'll find a few slick megachains like Starbucks and Pasqua, most Bay Area coffeehouses are either family-run or local chains with no more than three or four branches. They come in every style imaginable, and sampling the range is part of the fun: You can drink your morning cappuccino in a cubbyhole with elegant sofas and classical music; savor your noon espresso in a postmodern warehouse space where Armani-clad admen mingle with mangled bike messengers; and linger over a late-night latte in a pillow-strewn, tapestried setting resembling an Ottoman sultan's chamber. If you're looking for the company of students, politicos, or New Age prophets, head to Berkeley. Otherwise, your scene awaits somewhere in San Francisco. Cafés are generally open from 6 AM or 7 AM to 11 PM on weekdays and until midnight (sometimes later) on weekends.

SAN FRANCISCO

San Franciscans have long been believers in the connection between coffee and the arts. Early acolytes of this philosophy included beat poets Jack Kerouac and Allen Ginsberg, who held all manner of performances at Caffè Trieste (*see below*), in North Beach. It's still a popular place to grab a demitasse on a rainy day, especially if you have someone with whom you can hold hands under the table. Postmodern hipsters will feel more comfortable in the cafés in the Mission or the Haight.

CASTRO DISTRICT

Café Flore. Flore is one of the Castro's premier gay gathering spots for pseudoartists, political activists, and trendy boys in black turtlenecks. If the outside seats are full, strike a pose until someone makes room—sharing tables is de rigueur. Expect plenty of noise, action, and, in the midst of it all, an incredibly attractive someone looking furtively your way. Preferred reading material: Jean Genet (just pretend to read). *2298 Market St., at Noe St., tel. 415/621–8579.*

WOULD YOU LIKE COFFEE WITH THAT?

Beyond the basic drinks like espresso, cappuccino, latte, and mocha, some café menus list a half dozen or more caffeine concoctions. Figuring out how to order can be tough: Gone are the days of small, medium, and large. Instead, you must decide between a single or double (bonus points for ordering a doppio) in sizes short, tall, or grande and with wet or dry foam. Occasionally, cafés adopt an absurdist mix-and-match attitude. If you are asked, "Would you like the doppio in a grande cup with dry foam?" you have our permission to move to a different venue.

Cup-a-Joe. This funky place with maroon walls has all the ingredients of a successful café: a mean cup o' joe, tasty pastries, and an art-student clientele. They occasionally hold spoken-word performances; call for details. *3801 17th St., at Sanchez St., tel. 415/487–1661.*

Jumpin' Java. Escape the see-and-be-seen chaos of Castro cafés in the quiet, tree-lined neighborhood of Duboce Triangle just outside the thick of things in the Castro. Although the *Bay Guardian* has deemed this "the best place to cruise nerdy gay guys," you'll also find a mix of students and gay and straight couples. *139 Noe St., between Henry and 14th Sts., tel. 415/431–5282.*

Morning Due. On the border between the Castro and Mission districts is a refreshingly airy, well-lighted café with a good selection of light meals and snacks. The studious crowds and mellow world-beat music make it a good place to enjoy a novel; they'll even sell you a book from their shelves. Aspiring poets and folk musicians show up for an occasional open-mike Saturday night. *3698 17th St., at Church St., tel. 415/621–7156.*

Pasqua Coffee. The friendly crowd at the Castro branch of this normally impersonal local chain sets it apart from all the rest. Toned, tanned locals come for the excellent scones and coffee and stay for the stylish social scene. *4094 18th St., at Castro St., tel. 415/626–6263.*

CIVIC CENTER/HAYES VALLEY

Mad Magda's Russian Tea Room and Café. Magda's has an otherworldly feel, a bit like the Mad Hatter's tea party in *Alice in Wonderland*: There are deep blue ceilings, red walls, and a "magic" garden in back. For $13 you can get an expert palm, aura, or Tarot card reading (Mon. and Tues. 1 PM–9 PM, Wed.–Sat. 1 PM–midnight, and Sun. until 7 PM). Preferred reading material: tea leaves. *579 Hayes St., between Octavia and Laguna Sts., tel. 415/864–7654.*

Momi Toby's Revolution Café. A Sunday-morning hangout for Hayes Valley locals, Momi Toby's encourages artistic expression by providing sketchbooks, crayons, and a working piano. Prefer to read quietly? You'll find quality literature shelved next to the counter. Beer, wine, and appealing snacks like tuna melts and Brie baguettes are on the menu. There's live music on some weekends. *528 Laguna St., between Hayes and Fell Sts., tel. 415/626–1508.*

DOWNTOWN

Cafe de la Presse. This café, near the German and French cultural centers, has a French-speaking staff and stacks of *Le Monde* (among other European newspapers) at the counter. You can enjoy your espresso outdoors under sidewalk umbrellas, but the Parisian fantasy ends there: One look at the snarl of traffic from Bush Street to the Chinatown Gate will remind you this is a West Coast metropolis. *352 Grant Ave., at Bush St., tel. 415/398–2680.*

Yakety Yak. The bright facade of this mellow coffeehouse makes a rebellious contrast to its gray surroundings. Portfolio-toting artists from the nearby Academy of Arts come here for a caffeine fix, a huge selection of fresh pastries, and a fast Internet connection. Open-mike poetry readings are held on Friday night 7–9. *679 Sutter St., at Taylor St., tel. 415/885–6908.*

HAIGHT-ASHBURY AND WESTERN ADDITION

Bean There. Set foot inside this airy, high-ceiling space, and you'll forget you're one block from grimy Lower Haight. Play a game of chess, have a snack, and sip your Caffè Duboce (latte with a dash of almond, caramel, or vanilla), the house specialty. On weekends neighbors laze at sidewalk tables with the Sunday crossword and the family dog. On weekday mornings locals line up for excellent organic coffees (sold by the pound). *201 Steiner St., at Waller St., tel. 415/255–8855.*

The Horse Shoe. For disaffected youths with tattoos, pierced body parts, and time on their hands, this is the place. Regulars come to play chess, shout over cranked-up music, or peruse the millions of posted flyers seeking band members or advertising obscure artistic events. *566 Haight St., between Steiner and Fillmore Sts., tel. 415/626–8852.*

Jammin' Java. This sunny, neighborly café one block south of frenetic Haight Street serves terrific, strong coffee drinks, decent snacks, and so-so desserts. The indoor and outdoor tables are populated day and night, and background music ranges from big band to hip-hop. *701 Cole St., at Waller St., tel. 415/668–5282.*

MISSION DISTRICT

Proper café etiquette includes busing your own table and tipping the counterperson.

Café Istanbul. The Syrian owner of this unique café serves authentic and delicious Middle Eastern food and beverages in an exotic tapestried setting. The floor is festooned with pillows, and intricately scrolled gold-color trays function as tabletops. Take off your shoes and settle down with some dolmas (stuffed grape leaves), baklava (pastry with honey and nuts), or cardamom-spiked Turkish coffee. *525 Valencia St., between 16th and 17th Sts., tel. 415/863–8854.*

Cafe Macondo. The Macondo proves that even in the trendiest part of the Mission, the down-to-earth, neighborly coffeehouse lives on. The walls are plastered with revolutionary posters from all over Latin America, and a mix of students, intellectuals, and revolutionaries sits at the heavy wooden tables to read, study, or talk politics over steamy cups of *café. 3159 16th St., between Valencia and Guerrero Sts., no phone.*

La Bohème. This Mission District institution draws a multiracial clientele that feasts on a variety of deli-style American, Greek, and Middle Eastern sandwiches. Weekend nights occasionally bring live guitar music. *3318 24th St., at Mission St., tel. 415/643–0481.*

Mission Grounds. Even though this place is near the popular Kilowatt club (*see* Live Music *in* Chapter 6) and other outposts of Mission nightlife, it isn't an evening café; come nightfall, it's just you and the dust bunnies. Crêpes and omelets are served all day. *3170 16th St., between Valencia and Guerrero Sts., tel. 415/621–1539.*

Radio Valencia. This friendly place is all about music, from the vintage instruments on the walls to the carefully chosen tunes playing over the speakers. The owner used to work in radio, and now he (and other staff members) draws up a fresh play list daily, displayed in a "menu" on each table. Come in for live bluegrass and swing Friday through Sunday nights. Besides coffee, there are a dozen or so microbrews on tap and excellent focaccia sandwiches and pizzas. *1199 Valencia St., at 23rd St., tel. 415/826–1199.*

Red Dora's Bearded Lady. A self-proclaimed "dyke café (everybody welcome)," this small coffeehouse is an outlet for San Francisco's young, energetic gay culture. Especially in the afternoon and on weekends the pierced-but-unpretentious come to lounge on mismatched furniture or in the lovely backyard garden. Dora's serves the usual café eats plus a tasty breakfast burrito and a tofu burger. Spoken-word and musical performances take place some Friday and Saturday at 8 PM after the café closes; call ahead to confirm. *485 14th St., at Guerrero St., tel. 415/626–2805.*

NORTH BEACH

Caffè Greco. A European crowd fills this airy, bustling, comfortable café, whose windows overlook Columbus Avenue, providing grand people-watching opportunities. Rich Italian espresso accompanies a variety of music—from Edith Piaf to Italian pop. You'll find a colorful selection of desserts; regulars worship the decadent tiramisu. *423 Columbus Ave., between Vallejo and Green Sts., tel. 415/397–6261.*

Caffè Trieste. This is the legendary home of the beat generation, where Kerouac and friends oozed cool from every pore. And it hasn't changed a bit since—including the '50s jukebox, which spouts opera.

OVERCAFFEINATED ON THE INFORMATION SUPERHIGHWAY

Leave your laptop at home? You can check your E-mail and surf the Web at several cafés around the city. Rates are usually steep (expect to pay $10 an hour), but that triple vanilla latte you just downed will probably help things go faster. You'll find Internet access at Yakety Yak (see Downtown), Muddy's (1304 Valencia St., at 24th St., Mission District, tel. 415/647–7994), Muddy Waters (521 Valencia St., near 16th St., Mission District, tel. 415/863–8006), Seattle St. Coffee (456 Geary St., near Mason St., Union Square, tel. 415/922–4566), and The Coffeenet (744 Harrison, near 3rd St., SoMa, tel. 415/495–7477).

Saturday afternoon at 2, local Italian performers serenade guests with sentimental Italian tunes accompanied by a live mini-orchestra. *601 Vallejo St., at Grant Ave., tel. 415/392–6739.*

Mario's Bohemian Cigar Store and Café. For more than 50 years this old-fashioned Italian café has been serving espresso, beer, and of course a nice Chianti—the perfect accompaniment to homemade focaccia sandwiches and Neapolitan pizza. Views of Washington Square Park and the Church of Saints Peter and Paul enhance the Florentine mood. *566 Columbus Ave., at Union St., tel. 415/362–0536.*

North End Café. The young and the restless congregate here over massive bowl-size cups of strong coffee. Beware: One cup will render you giddy, two will leave you babbling incessantly. If that's not enough of a stimulant for you, the sheer number of beautiful people should give you a wake-up jolt. *1402 Grant Ave., at Green St., tel. 415/956–3350.*

Steps of Rome. Well-dressed—correction, make that *very* well dressed—young urbanites crowd this large, bright café. The music is loud, the conversation (ranging from intellectual banter to cheesy come-ons) louder, and the waiters might make a pass at your girlfriend or break into spontaneous song. *348 Columbus Ave., near Grant Ave., tel. 415/397–0435.*

SOUTH OF MARKET

Brain Wash Café and Laundromat. Where else can you drink beer, listen to live music, play pinball, and wash your clothes, all at the same time? The decor is hip and Jetsons-like, making it fun to come here, even sans dirty socks, for a two-egg breakfast, or just to sip coffee and stare through big windows at lonely warehouse-lined Folsom Street. There is live music (from acoustic to punk) Tuesday–Saturday at 10 PM, no cover. *1122 Folsom St., between 7th and 8th Sts., tel. 415/861–3663 or 415/431–9274.*

Café Natoma. In the shadow of the Museum of Modern Art and the impressive 1925 Pacific Telephone and Telegraph office tower, this place draws lunchtime museum goers and office workers (it closes daily at 4). Sandwiches are named after SoMa streets and alleys: Try the Natoma Street Original (smoked ham) or the Yerba Buena (veggie). *145 Natoma St., at New Montgomery St., tel. 415/495–3289.*

Caffè Centro. Young graphic artists, designers, computer programmers, and other denizens of "multimedia gulch" snag the sidewalk tables of this café overlooking South Park—a beautiful patch of green surrounded by trophy homes. It's most popular at lunchtime (it closes at 6:30 during the week, 4 on weekends). Preferred reading material: *Wired* magazine. *102 South Park Ave., between 2nd and 3rd and Bryant and Brannan Sts., tel. 415/882–1500.*

Mr. Ralph's. At this offbeat coffeehouse in a bright green tiled building you can unwind with a mellow, artsy professional crowd after cultural overload at the MOMA. Happy hour (weekdays 4:30–6:30) brings $2.50 pints (of beer, that is); Friday evening there's free live jazz. *90 Natoma St., between 1st and 2nd Sts., tel. 415/243–9330.*

OUTLYING NEIGHBORHOODS

Even beyond the parts of the city where espresso bars run two to a block, there are still places to get your caffeine fix in almost every neighborhood.

Blue Danube. Bring your purchases from nearby Green Apple Books and Music (*see* Chapter 3) and enjoy an afternoon in the Richmond District with college students, resident youth, and thirtysomethings who still remember how to relax. On sunny days the wide-open windows are perfect for people-watching. *306 Clement St., between 4th and 5th Aves., tel. 415/221–9041.*

Cool Beans. Like the bar on *Cheers,* this brightly painted Inner Richmond café is a home away from home. Owners Sam and Henry—one of whom is usually behind the bar—will learn your name by your second visit, and it's easy to make the acquaintance of the locals who spend many of their daylight hours here. They also serve homemade soups and great sandwiches. *4342 California St., at 6th Ave., tel. 415/750–1955.*

Farley's. You'll find all the classic features of a good café at this Potrero Hill favorite: strong coffee, plenty of sidewalk tables, and paintings on the walls by neighborhood artists. And they offer a few bonuses, like a stack of board games, a magazine rack with more than 200 titles, and occasional music nights. *1315 18th St., between Texas and Missouri Sts., tel. 415/648–1545.*

Java Beach. What do surfers at Ocean Beach do when the waves are blown out? They go to Java Beach, the only decent café in the Outer Sunset, to swap tales of conquered swells. Nonsurfers come to read, chat, study, or catch some of the occasional live music. *1396 La Playa St., at Judah St., tel. 415/665–5282.*

Royal Ground Coffee. Patrons here (mostly families and twentysomethings) insist on calling this neighborhood Lower Pacific Heights to distinguish it from the seedy stretch of Fillmore south of Geary. Wherever it is, it's a terrific place to stop and refuel after exploring Japantown or Fillmore Street. *2060 Fillmore St., at California St., tel. 415/567–8822.*

Tart to Tart. The friendly owners of Tart to Tart whip up a mean cup of coffee and plenty of excellent desserts and sandwiches for Inner Sunset locals and UCSF medical students. *641 Irving St., between 7th and 8th Aves., tel. 415/753–0643.*

EAST BAY

The "People's Republic of Berkeley" would collapse without cafés. Students would have nowhere to be seen while "studying"; skate punks would have nowhere to hang while cutting class; artists and poets would have no place to share their angst. Around **Telegraph Avenue** south of campus and **Euclid Avenue** north of campus you'll find cafés crowded day and night with students; the crowds downtown and on **College Avenue** are more mixed. Oakland isn't exactly a latte town, but locals do gather at the cafés in the **Rockridge, Piedmont Avenue,** and **Grand Lake** areas, especially on sunny weekends. Smokers should take note: In 1994 Berkeley banned smoking in all indoor *and* outdoor cafés.

BERKELEY

Au Coquelet Café and Restaurant. There *is* life in Berkeley after midnight, and you'll find it here, a couple doors down from the UC Theatre (*see* Chapter 6). Au Coquelet stays packed late into the night with hungry, caffeine-craving moviegoers and students. Sunday is also busy; brunch is served weekends until 3 PM. *2000 University Ave., at Milvia St., tel. 510/845–0433.*

Café Fanny. Opened by Alice Waters, the chef-owner of famed Café at Chez Panisse (*see* Chapter 4), and named for her daughter Fanny, this west Berkeley café beckons yuppies of every generation to its trellised patio. The food is delicious though not cheap, and the portions are small—stick with buckwheat crêpes or cinnamon toast if money's tight. Come early: The café closes at 3 PM Sunday–Friday and Saturday at 4. *1603 San Pablo Ave., at Cedar St., tel. 510/524–5447.*

Caffè Strada. Strada's sprawling outdoor patio attracts a social mix of students and visiting foreigners (residents of International House, across the street). Relax in the sun with a newspaper or eavesdrop on your neighbors while sipping a Strada Bianca or a Strada Bianca Mocha—both are made with white chocolate, the house specialty. *2300 College Ave., at Bancroft Way, tel. 510/843–5282.*

Espresso Roma. Though it's in the sleepy Elmwood neighborhood, Roma is one of Berkeley's favorite late-night hangouts—the large café is always packed on weekends with locals from all walks of life. They serve a variety of beers and some overpriced salads and sandwiches. *2960 College Ave., at Ashby Ave., tel. 510/644-3773.*

Mediterraneum Caffè. The Med was featured in *The Graduate* and is a longtime hangout for Berkeley's resident thinkers, dreamers, and revolutionaries. There are reasonably priced sandwiches and pastas as well as the usual coffee drinks. *2475 Telegraph Ave., between Haste St. and Dwight Way, tel. 510/ 549-1128.*

Nefeli Caffè. This Greek coffeehouse in north Berkeley is popular with students and professors for its "secret recipe" Italian-roast coffee and an innovative, reasonably priced menu. Try their eggplant, roasted pepper, feta, and kalamata olive spread sandwiches, or sip a glass of retsina (Greek wine). *1854 Euclid Ave., at Hearst St., tel. 510/841-6374.*

Peet's Coffee & Tea. What is now a coffee empire began in the '60s with this single unassuming café. Peet's now distributes its roasts worldwide and has more than a dozen cafés in the Bay Area, providing superstrong blends to experienced coffee swillers. *2124 Vine St., at Walnut St., tel. 510/841-0564.*

Red Café. Redbrick walls, exposed beam ceilings, and a massive skylight create a mellow setting for an artsy, postgrad crowd. The full kitchen serves vegetarian sandwiches, salads, and pastas, and the café has a fine selection of beers. Though there's frequent live jazz, it's not a late-night hangout: Be prepared to clear out at 7 PM on weekdays, 5 PM Saturday. *1941 University Ave., at Bonita St., tel. 510/843-8607.*

OAKLAND

Gaylord's Café Espresso. If the Piedmont area has a central gathering spot, Gaylord's is it. Consistently named "Best Café in the East Bay" by the *East Bay Express,* Gaylords gets points for its lively space, late hours, and tasty ice cream. Word to the wise: Avoid their mediocre baked goods. *4150 Piedmont Ave., at 41st St., tel. 510/658-2877.*

Royal Coffee. Plentiful sidewalk seating and some of the strongest brew in the Bay Area draw locals to this understatedly hip Rockridge favorite. Rich with people-watching opportunities, Royal is a friendly place to while away an afternoon. Beans are sold here in bulk as well; if you like the strength of Peet's homebrew, try a pound of Royal's roast. *6255 College Ave., at 63rd St., tel. 510/653-5453.*

AFTER DARK 6

REVISED BY DENISE M. LETO, CHRIS BATY, AND LOTUS ABRAMS

T hough die-hard night owls may find the Bay Area's nightlife a bit on the tame side, most admit that what the area lacks in high-intensity late-night energy, it makes up for with its sheer variety of options. If you can't find your scene in one of the thousands of bars throughout the city and surroundings, you can see a movie classic in a funky theater, check out a live show at a local club, watch some unbridled genius at a performance space, or dance all night at an underground party.

In this chapter nightspots have been broken down into bars, live music, and clubs, but these distinctions are not hard and fast. More often than not, your favorite café will also serve beer, host a local band, and cater to groups of various sensibilities depending on the night. The city's live-and-let-live attitude extends to its nightlife, which means you can always find your niche in the local club scene. Check the free *SF Weekly* or *Bay Guardian* (both available at newsstands and cafés citywide), or the *SF Chronicle's* Sunday "Datebook" section for listings of current happenings after dark. The free weeklies *Bay Times* and *Bay Area Reporter* are good sources for gay and lesbian listings.

SAN FRANCISCO

BARS

CASTRO DISTRICT

This safe, very gay quarter of San Francisco hosts some of the wildest festivals in the city. You're far more likely to kindle a romance here if you're enamored of the same sex, but open-minded straight folks frequent a few of the less intense pickup bars after an evening at the grand old Castro Theatre (*see* Movie Houses, *below*). Bars in this neighborhood tend to get busy early: By 2 PM on Saturday many are already full of an intensely social crowd whiling away the afternoon.

Bar on Castro. With a newly redesigned, coolly industrial interior, the bar attracts a well-heeled, almost exclusively male clientele. Glass doors lend the front section an airy feel (or a strong similarity to Macy's show windows), while beautiful boys eye one another in the darker reaches toward the back. *456-B Castro St., between 17th and 18th Sts., tel. 415/626–7220.*

IMBIBING OUTSIDE

Most evenings in San Francisco are so cold and damp they'll leave you running for a fireplace and a hot toddy, but on those rare balmy days just begging for a bar with a patio, try the following spots.

In the otherwise sedate Noe Valley, the Rat and Raven (4054 24th St., tel. 415/285–0674) attracts a mostly postcollegiate crowd to its patio, which is open from noon to about 9. Zeitgeist (199 Valencia St., tel. 415/255–7505), probably the city's friendliest biker bar, has an outdoor patio where you can hear the traffic whizzing by. In Cole Valley try the locals' favorite, Finnegan's Wake (937 Cole St., tel. 415/731–6119). And if the young, black-clad crowd at Café du Nord is too trendy for you, head a few doors down to Lucky 13 (2140 Market St., tel. 415/487–1313), where a laid-back tattooed-and-pierced set drinks the many beers available on tap.

The Café. A longtime Castro anchor, this large, lively bar with mirrored walls and neon lights welcomes a large lesbian contingent, though you'll find plenty of men here as well. If there's no room on the dance floor, you can hang out on the balcony and watch the Castro strut by. *2367 Market St., near Castro St., tel. 415/861–3846.*

Cafe Flore. This bar/café's prime corner location and greenhouse feel make it a Castro favorite. A friendly mixed crowd sits inside at closely spaced tables, sipping beer or coffee from the counter. The glass-enclosed patio, popular on sunny days and the rare warm San Francisco evening, is one of the few in the city where smoking is allowed. *2298 Market St., at Noe St., tel. 415/621–8579.*

The Detour. Minimally decorated with a chain-link fence and pool table, this bar attracts a young, good-looking crowd on the prowl. Urgent techno music and Saturday-night go-go dancers set the racy mood. If you forget the address, listen for the music, since the black-on-black sign is impossible to see at night. *2348 Market St., between Castro and Noe Sts., tel. 415/861–6053.*

Harvey's. One of the Castro's most mixed crowds comes to Harvey's for its casual, no-pretense atmosphere, potent drinks, and prime corner location. Pull up a stool at one of the copper-topped window tables and watch the Castro parade by. A tribute on the wall honors the bar's namesake, Harvey Milk, San Francisco's first openly gay city supervisor, murdered (along with Mayor George Moscone) in 1978. *500 Castro St., at 18th St., tel. 415/431–4278.*

Midnight Sun. Two large video screens that show a mix of campy TV shows and current music videos help alleviate the need for conversation in this crowded, colorful bar. The thirtysomething crowd tends toward the clean-cut and upscale. *4067 18th St., near Castro St., tel. 415/861–4186.*

Orbit Room. The Orbit has a smart-looking high-ceiling drinking area with artsy, slightly uncomfortable bar stools and a mostly straight crowd. The subdued lighting, stucco walls, and innovative design scheme make you feel as if you're on display at some swank art gallery. Drinks of choice? Cocktails or espresso. *1900 Market St., at Laguna St., tel. 415/252–9525.*

Twin Peaks. David Lynch has nothing to do with this casual, loungelike gay bar; in fact, the Peaks has been around since the early eighties and proudly claims to have been the first gay bar in the city with clear—as in, not tinted—floor-to-ceiling windows. Twin Peaks enjoys its high visibility on the corner of Market and Castro; on weekends expect big crowds of both newcomers and an older, established clientele. *401 Castro St., at Market St., tel. 415/864–9470.*

CHINATOWN

By day a maelstrom of gaudy souvenir shops, pungent markets, and overcrowded sidewalks, Chinatown transforms into a quieter neighborhood at night, when most people on the streets are en route to or from one of the neighborhood's many Chinese restaurants. Step into one of the local bars for a reminder of whose part of town this is.

Li Po's. The dark, cavernous setting and incense-burning altar lend an oddly mystical feel to Li Po's. By 1 AM the coveted back booths are filled with boisterous escapees from the North Beach scene, who are almost daring enough to join in the occasional karaoke. *916 Grant Ave., between Jackson and Washington Sts., tel. 415/982–0072.*

Mr. Bing's. A heterogeneous mix of drinkers lines the narrow V-shape bar at this hangout on the edge of Chinatown. The scenery includes ubiquitous video poker machines and a jukebox that plays scratchy Sinatra tunes. *201 Columbus Ave., at Pacific Ave., tel. 415/362–1545.*

DOWNTOWN AND CIVIC CENTER AREA

Beware of this area after sundown: Prostitution and drug dealing are common on many corners—especially in the Tenderloin, which is loosely bordered by Larkin, O'Farrell, Mason, and Market streets. Nevertheless, there are a few bars worth braving if you have door-to-door transportation (when in doubt, call a cab).

Backflip. A mixed international crowd packs this chic bar, which manages to feel space-age and retro at the same time. Tucked into the Phoenix Hotel (*see* Chapter 7), the bar is in the middle of a small dance area that leads to a more spacious lounge section. Don't miss the glassed-in waterfall in the wall—one of many interesting touches in this surprisingly unpretentious spot. A cab is a wise choice in this part of the Tenderloin. *601 Eddy St., at Larkin St., tel. 415/771–3547.*

Edinburgh Castle. This diamond in the rough was established before the Tenderloin earned its reputation for squalor. A Scottish pub with a beautiful bar, it's a great place to play darts, make friends with thick-accented U.K. types, eat fish-and-chips, and down pints of Guinness or Bass—it also has the best single-malt collection in the Bay Area. Local bands make occasional appearances; if you're lucky, you might catch a reading by such authors as Patrick McCabe. *950 Geary St., between Polk and Larkin Sts., tel. 415/885–4074.*

Diva's. This Tenderloin landmark is the city's most popular transvestite haven, although there's no "dress" code posted at the door. The area is often dangerous and the crowd occasionally seedy, but the flamboyant patrons provide an energetic, entertaining night of thrills. Come for the free drag shows on Friday and Saturday nights—but please refrain from gawking. *1081 Post St., between Polk and Larkin Sts., tel. 415/928–6006.*

Place Pigalle. The vibes are hip and European (but definitely not pretentious) at this sleek, low-key, French-owned Hayes Valley wine bar and gallery space. Stop in for a glass of wine after work and stay for the evening; there's live jazz from Thursday through Saturday nights and occasional spoken-word performances during the week. *520 Hayes St., between Octavia and Laguna Sts., tel. 415/552–2671. Cover: up to $5.*

HAIGHT AND THE WESTERN ADDITION

Always hot on the heels of the latest trend, the Haight has some good bars that capitalize on the city's passion for retro cocktail emporiums. The neighborhood is especially popular with cocktail-quaffing consumers who have just loaded up on pricey flower-child togs, as well as a sprinkling of middle-aged hippies and slacker kids. When you want a watering hole that's slightly rougher around the edges, head for the Lower Haight, where you're likely to find local barflies in their twenties.

The Deluxe. The year is perpetually 1945 at this slick retro bar in the Upper Haight. Patrons enjoy donning their finest '40s duds (hairdos and shoes included), sipping martinis, and acting *very* cool. You'll usually find a crooner, complete with backup swing band, or at least owner Jay Johnson doing Sinatra his way. *1511 Haight St., between Ashbury and Clayton Sts., tel. 415/552–6949. Cover: $3–$5.*

Mad Dog in the Fog. This British-style pub in the heart of the Lower Haight is frequented by neighborhood folk in search of cold beer and televised rugby. For lukewarm rugby fans there are other diversions: a dartboard inside, a beer garden outside, and trivia competitions for beer and cash prizes on Monday and Thursday. Mornings there are greasy breakfasts like the Greedy Bastard (bacon, sausage, baked

Forget bars; for an hourly fee you can practice your bank shot at one of San Francisco's pool halls. At Hollywood Billiards (61 Golden Gate Ave., near Market St., tel. 415/252–9643), every Sunday you can play up to three hours for $6 an hour, but beware—it's not in the best neighborhood. At the upscale Chalkers (101 Spear St., at Mission St., tel. 415/512–0450), yuppies in business suits are the norm. The hall features 30 tables, a full bar, and a grill menu. Its rates are $10 an hour for two Monday through Thursday, $12 on Friday and Saturday, and $8 on Sunday.

beans, scrambled eggs, and tomato; $6.50)—and all dishes more than $6 include a free pint until 2:30 PM. *530 Haight St., between Fillmore and Steiner Sts., tel. 415/626–7279.*

Molotov. Young, tattooed, Lower Haight types come here to drink beer and play pool. Arrive early on weekends to snag the lone table, as the crowd can be fierce in the standing room. *582 Haight St., between Fillmore and Steiner Sts., tel. 415/558–8019.*

Murio's Trophy Room. Murio's, in the Upper Haight, is often overcrowded with bikers and Haight Street slackers, but it can be fun and low-key on weekdays. When the conversation lags, amuse yourself with the pool table, jukebox, and TV. *1811 Haight St., between Shrader and Stanyan Sts., tel. 415/752–2971.*

Noc Noc. Step inside this Lower Haight institution and you'll find yourself in a postmodern cave complete with chunky Flintstones-style furniture and a very eclectic music repertoire. Expect a healthy variety of beers and a couple kinds of wine including sake—but no hard liquor. *557 Haight St., between Fillmore and Steiner Sts., tel. 415/861–5811.*

The Toronado. A narrow, dark Lower Haight dive, the Toronado attracts a leather-clad set with one of the widest selections of microbrews in the city. The jukebox blares a refreshing mix of kitschy country and western in addition to the standard grunge anthems. *547 Haight St., between Fillmore and Steiner Sts., tel. 415/863–2276.*

MARINA DISTRICT/COW HOLLOW

The nightlife in this affluent neighborhood is typified by the bevy of bars in the Triangle, the intersection of Fillmore and Greenwich streets, which attract hordes of sporty young professionals. The crowds are clean-cut, and the neighborhood is one of the safest in the city.

Blue Light Cafe. If the modern industrial decor (including, of course, blue neon) doesn't seem like that of a sports bar, the TVs will eventually clue you in. Beloved by Marina and Cow Hollow singles, the Blue Light packs in the young and sporty every evening. *1979 Union St., at Buchanan St., tel. 415/922–5510.*

City Tavern. An elegantly casual thirtysomething crowd gathers around the oval-shape bar to enjoy expertly mixed drinks, the mellowing effect of incense, and music soft enough to allow for conversation. Warm-color walls and subdued light from blue lamps take the edge off the industrial cement floor, making this tavern, mainly a restaurant, a pleasant spot for a drink before a night on the town. *3200 Fillmore St., at Greenwich St., tel. 415/567–0918.*

Comet Club. Marina hipsters who don't feel like trekking to the Mission head into this cavelike bar. Kids in expensive leather jackets snuggle in the half-moon booths lining the wall across from the bar and listen to the throbbing sounds of soul, techno, and R&B. After 10 o'clock the small dance floor in the back starts jumping. *3111 Fillmore St., at Filbert St., tel. 415/567–5589.*

Union Ale House. Head downstairs into this friendly English-style pub and have a pint with Cow Hollow's postcollegiate crowd. Or make your way to a table in the large back room, where a tropically colored wall-sized mural counteracts the subterranean locale. Loud music and the popularity of this watering hole can make for a high-decibel experience on weekend evenings. *1980 Union St., between Buchanan and Laguna Sts., tel. 415/921–0300.*

MISSION DISTRICT

A young bohemian crowd dressed in fashionable black clothes and chunky platform shoes frequents the many bars, cafés, restaurants, and clubs in this hip neighborhood, which not so long ago had a shady reputation. The poorly lighted side streets are still dicey: If possible, stay on 16th or Valencia streets, where dense clusters of bars and restaurants make for heavy foot traffic.

The Albion. Elbow your way into this cramped bar and fight for a seat under the glow of pink neon lights. If you're left standing, you can always shoot some stick or edge your way closer to the occasional live music. *3139 16th St., between Valencia and Guerrero Sts., tel. 415/552–8558.*

Beauty Bar. This cramped New York import is themed to the gills. Designed to resemble a 1950s beauty salon, the bar features a row of salon seats with old-fashioned hood hair dryers, a manicurist on duty, and drinks with names like Prell (with creme de menthe). A funky see-and-be-seen crowd packs the bar and jockeys for space at one of three coveted tables. *2299 Mission St., at 19th St., tel. 415/285–0323.*

Dylan's. Welsh memorabilia decorate the walls of this Potrero Hill pub named after Wales's most famous poet. You may not understand the bartender's thick accent, but he'll understand you when you order a pint. Jazz music on Wednesday night draws a big crowd. *2301 Folsom St., at 19th St., tel. 415/641–1416.*

If you prefer cocktails to coffee with your sunrise, head to Vesuvio (see below) or Diva's (see above), which open at 6 AM, or the Peaks (1316 Castro St., near 24th St., tel. 415/826–0100), which opens at 8 AM for your drinking pleasure.

500 Club. Here's a little slice of Americana—complete with a huge neon martini sign, two cramped pool tables, and three comfy vinyl booths. The hard-drinking regulars are joined by younger patrons on weekends, when it's difficult to find a place to stand. *500 Guerrero St., at 17th St., tel. 415/861–2500.*

Hush Hush Lounge. This new dark lounge off the Mission's beaten track features red banquettes and booths and blue accents—check out the funky blue mural of the scantily dressed woman in the moon. Laid-back twenty- and thirtysomethings listen to hipster lounge-lizard tunes from the old-fashioned jukebox and play pool at the table in back. Even on a Saturday night, at least until word gets around, it's a good bet you'll get a seat. *496 14th St., at Guerrero St., tel. 415/241–9944.*

Lexington Club. Tucked on a quiet stretch of mostly residential 19th Street, the city's only seven-day-a-week lesbian bar is a supremely comfortable affair. The crowd, mostly women in their twenties and thirties (though men are made to feel welcome), lounges against dark red walls under provocative art. The well-scuffed, bare wooden floor attests to the popularity of this intimate space. *3464 19th St., at Lexington St., tel. 415/863–2052.*

The Liberties. One of the newest bar/restaurants on the Mission scene isn't quite of the scene. The simple, elegant decor and gorgeous dark-wood bar give this Irish pub a more upscale, grown-up feel than most in this hipster 'hood, offering respite to a crowd more mellow and older than the typical Mission-bar denizen. And unlike many other watering holes, it's busiest at dinner and in the early evening hours, then empties out as the night progresses. *998 Guerrero St., at 22nd St., tel. 415/282–6789.*

Lone Palm. Push open the huge black door, and you will enter a classy oasis. Dimly lighted tables, a retro '40s atmosphere, and skilled cocktail shakers behind the bar combine to make this an intimate setting in which to sip martinis with that special someone. *3394 22nd St., at Guerrero St., tel. 415/648–0109.*

Make Out Room. The dark, quiet street and beckoning marquee may have you convinced this is some shady strip joint. In fact, it's a perfectly reputable, popular bar with a spacious floor, which means you won't get jostled too unmercifully on crowded weekend nights. Expect to pay a cover for occasional live band performances. *3225 22nd St., between Mission and Valencia Sts., tel. 415/647–2888. Cover: $3–$7.*

McCarthy's. This large, brick-walled bar and restaurant reminiscent of a New England saloon attracts a boisterous postcollegiate crowd—you'll see more white button-downs than vintage black leather. Stairs lead from the back pool room up to tables perfect for a quiet(er) tête-à- tête. The menu, more than one step up from average pub grub, comes courtesy of the folks at the Haight's Caribbean tapas favorite, Cha Cha Cha (*see* Food chapter). *2327 Mission St., between 19th and 20th Sts., tel. 415/648–0504.*

The Rite Spot. The piano in the corner, candlelighted tables, and understated decor all lend a sense of timelessness to this outer Mission bar that's a favorite among locals. They also serve light meals, so you won't have to leave if you get the munchies. *2099 Folsom St., at 17th St., tel. 415/552–6066.*

The Uptown. Sit at the long oak bar and get rowdy with friendly barflies, grab a game of pool with neighborhood hipsters, or stand outside watching the sometimes sordid street life. Several well-worn couches in back make you feel right at home. *200 Capp St., at 17th St., tel. 415/861–8231.*

Zeitgeist. This is the original no-frills biker bar—albeit a bit trendier and friendlier—for every kind of biker. In the afternoon it fills with bike messengers relating the day's near encounters with the Big Grille in the Sky; by night BMW motorbikers clog the outdoor deck, waiting their turn at the lone pool table. *199 Valencia St., at Duboce Ave., tel. 415/255–7505.*

NOB HILL AND RUSSIAN HILL

Nob Hill's bars are mainly lounges in the luxury hotels that make this neighborhood famous; you'll have to dress up and pay a lot to enjoy the ambience. Russian Hill, on the other hand, is largely populated by the city's young, upwardly mobile professionals. This isn't the right place to look for casual dives, but you just might be able to find a financially solvent date in one of Russian Hill's singles bars.

Red Room. A trendy clubbing crowd frequents this lounge-y cocktail bar attached to the Commodore Hotel. Its impressive entrance opens to a curved wall of red bottles stacked to the ceiling and a shockingly red interior. Prepare to match wits against the top 10% of the social food chain. *827 Sutter St., at Jones St., tel. 415/346–7666.*

Tonga Room. Nostalgic for 1950s-style kitsch? Come to the Fairmont Hotel to sip on tropical drinks that are filled with paper umbrellas and Polynesian paraphernalia. Every 30 minutes or so, a simulated rainstorm blows through the bamboo-and-palm-filled room, and at 8 most nights an almost comically bad soft-rock band performs from a thatched hut in the middle of a lagoon. Even during happy hour (5–7) drinks cost $4–$6, and the greasy all-you-can-eat buffet is an additional $6—but where else will you find such Tiki treats? Enter the hotel on California Street between Mason and Powell streets and turn right down the first hall. *Fairmont Hotel, California and Mason Sts., tel. 415/772–5278.*

NORTH BEACH

North Beach is famous for its Italian restaurants, cafés, and tiny cobblestone alleys. Although it does have a small red-light district on Broadway, the generally civil crowd, which usually includes a number of out-of-towners, is more attracted to the bars, cafés, and jazz clubs that line Columbus and Grant avenues.

Blue Bar. Every night the strains of live jazz fill this tiny bar tucked below the trendy Black Cat restaurant. True to its name, the space is all blue, from the lighting to the '50s-style Formica tables. A laidback, broadly mixed crowd knows that this is an excellent choice for a lively evening away from the frenzy of some North Beach spots. *501 Broadway, at Kearny St., te. 415/981–2233.*

Hi-Ball Lounge. Found near the Wall-to-Wall Sex Parlor, this swank bar features some of its own red-light-district furnishings—leopard-skin drapery and red-velvet booths—but none of the sleazy clientele. Before the Hi-Ball days, this spot was a hangout for such jazz greats as John Coltrane and Miles Davis, and the bar tries to maintain that legendary atmosphere with live swing bands. Unfortunately, the tiny dance floor is too cramped for dancing; instead, slip into your favorite cocktail attire and swill smooth martinis. *473 Broadway St., near Columbus Ave., tel. 415/397–9464. Cover: $2–$8.*

San Francisco Brewing Company. A thirtysomething crowd that is equal parts jazz lovers and beer connoisseurs frequents this popular brewery. The daily brews on tap are always good, and the frequent mellow jazz ensures they go down smoothly. The improv comedy performed on some weeknights is a mixed bag—take your chances. *155 Columbus Ave., tel. 415/434–3344.*

Savoy-Tivoli. This cavernous North Beach institution caters to an amorous set recuperating from a hard day in the Financial District. The large, covered front patio opens when the weather's nice, making the Savoy prime territory to drink wine, watch the world go by, and make believe you're in Italy. If it's raining, shoot pool in the back. *1434 Grant Ave., between Union and Green Sts., tel. 415/362–7023.*

Specs'. Its given name is Specs' Twelve Adler Museum Café, but this classic North Beach hangout for the perennially half-sloshed is popularly known as Specs'. It's a jovial, divey, no-attitude sort of place where you can gaze for hours at the quirky memorabilia papering the walls. *12 Saroyan Pl., tel. 415/421–4112. Off Columbus Ave., next to Tosca (see below), between Broadway and Pacific Ave.*

Tosca. A mostly opera jukebox and a beautiful old espresso machine create a worldly environment—no wonder celebrity patrons (including Francis Ford Coppola and Mikhail Baryshnikov) are occasionally spotted in the enormous red booths. Try one of the excellent liqueur-laced coffee drinks. *242 Columbus Ave., near Broadway, tel. 415/391–1244.*

Vesuvio. A bohemian hangout during the beat era, Vesuvio is the ideal place to sip a glass of red and peruse the copy of *Howl* you just bought next door at the City Lights bookstore. The best seats are upstairs and all the way back, where large windows look out on Columbus Avenue. *255 Columbus Ave., near Broadway, tel. 415/362–3370.*

SOUTH OF MARKET

A once-roughshod but increasingly upscale area of warehouses, outlet stores, and artists' studios, South of Market has plenty of dance clubs and upscale supper clubs (*see box,* Music to the Mouth, *below*), plus several standout drinking holes you should go out of your way to try–come early and toss back a few before the sweaty postclub crowds invade.

Café Mars. Although it's situated in a somewhat removed area of SoMa, Mars is a happening bar and frequently fills to the gills with an increasingly upscale crowd—patrons are likely to have come from the Marina or Russian Hill. On Wednesday it becomes the Cosmic Lounge as DJs spin the latest spacey jazz. Other nights you can shoot pool in the back and enjoy Martian Martinis, made with cranberry vodka with a dried cranberry twist, and delicious tapas from the kitchen. *798 Brannan St., near 7th St., tel. 415/621–6277.*

Hotel Utah. All manner of local rock, jazz, and acoustic sounds reverberate off the woody interior of this casual SoMa bar. If you don't want to hang in the tiny music room, take a seat at the long mahogany bar (shipped from Belgium during the Civil War) and avail yourself of the fine assortment of beer and liquor. The friendly crowd ranges from lawyers to bikers to dogs (yes, dogs); the wooden floor occasionally creaks; and a fine view of a U.S. 101 off-ramp is yours through the front windows. *500 4th St., at Bryant St., tel. 415/421–8308.*

Julie's Supper Club. Past music greats (captured in black-and-white photos) gaze down at professionals and clubsters nibbling interesting appetizers and sipping cocktails. As the name implies, Julie's is a place to dine, but the art-deco-style interior and innovative munchies, including calamari and quesadillas, make this a good place for an after-work or preclub cocktail as well. *1123 Folsom St., near 7th St., tel. 415/861–0707.*

20 Tank Brewery. With a large selection of microbrews and some hearty appetizers and pizzas, this former warehouse is a good place to fuel up before heading across the street to DNA or Slim's. On weekends it can feel like a frat party right down to the cheesy '80s tunes. *316 11th St., near Folsom St., tel. 415/255–9455.*

LIVE MUSIC

Although not at the forefront of any musical revolution, San Francisco has an eclectic and energetic music scene. Bars and clubs feature live music on any given night of the week, usually for a modest cover, and sometimes you can see talented bands for free in parks, music stores, bars, and cultural centers. For a price, you can also see the kinds of national and international acts that you'd find in any world-class metropolis. Your best bets for up-to-the-minute music listings are the *SF Weekly* and the *Bay Guardian*.

The **Great American Music Hall** (859 O'Farrell St., between Polk and Larkin Sts., tel. 415/885–0750), a gorgeous old theater that serves as a midsize concert venue, books an innovative blend of rock and world music. Tickets cost around $7–$18. Boz Scaggs's club, **Slim's** (333 11th St., tel. 415/522–0333), specializes in bluesy rock icons, roots music, and the occasional indie band; tickets are $5–$16. MTV-friendly bands often play at the **Warfield** (982 Market St., between 5th and 6th Sts., tel. 415/775–7722) or at the historic **Fillmore** (1805 Geary Blvd., at Fillmore St., tel. 415/346–6000), where tickets run about $15–$30. To avoid paying steep service charges for events at both venues, stop by the Fillmore box office on Sunday 10–4. **Bimbo's 365 Club** (1025 Columbus Ave., at Chestnut St., tel. 415/474–0365), a stylish concert venue swathed in red draperies, books a lot of big names in jazz, swing, and world music; tickets are $10–$25, usually with a two-drink minimum.

WHERE TO WHISPER SWEET NOTHINGS

Tired of elbowing your way into a crowded club just so you can shout to your date over the blare of speakers? This most romantic of cities also has the most romantic of bars. To enjoy the following places, put on your classiest duds and prepare to nurse an expensive drink while gazing longingly into your date's eyes.

Ovation (333 Fulton St., at Franklin St., tel. 415/553–8100), in the Inn at the Opera, has plush Victorian decor, low lighting, and a crackling fireplace, which make up for high drink prices and slightly snooty service. Forget about trying to get in before or after an opera or symphony performance. Quiet jazz music is performed at the Art Deco Redwood Room (Taylor and Geary Sts., tel. 415/ 775–4700), in the Clift Hotel. The older crowd tends to be stuffy, but with any luck you'll be so engrossed with your date you won't notice. Harry Denton's Starlight Room (450 Powell St., tel. 415/395–8595), on the 21st floor of the Sir Francis Drake Hotel, is the most romantic of the city's skyline bars. Plush velvet booths and dim lighting set the mood for live or recorded jazz, with a heavy emphasis on Sinatra tunes.

ROCK

Bottom of the Hill. Squeeze into this classic dive bar at the bottom of Potrero Hill to hear promising local talent and touring bands. On Sunday afternoon, $3 will gain you admission not only to the live music but also to the all-you-can-eat barbecue (served at 4). *1233 17th St., at Texas St., tel. 415/626–4455. Cover: $3–$6.*

Kilowatt. Weekends this Mission bar hosts local alternative-rock bands reaching maximum noise levels. The dark, smoky bar is usually filled with a mix of neighborhood locals. *3160 16th St., between Guerrero and Valencia Sts., tel. 415/861–2595. Cover: $5–$7.*

Paradise Lounge. The Paradise is like a carnival fun house with something unexpected around every corner: three different musical stages from which to choose, Sunday-night poetry slams, Tuesday-night open mikes, pool tables, free-flowing booze, and a constant flow of people. Although the quality of music varies widely (to put it kindly), it's almost always a reliable weekend destination. *1501 Folsom St., at 11th St., tel. 415/861–6906. Cover: $5–$10.*

JAZZ

San Francisco's jazz scene has exploded of late, with a rash of local bands who have taken it upon themselves to fuse the edges of funk, hip-hop, and jazz to create a distinctive new sound. Venues like the Elbo Room (*see below*), Café du Nord (*see below*), and Bruno's (*see below*) devote much space to these new acts: Look for the **Broun Fellinis** (freestyle jazz with a funky bass line), **Alphabet Soup** (upbeat, reggae-influenced jazz along with a pair of rappers), the **Supernaturals** (a lounge-y new direction taken by former members of the band the Loved Ones), and the **Charlie Hunter Trio** (traditional jazz). Oakland has more mainstream big-name acts.

Bruno's. Divided into a full-scale restaurant and a lounge-y bar, Bruno's has been wildly popular since it reopened in 1995. Nightly the intimate club showcases local jazz and swing acts, many of them up-and-coming stars of the San Francisco scene—though sometimes the patrons here are too busy being fashionable to pay much attention to the band. Relax in the red-vinyl booths with a martini or squeeze up closer (if that's possible) to the band. *2389 Mission St., between 19th and 20th Sts., tel. 415/550–7455. Cover: $3–$10.*

Café du Nord. The specialty at this large, crowded Castro club is jazz you can afford. Friday night often features the sultry crooning of local faves LaVay Smith & Her Red Hot Skillet Lickers. Other nights feature lounge, salsa, swing, big-band music, and fine local talent such as Latin jazz master Josh Jones. Those more interested in playing pool or socializing can do so in the front of the bar, while music lovers groove uninterrupted in the back. Dinner is served Wednesday–Saturday. *2170 Market St., at Sanchez St., tel. 415/861–5016. Cover: $3–$7.*

CoCo Club. A variety of acts comes through this small woman-owned restaurant and performance space South of Market—everything from acoustic rock to avant-garde jazz and blues. The tiny, comfortable interior also hosts a few lesbian events each week, though other nights men are welcome. The entrance is on Minna Street. *139 8th St., between Mission and Howard Sts., tel. 415/626–2337. Cover: $3–$7.*

Elbo Room. This stylish Mission watering hole becomes unmanageably popular as the night progresses. Head upstairs for some of the best local live jazz and hip-hop acts, as well as occasional DJs. Forgot your dancing shoes? Join the locals packed around the pool table—the drinks are cheap enough to keep you around until closing. Happy hour stretches from 5 to 9, and you can often win tickets to shows at their Web site, www.elbo.com. *647 Valencia St., near 17th St., tel. 415/552–7788. Upstairs cover: $4–$7.*

> *Folks say the city's best margaritas are mixed at Puerto Alegre (546 Valencia St., near 16th St., tel. 415/626–2922), about a block from the Elbo Room.*

Jazz at Pearl's. This sedately romantic North Beach joint generally showcases mainstream, traditional jazz in a dimly lighted setting. However, if you stick around late, you just might catch some smokin' improvisational jams. During shows there's a two-drink minimum. *256 Columbus Ave., at Broadway, tel. 415/291–8255. No cover.*

Noe Valley Ministry. An adventurous booking policy draws some serious talent—from experimental jazz and blues artists to well-known world-music acts—into this church in Noe Valley that moonlights as a performance space. Call ahead for tickets ($10–$20) if you don't want to be disappointed at the door. *1021 Sanchez St., between 23rd and Elizabeth Sts., tel. 415/282–2317.*

Up and Down Club. Sleek deco digs give this multilevel SoMa supper club the feel of a New York lounge. Upstairs you'll find a DJ laying down tracks but little room in which to dance. Downstairs, jazz, including Latin and acid varieties, heats up the room. The club is closed Tuesday and Sunday. *1151 Folsom St., between 7th and 8th Sts., tel. 415/626–2388. Cover: about $5.*

BLUES

Although Oakland's blues scene is more renowned, San Francisco's devoted blues followers are pros at supporting local acts. Several venues, most notably **Slim's** (*see above*) and the **Great American Music Hall** (*see above*), are often stops for traveling blues legends.

Blue Lamp. This friendly downtown bar books a variety of blues, jazz, folk, and rock bands nightly and attracts an equally diverse mix of patrons. Arrive early to stake your spot near the fireplace. *561 Geary St., between Taylor and Jones Sts., tel. 415/885–1464. Cover: up to $5.*

Boom Boom Room. Posters of blues legends hang on the wall at John Lee Hooker's club, and the man himself has been known to stop by on occasion. Quality live blues bands play every night of the week to an enthusiastic mixed crowd. This lower Fillmore club is not in the best of neighborhoods. *1601 Fillmore St., at Geary Blvd., tel. 415/567–3227.*

Grant and Green Blues Club. This dark, smoky bar hosts some raucous blues shows—a welcome contrast to the very civilized cafés and coffeehouses that dominate North Beach. *1371 Grant Ave., at Green St., tel. 415/693–9565. No cover .*

CLUBS

In San Francisco hard-core club hoppers often take their nightlife more seriously than their jobs. Spaces large and small play music for every age, style, and level of rhythmic ability. There's a huge variety of

MUSIC TO THE MOUTH

The old concept of supper clubs combines live music, classy duds, and fancy food. For an extremely classy (and expensive) night out, nothing can touch gorgeous Art Deco Bix (56 Gold St., between Jackson St. and Pacific Ave., Montgomery and Sansome Sts., tel. 415/433–6300), where a swank crowd dressed to the nines enjoys excellent New American cuisine and nightly jazz. 330 Ritch Street (330 Ritch St., off Townsend St. between 3rd and 4th Sts., tel. 415/522–9558), with its jazz, salsa, and swing, attracts a classy crowd; tapas and dinner are served Wednesday through Saturday. Also check out Julie's Supper Club (see Bars, above), which serves California cuisine in a 1950s-style setting; and Bruno's (see Jazz, below), where meals are expensive but the setting refined.

quite cheap and casual dance venues, as well as some that ooze pretension. Dance purists can even find spaces that don't allow alcohol or smoking. On the other end of the spectrum are raves and dance parties—still going strong in warehouses and fields—where substance abuse is by no means limited to alcohol and smoking.

For flyers on the club scene, check smaller, more alternative retail and record shops. Many spaces host various clubs on different nights of the week; the *Bay Guardian* and *SF Weekly* have complete listings of the Bay Area's rotating club nights (call ahead because the hot spots change quickly.) For current listings of gay and lesbian clubs (as well as the latest gossip), flip through the free monthlies *Odyssey* and *Oblivion*, available in cafés and bookstores around the Castro District.

PREDOMINANTLY STRAIGHT

Bahia Cabana. A multigenerational international crowd comes to samba at this tropical downtown supper club. Thursday, Friday, and Sunday are salsa nights; Saturday brings live Brazilian music. Other evenings expect various Latino bands and on Monday techno trance. *1600 Market St., at Franklin St., tel. 415/626–3306. Cover: $5–$10.*

The Cat Club. On Wednesday only the Cat Club hosts the oldest fetish dance party in California: "Bondage A Go-Go." It's a light introduction to the real S&M subculture, where you may engage in acts of light bondage, get whipped by a professional dominatrix, or just stand to the side and gawk. The small back room of this mostly after-hours club in SoMa features everything from jazz to jungle to ambient house. *1190 Folsom St., near 8th St., tel. 415/431–3332. Cover: $5–$10.*

DNA Lounge. This dependable choice for after-hours dancing (Friday and Saturday until 4 AM) has eclectic acts that range from rockabilly nights to tattoo and piercing shows. The crowd isn't afraid to break a sweat on the dance floor, but many come just to kick back in dimly lighted corners downstairs. On Friday dance to the '70s retro band Grooveline. DJs usually come on after the live music. *375 11th St., at Harrison St., tel. 415/626–1409. Cover: $5–$15.*

El Río. This casual neighborhood hangout in the Mission attracts a healthy mix of men and women, straight and gay and in between, with different dance parties every night. On sunny afternoons nothing is more relaxing than a cold brew under the palm tree in El Río's back patio, and if you come on a Sunday, you can work off the beer with some fiery dancing to live salsa music. The neighborhood isn't the best; women especially should avoid walking alone on Mission Street at night. *3158 Mission St., at Precita Ave., tel. 415/282–3325. Cover: $5–$7.*

Nickie's BBQ. Red-vinyl booths and Christmas lights decorate this urban Lower Haight hole-in-the-wall that's entirely lacking in pretension. Nightly you can listen to '70s funk, soul, hip-hop, reggae, Latin, and world-beat booms. This is the cool venue pictured on the album cover of the sizzling, modern dance-floor jazz compilation *Home Cookin'* (Ubiquity Records). *460 Haight St., between Webster and Fillmore Sts., tel. 415/621–6508. Cover: $3–$5.*

Polly Esther's. Featuring two dance floors focusing on two decades—the '70s and the '80s—this branch of the New York club chain attracts a bubble-gum mainstream crowd to its retro theme park. Open Thursday, Friday, and Saturday only, the club is so cavernous that the decor alone will keep you entertained for hours. *181 Eddy St., at Taylor St., tel. 415/885–1977. Cover: $10.*

Roccapulco. This popular salsa club and restaurant features Latin drag shows on Tuesday, salsa on Friday and Saturday, and mariachi music on Sunday. Serious salsa steppers heat up the floor later in the evening. *3140 Mission St., near César Chávez (Army) St., tel. 415/648–6611. Cover: about $10.*

Sound Factory. This club is tame and mainstream by city standards, but Friday night's deep-house dance extravaganza has been embraced by all-nighters as a favorite after-hours hangout. Modeled after the clubs in New York and Los Angeles, the enormous SoMa space has a literal maze of pulsating rooms. Call for upcoming clubs and events. Open until 4 AM Friday and Saturday only (summer also Thursday). *525 Harrison St., at 1st St., tel. 415/243–9646. Cover: $12–$15.*

PREDOMINANTLY
GAY AND LESBIAN

The Box. This Thursday-only artsy-industrial SoMa club plays hard-core hip-hop, funk, soul, and house without attitude. For an extra treat, go-go platforms mounted on the walls showcase dancers who gyrate at full throttle. The city's most accomplished DJs—including "Mixtress" Paige Hodel, San Francisco's most famous gay DJ—and club dance troupes appear here. Although the club is lesbian-run, the multicultural crowd includes straights, too. *628 Divisadero St., tel. 415/647–8258. Cover: $7.*

All aboard for some serious salsa. Friday and Saturday nights the Mexican Bus winds its way through the city depositing dancers at various Latin Clubs. Join the fun for $33 (cover charges included). Call 415/546–3747 for details.

Club Townsend. This vast SoMa disco hosts the high-energy Sunday "Pleasuredome," with local DJs churning out sounds for a largely male crowd followed by a where-do-they-get-the-energy Sunday tea dance until 6 AM. "Club Universe," on Saturday, is less gender-specific, and the artsy decor changes to create a stunning new illusion each week. *177 Townsend St., between 2nd and 3rd Sts., tel. 415/974–1156. Cover: $7–$12.*

Covered Wagon. Black light illuminates the Western decor on the walls as well as the lint on your shirt at this dark SoMa bar. Afternoons the CW sees a lot of bike messengers taking a breather, but at night it caters primarily to gay women, with live funk, soul, and ska some nights, DJs and dancing on others. Thursday the bar hosts the infamous "Stinky's Peep Show," when large-size go-go dancers engage in provocative acts. *911 Folsom St., at 5th St., tel. 415/974–1585. Cover: $3–$6.*

The EndUp. Home of the "misplaced weekend," this primarily gay bar has an outdoor patio, a pool table, a gazebo, and a waterfall, all surrealistically situated almost directly beneath U.S. 101. The elevated dance floor couldn't possibly accommodate everyone, so the sweaty crowd gets down wherever it pleases. Come at 5:30 AM for the "Sunday T Dance," a tradition for a quarter of a century. On Monday night the EndUp hosts "Club Dread," a DJ'ed reggae dance party; "Fag Fridays" feature go-go dancers and some of the best-looking boys you'll see all week; and Saturday is "G-Spot," a women-only party including outdoor barbecues. *401 6th St., at Harrison St., tel. 415/357–0827. Cover: $5–$10.*

Esta Noche. Tucked away in the Mission, Esta Noche plays a good mix of hard-pumping Latin, house music, and '70s disco. The crowd consists mostly of Latino drag queens and their admirers, and Anglo patrons are respectfully requested to refrain from doing the cha-cha. Women, though few, will not feel unwelcome. *3079 16th St., at Valencia St., tel. 415/861–5757. Cover: $5–$8, weekends only.*

The Stud. This SoMa club is a San Francisco legend and a good watering hole any night of the week. Dress up or come as you are and have fun flirting with innocent out-of-towners. Friday night is often set aside for lesbian events; on Wednesday the club draws in a postcollegiate crowd for dancing to '70s and early '80s classics. The Tuesday-night club, "Trannyshack," for "makeup tips and cheap cocktails," is especially popular. *399 9th St., at Harrison St., tel. 415/252–7883. Cover: $3–$6.*

SHALL WE DANCE?

If you find yourself stumbling over two left feet instead of cutting a rug, get theeself to the dance club. At Café du Nord (see Live Music, above) samba, mambo, and cha-cha lessons are included in the $5 cover Tuesday at 9 PM, while Sunday means swing lessons at 8 PM (included in the $5 cover). Head to 330 Ritch Street (330 Ritch St., off Townsend St. between 3rd and 4th Sts., tel. 415/522–9558) for free swing instruction from Work That Skirt Wednesday at 8:30 PM. Follow the same instructors to the Verdi Club (2424 Mariposa St., at Portrero, tel. 415/905–5712) for swing lessons Friday at 8:45 PM and take a turn on this recently reopened club's huge dance floor. Thursday at 7 PM at the Verdi mean Argentine tango lessons. Barring the above, a coy glance and a polite inquiry might enlist the company of a willing and—you hope—capable partner.

MOVIE HOUSES

The Bay Area is fortunate to have more than a handful of tiny independent theaters, where fervent buffs insist on viewing "films" and not "movies." San Francisco also happens to be one of the nation's most prolific cities for independent filmmaking—in particular, documentaries, shorts, and experimental and avant-garde films. The **Artists' Television Access** (992 Valencia St., at 21st St., tel. 415/824–3890), a nonprofit media arts center in the Mission, screens offbeat films for $5.

During spring and summer five big film festivals roll through town, starting in early March with the **San Francisco International Asian-American Film Festival** (tel. 415/863–0814), during which most films are shown at the Kabuki (*see below*). In mid-April look for the **San Francisco International Film Festival** (tel. 415/931–3456), which features quality films from all over the world. During the last two weeks in June the much-loved **International Lesbian and Gay Film Festival** (tel. 415/703–8650) coincides with Gay Pride Week and is the largest such event in the world. The **Jewish Film Festival** (tel. 415/621–0556) breezes into town—one week at the Castro Theatre in San Francisco and one week at the UC Theatre in Berkeley—at the end of July and beginning of August. September brings the relatively small but increasingly popular **Festival Cine Latino** (tel. 415/553–8135). Finally, in November the Bay Area's independent and documentary-film talent takes center stage at the **Film Arts of Independent Cinema** festival (tel. 415/552–8760).

For new releases everyone goes to the **AMC Kabuki 8** (1881 Post St., at Fillmore St., tel. 415/931–9800), even though some of the multiplex's eight screens are tiny and seating is limited. Tickets run $7.50. Take advantage of the validated parking in Japan Center, since this isn't the safest place to leave your car. **Landmark Theaters** (tel. 415/352–0810 for show-time information) runs a number of artsy and foreign film houses in the city, including the Embarcadero Center Cinema (One Embarcadero Center), Clay Theatre (2261 Fillmore St., at Clay St.), Lumière Theatre (1572 California St., at Polk St.), Opera Plaza Cinema (601 Van Ness Ave., at Golden Gate Ave.), and Bridge Theatre (3010 Geary Blvd., at Blake St.). If you've just *got* to see a loud action flick, the **United Artists Coronet** (3575 Geary Blvd., at Arguello St., tel. 415/752–4400) impresses with its huge capacity, large screen, and Sony Dynamic Digital Sound. The new Sony **Metreon** multiplex-cum-IMAX (see South of Market in Chapter 2) is also expected to be a popular theater. The *Bay Guardian* and *SF Weekly* have complete listings and reviews for both first-run theaters and rep houses.

Casting Couch Micro Cinema. Come to this deluxe 46-person screening room for an intimate and unique viewing experience. Sink into one of the sofas and let the waitstaff bring you cookies while you check out their roster of all-independent films. Arrive 15 minutes before show time to secure a seat. *950 Battery St., between Green and Vallejo Sts., tel. 415/986–7001. Admission: $8.50.*

Castro Theatre. An Art Deco gem built in 1922 and still the most beautiful place to see a film in San Francisco, the Castro shows a wide selection of rare, foreign, and unusual films, which play anywhere from a night to a week or two. The specialties here are camp, classics of all genres, and new releases of interest to lesbian and gay viewers. The man who rises out of the floor playing a Wurlitzer organ is guaranteed to make you giggle. *429 Castro St., between Market and 18th Sts., tel. 415/621–6120. Admission: $6.50.*

Red Vic. Films at this co-op range from the artsy to the cultish to the rare, and you can have your herbal tea in a real mug to accompany your popcorn sprinkled with nutritional yeast. If you get here early, snag one of the couches before lovebirds beat you to it. *1727 Haight St., between Cole and Shrader Sts., tel. 415/668–3994. Admission: $6.*

The Roxie. This slightly run-down Mission theater shows political, cult, and otherwise bent films of widely varying quality. Though some real winners pass through here, they also play a lot of silly old flicks that might just as well be forgotten. *3117 16th St., at Valencia St., tel. 415/863–1087. Admission: $6.*

San Francisco Cinemateque. Dedicated to the perpetuation of experimental filmmaking, the San Francisco Art Institute's nonprofit theater screens rare avant-garde films, documentaries, and independent films. Screenings usually take place Thursday at the Center for the Arts at Yerba Buena Gardens (*see* Multimedia Performance Spaces, *below*) and Sunday at the Institute. *San Francisco Art Institute, 800 Chestnut St., between Jones and Leavenworth Sts., tel. 415/558–8129. Admission: $6.*

THEATER

Some of San Francisco's best theater talents can be found in its smaller multicultural and experimental ensembles. Local troupes worth watching include the **Sick and Twisted Players,** a mostly gay group that specializes in campy staged interpretations of films like *The Rocky Horror Picture Show.*

For more mainstream tastes, **ACT** (American Conservatory Theater), the city's major theater company, presents about eight plays annually, from October through late spring, at the Geary Theater (415 Geary St., at Mason St., tel. 415/749–2228). Broadway-type shows usually appear at the downtown **Curran Theater** (445 Geary St., at Mason St., tel. 415/551–2000). The 2,500-seat **Orpheum** (1192 Market St., near the Civic Center, tel. 415/551–2000) is used for the biggest touring shows. For discounts try TIX Bay Area (251 Stockton St., between Post and Geary Sts., tel. 415/433–7827), a same-day half-price ticket booth on Union Square. Most venues also provide discounts for students with ID.

The productions ($10–$12) at **Josie's Cabaret & Juice Joint** (3583 16th St., at Market, tel. 415/861–7933), an established gay cultural center, lean toward campy cabaret and riotous stand-up, though you'll see the occasional serious piece as well. At **Climate Theater** (285 9th St., at Tehama St., tel. 415/978–2345), you can catch small ensembles and solo performers doing original work. Tickets are $7–$10.

If you're interested in modern theater, don't miss the **San Francisco Fringe Festival** (tel. 415/931–1094), which brings local, national, and international experimental theater to venues throughout the city just after Labor Day. Another event to watch for is the **San Francisco Shakespeare Festival** (tel. 415/422–2222), performances of the Bard's work in parks throughout the Bay Area weekends from August to October. San Francisco performances are held in Golden Gate Park, usually in September.

Asian American Theater Company. This company presents plays by Asians and Asian-Americans and works extensively with local actors. Tickets go for $8–$21. *Administrative office: 1840 Sutter St., Suite 207, at Webster St., tel. 415/440–5545.*

Beach Blanket Babylon. This zany San Francisco revue has been selling out most nights since it opened in 1974, with talented musicians, polished performers, impeccable timing, extralarge headgear, and a zesty, zany script that changes to incorporate topical references and characters (not to mention an ongoing love affair with the British royal family). A significant chunk of your $20–$45 ticket cost goes to local charities. Those under 21 may attend Sunday matinee performances only (because alcohol is served at other times). *Club Fugazi, 678 Green St., at Powell St., tel. 415/421–4222.*

BRAVA! Brava! For Women in the Arts is the official name of this resident theater company, a stronghold of women's stage work. The mostly experimental programming includes local playwrights and performance artists and frequently showcases the work of the Latina community. Tickets cost up to $16. *2789 24th St., at York, tel. 415/826–5773.*

SOUNDS FOR SILENT SCREENINGS

Defying classification in any musical category, the Club Foot Orchestra consists of nine musical adventurers with backgrounds in orchestral, popular, and world music. Though they started off playing in clubs South of Market, today they're best known for writing scores to classic silent films and performing during the screenings. If at all possible, see them when they're accompanying a film at the Castro Theatre, when tickets are usually $10; they also play at Bruno's (see Live Music, above). Check the papers for their schedule.

Exit Theatre. One of the best venues downtown is this two-stage black-box café-theater, which annually presents a season of absurdist works. In addition, small but imaginative productions sometimes draw on video, music, or other media. Political satire is a favored topic of many productions, and no one is safe from their far-reaching comedic jabs. Tickets range from $6 to $15. *156 Eddy St., at Mason St., tel. 415/673–3847.*

Lorraine Hansberry Theatre. A consistently high-quality locus of African-American theater, the Lorraine Hansberry performs experimental, musical, and classical works by African Americans and other writers of color. The work of talented young playwrights is often premiered at the theater. Tickets cost $20–$24. *620 Sutter St., at Mason St., tel. 415/474–8800.*

Magic Theatre. The Magic is San Francisco's standby for the modern and mildly experimental. Sam Shepard wrote a lot of his plays for this venue in the late '70s and early '80s; the theater continues to premiere innovative American works, and Sam himself returns from time to time. Tickets for performances run $18–$32. *Fort Mason Center, Bldg. D, tel. 415/441–8822.*

The Marsh. This self-described "breeding ground for new performances"—get it?—hosts primarily new works by local artists. Though the shows are not consistently excellent, they are almost always intriguing. The 99 house seats include a cozy corner of sofas. The "Monday Night Marsh New Works Series" ($6) presents works in progress, and the "Growing Stage" program presents performances and workshops for children. Most performances cost $8–$15, though children's programs are usually less. *1062 Valencia St., near 22nd St., tel. 415/826–5750.*

San Francisco Mime Troupe. Since 1961 this provocative ensemble has been staging free scathing political comedies and musicals in Golden Gate and other Bay Area parks on weekends at 2 PM from July 4 through Labor Day. Call for its current whereabouts. *Tel. 415/285–1717.*

Theater of Yugen. This theater's mission is to bring the Japanese aesthetic to Western audiences. Of the four East-West fusion works staged each year, three are primarily in English and deal with Japanese stories or themes, while the fourth is *kyogen,* traditional Japanese comedy, performed in Japanese on a simple black-draped stage. Tickets cost $10–$15, with reduced rates for previews. Performances take place both at the Noh Space (2840 Mariposa St., at Alabama St., tel. 415/621–7978) and the Cowell Theater, at Fort Mason (Pier 2, Laguna St. at Marina Blvd., tel. 415/441–5706).

Theatre Rhinoceros. The only strictly gay and lesbian theater company in San Francisco stages reliably good plays in its tiny Mission District hall. Though you can catch dramas here, you're more likely to see a comedy with a wry twist: Witness *The Big Drag,* advertised as "a hard-boiled yarn of girls, guns, and genre dysphoria." Ticket prices are $12–$20. *2926 16th St., tel. 415/861–5079.*

MULTIMEDIA PERFORMANCE SPACES

As technology has increasingly affected theater, video, dance, and music, it has also become a powerful medium in itself. The following venues are committed to exploring the evolving relationships among performance media.

Audium. This theater of sound-sculpted space explores the relationship between music and space. You sit in pitch darkness surrounded by 169 speakers that saturate you with sounds; the effect of the 72-minute performance is both intense and unsettling. The show's affable composer, Stan Shaff, who handles the controls during the shows, is happy to discuss his art afterward. This small theater—just 49 seats—is open Friday and Saturday only; shows start promptly at 8:30 PM. *1616 Bush St., at Franklin St., tel. 415/771–1616. Admission: $10.*

Center for the Arts at Yerba Buena Gardens. The bright yellow and red of this modern theater's lobby give way to the more metallic luster of the interior space. The center's ambitious mission draws top dancers, musicians, and dramatists and sometimes combines them in large-scale ways. The theater itself has superb acoustics and souped-up technological gadgets. Despite the 750 seats it feels like an intimate space. Tickets start at $9. *701 Mission St., at 3rd St., tel. 415/978–2787.*

George Coates Performance Works. Technological wizard George Coates mixes the latest computer technology with the stage. Performances, held under the soaring vaulted ceiling of a former church, involve music, video, and motion and use only a scrim and special lighting to create "virtual" sets. Tickets cost $10–$35. *110 McAllister St., at Leavenworth St., tel. 415/863–8520.*

Intersection for the Arts. This stark stone-walled space in the Mission seats 65 for viewing performance art, performative readings, competitive "Poetry Slam Finals," workshops, chamber operas, and lectures. The gallery space upstairs features intriguing sound and visual installations. Opened in 1967, the Intersection is San Francisco's oldest alternative art space, and its shows are consistently good. Ticket prices vary widely but are usually around $10–$20. There's free evening parking at 670 Valencia Street. *446 Valencia St., between 15th and 16th Sts., tel. 415/626–2787.*

Luna Sea (2940 16th St., Room 216C, tel. 415/863–2989) is a women's group upstairs from Theatre Rhinoceros, in the Mission; they sponsor readings, music, and other events, often as benefits.

New Langton Arts. This far-reaching organization has been around since 1975, providing local performance and installation artists with grants to complete their work and an audience to appreciate it. New Langton's work is similar to that of Theater Artaud (*see below*) but on a smaller scale. Upstairs is a bright, continually changing gallery; downstairs is a 75-seat well-equipped multimedia theater. Admission is $5–$8. *1246 Folsom St., at 8th St., tel. 415/626–5416.*

Theater Artaud. Artaud has one of the most interesting performance halls in town: a cavernous converted cannery. The 300-seat space creates eerie echoes that generally add to the effect. The excellent local and traveling shows—often dance, drama, and music all at once—provide insight into the experimental scene both in San Francisco and internationally. Tickets run $10–$25 and are cheaper weeknights. The neighborhood is seedy, but the experience is worth it. *450 Florida St., between 17th and Mariposa Sts., tel. 415/621–7797.*

Venue 9. Energetic performers stage a variety of events at this South of Market venue run by the Foot-Loose Dance Company. For example, their "Women's Work" series featured musical, theater, dance, and comedy performances, as well as provocative films made by women. Admission varies from $5 to $12, with many shows charging from $6 to $10 on a sliding scale. *252 9th St., at Folsom St., tel. 415/626–2169.*

CLASSICAL MUSIC

Herbst Theatre. World-class soloists and occasional groups play at the elegant Herbst, in the Veterans Building downtown, usually charging $20 and up per seat. Though the theater is plush, the acoustics are mediocre. *401 Van Ness Ave., tel. 415/392–4400.*

San Francisco Conservatory of Music. The city's major music school has something going on almost nightly, whether it's performed by students, faculty, or the Conservatory Orchestra. Quality is unpredictable, but with the school's fine reputation, odds are you'll see something worthwhile. General admission is $10; most student recitals are free. *1201 Ortega St., at 19th Ave., tel. 415/759–3477.*

San Francisco Contemporary Music Players. The biggest name of any contemporary company in the area hosts only about six performances a year at the Center for the Arts (*see* Multimedia Performance Spaces, *above*) in both the main theater and the intimate 300-seat Forum Theater. Concerts generally feature brand-new works by contemporary composers, with some by "oldies" like John Cage. Tickets are $18 for general admission, and prices include a preconcert discussion with composers and other guests. *701 Mission St., at 3rd St., tel. 415/978–2787 or 415/252–6235 for programming information.*

San Francisco Opera. The opera's grand-scale performances each season at the beautifully restored War Memorial Opera House usually include one exorbitantly lavish production each year: 1999's program included a four-program series of Wagner's *Ring* cycle. Prices are equally exorbitant, ranging from $20 to $100. Flash a student or senior ID (or anything that looks like one) two hours before curtain time and you may score tickets for $15–$20; call ahead to make sure discount tickets are available. *301 Van Ness Ave., at Grove St., tel. 415/864–3330.*

San Francisco Symphony. Under the baton of American-born conductor Michael Tilson Thomas, the symphony performs at Davies Symphony Hall, where the interior architecture looks odd but creates good acoustics for even the cheapest balcony seats ($25). The best deals, though, available for most but not all performances, are the $10–$12 center terrace seats: A limited number are available in advance but sell out quickly; 40 more go on sale two hours before the show. The seats hover directly over the orchestra, yielding an off-balance sound but a fantastic face-on view of the conductor and an intimate look at the musicians' work. *Davies Symphony Hall, 201 Van Ness Ave., at Grove St., tel. 415/ 864–6000.*

San Francisco Women's Philharmonic. After a nearly two-year hiatus, this talented group of performers resumed advancing the work of women composers, conductors, and performers in 1997. Their performances, held at the Herbst Theatre and the Center for the Arts, are often preceded by a discussion with the artists. Tickets cost $20–$35. *44 Page St., Suite 604D, tel. 415/437–0123 or 415/392–4400 for reservations.*

DANCE

The world's very best dance troupes pass through the Bay Area, many stopping at **Zellerbach Hall** (*see* Classical Music *in* East Bay, *below*) or at the neoclassical **Palace of Fine Arts** (3301 Lyon St., San Francisco, tel. 415/567–6642). Modern dance has been embraced locally with a fervor, and the Bay Area has quite a few progressive and experimental companies, many of which take a turn at Theater Artaud and the Center for the Arts (*see* Multimedia Performance Spaces, *above*). Probably the most important entry on the Bay Area's dance calendar is the **San Francisco Ethnic Dance Festival** (tel. 415/474–3914), held for several days in June. The auditions, in mid-January, are the best dance bargain of the year: $5 for a full day of entertainment. Call ahead for the exact dates and times. Check the *Bay Guardian* for schedules and dependable recommendations.

Dancer's Group/Footwork. This small but well-respected company packs its informal space to capacity most Friday and Saturday nights, with avid audiences enjoying the vibrant creativity of local choreographers. Many performances incorporate text with music and movement to examine a variety of personal and political themes. Intermediate and advanced dance lessons are offered at $9 a session. *3221 22nd St., at Mission St., tel. 415/824–5044.*

Lines Contemporary Ballet. Led by Artistic Director Alonzo King, Lines pushes the boundaries of dance, often collaborating with such musical luminaries as tabla master Zakir Hussein and jazz saxman Pharoah Sanders. The troupe performs at the Center for the Arts. *50 Oak St., tel. 415/863–3040.*

San Francisco Ballet. Though this company has never been known for cutting-edge performances, its reputation for expert classical performances continues to grow—Artistic Director Helgi Tomasson's new productions of *Giselle* and *Romeo and Juliet* garnered rave reviews. The ballet's repertoire also includes works by such master modern choreographers as George Balanchine and Mark Morris. Ticket prices can be steep, ranging from $18 to $85. *301 Van Ness Ave., tel. 415/865–2000.*

EAST BAY

East of the Bay Bridge you'll find plenty of bars and a handful of live music venues: Come to Oakland to sample world-class blues and jazz and a burgeoning improv scene or to Berkeley to drink with a predominantly collegiate crowd. Pore through the free weekly *East Bay Express* for a complete events calendar, including films, lectures, readings, and music.

BARS

BERKELEY

Berkeley has very few high-concept bars, but you'll find plenty of casual places to have a beer. The bars along Telegraph Avenue can't help but appeal to student tastes and budgets. To peer more deeply into Berkeley's psyche, head to one of the watering holes scattered along San Pablo Avenue, which tend to be seedier but more genuine despite the diminished collegiate contingent.

The Albatross. This no-nonsense watering-hole attracts students and working folk. The draft beers taste even better with the bottomless bowl of 25¢ popcorn, and there is a cozy fireplace and a whole row of dartboards occupying a good-size portion of the bar. This is the sort of place where grad students borrow the bar's Scrabble game and settle in for a quiet evening. *1822 San Pablo Ave., between Hearst Ave. and Delaware St., tel. 510/849–4714. From Berkeley BART, Bus 51 west to San Pablo Ave., walk 1½ blocks north.*

Le Bateau Ivre. Beautifully decorated in French provincial style, this elegant establishment nevertheless felt compelled to install a neon sign with the decidedly unalluring English translation of its name (from an Arthur Rimbaud poem): THE DRUNKEN BOAT. Still, it remains a place both romantic and subdued, complete with fireplace and candlelighted tables—the perfect setting for one of the creamiest pints of Guinness this side of Dublin. On summer evenings the outdoor patio feels like a Parisian sidewalk. *2629 Telegraph Ave., at Carleton St., tel. 510/849–1100. 6 blocks south of UC campus.*

Bison Brewing Company. Homemade stout, cider, ale, and snakebites bring in a mixed crowd of Berkeley frat boys and tattooed types—especially during happy hour (4–6 weekdays, 3–8 during daylight savings time). Live bands ranging from blues to Irish folk entertain from Thursday through Saturday: Shout over the music or steal away to the upstairs patio if you need a quiet moment. There is often free live jazz on Sunday afternoon. *2598 Telegraph Ave., at Parker St., tel. 510/841–7734. 5 blocks south of UC campus. Cover: $1–$2.*

Ivy Room. This self-styled dive bar attracts a congenial mix of students, working-class folks, and retired bikers with its live, mostly bluesy music and $2 Buds. The welcoming bar staff and colorful cast of regulars make for excellent company when you're out to pull a few pints, even on a weeknight. *858 San Pablo Ave., at Solano Ave., tel. 510/524–9299. From Berkeley BART, Bus 43 west to Solano Ave.*

Jupiter. This spacious bar across from the Berkeley BART station is one of the city's finest, popular for its sizable outdoor beer garden, 20 microbrews on tap, and free live jazz on weekends. The end of the week draws large down-to-earth crowds, but it's almost always mellow enough to allow for conversation. *2181 Shattuck Ave., near Center St., tel. 510/843–8277.*

The Pub. Officially titled Schmidt's Tobacco & Trading Co., the Pub is a cozy gathering spot for cheap pints and thick coffee. Overstuffed sofas, oak tables, and a pipe-tobacco aroma complement a game of chess or a good novel: If you forgot your book, borrow one of theirs. Weekend nights are busy and loud, but during the week you'll find studious types drinking hot chocolate and poring over their books. *1492 Solano Ave., tel. 510/525–1900. From Berkeley BART, Bus 43 north to Santa Fe Ave.*

Pyramid Brewery and Alehouse. A huge, block-long facility opened in 1997, Pyramid pumps out 80,000 barrels of beer a year to be shipped to California stores and imbibed on the premises. From the spacious bar, filled with copper-top tables and dark-wood decor, you can watch the brewers through the windows—and smell the works in progress. *901 Gilman St., at 7th St., 4 blocks west of San Pablo Ave., tel. 510/527–9090.*

Spats. The inventive drink selection here rivals anyone's anywhere: Choose from concoctions like the Borneo Fogcutter (rum, brandy, fruit juices, and liqueurs) or the Nutty Buddy (Frangelico, cream, and crème de cacao)—then settle into a cushy old Victorian sofa in the parlorlike bar. Messy nachos and other appetizers keep people here through happy hour and into the dinner hour. *1974 Shattuck Ave., tel. 510/841–7225. 2 blocks north of Berkeley BART.*

Triple Rock Brewery. The 1950s reign supreme at this popular microbrewery, where vintage posters and nostalgic knickknacks line the walls. The crowd is noisy in a collegiate sort of way, but folks are friendly. The outdoor patio area is the best place to enjoy one of their home brews and the excellent munchies. *1920 Shattuck Ave., at Hearst Ave., tel. 510/843–2739. 3 blocks north of Berkeley BART.*

OAKLAND

Oakland's bars are generally cheaper and rougher around the edges. Rockridge bars, however, often fill with students—from UC Berkeley and the nearby California College of Arts and Crafts—and are barely distinguishable from those in Berkeley. Downtown bars, near Jack London Square and off Broadway between 10th and 20th streets, appeal mostly to the gainfully employed and get hopelessly crowded on weekends. The farther you venture from central Oakland, the seedier the bars become; be careful when walking around at night.

The Alley. This is the only bar in Oakland where you can sit at a piano and sing along with your drunken *compadres*. It's been in business since the late 1940s and has the clientele and bar staff to prove it. Dark, musty, and unassuming, it's a great place to hang out with low-key locals. Live piano music usually begins at 9 PM. *3325 Grand Ave., 3 blocks east of Lake Merritt, tel. 510/444–8505. From 19th St. BART, Bus 12 east to Santa Clara Ave.*

George and Walt's. G&W's celebrated its 50th anniversary in 1996, and its regular clientele remains loyal (though whether to its dim, comfortable bar or to its big-screen TV remains undecided). Students and sports fans swear by their beers on tap. *5445 College Ave., tel. 510/653–7441. 5 blocks south of Rockridge BART on College Ave.*

Pacific Coast Brewing Company. In old downtown Oakland, this brewpub serves four home brews and has 15 other beers on tap. Its polished appearance attracts a clean-cut thirtysomething crowd. The beers are top drawer. *906 Washington St., near 10th St., tel. 510/836–2739. From 12th St. BART, 3 blocks southwest on Broadway, 1 block west to Washington St.*

LIVE MUSIC

The East Bay's music scene is sporadic: Some nights the great number of events taking place in the area make it difficult to choose; others will leave you hunting for something to do. Berkeley is better known for its student bars and cafés than for its music venues. Though rock, folk, jazz, and world music are prevalent in the East Bay, it's the soulful sounds that lure people into the depths of Oakland, home of the West Coast blues.

ROCK

924 Gilman Street. This all-ages alcohol-free cooperative features local hard-core garage and punk bands. Green Day got its start here (and has brought the place a fair amount of renown), but now that they're famous, you're not likely to find them playing here. Most shows cost $5, and you have to buy a $2 membership (valid for one year) to get in the first time. *924 Gilman St., at 8th St., Berkeley, tel. 510/ 525–9926. From Berkeley BART, Bus 9 north to 8th St.*

Stork Club. It would seem that only hard-core boozers would be drawn to the tinsel-and-Christmas-light decor, but this bar has gained a reputation for booking innovative local bands. The crowd neatly divides itself in half by the bar, which runs down the middle: The younger, hipper music-loving crowd is on the right, and the barflies who arrived for the 6 AM opening are on the left. *380 12th St., tel. 510/444–6174. 1½ blocks east of Broadway. Cover: $5.*

JAZZ

Jazz greats come through Oakland on a regular basis, making appearances at established venues and putting on special shows.

Kimball's East. In Emeryville, a small community tucked between Berkeley and Oakland, look for this excellent jazz and supper club, which books well-known jazz musicians from Wednesday through Sunday. Downstairs, **Kimball's Carnival** draws big names in Latin jazz and Caribbean music, with an audience of mostly older professionals. *5800 Shellmound St., Emeryville, tel. 510/658–2555. From MacArthur BART, Bus 6 or 57 west on 40th St. to Pacific Park Plaza. Cover: $15–$30.*

Yoshi's. A well-respected club and restaurant near Jack London Square, Yoshi's serves up sushi and jazz in sophisticated style. The clientele knows its music, and past acts have included Cecil Taylor, Anthony Braxton, and Ornette Coleman. *510 Embarcadero, Oakland, tel. 510/238–9200. From Oakland City/Center 12th Street BART, take Bus 58 or 59 to Embarcadero and Washington St. Cover: $5–$100.*

BLUES

In the years following World War II, Oakland gave birth to the gritty, hurts-so-bad-I'm-gonna-die music known as the West Coast blues. More than 50 years later it still flourishes in clubs and bars all over town. Dedicated to the preservation of blues, jazz, and gospel, the **Bay Area Blues Society** (tel. 510/836–2227) sponsors shows and festivals year-round and is a wellspring of information about West Coast blues. These folks are also the ones to call for information on the famed **Oakland Blues and Heritage Festival,** which takes place every September.

Blake's. This restaurant and live music joint has been a Berkeley institution since it opened in the late 1940s. The sunny ground-floor dining room serves tasty "my parents are in town and I have to take them somewhere" food, and the upstairs bar (Leona's) provides brews and free popcorn to a sedate postcollegiate crowd. The real reasons to come, though, are the fully stocked bar (a rarity this close to campus) and the cramped dark basement downstairs—a no-frills bar with a sawdust-covered floor where you'll find some of the best funk acts in the area plus the occasional alternative rock band. If you venture downstairs to use the bathroom, you'll get an earful of the band, and you can decide if they're worth the cover charge. *2367 Telegraph Ave., near Durant Ave., Berkeley, tel. 510/848–0886. 1 block from UC campus. Cover: $3–$6.*

Eli's Mile High Club. The reputed birthplace of West Coast blues remains a consistently good bet, continuing to highlight promising local acts plus more renowned performers. It's a small club with a pool table, soul food, and music from Thursday through Saturday. The club opens at 8 PM, and the music usually starts around 9:30. *3629 Martin Luther King Jr. Way, Oakland, tel. 510/655–6661. From Berkeley, Bus 15 south on Martin Luther King Jr. Way. Cover: $4–$8.*

Fifth Amendment. High-quality blues and jazz acts play to a largely African-American crowd of professionals, students, and local old-timers. Dress up a bit for some absolutely searing music. *3255 Lakeshore Ave., Oakland, tel. 510/832–3242. From MacArthur BART, Bus 57 to corner of Lakeshore Ave. and Lake Park Way. No cover.*

FOLK

Freight and Salvage. At this smoke- and alcohol-free coffeehouse you'll find Berkeley's thriving (and aging) folk music community enjoying a wide variety of entertainment—everything from world-class accordionists to spoken-word performers to lefty singer–songwriters. Certain Tuesdays are open-mike nights ($2.50). *1111 Addison St., near San Pablo Ave., Berkeley, tel. 510/548–1761. From Berkeley BART, Bus 51 west to San Pablo Ave., 1 block south to Addison St. Cover: $7–$15.*

Starry Plough. This popular Irish pub near the Berkeley–Oakland border has an eclectic mix of folk music and not-too-extreme rock bands. Join the older, politically left crowd for a pint or two of Guinness, Bass, or Anchor Steam and a game of darts. On Monday at 7 PM pros and amateurs take part in free Irish dance lessons. *3101 Shattuck Ave., at Prince St., Berkeley, tel. 510/841–2082. From Ashby BART, walk 3 blocks south. Cover: up to $6.*

WORLD MUSIC

Ashkenaz. In December 1996, owner David Nadel was shot and killed outside this beloved Berkeley club—an event that shocked the East Bay community all the more because this world-music emporium has been a fixture here since the early '70s. After some touch-and-go times, Askenaz reopened and resumed its wonderfully eclectic programming. Winner of the *East Bay Express*'s "Best Place to Dance" award in 1998, the club offers a different live beat every night, from African to zydeco to Bulgarian folk. *1317 San Pablo Ave., Berkeley, tel. 510/525–5054. From Berkeley BART, Bus 9 west to San Pablo Ave. Cover: $5–$10.*

La Peña. This Latin American cultural center offers a wide selection of live music, political lectures, performance pieces, and workshops on Central and South American issues. Many shows are benefits, so covers often masquerade as donations, ranging from a few bucks to $15. *3105 Shattuck Ave., Berkeley, tel. 510/849–2568. Next to Starry Plough (see above).*

CLUBS

With San Francisco just across the bay, there was never a need for the East Bay to develop a dance club scene of its own: East Bay clubbers make the trek to the city when they want serious after-hours danc-

CLASSICS ON THE CHEAP

On summer Sundays, the Stern Grove Midsummer Music Festival (tel. 415/ 252–6252) brings various performing artists to Stern Grove in San Francisco for 2 PM shows. The Brown Bag Opera series (tel. 415/565–6434) pitches divas against traffic noise: Performances are held at 12:15 at 1 Bush Street, among other Bay Area locations. You can also find free, or nearly free, concerts at local universities: Berkeley's free Wednesday Noon Concerts (Hertz Hall, tel. 510/ 642–4864) showcase talented professors and students; Oakland's Mills College (see below) is well known for its sometimes-free contemporary music program; and the San Francisco Conservatory of Music (see above) hosts free amateur performances.

ing. But if you're intent on staying away from the big city, **Blake's** (*see* Live Music, *above*), a sweaty basement ruled by funk, soul, hip-hop, and rare grooves, should serve your dance needs just fine.

Caribee Dance Center. Occasional live music is supplemented six nights a week (closed Thursday) with dancing to reggae, salsa, and African music. Drinks cost $2–$5. *1408 Webster St., Oakland, tel. 510/ 835–4006. From 12th St. BART, 2 blocks east on 14th St. Cover: $5–$10.*

White Horse Inn. Get down under a gleaming disco ball at this easygoing place on the Oakland–Berkeley border. Most patrons are gay or lesbian, but other fun seekers are welcome. A DJ is in the house Thursday–Saturday after 9 PM, and the bar's open daily until 2 AM. *6551 Telegraph Ave., at 66th St., Oakland, tel. 510/652–3820. From MacArthur BART, Bus 40 south on Telegraph to 66th St. No cover.*

MOVIE HOUSES

Of the several big cinema complexes that show first-run releases in the East Bay, the **Grand Lake Theatre** (3200 Grand Ave., near I–580, tel. 510/452–3556), just east of Oakland's Lake Merritt, is by far the most stylish, and no wonder—it dates from 1926. Just around the lake from the Grand Lake, the popular **Parkway Theater** (1834 Park Blvd., at E. 18th St., tel. 510/814–2400) offers a mixed program of recent-run blockbusters and art films. Admission is only $5; and Wednesday is two-for-one night. Best of all, microbrews and pizza are available at the concession counter. In Berkeley, Landmark's **UC Theatre** (2036 University Ave., between Milvia St. and Shattuck Ave., tel. 510/843–6267), in operation since 1917, shows foreign films and classics; double features are juxtaposed with great creativity, and billings change daily. The theater is cavernous, the seats lumpy, and you get to see John Waters ask you not to light up.

Pacific Film Archive. Housed in the UC Berkeley Art Museum, the PFA caters to hard-core film enthusiasts with its impressive collection of rare and foreign titles. Films change nightly and often center around a certain theme—past offerings have included "Space, Time, and Memory" and "An Evening with Ingmar Bergman." Filmmakers often show up to discuss their work before the show. *2625 Durant Ave., tel. 510/642–1412. Admission: $6.*

Paramount Theatre. An Art Deco landmark in downtown Oakland, the Paramount Theatre is a beautifully restored motion picture palace that now houses both the Oakland Symphony and the Oakland Ballet (*see below*). Classic and silent films are featured intermittently on Friday and Saturday evenings, complete with preshow organ music and old newsreel clips; live rock and jazz performances also take place here. Seating is reserved; buy tickets early since the seats toward the back are in the stratosphere.

Tours of the theater are available for $1 on the first and third Saturdays of the month at 10 AM. *2025 Broadway, near 19th St., tel. 510/465–6400.*

THEATER

Berkeley Repertory Theatre. Berkeley is currently cultivating an arts movement downtown, with the Berkeley Repertory Theater, which stages performances every night except Monday, as its keystone. The company also has some matinees in the smaller theater. The works are rarely experimental, but they are meticulously produced and well worth the $20–$45 ticket price. A limited number of half-price tickets are available at the box office on the day of performance starting at noon. *2025 Addison St., tel. 510/845–4700.*

Black Repertory Group. Founded in 1965, this Oakland company continues to be committed to the production of works by black authors and the celebration of black culture in the United States. The words of the likes of Langston Hughes and James Weldon Johnson are frequently represented in amateur but heartfelt musical and dramatic productions. Admission is $10, or $5 for the Saturday matinee. Some of the most interesting works are the one-act plays, shown for $3 on Sunday. *3201 Adeline St., tel. 510/652–2120.*

CLASSICAL MUSIC

Although the East Bay puts on fewer major productions than San Francisco, you can easily find an inexpensive venue for a concert. For chamber music, jazz, or world music in a beautiful, intimate setting, try the **Maybeck Recital Hall** (1537 Euclid Ave., at Buena Vista, Berkeley), designed by revered Berkeley architect Bernard Maybeck. UC Berkeley's **Zellerbach Hall** (Lower Sproul Plaza, tel. 510/642–9988) presents solo recitals, as well as chamber, orchestra, and contemporary renderings of classical works by some of the finest names in the world.

For $25 the PFA will set you up in a private screening room with a film of your choice: Choose from their vast library—particularly strong in Soviet and Japanese films—of 16-millimeter films. Call their reference line (tel. 510/642–1437) for details.

Berkeley Opera. If you think opera is a stuffy affair, this 20-year-old company may change your mind. For example, in 1997 they performed a new translation of Rossini's *The Italian Girl in Algiers,* retitled *The Riot Grrrl on Mars.* Many of its lead singers come from the San Francisco Opera Chorus; a few have reportedly gone on to the Met. The opera performs about three operas each season in the intimate Julia Morgan Theater (2640 College Ave.); tickets cost up to $28—a reasonable investment for opera lovers who have experienced only large houses. Tickets can be purchased by phone or at the opera venue. *Tel. 510/798–1300.*

Berkeley Symphony Orchestra. By an unbelievable stroke of luck, the Berkeley Symphony Orchestra has managed to hang on to Kent Nagano, a world-famous conductor who spends part of the year with Berkeley, part with the renowned Lyon Opera in France. His inspired performances—often featuring music by 20th-century composers—are well worth the $19–$35 ticket price. *Tel. 510/841–2800.*

Mills College. One of the hottest places around for contemporary composition and performance, Mills College hosts an extensive season of classical and experimental concerts during the academic year. Their whimsical and outlandish hall is in the Oakland hills; if you're coming by car, call ahead for directions. Many shows are free; some run $5–$10. *5000 MacArthur Blvd., Oakland, tel. 510/430–2296. From Coliseum BART, Bus 56 west.*

DANCE

One Oakland-based troupe to watch for is the **Dance Brigade** (tel. 510/652–0752), a casually feminist troupe that delights in subverting the classics. Also in Oakland, look for **Dimensions Dance Theater** (1428 Alice St., third floor, tel. 510/465–3363), a young, vibrant company that produces "choreo-dramas" teeming with African influences.

Oakland Ballet. Thirty-four years in the business hasn't corrupted this company. Though it's a classical troupe, company productions often bear a heavy thematic weight, exploring the outer boundaries of classicism. Seasons often feature revivals of early 20th-century classics as well as new works set to contemporary music. Performances are held in the grand old Paramount Theatre downtown (*see* Movie Houses, *above*); tickets run $11–$39. *1428 Alice St., tel. 510/452–9288.*

MARIN COUNTY

Quiet, residential Marin is not the place for night owls. If you do find yourself in Marin after sundown, head to the Sweetwater in funky Mill Valley (*see below*) or to any of the many fine bars and clubs in San Rafael.

LIVE MUSIC

Fourth Street Tavern. A fireplace contributes to the mellow atmosphere at this no-attitude bar that books mainly R&B and rock. *711 4th St., near Lincoln St., San Rafael, tel. 415/454–4044. Cover: none–$10.*

New George's. New George's routinely wins Bay Area polls for "Best Nightlife in Marin." Check out the live jazz, R&B, and acoustic entertainment, heavy on local talent and touring old favorites. *842 4th St., at Cijos St., San Rafael, tel. 415/457–1515. Cover: $5–$12.*

Sweetwater. This tiny Mill Valley club is a favorite hangout of famous locals like bluesman Roy Rogers who often stop by to jam. It's been called the "best little roadhouse west of Texas," and it attracts some of the finest jazz and R&B talents in the country. There's a two-drink minimum in addition to the cover. *153 Throckmorton Ave., at Miller Ave., Mill Valley, tel. 415/388–2820. Cover: $5–$20.*

THEATER

Marin Theatre Company. Drawing on the North Bay's formidable talent pool, this award-winning theater company (established 1967) runs from September through June, with a compelling mix of contemporary comedies, musicals, and dramas. *397 Miller Ave., at Evergreen St., Mill Valley, tel. 415/388–5208. Tickets: $10–$38.*

SOUTH BAY

Like any big city, San Jose has a big nighttime scene and a busy cultural calendar. Look for nightclubs and dance floors within the larger hotels, as well as a burgeoning cluster of small clubs in an area called SoFA—the South of First Area—along 1st and 2nd streets south of San Carlos Avenue.

Palo Alto is a different story. As any Stanford student will lament, the town is seriously hurting in the nightlife department. Still, Stanford University is surrounded by a few lively bars and clubs that draw an affluent student crowd, and there are some local favorites as well.

BARS

In Palo Alto, you can shoot pool, down suds, and meet locals at the **Blue Chalk Café** (630 Ramona St., tel. 650/326–1020), where a twentysomething group comes for espresso and beer. More trendy and with a notably impressive beer selection is **Gordon Biersch Brewery** (640 Emerson St., tel. 650/323–7723), where the young and beautiful mix and mingle. In San Jose, join the hip young crowd at **Café Matisse** (371 S. 1st St., at San Carlos St., tel. 408/298–7788), open daily until midnight.

Antonio's Nut House. At deliciously divey Antonio's, you can get Guinness on tap, free peanuts dispensed by a mechanical gorilla, and drinks until 2 AM nightly—a rarity around here. *321 California Ave., at Birch St., Palo Alto, tel. 650/321–2550. 2 blocks north of El Camino Real.*

Rose and Crown. Suburban Anglophiles, Stanford graduate students, and young professionals flock to this clubby British pub in Palo Alto. They serve everything from creamy pints to 20-year-old port, but the back room's dartboards are what really bring in the crowds. *547 Emerson St., at University Ave., Palo Alto, tel. 650/327–7673.*

South First Billiards. This warehouse-size pool hall (almost 30 tables) in the SoFA district of San Jose fills up quickly on weekends. In addition to 45 beers (15 on tap), the bar area has snacks, video games, and a Foosball table. *420 S. First St., at San Salvador St., San Jose, tel. 408/294–7800.*

Trial's Pub. When you tire of San Jose's trendy SoFA scene, head to this quiet British pub for a pint of Guinness or hard cider. The 1898 structure has a storied past—among other things it has been a jail, barbershop, hotel, and saloon—so it's understandable that it's a little worn. But it's comfortable thanks to cozy couches in the front and darts and a newly installed fireplace in the back. *265 N. First St. at Julian St., San Jose, tel. 408/947–0497.*

LIVE MUSIC AND CLUBS

Agenda. You have two options at this sizzling nightspot in downtown San Jose's trendy SoFA district: The Cellar spins dance music from the '70s, '80s, and '90s, Friday and Saturday. Upstairs, a swank Parisian-style lounge grooves Wednesday–Saturday to live jazz, R&B, and swing, with DJ'ed music the rest of the week. *399 S. 1st St., at E. San Salvador St., San Jose, tel. 408/287–4087. Cover: $3–$5.*

B-Hive. The crowd is always dressed to be noticed, and the air is thick with attitude, just as you'd expect at a slick SoFA spot. But pounding hip-hop, R&B, and dance mixes Wednesday–Saturday on two dance floors makes the bump-and-grind vibe contagious. If the scene is too much, you can always play pool at one of two tables near the bar. *372 S. First St. at San Carlos St., San Jose, tel. 408/298–2529. Cover: $5–$15.*

Cactus Club. The Cactus Club isn't fancy, but for years it's been the best spot in San Jose for indie rock, particularly up-and-coming local bands. As if that weren't enough, there's DJ'ed dancing on Monday (country music), Tuesday (retro modern rock and disco), and Thursday (Gothic/industrial); live music on other nights; and darts, video games, and snacks whenever your dancin' feet need a break. *417 S. 1st St., at E. San Salvador St., San Jose, tel. 408/491–9300. Cover: $2–$10.*

Café Borrone. Students come here in droves to listen to free Dixieland jazz on Friday nights. Hang out inside or out back on the brick patio. *1010 El Camino Real, near Ravenswood Ave., Menlo Park, tel. 650/327–0830. No cover.*

The Edge. No wonder it wins "Best Club" in the *Metro* year after year: The South Bay's hottest venue for live music has three huge floors and a great sound system. National rock acts play here, and some of the 'burbs' best DJs spin funk, techno, new wave, and disco on Tuesday, Friday, and Saturday. The Edge has even been known to lure hipsters out of San Francisco. *260 California Ave., at El Camino Real, Palo Alto, tel. 650/324–3343. Cover: $2–$20.*

Garden City. This classy jazz club, with its dizzying A-frame peak, has free live jazz seven nights a week. Some of the world's most talented acts have played on the club's intimate stage, including Miles Davis, Ray Brown, Mundell Lowe, and Mose Allison. *360 Saratoga Ave., at Stevens Creek Blvd. off I–880, San Jose, tel. 408/244–3333. No cover.*

JJ's Blues. This tiny family-run joint can't be beat when you're hankering for good ole Chicago-style blues (they also book jazz and Latin rock). Open since 1983, it's drawn legends like Albert Collins and John Lee Hooker. There are free popcorn and live music nightly, with a jam at 6 and a band at 9. *3439 Stevens Creek Blvd., between Winchester and Cypress Sts., Santa Clara, tel. 408/243–6441. From downtown San Jose, take W. San Carlos St. (which becomes Stevens Creek Blvd.) 1 mi west. Cover: $7– $12 Fri.–Sat.*

Jose's Caribbean Restaurant & Nightclub. A refreshing departure from Palo Alto's prolific student bars, this festive spot draws a varied crowd for its high-energy salsa and merengue dance nights and its tasty Caribbean cuisine. Beginners show up at 8:30 Friday and Saturday nights for lessons, while the pros trickle in later. Argentine tango lessons are on Tuesday nights at 7. *2275 El Camino Real near California Ave., Palo Alto, tel. 650/326–6522. From Embarcadero Rd. exit U.S. 101, head west to El Camino Real; turn left and continue a few blocks. Cover: $8–$10.*

Q Cafe. Students and twentysomething professionals flock to this spacious, well-designed club and pool hall that's open every night until 2 AM. The crowds show up for frenzied dancing on the split-level dance floor to DJ'ed techno on Thursday and hits from the '70s, '80s, and '90s on Friday and Saturday. The back is a whole different scene, with six regulation-size pool tables and a more laid-back atmosphere. *529 Alma St., between University Ave. and Hamilton Ave., Palo Alto, tel. 650/322–3311. From Hamilton Ave. heading west (1 block south of University), make a right on Alma St. Cover: $5 Thurs.–Sat.*

MOVIE HOUSES

Stanford Theatre. Founded and financed by Hewlett Packard Jr., this 1920s-style movie palace has all the trappings of the grand old days, right down to the velvet seats. It screens exclusively Hollywood classics, including silent films accompanied by the theater's mighty Wurlitzer organ. *221 University Ave., Palo Alto, tel. 650/324–3700. Admission: $6. Call for a schedule.*

THEATER AND CLASSICAL MUSIC

Big Lil's Barbary Coast Dinner Theater. You can hiss at villains and cheer for heroes at this old-fashioned melodrama and vaudeville venue. Hand-painted murals depicting San Francisco's wild Barbary Coast days, crystal chandeliers, and ragtime piano contribute to the nostalgic atmosphere. Shows are Friday and Saturday nights. *157 W. San Fernando St. between Market St. and Almaden Blvd., San Jose, tel. 408/295–7469. Dinner and show: $33.50, show only: $15.*

San Jose Center for the Performing Arts. Designed by the Frank Lloyd Wright Foundation, this 2,700-seat venue is home to the acclaimed **San Jose Symphony** (tel. 408/288–2828), the **San Jose Cleveland Ballet** (tel. 408/288–2800), and the **American Musical Theatre of San Jose** (tel. 408/453–7108). All perform from September through May. Summer months are devoted to traveling productions such as *Les Miserables. 255 Almaden Blvd., at W. San Carlos St., San Jose, tel. 408/277–3900.*

San Jose Repertory Theatre. The only professional resident theater company in Silicon Valley is considered one of the Bay Area's best. Each season (September through June) it stages six major contemporary and classical works in its 528-seat facility. *101 Paseo de San Antonio, near San Carlos St., San Jose, tel. 408/291–2255. Tickets: $16–$32.*

WHERE TO SLEEP 7

REVISED BY MELISSE GELULA AND LOTUS ABRAMS

S an Francisco's lodgings are as varied as its neighborhoods, although prices are rising quickly across the board. If mainstream isn't your style, you can opt instead for an artist's bed-and-breakfast complete with easels and plenty of light, a Haight District landmark whose nightly accommodations include the Summer of Love Room, a gay B&B in the Castro, or a funky, '50s resort-style motor lodge. For true affordability, though, you'll probably end up in one of the many hostels. Those in search of scenic open space outside the city will find it in Marin County's woodsy hostels and campgrounds, where beach campsites often cost less than $12. The San Mateo County coast has plenty of hostels and campgrounds that are as beautifully situated as those in Marin, and much less populated. To add to your choices, there are scores of motels in the East Bay, bed-and-breakfasts in Marin, and business-oriented chain hotels in the South Bay.

SAN FRANCISCO

The city proper has a surprisingly large assortment of reasonably priced accommodations, even if the 14% hotel tax does take an extra bite out of your wallet. For a great no-frills deal, stay in one of nine hostels, where a bed costs a mere $12 or so, or in one of the residential hotels that populate downtown and North Beach. For a bit more ($40–$60 a night), many small downtown hotels have charming European-style rooms (translation: the toilet's down the hall)—an option worth considering, since downtown is also the public transportation hub.

If you don't reserve a month in advance in summer, you may be exiled to the strip of generic motels along Lombard Street in the Marina District. These motels are about a 20-minute bus ride from downtown (on Bus 76) but are quite close to Fisherman's Wharf, the Marina Green, and the Golden Gate Bridge. On Lombard you'll pay $60–$80 for a double—stay here only if you're desperate. The area South of Market has its share of similar last-resort places on 6th Street, but the neighborhood can be unsafe; if you do want to stay in SoMa, try a hostel.

All prices listed are for a standard double room in high season (you'll find that "low season" means little difference in room rates with some hotels, but with others can prices can drop considerably), excluding tax.

HOTELS AND MOTELS

Directions below are given from the downtown BART/Muni stations along Market Street. To reach the stations from San Francisco International Airport, take SamTrans (see Bus Travel in Chapter 1): The 7F is an express bus with luggage limits, and the 7B is a local bus that allows heavy bags. Either will drop you on Mission Street one block south of Market Street; just ask the driver for the stop nearest your station.

THE CASTRO

Not surprisingly, the most prominent gay neighborhood in the United States offers a wide variety of accommodations tailored to gay and lesbian travelers, though all travelers are welcome almost everywhere. The hotels nearest Castro Street are pricey, but those on upper Market are more affordable; the entire neighborhood is generally safe at night. **Beck's Motor Lodge** (2222 Market St., 94114, tel. 415/621–8212) is a passable, love-in-the-afternoon budget option, with doubles for $95 and free parking. Those in search of a women-only atmosphere should call the **House O' Chicks** (tel. 415/861–9849; call for address), where the proprietors like to speak with potential guests before accepting reservations for their two rooms ($75–$100) with shared bath. To stay in the Castro in June, reserve far in advance, as thousands of visitors arrive in the area for the San Francisco Lesbian, Gay, Bisexual, Transgender Pride Celebration—San Francisco Pride, for short (formerly known as the Gay and Lesbian Freedom Day Parade). For a map of Castro lodging, see the Haight and Castro Lodging map, below.

UNDER $60

Twin Peaks. Transportation lines to downtown, the Marina, Golden Gate Park, and just about every other part of the city are within a block or two. The tiny but tidy rooms are nondescript, and there are no in-room phones, but the price is right: doubles range from $45 to $59 for those with a bath. Affordable weekly rates are also available. 2160 Market St., between Church and Sanchez Sts., 94114, tel. 415/621–9467, fax 415/863–1545. From Montgomery St. BART/Muni, Muni F, K, L, or M streetcar to Church St.; walk 1 block southwest on Market St. 60 rooms, 3 with bath. In-room safes.

UNDER $100

Inn San Francisco. One of a precious few remaining Victorians left untouched by the fire of 1906, this Italianate mansion has dimly lit rooms filled with antiques and amenities including feather beds, robes, chocolates, and, to leap ahead a century, a redwood-enclosed Jacuzzi out back. Continental breakfast is included ($85–$105 double with semiprivate bath; $125–$175 double with private bath), which you can take in the double parlor or in the garden. Ask the innkeeper, Marty Neely, to interpret the historical photos that line the downstairs hallway. 943 Van Ness Ave., between 20th and 21st Sts., the Mission, 94110, tel. 415/641–0188 or 800/359–0913, fax 415/641–1701. From 24th St./Mission BART/Muni, walk 1 block east on 23rd to Van Ness and take a left; walk 2 blocks north. 22 rooms, 2 with shared bath. Mini-refrigerators.

24 Henry. Walter, the friendly proprietor, caters to a mostly gay and lesbian clientele, but everyone is welcome. The rooms are colorful and cozy, the showers are big enough for two, and a complimentary breakfast is served in the Victorian-style parlor. Singles are $60–$95 per night, doubles $80–$95, and suites for three people with kitchens $105–$135. A second guest house on 18th Street near Castro was acquired in June 1999 and has five newly furnished bedrooms that are served through the main house. 24 Henry St., between 14th and 15th Sts., 94114, tel. 415/864–5686 or 800/900–5686, fax 415/864–0406. From Powell St. BART/Muni, Muni train E, J, K, L, or M to Church St., or F streetcar to Sanchez or Noe and Market Sts.; walk 3 blocks north to Henry St. 11 rooms, 4 with bath.

UNDER $130

Dolores Park Inn. Consistently rated one of San Francisco's 10 best by the San Francisco Chronicle, this 1874 Victorian is on a sedate street between the Mission and the Castro, one block north of Mission Dolores Park. Singles are $89, doubles $119–$189, including breakfast, afternoon beverages, and access to the garden and parlor. There's a two-night minimum stay. 3641 17th St., near Dolores St., 94114, tel. 415/621–0482. From any downtown BART/Muni station, Muni J streetcar to 16th and Church Sts.; walk 1 block south on Church St. to 17th St. 3 rooms, 1 with bath, suite with kitchenette.

Inn on Castro. Hyper '70s pop-art decor brings a cheery look to this immaculate B&B in a restored Edwardian. The low-slung couches around the fireplace are a cozy place to sip your complimentary brandy. Prices range from $100 for a double with shared bath to $175 for a suite with private bath and sundeck—all include a full breakfast of fruit, muffins, and pancakes or omelets. *321 Castro St., near Market St., 94114, tel. 415/861–0321. From Montgomery St. BART/Muni, Muni F, K, L, or M streetcar to Castro St.; walk 1 block north. 8 rooms, 7 with bath.*

CHINATOWN

Its narrow sidewalks lined with storefront meat and produce markets, Chinatown is almost as quiet at night as it is busy during the day. Bounded by North Beach, the Financial District, and Union Square, it's in the heart of the city, and it's chock-full of inexpensive restaurants, making it a smart place to be near. It's women only at the **Gum Moon Women's Residence** (940 Washington St., at Stockton St., 94108, tel. 415/421–6937), where doubles run $27 per night or $110 per week; guests have access to a full kitchen (although you'll need your own cooking utensils) and laundry facilities, as well as two spacious common rooms, each with TV. For a map of Chinatown hotels, *see* Downtown San Francisco Lodging map, *below*.

UNDER $45

Hotel Astoria. Steps from the Chinatown Gate, this hotel can be a real bargain—provided you're willing to share a bathroom. Singles with TV cost $38 a night; doubles with two twin beds are also $38, or $56 with bath. Rooms are decent and clean, and the neighborhood is prime. *510 Bush St., at Grant Ave., 94104, tel. 415/434–8889 or 800/666–6696, fax 415/434–8919. From Montgomery St. BART/Muni, walk 2 blocks west on Post St., 2 blocks north on Grant Ave. 70 rooms, 50 with bath. In-room safes.*

UNDER $75

Grant Plaza. This large hotel on a lively Chinatown thoroughfare (just a block from the Ritz) offers a bargain for groups of four—two double beds for $95. All rooms (singles $58, doubles $68) have private bath, color TV, phone, free toothbrushes, and use of hot pots at the front desk. It's a favorite with families and older travelers. *465 Grant Ave., between Bush and Pine Sts., 94108, tel. 415/434–3883 or 800/ 472–6899, fax 415/434–3886. From Montgomery St. BART/Muni, walk 2 blocks west on Post St., 2½ blocks north on Grant Ave. 72 rooms with bath.*

CIVIC CENTER

The area around the Civic Center *should* be a great place to stay: Davies Symphony Hall, the Opera House, and a slew of theaters, museums, and galleries are all within easy walking distance, and many of the city's public transport lines converge here. Unfortunately, the Civic Center can be quite dangerous, especially at night, due to an active drug and prostitution scene in the Tenderloin. After dark solo travelers—particularly women—should steer clear of the triangle formed by Market, Polk, and Geary streets; the section of Jones Street that runs through here is especially nasty and should be avoided even during the day. For a map of Civic Center hotels, *see* Downtown San Francisco Lodging map, *below*.

UNDER $55

YMCA. Although it's in one of the shadiest parts of the Tenderloin, the Y is a good bet for clean, safe accommodations, and the amenities might make you forget the sketchy surroundings. Guests have free access to a full-size swimming pool, a sauna, a fully equipped weight room, aerobics classes, and morning danish and coffee. Tired-looking singles with shared bath and clean sheets start at $42; doubles are $52. The few rooms with private baths go fast at $62. The cheapest sleeps are the 12 dorm-style bunk beds where, for $30, you can listen to the guy below you snore. *220 Golden Gate Ave., at Leavenworth St., 94102, tel. 415/885–0460, fax 415/885–5439. From Civic Center BART/Muni, walk 1 block east on Market St., 1 block north on Leavenworth St. 106 rooms, 6 with bath. Laundry.*

UNDER $60

Aida Hotel. Tourists from all over the world sleep at this centrally located hotel one block from the Civic Center BART station. Doubles with TV, phone, and private bath cost $59, but if you show this book to the desk staff, you'll get a $5–$10 discount. Although the highbrow name invokes Verdi's opera, the low-grade motel decor won't satisfy a true diva; but the rooms are surprisingly large, and those on the top floor are full of sunlight. Since there are 174 rooms, you can probably get something at the last minute, even dur-

ZEN AND THE ART OF SLEEPING

The San Francisco Zen Center, between the Civic Center and the Lower Haight, has four rooms for visitors with an honest interest in enlightenment. For $45 (single) or $55 (double with shared bath) you get a spotless, nicely furnished room overlooking a courtyard, plus a hearty breakfast. This working temple also has a longer-term guest-student program. Reserve in advance, especially during summer. 300 Page St., at Laguna St., 94102, tel. 415/863–3136. From Market St. downtown, take Bus 6, 7, or 71 west to Page and Laguna Sts.

ing high season. *1087 Market St., at 7th St., 94103, tel. 415/863–4141 or 800/863–2432, fax 415/863–5151. From Civic Center BART/Muni, walk 1 block northeast on Market St. 174 rooms, 100 with bath.*

UNDER $100

Abigail Hotel. There's nothing on this block but the Abigail and its terrific upscaleish vegetarian restaurant, Millennium (tel. 415/487–9800; dinner only), but it's a mere block or two from the area's cultural sites. When you've exhausted yourself with all the art, cross the lobby's tessellated floor in your opera heels and gown and retire to your room, making sure to enjoy its antique furnishings and down comforters. Your mornings here will be as nice as your evenings, as newspapers and continental breakfast are included in the room rate ($89–$99). *246 McAllister St., between Hyde and Larkin Sts., 94102, tel. 415/861–9728 or 800/243–6510, fax 415/861–5848. From Civic Center BART/Muni, walk 2 blocks north on Hyde to McAllister, turn left. 60 rooms with baths, 1 suite.*

Phoenix Hotel. This lively hotel is a tropical paradise on the edge of the Tenderloin, with bamboo furniture and piped-in poolside jungle sounds. But it's cool in that ironic way, a fact proven by such hip and illustrious past guests as R. E. M., the Red Hot Chili Peppers, and Pearl Jam. In keeping with the hipness, the front desk provides complimentary condoms *and* dental floss. During high season you'll pay $90 for a single or double (Continental breakfast, cable, and parking included) and have to book well in advance. Check out Backflip, the hotel's suburbia–gone–space age cocktail lounge and restaurant. *601 Larkin St., at Eddy St., 94109, tel. 415/776–1380 or 800/248–9466, fax 415/885–3109. From Powell St. BART/Muni, Bus 31 west on Eddy St. 41 rooms with bath, 3 suites. Restaurant.*

UNDER $125

Albion House. Opened as a saloon in 1906, this charming B&B is conveniently close to Market Street, city hall, and the Hayes Valley shopping and dining strip; the area is also relatively safe at night. Afternoon tea and evening wine and brandy are served in the old-fashioned drawing room, where a marble-columned fireplace and a baby grand piano complete the nostalgic mood. The smallish, well-appointed doubles start at $115, including full gourmet breakfast, and a room with two queen beds runs $165; ask about off-season discounts. *135 Gough St., between Oak and Page Sts., 94102, tel. 415/621–0896, or 800/625–2466, fax 415/621–3811. From Civic Center BART/Muni, walk 3 blocks southwest on Market St., right on Gough St. 10 rooms with bath. Restaurant, laundry.*

DOWNTOWN

This fog-shrouded neighborhood is home to San Francisco's Theater District, some shady local bars, and a handful of snazzy restaurants. Its many turn-of-the-century and Victorian buildings lend the area an old-world charm, and its central location affords easy access to North Beach, the Financial District, and Chinatown. Downtown, however, also adjoins the Tenderloin: Be cautious of the suspect characters who linger day and night. The safest area is west of Mason Street and north of Sutter Street.

UNDER $65

Adelaide Inn. On a short, dead-end street just minutes from Union Square, this sunny place attracts Europeans with its off-kilter, mismatched decor. Rates include continental breakfast; some kitchen facilities are also available. Rooms with queen beds start at $58. It's $64 for those with two double beds. *5 Isadora Duncan La., near Taylor St., 94102, tel. 415/441–2261, fax 415/441–0161. From Montgomery St. BART/Muni, Bus 38 northwest to Geary and Taylor Sts.; walk ¾ block north on Taylor St. and turn left. 18 rooms without bath.*

UNDER $90

Biltmore Hotel. Run by the same folks who run the Amsterdam next door (*see below*), the Biltmore has sunny rooms, some with great downtown views, for $79–$89 (doubles) nightly, and $475–$550 weekly. If you're quick and somewhat flush, you can have a deluxe suite with wet bar, microwave, and refrigerator. *735 Taylor St., 94108, tel. 415/775–0630, fax 415/673–0453. From Montgomery St. BART/Muni, Bus 2, 3, or 4 west to Sutter St. 60 rooms with bath.*

Brady Acres. Studios at this small, comfortable hotel near the Theater District are fully decked out, with in-room microwaves, toasters, silverware and dishes, coffeemakers, and mini-refrigerators filled with chocolates and jam—plus answering machines, cable TVs, radio/cassette players, and apricot and papaya shampoos in the bathrooms. Singles and doubles are $79 and $89–$109, respectively; if you pay for six nights, the seventh is free. *649 Jones St., between Post and Geary Sts., 94102, tel. 415/929–8033 or 800/627–2396, fax 415/441–8033. From Montgomery St. BART/Muni, Bus 38 west to Geary and Jones Sts. 25 rooms with bath. In-room safes, kitchenettes, laundry.*

> *A special legal exemption was obtained for the Phoenix's swirling black-tile swimming pool floor, since an obscure state law requires pool bottoms to be a certain shade of blue.*

San Francisco Residence Club. At the top of Nob Hill, this friendly family-owned pension built in 1910 offers a great deal: Breakfast and dinner (except Sunday) are included with a night's stay. Clean, spacious rooms have Victorian furnishings, and some see out to Angel Island. Even if your room doesn't come with a view, you can still enjoy the sunny garden or dabble on the lobby's Steinway. Doubles are $78–$148 nightly, $500–$795 weekly. *851 California St., at Powell St., 94108, tel. 415/421–2220, fax 415/421–2335. From Powell St. BART/Muni, walk 8 blocks north or take cable car to California St. 84 rooms, 6 with bath. Laundry.*

UNDER $110

Amsterdam. This comfortable, clean Victorian B&B is two blocks from Nob Hill. Singles with queen beds are $89; doubles start at $99–$109; deluxe doubles with a king-size bed, private Jacuzzi, and outdoor patio go for $139. The sunny, cloistered deck garden is a great spot to enjoy the complimentary breakfast. *749 Taylor St., between Sutter and Bush Sts., 94108, tel. 415/673–3277 or 800/637–3444. From Montgomery St. BART/Muni, Bus 2, 3, or 4 west to Sutter St. 34 rooms with bath.*

The Andrews Hotel. This 1905 Queen Anne–style Victorian building has small, pretty rooms with iron bedsteads, fresh flowers, and gracious service. A buffet-style continental breakfast is served in the hallway of every floor each morning, and complimentary wine is served in the hotel restaurant in the evening. Doubles are $92–$109; and suites with bay windows and juice bars are $142–$152. *624 Post St., at Taylor St., 94109, tel. 415/563–6877 or 800/926–3739, fax 415/928–6919. From Powell St. BART/Muni, walk 4 blocks north on Powell, left on Post St. 48 rooms with bath. Restaurant.*

Cornell. This small French country–style hotel on Nob Hill has flower- and lace-filled singles for $95–$110 and doubles for $110–$135. The French owners also operate a small restaurant in the cellar with a $27 prix fixe menu, stained glass, and medieval accoutrements on the walls. But leave your Gauloises at home; no smoking's allowed. *715 Bush St., between Powell and Mason Sts., 94108, tel. 415/421–3154 or 800/232–9698, fax 415/399–1442. From Powell St. BART/Muni, walk 5½ blocks north on Powell St., left on Bush St. 58 rooms, 48 with bath. Restaurant, in-room safes.*

Hotel David. David's famous New York–style deli has been selling knishes on Theater Row for more than 40 years. Not surprisingly, then, he's given thought to guest meals and deals at the hotel: A night in an immaculate single or double ($79–$139) includes breakfast and a 15% discount on lunch and dinner. The hotel also provides free pickup from San Francisco International Airport for guests who stay two nights or more. Two floors are reserved for nonsmokers. *480 Geary St., at Taylor St., 94102, tel. 415/*

MARINA

Chestnut St.
Lombard St.

① ②

③

Octavia St.
Gough St.
Franklin St.
Van Ness Ave.
Polk St.
Larkin St.

101

④ Chestnut St.
⑤ Lombard St.

⑥

Chestnut

Lombard

Greenwich St.
Filbert St.
Union St.

NORTH BEACH

Columbus Ave.

RUSSIAN HILL

Green St.
Vallejo St.

Broadway

PACIFIC HEIGHTS

Broadway Tunnel
Pacific Ave.
Jackson St.

Hyde St.
Leavenworth St.
Taylor St.
Mason St.
Powell St.

⑫

⑨

101

Lafayette Park

Washington St.
Clay St.
Sacramento St.
California St.

NOB HILL

Waverly
CHI

㉘

Webster St.
Buchanan St.
Laguna St.

Pine St.
Bush St.

Leavenworth St.
Jones St.

JAPANTOWN

Gough St.
Franklin St.
Van Ness Ave.
Polk St.
Larkin St.
Hyde St.

POLK GULCH

⑭ ⑬

㉗

Sutter St.
Post St.

㉖

UNION SQUA

Union Square

Geary Expressway

Geary St.
O'Farrell St.
Ellis St.

⑮

㉕

㉔

㉜

Eddy St.

㉞

Powe
ba BART

⑯

Turk St.
Golden Gate Ave.

⑳

McAllister St.

㉓

Market St.

Missi
5th St.
6th St.
7th St.
Howard St.

City Hall

CIVIC CENTER

Fulton St.

Grove St.

Hayes St.

⑦

⑧

⑰

⑱ ⑲

㉑

㉒

ba Civic Center BART Station

8th St.

⑳

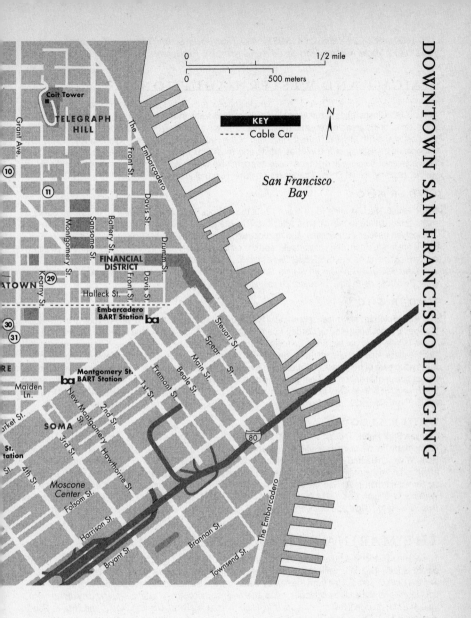

KEY
----- Cable Car

San Francisco
Bay

Coit Tower
TELEGRAPH
HILL

Grant Ave.

10
11

Montgomery St.

Sansome St.

Battery St.

Davis St.

The Embarcadero

Front St.

Drumm St.

FINANCIAL
DISTRICT

29

ATOWN

Kearny St.

Halleck St.

Davis St.

Front St.

Embarcadero
BART Station ba

30
31

RE

Montgomery St.
BART Station ba

Maiden
Ln.

rket St.

Stewart St.

Spear St.

Main St.

Beale St.

Fremont St.

1st St.

2nd St.

New Montgomery St.

Hawthorne St.

SOMA

3rd St.

St.
tation

St.

4th St.

Moscone
Center

Folsom St.

Harrison St.

Bryant St.

Brannan St.

Townsend St.

The Embarcadero

80

0   1/2 mile
0   500 meters

N

771–1600 or 800/524–1888, fax 415/931–5442. From Powell St. BART/Muni, walk 2½ blocks north on Powell St., 2 blocks west on Geary St. 54 rooms with bath. Restaurant.

HAIGHT AND WESTERN ADDITION

During its heyday in the '60s and '70s, the Haight saw rock bands (the Grateful Dead, Janis Joplin), poets (Allen Ginsberg), and runaway hippie children all settle in at various times. Staying here will give you a sense of the area's history and transformation; it will also put you close to other neighborhoods like the Castro and the Mission District. Northeast of the Haight, the once-seedy Western Addition is now undergoing something of a revival as artists and musicians discover its (relatively) cheap rents. Still, both areas can be dicey at night; be especially careful in the Western Addition west of Webster Street as well as all along Haight Street—particularly between Laguna and Pierce streets.

UNDER $60

Metro Hotel. The first thing you'll notice about the Metro is its neon sign lighting up Divisadero Street, a major thoroughfare in the Western Addition. This is a good middle-range option; it's popular with gay and lesbian travelers, Europeans, and the occasional rock band. The high-ceiling rooms (doubles $55–$104) are large, clean, and comfortable, and the café downstairs serves breakfast and lunch on a sunny outdoor patio behind the hotel. *319 Divisadero St., between Oak and Page Sts., 94117, tel. 415/861–5364, fax 415/863–1970. From Market St. downtown, Bus 7 or 71 west to Divisadero and Haight Sts.; walk 1½ blocks north on Divisadero. 24 rooms with bath. Restaurant.*

UNDER $90

The Red Victorian. An immensely popular Haight Street landmark, the Red Vic has rooms with various themes: Try the Japanese Tea Garden Room (single $86, double $96) or the nostalgic Summer of Love Room (single $76, double $86), complete with a tie-dye canopy and authentic '60s concert posters. Double-glass windows ensure that even street-side rooms are tranquil, and proprietress Sami Sunchild takes good care of her guests, right down to the free continental breakfast. Stays of three days or longer garner substantial discounts. Contrary to what you might expect from the neighborhood, this is a smoke-free hotel. *1665 Haight St., between Belvedere and Cole Sts., 94117, tel. 415/864–1978, fax 415/863–3293. From Market St. downtown, Bus 7 or 71 west to Haight and Cole Sts. 18 rooms, 6 with bath.*

UNDER $120

Stanyan Park Hotel. Though somewhat sterile, this hotel nevertheless offers a respite from the Haight's hippy-dippy hoopla of incense and tie-dye and is an excellent starting point for forays into Golden Gate Park. Wide, characterless hallways lead to immaculate doubles ($110–$160, including breakfast and afternoon refreshments). The $185 suites, which can sleep four adults and two kids, are bigger and better furnished than most San Francisco apartments and have full kitchens. *750 Stanyan St., between Waller and Beulah Sts., 94117, tel. 415/751–1000, fax 415/668–5454. From Market St. downtown, Bus 71 west to Haight and Stanyan Sts.; walk 2 blocks south on Stanyan St. 36 rooms with bath.*

THE MARINA AND PACIFIC HEIGHTS

The Marina District is a quiet, safe residential neighborhood popular with young folks climbing the corporate ladder. It's a long walk from North Beach, Chinatown, and downtown, but the views of the bay and the Golden Gate Bridge from the nearby waterfront are tremendous. Posh Pacific Heights sits above the Marina and shares its spectacular vistas; this neighborhood, too, is safe, quiet, and very dull at night, though a star-studded cast slumbers within its confines (Meg Ryan, Danielle Steele, and Nicolas Cage, to name a few). Union and Fillmore streets have a good selection of yuppified restaurants and singles bars. Unfortunately, most cheap lodgings in this area lie along busy Lombard Street (not on the "world's crookedest" part), a major thoroughfare leading to the Golden Gate Bridge. The **Travelodge** (1450 Lombard St., at Van Ness Ave., 94123, tel. 415/673–0691) isn't too bad—in a last resort kind of way—with clean singles ($99) and doubles ($125), which are cheaper on weekdays and during low season. Some of the smaller motels closer to Van Ness Avenue attract drug dealers, prostitutes, and other shady types, so look carefully before checking in. For a map of Marina and Pacific Heights hotels, *see* Downtown San Francisco Lodging map, *above.*

HAIGHT AND CASTRO LODGING

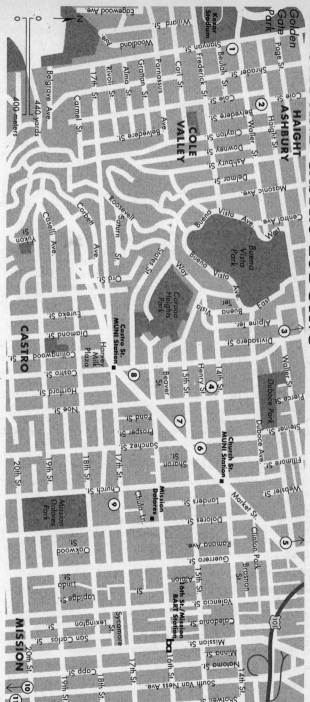

HAIGHT ASHBURY

Golden Gate Park

COLE VALLEY

Kezar Stadium

Buena Vista Park

Corona Heights Park

CASTRO

Castro St. MUNI Station

Harvey Milk Plaza

Church St. MUNI Station

Mission Dolores

Mission Dolores Park

16th St./Mission BART Station

MISSION

24 Henry, **4**
Beck's Motor Lodge, **7**
Dolores Park Inn, **9**
Inn on Castro, **8**

Inn San Francisco, **11**
Metro Hotel, **3**
The Red Victorian, **2**
San Francisco International Guest House, **10**

San Francisco Zen Center, **5**
Stanyan Park Hotel, **1**
Twin Peaks, **6**

165

UNDER $100

Holiday Lodge. At this '50s resort-style motor lodge, simply furnished rooms overlook the award-winning landscaped courtyard, making it hard to believe the very urban Van Ness address. Rooms in each of the two buildings are priced right ($89–$109), and those with kitchenettes (microwaves and mini-refrigerators) are a deal, since you can eat in. Kids can borrow board games when they're not splashing about in the heated pool. With so many perks you'll feel guilty whining about the flowery bedcovers; but you, your kids, and your car will be happy here, since parking is not only available, it's also free. *1901 Van Ness Ave., at Washington St., 94109, tel. 415/776–4469 or 800/367–8504, fax 415/474–7046. From Civic Center BART/Muni, Bus 47 or 49. 75 rooms with bath, 2 suites.*

Marina Motel. This quiet, family-owned motel is an excellent alternative along the generally bland Lombard strip. Built as little apartments in 1939, most rooms (doubles $95–$129) include fully equipped kitchens, garage parking, and views of a courtyard garden resplendent with pink bougainvillea and colorful murals by local artists. Off-season you can rent by the week for $375–$400. The multilingual staff will give you breakfast discount coupons for nearby Judy's Cafe. *2576 Lombard St., at Divisadero St., 94123, tel. 415/921–9406, fax 415/921–0364. From Embarcadero BART/Muni, Bus 30 northwest to Chestnut and Divisadero Sts.; walk 1 block north. 38 rooms with bath. Kitchenettes.*

UNDER $110

Hotel Del Sol. This new very colorful, very California motor lodge could be confused with its sister establishment, the Holiday Lodge (*see above*), if it weren't for the distinctive use of yellow and orange on the building's facade and courtyard and the capricious, possibly disorienting ("Am I in Ikea?") room furnishings. Doubles are $99–$139, and one of the 10 suites ($159–$219) has a bunk bed for kids. There's also a pool and sauna. *3100 Webster St., at Greenwich, 94123, tel. 415/921–5520, fax 415/931–4137. From Embarcadero BART/Muni Bus 45. 57 rooms with baths, 10 suites. Outdoor pool, sauna.*

UNDER $130

Art Center Bed and Breakfast. The owners like to call this place a country inn with a city built around it; when you see it, you'll understand why. The "inn," near the Presidio and the singles bars of Union Street, is cluttered with paintings of the big-eyed-animal-and-children type. If you want to take brush to canvas, the proprietors will be glad to set up an easel for you, and you can go to the garden in back for inspiration. Three studios ($105) and a pair of two-room suites ($125) have queen beds, TV, radio, and access to a small community kitchen. A three-room apartment with the same amenities and a private entrance runs $145. *1902 Filbert St., at Laguna St., 94123, tel. 415/567–1526. From Embarcadero BART/Muni, Bus 41 northwest to Laguna St.; walk 1 block north and turn left. 5 rooms with bath. Laundry.*

NORTH BEACH

North Beach—where Italian immigrants and beat poets once converged on narrow sidewalks—is a uniquely San Francisco experience and a great place to stay. Near downtown, Chinatown, and Fisherman's Wharf, this is also where most tourists congregate, and hotel rates are accordingly high. Although North Beach is close to many of the city's most popular restaurants, bars, and cafés, you should also be aware of a row of tacky strip joints along Broadway. An appealing, low-cost lodging option is the **Green Tortoise Guest House** (*see* Hostels, *below*). For a map of North Beach hotels, *see* Downtown San Francisco Lodging, *above*.

UNDER $75

San Remo Hotel. A short walk from Fisherman's Wharf and North Beach, the friendly San Remo is an incredible bargain in a pricey area. Quiet, spotless doubles with shared bath (but in-room sinks), redwood antique furnishings, and stained-glass windows cost $60–$80; the more you spend, the better your view. *2237 Mason St., between Francisco and Chestnut Sts., 94133, tel. 415/776–8688 or 800/352–7366, fax 415/776–2811. From Montgomery St. BART/Muni, Bus 15 north to Chestnut St.; walk 1 block west to Mason St. 64 rooms, 1 with bath. Restaurant, bar.*

UNDER $130

Hotel Bohème. Down the street from City Lights Bookstore and overlooking the outdoor cafés that sidle up to Columbus Avenue, Bohème re-creates the artsy ambience of the beat scene. Plush striped carpeting and black-and-white snapshots on the hallway walls will make you feel as if you've just stepped into a smoky, suspenseful scene from an old private-eye flick—minus the smoke (all rooms are no-smoking). Doubles cost $129; there's also one suite that goes for $154 (for three) or $159 (for four). *444 Columbus Ave., at Vallejo St., 94133, tel. 415/433–9111, fax 415/362–6292. From Montgomery St. BART/Muni, Bus 41 north to Vallejo St. 15 rooms with bath.*

HOSTELS

Hostels affiliated with American Youth Hostels (AYH), the American branch of Hostelling International (HI), promise a certain welcome predictability (for example, all have guest kitchens), but private hostels are often cheaper and filled with a more diverse crowd. Although some hostels require proof that you are a traveler, they don't have "youth" requirements, and both families and seniors can often be found among the backpacking college types. Due perhaps to the dearth of budget lodging in the area, hostels are extremely popular; make reservations before you arrive. In a pinch you can also try to get one of 12 dorm beds at the YMCA (*see Civic Center, above*).

AYH Hostel at Union Square. This huge hostel one block from Union Square sleeps 230 people—mostly international students—in rooms with one to four beds (in summer, $19 for members, $21 for nonmembers). The interior is bright and pleasant; amenities include a TV room, a smoking room, a library, and a kitchen (with microwaves, toasters, and refrigerators). Bulletin boards are covered with information on San Francisco nightlife and other attractions. About 40% of the rooms are set aside for reservations (a credit card is required), which must be made at least 48 hours in advance. *312 Mason St., between O'Farrell and Geary Sts., 94102, tel. 415/788–5604 or 800/909–4776, ext. 02. From Powell St. BART/Muni, walk 1½ blocks north on Powell St., 1 block west on O'Farrell St., turn right. 230 beds. Reception and check-in daily 24 hrs. Kitchen.*

European Guest House. A good choice for fans of SoMa nightlife or those departing on an early-morning Greyhound, this midsize hostel has decent bunk-bed lodgings in four-person dorms and first-come, first-served doubles ($18 per person). A sundeck, a common room, a kitchen, and laundry facilities make up for the less-than-savory showers: Bring your flip-flops and close your eyes. *761 Minna St., near Mission St. between 8th and 9th Sts., 94103, tel. 415/861–6634, fax 415/621–4428. From Civic Center BART/Muni, walk 2 blocks south on 8th St., turn right on Minna St. 24 beds. Reception and check-in 24 hrs. Kitchen, laundry.*

Fort Mason International Hostel. Perched high above the waterfront, this AYH hostel will dazzle you with its views of the bay and the Golden Gate Bridge. Reservations must be made at least 24 hours ahead with a credit card or a one-night deposit. Get here early if you don't have a reservation, as available space often sells out by 8 AM. Beds are $18 a night (no AYH membership card is needed), and everyone is required to perform a chore each day. *240 Fort Mason, 94123, tel. 415/771–7277 or 800/444–6111, fax 415/771–1468. From Transbay Terminal, Bus 42 to Van Ness Ave. and Bay St.; turn right on Bay St. and follow signs to Larkin. 150 beds. Reception and check-in 24 hrs. Kitchen, laundry.*

Globetrotter's Inn. The lack of restrictions and small size (it sleeps only 48 people) are among the strengths of this independent hostel on the edge of the down-and-out Tenderloin District. It's not as new or as sunny as some others, but the staff has done its best, putting artwork on the walls and creating a comfortable common space with a TV, plants, and a 24-hour kitchen. A space in a double or in a four- or six-person dorm costs $13; the 16 singles are $26. *225 Ellis St., between Mason and Taylor Sts., 94102, tel. 415/346–5786. From Powell St. BART/Muni, walk ½ block north on Powell St., 1½ blocks west on Ellis St. 48 beds. Reception and check-in 8 daily AM–midnight. No reservations. Kitchen, laundry. Cash only.*

Green Tortoise Guest House. From the people who brought you budget bus travel comes one of the best hostels in San Francisco. Green Tortoise is just steps from North Beach on the neon Broadway strip, a few blocks from downtown and Chinatown. European student backpackers book most of the rooms, which are clean, spacious, and rarely vacant—call ahead (no reservations are taken May–Sept.). There's no curfew or lockout, and the managers are friendly and mellow. Single bunks cost $18 per night and private doubles are $50. Rates include breakfast, and guests also have access to a sauna. *494 Broadway, between Montgomery and Kearny Sts., 94133, tel. 415/834–1000, fax 956–4900. From Montgomery St. BART/Muni, Bus 15 or 9X north. 40 rooms (110 beds). Reception and check-in 24 hrs. Kitchen, laundry. Cash only.*

Interclub Globe Hostel. Intended for international travelers (though passport-carrying Americans are not turned away), this SoMa hostel has few rules and a warm, relaxed atmosphere—not to mention a pool table and a sundeck with a grand view of the city. Dorms ($14 per bed) sleep four or five, and each has a bathroom; two floors are reserved for nonsmokers. During nonsummer months there are seven private rooms (doubles $40) that also rent by the week for $246. At the lively adjoining canteen, you can get dinner for less than $5. Older travelers and families will feel comfortable here. *10 Hallam Pl., near Folsom St. between 7th and 8th Sts., 94103, tel. 415/431–0540, fax 415/431–3286. From Civic Center BART/Muni, walk 3 blocks south on 8th St., turn left on Folsom St. 120 beds. Reception and check-in 24 hrs. Laundry. Cash only.*

New Central Hotel and Hostel. This former flophouse has been transformed into a decent hostel; the location is still seedy but central. Dorm space costs $15 per night ($95 per week); singles are $25 per night, doubles $35. Other perks include an exercise room, free coffee, breakfast, social events, a pool table, a jukebox, table tennis, and TV rooms. All visitors, even Americans traveling within the United States, must show travel documents to stay here. *1412 Market St., at 10th and Fell Sts., 94102, tel. 415/703–9988, fax 415/703–9986. From Van Ness Ave. Muni, walk 1 block northeast on Market St. 250 beds. Reception and check-in 24 hrs. Kitchen, laundry.*

Pacific Tradewinds. This extremely friendly, homey place in Chinatown has 28 dorm-style beds with kitchen access and a TV-less common room that's great for meeting fellow travelers. Thanks to recent renovations, there are new carpets, new bathroom fixtures and tiling, and nearly everything has a fresh coat of paint. If you want to come in after midnight, the proprietors will give you a key (with a $20 deposit). Beds are usually $16 per night, but ask about off-season discounts such as the wintertime special where you can stay seven nights for the price of six. *680 Sacramento St., near Kearny St., 94111, tel. 415/433–7970, fax 415/291–8801. From Montgomery St. BART/Muni, walk 1 block west on Post St., then Bus 15 north on Kearny St. 28 beds. Reception and check-in daily 8 AM–midnight. Kitchen.*

San Francisco International Guest House. Tucked away on the outskirts of the Mission District in a building that dates from the 19th century, this nicely maintained hostel has a five-day minimum-stay requirement that's known to breed—how shall we say it—intimacy; although there are no age restrictions, seniors, couples, and families may feel more comfortable elsewhere. There are two full kitchens, a TV room, and a funky, orange-color reading room. Rooms of two to four people go for $13 per person ($11 if you stay more than 28 days and pay in advance). International travel documents are required. *2976 23rd St., at Harrison St. (next to the Laundromat), 94110, tel. 415/641–1411. From 24th St. BART/Muni, walk 1 block north on Mission St. to 23rd St., then 6½ blocks east. 28 beds. Reception and check-in 24 hrs. Kitchen.*

San Francisco International Student Center. Right in the middle of SoMa, the student center has 16 dorm rooms, a small kitchen, a common room, and an owner who doesn't believe in television. There are no age restrictions, but the atmosphere is decidedly young and funky. Beds cost $13 a night, $84 a week. *1188 Folsom St., near 8th St., 94103, tel. 415/255–8800, fax 415/487–1463. From Civic Center BART/Muni, walk 3 blocks south on 8th St. to Folsom St. 38 beds. Reception and check-in 9 AM–11 PM. Kitchen. Cash only.*

EAST BAY

BERKELEY

Lodging in Berkeley is often either shabby or downright expensive—sometimes both. If that isn't enough, it's also often hard to come by: In mid-May, when thousands of graduating Berkeley students don caps and gowns, reservations become absolutely essential, since most of the nicer hotels sell out four to five months in advance. To add insult to injury, all Berkeley lodgings add 12% tax to the prices listed below.

Most of the city's motels are on **University Avenue** west of campus, and most of these are not recommended. Your life wouldn't necessarily be in danger here, but expect a general air of seediness (i.e., velvet curtains, the reek of cheap perfume . . .). It's best to stick to the campus end of University Avenue; the farther west you go, the shoddier the surroundings become. To reach all the motels in the vicinity from Berkeley BART, walk two blocks north to University Avenue and head west, or take Bus 51.

Berkeley has no youth hostels, but the **YMCA** (2185 Milvia St., 94704, tel. 510/848–6800, fax 510/848–6835)—open to both men and women—is cheap and within easy reach of Berkeley's sights. Clean dorm-style singles with shared bath cost $25; there are also a few doubles ($33) and triples ($40). After 14 days you're eligible to stay longer (in single rooms only) for around $100 per week. Guests have access to a kitchen and to a basketball court, weight room, and Olympic-size swimming pool at the fitness center next door.

UNDER $70

Campus Motel. The bright blue South Pacific–style sign out front is the best thing about this hotel on noisy University Avenue. Still, it's close to campus (six blocks west), and the rooms are tidy, plain, and cheap, with cable TV and coffeemakers. Singles are $55, doubles $60–$70. *1619 University Ave., between McGee Ave. and California St., 94703, tel. 510/841–3844, fax 510/841–8134. 23 rooms with bath.*

Golden Bear Motel. One of the nicer budget lodgings in town, the Golden Bear has clean doubles with two queen beds for $58–$99. Self-inclusive cottages ($145) sleep four and have everything you'll need to dine in except food. The surrounding neighborhood is a little shady, so be careful walking around at night. Bus 52, across the street, will whisk you to Telegraph Avenue and the Berkeley campus. *1620 San Pablo Ave., 94702, tel. 510/525–6770, fax 510/525–6999. From North Berkeley BART, walk 3 blocks west to San Pablo Ave. and turn right. 40 rooms with bath, 4 cottages. Restaurant.*

Travel Inn. Another pink motel on University, this place is cheap, clean, and far enough from the street to escape traffic noise. Though the rooms are generic, they have new TVs and phones. Singles cost $56, doubles $70. *1461 University Ave., between Sacramento and Acton Sts., 94702, tel. 510/848–3840, fax 510/848–3846. 3 blocks south of North Berkeley BART. 42 rooms with bath. In-room safes, laundry.*

UNDER $80

Flamingo Motel. True to its name, this plain, kinda old, but functional motel on University Avenue is painted pink. A room with one double bed is $65, and four-person, two-bed rooms cost $95. *1761 University Ave., at Grant St., 4 blocks from the Berkeley BART station, 94703, tel. 510/841–4242, fax 510/841–4449. 29 rooms with bath.*

Travelodge. If you're not concerned about price or atmosphere, you can always settle for the generic blue-and-white Travelodge, three blocks from campus, where basic, very clean doubles start at $78. *1820 University Ave., near Grant St., 94703, tel. 510/843–4262, fax 510/848–1480. 30 rooms with bath.*

UNDER $100

Beau Sky Hotel. This small hotel on the southern edge of campus has a porch overlooking colorful Durant Avenue. The large rooms (singles from $85, doubles from $95) are functional and clean, even if the decor is secondhand hodgepodge. Some rooms have balconies, and all have cable TV and telephone. Continental breakfast is included. *2520 Durant Ave., 94704, tel. 510/540–7688, fax 510/540–8089. From Berkeley BART, walk 3 blocks south on Shattuck Ave., turn left on Durant Ave., continue 4 blocks. 20 rooms with bath.*

Berkeley City Club. This landmark building with gorgeous high ceilings and Moorish-Gothic architecture was designed in 1927 by famed northern California architect Julia Morgan. It is now a private social club and hotel with rather spartan singles and doubles for $95 (Continental breakfast, parking, *and taxes* included). Many rooms have bay views, and guests have access to the club's fitness center and pool. *2315 Durant Ave., 94704, tel. 510/848–7800, fax 510/848–5900. From Berkeley BART, walk 3 blocks south on Shattuck Ave., turn left on Durant Ave. 42 rooms with bath. Restaurant, bar, laundry.*

French Hotel. This little hotel in north Berkeley is close to boutique shopping and several of Berkeley's best gourmet restaurants, including Alice Waters's world-famous Chez Panisse (*see* Chapter 4). Doubles with a minuscule patio cost $95; those without patio include a complimentary breakfast for the same price. Guests can take breakfast in the cozy brick-walled café downstairs. *1538 Shattuck Ave., between Cedar and Vine Sts., 94709, tel. and fax 510/548–9930. From Berkeley BART, walk 6 blocks north on Shattuck Ave. 18 rooms with bath. Restaurant.*

UNDER $110

Rose Garden Inn. Though this stretch of Telegraph Avenue is heavily trafficked and short on trees, this rambling Victorian hideaway does its best to make everything look rosy. Open the gates, and you'll enter a wonderland of flower beds, cute stone paths, and chintz. Doubles in the main house are $109. The larger, king-bed rooms in the Cottage or Garden houses run $145–$165. Many rooms have fireplaces and balconies, two have bay views, and all include a hearty breakfast. *2740 Telegraph Ave., at Stuart St., 94705, tel. 510/549–2145, fax 510/549–1085. From Ashby BART, walk 5 blocks east on Ashby Ave., turn left on Telegraph Ave. 40 rooms with bath.*

UNDER $150

Hotel Durant. An elegant lobby, a friendly staff, and a convenient location one block from campus make this hotel a popular choice with visiting parents and Cal Bears fans (book ahead for big football games). The rather small rooms all have big beds, mahogany writing tables, and forest green thick-pile carpet. Singles cost $120, doubles $140. Ask about available discounts. *2600 Durant Ave., at Bowditch St., 94704, tel. 510/845–8981 or 800/238–7268, fax 510/486–8336. From Berkeley BART, walk 3 blocks south on Shattuck Ave., turn left on Durant Ave., continue 5 blocks. 140 rooms with bath. Restaurant, bar.*

UNIVERSITY HOUSING

University Summer Visitor Housing (2601 Warring St., 94709, tel. 510/642–5796, 510/642–5925 June 1–Aug. 9), fax 510/642–9701) has summer dorm accommodations at Stern Hall (Hearst Ave. and Highland Pl). for $41 (single) and $54 (double) per night. Rooms have the basics: bed, desk, chair, and phone, and bathrooms are shared. But you'll get linens, soap, free local calls, and parking (fee). The dorms are a very safe place to stay, and every seventh night is free.

OAKLAND

Travelers concerned about price and safety should consider staying in San Francisco since Oakland's budget lodging scene is pretty bleak. Hotels are either geared toward executives with expense accounts, or they're in the middle of dicey neighborhoods. And, sad to say, Oakland has no youth hostel. If you're desperate, there are faceless chain motels in downtown Oakland and near the airport with rooms for $50–$75 per night.

UNDER $110

Best Western Inn at the Square. Traveling theater companies appearing at the nearby Paramount Theater often stay at this squeaky clean hotel. Just a block from the waterfront shopping and dining of Jack London Square and a short walk from the ferry pier, all rooms (singles $85, doubles $105–$125) have cable TV, coffeemakers, and phones; some have balconies. Especially nice is the sweeping, sunny courtyard with a pool and deck furniture, perfect for sunbathing. *23 Broadway, at 3rd St., 94607, tel. 510/452–4565 or 800/633–5973, fax 510/452–4634. From 12th St. BART, walk west on Broadway 9 blocks. 102 rooms with bath.*

CAMPING

Anthony Chabot Regional Campground. Perched above Lake Chabot southeast of downtown Oakland, this is one of the East Bay's most scenic sleeping options. Tent sites in a pleasant wooded area are $15 per night, plus a $6 reservation charge, and check-in is between 2 and 10 PM. The campground is close to hiking and biking trails (*see* Hiking and Biking *in* Chapter 8), and the lake is great for boating and fishing. Reserve ahead in summer. The nearest bus stop is 1½ mi from the park entrance; from there you'll have to hike a ways longer to get to the campground (if you have a car, you can park about 500 ft from the closest sites). *Tel. 510/562–2267. From I–880, I–580 east to Redwood Road exit; turn left and follow Redwood Rd. 4½ mi to park gate (it's another 2½–3 mi to campground). 63 sites. Drinking water, fire grates, flush toilets, picnic tables, showers.*

MARIN COUNTY

Across the Golden Gate Bridge from San Francisco, Marin County is home to a couple of idyllic hostels and plenty of breathtaking campgrounds. In addition, the **Bed and Breakfast Exchange of Marin** (tel. 415/485–1971) books brief or extended stays in private homes and B&Bs; expect to pay $65–$150 per night. They can also arrange a quintessential Marinite experience for you: lodging for four to six people in a houseboat (about $225 per night).

ALONG U.S. 101

SAUSALITO

Though tourists crowd Sausalito's streets during the day, all but the deepest of pockets have to find somewhere else to spend the night. Luckily, an excellent hostel and free camping are only a 10-minute drive away.

UNDER $90

Alta Mira Continental Hotel. This Spanish-style hotel in the Sausalito hills is well worth the price for the extraordinary bay and city views and is within walking distance of central Sausalito (albeit up a steep hill). Doubles start at $85; rooms with a view (some with private deck) are closer to $135. Even if you stay in one of the cheaper rooms, you can still enjoy the view of the bay from the hotel terrace. Every guest room has a TV and a telephone. *125 Bulkley Ave., 94965, tel. 415/332–1350, fax 415/331–3862. From U.S. 101, Sausalito exit, follow signs onto Bridgeway, turn right at Princess Ave. (the 9th stoplight), continue 3 blocks. 29 rooms with bath. Restaurant.*

HOSTEL

Golden Gate AYH-Hostel. Built in 1907, this friendly hostel is in the historic Fort Barry section of the Marin Headlands, just up the hill from the visitor center. In addition to endless hiking trails and breathtaking scenery, guests enjoy a communal kitchen, a laundry room, a tennis court, a Ping-Pong table, a pool table, and a common room with a fireplace. Dorm beds cost $12 per night; in another building private rooms are available for couples and families, starting at $35. No membership card is required to get this rate. Getting to the hostel by public transit is tricky: From San Francisco catch Golden Gate Transit Bus 10 or 50 from the Transbay Terminal and ask to be let off at the bottom of the Alexander Avenue off-ramp; from here it's a stiff 5-mi hike. On Sunday only Bus 76 goes from the Transbay Terminal all the way to the Marin Headlands Visitor Center, one block from the hostel. *Fort Barry, Bldg. 941, 94965, tel. 415/331–2777. From U.S. 101, Alexander Ave. exit, cross under freeway, make first right after MARIN HEADLANDS sign; continue 1 mi, turn right on McCullough Rd., left on Bunker Rd.; follow signs to visitor center. 103 beds. Lockout 9:30–3:30, reception open daily 7:30 AM–11:30 PM. Kitchen, laundry.*

CAMPING

Marin Headlands. There are three areas for tent camping, all available at no charge, in this beautiful section of the Golden Gate National Recreational Area, just a few miles north of San Francisco. Hawk Camp (three sites) is the most primitive; getting there requires a 3½-mi hike. Campers can drive within 100 yards of the sites at Bicentennial (three sites). At Haypress (five sites) you'll have a comfortable ¾-mi walk in. None of these campgrounds have water, fires are not allowed, and backcountry permits are required. To reserve a site and for permit information, call between 9:30 and noon no more than 90 days in advance. *Tel. 415/331–1540. Call anytime for directions. 11 sites. Pit toilets, food lockers, picnic tables (Haypress only).*

TIBURON AND ANGEL ISLAND

Tiburon has no cheap lodging. If you don't want to head to the Golden Gate Hostel a few miles south (*see above*), consider a ferry trip to Angel Island for a night of camping.

CAMPING

Angel Island State Park. Here you can get away from it all without losing sight of the city. Nine shower-less, primitive sites ($10 Sunday and Monday, $11 Friday and Saturday) are scattered around the island. Sites 3 and 4, with views of the Golden Gate Bridge, are the most popular; Sites 1 and 2, sur-rounded by pine trees and with a view of the East Bay, offer more privacy and shelter from the wind. Wherever you camp, prepare for a 2-mi hike. Reserve a few weeks ahead for a weekend stay; on week-days you can almost always get a site on the same day. For directions, *see* Tiburon and Angel Island *in* Chapter 2. *Tel. 415/435–1915 for information or 800/444–7275 for reservations. 9 sites. Barbecues, drinking water, pit toilets, food lockers, picnic tables.*

SAN RAFAEL

Although the hotels in this very down-to-earth town could hardly be called budget, they're more afford-able than the rest of Marin County. Smokers, be forewarned that San Rafael is an adamant no-smoking town—even lighting up in the privacy of your hotel room is an infraction subject to fine.

UNDER $55

Panama Hotel. In this rambling, circa-1920s Spanish ranch–style hotel you'll find individually furnished rooms—the Bordello Room has a bidet; the Roy Rogers Room is cowboy kitsch—some with canopy beds and claw-foot tubs. Rooms without bath start at $65 ($90–$145 with bath), including breakfast. The hotel restaurant has a trellised outdoor seating area that's perfect for enjoying your lattes and scones. *4 Bayview St., 94901, tel. 415/457–3993 or 800/899–3993, fax 415/457–6240. From U.S. 101, Central San Rafael exit, left on 3rd St., left on B St., continue 4 blocks to where B St. becomes Bayview St. 15 rooms, 9 with bath. Kitchenettes.*

UNDER $100

425 Mission. The homey rooms in this wood-shingled cottage come complete with antiques, rosewood and wicker furniture, and the occasional claw-foot tub. You can hang out on the redwood deck or in the backyard porch swing when the weather is nice or lounge in the comfortable downstairs living room. Rooms run $85–$105, including a gourmet breakfast; Dutch baby pancakes are the specialty. Guests have access to the hot tub, and if you stay a while, the innkeeper will do your laundry for free. *425 Mis-sion Ave., 94901, tel. 415/453–1365. From U.S. 101, Central San Rafael exit, continue 5 blocks to Mis-sion Ave., turn right. 4 rooms, 2 with bath.*

CAMPING

China Camp State Park. The trappings of civilization fade as you enter the 1,600-acre China Camp State Park, 4 mi northeast of San Rafael near San Pablo Bay. The 30 walk-in sites aren't far from the parking lot or from each other, but they're well sheltered by oak trees. And you get hot water (and coin-operated showers) to boot. Sites are $16 per night ($12 off-season), for up to eight people. *Tel. 415/ 456–0766 or 800/444–7275 to reserve. From U.S. 101, N. San Pedro Rd. exit, follow signs. 30 sites. Drinking water, fire grates, flush toilets, food lockers, picnic tables, showers.*

COASTAL HIGHWAY I

MT. TAMALPAIS

Hard-core hikers will be happy with the Pantoll campsites (*see below*), which are near the Mt. Tamal-pais ranger station and many trailheads. The Steep Ravine cabins, perched along the rocky coast, are better suited for those who want to escape civilization and its trappings—including roads and flush toi-lets. Both are supremely worthwhile.

CAMPING

Pantoll. Fifteen campsites, relatively close together but well sheltered by trees, are about a 100-yard walk from the parking lot of the Pantoll ranger station in Mt. Tamalpais State Park. The fee is $15 ($16 on weekends) per night. A 16th site ($3 per person) is reserved for those without a car. All sites are avail-able on a first-come, first-served basis. *Tel. 415/388–2070. From Hwy. 1, follow signs to Mt. Tamalpais*

State Park, then Panoramic Hwy. to Pantoll ranger station. 16 sites. Barbecues, drinking water, flush toilets, food lockers.

Steep Ravine Environmental Campground and Cabins. Off Highway 1 in Mt. Tamalpais State Park, Steep Ravine has six walk-in campsites for $9 per night, $7 off-season. Cabins with two double beds (read: wooden platforms—bring a sleeping bag) and two small bunk beds, as well as an indoor wood stove and outdoor barbecue, cost $30 per night. If you can deal with a pit toilet, this place is unbeatable—just you and a few other guests with an endless view of the dramatic coastline. Unfortunately, Steep Ravine is not an unknown gem, so cabins are fully booked well in advance, except in winter. *Tel. 800/444–7252 or 800/444–7275 for reservations. From U.S. 101, Stinson Beach/Hwy. 1 exit, follow Hwy. 1 until you see signs. 10 cabins. Drinking water, pit toilets, food locker. No pets.*

UNDER $150

Mountain Home Inn. The panoramic view from this romantic hiker's haven between the San Francisco Bay and ocean is breathtaking. *Every* room at the secluded B&B has a view and many have decks, fireplaces, and Jacuzzis. Hiking trails are everywhere, Muir Woods and the beach are 10 minutes away, and the inn's restaurant serves delicious food. You'll be spending $140—$260 for your room and full breakfast in your rustic-chic retreat. *Tel. 415/381–9000, fax 415/381–3615. From U.S. 101, Stinson Beach/Hwy. 1 exit to Hwy. 1, take left at first light; take right onto Panoramic Hwy, at four-way intersection, take road to Mt. Tamalpais for 2 mi. 10 rooms with baths. Restaurant, bar, deck, hiking.*

STINSON BEACH

Stinson Beach is full of B&Bs that are quaint in every detail except price. Expect to pay upward of $90 a night.

UNDER $75

Stinson Beach Motel. One of Stinson's few affordable lodging options consists of six endearing 1912 cottages (all without phone) surrounding a gravel courtyard abundant with star jasmine, climbing geranium, and lilac. Doubles are $60, and two four-person apartments with kitchens go for $80. If you can't get a room here, try the Redwoods (tel. 415/868–1034) just next door, where a double room including breakfast will cost you about $60. *3416 Hwy. 1, 94970, tel. 415/868–1712. Take 101 north to Tam Junction intersection; turn left onto Shoreline Hwy (Hwy 1 north), and continue about 6 mi. 6 cottages.*

POINT REYES

In addition to its excellent hostel, Point Reyes National Seashore has four free campgrounds, open to backpackers only, in isolated wilderness areas. You may have to hike in as far as 6 mi to reach one—but in these surroundings that's hardly a chore.

HOSTEL

Point Reyes AYH-Hostel. Eight miles west of the Point Reyes Visitor Center and surrounded by hiking trails, this place makes a great base camp—which is why it's so popular with both foreign travelers and weekenders from San Francisco. The two common rooms have wood-burning stoves and plenty of reading material. Beds cost $12; there is one private room for families with small children. *Mailing address: Box 247, Point Reyes Station, CA 94956, tel. 415/663–8811. From Hwy. 1, head left (west) on Bear Valley Rd. (1 block beyond stop sign in Olema), continue 1½ mi, turn left at LIGHTHOUSE/BEACHES/HOSTEL sign, left after 6 mi onto Crossroads Rd. 44 beds. Lockout 9:30–4:30, reception open daily 7:30 AM–9:30 AM and 4:30 PM–9:30 PM. Kitchen.*

CAMPING

To reserve a campsite up to two months in advance in Point Reyes ($10 per site), call the **Bear Valley Visitor Center** (tel. 415/663–8054) weekdays between 9 and 2. Trails to the campgrounds leave from the visitor center, which is on the entrance road (turn left off Highway 1 just past Olema on Bear Valley Road). All sites have barbecues, food lockers, picnic tables, and pit toilets.

Coast Camp is a 2-mi hike from the youth hostel parking lot (*see above*) or an 8-mi trek from the visitor center, but you'll sleep within a stone's throw (100 yards) of the ocean at any of the 14 sites. People tend to avoid the 12 sites at **Glenn Camp** because it's 5 mi from the nearest road, but it's in a quiet valley surrounded by trees, perfect for those who want to get away from civilization. The two group and 12 individual sites at **Sky Camp** are the most popular; they're a 2½-mi walk from the visitor center and 2 mi from the nearest parking area. The campground is perched on a small mountain ridge with an outstanding view. For the true misanthrope, **Wildcat Camp,** a stiff 6½ mi from the nearest road, has seven sites on a bluff, just a short walk from the beach. Privacy is never a problem.

Samuel P. Taylor State Park. This is a good choice if all the campgrounds in Point Reyes are full—or if you need creature comforts such as hot showers, flush toilets, and easy access to the road. Six miles east of Point Reyes on Sir Francis Drake Boulevard, 60 campsites are available for $12–$16 per night (hike-in and bike-in sites cost $3 per person). Reservations can be made through Reserve America (tel. 800/444–7275); during summer even weeknights are booked in advance. Golden Gate Transit Bus 65 stops at the park on weekends and holidays (*see* Bus Travel *in* Chapter 1). *Tel. 415/488–9897. From U.S. 101, take Sir Francis Drake Blvd. about 15 mi west. 60 sites. Barbecues, fire grates, flush toilets, food lockers, picnic tables, showers.*

SOUTH BAY

Though the area along U.S. 101 is crowded with strip malls, fast-food restaurants, and chain motels where double rooms invariably cost $50–$70 per night, there are a few decent lodgings in Palo Alto. San Jose offers little to choose from between uninspired budget motels and luxury accommodations. Many of San Jose's nicest hotels empty on weekends, however, when business travelers disappear, so check for rates that often dip below $100 a night. For a cheap weekend getaway, the San Mateo County Coast has two excellent hostels and several secluded campgrounds.

PALO ALTO

Although Palo Alto isn't exactly a mecca of budget accommodations, it's the most happening place to stay in the South Bay—a healthy number of upscale restaurants, bars, and cafés cater to the Stanford University community. Most of Palo Alto's budget motels are along **El Camino Real.**

UNDER $70

Coronet Motel. Traffic on El Camino Real makes it noisy, but the Coronet wins points for location and value (there's even a tiny pool). It's only a few blocks from Stanford University, and the Stanford Shopping Center is a short drive away. Doubles are $60–$65, and the rooms—many with kitchenettes—are comfortable, if not exactly modern. *2455 El Camino Real, between California Ave. and Page Mill Rd., 94306, tel. 650/326–1081. From U.S. 101, take Embarcadero Rd. exit west, turn left on El Camino Real. 21 rooms with bath.*

Cowper Inn. The spacious, airy rooms in this Victorian B&B are filled with antiques, and all have phone and cable TV. Doubles start at $65 with shared bath, $130 with private bath and/or kitchenette (breakfast included). Sip sherry and munch on almonds in the parlor after spending the day exploring the nearby San Mateo Coast. *705 Cowper St., at Forest Ave., 94301, tel. 650/327–4475, fax 415/329–1703. From U.S. 101, take University Ave. west 2–3 mi, turn left on Cowper St., continue 2 blocks. 14 rooms, 12 with bath. Kitchenettes.*

HOSTELS

Hidden Villa Hostel. This is an actual working farm, complete with animals and organic gardens. Set in a 1,600-acre canyon in the Los Altos Hills between Palo Alto and San Jose, it's surrounded by hiking trails and peaceful dirt roads. Large, rustic dorm-style cabins dot the canyon, and each cabin has communal bathroom facilities. HI members pay $11 per night, nonmembers $14. You can also reserve a private room for $25. There's no curfew, but lockout is 9:30–4:30. *26870 Moody Rd., Los Altos Hills 94022, tel. 650/949–8648. From San Francisco, I–280 south past Palo Alto to El Monte/Moody Rd. exit, turn right on El Monte Ave., left on Moody Rd. (at stop sign), continue 1¾ mi. Or from San Francisco, take SamTrans Bus 7F from Transbay Terminal (see Bus Travel in Chapter 1) to Palo Alto, then SamTrans Bus 35 to Foothill College; walk 2 mi to hostel. 35 beds. Reception open daily 8–9:30 and 4:30–9:30. Closed June–Aug.*

Sanborn Park Hostel. This is one of the most attractive hostels in California, perfectly situated for avid hikers and bicyclists and easily reached by public transit. The main cottage, a log cabin that dates from 1908, is surrounded by the dense 300-acre redwood forest of Sanborn Park, also home to a nearby nature museum. Hostelers stay in a large hall and have access to a volleyball court, a grill, laundry facilities, and the standard HI kitchen—all for $8.50 per night ($10.50 for nonmembers). Bring your own food, since the only restaurants and grocery stores are 4 mi away in downtown Saratoga. Sheet rental costs 50¢. *15808 Sanborn Rd., Saratoga 95070, tel. 408/741–0166. From San Francisco, I–280 south to Saratoga/Sunnyvale exit, turn right, go 5½ mi to Hwy. 9, turn right (toward Big Basin), go 2½ mi, turn left at* SANBORN SKYLINE COUNTY PARK *sign, go 1 mi, and turn right. Or from Sunnyvale CalTrain station, take Santa Clara County Transit Bus 54 to Saratoga post office; call hostel for ride. 39 beds. Curfew 11* PM, *lockout 9–5, reception open daily 7* AM–9 AM *and 5* PM–11 PM. *Kitchen, laundry. Cash or checks only.*

SAN JOSE

When midweek conference goers leave San Jose, weekend specials abound at some of San Jose's fancier hotels, like the full-service **DoubleTree Hotel** (2050 Gateway Pl., 95110, tel. 408/453–4000), which offers weekend rates starting at $89. The hotel has a sprawling lobby with its own sushi bar, a large pool with a hot tub and sauna, modems in every room, and a feature Silicon Valley types appreciate: portable phones that work anywhere in the hotel.

UNDER $70

Vagabond Inn San Jose. This motel is nothing fancy, but it's located right across from a light rail stop, making it easy to get downtown. All rooms, which start at $69, have refrigerators, hair dryers, coffeemakers, and modem lines; a continental breakfast is included. The motel's best features are a 24-hour restaurant and a pleasant outdoor pool and spa area surrounded by palm trees. *1488 N. First St., at Gish Rd., 95112, tel. 408/453–8822, fax 408/453–0559. From US 101, exit First St. and go south to Gish Rd. 76 rooms.*

UNDER $75

San Jose Sports Arena Travelodge. The streets close to the sports arena are lined with motels, and this one is a notch above the rest. The small, barren pool area is rather dismal, but the rooms are pleasantly decorated, reasonably sized, and maintained in excellent condition. Rooms start at $70 and come with a microwave, refrigerator, and coffeemaker. *1041 Alemeda, at Race St., 95126, tel. 408/295–0159, fax 408/998–5509. Take Santa Clara St. east from downtown (it turns into Alemeda). The motel is located just a few blocks past the arena. 62 rooms.*

UNDER $80

Madison Street Inn. This affordably priced B&B in Santa Clara achieves a homey feeling with its Victorian-decorated rooms, sunny backyard garden (with pool and hot tub), and cozy parlor (where sherry and port are always available). Rooms with shared bath go for $75 a night, and rooms with private bath cost $95–$125. Breakfasts may include Belgian waffles or baked apples and are often served in the garden in summer. The only minus is that you are 15 minutes from downtown San Jose. *1390 Madison St., at Lewis St., Santa Clara 95050, tel. 408/249–5541. From U.S. 101, take De La Cruz Blvd. exit south (it becomes Lewis St.). 6 rooms, 2 with shared bath.*

San Jose Convention Inn. A spring 1999 remodeling gave the rooms at this downtown motel some much-needed attention, and the fitness center was upgraded as well. Rates start at $75 and include breakfast. All rooms have refrigerators, and the motel has a pool, hot tub, and sauna. But the best thing about it is the location—right downtown, just a few blocks away from San Jose's major attractions and the South of First Street nightlife scene. *455 S. Second St., between San Salvador and William Sts., 95112, tel. 408/298–3500, fax 408/298–2477. 72 rooms.*

UNDER $105

The Briar Rose Bed and Breakfast. If you want to escape the characterless budget motels in San Jose and spend a little extra, try this charming B&B in an 1875 Victorian farmhouse on nearly half an acre of gardens. The cozy front parlor is welcoming with its marble fireplace, and rooms ($100–$140, all with private baths) are decorated with antiques and have special touches like feather mattresses. For breakfast you might have quiche, crêpes filled with caramel apples, or an omelet with vegetables straight from the garden. *897 Jackson St., at 19th St., 95112, tel. 408/279–5999, fax 408/279–4534. From U.S. 101, take the 13th St. exit south, turn left at Jackson St. 6 rooms with private bath.*

SAN MATEO COUNTY COAST

The desolate coastline south of San Francisco has some of the area's most striking scenery. **Half Moon Bay,** the largest and most centrally located town, is not the best choice for budget accommodations. Instead, head for Montara or Pescadero, where the Bay Area's two best lodging deals await you.

PACIFICA AND MONTARA

The hostels here are far more memorable than the generic budget motels. Of the latter, the **Sea View Motor Lodge** (2160 Francisco Blvd., 94044, tel. 650/359–9494) is a step above the others: Airy, comfortable doubles, many with an ocean view, go for $50 ($70 for a quad with a kitchenette). Highway 1 is distressingly close, but you're within walking distance of the beach and old town.

HOSTEL

Point Montara Lighthouse AYH-Hostel. This functioning lighthouse and its adjoining hostel are perched on a cliff a half mile south of Montara State Beach. Best of all, you get incredible views of the coastline and access to a beach and tide pools. Inside, there's a fireplace in the comfortable living room, a communal kitchen, a dining area, and an outdoor hot tub ($6 per person per hour, two-person minimum). Beds go for $13 per night ($16 for nonmembers), and everyone must perform a small chore. Reservations can be made up to six months in advance with a night's deposit. *Hwy. 1 at 16th St., Montara 94037, tel. 650/728–7177. From Daly City BART, SamTrans Bus 1L or 1C southbound; ask driver to let you off at 14th St. 45 beds. Curfew 11 PM, lockout 9:30–4:30, reception open daily 7:30–9:30 and 4:30–9:30. Kitchen, laundry.*

HALF MOON BAY

On the southern outskirts of town, the distinctly European **Cameron's Inn** (1410 S. Cabrillo Hwy., 94019, tel. 650/726–5705) has three clean, simple doubles, two with shared bath ($90), that are as cheap as you'll find in the area. Big beds and fine-art prints lend some style to the rooms, but that does not diminish the noise of big rigs downshifting on the highway. The **San Benito House** (356 Main St., 94019, tel. 650/726–3425), built at the turn of the century, has 12 rooms with a beautiful backyard garden and a pricey restaurant overlooking Main Street. Nightly rates are $60 (shared bath), $75–$95 (private bath), with a 20% weekday discount. If all else fails, a 20-room **Ramada Inn** (3020 Hwy. 1, 94019, tel. 650/726–9700 or 800/272–6232) at the north end of town has doubles starting at $85 weekdays, $95 weekends, including breakfast.

UNDER $130

Old Thyme Inn. If you're going to splurge on coastal accommodations, head to this romantic 1899 Victorian inn. The Laura Ashley–clad rooms, each named after a different herb, are all decked out with fresh-cut flowers, charming antiques, and the innkeepers' collection of fine art. All this for $125–$180 ($210 and up for a fireplace and a whirlpool bath). A bountiful breakfast is served in the parlor, where sherry and snacks of candy or cheeses await you every evening. *779 Main St., 94019, tel. 650/726–1616 or 800/720–4277, fax 650/726–6394. From State 92 make a left on Main St. in Half Moon Bay. 7 rooms with bath.*

CAMPING

Half Moon Bay State Beach. Because of its proximity to downtown Half Moon Bay, this place attracts teenage partyers and weekend warriors, especially during summer. You'll fall asleep to the sound of waves and arise to the smell of the sea, but it's hardly the great outdoors. At the base of a small sand dune, the 56 characterless sites cost $16 per night; all sites are doled out on a first-come, first-served basis. *95 Kelly Ave., 94019, tel. 650/726–8820. From Hwy. 1, Kelly Ave. west. 56 sites. Barbecues, drinking water, fire grates, flush toilets, food lockers, picnic tables.*

LA HONDA

Outdoorsy types have four excellent lodging choices in La Honda.

HOSTEL

Hiker's Hut. This A-frame cabin in Sam McDonald County Park sits atop a ridge 1½ steep mi above the parking lot—from the deck you can see the ocean on a clear day. There's sleeping space for 14 people; the fee is $10 per night per person ($8 for Sierra Club members). Reservations require a 50% check deposit and must be made well in advance, especially for summer weekends. Reserve through the Loma Prieta chapter of the Sierra Club (3921 E. Bayshore Rd., Palo Alto 94303, tel. 650/390–8411). *Take Hwy. 84 ½ mi west of La Honda, turn left on Pescadero Rd., drive 2 mi to Sam McDonald parking lot (follow signs). Kitchen, pit toilets.*

CAMPING

Memorial County Park has 156 quiet sites ($15), with picnic tables, fire pits, and hot showers, in a thick old-growth forest. Although popular with car campers on summer weekends, the campground is sparsely visited at other times. Sites are allotted on a first-come, first-served basis. In **Portola Redwood State Park,** the 53 family sites and seven hike-in sites ($17–$18) see little light in their cool berth beneath the redwoods. The family sites have running water, showers, fire pits, and picnic tables. Reserve through Reserve America (tel. 800/444–7275). **Pescadero Creek County Park** has 15 hike-in sites (free) in the midst of a dense second-growth forest along the river. Contact the rangers at Portola Redwood State Park (tel. 650/948–9098) to secure a spot. For directions to these parks and information on exploring them, *see* South Bay *in* Chapter 2.

PESCADERO

This pristine town overlooks miles of unblemished coastline; an enchanting hostel and peaceful campgrounds are situated among the redwoods.

HOSTEL

Pigeon Point Lighthouse Youth Hostel. Perched on a small bluff 5 mi south of Pescadero State Beach are four bungalow-style dorms, plus an outdoor, bluff-side hot tub ($3 per person per half hour). Tours of the historic lighthouse on the grounds are available for $2. One night in any of the 52 comfortable beds costs $13 ($16 for nonmembers); another $12 secures a private room for two. All guests must do a chore each day of their stay. The maximum stay is three nights. *210 Pigeon Point Rd. and Hwy. 1, 94060, tel. 650/879–0633. From Daly City BART, take SamTrans Bus 1L to Half Moon Bay, then Sam-Trans Bus 96C. Curfew 11 PM, lockout 9:30–4:30, reception open daily 7:30–9:30 and 4:30–9:30. Kitchen.*

CAMPING

Surprisingly few visitors venture out to the 21 campsites and 18 hike-in sites ($16 weekends, $15 weekdays) in quiet **Butano State Park** (tel. 650/879–2040). All sites have fire rings, picnic tables, and food lockers. Reservations can be made through Reserve America (tel. 800/444–7275) up to eight weeks in advance but are usually not necessary. None of the sites has showers. For directions to Butano and information on the park, *see* The San Mateo County Coast *in* Chapter 2.

THE GREAT OUTDOORS

REVISED BY LISA HAMILTON

I t's no surprise that Bay Area residents have a discriminating palate for the outdoors—many people choose to live here precisely because some of the country's most spectacular natural attractions are within easy reach of the city. The cool, moist woodlands of Marin County are prime territory for hikers, bikers, horseback riders, and bird-watchers. Afternoon breezes make San Francisco Bay ideal for windsurfing. And when the summer winds die down, you can put away your sail and dust off the surfboard for the winter waves. Rock climbers, in-line skaters, mountain bikers, and sea kayakers will have no trouble finding new challenges in the Bay Area. This is California, after all, where even Silicon Valley professionals surf more than the Internet.

A great place to get the inside scoop on the outdoors is at **Outdoors Unlimited** (OU; 550 Parnassus Ave., at 3rd Ave., tel. 415/476–2078), where volunteers teach everything from fly-fishing to CPR, organize backpacking and cycling outings, lead moonlight kayak trips, and rent out top-notch equipment. The office is open Monday and Friday 11:30 AM–1:30 PM and 5 PM–8 PM, Tuesday–Thursday 5 PM–8 PM. Berkeley's **Cal Adventures** (2301 Bancroft Way, tel. 510/642–4000 or 510/643–8029), on the UC campus, offers a wide variety of affordable outings and lessons in such sports as sailing, kayaking, windsurfing, backpacking, and rock climbing. It also rents equipment at low prices. The office is open weekdays 10–6.

The nonprofit **Environmental Traveling Companions** (ETC; Fort Mason Center, Bldg. C, tel. 415/474–7662) leads sea kayaking, river rafting, and cross-country skiing expeditions in and around the Bay Area for people with special needs—physical as well as financial—as well as for the population at large (*see* Disabilities & Accessibility *in* Chapter 1).

The best places to stock up on sports-related pamphlets, books, and maps are San Francisco's **Rand McNally** (595 Market St., at 2nd St., tel. 415/777–3131), Oakland's **Sierra Club Bookstore** (6014 College Ave., tel. 510/658–7470), and Berkeley's **REI** (1338 San Pablo Ave., tel. 510/527–4140), which also hosts free wilderness lectures, book signings, and slide presentations. **Transit Outdoors,** published by the Bay Area Open Space Council, is a free guide to reaching Bay Area parks and trailheads via public transportation; it's available at public libraries and park districts. Also check out www.transitinfo.org/outdoors.

BODYWORK

The Bay Area counterculture of the 1960s left behind a legacy of varied value, but one certain blessing is today's network of body-work and healing-arts professionals and the inexpensive services they provide. Massage is offered in quick, cheap doses throughout the city, every place from health food markets to street fairs. The area's many massage schools offer low-cost, full-body rubdown clinics conducted by students but always supervised by experts. **Alive and Well! Institute of Conscious Body-work** (100 Shaw St., San Anselmo, tel. 415/258–0402; take Golden Gate Transit bus 18 or 20 from San Francisco or 19 from the Larkspur Ferry) holds the area's cheapest clinic on Monday, Thursday, and Saturday and charges $18 for 50 minutes. Friday from 4 to 7 PM the workweek winds down with Swedish and vibrational massage at the **World School of Massage and Advanced Healing Arts** (401 32nd Ave., tel. 415/221–2533); one hour costs $25. For the same price ($20 an hour for those 55 and older), students at the **National Holistic Institute** (5900 Hollis St., Suite J, Emeryville, tel. 510/547–6442) will practice their Swedish and shiatsu techniques on you. Their clinics are held daily, but times vary so be sure to call first.

New, fancy yoga centers seem to spring up daily, but, considering that this art has been around longer than Western civilization, you really don't need more than the basics. San Francisco's best-known center is the **Integral Yoga Institute** (770 Dolores St., at 21st St., tel. 415/824–9600), where hatha yoga classes cost $8, or $5 for first-timers and those over 62 or HIV+. University of California's **CalFIT Yoga** (Recreational Sports Facility, 2301 Bancroft Way 4420, Berkeley, tel. 510/643–5151) offers no-frills vinyasa yoga classes for $4.50. The best deal in the Bay Area is at the **Happy Belly Deli and Café** (30 Jack London Sq., Shop #216, Oakland, tel. 510/835–0446), where every Monday at 6 PM there's a free Astanga and Iyengar class. The **World Gym** (see Fitness Centers and Pools, *below*) includes Bikram yoga classes within its $10 day pass rate.

GOLF

The Bay Area isn't lacking for fairways, but each has its place and time in (and out of) the sun. Ocean-side courses are reliably beautiful but also reliably windy, so unless you have an industrial strength wind-breaker (and a heavy driver), these courses are frustrating on all but the calmest days. Inland courses in Marin and the East Bay are sunny from April to November, while San Francisco greens are best in spring and fall (though fog-lovers will enjoy them year-round).

San Francisco's **golf information line** (415/750–4653) gives detailed information on prices and offers advance booking for the city's public courses. Though usually fogged in, **Harding Park** (Harding Rd. and Skyline Blvd., tel. 415/664–4690) is the city's best place to play golf, with a heavily forested and well-trapped par-72 course whose illustrious past includes several international tournaments. The 18-hole, par-68 course at **Lincoln Park** (34th Ave. and Clement St., tel. 415/221–9911) has a weaker lay-out but makes up for it with stunning views of the Golden Gate Bridge and the Pacific Ocean. Beginners will appreciate the 9-hole, par-27 at **Golden Gate** (47th Ave., between Fulton St. and John F. Kennedy Dr., tel. 415/751–8987). Arnold Palmer's 18-hole, par-72 **Presidio Golf Course** (300 Finley Rd., near W. Pacific Ave. and Arguello Blvd., tel. 415/561–4653) is privately maintained, so it's better groomed than city courses and consequently more expensive. The challenging **Gleneagles International Golf Course** (2100 Sunnydale Ave., tel. 415/587–2425), in McLaren Park, offers nine holes at a par-36.

FITNESS CENTERS AND POOLS

In this city of beautiful bodies, you'll have only to walk a block or two to pump iron, swim laps, or aero-bicize. Although some clubs are members-only, most facilities sell day passes for an average charge of $10 to $20. The **Embarcadero YMCA** (169 Steuart St., tel. 415/957–9622) has racquetball, a 25-meter swimming pool, and aerobics classes. The $12 drop-in fee includes use of the sauna, steam room, and whirlpool, plus a magnificent view of the bay. The various branches of **24-Hour Fitness** (1645 Bryant St., tel. 415/437–4188; 1200 Van Ness Ave., tel. 415/776–2200; 350 Bay St., tel. 415/583–3535; 100 California St., tel. 415/434–5080; 2nd St. at Folsom St., tel. 415/543–7808) are open to the public for a $15 drop-in fee. Most branches have saunas, Jacuzzis, and steam rooms, plus aerobics classes and a complete line of fitness equipment. The **World Gym** (290 De Haro St., at 16th St., tel. 415/703–9650), though a bit off the beaten track, is a must-see for bodybuilding enthusiasts; what it lacks in spa facilities it makes up for in extensive weight-training and aerobic equipment. The day rate of $10 includes aerobics classes.

The facilities at some hotels are open to nonguests for a fee. Try the swanky clubs at the **Hotel Nikko** (222 Mason St., tel. 415/394–1153) or the **Fairmont** (950 Mason St., tel. 415/772–5000), where the fees are $20 and $15, respectively.

If you're more inclined to work out in water, try the San Francisco Recreation and Park Department's (tel. 415/831–2700) one outdoor swimming pool and eight indoor pools throughout the city. Fees are $3 for adults over 18. The **Sava Pool** (19th Ave. and Wawona St., tel. 415/753–7000) is one of the more popular (and crowded) pools. **Hamilton Pool** (Geary Blvd. and Steiner St., tel. 415/292–2001) is a favorite among serious lap swimmers. The **Embarcadero YMCA** (see above) has a 25-meter pool, gym, and spa facilities for a $12 day fee. The University of San Francisco's **Koret Health and Recreation Center** (Parker Ave. at Turk St., tel. 415/666–6820), a few blocks from the Golden Gate Park panhandle, has an especially well maintained Olympic-size pool and a fitness center. Visitors have access to both facilities for an $8 day fee if they arrive before 2 PM. The Bryant Street branch of **24-Hour Fitness** (see above) has a 25-meter pool with three lanes; the $15 fee covers the pool as well as the fitness center. The **Sheehan Hotel** (620 Sutter St., tel. 415/775–6500), a few blocks from Union Square, has a four-lane lap pool that's open to the public for a $10 fee.

HIKING AND BIKING

If you want to hit the trail with just your feet, contact the **Golden Gate Hikers,** sponsored by Hostelling International. You don't have to be an HI member to hike—just bring a buck for each event, a bag lunch, and a $3–$5 carpool fee. For free information on upcoming hikes, write to 1717 Cabrillo St., San Francisco 94121 or call the **Hikers' Hotline** (tel. 415/550–6321). At **Outdoors Unlimited** (see chapter introduction), in a truly cooperative spirit, all the hiking trips are free—save the cost of transportation. Anyone may sign up on the trip sheet posted at the OU office on the UCSF campus (550 Parnassus Ave., tel. 415/476–2078) up to 11 days prior to a scheduled jaunt. The **Sierra Club** also sponsors hikes all over the Bay Area. They're free, though a donation may be requested, and carpoolers are expected to share gas, parking, and bridge tolls. Pick up a schedule at the Sierra Club Bookstore (see chapter introduction).

Northern Californians literally reinvented the wheel with the creation of the mountain bike. If you want to rub rims with other cyclists on a planned recreational ride, check out the calendar of events in the free monthly *Northern California Bicyclist,* available at bike shops. The **Sierra Club** organizes group rides on terrain that ranges from farmland to challenging hills. You need at least a 10-speed bike for all but the most level routes, and you must wear a helmet. Pick up their activities schedule at the Sierra Club Bookstore (see chapter introduction) for a list of planned rides. The best guides to biking in the Bay Area include *Bay Area Bike Rides,* by Ray Hosler (Chronicle Books, $10.95); *Cycling the San Francisco Bay Area,* by Carole O'Hare (Bicycle Books, $12.95); and *Marin County Bike Trails* (Penngrove Publications, $11.95).

SAN FRANCISCO

HIKING

The **Coastal Trail** follows 9 mi of San Francisco's shoreline, from the cliffs near Golden Gate Bridge over dirt roads, onto residential sidewalks, around craggy headlands, and along the beach all the way down to Fort Funston. Begin at the **Golden Gate Bridge** toll plaza parking lot. Walk west underneath the toll plaza, turn left onto Merchant Road, and continue west to find the trailhead. After about 10 minutes you get your first hint of why this hike is not to be missed: The view takes in 200-ft cliffs, the Golden Gate Bridge, and the Marin Headlands all at once. The trail then heads inland; when the path ends on Lincoln Boulevard, take the dirt road to the right that leads to the sandy dunes and salty air of **Baker Beach**; cross the parking lot and head into the forest (keep to the right every time the trail forks). About five minutes later, the trail spits you out onto **El Camino del Mar,** which travels through the extravagant **Seacliff** neighborhood. The dirt trail begins again on the right just where the houses end. The next 1.7 mi of the trail passes through **Lands End,** San Francisco's wildest little corner, full of rocky cliffs, grassy fields, crashing surf, and magnificent views. Wise hikers will heed the warning signs and stay off the unstable cliffs. The dirt trail ends in a parking lot overlooking the **Sutro Baths** ruins; head downhill past the aptly named **Cliff House** to **Ocean Beach.** From here to **Fort Funston** (4.7 mi south) you'll pass **Golden Gate Park** and the **San Francisco Zoo** on your left. If you make it all the way to Fort Funston, you'll find pic- nicking areas with great views of the ocean and local hang gliders practicing their craft. Once you hit Ocean Beach, you can catch a bus back to downtown at almost any cross street. For a map, call or visit the **Golden Gate National Recreation Area Visitor Center.** *West end of Point Lobos Ave. at the Great Highway, under the Cliff House, tel. 415/556–8642. From Montgomery BART, Bus 38, 38L, or 38AX to Cliff House. Open daily 10–5.*

For a less strenuous and time-consuming urban stroll, try the **Golden Gate Promenade.** Starting from the same parking lot as the Coastal Trail, head east down the stairs that lead to **Fort Point National Historic Site.** From here follow the 3½-mi mostly asphalt path, which traces the bay from Fort Point to the **Hyde Street Pier.** The popular jogging route takes you by the windsurfers at Crissy Field, around the yacht har- bor, past Marina Green, and over the hill of Fort Mason to Aquatic Park, near Fisherman's Wharf.

For a taste of green San Francisco, try **the Presidio** (*see* Neighborhoods *in* Chapter 2). The 2-mi **Ecol- ogy Trail** starts at the southeastern corner (Presidio Blvd. and Pacific Ave.) of the Presidio and travels through cool, springy forest beds, providing an intimate intro- duction to some of San Francisco's most distinctive plant life. For information on this and other Presidio trails, as well as a schedule of guided tours offered by the National Park Service, stop at the **Presidio Visitor Information Center.** *Montgomery St., Bldg. 102, tel. 415/561–4323. Open daily 9–5.*

On the third Sunday in May crowds of costumed carousers and competitive runners race across the city, from the bay to the ocean (12k), in the annual Examiner Bay-to-Breakers *(tel. 415/512– 5000, ext. 2222).*

BIKING

If you plan to do a lot of riding, pick up a copy of the free *San Francisco Biking/Walking Guide* at the Berkeley TriP Com- mute Store (*see* Transportation *in* Chapter 1); the comprehen- sive map shows street grades and bike-friendly routes. **Park Cyclery** (1749 Waller St., at Stanyan St., tel. 415/751–7368) rents mountain bikes for $5 an hour or $25 a day. **Adventure Bicycle Company** (968 Columbus Ave., at Chestnut St., tel. 415/771–8735) has bikes for the same price and includes any and every accessory.

Bike enthusiasts can join the local pedaling scene at the **Critical Mass** ride on the last Friday of every month. While the ride began as a lighthearted group commute of just 45 riders in 1992, the crowds now can number in the thousands, and the attitudes range from friendly to revolutionary as traffic lights and motorists defer to the power of this unstoppable procession of cyclists. To join the ride, meet at 5:30 PM at Justin Herman Plaza (The Embarcadero at Market St.).

One of the best rides in San Francisco takes you through Golden Gate Park, into the Presidio, across the Golden Gate Bridge, and along the coast, for a total distance of 21 mi. Start at the west end of Golden Gate Park, where **John F. Kennedy Drive** hits the Great Highway. Follow JFK Drive along a slight incline to the east end of the park, turn left on **Conservatory Road,** left again on **Arguello Boulevard,** exit the park, and head through residential neighborhoods and onto the curvy, downhill roads of the **Presidio.** Hang a right on Moraga Avenue, then take another right onto **Presidio Boulevard** for a quick tour of the historic former military base. Make a hard left onto **Lincoln Boulevard** almost immediately; it leads to the windy view area and toll plaza of the Golden Gate Bridge, where signs tell you how to cross accord- ing to the time and day of the week. When you return, follow Lincoln Boulevard west; it turns into **El Camino del Mar** and runs through the beautifully grand **Seacliff** neighborhood. At the Palace of Legion of Honor, the road veers right and becomes **Legion of Honor Drive** before dumping you back onto **Clement Street.** Turn right on Clement, and when it dead-ends, take **Point Lobos Avenue** past the **Cliff House** back to the Great Highway, where you can either collapse on the beach for some well-earned rest, continue down the coast, or head back into Golden Gate Park. Another option at the Presidio is the sporadic **"Pedaling the Presidio"** tour, a 6-mi ride that includes stops at several historic and scenic spots; check at the visitor information center for details.

EAST BAY

The extensive **East Bay Regional Park District** (tel. 510/562–7275) spans two counties, includes 90,000 acres of parkland, operates 56 regional parks, and provides a varied terrain of dark redwood forests, blustery hills with ocean views, lakes, and grassy fields. At any one of six visitor centers you can get free maps and the useful "Regional Parks" brochure, which includes information on all the parks and attractions. Parking and admission to all East Bay parks is free unless otherwise noted. For bike rentals, try **Missing Link Bicycle Co-op** (1988 Shattuck Ave., Berkeley, tel. 510/843–7471), where a mountain bike goes for $35 a day.

The 31-mi **Skyline Trail** connects the six East Bay Regional Parks running through the Berkeley-Oakland hills. From the north trailhead in **Wildcat Canyon Park,** the trail snakes south through **Tilden Regional Park** (see below); **Sibley Volcanic National Reserve,** with its volcanic dikes and peaks made of lava and volcanic debris; **Huckleberry Botanic Regional Reserve,** known for its endangered and rare plant life; and **Redwood Regional Park** (see below); the southern trail terminus is at **Anthony Chabot Regional Park** (see below).

TILDEN REGIONAL PARK

Named after Major Charles Lee Tilden, first president of the park district board, Tilden Park contains 2,078 acres of eucalyptus trees and rolling hills, filled with hikers, cyclists, picnickers, and poison oak. As in most Bay Area parks, mountain bikes are limited to the fire trails. To reach Tilden Park, take University Avenue east from I–80 to Oxford Street; go left on Oxford, right on Rose, and left on Spruce Street to the top of the hill. Cross Grizzly Peak Boulevard, make an immediate left on Canon Drive, and follow the signs. From the Berkeley BART, AC Transit Bus 67 gets you as far as Spruce and Grizzly Peak on weekdays and directly to **Lake Anza** on weekends. In summer AC Transit Bus 65 will transport both you and your bike from the Berkeley BART station to Grizzly Peak at the top of Spruce Street. To reach **Inspiration Point** by car from University Avenue, turn left on Oxford Street, right on Rose Street, and left on Spruce Street. Follow Spruce to the top of the hill, then turn right on Wildcat Canyon Road; the Inspiration Point parking lot is on your left after about 15 minutes. Stop by the **Environmental Education Center** (tel. 510/525–2233), at the north end of the park, for maps and information.

HIKING • Tilden contains two of the highest points in the East Bay: **Volmer Peak** (1,913 ft) to the south, and **Wildcat Peak** (1,250 ft) to the north. You can hike to Wildcat Peak from **Inspiration Point** along **Nimitz Way,** a 4½-mi road with views of the bay and of the San Pablo and Briones reservoirs.

To avoid poison oak and brambles, head to the central part of the park. Starting at the Lake Anza parking lot, walk northeast on the **Lake Anza Trail,** which encircles the lake. When you reach the far northeast corner of the lake, look for the **Wildcat Gorge Trail,** which will be on your left. The initial steep descent past a century-old springhouse is no indication of things to come: The trail tunnels through a wide, rocky gorge but eventually rises to 80 ft above the creek that carved it. Continue for a half mile until the trail forks. To the right, the **Curran Trail** rises sharply for about ¾ mi to Inspiration Point. Otherwise, the Wildcat Gorge Trail, one of the nicest in Tilden, continues on through groves of California bay laurels. About a third of a mile up the trail on your right, you'll pass a hill with a practically vertical path upward (this isn't on the official Tilden map). At the top of the hill you'll have a 360-degree view of the park. Return to the Wildcat Gorge Trail and backtrack to Lake Anza for an easy to moderate 1½-hour hike.

The moderate 1½-mi, 800-ft climb through woods and fields to the top of Wildcat Peak begins at the Environmental Education Center: Head east on the **Laurel Canyon Trail,** cross the fire road, continue uphill, and turn left onto the **Wildcat Peak Trail.** A turnoff to the right leads all the way to the top, where you can look out over Oakland, San Francisco, and Marin. Head back down the way you came, turn right onto Wildcat Peak Trail, and go left on the **Sylvan Trail,** which leads back to the nature center.

BIKING • To escape the asphalt obstacle course of Berkeley's streets, take this strenuous 7-mi loop along the ridge of the Berkeley Hills and into Tilden Park. From the intersection of **Grizzly Peak Boulevard** and **Spruce Street** in north Berkeley, head south up Grizzly Peak Boulevard. This is the hardest part of the ride; at times this winding, steep street has only a narrow shoulder, and riding on it can be hairy. Not far beyond the two lookouts, make a left on **South Park Drive,** which takes you down through Tilden Park and past several picnic grounds. The street dead-ends at **Wildcat Canyon Road;** go left and ride over rolling hills past Lake Anza and back to the intersection with Grizzly Peak Boulevard. Taking this loop in the opposite direction involves potentially dangerous sharp curves and limited visibility. Spruce Street is the main access road to Grizzly Peak Boulevard north of town; **Tunnel Road,** which goes up into the hills past the Caldecott Tunnel, is the main access road to the south.

A beautiful, moderately strenuous 13⅓-mi loop through both Tilden and Wildcat Canyon Park begins just west of the Inspiration Point parking lot (see above). Head down the rocky **Meadows Canyon Trail,** which starts to the left of the paved Nimitz Trail; when you come to **Loop Road,** hang a left, which will lead you to the **Environmental Education Center.** On the west side of the EEC, pick up the **Wildcat**

Creek Trail, and 6 mi farther head right on the **Belgum Trail** for a steep and often muddy ascent of just less than a mile. Make another right onto the **San Pablo Ridge Trail,** a steep uphill grade that affords spectacular views of the bay. From here you can pick up the paved **Nimitz Way Trail,** which leads back to Inspiration Point. For a shorter ride that avoids the most challenging stretch of the Belgum Trail, turn right off Wildcat Creek Trail onto the **Conlon Trail.**

WILDCAT CANYON REGIONAL PARK

Not nearly as developed or crowded as Tilden, Wildcat Canyon has the feel of a forgotten country back road; here you'll share the grassy hills and stunning views of San Pablo Bay with grazing cattle. The main entrance is on Park Avenue, at the north end of the canyon; this is also the site of the park visitor center (tel. 510/236–1262). To get here, take I–80 to the Solano/Amador exit. Turn left on Amador, and at the second stop sign turn right on McBryde Street and follow signs to the park office. From the El Cerrito del Norte BART station, take AC Transit Bus 68, which stops a few hundred feet from the park entrance.

HIKING • The best trail loop is a moderate 4-mi hike: From the **Wildcat Creek Trail**—which starts at the EEC in Tilden Park (*see above*) and is different from the Wildcat *Peak* Trail—go 1½ mi up through the tall grass on the **Mezue Trail** for an excellent view; then turn right and continue for ¾ mi along the paved **Nimitz Way.** Turning right onto the **Havey Canyon Trail** will return you to the Wildcat Creek Trail on a winding 1½-mi path.

Since Huckleberry Botanical Preserve is outside the fog belt, it's a good place to see the first blossoms of the season. Hike the nature trail there in early spring. To reach Huckleberry, follow the directions for Redwood Regional Park.

REDWOOD REGIONAL PARK

More than a hundred years ago sailors entering San Francisco Bay used the giant redwood trees growing on the hills east of Oakland as a landmark. Unfortunately, most of those trees were mowed down at the start of the California gold rush. Only a few virgin redwoods remain in Redwood Regional Park, but the second-growth forest is still impressive.

Free trail maps are available at the **Skyline Gate entrance.** To get there, take I–580 to Highway 24, then head east to Highway 13S. Exit north on Joaquin Miller Road and turn left on Skyline Boulevard; the Skyline Gate entrance is about 4 mi farther on the right. From the Coliseum BART station, AC Transit Bus 46 takes you to Skyline Boulevard; from there head up the hill a third of a mile to the park. To get to **Redwood Gate,** take I–580 east toward Hayward and exit at 35th Avenue/MacArthur Boulevard. Take 35th Avenue, which becomes Redwood Road, east past Skyline Boulevard. The park entrance is about 3 mi farther down the road. Parking inside costs $3 on weekends, but you can park along the road for free. There is no public transit to Redwood Gate.

HIKING • Connecting the north and south entrances are two main trails, the **East Ridge Trail** and the **West Ridge Trail.** Both, along with the **Stream Trail,** start at the Skyline Gate parking lot. The West Ridge Trail is the main thoroughfare through the park, and too much time on its broad path may get you flattened by a charging mountain biker (most other trails are limited to hikers). From the Skyline Gate entrance, take the 3-mi Stream Trail, which after a steep (and often hot and dry) descent to the valley floor meanders through the redwoods. If you'd rather have shade and the company of redwood groves on your way down, follow the West Ridge Trail a little farther, to the strenuous **French Trail.** To return to the Skyline Gate entrance from the valley floor, simply follow any trail heading up and to the right; you'll soon connect with the West Ridge Trail, which will lead you back to the park entrance.

BIKING • The 9-mi bike loop through the redwood forest is moderately difficult, with some strenuous areas. From **Redwood Gate** follow the road past the picnic areas to the trailhead. **Canyon Trail** begins with a steep climb (which gets nice and muddy in the rainy season). After a half mile bear left on the **East Ridge Trail** for a gentle 3½-mi ascent to the **West Ridge Trail.** The road levels for a bit, but the downhill stretch has plenty of danger zones, so watch your speed. After about 5 mi, the West Ridge Trail becomes the **Bridle Trail,** which runs into the Fern Dell picnic area. From here turn right and take the **Stream Trail** all the way back.

ANTHONY CHABOT AND LAKE CHABOT REGIONAL PARKS

South of Redwood Regional Park and only 20 minutes from downtown Oakland, Anthony Chabot covers almost 5,000 acres. One of the few East Bay parks with a campground (*see* Chapter 7), this is conveniently adjacent to the blue waters of Lake Chabot. The flat 9-mi walk around the lake's perimeter gives you a close-up view of the wildflowers and waterfowl that abound in this habitat. There's no swimming allowed, but you can rent a rowboat, a canoe, or a pedal boat ($12 per hour, $32 per day, plus a $30 deposit). For hiking, biking, and camping information, call 510/562–2267; for lake information dial 510/582–2198. To get to Lake Chabot from I–580E, exit at 150th Avenue/Fairmont Drive East, which merges with Lake Chabot Road; then follow the signs. Avoid the $3.50 parking fee by stationing your car somewhere along the road. To reach Anthony Chabot Park, take I–580W to Highway 13N. Exit at Carson Street/Redwood Road, then follow Redwood Road to the park's entrance.

The hilly 14-mi loop around Chabot Park passes over all sorts of great biking terrain. From the parking area at the marina, take the **East Shore Trail.** Cross the bridge and turn right on the **Live Oak Trail** for a steep, rutted ascent of just under a mile that will deter any 10-speeder and even a few mountain bikers. Then turn right on the **Towhee Trail** to the **Red Tail Trail.** Follow Red Tail—where you will be serenaded by the sounds of gunshots from the local rifle range—until you meet the **Grass Valley Trail.** Follow the **Brandon Trail**—a U-turn after the gate at the end of the Grass Valley Trail—to the **Goldenrod Trail;** if you make it this far, your reward is a drinking fountain for cows and humans to share. Next is the **Bass Cove Trail,** another rain-rutted trail that ends up on the **West Shore Trail,** which takes you back to the lake.

MARIN COUNTY

Just over the Golden Gate Bridge you'll find virgin redwoods, grassy mountain fields, and beaches where the roaring Pacific crashes against the cliffs. Many of Marin's best hiking and biking areas—Muir Woods, Mt. Tamalpais, and Point Reyes National Seashore—lie along Highway 1, which snakes its way up the coast.

The birthplace of the mountain bike is now a battleground, with bikers squaring off against hikers who want to keep the two-wheelers off the trails. Marin County has been particularly zealous about curtailing the use of mountain bikes: Trails that haven't been closed to bikers have a 15 mph speed limit (5 mph around turns), and rangers aren't shy about giving out hefty tickets ($180–$200) for violations.

There are bike shops all over Marin, and those offering rentals are strategically placed near favorite routes. One good option is **Start to Finish Bicycles** in San Rafael (1820 4th St., at H St., San Rafael, tel. 415/459–3990), where mountain bike rentals run $7 per hour, $30 for 24 hours, or $50 a day for full-suspension bikes.

MARIN HEADLANDS

Part of the **Golden Gate National Recreation Area,** the headlands are home to rolling hills covered with coyote bush, low-lying grasses, precipitous bluffs, hardy wildflowers, and sandy beaches—dress in layers, as wind and fog are always present. You can easily get here by bike—just hop on the Golden Gate Bridge and take the first exit (Alexander Avenue). If you're driving, pass under the freeway at Alexander Avenue, turn right before the entrance to U.S. 101S, and follow the signs to the **visitor center** (tel. 415/331–1540); it's open daily 9:30–4:30. Here you can see natural history exhibits, pick up a free trail map, purchase more detailed guides, and get trail suggestions from the staff. Most trails start here, and parking is free. On Sunday and holidays only, Bus 76 travels from the Transbay Terminal to the visitor center.

HIKING • Skirting the 1½-mi perimeter of **Rodeo Lagoon** makes for an easy stroll. For something more substantial, head north up the **Coastal Trail.** From the visitor center parking lot go up the closed-off road (*not* the left stairway). Persevere for about 2 mi, turn right onto the **Wolf Ridge Trail,** and head up the grassy hill (alias Wolf Ridge) for 1½ mi to the top, where you can look down on Tennessee Valley. Then continue less than a mile down the verdant leeward side of the hill until it hooks up with the **Miwok Trail,** which you follow south. The trail wanders above the edge of grassy Gerbode Valley, where you may spot a black-tailed deer or a bobcat basking in the chaparral. Two miles later you'll be back at the visitor center.

The **Tennessee Valley Trail,** at the end of Tennessee Valley Road (from U.S. 101N take the Highway 1 exit west and make the first left), is a broad path that meanders next to a small creek and through grassy fields for an easy 2 mi. In no time you'll be on **Tennessee Beach,** in the company of many families. Here, during very low tide, you may be able to glimpse the namesake of the valley—the shipwreck of the S.S. *Tennessee.* For a more strenuous, 8-mi round-trip hike, follow the Tennessee Valley Trail about a mile from the parking lot and veer right onto the **Coastal Trail.** After ¾ mi, the trail wildly snakes above the secluded **Pirates Cove** for about 2 mi, with stunning views of the jagged coast, and eventually leads you down to **Muir Beach.** Before you make your way back, relax a while at the pub of the **Pelican Inn** (*see* Muir Beach *in* Chapter 2). On your return see the less dramatic side of the Tennessee Valley by turning left off the Coastal Trail at **Coyote Ridge Trail** after a mile. Keep your eyes peeled here for deer, bobcats, hawks, and great horned owls. Continue for 1½ mi and take the **Fox Trail** back to the Tennessee Valley Trail. You complete the 8-mi round trip with a short walk north back to the parking lot.

BIKING • A popular series of fire trails gives you intermittent views of the Golden Gate and the Pacific. Take the **Miwok Trail** (from the parking area near the visitor center) to the **Bobcat Trail** and continue 3½ mi uphill to the **Marincello Trail.** This gravelly downhill run drops you on **Tennessee Valley Road,** which leads to the beach. To return, go back up Tennessee Valley Road and pick up the **Old Springs Trail,** which picks up on the road leading into Miwok Stables. Once you get back to the Miwok Trail, hang a right and head back down to the trailhead. The entire trip is 11½ mi and is mostly moderate, with a few steep sections. Rangers sometimes lead mountain-biking tours along this route; call for details.

ANGEL ISLAND

Almost all 750 acres of this island in San Francisco Bay are covered with forest or sweeping grasses, throughout both of which the spring wildflowers are spectacular. **Perimeter Road,** which circles the island, is very steep and gravelly in some places. For information on ferry travel to the island, *see* Tiburon and Angel Island *in* Chapter 2. For recorded information call 415/435–1915; dial 415/435–5390 to speak to a ranger.

HIKING • All trails lead in from Perimeter Road. On the **Sunset Trail,** immediately southeast of park headquarters (behind the picnic area, west of the ferry landing), 2 mi of ascending switchbacks afford stunning views of San Francisco to the west. As you circle the 781-ft summit, called **Mt. Caroline Livermore,** you'll reach a crossroads; take a left up the paved road to the top for a 360-degree view of the Bay Area. After you backtrack to the crossroads, return to the ferry via the **North Ridge Trail** to view the east side of the island. The entire loop takes 2½–3 hours.

In the annual 7-mi Dipsea Race, usually held the second Sunday in June, runners sprint from Mill Valley over Mt. Tamalpais, ending up at Stinson Beach. The race originated in 1905 and now has almost a cult following.

BIKING • The few areas not closed to cyclists are great for scenic, easy spins. **Perimeter Road** is a 5½-mi twirl around the island; the **Fire Road** is a 3½-mi elevated loop. You can bring your bike over on the ferry; otherwise, rent a mountain bike by the ferry landing for $10 (including helmet); here you can also pick up a free trail map.

MUIR WOODS

The good news: This is one of the few places in the world where you'll find ancient, towering redwoods (the oldest has been around more than 1,200 years). The bad news: Droves of tourists are aware of this. An estimated 1.5-million sightseers shuffle past the redwoods annually (8,000–10,000 daily in summer), but happily, fewer than 10% venture onto the network of hiking trails that start here. You can make a quick escape by following any of the trails that head up from the valley floor and connect with the 60 mi of trail in Mount Tamalpais State Park. The trail guide for sale at the park entrance ($1) provides great explanations of various flora and fauna. Cyclists are prohibited on everything but fire roads; you'll find free bike maps at the Muir Woods Visitor Center/Kiosk detailing where you can and cannot go. For recorded information call 415/388–2596.

For a spectacular view and workout, head up the **Ben Johnson Trail** after crossing the fourth bridge from the park entrance. You'll climb up through the forest for 2 mi (the last half mile is quite steep despite the switchbacks) until you reach the top of a hill with postcard views of several canyons and the Pacific. You can either head east on the **Dipsea Trail** to complete a 4½-mi hike or follow it 2 mi west down a steep gulch to **Stinson Beach.** The 9-mi round-trip hike is one of the best around. Weekends and holidays only you can shorten the hike back by hopping on the hourly Golden Gate Transit Bus 63 (*see* Stinson Beach *in* Chapter 2) at the Stinson Beach park entrance. This will take you to the Mountain Home Inn, from which you can pick up the **Panoramic/Ocean View Trail,** which leads 2 mi downhill to the parking lot. *Tel. 415/388–2596. From U.S. 101, follow signs from Stinson Beach/Hwy. 1 exit.*

MT. TAMALPAIS

Home to Miwok Native Americans for thousand of years before the first European explorers arrived, "Mt. Tam" is now a playground for hikers and bikers. About 50 mi of trails crisscross the park, and more than 750 species of plant life provide endless scenery. The 2,571-ft summit dominates the Marin skyline; on a clear day you can spot the Sierra Nevada from the top.

HIKING • Of all Mt. Tam's well-worn trails, the 3-mi trip to the top is the most popular. Park at the Boot-jack day-use area (5 mi from Panoramic Highway, *see below*) and head north on the **Bootjack Trail** (which also connects Mt. Tam to Muir Woods). At the Mountain Theater turn right onto Ridgecrest Boulevard, following the well-marked paths to the summit. If you want to drive up most of the way, park at the free East Peak parking lot. From there an easy mile on a paved road gets you to the top for a hum-bling view. Those traveling by bus may take Golden Gate Transit Bus 10, 20, or 50 from the Transbay Terminal and transfer at the Marin City Transfer Center to Golden Gate Transit Bus 63. This deposits you at the Pantoll ranger station.

The 2-mi **Steep Ravine Trail** follows a redwood-lined creek down to the ocean, with waterfalls all along the way. The trail begins at the west end of the parking lot at the **Pantoll ranger station** (tel. 415/388–2070), where you can pick up an excellent trail map ($1). It's all downhill to **Stinson Beach**; take the brutal but scenic 1½-mi **Dipsea Trail** or stick to the trail that leads to **Rocky Point** and the **Steep Ravine Environmental Camp** (1 mi south of Stinson Beach on Highway 1), where you can view seals, sea lions, star fish, and beach crabs. The less strenuous **Rock Spring Trail** starts at the Mountain Theater—an amphitheater with stone seats cut into the hillside—and climbs gently up to the West Point Inn, where you can relax and enjoy a lemonade before returning to the theater or charging uphill another 2 mi to the Middle Peak. To get to the Pantoll ranger station from U.S. 101, take the Stinson Beach/Highway 1 exit, turn left at the first traffic light onto Highway 1, and then turn right onto Panoramic Highway. Park-ing at the station is $5, but is free at roadside pullouts.

BIKING • Before you embark on two wheels, get a map from the **Pantoll ranger station** to find out which trails are legal. From there you can set out for Mt. Tam's **East Peak;** the long but gradual uphill climb pays off at the top, where you get an exhilarating view. If you continue past the East Peak, you're in for an all-day journey. From the ranger station take the **Old Stage Road** uphill a half mile to West Point Inn, where you can grab a glass of lemonade. From the inn go left on the **Old Railroad Grade,** which runs for 2 mi almost to the top of Mt. Tam. It's one of the most popular riding paths on the mountain and gets quite crowded on weekends.

From the top you can either head back the way you came or turn your ride into a 20-mi loop that takes you back down Mt. Tam and halfway up again. If you've got the stamina, go down **East Ridgecrest Drive** and pick up the **Lagunitas–Rock Springs Trail,** which begins on the other side of the dirt parking lot. After a short climb, the trail descends to Lake Lagunitas, where you'll turn right to circle the lake. Turn right again on **Lakeview,** and eventually you'll meet the **Eldridge Grade,** where you start another ascent. Go left at **Indian** and enjoy a steep and bumpy downhill ride. Turn right on **Blithedale Ridge** (past the Hoo Koo E Koo Trail) and take either of two spurs that drop down to the right toward the **Old Railroad Grade.** When you hit West Point Inn—last call for lemonade—go left on **Old Stage Road** and head back to the ranger station.

BOLINAS

The 45-mi **Coast Trail** stretches from the Palo Marin trailhead in Bolinas (*see* Marin County *in* Chapter 2) into the middle of the Point Reyes National Seashore. The trailhead is at the end of Mesa Road, just past the bird observatory. For a healthy day hike follow the trail to **Bass Lake** (5½ mi round-trip) or **Pel-ican Lake** (7 mi round-trip). Either way you'll walk through eucalyptus groves and untamed wetlands and along the edge of the cliffs that overlook the Pacific Ocean. Camping along the trail is allowed only within the boundaries of the national seashore and in designated campgrounds; permits are required.

POINT REYES

Though it's close to the city, Point Reyes seems a world away. Gazing at the rest of Marin County from this national seashore, you'll feel as if you're on a separate island—which is almost true, except that the Tomales Valley joins the little peninsula to the mainland. The San Andreas Fault runs right through the valley, putting Point Reyes on a different tectonic plate than the rest of the continent. Within the penin-sula the geography varies greatly; in just a few miles you can see meadows, forests, peaks with panoramic vistas, craggy cliffs overlooking the ocean, and isolated coves. The area erupts with wild-flowers from mid-February through July; and though winter sees a lot of rain, that's when the rivers and ponds teem with life and the whales migrate south.

The **Bear Valley Visitor Center** (tel. 415/663–1092) has trail maps, exhibits, and an informative slide show about the park; from there a 1½-mi path leads to **Kule Loklo,** a reconstructed Miwok village. To get to the visitor center, take Bear Valley Road off Route 1, just west of the village of Olema. On weekends only Golden Gate Buses 50, 70, or 80 from the Transbay Terminal connect with Bus 65, which takes you as far as the visitor center. Call ahead for bus schedules—Bus 65 runs only once a day in each direction. Its schedule gives you six hours at Point Reyes, but the trip can take more than two hours each way, so consider reserving a campsite and spending a night under the stars (*see* Marin County *in* Chapter 7).

HIKING • For a hike along a narrow peninsula, with the Pacific crashing on one side and Tomales Bay gently lapping the other, head all the way north to **Tomales Point.** From the visitor center take Bear Valley Road, go left at the stop sign on Sir Francis Drake Boulevard, and bear right at Pierce Point Road, which ends at the historic Pierce Point Ranch. The **Tomales Point Trail** picks up here and heads right through the Tule Elk Range; keep your eyes peeled for these graceful animals. Three miles down the road, the official trail ends, and the sandy footpaths to the cliffs (1½ mi) begin.

It's a steep, strenuous hike to the highest point in the park, Mt. Wittenberg (1,407 ft). Beginning just off the Bear Valley Trailhead, at the south end of the park, the **Mt. Wittenberg Trail** rises 1,250 ft; the final push follows an unmaintained offshoot up to the peak, where you'll be rewarded with a panorama of land and sea. To get down, head back to the Mt. Wittenberg Trail, turn right, and take the **Horse Trail** to the Bear Valley Trail, where another right completes your 6-mi loop.

BIKING • Most of the pristine trails in Point Reyes National Seashore are closed to bikers, but a few open paths and the park's paved roads make for scenic riding. For an easy, beautiful ride, take the **Bear Valley Trail** from the south end of the parking lot. About 3 mi into the ride you'll reach a rack where you can lock your bike while you hike about a mile out to the coast.

A more strenuous, 13-mi ride leaves from Five Brooks, a well-marked parking area off Highway 1, about 3 mi south of Olema. Pick up the **Olema Valley Trail,** which leads to the **Randall Trail** (on the left); cross Highway 1, ascend to Bolinas Ridge, and go right on the **Bolinas Ridge Trail.** About 1½ mi down the road, pick up the **McCurdy Trail,** cross Highway 1 again, and take the Olema Valley Trail all the way back.

SOUTH BAY

The gently rolling hills that shelter the San Mateo County Coast provide excellent opportunities for hiking and biking. The area is much less crowded than Marin County, and its small towns and farms give it a sleepy country feel. Plan on driving to these parks since most are inaccessible by public transit. The inland town of **La Honda,** on Highway 84 (*see* The San Mateo County Coast *in* Chapter 2), is a good place to stop for picnic supplies on your way to the nearby state or county parks.

PACIFICA

Biking is prohibited on most trails around here, but hiking opportunities abound. The hike along **Sweeney Ridge** is mediocre, but its proximity to the city and an amazing view of the coastline make it a worthwhile getaway. To reach the peak, hike 2 mi up a moderate grade through coastal scrub and grasslands that bloom with wildflowers in spring; the trailhead is at the end of Sneath Lane. A monument to the Spanish captain Gaspar de Portola, who supposedly discovered San Francisco Bay from this point in 1769, stands atop the peak. Most people are content to contemplate the view from here, but if you want to keep going, you can hike the **Baquiano Trail** about another 2 mi down to Pacifica (be prepared for wind and zero visibility on foggy summer afternoons). To get here, take I–280 or Skyline Boulevard (Highway 35) to the Sneath Lane exit in San Bruno. Follow Sneath Lane west to the Sweeney Ridge Gate, about a 10-minute drive.

San Pedro Valley County Park has several mellow hiking trails that take you through shady woods and meadows exploding with wildflowers. In winter and spring the half-mile **Brooks Falls Overlook Trail** affords great views of a three-tiered 275-ft waterfall. The even-shorter **Plaskon Nature Trail** abounds with plants and wildlife. For more tips or a detailed guide to the nature trail, stop by the **visitor center** (600 Oddstead Blvd., tel. 650/355–8289), open weekends 10–4 only. The park entrance fee is $4, though it's usually not collected on weekdays. To reach the park, take Highway 1 into Pacifica and turn east on Linda Mar Boulevard. When it dead-ends, make a right onto Oddstead Boulevard; the entrance is 50 yards up on the left.

LA HONDA

Eleven miles east of Highway 1 along Highway 84 lies the beautiful and secluded **Portola Redwood State Park.** Stop by the **visitor center** (tel. 650/948–9098) at the entrance, where you must pay a $6 per-car day-use fee (walk-ins are free). Here you can also purchase a trail map for $1 or get information on guided nature walks and other activities.

HIKING • For a moderately difficult 4½-mi hike through towering redwood groves, catch the steep **Coyote Ridge Trail,** just north of the visitor center. Follow it to Upper Escape Road, where you'll turn left; then turn left again onto the **Slate Creek Trail,** shoot downhill on the steep **Summit Trail,** and follow the service road back to the visitor center. To reach Portola, take I–280 to Highway 84W to Skyline Boulevard (Highway 35). Go south 7 mi, then turn west on Alpine Road.

BIKING • Some of the best mountain biking in the area is found in **Pescadero Creek County Park,** near La Honda. You can access the trails from nearby **San Mateo County Memorial Park** (9500 Pescadero Rd., Loma Mar, tel. 650/879–0212): From Memorial's visitor center take Pescadero Road back toward La Honda, turn right on Wurr Road, cross the bridge, and you'll come to the well-maintained dirt-and-gravel **Old Haul Road,** where you can ride to your heart's content.

BUTANO STATE PARK

This little-known state park in the Santa Cruz Mountains occupies a small canyon heavily forested with redwoods and ferns. Even when its campsites are full, you can still find solitude in Butano. Be sure to buy the 50¢ map available at the entrance station: In addition to marking the trails, it has information on the park's wildlife communities.

HIKING • A great hike that will introduce you to the park's beautiful terrain starts at the **Año Nuevo Trail,** to the right of the entrance station (watch out here for stinging nettles and poison oak). Less than a half mile up the steep ascent, you'll come to the **Año Overlook,** which on a clear days has views all the way south to Año Nuevo Island. Continuing on, you'll run into **Olmo Fire Road.** Turn left and then left again on the **Goat Hill Trail** for a 2-mi walk through the quiet forests. When the trail hits the main road, follow it to the right for the highlight of the hike: **Little Butano Creek Trail,** where the trail meanders along Little Butano Creek, which is crisscrossed by fallen redwoods. At the end of the trail turn right onto the main road, right again onto **Mill Ox Trail,** then left onto **Jackson Flat Trail,** which takes you through forests and fields of wildflowers while the creek rushes along far below. Jackson Flat will deposit you back at the entrance station—for a total hike of about 7 mi. For a gentler introduction to Butano, join one of the ranger-led 1½-hour nature walks, which leave from the park entrance every Saturday and Sunday at 2.

To get to Butano, take Highway 1 about 15 mi south from Half Moon Bay to Pescadero; turn left on Pescadero Road, right on Cloverdale Road, and go about 5 mi to the park entrance. It costs $6 to park within the grounds, but you can usually leave your car for free at the turnoff just south of the Cloverdale Road entrance.

BIKING • You can ride on the 10 mi of fire roads, though mountain bikes are forbidden on trails. Your best bet is to park at the entrance gate near the corner of Cloverdale and Canyon roads, about a mile north of the main park entrance, and ride **Butano Fire Road.** If you're in good shape, you can take it all the way to **Olmo Fire Road,** which leads back to the park's main road, and pedal back to your car.

IN-LINE SKATING

On Sunday, **Golden Gate Park** closes to motor vehicles to make way for a confluence of skaters and cyclists that glide through the park. With its great views of Marin and the Golden Gate Bridge, **Marina Boulevard** is another hotbed for bladed youths on weekday afternoons and weekends. The numerous parks around the Bay Area are agreeable for sport blading (skating on unpaved surfaces), and devotees highly recommend **Angel Island**—but it's bumpy going for novices. Experienced (and fearless) East Bay skaters head to **Tilden Park** (see above). Nimitz Way provides almost 9 mi (round-trip) of paved path, some of it with distant views of San Francisco Bay.

Skates on Haight (1818 Haight St., tel. 415/752–8375) rents in-line skates ($8 per hour, $28 per day) right outside the entrance to Golden Gate Park. **Skate Pro Sports** (3401 Irving St., at 35th Ave., in the Sunset District, tel. 415/752–8776) charges $5 an hour, $20 a day. If you want to skate along the Marina Green boardwalk, rent skates from **Marina Skate and Snowboards** (2271 Chestnut St., near Scott St., tel. 415/567–8400), where the rate is $7 an hour, $20 a day. Rentals include padding and helmets. All rental stores give free lessons; Marina Skate and Snowboards and Skate Pro Sports even throw in a free rental for the duration of the lesson.

PICKUP GAMES

BASKETBALL

The following San Francisco courts usually get going weekday afternoons as well as weekend mornings between 8 and 11. **Grattan Playground** (Grattan and Stanyan Sts.), near Golden Gate Park, sees casual play weekday afternoons around 3:30; weekends draw larger crowds and more ferocious competition. In the Marina, the popular **Moscone Recreation Center** (Chestnut and Laguna Sts.) has courts with night lighting and unforgiving double rims. Games at the **Potrero Hill Recreation Center** (Arkansas and 22nd Sts.) get highly competitive, especially Monday and Thursday nights. Relatively low-key four-on-four games begin early on weekends at the two full-length courts of Noe Valley's **James Lick Middle School** (Clipper and Castro Sts.). The small courts in the Panhandle of Golden Gate Park, between Oak and Fell streets, have competitive games going all the time.

In north Berkeley the short court at **Live Oak Park** (Shattuck Ave. and Berryman St.) hosts weekend three-on-three games, but the number of people waiting to play can be considerable. A more intimidating game goes on at **Ohlone Park** (Hearst Ave. near California St.). In south Berkeley the court at **People's Park** (Haste St. between Telegraph Ave. and Bowditch St.) is always hopping, usually with UC students cutting class. If you *really* want to get serious, you'll find competitive players on the courts at the **Recreational Sports Facility** on the UC Berkeley campus (2301 Bancroft Way, tel. 510/643–8038), but you'll have to shell out $8 for a gym day pass to play.

Friday nights you can watch nearly 500 in-line skaters flying through San Francisco on a 13-mi, figure-eight loop. The Midnight Rollers meet at the Ferry Building at 8 PM. Join them, or just observe. Contact David Miles (tel. 415/ 752–1967) for information.

SOCCER

Sunday mornings year-round a crowd gathers at Golden Gate Park's **Polo Field** (Middle Dr. W near Martin Luther King Jr. Dr.) for impromptu soccer games, where the players—almost exclusively male—represent a wide range of skill levels. League teams square off at the three fields behind the **Beach Chalet,** at the westernmost edge of the park. You'll find women's teams there on Saturday and men's on Sunday. Wednesday after work postcollege footsters play at the **Marina Green** (Marina Blvd. and Fillmore St.), where lack of night lighting means less play on shorter winter days.

In Berkeley the field at the top of **Clark Kerr Campus,** also known as **Dwight/Derby** (off Dwight Way east of Warring St.), has coed pickup games weekday evenings, women's (usually) Tuesday or Thursday evening, and mostly men's on weekend mornings; the courts quiet down when the university is not in session. Down the hill, **Willard Park** (Derby St. between Hillegass Ave. and Regent St.) usually has Friday-afternoon pickup games from 2 or 3 until 6. In winter a casual mixed game can often be found between Russell and Oregon streets, just off Martin Luther King Jr. Way, at 10 AM Sunday. Serious, testosterone-charged pickup games take place weekdays at 5 and weekends at 4 on **Kleeberger Field's** AstroTurf (Piedmont Ave. at Stadium Rim Way).

ULTIMATE FRISBEE

The rules of ultimate Frisbee combine those of football and soccer, except that ultimate is a noncontact sport with no referees, and players call their own fouls. For the latest on pickup games in Berkeley and Oakland, call the **East Bay Ultimate Hotline** (tel. 510/464–4494).

Sharon Meadow, off Kezar Drive in Golden Gate Park, sometimes sees coed pickup games of up to 40 people. Frisbee fanatics gather here every Tuesday and Thursday evening while it's still light out and on late mornings every weekend. **Julius Kahn Playground** (W. Pacific Ave. between Spruce and Locust Sts.), near the southeast corner of the Presidio, hosts pickup games Wednesday evening and Saturday morning. Other popular places to play are in the East Bay at **Cedar Rose Park** (Oxford St., between Cedar and Rose Sts.), which hosts games Sunday morning at 11 and, in summer, Thursday at 6 PM, and **Oakland Tech High School** (4351 Broadway, at 43rd St.), where games take place weekends at 1 PM.

VOLLEYBALL

On weekends in San Francisco people set up their own nets at the **Marina Green** (*see* Soccer, *above*) and nearby at the **Moscone Recreation Center** (*see* Basketball, *above*). At both locations you'll usually

SADDLE SORES

Golden Gate Park Stables (JFK Blvd. at 36th Ave., in Golden Gate Park, tel. 415/668–7360) has daily one-hour guided rides for $26. For $35, Las Trampas Stables will guide you on horseback along the woodsy ridges of Las Trampas Regional Wilderness for spectacular view of San Francisco and the Central Valley. They also offer a sunset barbecue ride every Friday. South of San Francisco on Highway 1 lies Sea Horse Ranch (tel. 650/726–2362); rent a horse ($25 an hour or $40 for two hours) for an unguided ride through 10 mi of verdant trails, ending in a stretch of sandy beach.

find high-skill two-on-two games. Also intimidating are the six-on-six weekend games at several spots along JFK Drive in **Golden Gate Park.** You can rent nets for $13 for the weekend at **Outdoors Unlimited** (*see* chapter introduction).

The **San Francisco Recreation and Parks Department** (tel. 415/753–7028) hosts friendly open play, usually on Monday night at 7 ($2); call ahead since times and locations vary. You'll also find games at the **South of Market Rec Center** (270 6th St., at Folsom St., tel. 415/554–9532), the **Glen Park Rec Center** (Bosworth St. and O'Shaughnessy Blvd., tel. 415/337–4705), and for women-only play, **St. Mary's Rec Center** (Murray St. and Justin Dr., tel. 415/695–5006).

In the East Bay, **People's Park** (*see* Basketball, *above*) has two outdoor sand courts, but you may have to fight for your right to play. Pickup games take place Tuesday night at the asphalt court in **Live Oak Park** (*see* Basketball, *above*). Players also set up on the grass in **Ohlone Park** (Hearst Ave. between Sacramento Ave. and Milvia St.) on Saturday morning. For $5 you can take part in open play on either indoor sand or hard courts in Emeryville, at **City Beach Sports and Recreation Center** (4701 Doyle St., at 47th St., tel. 510/428–1221).

ROCK CLIMBING

REI (*see* chapter introduction) is a good place to go for the essentials; they also rent climbing shoes (but not harnesses) for $10 the first day, $6 for each subsequent day. **Marmot Mountain Works,** in Berkeley (3049 Adeline St., tel. 510/849–0735), has a knowledgeable staff that can outfit you with the climbing basics.

Indoor climbing gyms are a good place to meet climbing buddies. **Cal Adventures** (*see* chapter introduction) offers all sorts of classes, from one-day rock-wall introductions ($60) to weekend climbing classes that include camping at Pinnacles National Monument ($150). Cal Adventures also has an outdoor climbing wall available to all those who can pass a belay test. You can rent equipment (shoes, harness, belay device, and a helmet) for $2; a day's access to the wall costs $8. **CityRock Gym,** in Emeryville (1250 45th St., tel. 510/654–2510), is in a 6,000-sq-ft warehouse with sculpted walls up to 40 ft high and a separate area for ropeless bouldering. A day spent climbing the walls will cost you $14, $20 if you need shoe and harness rentals. They also have a full-service climbing school, offering private lessons for $40 an hour and a belay class for $25. **Class 5,** in San Rafael (25B Dodie St., tel. 415/485–6931), has 35-ft walls ($14 day fee) and rents shoes and harness ($6) for in-house use; they also conduct climbing classes. The **Mission Cliffs Climbing Gym** (2295 Harrison St., tel. 415/550–0515), with 50-ft walls, sells day passes for $16 and rents equipment for $6. And, finally, if you already know what you're doing, you can hoist yourself up the climbing wall at **REI** for free (*see* chapter introduction) Thursday 5 PM–8 PM and Saturday 10–noon.

You can't rent ropes anywhere for liability reasons, so for outdoor climbing we recommend that you meet a rope-toting local. One of the best places for new climbers to practice and meet seasoned veterans is **Indian Rock Park,** in north Berkeley, where Shattuck Avenue dead-ends (*see* East Bay *in* Chapter 2).

When Indian Rock gets too crowded, more experienced climbers head to Morter Rock, a few hundred feet uphill. Arid **Mt. Diablo State Park** has excellent climbing up to 120 ft high in some areas. The sandstone rock varies in hardness, with new routes simply waiting to be discovered. The two main climbing areas are the more charted Boy Scout Rocks, in the southeast corner of the park, and Pine Canyon, just past the North Gate fee station, which is closed from early February to late June for the raptor nesting season. Head east on Highway 24 toward Walnut Creek, then south on I–680. Exit at Diablo Road, follow it to the park entrance ($5 day-use fee), and look for the Rock City parking lot to the right.

Castle Rock State Park, in a beautiful wooded area of the Santa Cruz Mountains, has sandstone rock, with some routes recommended for novices. To get here, take I–280 south past Palo Alto, continue south on Route 85, west on Big Basin Road, and then turn left on Skyline Boulevard. After 2 mi look for the parking lot to the right. Directly south of Stinson Beach along Highway 1—look for the dirt pullout about a mile south of Stinson—**Mickey's Beach** is popular with nude bathers as well as serious rock climbers. The greenstone rock edges its way toward the ocean, making 30–65 ft of spectacular climbing on well-established routes with names like Endless Bummer. The rocky outcropping to the north is suitable for bouldering. For information on other locations, including route maps and difficulty levels, look for *Bay Area Rock,* a guidebook by local expert Jim Thornburg, available at CityRock and other stores ($9.95).

WATER SPORTS

Don't surf at Mavericks in Half Moon Bay unless you know what you're doing. Its 35- to 40-ft waves are some of the biggest in the world and can be lethal—as they were for Hawaiian expert surfer Mark Foo.

SAILING

The San Francisco Bay has a remarkably consistent westerly wind, making it one of the most challenging places in the country to sail. If you're up for testing the winds, you can rent a 15-ft Coronado from **Cal Adventures** (*see* chapter introduction). Another option is to sign up for a one-day excursion with one of the local sailing clubs; most start from the Berkeley Marina, at the west end of University Avenue. AC Transit Bus 51M heads to the marina from downtown Berkeley. The **Olympic Circle Sailing Club** (1 Spinnaker Way, near the Berkeley Marina, tel. 800/223–2984) conducts a variety of afternoon sails ($65) year-round and a two-hour Wednesday night sail ($35) April to October. **Spinnaker Sailing/Rendezvous Charter** (Pier 40, South Beach Harbor, San Francisco, tel. 415/543–7333) has a two-hour sunset sail ($22.50) on Wednesday, Friday, and Saturday, as well as Sunday-afternoon excursions.

SEA KAYAKING

The Bay Area's many lagoons, estuaries, inlets, and of course ocean waters allow both novices and experts to roll their kayaks gleefully year-round. Check the quarterly bulletin published by **Outdoors Unlimited** (*see* chapter introduction) for listings of free kayak and canoe workshops and volunteer-led trips. Berkeley's **Cal Adventures** (*see* chapter introduction) has instruction, rentals, and trips, including sunset/full-moon-rise paddles open to kayakers of all levels of expertise ($30 per person). **California Canoe and Kayak** (409 Water St., Jack London Sq., Oakland, tel. 510/893–7833 or 800/366–9804) offers the widest range of classes and trips. A one-day introductory class runs $89 and outings begin at $50 per person. **Sea Trek** (Schoonmaker Point Marina, Sausalito, tel. 415/488–1000 or 415/332–4465) also has classes and rentals, and they offer special kayak trips with naturalist guides through San Francisco Bay and around Tomales Bay in Point Reyes National Seashore. Sea Trek rents equipment for about $7–$12 an hour, and a seven-hour introductory class costs $95. Other outings include a full-day trip to Angel Island for $95.

A good place for beginners is **Richardson Bay,** between Tiburon and Sausalito in Marin County. With its calm waters, gorgeous setting, and bird-watching opportunities, Richardson also makes a good launching point for an intermediate-level trip to Angel Island or an advanced trip through the rough and dangerous currents under the Golden Gate Bridge. For even calmer waters head farther north to **Bolinas Lagoon,** a protected estuary where you'll paddle past egret nesting sites. **Drake's Estuary,** another bird-infested spot, is a beautiful bay on the Point Reyes peninsula with calm waters for beginners. The placid waters of **Tomales Bay,** also off the coast of Point Reyes National Seashore, claim a resident flock of white pelicans as well as jellyfish and starfish. Beginners and intermediates will feel comfortable in the western part of the bay, with its stunning views of coves and beaches on shore.

SURFING

Throughout the Bay Area, swells are best during fall and winter, when storms far out at sea send ripples across the Pacific. For conditions at Stinson Beach call the **Livewater** surf shop (*see below*); for Santa Cruz conditions call the **O'Neil Surf Shop** hot line (tel. 831/475–2275); for Pacifica conditions call the **Nor-Cal** surf shop (*see below*). The **Surfrider Foundation** sponsors surfer-oriented events from paddles to cookouts to educational programs and provides information on water contamination at popular breaks. Contact the San Francisco chapter at 415/665–4155 or the Santa Cruz chapter at 831/476–7667.

Two world-class surfing instructors offer lessons near Santa Cruz. Champion surfer Richard Schmidt (tel. 831/423–0928) teaches classes through the **Santa Cruz Parks and Recreation Department** (tel. 831/420–5250): A two-day group lesson, two hours each day, costs $84. You can also sign up for private lessons with Schmidt; for $60 an hour (equipment included), he guarantees first-timers will ride their boards. Or head to Cowell Beach, where instructor Ed Guzman conducts **CLUB ED Surf School** (tel. 800/287–7873) in front of the Dream Inn. A two-hour group lesson ($70) starts you off on an oversize board, perfect for beginners who don't yet have their balance. If you don't get the hang of it the first time, you can come back for another two-hour lesson for only $45. Ed also rents a variety of boards for about $25 a day, wet suits for $10, and booties for $3.

At **Outdoors Unlimited** (*see* chapter introduction), weekend wet-suit rentals run $17–$21. **Livewater** (3450 Hwy. 1, Stinson Beach, tel. 415/868–0333) rents surfboards for $25 a day, wet suits for $10. To the south, local surfers staff the **Nor-Cal Surfshop** (5460 Cabrillo Hwy., Pacifica, tel. 831/738–9283), where you can rent a soft board for $15 a day. In Santa Cruz, the **O'Neil Surf Shop** (1149 41st Ave., tel. 408/475–4151) rents boards for $10 a day and wet suits for $8 a day. Santa Cruz's women-owned **Paradise Surf Shop** (3961 Portola Dr., tel. 831/462–3880) has all of the gear (including women's wet suits up to size 13 and clothes cut for athletic women) but none of the attitude that can make surf shops unbearable. Everyone is genuinely welcome to hang out on the porch here between swells and trade big-wave stories with the friendly staff and mellow contingent of local longboarders.

Surf's up at **Ocean Beach,** west of Golden Gate Park, but you may wish it would go back down. Winter waves get as big here as almost anywhere in the world (20–25 ft), but experienced surfers complain about their shape. Even when the swells are manageable, the current is strong. You don't have to be an expert to surf Ocean Beach, but it's not a place to learn unless you're into self-abuse. Waves are cleaner at **Fort Point,** beneath the Golden Gate Bridge on the southeast side. Though the current and rocks may deter beginners, the seals seem to enjoy themselves.

Beginners will have better luck outside the city. Drive north along Highway 1 to **Stinson Beach,** where shallow beach break is not demanding, and the waves are neither fast nor big. This is a popular beach for sunbathing, but the water is rarely crowded. Or drive 45 minutes south of San Francisco along Highway 1 to **Pacifica State Beach,** also known as **Linda Mar Beach.** Pacifica breaks best at high tide, with smaller waves for beginners at the south end of the beach. Just north of the rocky promontory, **Rockaway Beach** has bigger waves, but it's more crowded and competitive. Adventurous types go to the isolated state beaches between Pacifica and Santa Cruz.

WINDSURFING

The San Francisco Bay ranks as the third-best spot for windsurfing in the United States, after Oregon's Royal Gorge and Maui. Summer is the season to tack across the bay: From April to August westerly winds provide optimal conditions for windsurfing almost anywhere in the Bay Area. Winds are sporadic during the rest of the year, blowing either north or south. During winter the air can be as cold as the water, and you'll need a full wet suit. Some summer days are hot enough to go bottomless (in regard to wet suits, that is).

Boardsports (2936 Lyon St., tel. 415/929–7873) rents high-performance Windsurfers for $45 a day, not including wet suit. Beginners will find more basic boards at the store's other branches: on Gilman Street in Berkeley (tel. 510/527–7873), Crown Beach in Alameda (tel. 415/925–0543), and Larkspur Landing in San Rafael (tel. 415/925–8585). Rates are generally $20 for two hours or $30 per day, including wet suit.

Cal Adventures (*see* chapter introduction) has cheap windsurfing lessons: Seven hours of instruction on the bay with an added hour of recreational windsurfing, board included, costs $65. Since conditions on the bay are harsh for a beginning windsurfer, however, you may want to consider learning on a lake. **Spinnaker Sailing** (3160 N. Shoreline Blvd., Mountain View, tel. 650/965–7474) offers beginner and advanced classes ($150 for two days) on an artificial lake. To learn on a real lake, make the half-hour drive east from Oakland to **Windsurf Del Valle** (Lake Del Valle, Livermore, tel. 510/455–4008), the country's largest windsurfing school. The $95 six-hour beginners' course usually lasts two days, but the instructors will give you additional days of instruction for free if you need more help.

The **San Francisco School of Windsurfing** (3Com Park or Lake Merced, tel. 415/753–3235) specializes in increasing your skill level quickly. Beginners start at Lake Merced, but you soon learn to tackle the more popular bay. The two-day beginning course costs $130 (equipment included). Rentals run $16 an hour, including wet suit, booties, and harness; all-day rentals are $40.

Alameda's **Crown Beach,** with easy access to shallow waters, has the best conditions in the East Bay for learning the sport. The wind is usually light and blows toward the shore, so if you zig when you should have zagged, you won't be lost at sea. The beach is 10 minutes from downtown Oakland: Drive south on Broadway, go through the Webster Street tube to Alameda, continue on Highway 61, turn right on 8th Street, and look for the sign. Or take Bus 51 south on Broadway from downtown to Webster and Santa Clara streets, then walk a quarter mile west to the water.

In Marin County, **Larkspur Landing** is good for mixed windsurfing abilities. The light wind close to shore accommodates beginners, while the more advanced windsurfer will be challenged farther out in the bay. Mornings are calmest and best for beginners; the wind picks up in the afternoon. The drawback: When the wind is light, you have to paddle out from the rocky shore while keeping a wary eye out for ferries. From U.S. 101 take the San Rafael/Richmond exit east and continue a quarter mile past the Larkspur Ferry terminal.

If you and your Windsurfer are swept out to San Quentin, just east of Larkspur Landing, you will be escorted off the property by some distinctly unamused prison guards.

The **Berkeley Marina,** at the west end of University Avenue, requires intermediate to advanced skills. Access to the water is problematic because you must launch off either the dock or the rocks—and big weekend crowds mean you may have to wait for even one of these spots. The windy and choppy conditions provide plenty of wave-jumping opportunities for experienced windsurfers who like to spend time in the air. From I–80 take the University Avenue exit west to the end.

Crissy Field, in San Francisco's Presidio, challenges even advanced windsurfers. Beach access makes getting into the water easy, but with the strong tides and currents, getting out is a task. The current could easily sweep an unprepared windsurfer under the Golden Gate Bridge and into the Pacific or take you across the bay to Treasure Island. In addition, boat and ship traffic makes the water tough to navigate. Proceed with caution: More rescues are required here than in all other Bay Area sites combined.

Flat water, strong winds, and easy bay access make **3Com Park** (formerly known as Candlestick) a favorite with windsurfers who want speed. Winds average 19–25 mph, but they can get as high as 55 mph. You have to be an expert to handle the offshore winds, which carry you right into the bay—if the wind dies, you'll be stranded there. Take U.S. 101 south to the 3Com Park exit.

Waves are choppy at **Coyote Point,** south of San Francisco International Airport. The wind is moderate close to the shore, but farther out the surf will challenge even the most experienced. The entrance fee for **Coyote Point Park** (tel. 650/573–2592) is $4, well worth it for the use of hot showers. Follow U.S. 101 south past the airport to the Poplar Avenue exit, take Humboldt Street, turn right on Peninsula Avenue, go right across the overpass, and bear left onto Coyote Point Drive.

SPECTATOR SPORTS

BASEBALL

The baseball rivalry between San Francisco and the East Bay is as intense as ever. The National League's **San Francisco Giants** (tel. 800/544–2687) have a brand-new 40,000 seat stadium at Willie Mays Plaza (corner of King St. and 3rd St.). Unfortunately, at press time they anticipated every game in the 2000 season to be sold out long before the day of the game; nonetheless, there is a small number of $10 bleacher tickets sold on game days. Call for more information. If you do go, don't bother driving because there's nowhere to park; take CalTrain or any bus to the CalTrain station at Fourth and King streets and then follow the hordes of people heading across the street. The American League's **Oakland A's** (tel. 510/638–0500) play at the **Oakland Coliseum.** Bleacher seats cost $5, and those on the plaza level are $10–$14. The stadium is connected via an elevated walkway with the Coliseum BART station.

EXTREME SWIMMING

Who needs to jump out of an airplane or ski down a sheer cliff face when you can swim in San Francisco Bay? Not as thrilling, you think? We'll see what you say when you hit the 55°F water. To minimize the dangers of boat traffic and strong tides, hook up with the members of the Dolphin Swimming and Boating Club (502 Jefferson St., tel. 415/441–9329) or the South End Rowing Club (500 Jefferson St., tel. 415/776–7372), both at Aquatic Park; they'll give you pointers and maybe even convince you to join in the biannual swims to Alcatraz Island—yikes!

BASKETBALL

When the **Golden State Warriors** secured first pick in the 1995 NBA draft, local fans hoped they might become a team worth watching. Though they're yet to be famous for their record, thanks to the hot tempers of ex-Warrior Latrell Sprewell and other players who have since been traded, the team continues to merit its name. Even if they don't win (which they probably won't), watching a Warriors' game can be fun simply to see who gets in a fight with the coach next. Tickets ($19.50–$60) go on sale in late September or early October and sell out fast; call BASS (*see* Football, *below*). The Warriors play at the Oakland Coliseum Arena.

FOOTBALL

The **San Francisco '49ers** have built a huge fan base from all over northern California, and tickets for home games at 3Com (née Candlestick) Park are nearly impossible to get. Season-ticket holders have a lock on most seats, and when the rest go on sale in July, they usually sell out within the hour, despite the $40 and up price tag. Call the ticket office (tel. 415/468–2249) to find out what date tickets go on sale (usually in mid-July); then call BASS (tel. 415/776–1999 or 510/762–2277) at 9 AM that day.

The **Oakland Raiders** returned from Los Angeles in 1995, a move that brought Raiders fans from all over the Bay Area out of hiding. The city of Oakland is also thrilled by the revenue and publicity raked in by that the popular team, which left Oakland for Los Angeles in 1982 (L.A. TRAITORS, newspaper headlines blared at the time). The Raiders play at the Oakland Coliseum. For ticket information, call 800/949–2626.

HOCKEY

The **San Jose Sharks** (tel. 408/287–4275) have a loyal following, and tickets to games in the 1993 San Jose Arena ($16–$80) sell quickly. The season runs October–April. From San Francisco, CalTrain will get you to the San Jose Arena. There's also a shuttle to and from parking lots in downtown San Jose.

SOCCER

In 1996, the **San Jose Clash** (tel. 408/985–4625) kicked off major-league soccer at **Spartan Stadium.** Since their first season in '96, San Jose has embraced the Clash with smaller crowds but equal zeal to that with which they cheer on the Sharks. The season runs April–September; tickets are $12–$35. Take CalTrain to the San Jose station, then take Bus 25 in the direction of East San Jose.

COLLEGE SPORTS

The Bay Area's two big universities, UC Berkeley (known as Cal) and Stanford University, in Palo Alto, have been arch rivals for close to a century—especially when it comes to football. The **Cal Bears** football team, which plays in Memorial Stadium on the east side of campus, has improved a bit in recent years, and you'll find that even the most blasé Berkeley bohemian may work up a sweat over the team's more important games. Tickets cost $14 for general admission and about $25 for reserved seating. The Cal men's and women's **basketball** teams are not exactly championship teams, but they, too, have a loyal fan base. Games are usually played at Harmon Gym on campus, and men's tickets (about $18) are usually snatched up the day they go on sale. (Games also occasionally take place at the Oakland Coliseum; for these, last-minute tickets are usually available.) Women's basketball tickets cost $5 general admission, $7 reserved. **Baseball,** played at Evans Diamond on the corner of Bancroft Way and Oxford Street, costs $5. To buy tickets for Cal sports, call 800/462–3277.

Stanford's spectator sports revolve mainly around their football team, the **Cardinal** (named for the color, not the bird), which plays at Stanford Stadium. The other strong team on campus is women's **basketball,** a consistent NCAA championship contender. For information on tickets for all Stanford sports, call 800/232–8225 weekdays 9–4. Football tickets cost $10 general admission, $25 reserved, and about $50 for the Big Game, and they go on sale at the beginning of June. Tickets to **men's basketball** games, played at Maples Pavilion, go on sale in September and cost $15 for reserved seats, $6 general admission. **Women's basketball** costs $13 reserved, $6 general admission. **Baseball games** are played at Stanford's Sunken Diamond. Tickets cost $5 and are available at the game.

DAY AND WEEKEND TRIPS

REVISED BY DEKE CASTLEMAN, LISA HAMILTON, CLARK NORTON,
AND MARTY OLMSTEAD

hether you're looking for a day at the beach or a weekend in the mountains, a New Age healing session or an isolated cross-country ski trail, odds are good you'll find what you want somewhere in the diverse and gorgeous country surrounding San Francisco. Perhaps more than any other major American city, San Francisco is distinguished by its proximity to dramatic natural terrain and interesting small towns. North of the city lies California's world-famous **Wine Country;** to the south, **Santa Cruz** is a gathering point for surfers, New Agers, and neohippies. Continuing south, **Monterey** brims with tourists, harbor seals, and an incredible aquarium, while **Big Sur** rewards hardy campers and hikers with its rugged beauty. An afternoon's drive east at the right time of year will bring you to that most un-Californian phenomenon: snow—in the mountains surrounding **Lake Tahoe** or in **Yosemite,** California's favorite national park. Tahoe is home to some of the country's best skiing, while Yosemite provides northern Californians with a place to rock climb, hike, and hang out with the bears and other wildlife of the Sierra Nevada. You can escape to any one of these world-class spots in no more than four hours if you've got access to a car, and with patience and a little pretrip planning, public transit will get you into the great wide open as well.

THE WINE COUNTRY

Believe it or not, California's Wine Country lives up to its reputation. It's that beautiful, that elegant, occasionally that snooty, and definitely worth the 50-mi northeast trek from San Francisco. Wine novices shouldn't feel intimidated—just drink away and ask questions. Choose carefully, though: A number of Napa Valley wineries charge a $3–$6 tasting fee, which can add up if you're making the rounds. Watch the alcohol intake, too.

Most vineyards are concentrated in the Napa and Sonoma valleys, but the Wine Country actually stretches north through Healdsburg and all the way into Lake and Mendocino counties. Vintners have been making wine here for well over 100 years, but it was only in 1976, when a cabernet sauvignon from

Stag's Leap won a blind taste test in Paris, that Californians began boasting and people all over the world began buying. Since then production has skyrocketed. Twenty-five years ago there were only about 25 wineries; now there are nearly 400.

Napa Valley has the greatest number of wineries. In the good old days before pretension set it, visitors were greeted with open arms—and flowing bottles—by jolly vintners thankful for even a trickle of business. These days you'll have to search out Napa Valley's back-road wineries to get this kind of reception. Alternatively, head to Sonoma, home to a greater number of small, family-run wineries. In both counties the farther you stray from the main drag, the better off you'll be. Remember to call ahead though, since many smaller wineries have tours by appointment only.

If you need a break from the wineries, you can luxuriate in the hot springs, mud baths, and bubbling mineral baths of Calistoga; loiter in the lovely Spanish mission and old adobes of Sonoma; or browse through the small museums devoted to former residents Jack London and Robert Louis Stevenson, both of whom wrote about the area. Be forewarned, though: An overnight stay in the Wine Country can take a monster-size bite out of your budget. Lodging tends to be even more expensive than in San Francisco, and food is pricey as well. Consider, instead, visiting the Wine Country in a day trip from San Francisco. Otherwise, you can economize by eating at roadside produce stands and sleeping in the state parks. You might not even notice the difference after a couple samples of wine.

VISITOR INFORMATION

The **Napa Valley Visitors' Bureau** (1310 Napa Town Center, 94559, tel. 707/226–7459), open daily 9–5, provides information and maps. (Note: They don't answer the phone on weekends.) The **Sonoma Valley Visitors' Bureau** (453 First St. E, Sonoma 95476, tel. 707/996–1090), open daily 9–5 (until 7 in summer), gives advice on what to see and do in the "other" valley. Additionally, most wineries carry *Spotlight's Wine Country Guide,* a free monthly with maps, coupons, and winery information.

WHEN TO GO

During the autumn harvest season you'll see some real action in the wine cellars. In both spring and fall wildflowers and mustard plants bloom amid the endless rows of manicured vines. Try to avoid the Wine Country in summer: The dry, dusty valleys become even drier and dustier, and the crowds can be suffocating. During the winter months, on the other hand, things are much quieter, and you may find yourself alone in the tasting rooms, especially on weekdays.

COMING AND GOING

BY CAR

Traffic can be heavy, especially on weekends and during rush hours (7–9 and 4–6). From San Francisco take **U.S. 101** north over the Golden Gate Bridge and connect with **Highway 37E,** near Ignacio. From here take **Highway 121** north to **Highway 12N** for Sonoma, or follow Highway 121 as it curves east toward **Highway 29** for Napa. If you're only visiting the Napa Valley or are coming from the East Bay, take **I–80** north and exit at Highway 37W, in Vallejo. Highway 37 joins up with Highway 29 north to Napa. Even when traffic is heavy, it shouldn't take more than two hours; on good days you'll be there in about an hour.

BY BUS

Golden Gate Transit (tel. 415/455–2000 or 707/541–2000) provides bus service from San Francisco and Marin County to towns throughout Sonoma County. Bus 90 makes the 90-minute trek from San Francisco to Sonoma ($5.30) twice every weekday. On weekends you'll have to take the bus to Petaluma and transfer to **Sonoma County Transit** (*see* Getting Around, *below*). **Greyhound** has service from San Francisco's Transbay Terminal (*see* Bus Travel *in* Chapter 1) once a day to Napa(2½ hours, $15 one-way) and Middletown (4¼ hours, $20 one-way); twice daily to Sonoma ($12), taking three or four hours depending on whether you change in Vallejo or Santa Rosa ($17 one-way). Tickets are cheaper midweek.

GETTING AROUND

Unless you've hit one winery too many, orienting yourself in the Wine Country shouldn't be too difficult: Both the Napa and Sonoma valleys have main north–south arteries (Highways 29 and 12, respectively) that connect towns and vineyards alike. **Highway 29** begins in the medium-size town of Napa and

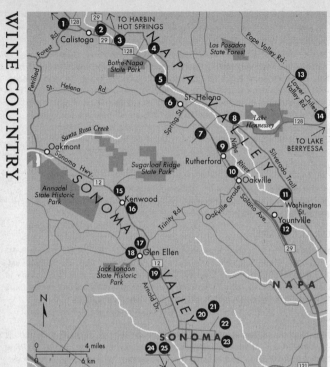

WINE COUNTRY

Bartholomew Park, **21**
Beaulieu Vineyards, **9**
Benziger, **18**
Beringer, **6**
Buena Vista, **22**
Château St. Jean, **15**
Clos Pegase, **2**
Field Stone, **1**
Freemark Abbey, **5**
Gundlach-Bundschu, **23**
Hakusan Sake Gardens, **25**
Kunde, **16**
Mumm Napa Valley, **8**
Nichelini, **14**
Niebaum-Coppola Estate, **7**
Ravenswood, **20**
Robert Mondavi, **10**
RustRidge, **13**
S. Anderson, **11**
Schug, **24**
Sterling Vineyards, **3**
Trefethen Vineyards, **12**
Valley of the Moon, **19**
Wellington, **17**
Wermuth, **4**

stretches north through Yountville, Oakville, Rutherford, St. Helena, and Calistoga, continuing north to Middletown and Clear Lake. A parallel route, **Silverado Trail,** avoids most of Highway 29's traffic lights (and jams), making for a more scenic and speedy ride. In the Sonoma Valley **Highway 12** runs north from Sonoma's main plaza, zigzagging east and then north through the towns of Glen Ellen and Kenwood before reaching Santa Rosa. East–west crossroads between the two valleys are **Highway 121** from Napa, the scenic **Oakville Grade/Trinity Road** from Oakville, and the **Petrified Forest Trail** from Calistoga.

BY CAR

In summer much of Napa's traffic can be avoided by staying off Highway 29 and exploring the less crowded and more scenic Silverado Trail, which parallels the highway about a mile to the east. Exit Highway 29 at any point between Napa and Calistoga and follow the Silverado Trail signs.

BY BUS

Seeing the Wine Country by public transit requires creativity, but that's half the fun. In particular, **Sonoma County Transit** (tel. 707/576–7433 or 800/345–7433) connects all cities in Sonoma County, with buses running weekdays 6 AM–6:30 PM (some until 10 PM), weekends 8–6. Fares are less than $2 to most places, and the routes get you within walking distance of a few wineries: Kunde, Château St. Jean, and Valley of the Moon, to name a few. **Napa Valley Transit** (1151 Pearl St., at Main St., tel. 707/255–7631) offers frequent service between Napa and Yountville ($1), St. Helena ($2), and Calistoga ($2) Monday–Saturday. In between you can be dropped off at Beaulieu, Beringer, Prager Port Works, and Sutter Home wineries.

BY BIKE

For a better workout, try pedaling up to Pope Valley in Napa or along the gently rolling hills of western Sonoma. The latter is less congested, but Napa is better for hard-core wine tasters, since the wineries there are closer together. Cyclists on Highway 29 must contend with traffic, especially on summer weekends—stick to Silverado Trail or Solano Avenue (an access road that parallels Highway 29 from Napa to

Yountville). In the town of Sonoma the best cycling route is along Arnold Drive, which splits off from Highway 12 about 4 mi south of town and rejoins the highway just south of Glen Ellen. **Napa Valley Bike Tours and Rentals** (4080 Byway E, at Trower Ave., tel. 707/255–3380 or 800/707–2453), at the north end of Napa, rents bikes for $7 per hour or $22 per day. Farther north, **St. Helena Cyclery** (1156 Main St., at Spring St., tel. 707/963–7736) charges $7 per hour, $25 per day, or $110 per week. **Sonoma Valley Cyclery** (20093 Broadway, Sonoma, tel. 707/935–3377), on Highway 12, can set you up with a mountain bike for $6 per hour or $20 per day. **Goodtime Bicycle Co.** (19503 Hwy. 12, Boyes Hot Springs, tel. 707/938–0453), on the north side of the town of Sonoma, is open daily and rents bikes for $5 per hour or $25 per day. All these shops offer biking maps and tour suggestions.

For an easy ride through Sonoma's fields and vineyards, take East Napa Street east from Sonoma's downtown plaza; turn left at the Sebastiani Winery (4th St. E), then right on Lovall Valley Road. From here follow signs to any of several wineries in the foothills, including **Bartholomew Park, Ravenswood,** and **Buena Vista** (*see* Wineries, *below*). For a longer ride, continue on Lovall Valley Road and turn right on Thornsberry Road, which leads to the **Gundlach-Bundschu** Winery (*see* Wineries, *below*). After you've tasted your fill, take Denmark Street back toward town. The entire trip is about 7 mi.

SONOMA VALLEY

Before stocking up on vino at a winery, check the local supermarket—it may have lower prices.

Although Napa Valley receives more of the hype, Sonoma Valley is the birthplace of California's wine industry. Unlike Napa, almost all of Sonoma's wineries offer free tastings, meaning you can sample to your heart's content without spending a dime. In addition, most of its wineries are small, family-owned concerns, more relaxed and less crowded than those in Napa. In summer the **Sonoma Valley Jazz Society** holds free concerts around town; call 707/996–7423 for details.

The town of **Sonoma** may have recently grown into an upscale bedroom community for San Francisco commuters, but behind the trendy restaurants and clothing boutiques lies some rich California history. It was here that Father José Altimira built the last and northernmost of the California missions, **Mission San Francisco Solano** (1st and Spain Sts., tel. 707/938–1519). The missionaries planted the region's first vines here in 1823, to make sacramental wine. For a $2 fee (also good for entrance to Lachryma Montis and the army barracks; *see below*) you can see the reconstructed priests' quarters and a collection of 19th-century watercolors by Chris Jorgenson. Catercorner to the mission lies grassy **Sonoma Plaza,** the largest such plaza in California and the epicenter of Sonoma life. Around the plaza are many adobe buildings dating to the days of Spanish and Mexican rule, including old army barracks and the restored **Toscana Hotel** (20 E. Spain St., tel. 707/938–5889). From Friday through Sunday between 1 and 4, kindly docents will recount the hotel's colorful past as a general store, a library, and a home to Italian stonemasons. Behind the hotel is Depot Park and the free **Sonoma Depot Museum** (270 1st St. W, tel. 707/938–1762), which chronicles Sonoma Valley history on and off the rails. It's worth a quick peek inside to see a pair of grizzly bear's feet worn by Ulysses S. Grant to a San Francisco masquerade ball in the 1860s. Three blocks west of the plaza lies **Lachryma Montis** (3rd St. W, off W. Spain St., tel. 707/938–1519), the ornate home of the last Mexican governor, General Vallejo. Vallejo named the home "Mountain Tears" after the area's many natural hot and cold springs. Admission to the grounds is $3.

WHERE TO SLEEP

Beds don't come cheap in the Sonoma Valley: Even at Sonoma's least expensive motel, **El Pueblo Inn** (896 W. Napa St., on Hwy. 12, 95476, tel. 707/996–3651 or 800/900–8844), a clean and attractive double will run you $80 weekdays, $94 weekends ($65 in winter), but at least it has a decent pool. The good news is there are plenty of appealing campgrounds. Alternatives are to make the half-hour drive north on Highway 12 to Santa Rosa, which has much more affordable lodgings, or consider staying at one of Sonoma's reasonably priced bed-and-breakfasts. **Hollyhock House** (1541 Denmark St., off 8th St. E, 95476, tel. 707/938–1809) is an old two-story farmhouse on a quiet country road, with geese, a friendly gray cat, and a comfy back porch. The two doubles cost $85 on summer weekends ($80 in winter), but you can lower the price of the cheaper room by $10 by staying more than one weekend night or coming on a weekday. In Glen Ellen, the **Jack London Lodge** (13740 Arnold Dr., at London Ranch Rd., 95442, tel. 707/938–8510) has comfortable doubles for $75; off-season specials can lower rates to $55–$60.

THE BEAR FLAG REPUBLIC

For a short period in 1846, Sonoma belonged not to Mexico, Spain, or the United States, but to the lesser-known Bear Flag Republic—the brainchild of Captain John C. Frémont and a ragtag group of Yankee trappers who decided to resolve tensions between the Mexican government and non-Mexican immigrants by throwing the Mexican general Mariano Vallejo in prison and creating their own country. The republic was broken up a month later when the U.S. Navy arrived, but the bear remains on the California state flag.

CAMPING • Sugarloaf Ridge State Park. Only 8 mi north of Sonoma on Highway 12, Sugarloaf has 50 campsites scattered around a large meadow. There are 25 mi of trails for hiking, biking, and horseback riding (*see* Outdoor Activities, *below*), and plenty of deer to be seen. Campsites cost $16 ($12 in winter). Reserve ahead through California Campsites (tel. 800/444–7275), especially in summer and on weekends. *2605 Adobe Canyon Rd., Kenwood 95452, tel. 707/833–5712. From Sonoma, Hwy. 12 north, right on Adobe Canyon Rd., which dead-ends at park. 50 sites. Barbecues, drinking water, flush toilets.*

FOOD

Sonoma is *the* place to get your fill of pesto this and roasted-goat-cheese that. Options for those long on gourmet taste but short on cash include the following: Put together a picnic at the **Sonoma Farmers' Market** Friday from 9 to noon in Depot Park or, from April until October, visit the market in the plaza Tuesday evening from 4:30 until dusk. You can taste free samples at the **Sonoma Cheese Factory** (2 Spain St., Sonoma, tel. 707/996–1931), where Sonoma Jack cheese is made. At the mellower family-owned **Vella Cheese Company** (315 2nd St. E, Sonoma, tel. 800/848–0505), watch cheese being rolled by hand Monday–Wednesday from 12:30 to 2:30. Or visit **Viansa** (25200 Arnold Dr., on Hwy. 121, tel. 707/935–4700), a slick commercial winery equipped with an Italian-style marketplace that puts out a spread of samples—chocolate sauces, preserves, mustards, oils, and, of course, wine.

For breakfast try the **Basque Boulangerie Café** (460 1st St. E, tel. 707/935–7687), where you can dunk award-winning, made-from-scratch Basque pastries into freshly brewed espresso. Come dinnertime, head down the alley east of the plaza to spirited **Murphy's Irish Pub** (464 1st St. E, tel. 707/935–0660) for homemade lamb stew and vegetables ($6.95), a pint of stout, and live Irish tunes (most weekends). For a Mexican-food fix, the roadside **Juanita Juanita** (19114 Arnold Dr., tel. 707/935–3981) serves homemade tortillas, all kinds of burritos and quesadillas, many in the $5 range, plus daily specials, and you can have your pick of more than 20 different hot sauces lined up on the counter.

For an excellent meal, trek out to the one-street town of Glen Ellen, where you'll find **Jack's Café** (14301 Arnold Dr., at Jack London Village, tel. 707/939–6111). It's open daily and serves breakfast—eggs Florentine, French toast, omelets—all day. Sandwiches and salads are $6.95–$8.95, special dinners, $8.50–$9.

WINERIES

It was in the Sonoma Valley that California began its upstart drive to compete with old-world wineries: In 1857 Count Agoston Haraszthy, the "father of California wine," brought thousands of European grapevine cuttings to the United States and started the **Buena Vista** Winery (18000 Old Winery Rd., Sonoma, tel. 800/926–1266). You can easily spend a leisurely day driving along Highway 12 through the 17-mi-long valley, stopping to sip wine, learn local history, have a picnic, and nap in the sun (the wineries below are listed north to south). Unless otherwise noted, wineries offer free wine samples all day long in their tasting rooms. If you're interested in touring a particular winery, call ahead to schedule an appointment.

Château St. Jean. The palatial grounds here include a fishpond, a fountain, and an observation tower with a spectacular view of the vineyard and surrounding area. Though tasting is free, the room is crowded, and the staff may be too busy to be very helpful. For a more relaxed time, kick back on the lawn with a picnic and a bottle of their excellent gewürztraminer. *8555 Hwy. 12, Kenwood, tel. 707/833–4134 or 800/543–7572. From Sonoma, Hwy. 12 north past Glen Ellen and look for sign on right. Open daily 10–4:30.*

Kunde. Kunde's claim to be the friendliest winery in the valley may well be true. Enjoy free tastings in their airy tasting room or take the half-hour tour through the vast cave cellars. If things are slow, you may even get a tour of the property, including the owner's duck sanctuary and the ruined stone winery where actress Geena Davis was married. *10155 Hwy. 12, Kenwood, tel. 707/833–5501. From Sonoma, Hwy. 12 north 7 mi; winery is on right, just past Glen Ellen. Open daily 11–5.*

Wellington. Run by a father-son team, this tiny winery opened its doors in 1994, and it's still obscure enough to escape the tourist hordes. Plant yourself in the tasting room—where a terrace looks out on the Sonoma Mountains—and sample unlimited wines. Be sure to try the Estate chardonnay, a combination of fruit and clove flavors that tastes like liquid Christmas. *11600 Dunbar Rd., Glen Ellen, tel. 707/939–0708. From Sonoma, Hwy. 12 north 7 mi, exit left at Dunbar Rd. Open daily 11–5.*

Benziger Family Winery. If all this wine tasting leaves you with a powerful thirst, visit this trendsetting winery, where some merlot vines are currently being torn out to make room for hops. On the free tram tour of the winery, a guide explains what happens in the vineyards. *1883 London Ranch Rd., Glen Ellen, tel. 707/935–3000. Open daily 10–4:30.*

Valley of the Moon. This totally renovated winery off the main drag is a breath of fresh air compared to the more crowded vineyards in the upper valley. Word hasn't gotten out about the gorgeous tasting room, which reopened in 1998, so the throngs have yet to arrive. The chardonnay and pinot noir are recommended, as are the free food pairings offered every weekend. *777 Madrone Rd., Glen Ellen, tel. 707/996–6941. From Sonoma, Hwy. 12 north 6 mi to Madrone Rd. Open daily 10–4:30.*

Ravenswood. The motto here is *Nulla Vinum Flaccidum* (No Wimpy Wines), and their merlots and zinfandels are definitely worth writing home about. If you didn't bring a picnic to eat on the terrace, try their inexpensive barbecued chicken or ribs with bread, coleslaw, and potato salad, available weekends in summer and early fall. *18701 Gehricke Rd., Sonoma, tel. 707/938–1960. From plaza, Spain St. east, turn left on 4th St. E, right onto Lovall Valley Rd., left on Gehricke Rd. Open daily 10–4:30.*

Bartholomew Park Winery. Oak-shaded picnic tables, 3 mi of marked hiking trails, and a thick blanket of spring wildflowers will make you wonder whether you came for the vino or the view. All the grapes here are hand-harvested, and you can sample the wares while wandering the adjoining viticulture museum. *1000 Vineyard La., Sonoma, tel. 707/935–9511. From plaza, Napa St. E, turn left on 7th St. E, turn left on Castle Rd., follow to winery entrance. Open daily 10–4:30.*

Gundlach-Bundschu. The motto of this family-owned winery, whose first harvest was in 1858, is "We make serious wines, but we don't take our wine too seriously." Indeed, in the main building (surrounded by trellised wisteria), old photographs of the family sit alongside a picture of Bacchus in shades. Then there are the corks, inscribed: LEAVE THE KIDS THE LAND AND MONEY—DRINK THE WINE YOURSELF. Call ahead for tickets to their summertime outdoor Shakespeare performances ($17). *2000 Denmark St., Sonoma, tel. 707/938–5277. From plaza, take E. Napa St. east, turn right on 8th St. E, left on Denmark St., and look for sign on left. Open daily 11–4:30.*

Schug. Walter Schug may personally pour you free tastes of his European-style wines at this mellow family-run winery. Afterward, explore the rooms where the wines are aged and bottled. *602 Bonneau Rd., Sonoma, tel. 707/939–9363, or 800/966–9365. From plaza, Hwy. 12 south, then Hwy. 121 west until it hits Hwy. 116 at stop sign; Bonneau Rd. is straight ahead. Open daily 10–5.*

OUTDOOR ACTIVITIES

Throughout Sonoma you'll find gentle hills covered with live oak and wildflowers. Spring and autumn are the best times for hiking and mountain biking in area parks. One of the more popular routes, either on foot or two wheels, is the Bald Mountain Trail, in **Sugarloaf Ridge State Park** (*see* Camping, *above*); you face a steep 3½-mi trek to the summit, but you'll be rewarded by a view that on a clear day stretches all the way to the Sierra Nevada. When the summer heat makes the backs of your legs stick to the car seat, head to **Morton's Warm Springs** (1651 Warm Springs Rd., off Hwy. 12 in Kenwood, tel. 707/833–5511), a low-key resort full of picnicking families and splashing kids. An entrance fee ($4.50, $6 weekends) gets you access to two spring-water pools, a small creek, a grassy picnic area, a snack bar, and a game room. Morton's is open daily from mid-May through August (weekends only in early May and September).

NAPA VALLEY

Although Sonoma is cheaper and more welcoming, it's Napa Valley, about a 20-minute drive east of Sonoma on Highway 121, that lures most visitors to the Wine Country. Though the crowds can be distressing, the scenery is still beautiful, the wine (in some cases) still free, and the town of **Napa** still lined with the attractive Victorian houses and California bungalows that make it all worthwhile. In summer the chamber of commerce sponsors free concerts in downtown Napa's **Veterans Memorial Park,** at the corner of 3rd and Main streets. One of the most popular is the **Napa Valley Jazz Festival,** held annually in mid-July.

Wine may take center stage in the Napa Valley, but a fair share of hedonists come here solely for a peaceful soak in the valley's hot springs and mud baths, most in or near Calistoga. Though you perhaps ought to hesitate before throwing yourself in any old roadside ditch and rolling around in the muck, folks in the Wine Country believe that mud baths and sulfur springs heal all manner of ills. Poverty, however, is not one of them: You'll pay a pretty penny for a day of pampering. On the bright side, you can spend the night at any of several low-key resorts for a decent price, and gain free access to mineral pools and Jacuzzis.

WHERE TO SLEEP

Although some of the most expensive lodging in the Wine Country is here in the posh Napa Valley, you'll also find campgrounds and inexpensive motels. In summer reserve at least three weeks ahead.

NAPA • One of Napa's cheapest options is the **Silverado Motel** (500 Silverado Trail, 94559, tel. 707/ 253–0892), where a tacky but fairly clean room is $45 weekdays, $65–$95 weekends. The **Napa Valley Budget Inn** (3380 Solano Ave., off Hwy. 29, 94558, tel. 707/257–6111) has clean but spartan doubles starting at $60 ($86 Friday or Saturday). The swimming pool is perfect after a long day at the wineries, many of which are within biking distance. At the **Wine Valley Lodge** (200 S. Coombs St., 94558, tel. 707/224–7911), where Elvis once slept, comfortable rooms cost $79 weekdays ($50 if you pick up a flyer at the visitor center), $99 weekends. Amenities include a pool and a barbecue in the courtyard.

Campers, take note: There isn't any public transportation to the campgrounds, so prepare to walk or bike back to civilization. If all else fails, head 20 mi east from Rutherford on Highway 128 to Lake Berryessa. The lake is divided into seven campgrounds, including **Pleasure Cove** (tel. 707/966–2172) and **Spanish Flat** (tel. 707/966–7700), for a total of 225 campsites (about $20 per site) near the water. Although you get direct access to swimming, fishing, picnicking, and waterskiing facilities, the area around the lake is barren, dusty, and very hot during summer.

Bothe-Napa State Park. This is the Wine Country's most attractive campground, in the Napa foothills amid redwoods, madronas, and tan oaks, only 5 mi north of St. Helena and its wineries. The sites are reasonably private, and the park is one of the few with a swimming pool (an additional $3 fee), much used on hot summer days. The campsite fee is $15–$20 from April through October or $12 off-season. Reserve through California Campsites (tel. 800/444–7275). *3801 St. Helena Hwy. N, Calistoga 94515, tel. 707/942–4575. From St. Helena, north on Hwy. 29. 48 sites. Drinking water, fire grates, flush toilets, picnic tables, showers.*

CALISTOGA • Pleasure seekers planning to hit both the wineries and the hot springs should consider staying in Calistoga. On the main drag, the **Calistoga Inn** (1250 Lincoln Ave., 94515, tel. 707/942– 4101) has clean, simple bed-and-breakfast rooms with full-size beds and shared baths for $55 ($68 Friday and Saturday); downstairs there's a restaurant and pub with fine home brews. For $54 (second night $5 off) you can get a cabin for two at the **Triple S Ranch** (4600 Mountain Home Ranch Rd., 94515, tel. 707/942–6730). There's no phone or TV, but the complex does have a swimming pool and a steak house. The ranch is north of Calistoga off Highway 128; take Petrified Forest Road west for 2½ mi until you reach Mount Home Ranch Road. Or try the **Holiday House** (3514 Hwy. 128, 94515, tel. 707/942–6174), 3 mi north of Calistoga; watch for the white picket fence. The three rooms here ($60 one night, $50 per night if you stay two) are a (slight) step above Motel 6.

Calistoga Ranch Club. A mere two minutes north of the Silverado Trail, the Ranch Club scores points for convenience and accessibility—not to mention its pool and laundry facilities. Although it's no isolated retreat, it *is* set off the main road with a fair amount of shade and greenery. Tent sites for four people run $20. You can also rent a rustic cabin (sleeps four) for $54—or for a slice of Americana, an Airstream trailer (sleeps five) with kitchen for $89. *580 Lommel Rd., Calistoga 94515, tel. 707/942–6565, 800/*

847–6272. From St. Helena, head north on the Silverado Trail. 58 campsites, 4 cabins, 2 Airstream trailers. Barbecue pits, drinking water, flush toilets, picnic tables, showers.

FOOD

Eating in Napa takes a close second behind wine tasting. The best way to eat well without breaking the bank is to stock up at one of the area's makeshift farmers' markets. One of the biggest is the **Napa Valley Farmers' Market**, held May through October on Tuesday mornings in Napa (West St., between 1st and Pearl Sts., tel. 707/252-2105) and Friday mornings in St. Helena (Old Railroad Depot, tel. 707/ 252-2105).

If you're spending the day in Calistoga, cruise down to the **Calistoga Roastery** (1631 Lincoln Ave., tel. 707/942-5757), great for bottomless cups of coffee and decadent ice cream lattes. For cheap Mexican food, head to the west end of Lincoln Avenue, where it dead-ends at the **Calistoga Drive-In Taquería** (1207 Foothill Blvd., tel. 707/942-0543).

Calistoga Inn. The California cuisine at this casual restaurant is excellent, and the portions fair for the price. If it's offered, try the Moroccan lamb stew with yams, apples, and raisins ($9.50), or cool off in the trellised garden with one of their award-winning home-brew ales or lagers—only $2.50 during happy hour (weekdays 4– 6). Dinner often brings live music in the front room. *1250 Lincoln Ave., tel. 707/942-4101.*

The Diner. Although several good restaurants line Washington Street in Yountville, this diner has been the best for the price for more than two decades. You can get huge plates of American or Mexican food for lunch and dinner or specialty eggs and pancakes for breakfast. *6476 Washington St., Yountville, tel. 707/944-2626. Closed Mon.*

If you've gone sour on the grapes, head to Hakusan Sake Gardens (intersection of Hwys. 12 and 29, tel. 707/258-6160), where $1 buys you samples of warm and cold sakes plus a view of a Buddhist sand-and-sculpture garden.

Pometta's Deli. This place is famous for its barbecued chicken platters ($7), but you can also get box lunches to go ($12.50–$15). Stick around after lunch to try your skills at the tournament horseshoe pits on the grounds. *Hwy. 29 at Oakville Grade, Oakville, tel. 707/944-2365.*

Red Hen Cantina. Enjoy a fajita ($25 for two people) or a hefty side dish (tamales, burritos, chili *rellenos*) on the outdoor patio. You'll be hard pressed to escape without indulging in one of the margaritas, which range in size from normal ($5) to *muy grande* ($40). *5091 St. Helena Hwy. (Hwy. 29), 5 mi north of Napa off Oak Knoll Rd., tel. 707/255-8125.*

WINERIES

If you're having trouble deciding which of the Napa Valley's hundreds of wineries to visit, first determine whether you prefer a more sophisticated tour at a big-name winery such as **Robert Mondavi** (1708 St. Helena Hwy., Oakville, tel. 707/259-9463) or the more intimate format at smaller, lower-profile wineries such as **Trefethen Vineyards** (1160 Oak Knoll Ave., Napa, tel. 707/255-7700). Some wineries are recommended for nonenological reasons: **Clos Pegase** (1060 Dunaweal La., tel. 707/942-4981) is worth seeing for its architecture and art collection alone; at **Sterling Vineyards** (1111 Dunaweal La., tel. 707/ 942-3300), you get the added bonus of a gondola ride and a dazzling view. Consider whether you mind paying the $3–$5 tasting fee that many wineries charge; if so, you might seek out the freebies at some smaller wineries, where the extra attention paid to the product often means better wine. Unless otherwise noted, the wineries listed below offer free wine samples and tours by appointment only (though their tasting rooms are open all day). Wineries are listed from north to south.

Field Stone. Although technically in Sonoma, Field Stone is easy to get to from Calistoga. The friendly staff may have to turn down the Bob Dylan when you arrive, but they will quickly set you up with free glasses of their award-winning wines. Don't be fooled by the casual, rural setting; their product is strictly top-notch. The many wine-barrel tables scattered throughout the grounds beg for cheese-and-fruit picnics. *10075 Hwy. 128, Healdsburg, tel. 707/433-7266. From Calistoga, 15 mi north on Hwy. 128. Open daily 10–5.*

Wermuth. Ralph Wermuth—equal parts vintner, philosopher, mad scientist, and stand-up comedian— will make your trip to Wermuth worthwhile. He proudly presents tastings of gamay accompanied by chocolate chips to "bring out the flavor," and colombard paired with that gourmet standby Cheez-Its. Wife and partner Smitty Wermuth designs the winery logos, which depict the old Italian basket presses still used here in the crush. *3942 Silverado Trail, Calistoga, tel. 707/942-5924. From Hwy. 29 north,*

TASTING NOTES

If you want to pass yourself off as a wine aficionado, you'll need to know some rules of tasting. First, move from light wines to dark, so you don't "clutter your palate." Begin by vigorously swirling an ounce of wine in your glass. Then, raise the glass to your nose and inhale deeply. In young wines you smell only the grapes, but with aging you get a more complex "bouquet" of aromas. Next, take a sip—you're encouraged to slurp because air helps you taste the wine—and swish it around in your mouth to pick up the more subtle flavors. Finally, notice the finish (or aftertaste) before coming to a judgment.

Hwy. 128 east to Silverado Trail; continue north past Bale La. and look for sign on right. Tasting fee $1. Open Wed.–Sun. 11–5.

Freemark Abbey Winery. In 1886 Josephine Tychson made history as the first woman to establish a winery in California. Today Freemark cabernets and estate-grown wines are still going strong. *3022 St. Helena Hwy. N, tel. 707/963–9694. Tasting fee $4. Open Mar.–Dec., daily 10–4:30; Jan.–Feb., Thurs.– Sun. 10–4:30; tours daily at 2.*

Beringer Winery. Thanks to a government license to make sacramental wine during Prohibition, Beringer has remained in continuous operation since 1876. A half-hour tour takes you through the winery's century-old caves and beautiful grounds. *2000 Hwy. 29, St. Helena, tel. 707/963–7115. Open Apr.–Oct., daily 9:30–5; Nov.–May, daily 9:30–4; tours daily every half hr on the half hr.*

Niebaum-Coppola Estate. Francis Ford Coppola fans won't want to miss this dramatic château where the director has been producing wine for decades. Created from vineyards once part of the old Inglenook estate, these wines are strictly first class. After you've tasted and toured, check out Don Corleone's desk and chair from *The Godfather* at the on-site film-history museum. *1991 St. Helena Hwy. (Hwy. 29), tel. 707/963–9099. Tasting fee $5. Open daily 10–5.*

Mumm Napa Valley. A joint venture of Mumm—the French champagne house—and Seagram, this is considered one of California's premier sparkling-wine producers, and its tour is particularly educational. An art gallery has a permanent exhibit of photographs by Ansel Adams that record the wine-making process. *8445 Silverado Trail, tel. 707/942–3434. Tasting fees $3.50–$6. Open daily 10:30–6, tours 11–3.*

Beaulieu Vineyards. Although Beaulieu has supplied wine to President Eisenhower and Queen Elizabeth, among other notables, the staff is far from snooty. If you like dessert wine, be sure to taste their lovely brandy-fortified muscat. Free, informative half-hour tours cover the wine-making process and BV's more than 100-year history. *1960 Hwy. 29, Rutherford, tel. 707/963–2411. Open daily 10–5, tours daily every half hr.*

S. Anderson. John Anderson, son of the late Stan (as in "S.") Anderson, does a wonderful job guiding you through his vineyards and candlelit stone wine caves, modeled after those in the Champagne region of France. The caves hold more than 400,000 bottles of sparkling wine, awaiting their "turn" (champagne bottles are turned by hand in a labor-intensive process that removes the yeast). *1473 Yountville Crossroad, Yountville, tel. 800/428–2259. From Hwy. 29 in Yountville, take Madison exit and follow signs for Yountville Crossroad. Tasting fee $3. Open daily 10–5, tours at 10:30 and 2:30.*

RustRidge. While you're traipsing through Napa's backwoods, check out this find—winery, ranch, and B&B ($105–$170). You'll probably be the only visitor indulging in the free tasters, served in a converted barn, with the family dogs and horses roaming nearby. You can picnic on the serene grounds of Catacula (Valley of the Oaks). *2910 Lower Chiles Valley Rd., St. Helena, tel. 707/965–9353 or 800/788–0263. From Hwy. 29N, Hwy. 128 east; cross Silverado Trail, left at fork (look for Pope Valley sign), first right on Lower Chiles Valley Rd. Open daily 10–5 (winter until 4).*

Nichelini. Napa's oldest family-owned winery (since 1890) lies 11 mi east of Rutherford and is worth every minute of the beautiful drive. Outside, under the shade of walnut trees and next to an old Roman grape press, you can sample several wines: Try one of their award-winning merlots. On summer weekends picnic to the strains of traditional Italian music on a hill overlooking the countryside. *Hwy. 128, St. Helena, tel. 707/963–0717 or 800/938–2783. Open May–Oct., weekends 10–6; Nov.–Apr., weekends 10–5.*

HOT SPRINGS

The majority of the Napa Valley's mud and mineral baths are in the curious little town of Calistoga, at the north end of the valley. The town's bubbling mineral spring became a spa in 1859, when entrepreneur Sam Brannan melded the word *California* with *Saratoga*, the name of New York's springs; Calistoga has been attracting health seekers ever since. Prices at the spas are uniformly steep, but you can pick up discount coupons at the **Calistoga Chamber of Commerce** (1458 Lincoln Ave., tel. 707/942–6333), open weekdays 9–5, Saturday 10–4, Sunday 10–3.

A cheaper option is open-air bathing at rustic retreats like Harbin Hot Springs or White Sulphur Springs (*see below*). You won't get to play human mud pie like at the outdoor spas, but you can bathe in natural springs and hike through rolling grounds far from the buzz of urbanity. Not only do these resorts offer many of the same amenities as the Calistoga spas, but you get an affordable room for the night to boot. If you opt for one of the indoor spas, call ahead for a reservation. Most accept walk-ins, but nothing is more stressful than being turned away from a longed-for massage.

> *They say, "Clothing optional," but you'll feel very out of place if you wear anything but a smile into the pools at Harbin Hot Springs.*

Golden Haven Hot Springs. Golden Haven is the only Calistoga spa to offer private coed mud baths (sorry lovebirds, there's still an attendant). The full treatment (mud bath, mineral Jacuzzi, blanket wrap, and 30-minute massage) will run you $64 per person. If you're too relaxed to make it past the front door, you can crash in one of their rooms for $65 ($49 Sunday–Thursday, September–June), which includes use of the swimming pool and hot mineral pool. *1713 Lake St., Calistoga, tel. 707/942–6793. From Lincoln Ave. east, left on Stevenson St., right on Lake St. Open daily 9–9.*

Harbin Hot Springs. Forty minutes north of Calistoga, this 1,200-acre laid-back community is run by the Heart Consciousness Church, a group that advocates holistic health and spiritual renewal. The retreat, popular with gay men, has three natural mineral pools, varying in temperature from tepid to *very* hot, and a cold spring-fed "plunge" pool, all open 24 hours. To use the pools, you must pay $5 for a one-month membership or $15 for a year (only one member per group required), plus an additional day-use fee ($13 Monday–Thursday, $18 Friday–Sunday and holidays). There's also an acclaimed massage school, whose graduates are happy to show you their skills ($46 per hour, $60 for 90 minutes). Rustic dorm beds start at $23 ($35 on weekends and holidays); you bring your own sheets or sleeping bag. Private rooms with shared bath are $60 ($90 on weekends), while campsites along the creek and in nearby meadows cost $14 per person ($23 Friday–Saturday, $17 Sunday). Guests at the resort are invited to use the vegetarian-only communal kitchen and to share the community's vegetarian meals ($8–$12). *Tel. 707/987–2477 or 800/622–2477 (northern California only). Hwy. 29 north to Middletown, turn left at junction for Hwy. 175, right on Barnes St.; go 1½ mi to Harbin Springs Rd. and turn left. Rides can be arranged for those taking Greyhound.*

Lincoln Avenue Spa. With pleasant stone-and-wood massage rooms and a central location, this spa is posh for the price. Their body mud treatment ($45) is the ideal alternative for those squeamish about wallowing in someone else's dirty mud: You get your choice of mud (herbal, sea, or mint) slathered over your body, a relaxing nap on the steam table, and a soothing facial mask. *1339 Lincoln Ave., Calistoga, tel. 707/942–5296. Open daily 9–9.*

Nance's Spa. Of the Calistoga spas, Nance's is one of the cheapest. Sixty-five dollars gets you the works: You begin by sliding into a tub of hot volcanic mud; then you shower and simmer in a bubbling mineral bath. Next you're swaddled in soft sheets and left to "set" like a human dumpling in preparation for a half-hour massage. Nance's facilities are sex-segregated and none too private: The amorous and the modest may opt to go elsewhere. *1614 Lincoln Ave., Calistoga, tel. 707/942–6211. Open weekdays 9–5, weekends 9–7.*

White Sulphur Springs. If you're planning to stay the night in Napa Valley, consider the bargain that is this longtime St. Helena resort. Along with a decent room for the night—either in the rustic, dormitory-

HUBCAPS AND MORE

Years ago, in Pope Valley, when Emanuelle "Litto" Damonte discovered that several hubcaps had been lost on a turn of the road near his property, he placed them on the fence for the owners to retrieve. Thirty years and more than 2,000 hubcaps later, his property is a registered California landmark and a tribute to American folk art. To reach the ranch from Highway 29, take Highway 128 east, cross Silverado Trail, and bear left on Chiles Pope Valley Road. When you reach Pope Valley, head onto Pope Valley Road—it's a couple miles farther on the right.

style carriage house ($95) or in the inn ($105, $115 weekends, where each room has a half bath—you and a friend can enjoy access to 300 acres of land, plenty of hiking and biking trails, a Jacuzzi, a natural mineral bath, and even a stand of redwoods. For day-trippers, a sulfur soak, a sauna, a Jacuzzi, and hiking trails are a bargain at $30. Reserve two weeks ahead. *3100 White Sulphur Springs Rd., St. Helena, tel. 707/963–8588. From Hwy. 29N, turn left on Spring St. in St. Helena and go nearly 3 mi. Note: Do NOT take Sulphur Springs Rd. from Hwy. 29.*

OUTDOOR ACTIVITIES

If you're determined to beat the heat, it's a half-hour drive from Napa or Rutherford to **Lake Berryessa** (*see* Where to Sleep, *above*), where you can rent almost any kind of water vessel—from a Jet Ski to a ski boat—at the lake's many resorts. At **Skyline Wilderness Park** (2201 Imola Ave., Napa, tel. 707/252–0481), the 2½-mi Lake Marie Trail runs along a shady creek and past overgrown orchards and ruined stone dairies. Swimming in Lake Marie isn't allowed, but you can try your luck fishing for bluegill and bass. If you're spending the day in Calistoga, pay a visit to **Robert Louis Stevenson State Park,** off Highway 29, 9 mi northeast of Calistoga. Here you can hike to the bunkhouse of the Silverado Mine, where the impoverished author honeymooned with his wife, Fanny Osbourne, in the summer of 1880. That stay inspired Stevenson's *The Silverado Squatters.* The park is perched atop Mt. St. Helena, said to be the model for Spyglass Hill in *Treasure Island.* Its 3,000 acres are largely undeveloped; picnicking is permitted, but overnight camping is not.

LAKE TAHOE

Straddling the border of California and Nevada on the northern flank of the Sierra Nevada range, Lake Tahoe is one of the West Coast's best-loved outdoor playgrounds, drawing up to 100,000 tourists at peak periods. During spring and summer, when temperatures hover in the 70s, the lake (about a 3½-hour drive east of San Francisco on I–80) becomes a recreation arena for boating, fishing, waterskiing, and jet skiing; and the mountains surrounding Tahoe Basin satisfy even the most demanding rock climbers, hikers, bikers, equestrians, and anglers. During the winter season (usually December–April, sometimes extending into May), attention shifts to downhill and cross-country skiing and snowboarding. Tahoe has earned a worldwide reputation for its "extreme" conditions, thanks to the sheer cliffs and steep faces of the Sierra Nevada, while the Donner Summit is famed for its challenging rock-climbing faces.

The lake itself is 6,225 ft above sea level, the highest altitude for a lake its size in the United States. The water is so clear you can see 75 ft below the surface, and, plunging to a depth of 1,625 ft, it holds enough water to cover the state of California to a depth of 14 inches.

Although it's a somewhat subjective division, the lake's locales are usually designated as belonging to either the north shore or the south shore. Thanks largely to the popularity of 15 or so ski areas (compared with two in the south), the north shore is the domain of Tahoe's athletic set, while the south shore is largely overrun with family vacationers and casino-bound gamblers. The north shore's largest town is **Truckee,** about a 30-minute drive (12 mi) north of the lake, with a modern downtown area to the west and an old town (complete with board sidewalks, wood-frame storefronts, and an ancient railroad) to the east. Donner Pass Road connects the two sides of town and serves as the main commercial boulevard. On the west shore of the lake, **Tahoe City** has a small-town warmth largely lacking in Truckee. On the south shore, the city center of **South Lake Tahoe** is packed with restaurants, motels, and rental shops. The pace never flags in summer, and in winter popular ski areas such as Heavenly keep the town jumping. Butting up against the east side of South Lake Tahoe is the prosaically named town of **Stateline,** Nevada, with its four major (and two minor) hotel-casinos.

BASICS

The **North Lake Tahoe Resort Association Chamber of Commerce** (245 Hwy. 89, Tahoe City, tel. 530/581–6900) lies north of the Bank of America across from the Tahoe City Y (the intersection of Highways 89 and 28 that is impossible to miss). This site has free guides and maps, lots of community and historical facts, information on kids' activities, resources for travelers with disabilities, and details on camping. The **North Lake Tahoe Resort Association Visitors and Convention Bureau,** in Tahoe City (950 North Lake Blvd., near the Safeway, tel. 530/583–3494 or 800/824–6348) has deals on activity and accommodation packages year-round. The **Lake Tahoe Forest Service Visitor Center** (Hwy. 89 between Emerald Bay and South Lake Tahoe, tel. 530/573–2674) has beach access and nature trails, and the staff will tell you all you want to know about the lake's natural and human history.

Going to the chapel? Then it might not surprise you that the wedding industry is second only to casinos for bringing the most business to the Tahoe area.

This is also the place to pick up campfire and wilderness permits for the Desolation and Mokelumne wilderness areas. Permits are free, but only a limited number are available.

The **South Lake Tahoe Women's Center** (3140 Lake Tahoe Blvd., tel. 530/544–2118) has Spanish and English services and also operates a crisis line (tel. 530/544–4444). Gay-friendly information on recreational activities, support groups, businesses, and accommodations is found through the **Tahoe Gay Hotline** (tel. 530/541–4297). **Disabled Sports USA of Northern California** (6060 Sunrise Vista Dr., Suite 2540, Citrus Heights, CA 95610, tel. 916/722–6447) has information on skiing, waterskiing, rafting, and other outdoor activities.

COMING AND GOING

BY CAR

Both routes to Lake Tahoe take 3½–4 hours from the Bay Area when road and traffic conditions are at their best. To reach the north shore, follow I–80 east all the way to Truckee, then turn south on Route 89 to Tahoe City or Route 267 to Kings Beach. For the south shore, take U.S. 50 east from Sacramento. You won't be allowed into the mountains without chains if it snows—a possibility almost year-round; bring your own, or you'll have to pay inflated prices for a set near the CalTrans checkpoint. Even if you bring your own, consider paying ($15–$20) to let someone else put them on for you. You will see swarms of jumpsuit-clad people with numbers on their backs at every checkpoint waiting to perform this service.

If snow doesn't slow you down, traffic might, especially on Friday and Sunday afternoon and during summer and holiday weekends. If you must drive to Tahoe on Friday, wait until 7 PM or 8 PM. Traffic is usually worst on I–80, so consider taking U.S. 50 even if you're headed for the north shore.

BY BUS

Greyhound Lines (tel. 800/231–2222) runs six buses a day between San Francisco and Truckee, a 5- to 10-hour trip that's $37 one-way, and 12 one-hour trips between Truckee and Reno ($14 one-way). If you're headed to the south shore, Greyhound makes the three-hour trip between Sacramento and the transit depot at the Y at South Lake Tahoe ($19 one-way) twice a day. Both Amtrak and Greyhound use the **Transit Depot** (Donner Pass Rd., in Old Town Truckee, tel. 530/587–3822), a safe place to wait for connections. You can pick up information at the tourist office here; there are also a few coin-operated lockers.

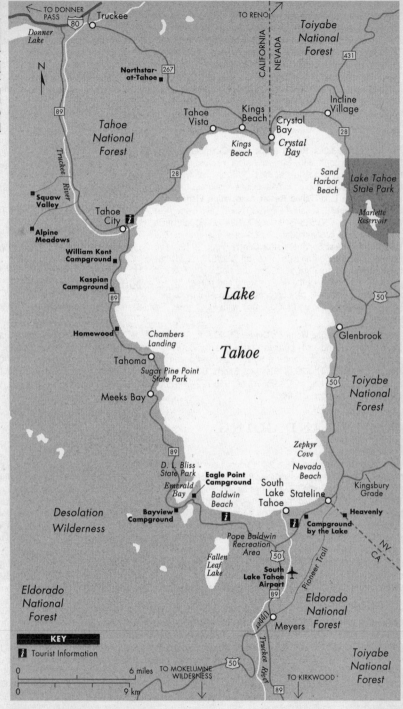

LAKE TAHOE

TO DONNER PASS
I-80
Truckee
Donner Lake
TO RENO
CALIFORNIA
NEVADA
Toiyabe National Forest
431

N

89
Northstar-at-Tahoe 267

Tahoe National Forest

Tahoe Vista
Kings Beach
Kings Beach
Crystal Bay
Crystal Bay
Incline Village
28

Sand Harbor Beach
Lake Tahoe State Park

Truckee River

28

Marlette Reservoir

Squaw Valley

Tahoe City

Alpine Meadows

William Kent Campground

Kaspian Campground

89

Lake

Tahoe

50

Homewood

Chambers Landing

Glenbrook

Tahoma

Sugar Pine Point State Park

50
Toiyabe National Forest

Meeks Bay

89

Zephyr Cove

D. L. Bliss State Park

Eagle Point Campground

Nevada Beach

Kingsbury Grade

Desolation Wilderness

Emerald Bay

Baldwin Beach

South Lake Tahoe

Stateline

Heavenly

Bayview Campground

Campground by the Lake

NV
CA

Pope Baldwin Recreation Area

Pioneer Trail

Eldorado National Forest

Fallen Leaf Lake

South Lake Tahoe Airport

50

Eldorado National Forest

89

Upper Truckee River

Meyers

Toiyabe National Forest

KEY
Tourist Information

0   6 miles
0   9 km

TO MOKELUMNE WILDERNESS

TO KIRKWOOD

50

89

BY TRAIN

Amtrak (tel. 800/872–7245) runs four train and bus routes a day between Emeryville and Truckee, with a transfer in Sacramento, a trip lasting five hours ($52 round-trip). If you're coming from San Francisco, take the free bus from the CalTrain Station at 4th and Townsend streets to the Emeryville Amtrak station (5885 Landregan St., at Powell St., tel. 510/450–1081). Amtrak also has six trains a week traveling the hour-long route between Truckee and Reno ($8 one-way). All trains arrive at the Truckee Transit Depot (*see* By Bus, *above*). Another train-and-bus combination serves South Lake Tahoe from Emeryville, again with a transfer in Sacramento, lasting five hours ($48 round-trip).

BY PLANE

At press time, no commercial airline had service to tiny **South Lake Tahoe Airport** (off Hwy. 89, about 2 mi south of the Y in South Lake Tahoe, tel. 530/542–6180). Your best bet is to get a flight to the **Reno-Tahoe International Airport** (2001 E. Plumb La., tel. 702/328–6499), then catch a **Tahoe Casino Express** bus (tel. 775/328–6400) to South Lake Tahoe. Fare is $17 one-way, $30 round-trip; buses depart from the airport up to 18 times a day.

GETTING AROUND

For recorded information on road conditions, call CalTrans at 800/427–7623 (in California only).

Three intersecting highways form a loop around the lake: **Highway 89** (a.k.a. Emerald Bay Road) skirts the west shore between Tahoe City and South Lake Tahoe; **U.S. 50** (a.k.a. Lake Tahoe Boulevard) intersects Highway 89 in South Lake Tahoe and follows the lake's east shore; and **Highway 28** (a.k.a. North Lake Boulevard or Lake Shore Boulevard) runs along the northern part of the shore back into Tahoe City. The intersections of Highways 28 and 89 in Tahoe City and Highway 89 and U.S. 50 in South Lake Tahoe are commonly referred to as the **Tahoe City Y** and the **South Lake Tahoe Y,** respectively.

The **Tahoe Area Regional Transit** (TART; tel. 530/581–6365 or 800/736–6365) has buses, most equipped with ski and bike racks, that serve the north and west shores of Lake Tahoe, traveling from Tahoma (Meeks Bay in summer) on the southwest shore to Incline Village in the north and up Highway 89 to Truckee. Fare is $1.25, and buses run from 6:30 to 6:30 year-round. Between **BUS PLUS** (tel. 530/542–6077) and the **South Tahoe Area Ground Express** (STAGE; tel. 530/573–2080), service runs 24 hours from the South Lake Tahoe Y to Stateline, Nevada; fare is $1.25 for STAGE. BUS PLUS ($3–$5) is for people who are too far from bus stops; if you call the number (*see above*), they will pick you up and drop you at the nearest STAGE stop. Schedules and maps are available from tourist information centers.

WHERE TO SLEEP

You'll face a mind-boggling number of options in choosing a place to stay in Tahoe. Hostels, motels, condominiums, cabins, and campgrounds abound. If you're just passing through for a night or two in summer, a motel or campground is the cheapest and most convenient alternative. But if you're coming for a week in winter to ski with a group of friends, consider a condominium or cabin on the north shore: It's more affordable than you might think (*see below*).

The quickest way to find a cheap (and perhaps fleabaggy) place to crash is to cruise the strip of U.S. 50 between South Lake Tahoe and Stateline—keep your eyes open for the neon. For a safer, quieter stay, opt for the area west of the South Tahoe Y, and travel up to the north shore. If you like to be in the middle of the action, look for cheap deals at the casinos on the Nevada side of both the south and north shores. No matter where you stay, reserve as far ahead as possible. On holidays and summer weekends everything is completely packed despite indiscriminate price hikes at most places. All the hotels and motels listed below have private bathrooms.

SOUTH SHORE

El Nido Motel. The excellent amenities here include a hot tub and small, modern rooms with TV, VCR, and telephone. Flawlessly clean doubles start at $47 weekdays, $55 on summer weekends; in winter prices are about $10 lower. Call for details on discount lift-ticket deals. *2215 Lake Tahoe Blvd. (U.S. 50), South Lake Tahoe 96150, tel. and fax 530/541–2711. 21 rooms.*

Emerald Motel. This well-maintained building dates to the 1960s and the proprietors are exceptionally friendly. Pope Beach and the woods are less than 2 mi away. Standard doubles start at $55 weekdays and $60 weekends, with rates $10 lower in winter. Rates are negotiable for stays of four nights or more. *515 Emerald Bay Rd. (Hwy. 89), South Lake Tahoe 96150, tel. 530/544–5515, fax 530/544–2510. 9 rooms.*

Ridgewood Inn. Set on a 2-acre lot you can explore, these clean, well-kept rooms, some with kitchenettes, are a swell deal. Doubles in summer are $50–$70, and a self-contained suite that sleeps five goes for $105. Some rooms have tubs, and there's also an outdoor Jacuzzi. *1341 Emerald Bay Rd., South Lake Tahoe 96150, tel. 530/541–8589, fax 530/541–8712. 12 rooms.*

NORTH SHORE

It's hard to find a budget motel on the north shore, especially in Truckee. For better prices and a better location, check out the smaller communities around the lakeshore, like Tahoe Vista or Kings Beach. One of the cheapest motels on the North Shore is in Kings Beach: the **Big 7** (8171 North Lake Blvd., 96143, tel. 530/546–2541), with weekday doubles $40–$50, weekends $65–$75.

North Shore Lodge. Across from Kings Beach, $60 gets you a double with a kitchen. The cabins are the best deal: One sleeps six ($115), and another sleeps eight for $125. Negotiate in winter: They've been known to take what they can get—sometimes as low as $25. In summer you have use of a heated pool. *8755 North Lake Blvd. (Hwy. 28) at Chipmunk St., Kings Beach 96143, tel. 530/546–4833, fax 530/546–0265. 11 rooms.*

River Ranch Lodge. The classy River Ranch Lodge is ideally situated beside the Truckee River between Truckee and Tahoe City. The rustic rooms (all no-smoking) were recently remodeled, with lodgepole pine beds and down comforters; half have small decks overlooking the river. Doubles start at $50 on spring and fall weekdays ($60 weekends), $60 on winter and summer weekdays ($85 weekends). Several of the noisier rooms above the bar go for $10 less, and there's a cheaper double facing the parking lot. Continental breakfast is included. *Hwy. 89 and Alpine Meadows Rd., Tahoe City 96145, tel. 530/583–4264 or 800/535–9900. 19 rooms.*

Tamarack Lodge Motel. The North Shore's best budget lodging is a short walk from the beach. Knotty pine paneling and bike-trail access are big selling points, as is the TART bus stop across the street. Doubles start at $36 weekdays, kitchenettes are $15 more, and rates go up by $10 in high season. *2311 North Lake Blvd. (Hwy. 28), Tahoe City 96145, tel. 530/583–3350 or 888/824–6323, fax 530/583–3531. 21 rooms.*

HOSTELS

Clair Tappaan Lodge. Managed by the Sierra Club and great for outdoorsy types, this coed hostel is about 45 minutes from Tahoe City. There are cross-country trails on-site, and they rent snowshoes and Nordic skis in winter. In summer they lead bird-watching, wildflower, and hiking workshops. Summer rates are $39 for nonmembers ($35 members) and include three meals per day. Rates in winter are about $6 higher. *19940 Donner Pass Rd., Norden 95724, tel. 530/426–3632, fax 530/426–0742. From Tahoe City, take Hwy. 89E, exit at Soda Springs/Norden. 140 beds. Check-in anytime.*

Doug's Mellow Mountain Retreat. At this laid-back private hostel about a mile from Heavenly and from the casinos, you can rent bikes for $10 per day and get your laundry done for $3. Doug invites guests to watch movies (he has more than 250), use his kitchen, and have barbecues on the deck. Beds in coed rooms go for $15. Reserve ahead; if you're a party of three, ask for the studio, which has its own kitchen, TV, and bath. *3787 Forest St., Box 2764, Stateline, NV 89449, tel. 530/544–8065. From South Lake Tahoe, U.S. 50 east, right on Wildwood Rd., left on Forest St. 15 beds. Check-in anytime.*

Squaw Valley Hostel. This privately run hostel, within walking distance of the Squaw Valley ski area, opens only during winter, usually from November 15 to April 15. During the week a dorm bed runs $23, $29 weekends. On weekends, when the hostel hosts groups, it's next to impossible to get a room unless you call well in advance. *1900 Squaw Valley Rd., Box 6655, Tahoe City 96145, tel. and fax 530/581–3246. From Truckee, Hwy. 89 south, right on Squaw Valley Rd. 100 beds. Check-in 4:30 PM–9 PM.*

WEEKEND AND WEEKLY RENTALS

As a rule of thumb, the more people in your group and the longer the stay, the more affordable rentals become. Contact the **Lake Tahoe Visitors Authority** (1156 Ski Run Blvd., South Lake Tahoe 96150, tel. 530/544–5050 or 800/288–2463) or the **North Lake Tahoe Resort Association** (*see* Basics, *above*) to find out about weekend or weekly rentals. You should be able to find a basic two- or four-person condominium for about $100 a night or $500 a week in the off-season, with prices rising roughly 10% in summer. **R. RENT** (tel. 530/546–2549) specializes in north-shore budget rentals. If you have the time, you can save a few bucks by arranging a rental directly through a property owner. To find out what's available, check the classified ads in the *Tahoe Daily Tribune* for south-shore listings or the *Tahoe World,* a north-shore weekly that comes out each Thursday.

CAMPING

You can hardly drive 5 mi in Lake Tahoe without bumping into a public or private campground, and almost all lie in beautiful pine forests. They close in winter until about Memorial Day. Temperatures can fluctuate widely in the region (from 60°F to below zero in a single 24-hour period), and many areas have snow until May. Call the Forest Service (*see* Basics, *above*) for advice and weather conditions before setting out. Free camping in the Tahoe area is restricted but still available at some lesser-known primitive campgrounds scattered around the lake. The Forest Service has maps, tips, and directions to free spots as well as a complete listing of campgrounds.

SOUTH SHORE • There are two inviting campgrounds just south of Emerald Bay on Highway 89. **Bayview,** on the inland side of Highway 89, has 10 first-come, first-served primitive sites amid the pines, with picnic tables and fire pits but no drinking water. A stopping-off point for journeys into Desolation Wilderness, it imposes a two-night limit on stays; but for those two nights you'll sleep for free. If all the sites in Bayview are full, head just up the road to beautiful **Eagle Point** (Hwy. 89, 1 mi south of Emerald Bay, tel. 530/525–7277 or 800/444–7275 for reservations). Here you'll find 100 well-spaced sites ($16–$18)— all with fire pits, barbecues, drinking water, picnic tables, food lockers, and access to bathrooms and showers—on a hillside covered with brush and pines. Some sites have incredible views of Emerald Bay.

Besides being deep and blue, Lake Tahoe is also mighty cold (40°F– 68°F throughout the year). You can swim in it, but most visitors just dip their feet and scamper back to shore.

NORTH SHORE • On the west shore dispersed camping is available near the Homewood ski resort, in **Blackwood Canyon.** From Highway 89 south of Tahoe City, look for a sign BLACKWOOD CANYON on the right. After 2½ mi, veer to the right on an unmarked dirt road, and camp anywhere you please.

William Kent Campground (off Hwy. 89, tel. 530/544–5994 or 877/444–6777 for reservations) is a 95-site National Forest campground set well off the highway, 2 mi south of Tahoe City; its $14 sites are in a moderately dense pine forest within walking distance of the lake. Sites are $12. Just down the road to the south, **Kaspian Campground** (tel. 530/544–5994 or 877/444–6777 for reservations) is squeezed in between a highway and the lake in Homewood village, on National Forest land. Its 10 sites cost $12 each and have piped water and flush toilets.

FOOD

On the south shore food stops are concentrated along U.S. 50 between South Lake Tahoe and Stateline, Nevada. In Stateline itself look for bargain eats at casino snack shops and all-you-can-eat buffets. On the north shore there are plenty of restaurants in downtown Truckee (especially on Donner Pass Road) and on Highway 28 in Tahoe City. For fresh organic produce and bulk foods, head to **Grass Roots** (2040 Dunlap Dr., at South Lake Tahoe Y, tel. 530/541–7788) on the south shore.

SOUTH SHORE

Ernie's Coffee Shop. An unpretentious greasy spoon serving breakfast and lunch only, Ernie's has a host of regulars who keep their personalized coffee mugs hanging on the wall. Breakfast is served all day in retro green-vinyl booths. Meals range from the standard two-egg-and-toast breakfast to more adventurous creations like the tostada omelet. *1146 Emerald Bay Rd. (Hwy. 89), at C St., South Lake Tahoe, tel. 530/541–2161. ¼ mi south of South Lake Tahoe Y.*

Hunan Garden. The friendly, sometimes wisecracking staff at this flower-festooned joint serves up a lunch buffet (11:30–2:30) for $5.50, and another at dinner (5–9) for $7.95. *900 Emerald Bay Rd. (Hwy. 89), just northwest of South Lake Tahoe Y, tel. 530/544–5868 or 530/544–7268.*

Sprouts. At South Lake Tahoe's small, cheery vegetarian paradise, you can feast on great sandwiches and fruit smoothies on an outdoor patio. The produce is largely organic. *3123 Harrison Ave., at intersection of U.S. 50 and Alameda Ave., South Lake Tahoe, tel. 530/541–6969.*

Taquería Jalisco. With a blaring jukebox and great food, this spot attracts Tahoe's sizable Latino population. Hidden behind Rojo's eatery, Taquería Jalisco sells burritos, nachos, and tacos (some vegetarian) for under $2.50. *3097 Harrison Ave., at San Francisco Ave., South Lake Tahoe, tel. 530/541–6516.*

NORTH SHORE

Bridgetender Tavern and Grill. Housed in an old wooden cabin with high, beamed ceilings and tree trunks poking through the roof, the Bridgetender is a worthy burgers-and-beer stop. Huge beef patties and tasty veggie burgers are served with hefty french fries until 11 PM weekdays and midnight weekends. Sit on a patio overlooking the Truckee River or drink beer and shoot pool inside. *30 Emerald Bay Rd. (Hwy. 89), Tahoe City, next to bridge at Tahoe City Y, tel. 530/583–3342.*

China Garden. One of Truckee's best restaurants serves up veggie dishes, seafood, and other Mandarin standards. There are lunch and dinner specials for $5–$10 and a $7–$9 Mongolian barbecue buffet. *11361 Deerfield Dr., tel. 530/587–7625. In Crossroads Center, off Hwy. 89 just south of I–80.*

Truckee River Coffee Company. This homey café has couches, a few tables, a piano, coffee, and dessert. Try the old-fashioned hot chocolate, or the Coffee Nut, made of hazelnut espresso, hazelnut syrup, and vanilla yogurt. *11373 Deerfield Dr., Truckee, tel. 530/587–2583. In Crossroads Center, just south of I–80/Hwy. 89 junction.*

AFTER DARK

Events on the south shore are covered in *Lake Tahoe Action,* a free weekly entertainment magazine put out by the *Tahoe Daily Tribune.* The *Tahoe–Truckee Review* covers the north shore. Both are available at most motels.

SOUTH SHORE

The south shore is surprisingly quiet by night. On the Nevada side of the border in Stateline, you'll find a number of casinos and the usual array of Las Vegas–style shows and headliners. Just north of the state line, the gay club **Faces** (270 Kingsbury Grade, just west of Hwy. 50, tel. 702/588–2333) has a relaxed, friendly atmosphere, with dancing three nights a week until 4 AM (no cover). The **Brewery at Lake Tahoe** (3542 U.S. 50, tel. 530/544–2739), 1½ mi west of the California–Nevada border, is a microbrewery and restaurant popular with the après-ski crowd. **The Island Café** (4093 Lake Tahoe Blvd., tel. 530/542–1142) is a gay- and lesbian-friendly spot with eight microbrews on tap, live music every night, and fresh food.

NORTH SHORE

Tahoe City is without a doubt the center of the lake's nightlife. Loud, crowded, and filled with hard-drinking youth, **Elevation** (877 North Lake Blvd., 1 mi northeast of Tahoe City Y, tel. 530/583–4867) features the best live indie music in the area most nights (cover $5–$20). When Elevation is sold out, the overflow crowd heads to **Rosie's Cafe** (571 North Lake Blvd., Tahoe City, tel. 530/583–8504), a large restaurant and bar housed in an old cabin full of Tahoe City memorabilia.

Catering to a mellower clientele, the **Naughty Dawg** (255 North Lake Blvd., ¼ mi northeast of Tahoe City Y, tel. 530/581–3294) has a good selection of high-quality beers, as well as surprisingly good salads, burgers, and pizza. **River Ranch Lodge** (*see* Where to Sleep, *above*) is an excellent place for a quiet drink, with a large deck next to the Truckee River and a stylish indoor bar. During the summer it hosts an outdoor concert series with eclectic bookings ranging from jazz to hard rock (cover $5–$25).

OUTDOOR ACTIVITIES

In addition to its excellent skiing, Lake Tahoe is full of opportunities for just about every fair-weather sport imaginable. An abbreviated list would include hiking, biking, fishing, sailing, waterskiing, jet skiing, rock climbing, hot-air ballooning, parasailing, horseback riding, and river rafting. Many of the more exotic adventures are pricey, but Tahoe is a great place to splurge. Tourist offices and the Forest Service (*see* Basics, *above*) have detailed information about all these sports. For equipment rentals, **Don Cheepo's** (*see* Equipment Rental *in* Skiing, *below*) carries everything from water skis to backpacks and other camping supplies. Also try **Alpenglow Sports** (415 North Lake Blvd., tel. 530/583–6917), in Tahoe City, for information and equipment. **Sports Exchange,** in Truckee (10095 W. River St., tel. 530/582–4510), is a good rock climbing resource.

HIKING

Almost every acre in the Lake Tahoe Basin is protected by some national, state, or local agency. **Tahoe National Forest** lies to the northwest, **Eldorado National Forest** to the southwest, and **Toiyabe National Forest** to the east. This means a whole lot of hiking trails for visitors, from easy scenic walks to strenuous climbs over mountain passes. The Lake Tahoe Forest Service Visitor Center (*see* Basics, *above*) has a complete list of day hikes.

One of the most interesting short walks is **Vikingsholm Trail,** a mile-long (one-way) paved path leading from the parking lot on the north side of Emerald Bay to the shoreline and the 38-room Vikingsholm Castle, a Scandinavian-style castle built in 1929. From the castle you can walk farther, to **Eagle Falls,** the only waterfall that empties into the lake. For something a little more woodsy, try the **Mt. Tallac Trail,** a half mile north of the Lake Tahoe Forest Service Visitor Center (follow the marked asphalt road opposite Baldwin Beach to the trailhead parking lot). A moderate hike takes you 2 mi through a beautiful pine forest to Cathedral Lake. For a serious daylong trek (with no potable water along the way), continue on the trail another 3 mi as it climbs past a series of boulder fields to the peak of Mt. Tallac, the highest point in the basin at 9,735 ft. At the top you'll enjoy excellent views of the lake and Desolation Wilderness. The trip up and back should take seven or eight hours.

For extensive backcountry camping and hiking the choices are limitless. Off the southwest corner of the lake, 63,473-acre **Desolation Wilderness** is filled with granite peaks, glacial valleys, subalpine forests, and more than 80 lakes. South of the lake, **Mokelumne Wilderness,** straddling the border of Eldorado and Stanislaus national forests, has terrain similar to Desolation without the crowds. Before you enter any wilderness area, whether for a day or for an extended visit, it's crucial to pick up a wilderness permit from the Lake Tahoe Forest Service Visitor Center (*see* Basics, *above*)—without one, you may actually be kicked off the trails.

BIKING

Lake Tahoe has enough mellow lakeshore trails, steep fire roads, and tricky single tracks to satisfy any two-wheeled explorer. The Forest Service has detailed trail information, and the North Lake Tahoe Resort Association (*see* Basics, *above*) puts out an excellent brochure called "North Lake Tahoe Mountain Biking" that lists bike tours, trails, bike parks, and bike shops for rentals. Several paved, gently sloped paths skirt the lakeshore: Try the 3.4-mi **Pope Baldwin Bike Path,** in South Lake Tahoe at the Pope Baldwin Recreational Center, or the **West Shore Bike Path,** which extends about 10 mi south from Tahoe City to Sugar Pine Point State Park, near the town of Tahoma. Also worthwhile are the path along the **Truckee River** between Alpine Meadows and Tahoe City and the **U.S. Forest Service Bike Trail,** an 8.5-mi paved path (through pine forest and rare aspen grove) that starts at Emerald Bay Road just west of the South Lake Tahoe Y and ends at the lake.

Experienced riders may dare the famous **Flume Trail,** a 24-mi ride past several lakes and along a ridge with sweeping views of Lake Tahoe. The trail begins at the parking lot of Lake Tahoe–Nevada State Park, just north of Spooner Junction on the lake's east shore (take Highway 28 east from Tahoe City). The *High Sierra Biking Map* ($6) and its accompanying book ($9) provide a detailed description of the Flume Trail as well as several dozen other excellent rides in the area. If you like the idea of riding downhill all day, **Northstar-at-Tahoe, Donner Ranch, Kirkwood, Squaw Valley,** and **Sugar Bowl** (*see* Skiing, *below*) all open a number of ski runs for mountain biking June–September. All-day tickets run $10–$21 (bike rentals $30–$45).

BIKE RENTALS • Dozens of shops around Tahoe rent mountain bikes, generally for $5–$7 an hour or $18–$25 a day. On the south shore there's **Don Cheepo's** (*see* Equipment Rental *in* Skiing, *below*), near the east end of the Pope Baldwin Bike Path. On the north shore try **Porter's** (501 North Lake Blvd., tel. 530/583–2314), on Highway 28, east of the Tahoe City Y.

BEACHES

Of the many beaches scattered around the lake's shore, two of the best are **Chamber's Landing,** south of Tahoe City, a favorite of young north-shore locals; and **Baldwin Beach,** a gorgeous and usually uncrowded sand beach between South Lake Tahoe and Emerald Bay. **Nevada Beach,** a more populated spot just across the Nevada border in Stateline, has great mountain views. **Sand Harbor,** a crescent-shape strand off Highway 28 south of Incline Village, is ideal for sunsets.

WATER SPORTS

Despite Lake Tahoe's often frigid waters, there's no lack of rental outfits specializing in sailing, waterskiing, jet skiing, windsurfing, kayaking, canoeing, and parasailing. Prices fluctuate a bit, but in general sailboats go for $35–$40 an hour, $90–$100 a day; Jet Skis run $60–$90 an hour; Windsurfers rent for $10–$15 an hour, $30–$40 a half day; and canoes and kayaks go for about the same. Parasailing rides, which usually last about 15 minutes, range from $40 to $60.

On the south shore the **Ski Run Boat Company** (tel. 530/544–0200), with motorboats, canoes, kayaks, and other toys, is one of several shops operating out of **Ski Run Marina,** off U.S. 50 about a half mile west of the California–Nevada border. On the north shore you'll find rental outfits in the **Sunnyside Marina,** about 2 mi south of Tahoe City on Highway 89.

FISHING

The most convenient area is **Lake Tahoe,** stocked occasionally with rainbow trout by the folks at the Fish and Wildlife Service; to find the section of the lake most recently stocked, call 530/355–7040 or 530/351–0832. Also popular is the stretch of the **Truckee River** between Truckee and Tahoe City—just pick a spot and cast your line. Wherever you fish, licenses ($10 a day, $28.70 a year) are required by law and available from most sporting-goods shops. For sportfishing on the lake, contact **Tahoe Sportfishing** (tel. 530/541–5448 or 800/696–7797), in the Ski Run Marina, or **Don's Sport Fishing** (tel. 530/541–5566), in South Lake Tahoe. The best deal is a half-day trip, generally starting at $65–$75; for full-day trips, you usually have to charter the boat.

SKIING

Whether you prefer downhill or cross-country, you've come to the right place. Unbelievably sheer faces, narrow chutes, and huge cliffs have attracted a new breed of downhill skier and snowboarder bent on pushing the sport to extremes. But novices shouldn't be intimidated: There are more than 24 ski resorts, and most have plenty of beginner-level slopes, both downhill and cross-country. In addition to the millions of discount rental and lift-ticket flyers you'll find all over the area, the tourist centers can give you the *Skier's Planning Guide,* the *Winter Travel Planner,* and the *Winter Visitors' Guide.* All have information on the various lift operators and advice about skiing in the area. Call the **North Lake Tahoe Resort Association** (*see* Basics, *above*) for tips on skiing specials—they change throughout the season.

EQUIPMENT RENTAL

Renting equipment from the shops run by the resorts will make it easier to get adjustments, repairs, or replacements midday. However, as a rule of thumb, the closer you get to the ski resorts, the higher the cost of renting equipment. For the cheapest rentals, try any one of the hundreds of stores crowding the lake's major roads. The best deal anywhere is the south shore's **Don Cheepo's** (3349 U.S. 50, about ¾ mi west of Heavenly, tel. 530/544–0356), where full downhill and cross-country rental packages (skis, boots, and poles) cost $7–$25. Snowboards rent for $17, including boots.

On the north shore, **Porter's** has low rates (full ski packages $13–$18, snowboards $15–$22) and three locations, including one in Tahoe City (501 North Lake Blvd., just east of Tahoe City Y, tel. 530/583–2314) and one in Truckee (in Crossroads Center on Hwy. 89, south of I-80, tel. 530/587–1500).

DOWNHILL SKIING

The "Big Five" ski resorts (*see below*) all charge about $45 a day, but if you're careful, you can avoid paying that price. Buying multiple-day or weekday tickets will save you $3–$7 per day; also scour local papers, motels, gas stations, and supermarkets (try Safeway) for discounts and deals. Beginners and intermediate skiers can save money and still get their money's worth at one of the smaller, less expensive resorts, some of which even offer midweek discounts. If you're coming from the Bay Area, you can save 30–45 minutes driving time by skiing at any of the Donner Pass ski resorts—Soda Springs, Sugar Bowl, Donner Ranch, Boreal, or Tahoe Donner. Of these five, **Sugar Bowl** (tel. 530/426–3847 for snow report), off the Soda Springs/Norden exit of I-80, is the largest and most beautiful. It's especially attractive for experienced skiers, with 50% of its runs designated advanced, including some of the best tree skiing in Tahoe. A few miles farther down the road, **Donner Ranch** (Soda Springs/Norden exit off I-80, tel. 530/426–3635 for snow report) is Tahoe's cheapest ski resort, with lift tickets starting at just $15 on weekdays and $23 on weekends. If you have more than a day for skiing, consider **Ski Homewood** (Hwy. 89, between Tahoe City and South Lake Tahoe, tel. 530/525–2992 or 530/525–2900 for snow report): From its 1,260 acres of varied terrain you can catch magnificent views of the lake. Lift tickets go for $36 for a full day, $26 for a half. Better still, Wednesday is two-for-one day, when you and a friend can ski for $18 each.

THE BIG FIVE • Squaw Valley (on Hwy. 89, 8 mi south of Truckee, tel. 530/583–6955 for snow report) is a vast resort with more than 8,000 acres of open bowls, 2,850 vertical ft, and more than 25 chairlifts. Though it's unofficially known as the home of extreme skiing, Squaw Valley is actually an all-around ski area—70% of the mountain is suited to beginning and intermediate skiers. **Alpine Meadows** (off Hwy. 89, 6 mi northwest of Tahoe City, tel. 530/581–8374 for snow report) has a high base elevation of 7,000 ft (allowing for a longer season) and 12 lifts servicing more than 100 runs. Alpine has built its reputation on the abundant snow and sunshine that its two mountains enjoy—most locals agree it's the best place for spring skiing. Alpine Meadows is also home to the **Tahoe Handicapped Ski School** (tel. 530/581–4161), the first school in the area to offer ski programs for the mentally and physically challenged. **Northstar-at-Tahoe** (Hwy. 267, 7 mi south of Truckee, tel. 530/562–1330 for snow report) has a breakdown of 25% beginner runs, 50% intermediate runs, and 25% advanced runs. It's worth coming here for a day, if only for the incredible views of the basin from the top of the 8,610-ft **Mt. Pluto. Heavenly** (west entrance off Lake Tahoe Blvd., in South Lake Tahoe, tel. 530/541–7544 for snow report) is officially the largest ski area in the United States, with more than 4,300 acres of skiable terrain, an incredible 3,500-ft vertical drop, and 25 lifts scattered over no fewer than nine peaks. **Kirkwood** (Hwy. 88E, off Hwy. 89 south from South Lake Tahoe, tel. 209/258–3000 for snow report) has the driest snow, which experienced skiers know means the best powder—all told, 85% of Kirkwood's runs are designated intermediate or advanced.

Alpine Meadows is one of the few resorts that does not allow snowboarders.

CROSS-COUNTRY SKIING

You'll have no problem finding a trail to suit your abilities at Tahoe's 13 cross-country ski areas, the most famous of which is the north shore's **Royal Gorge** (Soda Springs/Norden exit south from I-80, tel. 530/426–3871 or 800/500–3871), the largest cross-country ski resort in the United States. You can choose from 200 mi of trails running along a ridge above the north fork of the American River; fees are $17.50 weekdays, with the best deal on Wednesday at $12.

Eagle Mountain (tel. 530/389–2254, $16.50 weekends, Tues. 2-for-1, Wed.–Thurs. $10) is strictly for skiers with at least some experience. With incredible vistas along 45 mi of trails, it's Tahoe's closest Nordic resort—about an hour west of Truckee. Exit I-80 at Yuba Gap and follow the signs. Two other cross-country resorts on the north shore, **Northstar-at-Tahoe** (tel. 530/562–1330), charging a $14 fee, and **Squaw Creek** (tel. 530/583–6300), which charges $10, are right next to downhill ski areas (*see above*), making them great choices for vacation groups with divided loyalties. Of the two, Northstar, with 40 mi of trails, is the more exciting destination.

On the south shore, only **Kirkwood** (*see above;* tel. 209/258–7248) has both alpine and Nordic ski trails, with more than 50 mi of cross-country for skiers of all levels ($12). **Hope Valley** (Hwy. 88E, off Hwy. 89, tel. 530/694–2266) occupies a beautiful valley of the Toiyabe (Toy-*ah*-bee) National Forest, on the grounds of Sorenson's Resort. Best of all, you can ski its 60 mi of trails for free (donation requested). The North Lake Tahoe Resort Association (*see* Basics, *above*) can also hook you up with packages, such as a $39 three-day ticket that can be used at any of seven resorts.

YOSEMITE NATIONAL PARK

For over a century tourists have been flocking to, awestruck by, and—all too often—abusive of Yosemite National Park. A hundred years ago this abuse came in the form of carved-up giant sequoias—making a hole big enough to drive a car through—and atrocities against the Native peoples; in today's era of ecotourism, damage is the result of too much attention. Between 1986 and 1996 the number of visitors to the park increased from 3 million to more than 4 million—most came in the summer, and most went straight to the 7-mi stretch called **Yosemite Valley.** They came to gawk at **Half Dome** and **El Capitan**— two breathtaking but treacherous granite formations—as well as at the **Yosemite, Bridalveil, Nevada,** and **Vernal falls.**

Though park officials have long known the undue traffic has been damaging the park (not to mention visitors' appreciation of it), little was done to alleviate the problem until August 1996, when nature took matters into her own hands. First came the Ackerson Complex fires—the most devastating in park history, they burned 59,000 acres north of Tioga Road. A government shutdown closed the park for a record 21 days, and an 80,000-ton rock slide behind the Happy Isles Nature Center left a cloud of granite dust hovering over the valley for a week. Then came the floods of January 1997, the biggest floods recorded in park history. They were most destructive along the Merced River, the central waterway in Yosemite Valley: Two campgrounds were destroyed; several sections of Highway 140 were washed out; and drinking water, sewage systems, and power lines went down.

The cleansing effect of the fires and flood were naturally beneficial, as any ranger will tell you. Now park officials are faced with decisions on whether to further "cleanse" Yosemite by limiting visitation and traffic in Yosemite Valley, especially in summertime; some cars have already been turned back during crowded holiday weekends (especially Memorial Day and July 4). Except for such holiday weekends, however, no restrictions are expected to be imposed before 2001 at the earliest. If there are further restrictions, it's anybody's guess what they might mean for the less visited, nonvalley areas of the park— the undisturbed, forested backcountry with its massive granite formations and plunging waterfalls. Will **Tuolumne Meadows** (say it: *twa*-lo-mee), along Tioga Road; the giant sequoias of **Mariposa Grove,** off Highway 41 in the southwest corner of the park; **Glacier Point,** near Badger Pass; and the **Hetch Hetchy Reservoir** (north of Big Oak Flat) remain untrammeled and enjoyed by those who know their solitary wonder? Or will the numerous turnouts and day-hike areas that make these areas fairly easy to reach from the highway eventually become crowded with overflow visitors from the valley?

Whatever the future holds, the natural disasters (or perhaps blessings) haven't for a moment dulled the natural, glorious sheen of this land, formed by glacial sculpturing and prehistoric activity at the earth's mantle. Slightly smaller than the state of Rhode Island, Yosemite is still packed with waterfalls, sheer granite cliffs, lush forests, and generous expanses of alpine meadows, and you can still find a quiet spot to call your own.

BASICS

VISITOR INFORMATION

For current events in Yosemite, check out the *Yosemite Guide,* distributed free at all entrance stations. The visitor centers stock maps and brochures and give out free wilderness permits (required for overnight camping in the backcountry; *see* Wilderness Permits, *below*). The **Yosemite Valley Visitor Center** (Shuttle Stops 6 and 9, tel. 209/372–0299) is 11 mi east of the Highway 140 entrance and open mid-June–early September, daily 8–7; early September–late October and April–mid-June, daily 8:30–5; and November–March, daily 9–4:30. The **Tuolumne Meadows Visitor Center,** open daily in summer only, 9–5, is toward the east end of the park on Tioga Road. The **Wawona Information Station,** at the south end of Yosemite on Highway 41, provides wilderness permits summer only, weekdays 8:30–4:30. The **Big Oak Flat Information Station,** at the Highway 120 west entrance, is open from May to Labor Day, daily 9–5. If you're not actually in the park, send a self-addressed, stamped envelope to the **Public Information Office** (Box 577, Yosemite National Park 95389, tel. 209/372–0265) for free brochures and maps or call weekdays between 9 and 5. This is the best phone number to use to talk to a real person for information about the park, including any of the areas listed above. For automated information call the **Yosemite National Park information line** (tel. 209/372–0200).

WILDERNESS PERMITS • In 1972 Yosemite had to institute a permit system to limit the number of backpackers on the trails each day. Half the park's permits are reserved, while half are distributed free on a first-come, first-served basis one day in advance. To make a reservation (available from two days up to 24 weeks in advance), you'll need to pay a reservation fee of $3 per person and send your dates of arrival and departure, specific trailheads of entry and exit, your main destination in the park, the number in your party, and alternative dates in case your first choices aren't available to **Wilderness Reservations** (Wilderness Center, Box 545, Yosemite National Park, 95389). You may also call 209/372–0740 to reserve by phone.

For free first-come, first-served permits the day before your hike, bring a detailed itinerary, including trails and estimated overnight stops, to the **Wilderness Center** (tel. 209/372–0740), which is two buildings east of the Yosemite Valley Visitor Center (*see above*). When the Wilderness Center is closed (November–March), go to the wilderness permit station nearest your planned destination. Permits go

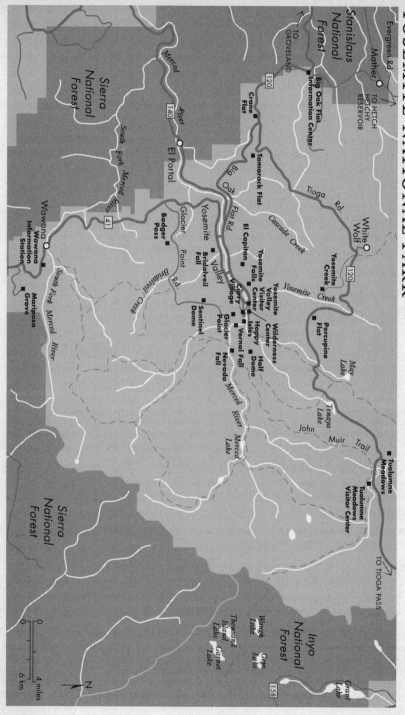

YOSEMITE NATIONAL PARK

quickly (some in just five minutes)—particularly for popular areas such as the valley and Tuolumne Meadows—so arrive early.

FEES

The park fee for one week is $20 per car or $10 per hiker or bicyclist. For $40 you can purchase an annual pass for unlimited access to the park.

WHEN TO GO

If possible, visit during spring or early fall, when crowds are less oppressive. Spring (late April–late May) is especially spectacular—the wildflowers are in bloom, and the waterfalls are at their peak of sound and fury as snow pack melts in the high country. Of the more than 4 million people who visit each year, 70% arrive during summer (June–August), when temperatures reach average highs of 90°F and lows of 40°F. In winter (November–March) temperatures drop to a chilly 45°F by day and a downright frigid 15°F by night—Tioga Pass and Glacier Point Road usually close by November due to snowfall, and typically don't reopen till late spring.

WHAT TO PACK

Rain gear is essential year-round; even a bright summer day could quickly give way to one of Yosemite's sudden tempests. Water-repellent shell pants and a warm jacket with polar-fleece lining are a smart idea, and don't forget wool or wick-dry socks—they'll keep you warm even when it's wet. If you plan to camp in winter, you'll need a subzero sleeping bag and a waterproof (or at least water-resistant) four-season tent. Hiking boots are a must for exploring the backcountry; bring snowshoes or crampons if you want to blaze your own trail in winter.

GENERAL STORES

If you're coming into the park from Highway 120, stop first at Oakdale's **Newdeal Market** (888 Hwy. 120, tel. 209/847–5919), open daily 7 AM–10 PM. If you're headed in on Highway 41, stock up at one of the major grocery stores in Oakhurst. Otherwise you're stuck with the grocery and camping stores in pricey Yosemite Village (at Shuttle Stops 3, 5, and 10). The **Village Sport Shop** (tel. 209/372–1286), open from spring to fall, has fishing and camping gear. Both the **Village Store** (tel. 209/372–1253), open daily 8 AM–9 PM spring–fall, 8–7 in winter, and the **Wawona Store** (Hwy. 41, near south end of park, tel. 209/375–6574), open daily 8–8, 9–6 in winter, stock groceries and basic camping supplies.

Badger Pass Ski Shop (tel. 209/372–8423), open daily 9–4:30 Thanksgiving through Easter (weather permitting), has ski clothing and equipment as well as limited picnic supplies. It's near the Badger Pass ski slopes, off Highway 41 on Glacier Point Rd. Curry Village, at the far-east end of Yosemite Valley (Shuttle Stop 14), has a fair selection of stores, including the **Curry Village Mountain Shop** (tel. 209/372–8396), where you can purchase rock-climbing supplies and topographic maps at inflated prices, and the **Yosemite Mountaineering School** (tel. 209/372–8344), where you can rent camping equipment including internal- and external-frame backpacks, day packs, sleeping bags, bear canisters, and foam pads at reasonable prices. Only climbing students can rent climbing shoes.

MEDICAL AID

The **Yosemite Medical Clinic,** in Yosemite Village, offers full medical services and 24-hour emergency care. *Between visitor center and Ahwahnee Hotel, tel. 209/372–4637. Open daily 8–5.*

COMING AND GOING

BY CAR

You can reach Yosemite on three routes: **Highway 41** from Fresno and the south, **Highway 140** from Merced in the west, and **Highway 120** from San Francisco (take I–580 east to I–205 and connect to Highway 120, a four-hour drive). Because of continuing extensive reconstruction after the 1997 floods, you may encounter moderate to severe delays along Highway 140, especially in nonsummer months. Highways 41 and 140 terminate in Yosemite Valley, and Highway 120 becomes Tioga Road inside the park; Big Oak Flat Road connects the latter with the valley. In spring and winter the eastern portion of Highway 120 (from Crane Flat east to the Tioga Pass and into Inyo National Forest and Lee Vining) is closed until Memorial Day weekend, assuming snows are cleared by then, as is Glacier Point Road. Summer traffic is frequently bumper to bumper, especially around July 4, Memorial Day, and Labor Day.

From late fall to early spring you should carry snow chains. The highways can get treacherous, and the California Highway Patrol often closes the roads to all traffic without snow gear. If you get stuck, you'll have to buy an expensive set of chains (about $60) from a gas station. For road and weather conditions call 209/372-0200, 916/445-1534, or 800/427-7623.

BY BUS AND TRAIN

There is no direct bus service to Yosemite from San Francisco; all lines stop either in Fresno or Merced, where you have to change coaches. Should the valley close to all car traffic, call 209/372-0265 to find out about the many bus services that will be shuttling visitors into the park from the surrounding towns. A cheap option from Merced is **VIA Adventures** (tel. 209/384-1315 or 800/369-7275), which runs several buses a day to Yosemite Valley ($20 one-way, $38 round-trip, park admission included) from Merced's Greyhound station on 16th and N streets, a 2½- to 4½-hour ride. In conjunction with VIA, **Amtrak** (tel. 800/872-7245) provides service from San Francisco/Oakland to the park and back for $68–$88, park admission included. The train stops in Merced, where you board the bus to Yosemite. All buses stop at Yosemite Lodge, Curry Village, and Yosemite Village. From San Francisco **Green Tortoise** (tel. 415/956-7500 or 800/867-8647) runs a three-day Yosemite and Eastern Sierra tour out of San Francisco that covers much of the park and surrounding forest. The tour costs $119, plus $31 for food (*see* Bus Travel *in* Chapter 1); Green Tortoise also has two-day winter trips for $79, plus $21 for food. The friendly folks at **Incredible Adventures** (tel. 415/759-7071 or 800/777-8464) lead three-day camping and hiking trips to Yosemite from San Francisco from mid-May to mid-October for an all-inclusive price of $185.

GETTING AROUND

Tioga Road (Highway 120) runs the entire 60-mi east–west length of the park, climbing 4,000 ft in elevation. If you're on a bicycle (*see* Biking, *below*), you may want to limit yourself to the valley, since both Highway 41 and Tioga Road are often narrow and winding, with extreme increases in elevation.

BY PARK SHUTTLE

Free shuttle buses operate throughout the year, though service hours vary according to season. The **Yosemite Valley Shuttle** travels every 20 minutes year-round, with stops at Curry Village, Yosemite Village, the Yosemite Lodge, and campgrounds and points of interest in between (*see* Where to Sleep, *below*). Starting in mid-April, the shuttle operates 7 AM–10 PM for most stops—excluding Happy Isles, the Mirror Lake Trail, and the North Pines campground, when service stops at 7:30 PM (campers in North Pines can easily walk from Shuttle Stop 19 at Lower Pines after 7 PM). In winter, hours are reduced to 9 AM–10 PM, and some stops receive no service at all. Check the *Yosemite Guide* for a current schedule. During ski season a free shuttle leaves Yosemite Lodge for the **Badger Pass** ski area in the morning and returns in the afternoon. Another shuttle ($10.50 one-way, $20.50 round-trip) runs three times daily from mid-May to early October (weather permitting) between Yosemite Lodge and **Glacier Point** (*see* Scenic Drives and Views, *below*). Tickets can be purchased at a **Yosemite transportation** desk, which is in all hotels. Stops are well marked; just look for the SHUTTLE BUS signs along the main roads. From July until Labor Day an early morning backpackers' shuttle ($14 one-way, $22 round-trip) runs once daily between Yosemite Lodge and Tuolumne Meadows. Call the Yosemite Lodge Tour Desk (tel. 209/372-1240) for schedules and reservations.

WHERE TO SLEEP

Close to the ground—that's the way to experience Yosemite, and camping and backpacking are the best ways to do it. If you must stay in a hotel, keep in mind that the privilege of four thin walls and a bed doesn't come cheap. Both beds and campsites go like hotcakes, and reservations are essential—especially in summer and fall.

One of the best-kept secrets of Yosemite accommodations is the **Yosemite Lakes Hostel** (31191 Hardin Flat, 17 mi east of Groveland, 95321, tel. 209/962-0121), 5 mi west of the park on Highway 120. It has all sorts of sleeping options: hostel rooms that sleep two ($31) or four ($41); deluxe rooms that sleep six ($51); cabins without private bath that sleep four ($35); fully equipped yurts (circular domed tents) that sleep four ($99, $89 after first night); and wooded tent sites ($16). Washing machines, a TV, and microwaves are on the premises. And—best of all—they often have space for walk-ins. The hostel, which has no age restrictions, is open from mid-May to September.

HOTELS AND CABINS

Hotel reservations can be made up to 366 days in advance, and believe it or not, most places actually fill up that far ahead. All lodging reservations are handled through **Yosemite Concessions Services Corporation** (5410 E. Home Ave., Fresno 93727, tel. 559/252-4848). Because Yosemite is so mobbed, especially in summer, you may not have a choice when it comes to your hotel accommodations. If you can find a single vacancy in peak season, consider yourself lucky. (One strategy, albeit risky, is to go to the park and hope for last-minute cancellations or no-shows—which do happen.) Otherwise, try the hostel (*see above*) or check out the nearby towns of El Portal, Fishcamp, and Oakhurst, all of which have reasonably priced lodgings.

If you don't think you'd make a happy camper, the **Yosemite Lodge** in Yosemite Valley has rooms for two with private bath starting at $92 in peak season (May–October) and $79 from November to March. Less expensive are accommodations in **Curry Village,** which include canvas tent cabins (starting at $40 in peak season and $34 in winter) and simple wooden cabins ($46–$59 without private bath, $69–$75 with private bath). Or seek out the valley shantytown called **Housekeeping Camp,** which consists of more than 260 identical concrete-and-canvas "tent" units open from April to late October. Though huddled close together and not particularly comfy, they're ideal for people who like a camp atmosphere but don't want to lug the equipment. Each structure can house four people in bunk cots for only $43 per night (extra cots are an additional $4 each). A grocery store, laundry, bathroom, and showers are nearby. The reservations number for all these accommodations is 559/252-4848.

CAMPING

Yosemite Valley's developed campgrounds share a number of characteristics: They're all large, flat, near a major road, and shaded by pine trees. Most have picnic tables, fire pits, flush toilets, piped water, and food lockers, but none has direct access to showers (for that you'll have to head to Housekeeping Camp or Curry Village). Unfortunately, another commonality is that they're all extremely crowded—and for most, reservations are a must. Campground reservations are available up to five months in advance (tel. 800/436-7275); call the 15th of the month for best pickings. (Call January 15 for dates through June 14, February 15 for dates June 15–July 14, March 15 for dates July 15–August 14, etc.). If you're stuck, show up at one of the campground kiosks (at Curry Village, Big Oak Flat, and Tuolumne Meadows) and put your name on the waiting list in case there's a cancellation; remember that without reservations you'll need to get a day-use permit in advance. The campground kiosks usually call off names once a day (around 3 PM) for cancellations and no-shows.

If you can't get a reservation at any major campground, you can try to land one of the park's first-come, first-served sites. In particular, check out the valley's only walk-in campground, **Sunnyside,** near Yosemite Lodge in Yosemite Valley. Its 35 sites ($3 per person), all with running water and toilets, are a favorite among hard-core rock climbers. For walk-ins outside the valley, try **Tuolumne Meadows** (*see* Outside Yosemite Valley, *below*), where 25 sites are reserved for backpackers with wilderness permits, and the rest are held for either advance or same-day reservations; check the visitor center (either in the valley or in Tuolumne) for availability. Other sites that operate on a first-come, first-served basis include: **Bridalveil Creek** (Glacier Point Rd.), with 110 sites ($10), open June–September; **Wawona** (Wawona Rd., at south end of park), with 100 sites that are nonreservation October–April only ($10); **Tamarack Flat** (Tioga Rd., just east of Crane Flat), with 52 sites ($6); **White Wolf** (Tioga Rd., about 10 mi east of Crane Flat), with 87 sites ($10); **Porcupine Flat,** with 52 sites ($6); and **Yosemite Creek,** with 75 sites ($6). The latter two are both off Tioga Road east of White Wolf. All the Tioga Road campgrounds close in winter, usually from mid-September or early October to early June. For information on backcountry camping, *see* Longer Hikes, *below*.

INSIDE YOSEMITE VALLEY • The 1997 floods knocked out a whopping 300-plus campsites in the valley—and two entire campgrounds (Upper and Lower River)—leaving the park just short of 1,500 total sites. The biggest valley campground is **Upper Pines,** with 238 tent and RV sites ($15 each), available year-round. It's conveniently located at Shuttle Stop 15, near trailheads to Mirror Lake and Vernal Fall, and gets predictably crowded. Across the street at Shuttle Stop 19, **Lower Pines** is open March–October, with 60 tent and RV sites ($15) sandwiched between the Merced River and Storeman Meadow. Expect the same pack of RVs and families you see at Upper Pines. **North Pines Campground,** with 85 sites ($15) available April–October, is conveniently located at Shuttle Stop 18. Open to both tent campers and RV owners, this campground gives you spectacular views of Yosemite Falls and has many sites along the sandy (sometimes soggy) shores of the Merced River. It's also a great starting point for the short hike to Mirror Lake.

OUTSIDE YOSEMITE VALLEY • Look for **Tuolumne Meadows,** an enormous riverside campground in some of the park's most beautiful country, perfect for exploring the east side of Yosemite. Its 314 sites ($15) lie along Tioga Road (Highway 120) and are usually open July–September, depending on the weather. This campground attracts its share of day hikers, but it's still one of the last to fill up. **Hodgdon Meadow,** just past Highway 120 at the Big Oak Flat entrance on the west side of the park, allows you to escape the chaos of the valley and still remain within striking distance (30–40 minutes). Its 105 sites ($15) draw nature-loving car campers year-round, except when snow closes the road.

FOOD

If you plan on camping, bring as much food as possible. Prices in Yosemite's stores (*see* General Stores, *above*) are predictably high. American eateries, from fast-food cafeterias to expensive sit-down restaurants, are the only other choice.

The **Yosemite Village** complex, 11 mi east of the Highway 140 entrance, has the largest selection of food in the park. **Yosemite Lodge** (Shuttle Stop 8, tel. 209/372–1274) has a year-round cafeteria where entrées are typically under $7. **Degnan's Pasta Plus** (Shuttle Stop 5, tel. 209/372–8381), which is closed in winter, is an inexpensive family-style restaurant serving basic pasta dishes, soups, salads, and roast chicken. Nearby, **Degnan's Deli** (tel. 209/372–8454), the valley's healthiest spot, has made-to-order sandwiches and salads.

Curry Village (Shuttle Stop 1 or 14, tel. 209/372–8333), on the west side of the valley near Happy Isles, has a cafeteria, a burger stand, a coffee-and-muffins bar, and a small pizzeria. The cafeteria, serving three meals a day in summer, has burgers, sandwiches, and breakfasts for less than $7.

If you're coming in on Route 41, at the south end of the park, be sure to stop at the majestic Mariposa Grove, Yosemite's largest stand of giant sequoias and home of the estimated 2,700-year-old Grizzly Giant, one of the largest sequoias in the world.

EXPLORING YOSEMITE

It can take anywhere from a few days to the rest of your life to familiarize yourself with Yosemite. To get a good overview in summer, drive along **Tioga Road** (Highway 120), stopping to take a walk or a hike wherever you're inclined. Scores of trails meander through the park, from relaxing strolls to highly demanding backcountry excursions, and many trailheads are easily reached by shuttle bus (*see* Getting Around, *above*). In winter be sure to check trail conditions with the rangers before heading out. Not all trails and roads are open year-round; trails in Tuolumne Meadows and Glacier Point may be inaccessible. Those venturing off the beaten path will need serious snow gear in the winter months.

ORIENTATION AND TOURS

The **Yosemite Valley Visitor Center** (*see* Basics, *above*) runs free periodic 30-minute slide shows. Also look for the center's documentaries about John Muir and Ansel Adams, shown in the late afternoon and in the evenings (call for schedules). Ranger-led programs in the valley—nature walks, storytelling, and the like—last anywhere from 30 minutes to more than an hour and are a great way to learn about the park; programs that are more in-depth, at Tuolumne, White Wolf, and Wawona, can last six hours.

All kinds of guided bus tours originate in the valley, from two-hour excursions ($17.50) along the valley floor (every half hour daily 9–4 in summer, six times daily the rest of the year) to a daylong grand tour ($45.25) of Mariposa Grove and Glacier Point (late spring to late fall). For reservations contact the **Yosemite Lodge Tour Desk** (tel. 209/372–1240) or go to one of the tour booths at Curry Village, the Ahwahnee Hotel, or the Village Store in Yosemite Village.

SHORT HIKES

Yosemite Falls, also known simply as the Falls, is the highest waterfall in North America and the fifth highest in the world. It's divided into the upper fall (1,430 ft), the middle cascades (675 ft), and the lower fall (320 ft). From the parking lot, a quarter-mile trail leads to the base. To reach the top, head to Sunnyside Campground and take the strenuous 3.6-mi (one-way) **Yosemite Falls Trail,** which rises over 2,700 ft; you'll be rewarded by breathtaking views. If you're not up to the full trek, which can take as long as six to eight hours round-trip, stop at **Columbia Rock,** just past the 1-mi trail marker. You'll still get a good workout and dizzying vistas of Half Dome and the valley. Get off at Shuttle Stop 7 and follow the signs.

At the east end of the valley, the 3-mi trail around **Mirror Lake/Meadow** (Shuttle Stop 17) is one of the gentlest in the park, so you'll probably encounter a steady stream of other hikers. From the Happy Isles Trailhead (Shuttle Stop 16), the difficult 6-mi round-trip trail to **Vernal Fall** (317 ft) and **Nevada Fall** (594 ft) takes a good six hours (bring a light picnic lunch), but the view from the top is phenomenal. The first half of the aptly named Mist Trail, in which steep steps climb right alongside Vernal Fall, is a great place to soak yourself on a hot day. A fantastic overnight hike (or extremely rigorous day hike) continues past Nevada Fall to Half Dome (*see* Longer Hikes, *below*). If you arrive in Yosemite along Highway 41, **Bridalveil Fall** will be your first view of the valley; it's a ragged 620-ft cascade that's often blown as much as 20 ft from side to side by the wind. The Ahwahneechee called it *Pohono* (Puffing Wind). An easy quarter-mile trail leading to its base starts from the parking lot. For fabulous views of some of Yosemite's finest, follow the strenuous **Pohono Trail.** The trek starts at Highway 41 at the Wawona Tunnel and terminates at Glacier Point. If you start on the west side of the tunnel, it's a mile to Inspiration Point, where looking eastward up the valley floor, you can bask in the shadow of El Capitan and Bridalveil Fall.

Numerous day hikes begin at **Tuolumne Meadows,** including an easy half-mile trail to **Soda Springs**—a potable naturally carbonated spring. In 1863 William Brewer of the California Geologic Survey called its water "pungent and delightful," though a more recent visitor said, "It tastes like flat seltzer." An arduous 1½-hour hike (5 mi round-trip) to emerald **Elizabeth Lake** wanders through mountain hemlock and lodgepole pine and across boisterous Unicorn Creek. These trails are less crowded than most originating in the valley.

LONGER HIKES

Though hundreds of possible day hikes beckon in Yosemite, to beat the crowds you'll need to do some serious backpacking in the wilderness, miles away from civilization. All trails are limited to a certain number of backpackers to prevent overuse, and free wilderness permits are required for overnight stays (*see* Wilderness Permits *in* Basics, *above*). A permit gives you access to 800 mi of trails crisscrossing Yosemite's outback. These often involve strenuous climbs along jagged paths no more than a foot wide, and some trails take upward of a week to complete. Fire rings are interspersed along the way, but you'll need to bring your own tent and provisions, including a water filter or iodine tablets to treat water. Park rangers highly recommend that you rent special 3-pound bear-proof canisters for $3 at the Village Sports Shop, Curry Village Mountain Shop, Crane Flat Grocery, Wawona Store, or Tuolumne Meadows Sports Shop (*see box* Some Things to Bear in Mind, *above*). Order maps and a pamphlet of hiking suggestions from the **Yosemite Association Bookstore** (Box 230, El Portal 95318, tel. 209/379–2648). At any of Yosemite's bookstores, you can buy topographic United States Geological Survey maps ($4), but experienced backpackers swear by Trails Illustrated's waterproof topographic map ($8.95), also available at the Wilderness Center in Yosemite Village (*see* Wilderness Permits *in* Basics, *above*).

If you're in top physical condition, take the hike out of Yosemite Valley, following either the John Muir or Mist Trail to **Half Dome.** Follow the trail to Nevada Fall (*see* Short Hikes, *above*) and continue past Little Yosemite Valley Campground to the Half Dome turnoff; then be prepared to climb an additional 2,700 ft for a total of 4,800 ft. This 17-mi round-trip hike takes from 10 to 12 hours and is not for those with vertigo; the last leg of the trip involves a steep area with guide-rail cables provided to help you keep your balance and to pull yourself up. At the top, if you can stomach it, lie belly down and hang your chin over the precipice. You can make the trek an overnighter by camping at **Little Yosemite Valley,** but you'll need a wilderness permit (*see* Wilderness Permits *in* Basics, *above*). You can leave your pack at the campground or just before the cables section and climb the last portion without extra weight.

Despite the massive dam (whose construction, completed in 1923, was said to have broken John Muir's heart) and the record-setting fires of 1996, the **Hetch Hetchy** area still retains much of its beauty. Here you'll find the wonderfully isolated, moderately difficult **Rancheria Falls Trail** (13 mi round-trip), which leads to the eponymous lonely falls. If you're in good shape, you can complete this trail in a day. If you have more time (five days) and excellent packing skills, go for the 52-mi **Rancheria Mountain and Bear Valley Loop,** a strenuous hike that rewards you with a terrific view of the grand canyon of the Tuolumne River and a secluded campsite near Bear Valley Lake. To reach the Rancheria Falls trailhead, exit the west side of the park on Tioga Road (Highway 120), turn right on Evergreen Road after 1 mi, and continue for 8 mi (you'll see signs).

The numerous trailheads near **Tuolumne Meadows** are great for backpackers who want to spend at least a few days in the wilderness. Serious hikers should consider the **Tuolumne Grand Canyon Trail,** accessed from either Tuolumne Meadows or White Wolf. Allow at least three full days for the strenuous 29-mi hike to White Wolf, beginning at Tuolumne Meadows. For the first 4 mi follow the river along the forest and then drop down along a series of waterfalls and cascades, where the trail gets steeper as it descends through the Muir Gorge into Pate Valley. From there it's a steep climb to White Wolf. Another popular trip out of Tuolumne Meadows from the John Muir Trailhead is the two- to three-day hike to **Vogelsang Lake,** about 30 mi round-trip: You'll hike up Lyell Canyon via the **John Muir Trail** to the **Rafferty Creek Trail,** which becomes steep and difficult. Get your permits early (*see* Wilderness Permits *in* Basics, *above*).

Yosemite is a mecca for world-class rock climbers; look around, and you'll understand why. Just watching climbers slowly ascend the sheer granite face of El Capitan is mesmerizing.

SCENIC DRIVES AND VIEWS

During summer you can drive up to **Glacier Point** for a spectacular view of the valley and surrounding mountains. The 16-mi road starts at the Chinquapin junction on Highway 41. Better yet, take a shuttle (*see* Getting Around, *above*) to the top and take Four Mile Trail (actually just under 5 mi one-way; allow three hours) back down into the valley, coming out on Southside Drive. **Tuolumne Meadows,** the largest subalpine meadow in the High Sierra and the site of several backcountry trailheads, is on Tioga Road, 25 mi west of Lee Vining and U.S. 395. This is a gorgeous part of Yosemite, with delicate meadows surrounded by huge granite formations, and it's usually much less crowded than the valley. Tioga Road is closed during winter and usually opens by late May, but harsh winters can force the road to remain closed into July.

OUTDOOR ACTIVITIES

For those who want to take it easy, the National Park Service rents binoculars ($3) for **bird-watching.** Free 1½-hour **photography walks,** which lead you to prime spots for shooting Yosemite, leave several times a week around 8:30 AM from the Yosemite Lodge or the Ahwahnee Hotel. **Horseback rides** (tel. 209/372–8384) originate at the stables in Wawona and Tuolumne (in summer) and in Yosemite Valley. Two-hour rides are $35, and half-day rides are $46. In summer (June and July) you can take a leisurely 3-mi raft trip down the Merced for $13. Sign up at the **rafting** area in Curry Village (tel. 209/372–8341), open daily 10–4. For more information on these and other outdoor activities, consult the *Yosemite Guide* or check with the visitor center (tel. 209/372–0299).

BIKING

Bikes are not permitted on any hiking trails, but Yosemite Valley has 8 mi of paved bike paths. Try the spectacular trail to Happy Isles, off the road to Curry Village; the easy 3-mi loop takes well under an hour unless you stop for a half-mile walk to Mirror Lake. Rent bikes ($5 per hour, $20 a day) from **Curry Village** in summer (tel. 209/372–8319) or **Yosemite Lodge** year-round, weather permitting (tel. 209/372–1208). Serious cyclists should consider the 15-mi round-trip from Tuolumne Meadows to Olmstead Point along Tioga Road. The grades are difficult and the roads narrow, but the views more than compensate.

ROCK CLIMBING

Basic and intermediate group lessons ($70–$80 per person) or private lessons (three people maximum) from $95 to $290 are available from mid-April to mid-October with the **Yosemite Mountaineering School** (tel. 209/372–8344). Prices include all equipment except climbing shoes, which you can rent for $6 a day. They organize trips from Yosemite Valley and Tuolumne Meadows. You can't rent climbing equipment in the park without enrolling in a class.

SKIING

Yosemite's ski season usually lasts from early December to March. Call 209/372–0200 for weather conditions.

DOWNHILL • Yosemite has a small and very reasonably priced ski area, **Badger Pass** (tel. 209/372–8430 or 209/372–1000 for snow report), which won't pose much of a challenge to accomplished skiers. It's a good place to learn, however, and there are enough relatively uncrowded trails to keep intermediate skiers entertained. It's open daily 9–4:30 Thanksgiving–Easter. Lift tickets cost $22–$28, depending on the number of lifts open, which in turn depends on snowfall. Badger Pass has five lifts, with three advanced runs and six intermediate runs. Ski rentals are $18 a day, snowboards $30 a day. Look for Badger Pass 6 mi east of Highway 41 on Glacier Point Road.

CROSS-COUNTRY • Yosemite has 90 mi of marked (and free) cross-country trails through the Badger Pass ski area to Glacier Point. A free shuttle from the valley runs to Badger Pass, departing twice in the morning and returning in the afternoon. **Glacier Point Road** is a good place to start: Beginners will enjoy the groomed track, and advanced skiers will get a workout if they take the whole 21-mi round-trip along the rim of the valley. The **Yosemite Cross-Country Ski School** (tel. 209/372–8444) offers two-hour lessons ($20) and four-hour lessons ($40, including rentals). Rentals alone are $12 half day, $15 full day. A guided overnight trip—including meals and lodging—is $110 per person. The **Tuolumne Grove of Giant Sequoias Trail** (3 mi round-trip), which starts at Crane Flat a few miles east of the Big Oak Flat entrance station, has a steep drop, but you get to ski among the largest living things on earth.

SNOWSHOEING

National Park Service naturalists conduct regular two-hour snowshoe walks from Badger Pass and sometimes at Crane Flat. These easy walks ramble around the ski areas and the Tuolumne Grove of Giant Sequoias; showshoes are available for $2. The **Yosemite Mountaineering School** (tel. 209/372–8444 in winter) rents snowshoes at Badger Pass for $11.50 per day.

SANTA CRUZ

Originally founded in the late 18th century as a mission town, Santa Cruz has long been considered a bastion of the California-bred cult of the individual. Old-time residents, many of Italian descent, still look askance at the liberal students and hippies who have been migrating to the town ever since the University of California opened its "alternative, no-stress" branch here in the 1960s. Back then Santa Cruz was a city-size incarnation of the hippie, and while that's no longer the case, the fact that people still call Santa Cruz a hippie town has somehow made it so.

These days Santa Cruz is subject to the conflicts of any sizable California community, particularly anti-immigration hysteria. As migrant farmworkers, mostly Mexicans and Mexican-Americans, move to Santa Cruz County in record numbers to work on nearby farmlands, these newcomers often find themselves made unwelcome by the largely homogeneous community.

Nonetheless, Santa Cruz holds on to its idyllic beach-town atmosphere better than many. The carnival-like **Boardwalk** is Santa Cruz at its flashiest, drawing legions of hormone-crazed teenagers from Salinas and San Jose every weekend. Beyond the town lies the stunning coast. The rocks off the craggy shore are favored perches for seals, the beaches are thronged with surfers and their retinue, and the surrounding hills fade into redwood forests.

If possible, visit in early August, when the **Cabrillo Music Festival** brings modern symphonic music and other live entertainment to town. Tickets cost $7–$25, depending on the performance and seating; call the Santa Cruz Civic Auditorium box office (tel. 831/420–5260). From mid-July to August U.C. Santa

Cruz hosts **Shakespeare Santa Cruz** (tel. 831/459–2121), six weeks of the Bard's works set against a backdrop of beautiful redwoods. Tickets ($15–$21) should be reserved a few days in advance.

BASICS

VISITOR INFORMATION

You'll find $2 maps at the **visitor information center** (701 Front St., tel. 831/425–1234). Gay and lesbian travelers can call the **Lesbian/Gay/Bisexual/Transgender Community Center Hotline** (tel. 831/425–5422) for listings of upcoming events and other resources.

COMING AND GOING

BY CAR

The most scenic route from either San Francisco, 1½ hours north, or Monterey, an hour south, is along **Highway 1.** San Jose is about 45 minutes away on curvy **Highway 17,** which meets up with I–280, I–880, and U.S. 101 and is the faster drive to San Francisco and the East Bay. Avoid Highway 17 weekend mornings, though, when the entire Silicon Valley seems to head for the beaches, and at night, when the sharp curves of the road are tricky.

Downtown has risen from the rubble of the 7.1-magnitude Loma Prieta earthquake of 1989, and many say the squeaky-clean new buildings symbolize a sea change toward conservatism. Still, Santa Cruz's sloppy individuality is still very much in place.

BY BUS

Green Tortoise (*see* Bus Travel *in* Chapter 1) lumbers from San Francisco to Los Angeles, stopping in Santa Cruz at the Safeway parking lot (2018 Mission St., at Younglove St.) once a week. Buses from San Francisco, a three-hour ride costing $10, arrive in Santa Cruz Friday at 11 PM. From Los Angeles buses arrive Monday morning, a 9- to 12-hour $35 trip. Reserve one week ahead in the summer. *Tel. 415/956–7500 in CA or 800/867–8647.*

Greyhound Lines (425 Front St., at Laurel St., tel. 831/423–1800) has direct service between Santa Cruz and San Francisco four times daily ($12 one-way weekdays, $13 weekends) and six times daily from Los Angeles, a 10-hour trip that costs $36 one-way at all times. **Amtrak** buses (tel. 800/872–7245) link the San Jose CalTrain depot and the Santa Cruz Metro Center roughly every hour between 4 AM and 10 PM for $5 each way ($8 for two tickets).

GETTING AROUND

The layout of Santa Cruz is insanity on a map and even more confusing in practice. On the edge of Monterey Bay and bisected by the San Lorenzo River, the town is full of crooked and puzzling streets, so keep a sharp eye on a map. Highway 1 becomes **Mission Street** when it enters Santa Cruz and resumes its old identity on the way out of town. **Bay Street** and **High Street** both funnel into U.C. Santa Cruz, which stands on a hill 2 mi northeast of downtown, while the Boardwalk is on **Beach Street,** just west of the river. The Boardwalk and downtown (which centers around **Pacific Avenue** and **Front Street**) are within comfortable walking distance (1 mi) of each other.

BY BUS

Bus service is efficient and fairly easy to use. The Santa Cruz Metropolitan District Transit (SCMDT), also known as Metro, operates from the **Metro Center** (920 Pacific Ave., at Laurel St.), adjoining the Greyhound station. Any bus in town will eventually take you to the Metro Center, where you can pick up a copy of "Headways," a free pamphlet that lists all bus routes. The fare is $1, but you can purchase a special all-day pass for $3 on any bus or at the Metro Center. Exact change, in coins or one-dollar bills, is required; change machines are available at the Metro Center. The center's phones are answered and the kiosk is staffed weekdays from 8 to 5, but you can pick up schedules and get exact change 24 hours a day. *Tel. 831/425–8600. Phones and information booth open weekdays 8–5.*

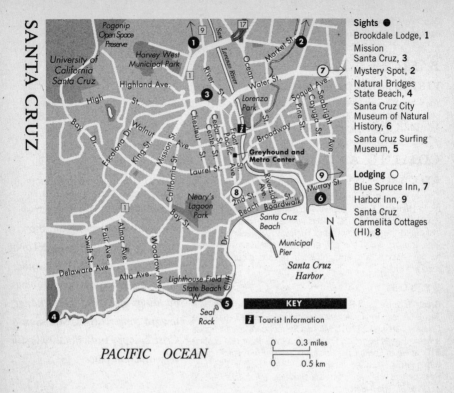

SANTA CRUZ

Sights ●
Brookdale Lodge, **1**
Mission
Santa Cruz, **3**
Mystery Spot, **2**
Natural Bridges
State Beach, **4**
Santa Cruz City
Museum of Natural
History, **6**
Santa Cruz Surfing
Museum, **5**

Lodging ○
Blue Spruce Inn, **7**
Harbor Inn, **9**
Santa Cruz
Carmelita Cottages
(HI), **8**

KEY

i Tourist Information

0   0.3 miles
0   0.5 km

PACIFIC OCEAN

BY BIKE

Biking is the best way to get around Santa Cruz. Many streets have wide bike lanes, and the weather is moderate, especially in spring and summer. If you can't bring wheels of your own, you can rent them at **The Bicycle Rental & Tour Center** (131 Center St., at Laurel St., tel. 831/426–8687). The bikes range from simple cruisers to full-suspension mountain bikes and start at $7/hour or $25/day. If you're in town for a few days, consider buying a bike at **Sullivan's Bicycle Shop** (417 Seabright, tel. 831/457–8554), and selling it back before you leave. Not only will you be able to find everything from a sleek mountain bike to a three-wheeler with a deep front basket, but all these pre-owned bicycles are in excellent condition and are surprisingly cheap (starting at $10 a piece, and averaging $40). Cyclophiles may want to stop in just to admire the funky selection and talk shop with the bike nut employees over a cup of espresso.

WHERE TO SLEEP

In summer, especially on weekends, finding a budget room in Santa Cruz is next to impossible. During the rest of the year hotels slash prices to rope in boarders. Year-round, the best deal is at the hostels—if you can get a bed (no age restrictions). Camping is popular in summer. If the campgrounds listed below are full, call the headquarters after 5 PM, when the Manresa and Sunset state beaches open overflow sites. Failing that, the Big Basin Redwoods State Park (*see* Near Santa Cruz, *below*) is 45 minutes away.

HOTELS AND MOTELS

The decently priced places to stay clustered on Mission and Ocean streets are comfortable and convenient if you have a car. Facing the Boardwalk on 2nd and 3rd streets and Riverside Avenue are some seedy motels that lie in an area with sketchy boundaries known as the Flats. These places rarely fill up. For a decadent treat, stay at one of several good B&Bs. The six-room **Blue Spruce Inn** (2815 Main St., Soquel, 95073, tel. 831/464–1137 or 800/559–1137, fax 831/475–0608) is within walking distance of downtown Capitola and a pleasant bike ride from Santa Cruz. The hot tub, private patios, and romantic rooms complete with plush feather beds and whirlpool bathtubs can serve as an entire night's entertainment, even for a single visitor. Innkeepers Pat and Tom O'Brien serve a hearty breakfast and make sure the cookie jar is always filled with homemade chocolate chip treats. Double rooms, which include breakfast, run $85–$175 per night.

UNDER $60 • Harbor Inn. In a residential area 10 minutes southeast of town, this inviting inn has doubles (starting at $55 in summer, $35 off-season) with a hodgepodge of old furniture and wooden beds. The inn often fills in summer, so call ahead for reservations. Most rooms have kitchenettes, and groups of four can get a suite ($85–$125, depending on the season). *645 7th Ave., 95062, tel. 831/ 479–9731, fax 831/479–1067. From downtown, cross river on Laurel St., right on San Lorenzo Blvd., left on Murray St., left on 7th Ave. Or Bus 67 or 6 to 7th Ave. 19 rooms, 14 with bath.*

HOSTEL

Santa Cruz Carmelita Cottages (Hostelling International). Two blocks from the Boardwalk on Beach Hill, these cottages are actually a cluster of houses made hosteler friendly ($13 for members, $16 for nonmembers). A curfew and a no-alcohol rule create a quiet atmosphere in the private and "family" rooms (from three to five people), which cost $30–$40, depending on the number of beds. Cyclists can use the on-site repair and tune-up shop. Eager beavers show up around 3 PM for the 5 PM first-come, first-served check-in; arrive in a car, and you get last dibs. Write two weeks ahead (Box 1241, Santa Cruz 95061) or call for reservations. *321 Main St., at 2nd St., 95060, tel. 831/423–8304. From Metro Center, Bus 7 to Main St. 25 beds. Curfew 11 PM, lockout 10–5. Reception open daily 8 AM–10 AM and 5 PM–10 PM.*

The forests around Santa Cruz are full of slimy little critters: Look for banana slugs (the UCSC mascot) and California newts, which have bright orange stomachs.

CAMPING

Henry Cowell Redwoods State Park. Five miles north of Santa Cruz, this 113-site campground is buffered by a redwood forest and rests under madronas and mixed pine trees near several trailheads. In summer RVs and screaming teens tend to overrun the place, but otherwise it's great. Bike campers share one large, shady site for $3 each. Make a reservation through Reserve America (tel. 800/444–7275). Both tent and RV sites are $17 weekdays, $18 weekends. 101 N. Big Trees Park Rd., Felton 95018, tel. 831/335–4598 or 831/438–2396. From Hwy. 1, Hwy. 9 north; from Metro Center, Bus 35. Drinking water, flush toilets, showers. Closed Dec.–Feb.

New Brighton State Beach. High above the ocean on a large cliff, this popular tents-only campground is in Capitola, 5 mi southeast of Santa Cruz. What it lacks in privacy, it makes up for in beauty: A few of its 112 sites enjoy an incredible view of the coast. A steep path leads downhill to the soft beach below. Reservations, available through Reserve America (tel. 800/444–7275), are a must between May and October. Sites go for $17 weekdays, $18 weekends. *1500 Park Ave., 95010, tel. 831/464–6330. Follow signs from Hwy. 1 or take Bus 71 to the corner of Soquel and Park Aves. and then make the long walk.*

Sunset State Beach and **Manresa State Beach.** Slightly more spacious and private than New Brighton, these two campgrounds, both about 10 minutes south of Santa Cruz, are short walks from wide, sandy beaches. Sunset has 90 campsites, all with fire rings, picnic tables, and hot showers. Spaces, reserved through Reserve America (tel. 800/444–7275), are $17 weekdays, $18 weekends. On the way to Sunset, you'll pass Manresa, which has 64 walk-in sites 100 yards from the parking lot and the same facilities, prices, and reservation system as Sunset. Sites are on a plateau above the beach or set back in a sparse sprinkling of trees. Both campgrounds open overflow sites when they're fully booked; the Manresa overflow accommodates RVs only, and Sunset puts tent campers in the picnic area. San Andreas Rd., tel. 831/763–7063 for Sunset and 831/761–1795 for Manresa. Hwy. 1 south to San Andreas Rd./Larkin Valley exit, right at bottom of ramp, right onto San Andreas Rd.

FOOD

Santa Cruz's hippie days have left a legacy of organic, largely vegetarian cuisine. For fresh produce head to the **farmers' market** held every Wednesday from 2 to 6 on the corner of Pacific Avenue and Walnut Street; then trot over to Lorenzo Park (River St., between Water St. and Soquel Ave.) for a picnic. Also, look for the markets along Mission Street.

SO YOU WANT TO DO A LITTLE HIKING

You can hook up with the Pacific Crest Trail out of Tuolumne Meadows and continue hiking for a few days, months, or a year by following the trail south to Mexico or north to Canada. Routed in 1928, the Pacific Crest Trail starts on the California–Mexico border and winds through 24 national forests, seven national parks, and 33 wilderness areas for a grand total of 2,638 mi, making it the longest complete trail in America.

UNDER $5

For a tasty slice of late-night pizza, head to **Uppercrust Pizza** (2415 Mission St., tel. 831/423–9010), on the west side of town near the Highway 1 turnoff for Natural Bridges State Beach. For heaping portions of Mexican food, hit **Taquería Vallarta** (608 Soquel Ave., 1 block east of Ocean St., tel. 831/457–8226).

Little Shanghai (1010 Cedar St., tel. 831/458–2460) not only serves tasty Chinese food, it offers a lunch special for $3.75 that includes rice or noodles, soup, spicy pickled cabbage, and two main dishes from a 12-item buffet including kung pao tofu and basil chicken. Even more remarkable, the price drops to $2.50 between 3 PM and the 3:30 PM closing time.

To be a surfer, or just eat like one, head to **Paula's** for a healthy carbo-load. The day's tides are written on the front door, the parking lot is filled with longboards, and there's only one menu item over $5; there are strict rules, however: You have to bus your own table and cell phones are verboten. *3500 Portola Dr., tel. 831/464–0741.*

UNDER $10

Dolphin Restaurant. Head to the end of Santa Cruz's municipal pier for crispy, freshly caught fish-and-chips. You can park yourself at the picnic tables adjacent to the Dolphin's serving window. *End of pier, tel. 831/426–5830. Cash only.*

Saturn Café. This Santa Cruz institution has been relocated to downtown, but otherwise it's the same: still decked out with theme tables (*Charlie's Angels,* Richard Nixon, and Madonna, to name a few) and flying saucer–like lamps. Try their stellar tomato-garlic pesto sauce over the pasta of the day or a bowl of soul-warming chili. *145 Laurel St., at Pacific, tel. 831/429–8505.*

Zachary's. A basic breakfast—two eggs, tasty home fries, and your choice of homemade breads—sells for a reasonable $5, but you might want to splurge on a huge stack of pancakes or homemade corned beef hash. Expect a wait of up to an hour on weekends. *819 Pacific Ave., between Laurel and Maple Sts., tel. 831/427–0646. Closed Mon.*

CAFÉS

In a town with more than 15,000 college students, the absence of nighttime diversions for the under-21 set has fueled a serious café scene. In addition to being popular hangout spots for college students, cafés are also frequented by locals looking for a lively debate or a place to read a good book. **Caffè Pergolesi** (418A Cedar St., at Elm St., tel. 831/426–1775) is inside a big, rambling Victorian house with a huge outdoor deck. The **Herland Book-Café** (902 Center St., at Locust St., tel. 831/429–6636), conceived as a safe haven for women, has books grouped in categories like "Women of the Wild West" or "Women Respond to the Men's Movement"—all female-authored. You can get organically grown tea and coffee at the **Jahva House** (120 Union St., near Cedar St., tel. 831/459–9876), which occupies a large, airy, comfortable warehouse softened by Oriental rugs and ficus trees.

EXPLORING SANTA CRUZ

To explore the jagged coast, you'll need a car or a mountain bike. However, most of Santa Cruz's sights are within a walkable area downtown. The **Pacific Garden Mall** consists of specialty stores, antiques shops, restaurants, and cafés. **Logos** (1117 Pacific Ave., near Lincoln St., tel. 831/427–5100) is Santa Cruz's premier used-book and music store. The **Mission Santa Cruz** (126 High St.)—built in 1791, destroyed by an earthquake in 1857, and rebuilt as a half-size replica in 1931—has grounds overrun with colorful gardens and fountains.

SANTA CRUZ BEACH BOARDWALK

Thick with the smell of suntan oil and hair spray, the Boardwalk provides the stickiest, most commercialized sun-and-sand carnival west of Coney Island. At center stage is the **Giant Dipper,** created in 1924—one of the oldest wooden roller coasters in the world. The ride affords you a brief panorama of Monterey Bay before plunging you down toward the beach. Another Boardwalk favorite is the Ferris wheel, which provides one of the best ocean views in Santa Cruz. *400 Beach St., tel. 831/423–5590 or 831/426–7433 for recorded information. From Front St. follow signs to the ocean. Rides open Memorial Day–Labor Day, daily from 11 AM; Labor Day–Memorial Day, weekends and holidays only; tel. 831/426–7433 for details.*

U.C. SANTA CRUZ

The beauty of the UCSC campus makes you understand why so many people choose to attend college in California. The **campus bookstore** (tel. 831/459–4544), at the center of campus, is woody and natural, resembling a ski lodge more than a student union. Investigate the **limestone quarry** near the bookstore—it's a nice spot for a picnic—and take a self-guided or docent-led tour of the 29-acre organic growing system at the **Farm and Garden Project** (tel. 831/459–4140), near the base of campus. The **admissions office** (tel. 831/459–4008), at the

At sunset go to It's Beach, immediately west of the lighthouse. Almost every summer evening locals gather here to drum and dance as night falls. You can hang back or jump right into the middle of the fun.

campus entrance, is open weekdays 8–5 and has maps and tour schedules. Avoid the on-campus parking fee by parking along Meder Avenue at the far west end of campus and catching the free shuttle at Bay and High streets. Otherwise take Bus 1 from the Metro Center to the west entrance of campus.

SANTA CRUZ CITY MUSEUM OF NATURAL HISTORY

The museum is small but full of information about the Ohlone Indians—the area's original inhabitants—and the local seals and sea lions. A slippery touch pool allows you to finger sea slugs and anemones. In January the museum sponsors the **Fungus Fair,** celebrating the mushrooms that blanket the forest floor. *1305 E. Cliff Dr., tel. 831/420–6115. From downtown, walk or drive east on Laurel St., cross river, turn right on San Lorenzo St. (which becomes East Cliff Dr.). Or take Bus 67 from Metro Center. $2 donation requested. Open Tues.–Sun. 10–5.*

SANTA CRUZ SURFING MUSEUM

At Lighthouse Point on West Cliff Drive, there's a tiny exhibit on surfing—from its Hawaiian origins to the present. Included in the display is a board bitten by a great white shark in 1987, testimony to the genuine shark danger along the coast from Santa Cruz to Pigeon Point. Plop down outside the lighthouse and watch the surfers on Steamer's Lane, one of the best surf spots in California. A little farther out you'll see Seal Rock, the summertime home of thousands of shiny barking seals. *Mark Abbott Memorial Lighthouse, West Cliff Dr., tel. 831/420–6289. Bus 3A to Lighthouse Field. Admission free. Open Mon. and Wed.–Fri. noon–4, weekends noon–5.*

NATURAL BRIDGES STATE BEACH

The mudstone bridgelike formation that gives this beach its name is a nesting spot for pelicans and an unusual sight for visitors. There's also a **monarch butterfly colony** on the grounds: You'll find thousands of the brightly colored creatures clustered in the trees from mid-October to February. Call ahead for the latest information (and to make a reservation for guided walks). Tidal pools, picnic tables, barbecue pits, and plenty of soft, warm sand round out the list of attractions. Park on Delaware Avenue just east of the park entrance to avoid the $6 parking fee. *West Cliff Dr., tel. 831/423–4609. From boardwalk, follow West Cliff Dr. 2 mi until you see signs. Or Bus 3B from Metro Center. Open daily 8 AM–sunset, nature center open 10–4.*

MYSTERY SPOT

This quirky little place lies in the redwoods 3 mi north of Santa Cruz and, in the minds of true believers, is at the center of a mysterious force that makes people taller and compels balls to roll uphill. It's kitschy, no doubt, but its gift shop is filled with everything you could ever want emblazoned with the Mystery Spot logo—from silver spoons to paperweights. Your $4 admission also buys you a Mystery Spot bumper sticker (that's why you see them everywhere). *465 Mystery Spot Rd., tel. 831/423–8897. From downtown, go south on Water St., left on Market St., go 2½ mi, then follow signs. Open Memorial Day–Labor Day daily 9–8:30; Labor Day–Memorial Day daily 9–5.*

AFTER DARK

Only a few bars in Santa Cruz feature live music; upcoming shows are listed in the weekly newspaper *Good Times.* Unless there's a big name playing, skip the **Catalyst** (1011 Pacific Ave., tel. 831/423–1336) and head straight to the **Kuumbwa Jazz Center** (320 Cedar St., at Laurel St., tel. 831/427–2227), which hosts jazz and blues shows throughout the year. Call for tickets ($6–$18) and scheduling information. Those with wheels might want to catch a double feature at the **Skyview Drive-In Theater** (2260 Soquel Ave., at Thurber La., tel. 831/475–3405) for $5 a head: Two first-run films and two not-quite-on-video-yet flicks play year-round starting around 7:30 in winter and 9 in summer.

The **Blue Lagoon** (923 Pacific Ave., across from Metro Center, tel. 831/423–7117) is Santa Cruz's premier (read: only) gay and bisexual nighttime hangout (straights are welcome, too). There's a $2 cover on weekends and Tuesday—a small price to pay for some of the best DJ'ed dance music in town. Despite its pastel-color stucco building and bland interior, the **Seabright Brewery** (519 Seabright Ave., at Murray St., 7 blocks east of the river, tel. 831/426–2739) is incredibly popular with locals, especially on Tuesday's Neighborhood Night, when homeowners mingle with renting students on the concrete patio, but out-of-towners are allowed to share the fun. Friday brings live rock and blues from 6 to 10. The **Red Room** (1003 Cedar St., at Locust St., tel. 831/426–2994) is a snazzy dive bar and a true UCSC institution, especially among the über-hip. Occasionally you can catch rockabilly and alternarock in the rear Crown Room for a minimal cover. Don't look for a sign out front; there isn't one.

OUTDOOR ACTIVITIES

HIKING AND MOUNTAIN BIKING

Some of northern California's best hiking and mountain-biking opportunities are found in the redwood-filled hills surrounding Santa Cruz. Two or three times a week the local chapter of the Sierra Club sponsors group outings—hikes, camping, and canoe trips. Stop by their office (1001 Center St., tel. 831/426–4453) for a listing of upcoming wilderness forays. If you're more hip to the solo experience, head directly to **Big Basin Redwoods State Park** (*see* Near Santa Cruz, *below*). Closer to town, the **Henry Cowell Redwoods State Park** (*see* Camping, *above*) has 20 mi of tamer trails, many of which meander through virgin redwood forests. Bikes are allowed on designated fire and service roads but not on hiking trails.

For a beautiful, albeit crowded, stroll among some of the park's tallest trees, take the **Redwood Grove Trail** (trailhead off Highway 9). For a longer hike, walk up Pipeline Road from the nature center and turn left on Ridge Fire Road, which heads 2 mi uphill to an observation deck; here you'll get a beautiful view of the valley. From downtown follow Highway 9 toward Felton.

The less-crowded **Forest of Nisene Marks** (tel. 831/763–7063) is a favorite among hiking and biking locals. Here, among creeks, redwoods, and steep trails, you can view the ruins of a Chinese labor camp or walk 2 mi to the epicenter of the 1989 Loma Prieta earthquake; the trail is clearly marked from the end of the park's drivable road. There are also a few trails that mountain bikers are allowed to ride—ask at the main gate. To get here, exit Highway 1 at Soquel and take Soquel Avenue a half mile east to Aptos Creek Road.

SURFING

Santa Cruz is the surf capital of northern California. **Steamer Lane,** between the Boardwalk and the lighthouse, hosts several competitions in the summer; consult the free quarterly *Ocean Life* for dates. The city's **parks and recreation department** (tel. 831/420–5250) has the best surf lesson deals: Four hours of lessons over two days for $84; surfboards are included, and wet suits can be rented for $10 per class (call ahead with your height, weight, and class number to reserve the accessories). **Cowell's**

Beach Shop (corner of Beach and Front Sts., across from the wharf, tel. 831/427–2355) also rents surfboards ($15) and wet suits ($15) by the day.

NEAR SANTA CRUZ

BIG BASIN REDWOODS STATE PARK

The first forest deemed a California State Park, Big Basin overwhelms you with acres of gigantic old-growth redwoods, lofty Douglas firs, rushing streams, and flowing waterfalls. All sorts of wildlife call the area home, including black-tailed deer, an occasional fox, bobcats, coyotes, and mountain lions. Just past the main entrance—where you'll pay a $6-per-car fee—you can pick up maps ($1) and trail information at the **park headquarters** (tel. 831/338–8860). If you have just an hour or so, head for the gorgeous **Silver Falls** and **Golden Falls,** about ¾ mi along the Skyline-to-the-Sea Trail. Here you can wade in the pools, shower in the falls, or skip across the creek on redwood logs. For a less crowded hike, try the **Howard King Trail** from the parking lot to Mt. McAbee. Along the way you'll pass through several different ecosystems before reaching the peak, which affords a supreme ocean view. You can return on Hammond Road for a round-trip of 5 mi in about two or three hours.

A river runs through the bizarre Brookdale Lodge (14 mi from Santa Cruz on Hwy. 9, tel. 831/338–6433), an oasis of drink during Prohibition. In those days a window behind the Mermaid Bar looked underwater into a swimming pool full of prostitutes.

The truly fit should tackle the 12.5-mi **Skyline-to-Sea Trail**—arguably the most scenic hike in the park—which travels over hill and dale all the way to the coast. Leave a second car at the trail's endpoint at Waddell Beach, and either pay scrupulous attention to a map or accept the possibility of getting lost, since several trailheads converge a few miles into the hike. Mountain biking is allowed only on fire roads in the park; there aren't many good loops, so your best bet is to follow North Escape Road a short distance from park headquarters to **Gazos Creek Road,** a 12-mi fire trail that stretches to the coast, and then return on Johansen Road via Middleridge Road.

COMING AND GOING • Big Basin is 23 mi northeast of Santa Cruz off Highway 9. Follow the highway north for 12 mi, then follow the signs for another 9 mi from Boulder Creek. If you're coming from the north on I–280, take Highway 85 south from Cupertino to Highway 9S, then pick up Highway 236 into the park. Bus 35 will take you 2½ mi short of the campgrounds; hike the rest of the way.

MONTEREY

Monterey—with the possible exception of Carmel—is California's tackiest and most unabashedly commercial seaside resort. John Steinbeck (1902–68) immortalized the busy fishing port in *Cannery Row* and *Sweet Thursday,* describing it as "a poem, a stink, a grating noise, a quality of light, a tone, a habit, a nostalgia, a dream." By the 1950s, however, the sardines were gone, along with much that was poetic. Visitors will still find the fascinating Monterey Bay Aquarium a worthwhile stop; unfortunately, much of the rest of the town has a Disneyland-by-the-sea feel—pricey gift shops sell plastic sardines, and lackluster restaurants feature "Steinbeck Specials." Still, Monterey's wealth has funded extensive public-space improvements—there's always a bench surrounded by a blooming garden just around the corner. And off Cannery Row and Fisherman's Wharf, historical conservation has preserved much of Monterey's past—it was the capital when Spain and Mexico ruled California, from 1775 to 1846.

BASICS

VISITOR INFORMATION

The **Monterey Peninsula Chamber of Commerce** (380 Alvarado St., at Franklin St., tel. 831/649–1770) provides free maps and information about the world-famous **Monterey Jazz Festival** (tel. 831/373–3366), held in late September, and the **Monterey Blues Festival** (tel. 831/394–2652), held in late June.

THE CAPITAL OF THE COAST

The ocean-side town of Capitola, along the coast about 5 mi southeast of Santa Cruz, has a wide, quiet sandy beach and a rickety wooden pier—a welcome change from the sometimes frenetic pace of Santa Cruz. After you've soaked up enough sun, head straight to Mr. Toot's (221 Esplanade, tel. 831/475–3679), a café full of old wooden tables, comfortable couches, and a deck overlooking the beach. Catch Bus 59 from Santa Cruz's Metro Center or take Highway 1 south to the Capitola/Park Avenue exit and head toward the Pacific.

COMING AND GOING

Greyhound Lines buses have regular service to Monterey from San Francisco (a four-hour trip, $16 one-way) and from Los Angeles (12 hours, $33 one-way) via Salinas. The Monterey **Greyhound station** (1042 Del Monte Ave., tel. 831/373–4735), in a gas station on the east end of town, is open daily 8 AM–10 PM.

Monterey-Salinas Transit (tel. 831/899–2555) makes regular connections to Carmel, Santa Cruz, and Salinas and a summertime-only connection to Big Sur ($1.50–$6). All buses depart from the downtown **Monterey Transit Plaza** (corner of Tyler and Pearl Sts.). For Big Sur, take Bus 22 (summer only); it will get you as far as the Nepenthe restaurant, on Highway 1.

GETTING AROUND

From Highway 1 the Pacific Grove/Del Monte Avenue exit will take you straight into downtown. The main drag is north–south **Alvarado Street,** with Fisherman's Wharf at the north end and Cannery Row (and the aquarium) 1½ mi farther northwest. Once in town, you can get around easily on foot or by bus. During summer and on holiday weekends, the shuttle bus **Wave** (tel. 831/899–2555) provides frequent service and stops throughout the downtown/Cannery Row area ($1, transfers free). Throughout the rest of the year, Bus 1 travels from the Transit Plaza to Fisherman's Wharf, Cannery Row, and the aquarium for $1.50. Because of summer tourism, both parking and crowds are a serious problem for drivers. The most reasonable parking garage downtown (between Alvarado, Franklin, Washington, and Del Monte Sts.) charges $1 an hour.

WHERE TO SLEEP

Monterey is almost devoid of cheap lodging—but if you're persistent (or if you have a tent), you may be able to scare up something reasonable. A slew of motels along North Fremont Street are close to downtown and accessible via Buses 9 and 10. The **Jabberwock** (598 Laine St., tel. 831/372–4777) is a unique treat located in a quiet residential area within walking distance of the aquarium. The exquisitely decorated rooms are named after the Lewis Carroll poem, and the innkeepers keep cognac available in the parlor around the clock. Eating the homemade breakfast while overlooking the garden from a sunroom table is a divine experience. Rooms start at $110. Across from Del Monte Beach and one block east of the Greyhound station, **Del Monte Beach Inn** (1110 Del Monte Ave., 93940, tel. 831/649–4410, fax 831/375–3818) is a small bed-and-breakfast with 18 rooms ($50–$60) decorated by a Martha Stewart disciple. Make sure to check in before 8 PM. The 46 flawlessly clean, albeit dull, rooms at **Lone Oak Motel** (2221 N. Fremont St., 93940, tel. 831/372–4924) cost $44 weekdays and a whopping $80 weekends—but the price includes access to a Jacuzzi and sauna room. Eight miles north of Monterey in the town of Marina (take Highway 1 north from Monterey to Del Monte Avenue, or Bus 7 to Beach Road), the **Paramount Motel** (3298 Del Monte Blvd., at Beach St., 93933, tel. 831/384–8674) looks shabby on the outside, but the proprietor is friendly and the six rooms ($35 for a double) are secure, clean, and comfortable. Reservations are not accepted, so arrive early.

CAMPING

Just five minutes from downtown, **Veteran's Memorial Park Campground** (Via del Rey, tel. 831/646–3865) is a first-come, first-served campground on a grassy knoll in a quiet valley. Although it's not exactly the great outdoors, its 40 tightly packed sites ($18) are well maintained. Hikers and cyclists share one large site for $3 per person. Showers are available, but bring your own food. From downtown take Jefferson Street west; or take Bus 3 from Transit Plaza.

FOOD

On Tuesday afternoons Alvarado Street downtown is closed off for a **farmers' market**; at all other times you can find a plethora of seafood and health-food restaurants here, but most are overpriced. At the **Lighthouse Bagel Bakery** (201 Lighthouse Blvd., at Reeside Ave., tel. 831/649–1714) you can load up on tasty bagels topped with cheese, avocado, or sandwich meat—all for less than $2. Minipizzas, salads, and sandwiches at the **Paris Bakery and Café** are all under $4, as are the many sugary desserts that taunt diners from the shining case running the length of the restaurant. Every day from 11:30 AM to 2 PM, **Totoya Sushi Bar** (867B Wave St., tel. 831/375–7024) offers an all-you-can-eat sushi buffet for $6.95. **Tillie Gort's Café** (111 Central Ave., Pacific Grove, tel. 831/373–0335) serves delicious Mexican and Mediterranean sandwiches with an emphasis on vegetarian dishes. **Fishwife** (1996½ Sunset Dr., Pacific Grove, tel. 831/375–7107) has fish dishes and pastas in the $10–$15 range.

EXPLORING MONTEREY

Monterey's main attraction is the justifiably world-famous **Monterey Bay Aquarium** (886 Cannery Row, tel. 831/648–4800), open daily 9:30–6 (10–6 in winter), where you'll find sharks and sea otters in convincingly natural habitats and a three-story kelp-forest aquarium. The outer-bay exhibit, featuring the world's largest viewing tank, is engineered to make visitors feel as if they've taken a dive—odd jellyfish drift by, and mackerel schools circle endlessly. These high-tech facilities clearly require a pretty penny—admission is $15.95. Avoid hour-plus waits during the summer by purchasing your tickets in advance from your hotelier or by phone (tel. 800/756–3737 or 831/648–4937). AAA members can find $5-off coupons in *VIA* magazine. From Highway 1 south follow signs from the Pacific Grove/Del Monte Avenue exit.

Cannery Row lies along the waterfront south of the aquarium, ending at **Fisherman's Wharf.** Both places have seen better days. The Laida Café—an "institution of commercialized love" in Steinbeck's time—is now a bright yellow ice cream parlor called **Kalisa's** (851 Cannery Row, no phone). To drown your sorrows over days gone by, head to **Bargetto Winery** (700 Cannery Row, tel. 831/373–4053), open daily 10:30–6, where tastings are free. Upstairs, **A Taste of Monterey** (700 Cannery Row, tel. 831/646–5446), open daily 1–6, charges $5 for a tasting of six of their 100-plus Monterey County wines—a bargain considering the superlative bay views.

Monterey's old buildings are fascinating and well preserved, though most tourists ignore them for the artificial flash of Cannery Row—a mistake you shouldn't make. Pick up "The Path of History Walking Tour" brochure from the chamber of commerce (*see* Basics, *above*) or take the $2 guided tour organized by **Monterey State Historic Park** (20 Custom House Plaza, tel. 831/649–7118). Don't miss Colton Hall, where the state constitution was written, and the Cooper Molera Adobe, or Custom House. Pay $5 at the first house you visit and you'll receive a pass good for admission to all sites for the remainder of the day.

Don't waste time at **Monterey State Beach,** where the wind will make you wish you'd worn thermals. It's nothing compared to **Asilomar State Beach** (tel. 831/372–4076), with its tide pools and enormous waves crashing on the rocky shore. Look for the beach 2 mi west of Monterey in the quiet town of **Pacific Grove** (Bus 1 will get you within walking distance). Here, between October and March, you can glimpse thousands of monarch butterflies who make their winter homes in **Washington Park,** at the corner of Pine Avenue and Alder Street. Pacific Grove is also home to the **Point Piños Light Station** (Ocean View Blvd., at Point Piños, tel. 831/648–3116), the oldest continuously operating lighthouse on the West Coast (established 1855). It's open Thursday–Sunday 1–4.

AFTER DARK

Skip the gimmicky clubs around Cannery Row and head instead to **Bulldog British Pub** (611 Lighthouse Ave., tel. 831/372–5565), a laid-back tavern tastefully plastered with British paraphernalia. Not

THE POOR MAN'S
17-MILE DRIVE

17-Mile Drive charges car owners a $6.50 toll to motor by Pebble Beach's manicured golf courses and multi-million-dollar homes; cars must head back to Highway 1 to drive between Monterey and Carmel without dropping greenbacks. Those in the know opt instead for the Poor Man's 17-Mile Drive, which is only 6 mi long but every bit as dramatic (and gratis). From Monterey head west on Ocean View Drive (just west of Cannery Row) and follow the road as it bends southward past Asilomar State Beach. Watch the sun set over wild sand dunes, and look for Lovers' Point, a grassy patch overlooking the ocean.

only is there expertly poured Guinness on tap, but breakfast is served until 3 AM Friday and Saturday. **Morgan's Coffee & Tea** (498 Washington St., at Pearl St., tel. 831/373–5601) is a café decked out like a medieval castle, offering excellent coffee, live music at least twice a week, and an eclectic selection of microbrews and wines by the glass. For information about local happenings not centered around the tourist industry, call the **Monterey Rock and Art Festival Hotline** (tel. 831/393–2787).

OUTDOOR ACTIVITIES

BIKING AND MOPEDS

Moped Adventures (1250 Del Monte Ave., at Sloat St., tel. 831/373–2696) rents beach cruisers ($20 a day) and mopeds ($20 for the first hour, then $10 an hour; $50 a day). Call ahead to reserve; a driver's license and deposit are required. For $22 a day you can rent a mountain bike from **Bay Bikes** (640 Wave St., 1 block inland from Cannery Row, tel. 831/646–9090) and make tracks for the 4-mi paved path that stretches from the wharf past Cannery Row and Lovers' Point. Another great idea is to pedal down 17-Mile Drive (*see box, below*) for free, then on into Carmel or back to Monterey. Cyclists don't have to stop at the pay booth and can catch quite a few spectacular ocean views between the ritzy homes. Bay Bikes lets you return bikes to their Carmel location (near the south end of the drive) for an extra $8, and from there you can take Monterey/Salinas Bus 22 or 24 back.

FISHING AND WHALE WATCHING

Contact **Chris's Fishing Trips** (tel. 831/375–5951), on Fisherman's Wharf, for half-day sportfishing trips ($30–$34); you'll pay another $17.50 for a license and equipment. Chris's also offers two-hour whale-watching trips ($15) between December and March, when Monterey Bay is filled with migrating gray whales.

KAYAKING

The kayaking off Cannery Row is superb, and you're sure to encounter a raft of otters, sea lions, or harbor seals. **Adventures by the Sea** (tel. 831/372–1807) can outfit you with a kayak, oars, wet suit, and a half-hour lesson for $25.

SNORKELING AND SCUBA DIVING

Monterey Bay attracts divers from around the world because of its vast kelp beds and magnificent underwater terrain. The bluffs and underwater caves off Ocean View Drive (between the aquarium and Asilomar Beach) are some of the best scuba and snorkeling spots in the area. Better yet are the pristine waters of Whaler's Cove, in Point Lobos. The **Aquarius Dive Shop** (32 Cannery Row, tel. 831/375–6605) has moderately priced equipment rentals for certified divers (about $70 the first day, $35 each additional day). No special training is required for snorkeling, and you can rent gear at Aquarius for less than $34. Snorkeling lessons and a tour cost $50.

BIG SUR

Of all the scribes who've attempted to capture Big Sur with pen and paper, locals call Henry Miller their patron saint. Miller, who lived in a shack in Big Sur for many years, wrote of the land as "a region where extremes meet, a region where one is always conscious of weather, of space, of grandeur, of eloquent silence." Spanish settlers in the 1770s had called this forbidding wilderness *el pais grande del sur* (the big country of the south), which got shortened to Big Sur in the early 1900s. Come here to see precipitous cliffs, rocky beaches, and redwood forests and to revel in the solitude of open space. The population is sparse, and the closest thing to a town is the group of stores surrounding the **Deetjen's Big Sur Inn** (Hwy. 1, tel. 831/667–2377), 22 mi south of Carmel. Locals head to the inn on Saturday night to hear live jazz or drum music; about a mile farther south, **Fernwood**, in Hwy. 1, tel. 831/667–2422) hosts live rock and roll on Saturday nights and boasts both a tranquil view of the Big Sur River and one of the world's few albino redwood trees.

Much of Big Sur lies within the 167,000-acre **Ventana Wilderness**, in Los Padres National Forest, whose deep, wide valleys, waterfalls, hot springs, natural pools, and perennial streams foster abundant wildlife; you'll find plenty of deer and a few bears. **Big Sur Station** (Hwy. 1, just south of Pfeiffer Big Sur State Park, tel. 831/667–2315), open daily 8–6 (until 4:30 in the winter), is loaded with information on camping and exploring the surrounding wilderness. For background information read *Hiking the Big Sur Country* ($16) or the latest issue of the free *El Sur Grande,* which contains a detailed map, hiking tips,

Jimi Hendrix made rock-and-roll history in 1969 when he burned his guitar in front of awestruck fans in Monterey. Later, horrified by the destruction of what he considered a sacred object, Indian sitarist Ravi Shankar almost refused to perform.

and history; both are available at the station. Park at one of Highway 1's turnouts to avoid paying $7 on state lots.

WHERE TO SLEEP

Camping at one of Big Sur's 1,000-plus sites is the most economical sleeping option. If you don't have camping gear, consider renting one of the tent cabins available at private campgrounds for $30–$40. One of the nicest is **Big Sur Campground and Cabins** (tel. 831/667–2322), 3 mi south of Andrew Molera State Park (*see below*), where cabins sleeping two start at $48. **Riverside Campgrounds and Cabins** (Hwy. 1., tel. 831/667–2414), 25 mi south of Carmel, provides the cheapest indoor accommodations in all of Big Sur. Five rooms with gorgeous redwood interiors start at $55, and two larger double cabins go for $95. You will find rustic, romantic cabins at **Deetjen's Big Sur Inn** (Hwy. 1, tel. 831/667–2377), secluded behind redwoods 3 mi south of the Big Sur station. Each of the 20 rooms ($75 and up) comes with a down comforter—which you'll need. There's also a great on-site restaurant.

CAMPING

One of the few access points to the interior of Big Sur, Nacimiento Road, 4 mi south of Lucia, twists and turns to reach eight $5 sites at **Nacimiento Campground** (11 mi from Hwy. 1) and 23 $15 sites at **Ponderosa Campground** (13½ mi from Hwy. 1). Both peaceful campgrounds lie on the bank of a babbling brook, but neither accepts reservations, neither has showers, and only Ponderosa has flush toilets; make sure to bring your own water or a purifier. Better yet, remember you can camp off any wide spot in the road (there are several great spots between Nacimiento and Ponderosa) for free as long as you walk 100 ft from your car and obtain a fire permit from the Big Sur Station (*see above*).

West of Highway 1, 10 mi south of Palo Colorado Road, **Andrew Molera State Park** has more than 4,000 largely undeveloped acres with beach access and camping. The 50 tents-only sites ($3) are first-come, first-served, but they never turn anyone away, which means the park can become a beehive when overflow campers from other campgrounds stack up on weekends. Though payment is on the honor system, rangers make their rounds at 8 AM to hand out $25 tickets to weasels. If you want to soak up a view of

SYKES HOT SPRINGS

If you have two days and backpacking gear on your hands, make the 10-mi trek to Sykes Hot Springs. After a six- or seven-hour hike up steep ridges and along a river valley crowded with redwoods, you can soak in the thermal spring and sleep under the stars before heading back the next day or continuing on into the depths of the Ventana Wilderness Area. On summer weekends you may have to vie for space in the rock-dam tubs—aim for the winter months. The trail begins at the Big Sur station parking lot; register and get a fire permit from the rangers here before heading out.

a tremendous valley among the majestic madronas and oaks of the Ventana Wilderness, trek to the 11 first-come, first-served campsites ($12) at **Bottcher's Gap,** 5 mi south of Garrapata State Beach, and east 8 mi on Palo Colorado Road. Though there are no phones and no showers, there is running water and all the peace and solitude you could want. Hikers and tent campers vie for one of two secluded primitive sites ($16) at **Julia Pfeiffer Burns State Park** (Hwy. 1, 38 mi south of Carmel), set in a cypress forest on bluffs overhanging the ocean. Even without potable water or flush toilets, these spots book early; reserve through Reserve America (tel. 800/444-7275). For information on both environmental and developed camping, call or stop by the Big Sur Station (*see above*).

FOOD

Wise travelers stock up at the supermarket in Carmel or San Luis Obispo. If you forget to pack the cooler, the **Center Deli** (Hwy. 1, tel. 831/667-2225), 30 mi south of Rio Road next to the Big Sur post office, has groceries, pasta salads, and the cheapest sandwiches around, as well as fruit smoothies in summer. The **Big Sur Village Pub** (Hwy. 1, next to Deetjen's Big Sur Inn, tel. 831/667-2355) has burritos and sandwiches for less than $6.

EXPLORING BIG SUR

Eleven miles south of Carmel, Palo Colorado Road winds its way east from Highway 1 through the Ventana Wilderness for 8 serpentine mi before ending at **Bottcher's Gap.** From the parking lot, **Skinner's Ridge Trail** climbs 4 mi (roughly three hours) to Devil's Peak, which affords incredible views of Ventana's dramatic wooded peaks and valleys. South off Skinner's Ridge Trail is the eight-hour round-trip hike to **Pico Blanco**—a rugged mountain peak that the Esselen Indians thought was the top of the world and the site of human creation. Winding partially through private property, the hike is not legal, but people do it anyway by trekking along the Boy Scout Service Road past the Boy Scout Camp and all the way up **Little Sur Trail.**

Back on Highway 1, south of Palo Colorado Road, look for the **Bixby Creek Bridge,** a 550-ft concrete span built in 1932. Just before the bridge, the circular **Old Coast Road** curves inland for 10 mi and meets back up with Highway 1 opposite the entrance to Andrew Molera State Park. This is California at its rugged best—craggy cliffs, majestic redwoods, and views of the Little Sur River running its way toward the ocean. If you're the four-wheeling type, you'll like the road's gravel- and mud-plagued inclines; a regular car should be fine if the weather's been dry.

Double back a half mile north from Andrew Molera to check out the **Point Sur Light Station** (tel. 831/625-4419), which was built in 1889 on a huge rock outcropping to prevent shipwrecks along this foggy and rocky stretch of coast. Tours of the lighthouse are available on weekends and on Wednesday May–October ($5). Call first for times and make sure to show up a half hour early so the docents can let you through the gate. **Andrew Molera State Park,** once the site of a Monterey Jack cheese factory and a dairy farm, now has more than 10 mi of hiking and mountain-biking trails. The strenuous hike up the **Ridge Trail** takes you through 4 mi of stunning coastal scenery to the top of a ridge. Savor the spectacular view of the Pacific before you head down the **Panorama Trail** to the **Bluffs Trail,** which is especially striking in spring when the wildflowers bloom.

About 5 mi south of Andrew Molera State Park, **Pfeiffer Big Sur State Park** (east side of Hwy. 1, tel. 831/667–2315) is one of the most popular camping and hiking spots on the coast, especially during summer. Don't waste your time at **Pfeiffer Falls**—the hike is crowded and the falls are less than spectacular. Just south of Pfeiffer on the same side of the highway, Big Sur Station (*see above*) is the starting point for the **Pine Ridge Trail,** a local favorite that leads into the Ventana Wilderness and **Sykes Hot Springs** (*see box, above*).

Sycamore Canyon Road, a mile south of the Big Sur station, is unmarked save for a stop sign. If you can find it, brave the road for 2 mi, and you'll land at **Pfeiffer Beach,** a turbulent, windswept cove with huge rock formations and an angry ocean not suitable for swimming. About 2½ mi farther south lies **Nepenthe** (tel. 831/667–2345), an expensive restaurant with an extraordinary view (also the last stop of Bus 22, which runs from Monterey in summer only).

Head south from Nepenthe to the **Henry Miller Library** (Hwy. 1, ¼ mi south of Nepenthe, tel. 831/667–2574). More like a book collector's attic, the tiny one-room library displays the bohemian author's artifacts (sorry, no steamy letters to Anaïs Nin) and has readings, events, and rotating exhibits on artists and writers associated with Miller or Big Sur. The library is open Wednesday to Sunday 11 AM to 5 PM.

More spectacular than Pfeiffer Big Sur State Park, **Julia Pfeiffer Burns State Park** (12 mi south of Big Sur Station, tel. 831/667–2315) has excellent and often less crowded hiking trails. Few people blink at the $6 entrance fee that's required to see **McWay Falls**—which was the most breathtaking sight in all of Big Sur before parking lots, postcards, and crowds demystified some of its natural wonder. From the parking lot, a half-mile path leads to a bluff with a phenomenal view of the creek

Locals scoff at the Esalen Institute's esoteric ideals, even though in the late '60s this was one of the first places to introduce Gestalt therapy. Today's classes have names like "Awakened Mind: Advanced Brainwave Training."

at the head of the falls. If you're looking for solitude, take the rugged 6-mi **Ewoldsen Trail** loop through one of the best vegetation samplings of the Big Sur coast.

Three miles south of Julia Pfeiffer, a sign on the right side of the road directs you to the world-famous **Esalen Institute** (tel. 831/667–3000), a onetime wacked-out hippie colony that specializes in the "exploration of human value and potentials." These days the grounds are closed to the public. Outsiders can use the famous hot springs perched on a cliff overlooking the ocean, but only in conjunction with a massage or enrollment in a workshop.

The southern stretch of Big Sur—between the tiny towns of Lucia and San Simeon—is less populated and has a gentler geography than the sometimes violently beautiful north. There's not much to see besides the continually unfolding coastline, but you will come across some choice beaches every now and then. Ten miles south of Lucia, **Jade Cove** is a secluded, rocky beach with sweeping views up and down the coast. Just north of Gorda, quiet **Willow Creek** is another local favorite.

OUTDOOR ACTIVITIES

The main activity in Big Sur is hiking (*see* Exploring Big Sur, *above*), but lots of people also bicycle along Highway 1. Cyclists should be experienced and unafraid of the highway and the lack of road shoulder. Most state parks offer cheap campsites (usually $3) to those on two wheels.

Andrew Molera State Park is the only Big Sur park with single-track trails for mountain biking. Mountain bikers in tip-top shape can take on the steep, strenuous **Ridge Trail,** which is more than 2 mi long and has elevation gains of 1,200 ft. For a more relaxing ride, try the **River** and **Cottonwood trails** (2 mi), both of which wind through the park's meadows. Most trails start at the parking area or a half mile away at the beach. Elsewhere in Big Sur, you'll have to stick to the fire and service roads or risk a fine. One possibility is to head up **Nacimiento-Ferguson Road,** 4 mi south of Lucia off Highway 1 (*see* Camping, *above*). Bikes are not allowed to the left into the Ventana Wilderness, but off the right side of the road you'll see a few trails, most of which are quite steep in sections.

INDEX